TEILHARD DE CHARDIN

PIERRE TEILHARD DE CHARDIN
Bronze head made in Peking in 1936/7 by Mrs Lucile Swan

TEILHARD DE CHARDIN

A Biographical Study

by

CLAUDE CUÉNOT

HELICON

Baltimore

Helicon Press, Inc.
1120 N. Calvert St.
Baltimore, Md. 21202

This translation of Pierre Teilhard de Chardin: les grandes étapes de
son évolution (*Librairie Plon*) *was made by* VINCENT COLIMORE
and edited by RENÉ HAGUE

Library of Congress Catalog Card Number 65-14382

Contents

Illustrations

Sources of the illustrations: 1, 2, 4, 16, Mlle J. Mortier; 3, M. François-Régis Teilhard de Chardin; 6 and 7, M. Marcel Légaut; 11, M. Maurice Penaud; 15, M. l'Abbé Lavocat.

Illustrations

CHAPTER ONE

The Formative Years

IN the heart of France's Massif Central lies the ancient province of Auvergne, its name derived from the Gaulish tribe of the Arverni, whose hegemony was already established there in the days of Julius Caesar. It is a country in which the traveller cannot fail to be impressed by a sense of both historical and geological antiquity. Man and nature are seen to have something in common: an appropriate homeland for a man whose whole life was to be a steady progress towards an all-embracing synthesis that integrated man with the planet on which he lives, with the universe in which they both evolved, and with the God to whom he proceeds.

Ancient, irregular, rambling, the house of Sarcenat is backed by the volcanic mass of western Auvergne; to the east it looks out on the valley of the Allier, with the twin cities of Clermont-Ferrand in the distance.

It was here, near Orcines, and a few miles west of Clermont, that Marie-Joseph-Pierre Teilhard de Chardin was born on 1 May 1881. The addition of Chardin to the family name came from his grandfather, Pierre-Cirice Teilhard, who in 1841 had married Victoire Barron de Chardin.[1] One of their two sons, Emmanuel, married in 1875 Berthe-Adèle de Dompierre d'Hornoy, a great-grandniece of Voltaire. Pierre was the fourth of their eleven children. His mother, who came from Picardy, was a woman of great piety and modesty, self-effacing, charitable, devoted to her husband, gentle but firm with her children. As one by one seven of these children died, she abandoned herself ever more fully to the will of God.[2] "To this dear

[1] The family traced itself back to Astorg Teillard, 1478–1549, ennobled in 1538.
[2] "There is no pain", Madame Teilhard de Chardin said to the parish priest who tried to console her for the death of one of her children. "Heaven lies ahead of us."

and sainted mother," Pierre said on learning of her death, "I owe the best part of my soul." On another occasion, writing on the feast of the Assumption, 1936, he acknowledges a more specific debt.

> I find a continual source of strength in recognizing that the evolutionary effort may be reduced to the justification of a love (God's love, in fact) and its development. This is just what my mother used to tell me. But it will have taken me a lifetime to integrate this truth into an organic vision of things.

Marguerite Teilhard-Chambon (Pierre's first cousin, who wrote under the name of Claude Aragonnès) has left an excellent picture of Alexandre-Victor-Emmanuel, the father:

> Uncle Emmanuel, with his great height, fine bearing, bright eyes and military moustache, used to terrify us and his own children too, I think, in his spells of taciturnity. When he did speak, it was in unexpected bursts of pungent but kindly humour. Fresh from the École des Chartes, he specialized in the history of his own province of Auvergne, and devoted his life to a patient study of the archives of Montferrand. . . . At the same time he was leading the full life of a "gentleman farmer", running several estates and subscribing to English periodicals that specialized in his favourite subjects: farming, hunting and racing. As a humanist with a strong cultural bent, he was a wide reader, particularly in history: he was a sound director of his children's reading, too, even superintending their Latin lessons until they were ready for secondary school. Another of his contributions to the formation of their minds was to inculcate in them an interest in natural objects, and to encourage them to make natural history collections, insects, birds and stones.[3]

Some of Pierre's brothers and sisters died very young; one brother went into the Navy, another into the Army, another into business, four others into engineering. One sister entered religion as a Little Sister of the Poor. His favourite sister, Marguerite-Marie, an invalid since her twentieth year, became in 1922 the leading spirit in the Catholic Union of the Sick.

For children at Sarcenat, life was regulated according to a kind of ritual at once easy-going and detailed. It began with rising at seven-thirty, breakfast in the governess's room, lessons (Latin from

---

[3] For much information concerning the years 1881–1923, and for some facts about later years, I am indebted to Mlle Marguerite Teillard-Chambon (Claude Aragonès). This quotation is from "Pierre Teilhard à Sarcenat", in *L'Auvergne littéraire, artistique et historique* (3rd quarter, 1957), p. 11.

their father, German from a Fräulein) and ended with six o'clock dinner and family night prayers at eight. On Sundays there was High Mass in the fourteenth-century church in Orcines; after Vespers the children played at charades, while the grown-ups drank tea in the drawing-room. The most severe winter months were spent at Clermont, where the family shared a thirteenth-century house with some cousins.

Spring brought them back to the country, to Sarcenat, or to Murol (near Maringues, on the banks of the Allier), where there was fishing and shooting. It was a simple, clannish, unpretentious family life, of which the only criticism that might be made was that it was somewhat too self-contained and sheltered.

A few remembrances survive of Teilhard's life as a child:

> I was just like any other child. I was interested specially in mineralogy and biological observation. I used to love to follow the course of the clouds, and I knew the stars by their names. . . . To my father I owe a certain balance, on which all the rest is built, along with a taste for the exact sciences.
>
> A memory? My very first! I was five or six. My mother had snipped of a few of my curls. I picked one up and held it close to the fire. The hair was burnt up in a fraction of a second. A terrible grief assailed me; I had learnt that I was perishable. . . . What used to grieve me when I was a child? This insecurity of things. And what used I to love? My genie of iron! With a plow-hitch I believed myself, at seven years, rich with a treasure incorruptible, everlasting. And then it turned out that what I possessed was just a bit of iron that rusted. At this discovery I threw myself on the lawn and shed the bitterest tears of my existence! Cut off from society and even from the times, my family lived in patriarchal simplicity.

One thing is certain, the deep impression made on Teilhard in childhood and boyhood, by the land of Auvergne.

> Auvergne moulded me . . . Auvergne served me both as museum of natural history and as wild-life preserve. Sarcenat in Auvergne gave me my first taste of the joys of discovery . . . to Auvergne I owe my delight in nature. Auvergne it was that gave me my most precious possessions: a collection of pebbles and rocks still to be found there, where I lived.

And it was to Auvergne that he would return, not only to see his family but also to draw fresh nourishment from his homeland.

More formal education began for Pierre in April, 1892, when he was enrolled in the secondary school run by the Jesuits at Notre-Dame de Mongré, Villefranche-sur-Saône (Rhône).⁴ He made a good start in his first year, with two prizes and three *proxime accessit*, and had no trouble in going through the whole curriculum. Noteworthy among his teachers, in his third (humanities) year was Henri Bremond, future author of the *Histoire littéraire du sentiment religieux en France*. One of his favourites was his physics teacher, Fr Desribes, whom he had in his fifth (philosophy) year, and who may well have sharpened his taste for scientific studies. Although no prodigy, Pierre achieved a high standard in a wide range of subjects, including Latin, Greek, German and Science. His last year (1896-7) was his most successful; he left with seven prizes, a *proxime accessit* and a special alumni award of a five-volume French biographical dictionary. In religious subjects, oddly, he did not do so well, but this seems to have been due not so much to lack of interest as to a certain nonconformist attitude (common enough in boys of that age) to rather narrowly catechetical instruction.⁵ As might be expected, he passed without trouble the two-part matriculation examination (*baccalauréat ès lettres*) of the University of Clermont-Ferrand.

Henri Bremond recalls:

Thirty years ago I had a little third-year pupil from Auvergne, very intelligent, first in every subject, but disconcertingly sophisticated. Even the most restive or dull-witted boys sometimes took a real interest in their work; a more lively lesson or a more exciting assignment brought a light to their eyes. Not so this boy: and it was only long afterwards that I learnt the secret of his seeming indifference. Transporting his mind far away from us was another, a jealous and absorbing passion—rocks.⁶

We know a good deal about his religious life. After making his

⁴ This was the rule in the Teilhard family. At ten or eleven the boys were sent to Mongré to school with the Jesuits and the girls went to Clermont under the Ursulines. Mongré was conducted by the Assumptionist Fathers after 1951. Auguste Demoment, S.J., the distinguished archivist of the Lyons province (to whom we owe so much), has written an excellent account of the school: "Le Collège de Mongré au XIXᵉ siècle (1852–1901)", in *Établissements des Jésuites en France depuis quatre siècles*, fasc. 18–19 (1957), pp. 170–91.
⁵ Cf. Henri Bremond, *L'enfant et la vie* (Paris: Bloud & Gay, 1953), pp. 163–6.
⁶ *Le charme d'Athènes* (Paris: Bloud & Gay), pp. 29–30.

first communion, on Ascension Day 1892, he was admitted to the Sodality of St Aloysius Gonzaga, and later (1895) to that of the Immaculate Conception, making his act of consecration to Our Lady on the feast of the Immaculate Conception. Next year he was elected by the boys first, secretary and then, prefect of the sodality.[7] The minutes he kept as secretary reflect the Jesuit concern for the interior life of their pupils:

> Father Bonnet, the philosophy teacher . . . showed us how we can attain holiness by the practice of the least showy virtues and by the simple performance of everyday duties just as well as by undergoing martyrdom or by miracles.
>
> Our director, Fr Charles Grognier, gave us a talk full of originality but very much to the point. He said the best way to show our love for the Blessed Virgin is to try to be men with a sense of duty, that is Christians. Then, when we leave school we can really work to bring France back to the road God has mapped out for it, and make it Christian again. If we do this we shall give back to Mary one of the brightest jewels in her crown, for as the old saying runs, *Regnum Galliae, regnum Mariae.*

Devotion to our Lady became deeply rooted in Pierre's heart. Mary was always to hold a special place in his thoughts, meditations and spiritual retreats: as a Jesuit, he would often associate the three feminines (*Marie, l'Église, la Compagnie*), Mary, the Church and the Society, and throughout his life he remained faithful to the recitation of the rosary.

On 20 March 1890 he entered the Jesuit novitiate at Aix-en-Provence. He explained later what impelled him to join the Society. It was neither his Jesuit education nor his family background, but a desire for perfection. "When I was seventeen, the desire for the 'most perfect' determined my vocation to the Jesuits."

He could not go direct from school to the novitiate for he was rather run-down in health, thin, and somewhat anaemic. His father wisely kept him at home in Clermont-Ferrand. Here, while recovering his health, he spent his weekdays in brushing up his mathematics under tutors, Sundays being devoted to excursions in search of mineralogical specimens.

[7] General René Ract-Madoux, who was his classmate in philosophy, wrote to us on 27 February 1957, "Simple, a good comrade, a worker, with a high sense of duty, of exemplary conduct and great piety, the young Teilhard was a model pupil, highly regarded by his schoolmates."

At Aix, until the end of September, 1900, he was "Brother Pierre", too absorbed in his new life as a novice to spend any time in picking up "pebbles".[8] In October, having completed his novitiate, he began his juniorate at Laval (Mayence), where he took his first vows on 25 March 1901. In a letter to his parents he expressed his thoughts upon assuming this first religious obligation and upon being

> at last entirely at the disposition of the Blessed Virgin . . . completely attached, forever, to the Society at the very moment when it is being so severely persecuted. . . . I shall never forget all you have done to assist my vocation. But keep on praying that I may continue to be equal to whatever God asks of me.

The juniorate is devoted to the study of language and literature. Teilhard proved an excellent classical scholar, composing Greek and Latin verses, reading Aeschylus, and composing for an entertainment a short play in Greek modelled on the *Frogs* of Aristophanes. During this period he was studying for his degree (the *licence ès lettres*).

1901, however, was the year of the *lois d'exception*, which restricted the activities of religious orders; and when in 1902, the accession of Combes to the Premiership marked the zenith of anticlericalism, French Jesuits left for England and the Channel Islands. Even as an old man Teilhard used to smile at some of the grotesquely comic incidents that lightened those sad days. The departure, for example, of the community from Laval. Having decided that lay dress would be more discreet, they had divided among themselves the assortment of clothing sent by their families, so that "grave fathers and young scholastics found themselves wearing a funereal top-hat with a light grey jacket, or a greenish old bowler with a long frock-coat, or a motoring cap with a black morning-coat".

---

[8] He made two friends here, Auguste Valensin, a fellow-novice, and Pierre Charles. Teilhard always retained his admiration for his "dear friend, the great Pierre Charles". Charles later taught at Louvain and constantly worked to have his friend's works printed. Teilhard's "dear good friend Auguste Valensin", remained to the end the chosen confidant, to whom a mere hint was always enough, and whose judgment was absolutely trustworthy (on Valensin, see the article in *Études* by A. Blanchet, February, 1955). It was Charles and Valensin who, in theology, opened Teilhard's eyes; for example, Teilhard would later mention and discuss Charles's hypothesis of a precosmic original sin. Charles, no mere textbook theologian, developed a deep and living understanding of Thomism. As for Valensin, he was himself profoundly influenced by Blondelian thought.

Thus it was on the island of Jersey that Teilhard resumed his studies as a junior. His environment there was a lively one, for he was a member of a small circle of active young minds: Doncœur, Demoré, Fontoynont, Burdo and Valensin. His "great friend, dear Auguste Valensin", a fine humanist deeply affected by the theories of Blondel, was to remain a chosen confidant and it was he who, with Pierre Charles, was to open Teilhard's eyes to the wonders of theology.

We have but one brief glimpse of his interior life at this time. While at school, he confided, he had felt obliged to reach some compromise between his attraction for nature and the evangelical teaching of the *Imitation of Christ* which supplied the spiritual nourishment for his prayers. Later, as a junior in Jersey, he thought seriously of giving up his study of rocks, an absorbing passion, and devoting himself entirely to "supernatural" activities. He adds:

> At that moment I would have gone off the rails if it had not been for the solid common sense of Père T. [Fr Paul Troussard, the Novice master]. What he did, in fact, was simply to assure me that my crucified God looked for a "natural" development of my being, as well as for its sanctification.[9]

From his first years in Jersey, Teilhard conceived an interest in the island's geology. From October, 1902, he devoted all the time he could spare from his philosophy studies and all his holidays to scientific excursions. He would be accompanied by some of his fellow-students and, from 1904 onwards, by Fr Félix Pelletier, a graduate in chemistry and mineralogy, who collaborated with him in a preliminary geological and mineralogical note of the island for the Jersey Society's annual bulletin.[10]

An unexpected break came in September, 1905, when he was sent to teach physics and chemistry at the Holy Family, the Jesuit

---

[9] At this time, too, his sister Françoise was going through a difficult period of spiritual trial before entering the Little Sisters of the Poor. Pierre, in words already characteristic, comforted her pessimism. "You look at your crucifix from the wrong side. It is not only the Cross you should see but Jesus Christ who is on the Cross.' (*Françoise Teilhard de Chardin, Petite Sœur des Pauvres*, p. 21.)

[10] At Jersey began what Teilhard called his "time of preliminary investigations of the earth" (1901–12): "...the chief result of these first studies had been to furnish samples and observations (many new species) to eminent geologists and palaeontologists" (*Titres et travaux*, p. 1). Teilhard at this time was still only an amateur.

secondary school in Cairo, where he was also in charge of the "museum", the jumble of collections assembled by the fathers of the school. His lessons seem to have been stimulating, but rather above the heads of the pupils, one of whom, now a Jesuit, recalled "when class was over I found myself impressed but not much the wiser". It was already apparent that what Teilhard was really suited for (apart of course from research) was higher teaching.

Anastasio Alfieri, secretary of the Egyptian Entomological Society, studied at that time under Teilhard and his friend and fellow-Jesuit Joseph Clainpanain, and remembers the expeditions they used to make into the desert, pursuing their interest in mineralogy and palaeontology. One expedition, to the red mountain of Abbassieh, was typical of Teilhard's contempt for comfort when it was a matter of scientific research. It was made in pouring rain, for Teilhard hoped that as the rain swept down the slopes it would expose some palaeontological specimens.

How far Teilhard progressed in science during his years in Jersey and Cairo it is difficult to say. This was before the theory of relativity, the quantum theory and refinements of the atomic theory. On his own admission it was simply elementary physics that he studied and taught. "In this field," he said later, "I was no more than an amateur, a layman." He considered beings as bound together principally by "matter" and he sought to find in the "elementary", in the mass of bodies, the point of balance and the principle of consistence in the universe.

But as a geologist, palaeontologist, and naturalist Teilhard enjoyed himself to the full in Egypt. At the beginning of April, 1907, in El Faiyum, at Kasr-el-Sagha, he filled his pack with

> fantastic fossils, said to be a symbiosis of hermit crabs and polyp colonies. . . . Alas, above the wall are marine deposits with the remains of whales; but a few miles further, sands with large pachyderms, and here are buried the monstrously horned skulls of *arsinoëtherium*. . . . But, for research here, a full-scale expedition would be required.

The following extracts from letters reflect some of the ardour of this hunt for fossils, minerals and rare insects:

> October 24 1907. At Behig, in the Mariout desert, I stumbled upon an abandoned quarry full of *Rumina, Buliminus Gaillyi, Helix philammia* (crenellated), not to speak of certain small

species of great interest to M. Pallary; *Orcula Scyphus*, and doubt-less some *Coecilianella* (a genus not reported in Egypt). In the large tufts of Graminaceae in the desert of Suez I collected two very odd species of grasshopper to add to the future work of Innes Bey.[11]

From Paris, M. du B. has been urging me to give some atten-tion to the *Chrysides* (Hymenoptera, blue and red)....I have sent him some rare ones: females where but males have been found, and vice versa.

I await impatiently the return of M. Couyat. In the Academy of Sciences publication for September 9 he has a note on our Celestine crystals. I am going to show him others more curious still, which some enormous radiolites from the Cretaceous de-posits of Abu-Roach are full of.

I have made the acquaintance of the viper of the pyramids—*echis carinata*—of which I am keeping two small specimens in alcohol. This snake, when threatened, rubs together the coils of its body, producing quite a loud noise.

March 12 1908. Here are my latest finds. M. Priem has a com-munication to the French Geological Society on the subject of my fish teeth from the Mokkatam mountain, and the jaw of the sirenian. At New Year I spent a week in Upper Egypt, and brought back from the deposits of Minieh a stock of echinoids which delighted M. Fourtau.[12] He is preparing an article on them.

Last Shrove Tuesday I picked up from the Cretaceous deposits of the Libyan Desert two small asteroida, which should now be on their way to Paris. Finally, I found on Mokkatam a deposit of fragments of Clypeaster, which may have as a result the re-assignment of the Mokkatam heights to the Upper Eocene. A month ago I met concretions of heavy spar, a new mineral, I think, for Cairo.

As a result of these researches Teilhard was already becoming known to a number of specialists. In 1908 he published his study on *The Eocene Strata of the Minieh Region*. He was already display-ing his leaning towards the Tertiary era, when mammals were becoming widespread and the primates were appearing. However, the Egyptian terrain led him to concentrate on marine fossils. He made contributions to entomology also, one incident he witnessed

[11] M. Pallary was a French scientist who lived at Oran; he specialized in Mediterranean conchology. Dr Innes, the director of the school of medicine in Cairo, owned some magnificent collections.

[12] M. Fourtau was a French engineer at Cairo. A member of the Institut Égyptien, he contributed more than anyone else to the geology of Egypt.

being described in a paper on "the spirited defence of an Acridian".
A lepidopteron, a hymenopteron, and a fossil (a variety of Gisopy-
gus) were named after him. He even feared that he might become
bogged down in a preoccupation with collections and collecting.
Although always eager to find new species and unusual specimens,
he remained primarily a keen observer.

Most important of all, however, for Teilhard was the discovery
of the East, "the lonesome waste of desert whose purple plains rose
and fell one after another to a vanishing point on the wildly exotic
horizon". His preference was for Upper Egypt, but his eight days
in El Faiyum made a deep impression on him, especially Lake
Moeris, the Birket Qarun.

> A sheet of steel-blue, almost gray, water, that the yellow cliffs
> of the desert suddenly confront. In the shallows, fishermen push
> their flat boats; they beat the water with great blows of their poles,
> to drive into their nets a species of carp.... On our side, the
> bottom drops imperceptibly, and for almost an hour we go for-
> ward slowly in the channel amid dwarf tamarisks, where we start
> herons and snipe, and stir to sibilant wakefulness the iridescent
> bee-eaters. At last we meet a band of tall reeds, and, once free
> from their thick clumps, slip into the open waters. Coots and
> ducks, covering the lake in dense flocks, start from and suddenly
> dive back into the grasses.... When we turn around to go back,
> it is already growing late. In the distance the pelicans, standing
> in a row to fish, look like a white line traced on the surface of
> the lake. The sun disappears and we glide on opalescent waters
> ringed by deep violet mountains.[13]

These impressions contributed to an increasing awareness of the
immensity of matter and the grandeur of Christ. The Orient meant
for Teilhard the East as a world opposed to the West and, the lure
of the exotic once exorcized, the challenge to effect the meeting of
these two worlds. This dialogue with the East, more specifically
with India and China, was to continue during the whole of Teilhard's life. It can never be sufficiently emphasized that however
often the dress of the explorer disguised the priest Teilhard was of
the blood and temper of the great Jesuit missionaries.

A Jesuit's training and studies are very lengthy. After the
Egyptian interlude Teilhard went through the customary four years
of theology at Ore Place, the Jesuit house in Hastings on the Sussex

[13] *Relations d'Orient*, December, 1907, pp. 276-8.

coast. On 24 August 1911, about a year before he had completed
these studies, he was ordained priest. His parents were present, and
on the next day received holy communion from his hands.

We know little about the priestly duties he then assumed, and no
details of his four-year course in theology. In a letter of 1 March
1954, written in English, Teilhard recalled those distant years.

> You know, at that time, I was a young student in theology—
> not allowed often to leave his cell of Ore Place (Hastings) and I
> did not know anything about anthropology (or even prehistory);
> my chief passion was the Wealdian bone-beds and their fossil
> teeth content.[14]

He speaks, however, of a week of parish work at Belle, not far
from Boulogne:

> ...my principal regret is at not having been able to visit
> Boulogne, nor the cliffs, nor a certain ichthyologist named
> Sauvage. But this did not keep me from passing an excellent
> week, in a charming countryside, where I was warmly received
> in a rectory simply lost in the open fields; here I was made to feel
> immediately at home. I did have some work to do, seeing that I
> had all the confessions in a parish which, though not large, is
> made up of regular communicants; but on the whole the work
> was light, as, indeed, it ought to be for a beginner.

At Paris (letter of 1 January 1913) he was to work among young
artisans—his first contact with the working class:

> In order to be not too much cut off from clerical activity, I go
> every other week among the glassworkers at Le Bourget (of whom
> I think I have already spoken to you). Last time, it was for Mid-
> night Mass. These poor people are very interesting, and show a
> lot of confidence in me, but you would not believe how much—
> even in a pretty small factory, and where the boss is excellent
> —those who refuse to go along with the gang get manhandled;
> there are a couple of youngsters (between fifteen and eighteen)
> here who are real heroes. I am certainly glad I accepted the week-
> end work here.
>
> For Passiontide I am to go to Gap, all by myself. There will be
> many sermons to preach (three a day between Palm Sunday and
> Passion Sunday), and the prospect scares me just a little. Well,

---

[14] He was pleased to discover in these bone-beds a molar tooth which he
gave to Smith-Woodward for study.

this will allow me to make my acquaintance with the neighbour-hood of the Alps.

Thanks to the liberal attitude of the Rector at Hastings, Teilhard was allowed to go more frequently on scientific walks and excursions, finding specimens to offer to the British Museum or the Museum at Hastings. He had now advanced beyond the amateur class, and was manifesting a clear bent towards the palaeontology of the vertebrates.

Another thing we know is that at this time Teilhard undertook (or went on with) the study of English. He was never to cease to improve his knowledge of this language. In China, he was to show himself already capable of drafting scientific articles in English, but less at ease in expressing philosophical ideas in it; yet towards the end of his life, in the United States, he could tackle in English the most abstract and difficult subjects, expressing himself with extreme facility. Paradoxically, it is in English, not French, that we have recordings of his voice (on American records). So well acquainted with English did he become that, when he was in China, we find him using both languages interchangeably in his notes and correspondence.

But religion was the chief matter of his studies during these years. It is possible that his education in Scripture and exegesis was insufficient. Teilhard was not inclined by temperament to exegesis, nor was his mind especially oriented towards biblical studies. This, however, needs some qualification. A certain offhand attitude that he sometimes displayed was much more apparent than real. If he thought that, in connection with certain difficult points in Genesis, theologians ought to take a step forward towards science, he urged scientists, in turn, to meet the theologians half-way so that the eventual encounter could be more quickly and gently achieved.

Earlier, as a novice, Teilhard had made the acquaintance of a Belgian, the future Father Pierre Charles, who was to become a teacher at Louvain. From the beginning of his studies, particularly under the influence of Father Scheuer, Charles's philosophical ideas had been formed along the lines of traditional Thomism, with a tendency towards an increasingly rigid dialectical conception. Thoroughly anti-Kantian, Charles never applied himself professionally to philosophy, and was scarcely aware of contemporary thought save incidentally, and indirectly. His intellectual activity was reserved almost exclusively for theology, and was exercised in this field with considerable vigour and originality, often lending new life to the exposition of traditional themes, without, however, departing at all from their substance.

For this "dear friend, the great Pierre Charles", Teilhard felt undying admiration; and Charles was wont to refer to his companion as "my friend Pedro". Contact between the two, broken off by World War I, was later resumed, and was then continuous. Charles grasped (doubtless under Teilhard's influence) the fact that one day human palaeontology would pose some very serious problems for theology. While Teilhard's superiors were still trying to decide upon what line of intellectual activity Teilhard should be directed to enter, the latter asked his friend Charles, "What do you think about it?" Charles's unhesitating answer was: the field of prehistory and allied sciences.

Teilhard sent regularly to Charles the famous typewritten sheets on which he recorded the new ideas he was developing. Charles found the ideas expressed in Teilhard's *Le milieu divin* entirely conformable to his own. And it was Charles who inspired the final pages (on sin) added to Teilhard's *The Phenomenon of Man*.

Though he was to remain long imbued with scholasticism, Teilhard soon left behind the categories of the Thomistic synthesis and the methods inherent therein, for he was never at home when arguing in traditional logical form and juggling with syllogisms.[15] He admired scarcely any of his teachers save Father Léonce de Grandmaison, whom he called "the divine Léonce". But he worked hard, and on 14 July 1912 passed the oral examination on the various theological theses which marks the close of undergraduate theological studies.

In summarizing this sketch of Teilhard's early life, we may recall a remark of Albéric's: "Our family was the glass-cased kind". For Teilhard did live under glass. After having known the joys of a family circle, he entered upon the joys of another family, which, though somewhat larger, continued to circumscribe his horizon,

---

[15] His first writings are filled with Thomism and a strong Thomistic background is required in order to understand them. On 10 January 1920, he could still write: "It would be very useful for me to be guided more by scholasticism, without thinking that there is no other path for an idea in the actual Church than the Aristotelian way." Even as late as 8 February 1955 he wrote: "...mounted as we are 'on the shoulders' of Plato, Aristotle and St Thomas...".

the Jesuits. Except for the Egyptian interlude, he had not yet met the world at large. He had gone through spiritual conflicts, but on the whole he had been happy and perfectly at ease in this larger family which had adopted him. For a long time a deep-running, secret life had been animating Teilhard, betraying itself by certain conflicts, by a certain amount of independence. His adult character was already formed. The young Jesuit was distinguishing himself by his intelligence and by his enthusiasm for science. And yet these qualities were still held in check by the discipline of his training. His genius was not yet free to flower.

Nevertheless, we can already distinguish much that was to be characteristic of his intellectual and spiritual outlook, and see the basis on which it lay. Son of an archivist-naturalist, he had pre-cociously felt a vocation to geology, as witnessed by his early love of iron, of crystals of quartz or amethyst, of fragments of chalcedony, of brute matter, resistant, invulnerable, hard. Teilhard was a son of the earth, and in earth's blind matter his being was rooted. This matter he loved, for he was of ancient stock, born of earth-bound gentry, whose life was attuned to the natural rhythm of the seasons.

As a scientist, he remained faithful to the experimental method. Consoling as he found the prospect offered by the supernatural gift of faith, this never excluded the stimulating and sensitizing function of experience. He had no taste for mere speculation or logic.

But if Teilhard was to become a rigorously methodical geologist, this was above all for a basically metaphysical reason; for his choice of a career as a scientist, while revealing certain mental aptitudes, conceals others which were more deeply ingrained. It was because Teilhard as a child had expressed his obscure need for the absolute in his appetite for the solid, the everlasting, the changeless, that he loved the rocks and the crystals that seemed to defy time and to mock human frailness.

To enumerate the basic components of Teilhard's thought is simple. They are three: the cosmic, the Christian, and the human. The cosmic, or sense of the totality and solidarity of the cosmos, and hence of human implication therein, was, for Teilhard, the continu-ation and extension of his love for the eternal. After having sought and loved the eternal in what was solid, that is, in an object which he took to be unalterable, and after then discovering that this object played him false, he proceeded to seek and love the eternal in the universe. For he had an increasingly conscious need of totality.

It would be incorrect to say that what took place here was the precocious mutation of the more primitive element (the orientation towards solidity), a transformation which would normally have been produced around the age of puberty, at the time when, under the force of sexual powers, an adolescent is drawn out of the magic circle of infantile egocentricism and becomes extroverted. Puberty in Teilhard seems to have been an increase in vigour much more than a development of sexual forces. These latter were, as is known from his private conversations, absorbed in the passion for the eternal.

Passionate lover of the physical world though he was, Teilhard was born into a Christian family, deeply and hereditarily Catholic, whose moral health and sincerity could provide no cause or justification for youthful revolt. In this sheltered country home everyone felt himself to belong primarily to God, and found it quite natural to sacrifice everything else to God's interest. More specifically, their piety was Christ-centred, and with them, therefore, devotion to the Sacred Heart occupied a central place. This devotion impressed upon the child Teilhard the fact that no one loves mere abstract love, and introduced into his piety the element of the personal, an element which might otherwise have been obliterated by his strong preference for the universal and the absolute and by his converse distaste for the individual and the contingent. Does not Christianity, in fact, boil down to a person-to-person contact? Since Teilhard's whole life was to be a progressive unfolding of his personal relationship with Christ, the apparently fragile Heart of Jesus, by its universal resonance, was to become for him the ever-constant centre of the cosmos. Christ was the great, the unique passion of this son of earth.

The sense of the human, the third component of Teilhard's thought, revealed itself in his capacity to perceive a single soul in the giant human molecules, so to speak, which are constituted by collectivities. Though this third component did not come into evidence till the time of World War I, all Teilhard's thought—or, more exactly, his spiritual life—may be resolved into the complicated play of these three basic components.

This leads us to the master idea which will henceforth serve us as guide: Spirit, for Teilhard, was above all a unity achieved by synthesis, by a rejection of airtight mental compartments, by allowing the free play of contrary influences, and the result, in Teilhard's own exceptionally endowed spirit, was unquestionably a synthesis in which some seemingly contradictory aspirations were to be found in harmony. In this synthesis the child of earth banded with the child of heaven, in a mystical union richer than that of monist, of pagan, or quietist, since it preserved the values of each of these without falling into their errors. The monist would annihilate his individuality in total unity, whereas it was in total unity that Teilhard would most fully realize his individualness. The pagan adores gods of palpable wood, stone, and metal; but for Teilhard these palpable things were but a ladder to Christ, the God-Man. Leaving the quietest gently rocked in a dream of the divine, Teilhard, like Jacob wrestling with the angel, spent his days strenuously wrestling with matter until it yielded the divine.

CHAPTER TWO

The Discovery of the Human

D URING the two years 1912–14 Teilhard, without losing contact with England and Jersey, applied himself to studying
science in Paris. After passing his theology examinations
around midsummer of 1912, he had his first interview with Marcellin Boule, professor of palaeontology at the Paris Museum. At the
time of the jubilee celebration for his old teacher in 1937, Teilhard
was to recall this first meeting:

> Do you remember our first interview, about the middle of July
> in 1912?... About two that afternoon I timidly approached to
> ring the bell at the door—since so often entered—of the laboratory
> on the Place Valhubert. You were busily clearing up your work
> before leaving on the very next day, for your vacation. Despite
> this Thévenin pushed his way in. But you took the time to talk
> with me. And ... you proposed that I should come to work with
> you at Gaudry. And so I began what has been my life ever since.[1]

At the reopening of the University year Teilhard enrolled in a
number of classes: Jean Boussac's at the Institut Catholique,[2] Haug's
(tectonics, mesozoic geology) and Cayeux's at the Collège de France
on the lithology of sediments. By his intelligence, his frankness and
his scientific ardour he soon, it seems, ingratiated himself with
everybody, even the formidable Boule. Boule, an Auvergnat, short,
sturdy, with something of the bulldog in him, was dictatorial in
manner, choleric, impatient of contradiction, with a biting tongue,
but he was a man, too, of rare intelligence, a fine geologist (particularly brilliant in comparative palaeontology) and one of the

[1] *L'Anthropologie*, 47 (1937), 599–600.
[2] Teilhard accompanied him on the excursion to the Alps of Dauphiné
which the latter led from 13 to 23 July 1914. Jean Boussac was the son-in-law
of Pierre Termier.

great specialists on Neanderthal man.[3] Later, Teilhard was not to be shy of crossing swords with Boule, though he continued to respect and love him, sentiments which Boule fully reciprocated. In 1922 he wrote of Teilhard:

> He ... possesses every quality required of a first-rate naturalist; an aptitude for work, penetrating observation, a combination— valuable as it is rare—of a keenness for minute analysis and a gift of wide synthesis, and great independence of mind. His career, though just begun, already gives promise of being among the most brilliant.[4]

This friendship with Boule led to another. For Boule was, at the I.P.H. (Institute of Human Palaeontology), the administrative superior of the Abbé Henri Breuil, later the great figure in pre-historical studies. These two priests, Teilhard and Breuil, hit it off at once and frequently discussed the scientific as well as the religious problems connected with the origin of man, and of sin. For Teilhard it was a happy time of intellectual and spiritual ferment in a world itself big with change. He was already revealing what were to appear as his fundamental traits of temperament: the need to march in the vanguard, an appetite for facts, a horror of controversy, the knack of bringing to light the best in another's mind, and, finally, a wholesome progressive quality of thought which prevented a reactionary attachment to the past and a myopic concern with the present, and prompted him to move, confidently and energetically, with the times.

Breuil was among the group with whom Teilhard, in late June of 1913, toured North-west Spain to visit the caves containing pre-historic paintings. They visited the caverns of Altamira (Santillana del Mar, Santander), Hornos de la Peña (San Felice de Buelna), Castillo (Puenteviesgo), the nearby Pasiega, and Pindal (Pimiango, Tina Mayor) near Oviedo. The company was as interesting as the

---

[3] Politically very broadminded, Boule gave the same welcome to the wife of a militant revolutionary and to a Jesuit, so long as they were good workers. This contact with the extreme left interested Teilhard deeply, but it did not disturb him. It was Boule who entrusted to him the collection on the origin of the phosphorites of Le Quercy that formed the basis of Teilhard's first two important publications: *Les Carnassiers des phosphorites du Quercy* (1914), and *Les primates des phosphorites du Quercy* (1916). 1912 to 1923 was the period that Teilhard called his "Phase of palaeontological research in Europe" (*Titres et travaux*, p. 1).

[4] *C. R. Somm. Soc. Géol. France*, meeting of 9 June 1922, pp. 130–1.

itinerary: besides Breuil there were Nels C. Nelson, Paul Wernert, Hugo Obermaier,[5] and Miles C. Burkitt—the same international research team with whom he was to delight to be associated later. Nelson, from the American Museum of Natural History in New York, has fortunately kept two fine snapshots taken—one by Obermaier and the other by Burkitt—in front of the Castillo cavern. In the first, Teilhard, seated in his shirtsleeves at the far left of the group, is holding a pickaxe as if he were about to dig with it; only the clerical hat, pushed to the back of his head, distinguishes him from a layman. The second is of a lunch party at the entrance to the cave, a spot which Obermaier had solemnly christened an inn, and designated "Zur Kröte"—"At the Sign of the Toad". Here Teilhard, in profile, looks thoughtful; Breuil, enthusiastic.

Teilhard, it seems, was always a little shy in the presence of Breuil, though not so much as to be kept from vigorously disputing questions of science with him, nor from choosing him, finally, as his intimate confidant.

A single reminiscence of Teilhard on this Spanish expedition survives, in a letter from Burkitt:

I excavated at the cave of Castillo in Northern Spain in 1912 and thereabouts and for some time Teilhard was with us. He was a fascinating person and full of life. Hugo Obermaier directed the "digs" and there were frequently Germans in the party, but the language spoken was French. I had no English books with me and began to find the continual foreign language tiring, so I went one day into Santander to get some English literature. The only book in the shop was Zola's *Lourdes*; Teilhard found me reading the volume and was furious! I explained it all to him but he said he would only let me continue reading it if I promised to visit Lourdes as soon as the season's "dig" was concluded, with a letter from himself to the *bureau de constatation*—note that at that time I was 22 years of age and a Protestant Englishman—I promised and of course went to Lourdes and was very interested and grateful to Teilhard. . . .

I don't know whether the little story interests you. It is all in character with his keen, vivid personality. My wife, who met him much later, wishes me to say how struck she was by his well-bred

---

[5] He is later called "H.O." in the correspondence. This German priest was a great friend of Breuil and specialized in the prehistoric archaeology of Spain. He was later a colleague of Breuil at the Institut de Paléontologie Humaine. He became professor at Madrid.

courtesy of manner. This fine courtesy was somehow deeply rooted in his personality and was that of the Christian mystic and gentleman combined.

This Spanish expedition was Teilhard's introduction to prehistory. His interest was sharpened by the now notorious "case of the *Eoanthropus*".

The story of the Piltdown Man began in 1912, when Charles Dawson, a local solicitor, and amateur archaeologist and geologist, arrived at the Natural History Museum in London with a certain number of specimens, which he entrusted to Sir Arthur Smith-Woodward, curator of the Museum's geology department. Among these specimens were some thick fragments of human cranial bone, chocolate-brown in colour, some hippopotamus teeth, and certain elephant fossils, along with some crude flint tools. They had been found, Dawson said, by some gravel-diggers at Barkham Manor, Piltdown, not far from Uckfield, in Sussex. The gravel had been deposited on that spot by a long-vanished river. Woodward agreed to accompany Dawson in late May and June of that year in making excavations at the site.

Upon excavating, they turned up further specimens: a fragment of a lower jawbone, simian in appearance, bearing two teeth; some other skull fragments; several teeth and bones of fossil animals; several flint tools; and, later, a remarkable implement fashioned out of bone. Then in August, 1913, there turned up an eyetooth, simian in appearance like the fossil found the year before, but with characteristic marks of wear associated not with the teeth of the large modern anthropoids, but with those of men. Finally, in 1915 the remains of a second Piltdown Man, or *Eoanthropus Dawsoni*, were reported to have come from a spot about two miles from the original site.

There would be no point in rehearsing the controversies which divided the world of science on the question of this astonishing discovery. The principal adversaries among the scientists were Smith-Woodward, who maintained that the ape jaw and the human skull belonged to the same individual, and Marcellin Boule, who insisted that they were parts of two individuals and that the ape jaw belonged, indeed, to an ape. Subsequent discoveries in Java, China, and South Africa could only (and with good reason) render *Eoanthropus* still more unclassifiable and baffling.

More recently (1949–55) the riddle of Piltdown Man was finally solved, in England, thanks to present-day techniques (and especially by analysis of the percentage of fluorine in the different pieces). The jaw of *Eoanthropus* is that of a modern orang-utan, with teeth artificially filed to simulate the wear characteristic of human teeth, and with a fossil-like colour imparted by dye. The skull pieces are human, and ancient, to be sure, but were smuggled from another site, were artificially dyed with iron oxide, and date back no further than the Neolithic period. As for the implement carved out of bone, the carving is revealed to have been done with a steel knife.

Dawson died before the hoax was exposed, and it is not clear what part he played nor what other persons were concerned. Teilhard met him by chance in the spring or summer of 1909 and the two became friends. Later, Teilhard worked with both Dawson and Smith-Woodward at Piltdown. He did not assist at the finding of the famous jawbone, but in August of 1913, after several courses under Marcellin Boule, he went back to England, stayed overnight at Lewes, and accompanied Dawson and Smith-Woodward on a tour of Piltdown to visit the site of the second find, where on Saturday 30 August he found one of the eyeteeth.[6]

It is not surprising that Teilhard should have been deceived. He had not yet graduated, and it was natural for him to have confidence in so eminent a scientist as Smith-Woodward. Later, when he had made his name in palaeontology, he always felt uneasy about the "Dawn Man", to whose name he always added a question mark or the epithet "puzzling". To Oakley, who finally unmasked *Eoanthropus*, Teilhard wrote, 28 November 1953, the following letter of congratulation (in English):

> I congratulate you most sincerely on your solution of the Piltdown problem. Anatomically speaking, *"Eoanthropus"* was a kind of monster. And, from a palaeontological point of view, it was equally shocking that a "dawn-Man" could occur in England. Therefore I am fundamentally pleased by your conclusions, in spite of the fact that, sentimentally speaking, it spoilt one of my brightest and earliest palaeontological memories.

August, 1914 . . . Father Teilhard was not yet called to the colours. He therefore continued his studies in science, and, after the Battle of the Marne, even began his tertianship at Canterbury. But he did

---

[6] Charles Dawson, in his article in the *Quarterly Journal of the Geological Society of London* (1913), p. 122, n. 1: commenting favourably on Teilhard's contribution.

not finish it, for the review board of December, 1914, classified him as "fit for duty". Called up almost at once and attached to the medical corps, he was sent, as he desired, to the front, where he appeared, 22 January 1915, as a stretcher-bearer in a Moroccan regiment of light infantry and Zouaves. The medical officer, Dr Salzes, himself an Auvergnat, describes his arrival:

> One morning... coming from Clermont-Ferrand, I saw, arriving by himself to serve as a regimental stretcher-bearer, a young man whose clear eyes reflected intelligence and kindliness. In order to become more "Arab" he had exchanged his field-service blue for the khaki of the African troops, and his képi for a red fez.... Such was my first meeting with Father Teilhard. (Letter to the author, 19 January 1957.)

Teilhard's regiment (the fourth combined light infantry and Zouaves) was the latest such regiment to be formed but the first to be awarded the right (for distinguished service) of wearing the red lanyard on the shoulder. General Guyot de Salins, commanding the 38th division, came to count them among his best troops.[7] In 1915 they were stationed first between the Oise and the Somme, then in the Ypres sector before taking part in the costly Champagne offensive.

Next year they distinguished themselves at Verdun; in 1918 they were in the second battle of the Marne[8] and then in the final counter-offensive, crossing, on 30 January 1919, the Kehl bridge into Germany.

Without reconstructing the details of his war career, we may note how conscious he was of the sounds and signs of war:[9]

[7] Cf. *L'histoire d'un régiment à fourragère rouge. Le 4e regiment mixte de zouaves-tirailleurs pendant la grande guerre* (Bizerta: Imprimerie française, 1919).

[8] Cf. letter of 8 April 1918: "I will not hide from you that to arrive in a region of complete panic is most disagreeable. It was tragic and moving to turn back the stream of fugitives toward an enemy who seemed to be advancing like an irresistible wave.... I have again seen villages in ruins that had been inhabited four days earlier.... We are living in cellars full of potatoes and cider-barrels. The cattle wander in the fields and we trample the green wheat... and this is not in Bocheland!"

[9] Nant-le-Grand, 14 October 1916; Ménil-sur-Saulx, 25 November 1916; Beaulieu-les-Fontaines (Oise), 13 August 1917; Mourmelon-le-Grand, Epiphany, 1918; Vertus, 15 January 1918; Strasbourg, Epiphany, 1919; Goldscheuer, Baden, 21 February 1919. The history of the regiment can fill in the gaps, as can the diaries of the medical officer, provided that one takes into consideration the individual furloughs of the parties concerned. For instance on 19 November 1917 Teilhard was in Paris.

The plain of Ypres in April 1915, when the air of Flanders reeked of chlorine, and the shells were cutting down the poplars all along the Yperlé ... the vast, silent expanse of Flanders fields, where opposing armies seem to sleep among the still waters ... the dismal slag-heaps rearing up amid the ruined mining villages.

Of Verdun he writes:

The burnt gully of Les Hauts-de-Meuse, where the heavy bursts of artillery fire wreathed the ground in smoke, as if from innumerable sulphur springs ... the stronghold, during those days of unforgettable chaos, where, amid the hurly-burly of dust and confused voices, rations, flares, and grenades were thrust hastily into the hands of the men preparing for the big attack.

And of the notorious Chemin des Dames:

Night had fallen, clear and still on this broken country of swamps and ridges. In the low places, under the poplars, still lingered the smell of the last gas attack. Higher up, on the wooded slopes, you would hear now and then the whirring, like a started woodcock's, of a descending bomb, which would burst with a sudden fleecy puff shot with fire. Yet through it all the concert of the crickets never ceased. ...

I had climbed at twilight up the hill from which you could look back at the sector we had just left, and which we should no doubt be soon climbing again. Ahead of me, across the now misting meadows, where you could still see the milky foam on the bends of the Aisne, the stripped ridge of Le Chemin-des-Dames stood out, clean as a whistle, against the gold and dappled sunset sky over Drachen. At long intervals you would see the swirl of silent smoke sent up by a mine. (*La nostalgie du front*, 1917.)

Although warfare hardly lends itself to intellectual pursuits, Teilhard got through a surprising amount of work. When not on duty, he filled whole notebooks in his quick, neat, handwriting; in spite of fatigue and surroundings ill suited to concentration he was already developing the richness and subtlety of his thought. From the same time, dates his friendship with the Bégouën brothers, both deeply interested in prehistory;[10] he completed a draft, too, of an

---

[10] On 5 September 1940, he spoke of them in a long letter (otherwise in English) as *"de vraies perles"*; cf. the testimony of Max H. Bégouën in the June, 1955, issue of *La table ronde*. In the period between the two wars Teilhard was an intimate friend of the Bégouën household and a frequent visitor at 6, rue Raynouard, Paris.

essay on the geological sections of the Thanetian deposits which he observed in the trenches near Rheims (where he gathered specimens, never suspecting that across no-man's-land the Germans in their dugouts were also picking up specimens to be sent to Munich for study by Max Schlosser).

"You gave me your mud, and of it I made gold", said Baudelaire of Paris, and so of the mud of the trenches Teilhard, too, made gold, for he had the supernatural gift of drawing from inanimate things and living things the nourishment by which he lived increasingly for God. The sight of ruins made him think less of the destruction of a venerable past and of centuries-old ways of life than of the chance to make all things new, to escape from the rut, and to save oneself from the passion for heirlooms: "As if any larger order had ever arisen save from the ruins of some smaller order!"[11] This was not insensitivity—Teilhard steeled himself against his natural distress—but the desire to turn his face towards a future more fair, in which being would take ascendancy over the passion for *having*.

He soon became known as a man who could be relied on in a difficult or dangerous situation. Persuaded that death is only a change of state, he would go out calmly to bring back the wounded under a hail of bullets. Though he came back from the war without a scratch, there was one time, on the eve of the battle of Douaumont, that he had a presentiment of death and that his body was doomed to a resting place in the wilderness.

Here is a first-hand account of one of his adventures. The episode took place in August, 1916, at the height of the battle of Verdun, in the Fleury-Ravin des Vignes sector:

> Word came to Lieutenant-Colonel Vernois that Captain Courtiaux was missing. It seemed likely that he had perished under German machine-gun fire, if he had not been blown to bits by a shell. Courtiaux, in civilian life, had been a secondary-school teacher in Tunis; we found him an excellent comrade, gentlemanly and courageous. Although an atheist he got on well with Teilhard. The Colonel, who wanted to make sure of Courtiaux's fate, and to retrieve his body if possible, gave orders for a search party, to be made up of volunteers. Teilhard, hearing of this, came to the Colonel to ask as a special favour to be allowed to go out alone and so spare a search patrol the risk. The Colonel hesitated at first, but finally agreed. While there was still light, they

---

[11] *La grande monade* (1918).

noted the spot where Courtiaux must have fallen—almost right in front of a German machine-gun post.

When it was dark, about ten it must have been, Teilhard crawled out on the field. Next morning, when you could just see light, he was back again, with the body of Courtiaux on his back. Our lines (if more or less connected shell-holes can be called lines) can't have been much more than two or three hundred yards from the Germans.[12]

His bravery won him a number of citations, the Croix de Guerre and Médaille Militaire.[13] About a year after his return to civilian life, 16 June 1920, he was made Chevalier of the Legion of Honour, upon a proposal sent by his former regiment and approved by all grades of command.

On 15 May 1915 he was promoted Corporal. The medical officer in command of his section described the special position that Teilhard won for himself:

I found my original impression of him was confirmed. . . . I had him posted a supernumerary stretcher-bearer, with rank of corporal; as such he was not confined to any one section. In billets, in the line, during operations, he was completely free to do his work as he thought best. (Letter to the author, 19 January 1957.)

When, however, General Guyot de Salins wished to appoint Teilhard chaplain to the 38th Division, with the rank of captain, he declined, urging that he was more useful in the ranks, where he could do more good. "Leave me," he said, "among the men."

He was popular with both officers and men. Since most of the men were Moslems, the section had no official chaplain, and Teilhard added this work to his own. In the army, his goodness, simplicity, and humility were as noticeable as his courage. One day when a certain stretcher-bearer was sentenced to pack-drill, it was Teilhard who interceded for him. In the trenches, of course, he shared the lot of the troops, and on marches insisted on shouldering his pack. Once, when they were moving camp, the major, walking along and chatting at his side, noticed that Teilhard seemed fatigued and suggested he put his pack on one of the wagons, if only until

---

[12] An account given by Lieutenant Jacquemot.
[13] On 29 August 1916, he was cited in divisional orders and on 17 September 1916, Army orders; cf. also *Journal officiel* of 2 May 1921. The Croix de Guerre was awarded on 1 September 1915 and the Médaille Militaire on 24 June 1917.

the next halt. Teilhard refused absolutely: "A corporal doesn't give a bad example."

True enough; but was it not the priest and Jesuit rather than the corporal who was answering? The number who received his spiritual ministrations was countless. He knew how to talk with soldiers, and knew just what to do and just what to say, at the proper time, to cheer up the men on duty. The way they addressed him reflected their respect for him. It was always "Monsieur Teilhard". As for the Moslems, who trusted him similarly, and for whom he was "le sidi Marabout" they sought his advice, and they wanted him near them when they were dying.

Lieutenant Jacquemot has preserved for us the memory of a Mass celebrated by Father Teilhard:

> We had just taken over the line (the front) opposite Nieuport-Ville, exactly in front of Lombaertzyde-Passchendaele—well into Flanders. Anyone acquainted with this part of Belgium knows that it presents the most uninvitingly swampy ground. It was impossible to dig a trench of any kind, because when you went a foot or two down you had water. The whole line, therefore, was constructed of sandbags filled with earth, which had to be dug from pretty far to the rear on account of the mud at the front.... Our makeshift shelters, pieced together with planks, logs, and whatever else could be found, could not offer more than three feet or so above ground to enemy fire. It was in one of these rat-infested shelters that Teilhard, upon the request of several Frenchmen with me, agreed to say a Mass for our families. This, if my memory serves, was in the beginning of January in 1916—about the 5th or 6th. Because it was impossible to stand upright in so low a structure, the celebrant had to say Mass—and we to hear it —kneeling down; there were six of us there all told. As Teilhard was replacing in his little case the vessels and vestments he had used at Mass, the Germans sent a hail of shells down on our sector. Not a one of us was touched by the bursts; Teilhard, in a calm and serious voice, said, "I had still my blessing to give you. God being with us, did not wish one of us to be hit." With that he gave us his blessing and returned to his aid post.

War served as his tertianship.[14] On 26 May 1918 at Sainte-Foy-lès-Lyon, Teilhard was allowed to take his solemn vows. One of his superiors was opposed to his doing so, but the other stood warranty

---

[14] A Jesuit spends two years as a novice. A third year is spent, after ordination, in a somewhat similar way, as a "tertian", before taking final vows.

for the soldier-priest. We happen to know, from a confidential source, with what full deliberation Teilhard pronounced these vows. When asked in what frame of mind he did so, he made answer in some such words as these: I am making a vow of poverty; never have I more clearly realized to what extent money can be a powerful means for the service and glorification of God. I am making a vow of chastity; never have I understood so well how a husband and wife complete each other in order better to advance towards God. I am making a vow of obedience; never have I better understood what liberation there is in God's service.

Had you not, he was asked, some little anxiety in making your vows? No, he answered, not even momentary misgivings; I placed my trust in God, certain that he would grant me the grace to do his will in my life as a religious and to be faithful to my vows.

Three passages from Teilhard's works offer a valuable commentary on these words; the first, written at the time of his profession, is the most significant.

> Lord, I dream of seeing extracted from the quantities of unused or misused richness all the power which they contain. To collaborate in this effort, that is the work to which I wish to consecrate myself. So far as my strength serves me, because I am a priest, I wish to be the first to be aware of what the world loves, and pursues, and suffers; the first to seek, to sympathize, to grieve; the first to offer myself and sacrifice myself, and to be more broadly human, more nobly of this world, than any of those who serve the world.
>
> I wish, on the one hand, to immerse myself in things, and by making them my own to wrest from them the last particle of whatever they contain of eternal life, "so that nothing may be wasted" (John 6. 13). And on the other hand I wish, by the practice of the evangelical counsels, to recover—by the very renouncement of them—whatever of the heavenly flame is contained in the three concupiscences, and to sanctify—in chastity, poverty, and obedience—the power contained in love, gold, and independence. That is why I have renewed both my vows and my priesthood in a spirit of acceptance and divinization of the Powers of the Earth; there lies my strength and my happiness.[15]

We may say, then, that Teilhard took his final vows with complete understanding, with perfect knowledge of the spiritual

---

[15] *Le Prêtre* (1918), obviously written on the occasion of these solemn vows.

potentialities contained in human love, in money and in free research, and with an unwavering will—thanks to total communion
with Christ—to reclaim these values by means of chastity, poverty,
and obedience.

The liberty he enjoyed in his life as a scientist and explorer
allowed him, in fact, to rise to those mysterious and unexplored
heights which are to be traced in *La messe sur le monde* (1923), *Le
milieu divin* (1926–7), and *Le Christique* (1955); and he often had
the opportunity to set forth—even to boards of directors—the nature
of the social and religious value of money:

> We may declare first of all that gold is something very beautiful
> in itself, something sacred, even. Why so? Because everywhere it
> represents, to human beings, material energy in an easily handled
> form. Gold, then, equals oil, or coal, or art, or books, or a library.
> It is, therefore, both the symbol and the medium of exchange of
> all these articles, and is thus the elementary factor of our economy.
> And so long as it is this, it is something wonderful.
> And yet the more it can do, the more wonderful it is, the more,
> too . . . does it require caution. Gold, which is blameless so long
> as it is busy in service and so long as it helps along the current of
> humanity, becomes corrupt as soon as it stands still. It is lack of
> motion that makes gold—a thing good in itself—first fester and
> then infect other things. The moment that a man arrests this
> energy to make it serve himself, or turns it aside from its normal
> flow—the moment that one renders it stagnant—it corrupts and
> becomes evil. . . . To abuse riches, to hoard riches, to make bad
> use of riches—this, I say, is not only a sin of injustice against your
> neighbour in need, but a sin against mankind, since for its proper
> life and development humanity has need of this material means
> in order to produce the spiritual. . . .[16]

On the subject of chastity Teilhard wrote:

> . . . Virginity is an advance upon chastity as consciousness is
> upon life.
> . . . At the present time physical union still has its value—indeed
> its necessity—for the race. But it is already creating and nourish-
> ing a type of higher union in which its spiritual quality will
> henceforth find realization. Love is in the process of undergoing
> a metamorphosis within the noosphere. And this process is a step
> towards the collective approach of the human to the divine.
> That is how I see the evolution of chastity. Such a transforma-

[16] A lecture to the Légaut group, at Chadefaud, 27 November 1930.

tion of love is possible—theoretically. It will be accomplished once the call of the divine, personal, centre is felt so strongly that it masters natural attraction.

What paralyses life is the failure to believe and the failure to dare. What is difficult is not solving problems, but formulating them; as we see it now, harnessing passion to make it serve the spirit must—on biological evidence—be a condition of progress. Therefore, sooner or later, despite our incredulity, the world will take that step. For everything that is more true does come about, and everything that is better is finally achieved. Some day, after mastering the winds, the waves, the tides, and gravity, we shall harness—for God—the energies of love. And then, for the second time in the history of the world, man will have discovered fire.[17]

Teilhard was demobilized on 10 March 1919. By Easter he was in Paris, and in August and September of the same year, on the island of Jersey, he was getting both work and rest, both contact with young people and solitude. He was working for his degree in natural sciences at the Sorbonne. Together with Pierre Lamare he attended Hérouard's and Robert's courses there, as well as special courses for those just released from service. In July of 1919 he passed the examination for the certificate of geology with a grade of "good"; the outcome in botany (October, 1919) and in zoology (19 March 1920) was less impressive. For though he attempted to apply the rule for Jesuit students which enjoins them to bring to their studies a burning desire for success (without, of course, any complacency in such success), Teilhard, who had already advanced to the research stage, was tired of such schoolboy tasks. Under the mentorship of his later friend Alfred Lacroix,[18] and with the encouragement of Pierre Termier he went back to Marcellin Boule at the Museum. It was then that he began his friendship with Paul Rivet, later founder of the Musée de l'Homme. Rivet, as soon as he was out of the service, conceived the idea of resuming relations with the Germans in the field of science. As he later wrote:

My very first visit was to the great Professor Marcellin Boule, who met the disclosure of my new plan with violent opposition (nor unfortunately, was he to be the only one to do so). So out of

[17] *L'évolution de la chasteté* (February, 1934).
[18] Lacroix was Professor of Mineralogy at the Museum in Paris; cf. letter of 19 June 1926, to Lacroix: "I do not forget your laboratory which in my memories makes up, together with just a few other rare spots, a place 'of election' where I have always felt happy."

countenance was I that I did not really notice a priest who was in the room but said nothing. But scarcely was I back in my own laboratory when there was someone at the door: it was the priest —Father Teilhard—bent on telling me at once of his perfect agreement with me. We fell to talking.... On that day there began a great friendship that has endured unclouded these thirty-five years.[19]

The Abbé Bremond has an interesting anecdote of this period:

When Barrès was shown our venerable ancestors in the Museum, he was visibly impressed, and, turning to Boule, his guide, he asked among other things what effect such startling discoveries might have upon religious belief in France. For answer, Boule simply smiled and pointed to a young Jesuit— it was Teilhard de Chardin—quietly making himself at home among these relics. It was going to take more than this to upset Revelation.[20]

Since Easter, 1920, Teilhard had been busy with his doctoral thesis, on the mammals of the Lower Eocene period in France and the deposits of these uncovered in the trenches at Rheims;[21] this thesis, handed in on 5 July, 1921, he was to defend successfully on 22 March, 1922, before an unusually large audience, and to the complete satisfaction of the examining board.[22] Boule, as a matter of fact, had shrewdly advised him to study the very fine material that had been got together by an elderly Rheims physician, Dr Victor

[19] France Observateur (21 April 1955), p. 17.
[20] H. J. and A. Bremond, Le charme d'Athènes et autres essais (Paris: Bloud & Gay, 1925).
[21] In a letter of 4 July 1920, he speaks of "my present modus studendi which involves being away from home from nine in the morning till six in the evening"; and a letter of 21 June 1921 states more specifically: "All my energy goes into field- or laboratory-work."
[22] The thesis was reported on by E. Haug, 3 July 1921. The eminent geologist had had the work in his hands since March. His analysis was most laudatory: "M. Pierre Teilhard de Chardin is no newcomer to palaeontology. ... The work of M. Teilhard ... from the importance of results obtained, does him the greatest credit and deserves, in consequence, permission to be printed." He added: "The defence only confirmed the excellent impression formed from reading the manuscript. The way in which the questions making up the second thesis were handled evidenced the professor's qualifications and the candidate's mental lucidity. The latter is certainly destined for a fine scientific future. The jury did not hesitate a moment in granting him the title of doctor with very honourable mention."
On Teilhard's first three major palaeontological publications, see the excellent notice by J. Piveteau in Bulletin de la Société Géologique de France (6th ser.), vol. 7, no. 6 (1957), pp. 788–90.

Lemoine, and deposited at the Muséum; this did not, of course, excuse the young scientist from field-work. A letter of 20 June 1920, speaks of his work in the sand-pits.

I have been putting in a good seven to eight hours every day on some digging I am doing three or four miles from here, and have been at it so hard that when I come home at night I have just one idea—sleep. Now you are not to think that some desperate need of money has led me to seek this employment; it is simply some excavating I am doing in the mountain of Berru, getting material for my dissertation ... yesterday I finished my search for small fossil teeth of Eocene mammals, so that I can now go back to Paris.[23]

This was Teilhard's third major project, the first two having been devoted to the Carnivora and Primates of the phosphorite beds of Le Quercy. At the same time he was keeping up and extending his contacts abroad. In August of 1920 we find him in England, excited at being shown the new fragment of cranium and the new fossil tooth "found" at Piltdown in 1915. In the early part of 1921 he first got in touch with the scientist Stehlin of Basle. He visited him at Basle on 7 or 8 August 1922, and was never to forget the warm welcome he received. In the same month he attended the Congress in Brussels, where he met Wong, co-director of the Chinese Geological Service.

Still another scholar abroad, the Englishman H. Plymen, had expressed admiration of Teilhard's *Notes on the Structure of the*

[23] This was not his only work in the field. We note, for example, a trip to Chelles on 13 March 1921; a journey from Épernay as far as Viz and Mont-Aimé on 21 June; the visit to Niaux on 6 September with Abbé Breuil and Dorothy Garrod, a student of Professor Sollas at Oxford. Miss Garrod became a fine prehistorian (excavations at Gibraltar and in Palestine) and taught at Cambridge. Recently converted to Roman Catholicism, she was at that time given to scruple and inquietude, and Père Teilhard was to do her much good in sending her the text of *Le milieu divin*. In 1922 Teilhard went to Ariège to visit the grottoes of Count Bégouën. On 31 July 1922 he was at La Fléchière, Thonon, Upper Savoy.

Hardly had he received his doctorate when he was awarded the Prix Viquesnel by the Société Géologique de France, of which he had been a member since 1912. Until the end of 1927 he remained an active member. From 1922 onwards he published book reviews in *L'anthropologie* and sent some communications to the Société d'anthropologie (21 March 1923; 17 March 1926). On 17 October 1924, he was elected a member of the Société de biogéographie to which, on 20 November 1925, he sent a note on the antiquity of certain components of continental fauna. In 1923 the Académie des Sciences awarded him the Prix Roux.

Island of Jersey, published in 1920, and offering an explanation of
the tectonics of that island. And an American, Granger (of the
American Museum), had met Teilhard in 1920. He showed Granger
the fossil remains of a very small Tarsioid. Since the origins of man
now occupied Teilhard's attention, he was interested in the hypothesis of the Tarsus group as containing distant ancestors of man,
and, drawn as he was to the problem of origins, he was by way of
becoming the chief European specialist in primitive types.[24] Another
new acquaintance was the Abbé Gaudefroy, an eminent mineralogist who had been a seminary friend of the Abbé Breuil's. It was
in fact Breuil who insisted that the two meet. Gaudefroy hesitated
but finally let himself be persuaded and followed Breuil up the
stairs to the top floor of 13 rue du Vieux-Colombier. Breuil, having
made the introductions, slipped away. Gaudefroy could hardly wait
to say, bluntly, that he mistrusted Jesuits, who he understood were
a secret society, with a rule they showed no one, and whose mail
was opened by their superiors.

Teilhard, with his characteristic laugh, pulled open a drawer on
the left side of his desk, pointed to the *Regulae Societatis Jesu*, and
said, "Look, here is my rule; I have no other," the gesture convinced
Gaudefroy, and the two developed a mutual trust.

This meeting with Gaudefroy had two effects upon Teilhard's
life. In 1919 Gaudefroy had been named to the Institut Catholique,
for the chair formerly held by the great geologist Albert de Lapparent, and now, appropriately, held by Lapparent's grand-nephew.
Gaudefroy, however, was a mineralogist, not a geologist (and among
specialists the two fields are considered rather widely separated).
He therefore asked that the chair be divided, and that he take
mineralogy for himself (it is still there on the ground floor of the
Institut Catholique), and Teilhard take geology (first and second
floors). His proposal was adopted, and from 1920 to 1923 Teilhard
taught at the Institut Catholique.[25] This was in the early days of
the Institute and there were not many students studying science; his

[24] His thesis was a decisive landmark in his connections with the United
States, in that he minutely compared the Mammalia of the French Lower
Eocene with the American Mammalia of the Palaeocene, which had just been
completely reclassified.

[25] Cf. letter of 20 June 1920: "It is probable that in the coming year I will
be assistant lecturer in palaeontology and geology at the Institut Catholique."
Some days later he was admitted to the staff. After the defence of his thesis,
Teilhard became a lecturer in geology at the École des Sciences.

1. Teilhard de Chardin at the age of five
From a pastel drawing in the Château de Sarcenat

2. Teilhard at the age of fourteen

Dressed in the uniform of the Collège de Mongré, with his two brothers Gabriel and Olivier. Photograph taken in the courtyard of the family house at Clermont-Ferrand

influence, therefore, was not widely felt. Two of his students, however, recall the deep impression he made on them:

> I was a student, in 1921 and 1922, of Father Teilhard de
> Chardin's. I still have a clear memory of his astonishingly lively
> and lucid teaching, which he made even more lively by proposing
> ideas which puzzled us and thus kept our curiosity awake.
> ... with a teacher like Teilhard everything became clear; and
> his fervour so enkindled our own that it happened sometimes that
> a class that started at five in the afternoon would end at eight
> or nine. During that time he would have given us a unified view
> of the whole Carboniferous period, without our feeling at any
> moment that we were getting out of our depth. In another way,
> the impression on the mind and heart, I feel that few of his
> students failed to be affected.

A second result of the meeting with Gaudefroy was the connection he formed with Gaudefroy's friend the Abbé Portal, a Lazarist
interested in student groups. Portal invited Teilhard to address a
number of students from the École Normale Supérieure, who
responded by asking for him again, year after year, as various groups
of students from the École Polytechnique were already doing,
captivated by the clarity and boldness of his thought.[26] The botanist
R. Franquet remembers hearing him preach to Catholic engineering
students a series of sermons of sustainedly high spirituality, out of
the ordinary, and not always easy to follow. We cannot sufficiently
insist upon the priestly activities of Teilhard, who, if he loved
science, worked at it in silence and humility as the means, above
all, to an effective apostolate.[27]

But it was Breuil who brought together Teilhard and Édouard
Le Roy, the distinguished professor at the Collège de France, as
proved by a note dated 19 October 1921.

[26] Cf. the letter of 16 March 1921: "My two principal resources ... are conversations with some friends (especially Doncœur and Abbé Breuil) and a
series of talks to engineers and to the students from the École Polytechnique
of Père Pupey-Girard—talks which force me to be precise and to adapt (to
external use) the aspirations that you know."

[27] Cf. letter of 26 May, 1925: "There is no need for me to tell you that
geology has a minor rôle, basically, in the begetting of this Gospel in me. I
need a contact with the Real to animate me and to nourish me—work with
the Real, too, so that I may participate in the 'human effort' and practise what
I preach, the alliance between Man and Christian. Geology has been this to
me. But I believe that any other experience would have had the same results
for me."

2*

Sir,

My friend M. l'Abbé Breuil has recently spoken to me of you in terms that have awakened my long-standing wish to meet you. If some day you have a few moments when we might exchange a certain number of ideas, I should be truly obliged to hear from you ...

—P. Teilhard.

Teilhard's influence was certainly beginning to spread further afield, even though he had had some doubts at first about the appointment to the Institut Catholique. He wrote:

... I should naturally have preferred a post as "prospector" at Beirut, Shanghai, or Trichinopoly, where I could get away from crowds. (Letter of 4 July 1920.)

But this regret did not last. Both as a scientist and as a priest he thought himself well placed in Paris, and considered it his duty to avail himself of the opportunities Paris afforded. The surest proof of his having taken root here was the homesickness he was always to feel for Paris, and the ease with which he resumed his apostolic activities whenever he returned there. At the same time, his connections with Belgium and with Belgian scientists continued for a long time, being hampered only by the force of circumstances. This is reflected in his published work. In 1924, we find him collaborating with L. Dollo on a note on the Palaeocene mammals of Belgium, and from 1925 to 1928 we find a variety of his papers, on the fossil mammals of Belgium, published in Belgian periodicals. Teilhard always kept up his connections with Louvain and with the *Revue des questions scientifiques*; and it is still in Belgium, both Walloon and Flemish, that his warmest admirers are to be found.

We may summarize Teilhard's adult career up to this point by dividing it into three distinct parts: first, his apprentice years as a student, teacher, and researcher; second, his war years as a stretcher-bearer, during which he seems to have arrived at a kind of self-appraisal; and third, his emergence, after the war, as a master of his profession, a period marked not only by the finishing of his doctoral studies, but also by the beginning of an intense mental activity, the first products of which were soon to appear.

It was in the period from 1912 to 1923 that matter, for Teilhard, began "to take on the tint of life", and that a series of basic spiritual discoveries began to take shape. At the same time his thought underwent fundamental change: from a belief in fixed species he became fully converted to evolutionism. Already during his years of theological studies at Hastings (1909–12) there had grown upon him, in such a way as to colour all his thoughts, his "consciousness of the radical drift, ontological and total, of the universal".

What influenced his conversion to evolutionism? His reading of Bergson's *L'Évolution créatrice* was but one occasion that made him realize where he stood, the coincidence of his own inner conviction with the need to understand the data of science, which only evolution could make intelligible. This twofold awareness blended into a single certitude.[28] Evolution, a simple hypothesis of nineteenth-century biology, revealed itself to Teilhard as a necessary condition of all scientific thought, since henceforth evolution (whatever might be the disputes among biologists about its mechanism and its modalities) was to invade and include every field, including physics, and was to dominate all cosmology. In his view, the unity of the world was of a dynamic or evolutive character, no longer an immobile cosmos, but a cosmogenesis, with everything unfolding in a biological space-time. In this Teilhard's view of evolution differed radically from Bergson's. Teilhard rejected the Bergsonian cosmos, which took the form of a *divergent* irradiation, originating at a central source, whereas his own was essentially *convergent*, and he rejected the Bergsonian idea of a vital impulse having no finality. Teilhard, although a vitalist—or, more exactly, a supporter of orthogenesis—did allow mechanisms their part (their very great part, particularly in elementary forms of life), but he credited them with only a minor role in complex forms of life—man above all— and maintained that life is, at bottom, of a psychic character.

If Teilhard's cosmology is indissolubly wedded to evolutionism, he deduced from the latter doctrine some original conclusions. By a purely apparent paradox—and in contrast with the philosophy of Herbert Spencer—his view of reality invalidated, in his mind, the hypothesis according to which the truly substantial is what is elementary and undifferentiated. The radical dualism of matter and spirit, of body and soul, dissolved before his eyes "like fog before rising sun". Matter and spirit seemed no longer two things, the latter

---

[28] On Teilhard and Bergson, see Madeleine Barthélemy-Madaule, *Bergson et Teilhard de Chardin* (Paris: Éditions du Seuil, 1963), and her article, under the same title, in *Études bergsoniennes* (Presses Universitaires de France, 1960).

reducible to the former, but two states, two aspects of one and the same cosmic "stuff". Spirit, which slowly emerges from matter, takes precedence of the physical and chemical, and it is in spirit, in the highly complex, that all substantiality, all "consistence" resides, so that to find it we must not "look backwards, to matter" but "forwards, to spirit".

This step towards "spiritualized evolution" was taken about 1914, and so coincided with Teilhard's introduction to war. From the first, life in the trenches seemed to act as a catalyst upon his mind; the first essay produced under its influence was *La vie cosmique* (24 March 1916), doubtless written in the vicinity of Nieuport. Teilhard's intention here was to voice his love of matter and of life, but in harmony with his adoration of the one, absolute, undevelopable divinity. His point of departure was the initial, basic fact that each one of us is connected by all the fibres of his being, material, organic, and psychic, with everything else around him; for the human monad, like every other monad, is essentially cosmic. He saw the problem, then, for a Christian, in these terms: Must one, in order to be united to Christ, detach one's self from the cosmic tide?

Teilhard had become convinced that the basis of our supernatural growth is not detachment from all the things that give charm and interest to our natural life. Thus we need not reject the impulses growing out of our awareness of the cosmos, provided we do not divorce from "sacred evolution" its orientation towards eternal hope and beatitude. In the section entitled "sacred Evolution" Teilhard speaks with happiness of his feeling of God's presence everywhere, of the mystic's total abandonment to God's will, and of the effort to communicate with the invisible through the visible world and so reconcile the claims of the Kingdom of God with love of the cosmos:

> Every force which moves through me, envelops me, or captivates me emanates from the divine will as its fundamental source, and, like a subtle, vital current, transmits the motion of that will. Thus every contact, whether it caresses me, pierces me, bruises me, jostles me . . . or crushes me, is a contact with one of the forms, multiple but in every case adorable, of the hand of God. God, too, is the source of all the elements of which I am constituted. By surrendering myself to the embraces of the visible and palpable universe, I can enter into communion with the invisible,

and its purifying power, and incorporate myself into the Spirit and its immaculate nature. . . . God is vibrant in the ether; and through it he penetrates to the very marrow of my material being. By the ether all material bodies are joined, influence one another, and support one another in the unity of the vast sphere whose ultimate boundary we cannot even imagine.

In life too, God is operative. He assists it, stimulates it, gives it the impulse that drives it on and provides it with the appetite that draws it and with the growth that transforms it. Thus I sense him, and touch him, and "see" him in the deep biological current that flows in my soul and carries it along. God shadows forth his being and his person in humanity, too. I bear him up when I support my fellow-man; I hear him speaking in orders from above; then again, as in a transcendent realm of the physical, I meet him and submit to the overwhelming and penetrating touch of his hand on the higher level of collective and social energies. The more deeply I descend into myself, the more conscious I am of God at the heart of my being; and the more I multiply the bonds that attach me to things, the closer does the Creator encompass me, continuing in me the work, long as the cycle of all centuries, of his Son's incarnation.

I am happy that "another girds me, and carries me where I go, not of my own will". I bless the vicissitudes, circumstances and all the turns of fortune, bright and dark, in my life. I bless my character, my virtues, my faults, my blemishes. I delight in the nature I have been given, and in what my destiny has made of it. Nay more, I strive to find and catch each slightest breeze that blows upon me, and to spread my sails wide to it. My will is that the divine will, which penetrates and fills all nature, may find my soul a monad at once transparent, pliable, and obedient.

Blessed passivities which entwine every strand of my body and my soul, sacred life, sacred matter—through which, at the same time as through grace, I am in communion with the genesis of Christ, since by surrendering myself to your vast coils I am afloat in the creative action of God, whose hand since the beginning has never ceased to mould the clay of human destiny into the Body of his Son—I swear loyalty to your domination; I surrender to you, I accept you, and I love you.[29]

[29] When he speaks of God being "personified in Humanity", he means, as the context clearly shows, that He "shines through human persons". The term "Genesis of Christ" or "Christogenesis" always means for Teilhard the begetting of the Mystical Body.

In *La vie cosmique* we find two basic ideas, one cosmological (governed by the evolutionist viewpoint), the other Christological, together with an early effort to combine the two. In fact in this early work Christ, as God-man who synthesizes all things, is already assigned a cosmic function, as is suggested in the conclusion:

> There is a communion with God, and a communion with the earth, and a communion with God through the earth.

The very title of a later essay is something of a shock: *La nostalgie du front* (September, 1917). That Teilhard could feel homesick for the ugliness and evil of the front line is explained by the fact that it was there that he was able to discover the third basic factor in his spiritual life. Until that time he had lived a sheltered, circumscribed life, at home, and as a young Jesuit, with few outside contacts. He now came up against man in the mass and realized that he was spiritually one with a wider humanity, a collective entity with riches past and future. This partial loss of individuality gave him an entrancing sense of a new freedom.

Moreover, the experience brought to him, as a priest, the revelation that, higher than the care of single souls, there is a universal function to be fulfilled, the offering to God of the entire world.

Teilhard had an exceptionally acute cosmic sense, an awareness, that is, of the solidarity of the cosmos and the ability to perceive the organic relationship that holds together the "molecular" structure of humanity. With this went the faculty of sympathizing with the masses. This is expressed in a passage written about New Year 1918, when the sight of the full moon rising over the barbed wire seemed to him a symbol of the earth endowed with thought, a first indication of his later concept of the noosphere:

> I have just been watching the moon rise over the crest of the nearby trenches. The timid slim crescent of earlier evenings has gradually grown to a full and shining disc. Solitary and majestic, the moon, which a fortnight before had been invisible, disengaged itself from the ridges of black soil, and seemed to glide across the barbed wire. In this shining body that hangs in the heavens I greet a new symbol . . . is it the moon that rises over the dark trenches this evening, or is it the earth, a unified earth, a new earth?

Although the spiritual significance of this period in Teilhard's life lay in his introduction to evolution and his new awareness of man, it would be a mistake to regard it as no more than his years of apprenticeship. His writing was already of sufficient importance to attract the attention of Maurice Blondel.

With Blondel I had been in touch (through Auguste Valensin) for about a year (soon after World War I, around 1920).[30] Certain features of his thought had certainly had their effect on me: the value of action (which became for me a quasi-experimental energetics of the biological forces of evolution), and the notion of pan-Christhood (at which I had arrived independently, without daring at the time, to name it so appropriately). (15 February 1955.)

But these contacts through an intermediary were to be inconclusive. The two men were not in accord on the nature of the supernatural; and Blondel did not share Teilhard's cosmic sense, much less Teilhard's notion of a universe in a state of cosmogenesis.

Some of Teilhard's writings at this time were brief essays in ontology; they were rough hewn, and the thought was sometimes incomplete, abstract, and uneven. Nevertheless, underneath this thin veneer of scholasticism an extremely original mind was at work, and we find the germ of a number of his more important themes. For instance, just as in the view of twentieth-century physicists matter is no longer an absolute, but merely a function of its own rate of motion, so, in Teilhard's view, *being* is no longer the fundamental concept, yielding its place to *uniting*. Creation, then, he considered above all an act of union; and it is this union that produces being. This idea was to underlie his whole metaphysics, as was still evident in 1948 in *Comment je vois*. To this same period belong some valuable meditations on the role of the priest and on "the mystic milieu", important as closely presaging *La messe sur le monde* (1923) and *Le milieu divin* (1926–7). In one of these we see the priest of today conceived as one who lives on a more intense level, a man whose burning ardour helps the layman to rediscover the sacramental significance of the universe:

Every priest, because he is a priest, has consecrated his life to the work of universal salvation. If he is conscious of his station, he must live no longer for himself but for the world, after the example of Him whom he is anointed to represent.

For me, Jesus, I feel that this duty has a more pressing urgency and a sharper significance than for many others who are much

[30] These contacts began in December, 1919, and afterwards never completely ceased; cf. letter of 13 October 1925.

better than I.... I should wish, Lord, in my very humble way, to be the apostle and, if I may ask so much, the evangelist of your *Christ in the Universe*. I should wish, by my thoughts, by my words, by the whole activity of my life, to bring to light and preach the continuousness that makes of the cosmos an all-embracing medium that is divinized by the incarnation, that divinizes by inter-communion, and is divinizable by our co-operation.

To bring Christ, by virtue of strictly organic connections, into the heart of realities that are considered the most fraught with danger, the least supernatural, the most pagan—such is my gospel and such my mission. Would not the reconciliation of our age with God be effected, if men were to see in themselves and in one another a part of the fullness of Christ? If they were to understand that the universe, with all its natural opulence and all its exciting reality, does not reach its full development save in Christ? And that Christ, for his part, does not reach full stature save through a universe pushed to the very limits of its potentialities? ... To those who are enthralled by the rich treasures the real offers, and overwhelmed by its immediacy, I should like to reveal the life of our Lord Jesus permeating all things, a veritable world-soul.

To those awed by the nobility of human effort, I should like to point out, on the authority of Christ, that men's work is sacred —made sacred by the purpose which it subjects to God, and by virtue of the tremendous task which, endlessly searching for the right road, it is accomplishing: the natural and supernatural liberation of the spiritual.

Those who are diffident, timid, undeveloped, or narrow in their religion, I should like to remind that Christ requires for his body the full development of man, and that mankind, therefore, has a duty to the created world and to truth—namely, the ineluctable duty of *research*.[31]

Sometimes Teilhard set down half-poetic, half-religious fancies, containing, however, clearly authentic philosophical intuitions, and thus useful as source-material to professional philosophers. Teilhard, however, was not a mystic who, out of modesty, presented his visions under the disguise of literature. His *Trois histoires comme Benson* are an exact depiction of things he himself experienced and understood. Such were two experiences he describes as follows:

You have often seen, at night, stars that can throw now a dart of red, now a dart of blue. You have seen too, the iridescence on

[31] *Le Prêtre* (1918).

the surface of a bubble.... In the same way, with a kind of indescribable shimmering, there played upon the changeless face of Jesus the brilliancies of all our beauties. I know not whether this came about through my wishing it, or by the disposition of Him who caused me to wish it. All I know is that all these changing aspects of majesty, of mildness, of irresistible attractiveness, succeeding one another, changing, and melting into one another, were wedded in a harmony which I found utterly gratifying.... And always, beneath this opalescent surface, supporting it, and binding it into one sovereign tonal unity, there streamed the incommunicable beauty of Christ.... This shining burst of all loveliness was so complete, so overwhelming, so amazing that my being, searched out and penetrated in all its faculties, at once thrilled to its very lowest notes in a diapason of triumph and of incomparable bliss.

In the third of the *Trois histoires* Teilhard has just uncovered the Blessed Sacrament and received Holy Communion:

I then summoned to my aid all my resources of recollection. I concentrated on the divine particle all the silence and love of which I was capable, I made myself limitlessly humble, tractable, pliant as a child so that I might not oppose in any way the slightest desires of the heavenly guest, that I might make myself indistinguishable from him, perfectly one, through obedience, with my limbs governed by his soul. Unrelentingly I cleansed my heart, to make my interior finally transparent to the light I harboured within me.

And still I fell short of this blessed goal.

Never could I overtake the host in concentration and quickening of desire, in the openness of my being to divine influences, in the purity of my affections.... By the abasement and continuous purification of my being I advanced further into it, as a stone drops into an abyss, but without ever reaching the bottom. Small as was the host, I was lost in it, without ever being able to grasp it, much less to fill it. Its centre, while drawing me on and on, was forever fleeing me.

The form of the *Trois histoires comme Benson* is of an unusual beauty, for in them he is the poet at once of earth, fire, and light. He takes anything as a starting point—a lamp of his cousin's, or one of those Saint-Sulpice pictures of the Sacred Heart—and proceeds to transfigure it. The lamp becomes the terrestrial globe, lighted by the translucent Christ; the Heart of Jesus (a childhood devotion that grew with him) flames out, shines forth, projects its rays into the darkest corners of matter, which is transformed thus into an immense Mount Thabor.

His quality as a poet is shown in the astonishing rhythms of *Le puissance spirituelle de la matière* (1919), *La messe sur le monde* (1923), certain passages in *Le cœur de la matière* (1950), and *En regardant un cyclotron* (1953). His lyric works rank with the finest of the world's religious poetry.

The inspiration of Teilhard's poetry was threefold: mystical, derived from the cosmic Christ revealed by St Paul; epic, derived from a palaeontologist's familiarity with the vast story of man, his origins, and the origin of the universe in which he lives; and finally eschatological, derived from his semi-prophetic view of man's future. We may think of him as continuing the great line of Hebrew prophets, as a Pascal freed from Jansenism and with no fear of the silence of infinite space, or as a Lucretius without the crude materialism of the *De Rerum Natura*.

His poetic talent was accompanied by the power to handle abstract ideas and construct a solidly framed argument. His thought, particularly in his early and late periods, was necessarily abstract, close-packed, difficult, at times almost cryptic, and expressed in a highly personal vocabulary. Under this complex exterior burned a volcano, which gave vigour and richness to his work, as the hot streams of lava enrich the grapes and olives that grow on the slopes of Vesuvius.

CHAPTER THREE

First Period in Tientsin
(1923–4)
Paris Interlude
(1924–6)

O N 13 August 1922, Fr Émile Licent wrote from the banks of
the Shara-Osso-Gol, in the great loop of the Yellow River,
inviting Teilhard to join him there. As a result, in 1923,
Teilhard was sent from the Institut Catholique with a subsidy from
the Museum to assist in excavations in central China. That year
marked a decisive turning point in his spiritual evolution, and
opened the longest and most fertile period of his life as a scientist.

Licent was a Jesuit of the Lille province. From his childhood he
had been an enthusiastic natural historian. After entering the
Jesuits at an early age, he had undergone his training as a religious
and pursued his university studies at the same time, dreaming the
while of founding, in pagan lands, a centre of scientific and Christian influence. After taking his doctorate, he obtained permission to
leave for China. Here he arrived in March, 1914, and began operations at Shienshien, in the grey and dusty monotony of the northern
plain. He began to learn the language, accustomed himself to the
ways of the country, habituated himself to long trips, trained a few
intelligent house-boys to serve as his assistants, and all this with but
slender resources. He was resolving to be at one and the same time
a geographer, geologist, naturalist, and ethnographer. His para-
mount ambition was to explore systematically the basin of the

Yellow River, and to create a combined museum and laboratory to house his collections and to provide a centre for research.

Learning to his cost the rude life of an explorer in lands infested with bandits, he traversed, in the course of the years, the great plain of Tcheu-Ly, the Mongol steppes, and the canyons of Shansi, and ventured even to the margin of the Tibetan plateau, all the time accumulating zoological, botanical, and mineralogical specimens for his collection. These had to be housed, and Licent chose Tientsin as the site of his Museum, which he named the Hwang-ho-Pai-ho Museum after the two great waterways of Northern China, the Yellow River and the White River.

As a by-product of his explorations, Licent had discovered some important fossil-bearing strata in the Pontiac deposits of the provinces of Kansu and Shensi. As usual, in order to identify the remains of fossil mammals he found, he resolved to consult specialists, and had sent off characteristic specimens to the Museum. Here Marcellin Boule, director of the palaeontological service, handed them over to Teilhard. Teilhard, in turn, wrote to Licent, seeking more detailed information. Early in July 1921, Licent began to urge Teilhard to come to China to see for himself.

It was arranged that the Paris Museum should bear the expenses of the expedition; Teilhard was to be given an official assignment by his superiors; Licent, in view of his nine years of experience, was to be in charge of the expedition; any unique finds were to be sent back to the Paris Museum, but the Hwang-ho Pai-ho Museum was to have any duplicates; finally, the expedition was to be called "The French Palaeontological Mission".

In February 1923, Teilhard telegraphed: "Coming for year. Leave when?" Licent's answer was equally laconic: "Arrive May 15". On 6 April Teilhard took ship at Marseilles and on 17 May was at Shanghai, arriving at Tientsin six days later. His *Lettres de voyage*[1] describe his journey, revealing the artist's interest in the various landscapes traversed, the zoologist's and botanist's reaction to Ceylon, besides numerous shipboard conversations which, both as an anthropologist and as a religious, he found rewarding. As a scientist he was also occasionally restive: on 5 May 1923 he wrote:

> Our trip continues without incident. But really, we are seeing too much water and not enough rocks (bar those that are too far away).

[1] Ed. Claude Aragonnès (Paris: Grasset, 1956). Eng. tr., *Letters from a Traveller* (London: Collins, and New York: Harper & Row, 1962).

But a few weeks later his attention was drawn to a spiritual problem:

> As a tentative summary, I may say that from the rapid view I have had of so many different kinds of people since I left Marseilles I retain above all the impression that the world is much more vast and more formidably complicated than I ever thought. Really, a journey to the Far East seems to represent a sort of "temptation of the multiple". How can one hope for the unification in mind and in heart of so many fragmentations of mankind, embracing every stage from savagery to a neo-civilization appreciably at variance with our Christian outlook?
>
> I am persuaded that at all costs we must cling to a faith in *some direction* and in *some destination* assignable to all this restless human activity. (27 May 1923.)

There was a strong contrast between the two Jesuits who met at Tientsin on 23 May 1923. Licent was a tough, thick-set Northerner, unconventional in dress, forbidding in manner. He had an intimate knowledge of the country and knew how to deal with the people, and to handle marauding bandits or lawless soldiery. He was a fine entomologist and geologist, but primarily a collector, and a jealous collector. He was a keen observer, but had little gift for classification, generalization or synthesis. At the same time, he was touchy, dictatorial, and quick-tempered. In the practical problems of life he was most competent.

At first, Licent was delighted to have Teilhard with him. Soon, however, they found themselves in disagreement. There may have been some jealousy of Teilhard, who had a wider knowledge of geology and palaeontology than Licent, and who, with his greater understanding of classification, was anxious to reorganize the museum in which Licent hoarded his collections.

Licent, again, preferred to work on his own. Teilhard, in contrast, was immediately drawn to teams already in the field—Swedish, American, and Chinese—and could see, furthermore, that, because of the awakening nationalist spirit in the country, all work without close collaboration with Chinese scientists would become impossible. Finally, the closer Teilhard's relations with the capital, Peking, became, the more his ties with Tientsin and with Licent were weakened.

Licent, however, was not basically disagreeable, and it is immensely to his credit that he gave a vigorous start to scientific research in North China before an official movement in this direction was so much as thought of. It was between the years 1929 and 1932 that differences between the two men were to grow most acute. On 16 June 1929 Teilhard wrote of "some rather painful brushes with Licent". He spoke of Licent, however, even at a time of serious tension (30 December 1929), as a "great-hearted and exemplary man". Earlier in that year, on 7 October, he gave a more detailed portrait of his former companion:

> The dark spot is still good old Licent, whom I cannot just drop (affection, gratitude, and prudence—in view of our common religious tie—all forbid it), but whose work, being too independent ...interests me less and less. The nearer I draw to Peking, the farther Licent withdraws from it. He is becoming nervy, and feels belittled. It's all a bit sad. You know, strictly speaking it's not vanity with Licent (though he clumsily gives that impression); it's only that he's tigerishly jealous of that museum of his, in which he sees an institution that it is his mission to keep up. I'm still hoping that we can arrive at a friendly *modus vivendi*. As a matter of fact, I haven't seen him since June. Each of us has been going his own way.

On 3 May 1931 Teilhard wrote again:

> As for Licent, he has decided to let the public in on the whole mass of his Neolithic material (found in part by me). I am a little afraid that it will amount to a great jumble, unanalysed, and displayed in assorted miscellanies. But I am not allowed in to look. Since the publication of my note on the Sang-kan-ho, in which, quite against my inclination, I was unable to rank the museum at Tientsin very high (because of the effect produced on Boule by the pamphlet you know), I am afraid that my services are no longer required at the museum. Well, in one way, this frees me. But I have the impression that, even in Licent's own interests, the estrangement has been pushed too far. He and I, of course, would never be easy shipmates together again (our ways of thinking are too different). But there is still plenty of room for fruitful collaboration, though Licent, his feelings being what they are, has closed his mind to it. Just a word from you, when you come by this way, will perhaps prove more helpful than all my overtures, which are accomplishing nothing.[2]

But the two men's differences were not irreconcilable, as proved by a charming letter from Licent in 1932, and the publication, in

[2] Cf. letters of 29 September and 30 December 1929, and 13 March 1932, written when the tension was most acute.

1936, of a note on which the two collaborated, "New Remains of Postschizotherium from S.E. Shansi". On 12 July 1938 Teilhard was noting still good-humouredly, on the occasion of Licent's final departure:

> I shall miss him like an old comrade. But I do believe that the work, in general, will go ahead more easily now.

It is to the credit of both Licent and Teilhard that they were able to patch up their differences. Moreover, Teilhard, who never learnt a word of Chinese and had no special preparation for work in China, owed a great debt to Licent's experience.

Teilhard was not slow to become acquainted at first hand with the geology of China. On 7 June 1923 he was at Peking, for a meeting of the Geological Society, where he gave a report (in English) on Licent's collections, made contact with the Chinese Geological Survey, and looked up young Wong again who, the year before, had still been studying at Brussels.

On the morning of 11 or 12 June he left Tientsin, with Licent, by rail for the vast plateau in western Mongolia contained in the big loop of the Hwang-ho. Here Licent had already been the year before. The working stage of the expedition commenced at Pao-Teou, west of Ville Bleu and north of the loop of the Yellow River. The party left in

> ...a caravan of ten mules with which we have been travelling since 22 June; we are half like mandarins, half like soldiers, are dressed in khaki, and are armed with several rifles. (15 August 1923.)

The ultimate destination was the Ordos desert. There were two reasons for the roundabout route: the absence of water and the activity of bandits on the direct road. Towards the end of March in the year a Belgian missionary, Fr Mostaert, had written to Licent:

> You will have received the message sent from Ningshia as well as the letter in which I gave you a report on the state of the countryside and advised you to put off your trip to the Ordos until some future time. The soldiers are continuing their policy of intimidation; they are circulating among missionized natives and saying that European priests are going to be killed. Lately some soldiers came and stood outside our gate and shouted insults at us.

A little later he wrote again:

> The soldiers are still hostile. Recently, a certain Colonel Feng
> said that the country will have to be rid of us—that we are to be
> killed, and our heads hung on the walls.

The chief fruit of the expedition was the discovery of traces of
Palaeolithic Man on 23 July on the Shui-tung, and in August on the
banks of the Shara-Osso-Gol, a strange little river which runs at the
bottom of a canyon over two hundred and fifty feet deep,

> ... near a Mongol settlement. It is carved in the midst of a table
> of hardened earth (cut out long ago by the Shara-Osso-Gol). On
> all sides are dunes and steppes, where horses and sheep browse
> side by side with gazelles, while at a distance long-haired Mongols
> in high boots keep watch. (15 August 1923.)

On the banks of the Shara-Osso-Gol extensive excavations were
made, for the two priests employed twenty workers, both Mongols
and Chinese, here, receiving unexpected help from an intelligent
Mongol named Wanschok, in extracting and sorting fossils.

At the discovery of the Palaeolithic deposit on the Shui-tung
K'eou, Teilhard exclaimed with joy:

> I believe this is the first discovery of this kind made in China,
> and even in the Far East. So it is perhaps a real find, and I cannot
> wait to tell Breuil and Boule of it. (26 July 1923.)

Fr Leroy adds the comment:

> In less than two weeks several cwt. of carved stone pieces were
> excavated from the principal deposit, the richest Palaeolithic bed
> then known in China. Found in formations of the Pleistocene age,
> these prehistoric implements ... are remarkable for their quality,
> their diverseness, and their quantity; edges and points, being of
> the Mousterian or Aurignacian type, were evident witness of the
> existence of Palaeolithic man in these regions.[3]
> ... The French Palaeontological Mission was returning with a
> valuable load. For the first time the existence of Palaeolitic man
> had been discovered south of the Yenisei River. And this discovery
> was a prelude to that, six years later, of Sinanthropus, which was
> to be the sensation of prehistorical studies in China.

---

[3] Expeditions from Communist China have since found more pieces of bone
(fragments of a parietal bone and a femur).

Part of the credit, of course, should be given to Père Licent, who had already (according to two Belgian missionaries, Père Mostaert and Père de Wilde) found some Palaeolithic fragments and fossil beds. Teilhard's contribution was his knowledge of geology and his gift for synthesis.

Teilhard's interest was not confined to geology and archaeology. He remarked how the Mongol women look you straight in the eye from under their headbands of coral beads. He noted the red colour of the pointed cap worn by the leading men. Landscapes, towns, vegetation, animals, everything interested him. How acute was his interest may be seen in the beginning of the *Letters from a Traveller* and especially in the marvellous descriptive notes entitled *"Choses mongoles"*, written under the canopy of a scow drifting and turning in the current, while on the left the high blue barrier of the Ala-Shan seemed to slide by; on the right the rust-and-grey plateau of the Ordos stood out, as the boat floated slowly between banks green with reeds, where wild geese sported by the hundreds on the mud-flats under a cold and misty sky. Here is a picture from Shensi:

> The north of Shensi is really a strange country. You can see where, comparatively recently, the loess has made a large pene-plain, slightly rolling. There then supervened the present phase of intense further erosion, which has traced in this peneplain a veritable maze of wide crevices, some of them over two hundred metres deep. The few folk who live here dwell in caves dug out of the loess; and in every spot that the erosion has not yet reached they sow millet, sorghum, and buckwheat. There is no getting about here save by the beds of the torrents, or following the trails that twist among the crevasses or else are scooped out in ledges (constantly crumbling away). In the middle of this loess you feel as lost as in the depth of a forest. (9 September 1923.)

Teilhard thought China headed for a fatal decadence (an idea which he was soon to change):

> ...I have not found in China (so far as I have seen it) the ferment whence I hoped we might draw the generous wine that would reinvigorate our West. So far, I have seen only races on their way to extinction, or primitives (the Chinese) who multiply without showing as yet any creativity. I firmly believe that it is our old Europe—and especially Paris—which is the promise of mankind today. This is not to say that I have been completely disappointed in what I have seen of the Far East. There were

once upon a time, in these countries here, certain men who perceived things (about the world) which decadent bonzes and lamas
have permitted to be lost (but which we may find again). And
there is still today, in the human ant-hill which borders the
Pacific, a disconcerting variety of spiritual tendencies.... I shall
return to France all the more convinced that the world is a far
bigger thing than we even dream. (15 August 1923.)

And on October 23 he adds:

I hope that upon returning from the Far East I shall be, indirectly at least, more the master of my ideas and better fortified
to defend them.

His *La messe sur le monde* gives further testimony to this spiritual
impulse. In fact, in the vast solitudes of Mongolia (which seemed
to him, from a human point of view, a region frozen and lifeless) he
saw the same thing as once upon a time he saw at the front (which
was, from the human point of view, a region where all life was at
the fullest), namely, that one single activity was in the course of
taking place in the world, and that it alone legitimized our individual activity: the deployment of some spiritual reality through the
medium of the struggle of our lives. As he rode along on his mule
for whole days, he repeated, as once before, for want of any other
Mass:

Since once again, Lord, as in another time in the forests along
the Aisne, I have neither bread, nor wine, nor altar, here on the
Asian Steppes I lift myself far above symbols, to the pure majesty
of the Real; and I, your priest, offer to you, on the altar of the
entire earth, the travail and the suffering of the world. Yonder
breaks the sun, to light the uttermost East, and then to send its
sheets of fire over the living surface of the earth, which wakens,
shudders, and resumes its appalling struggle.[4]

Teilhard had not gone to China simply to take part in an expedition. Ideas were more interesting to him than geology. And he
feared, while winter-bound in Tientsin, that he was losing precious
time that he could have employed profitably in furthering his
researches at the Paris Museum. In this perplexity he decided to

---

[4] *La messe sur le monde* is signed "Ordos, Easter, 1923". At that date Teilhard had not yet reached the Ordos, but he represents himself as celebrating
the feast in the solitude of Mongolia. This is the only occasion on which the
dating of a text may be misleading.

sound out Baudrillart, Rector of the Institut Catholique. While confessing that he would rather not stay too long in China, he declared his readiness to accept the decision of the Museum, should the latter advise undertaking another trip in the spring (with a return to Paris in August or September of 1924). From these facts, attested to by two letters (18 August and 23 October 1923) it follows that Teilhard was not planning to make China his permanent scene of activities, that there was nothing to hinder his return to Paris, and that the only question was whether his mission should include a trip to be made in the following spring. Both Boule and Baudrillart replied that Teilhard was to extend his stay for the spring trip.

While Teilhard awaited the coming of the Chinese spring ("everlasting dust storms", he noted, "with white flowers below and blue skies above") he was busy sorting the sixty cases of specimens brought back from the Ordos, writing up notes, completing (thanks to a friend in Paris) the furnishing of the Museum, and answering Vialleton's book in which the standard doctrine of transformism was attacked.[5] Teilhard was charitable and indeed friendly towards Vialleton, of whom he wrote (7 January 1930), "Vialleton's death grieves me: apart from his philosophical ideas he was a true scholar, and a most warm-hearted man". The book not only roused Teilhard's controversial ardour, but forced him to clarify his own position and made him an even more convinced evolutionist.

During this same winter of 1923-4 Teilhard was able to spend a good deal of time in Peking. He met American anthropologists, palaeontologists, and geologists, and was greatly interested in Dr Walter Granger, palaeontologist in the big American expedition into the Gobi. In early January he took part in a meeting of geologists:

> To start with, I went to the charming city of Peking to spend six days there on the occasion of the little convention of geologists I told you of. There were quite a number at the meeting, and the members, though a considerable mixture (Americans, Chinese, Frenchmen, Englishmen, Swedes, and Russians), were extremely cordial. A number of papers were read, nearly all giving new and important facts.

[5] *Membres et ceintures des vertèbrés tétrapodes, critique morphologique du transformisme* (Paris, 1924). Vialleton was a member of the faculty of medicine in Montpellier. He renewed his attack in 1929 with *L'origine des êtres vivants, l'illusion transformiste.*

What a difference between geology as one can pursue it here and as it is in the limestone of the Paris basin! And it is still the golden age of geological research in China.

And yet, here as elsewhere, the inventory of deposits and fossils will soon be completed in broad outline; and I often tell myself that within a generation the science I am concerned with will begin to wither away if it does not succeed in widening its subject matter and changing its methods. It will have to devise some means for tackling the study of the earth in a more radical and comprehensive fashion, and for looking at it as a whole, endowed with specifically terrestrial, mechanical, physical, and chemical properties. It is these specifically terrestrial properties, it seems to me, that we must determine, instead of burying our noses in a detailed study of the action of very limited causes, which influence only very limited parts of the earth.

If I had to start again I should go in for geodynamics or geochemistry.

But to come back to Peking: This visit left me no more time than earlier ones for sightseeing. I foresee having to return to France without ever having got inside the Imperial Palace and the Temple of Heaven. Yet this I but half regret. To be in the atmosphere of these ancient things is more gratifying to me than to go right up to them and peer at their details. What I like, at Peking, is the feeling of being at the heart of old China. My finest memories of the place may be recollections of coming home at night sometimes in a rickshaw through dark and twisting little streets under magnificently starred skies, against which there loom, just like "Chinese" shadow-pictures, the little curved roofs, and the gnarled and ancient trees covered with ravens' nests. (14 January 1924.)

At other times Teilhard went farther afield. The correspondence gives accounts of three trips, the first in January, the other two in February, of 1924. The first was to the coal-mines of Kai-Ping (three hours from Tientsin on the Mukden line)—his first acquaintance with the Primary formations in China. The second was a courtesy visit to the episcopal centre of the Jesuit Missions, in the Cheli plain at Sienhsien, a hundred and twenty-five miles south of Tientsin. But the third, like the first, was a geological tour; it brought him into the mountains which bound the Cheli plain at the Honan-Shansi border, two hundred and fifty miles south of Peking on the Peking-Hankow railway. Sienhsien was not easy to reach:

... three hours on the train, such accommodation overnight as the country provides, then six hours of bumping in a boxlike cart with cylindrical roof and no springs. (26 February 1924.)

The place gave the appearance of a vast monastery, as it might be Trappist, with numerous annexes (high school, seminary, convent, printshop, etc.):

... once there, you begin to realize what it means to be in the midst of China and in the midst of the Chinese. As far as the eye can see, there is nothing but the grey earth, cultivated to the last square inch, and recultivated the whole winter, so that not one wisp of straw may be lost. Over this stripped wasteland stretches a close network of earthen villages surrounded by small trees (they are never given time to grow up) and of endless cemeteries (they often take up half the village lands!). Inside the villages, swarming like ants are the Chinese—not evil, but primitive, inert, earthy, leading their humdrum lives in a mental twilight, and instinctively hostile to Occidentals, whose benefits they avail themselves of, but whom they regard basically as undesirables and trouble-makers.

When you have taken the plunge into this land and into this society you have the sensation of being absorbed or of being stifled. All missionaries have this experience and recognize it as the gravest of their afflictions. Of course, they love their work, and their calling, because they recognize their ultimate importance. But here and now they are immersed in the human mass without encountering any solid ground and without eliciting any interest or any appreciable affection. The labours that they give to God are aggravated for each of them by a feeling of being *apparently* abandoned. With nothing to grasp but this vague, yielding, elusive insubstantiality, one's mental grasp tends to weaken. (1 March 1924.)

The third trip provided another experience:

This trip enabled me to see, this time, not a big central mission residence but the little mission posts, and life as lived in these posts, lacking in comforts, and (what is worse) prey to the sociability (or outward signs thereof) of Chinese hangers-on, sometimes offensive, sometimes over-familiar. Travelling with Licent, we used to go about like soldiers or demi-mandarins—that is, aloofly. This time I had a taste of contact with the masses. (28 February 1924.)

Teilhard's first judgement of the Chinese was rather severe. He wrote:

> The Chinese soul is naturally turbid, vague, unstable, elusive (even to itself), and also, as if by nature, materialistic, down to earth, and agnostic. (26 February 1924.)

Yet his reaction, to a people whose very language he did not know, was far from negative:

> Note carefully that I have not really taken a dislike to these people ... and I believe that my predominant feeling toward the great number of Chinese is one of pity—that vast and elevating pity, philanthropic in the etymological sense, which is doubtless one of the most convincing manifestations of the potentialities still dormant in our subconscious. I have merely given you the raw data of what I have seen and experienced.
>
> I think, still in the light of personal experience, that the problem of the apostolate, and its difficulties, is very different in the case of Chinese of the educated, Europeanized classes. With them, Chinese vagueness, and the resulting inscrutability to Western eyes, is much less marked. (With two or three men of this category I have spoken as I would with friends in Paris!) With them, admittedly, I do run into an agnosticism, and one no longer instinctive, but systematic.
>
> No matter; if Christianizing such people is more difficult for the time being, there is a better chance that it will be more solid. (1 March 1924.)

Teilhard, in fact, was soon to build some lasting friendships among his Chinese colleagues. He witnessed with approval the nationalist awakening of China, and later, in his essay on *L'apport spirituel de l'extrême Orient* (1947), he paid tribute to the Chinese mind.

The spring trip (April–June, 1924) was approaching. There were considerable difficulties: threats of war between Mukden and Peking, the question of money, lack of water, and bandits. The region the explorers had in mind was the eastern edge of the Gobi (Dalai Nor and Shiling-Gol region) west of Mukden. Teilhard would have preferred to penetrate into the interior of the Ordos, which so far he had only skirted, or to study the mountain pass of Lang Shan (edge of the Gobi, north of the north-west turn of the arm of the Yellow River). The Japanese had already studied this part of the great Mongolian desert but with an eye to its industrial and military possibilities. It was not included in the plans of the American mission, so that the French and American expeditions would complement one another.

In *Letters from a Traveller* Teilhard records his impressions of Mongolia; on 30 June 1924 he wrote:

> From the top of a hill that overlooks the neighbourhood from a height of some five hundred feet, I was faced by a most unusual scene—a rolling succession of white waves, tipped with green, which filled a semi-circle of the horizon and ran away into the distance as far as the eye could see—just like the sea. Three or four miles to my left lay a large Nor, to my right, at about the same distance, a string of five or six still larger Nors. Behind me, the line of green mountains we'll be crossing tomorrow. Finally, all around me, a grassy hill, with ancient twisted elms, dotted about like apple trees in an orchard over an area of four square miles or so. And with this, not a sound, not a living soul.

Until the end of April the expedition found little of interest except some Neolithic remains, generally on the surface. Then, on 28 April, on the latitude of the Dalai Nor and the longitude of Kalgan, they came upon a wide Mio-Pliocene basin:

> No fine exhibition specimens, but many that point conclusively, for both beds (Miocene and Pliocene) to a varied fauna scarcely known in Mongolia. (25 June 1924.)

More important still were the geological implications of the basaltic *coulées* above the beds, surmounted by a sixty-mile chain of Quaternary volcanoes as recent as the Puys familiar to Teilhard in Auvergne.

By 10 September Teilhard was back in Shanghai, where he visited the grave of his elder sister Françoise (in religion Sister Marie Albéric of the Sacred Heart), who had been superior of the old people's home founded there by the Little Sisters of the Poor, and had died of smallpox at the age of thirty-two.[6] On 13 September Teilhard left China.

China had been to him only an interlude and he was anxious to get back to Paris and the Museum. On the other hand, he had formed valuable friendships with American, Swedish and Chinese

---

[6] Cf. *Françoise Teilhard de Chardin, Petite Sœur des Pauvres* (Clermont-Ferrand; Imprimerie L. Billet, n.d.), and *Sœur Marie-Albéric du Sacré Cœur* (Montreal, De La Salle Bureau, 1949). Both, though published anonymously, are by Marguérite-Marie Teilhard de Chardin.

scientists, and the work he had done had given him more standing. Research was to him "a vital and sacred function, the basis of all man's higher, mystical, life". And he adds,

> Never have I more advisedly and fully believed in the divine and Christian value of ever-increasing knowledge, nor felt such contempt for those who would arrest or limit its growth.

On 15 October 1924 he was in Marseilles, whence he went on to Paris. We know little of his life from November, 1924, to April, 1926. During that time he made a retreat at St-Étienne (Fr Valensin was with him part of the time) in July, 1925; and a letter of 16 August, dated at Sarlat (Dordogne) speaks of a trip through Lyons (to see the Jesuit Provincial) and Clermont-Ferrand, and his intention of spending another fortnight in the neighbourhood. That he did stay appears from a letter to another correspondent, dated from Sarlat, 22 August, in which he says that Boule is to pick him up in a car for a tour of the Périgord caverns. In September 1925 a geological excursion brought him to the convent of Ste-Odile, in the Vosges.

He soon resumed his scientific connections in Europe—with Belgium and Louis Dollo, and especially with England. He made a trip to the latter, for we find him there with Breuil and Dorothy Garrod: April 3 1925 he visited the Ipswich Museum and the Crag deposits where Reid Moir had discovered the highly contested "eoliths". Between April 6 and 9 he examined the glacial and interglacial cliffs of Cromer. Yet China remained his preoccupation. Thanks to the material (books, specimens) available at the Paris Museum, Teilhard was able to unify his various notes, with the help of Breuil, who made a study of the Palaeolithic instruments.

> ...I am beginning to change my mind about my Ordos "Pliocene" (beds of San-tao-ho or of St Jacques, marked "A" on the map below)... I have therefore practically decided to date the formation later, subject to bringing down to the Eocene division all the underlying red earths (without fossils) of the Ordos north of the Arbous Oula: imprudently relying on instinct, I had been looking on them as Pontian.... By this same post I am sending (pending something better) the proofs of a preliminary paper on my 1923 trip. It was written a year ago, and is based on my earlier estimate that the sands of St. Jacques are Pliocene. I am beginning to doubt, too, whether we should identify a Hercynian phase of

flexure in the Arbous Oula. You see what comes of writing too fast. (November, 1924.)

From the many notes and memoranda that Teilhard was composing about this time, it is apparent that his chief interest as a specialist in mammals was in the Tertiary, and even more the Quaternary, periods. On 20 July 1925 he writes that he is particularly busy with fossil rodents (*Siphneus, Prosiphneus*).[7] He continued to work on these ("a group often neglected"—10 August 1929), and developed important conclusions about orthogenesis in the Siphnoids. Although this work was too technical to attract much public attention, it won him an assured position as a specialist in this field.

Teilhard still kept up his contact with China, and especially with Licent. Licent wrote to him of his projects for 1926, sent him fossils, and kept him informed of the diggings near Kalgan, in the valley of the Sang-kan-ho, carried on in partnership with the distinguished Scots geologist George B. Barbour, at that time professor at Peking. Teilhard's gift for synthesis was already making itself felt. It seemed to him increasingly clear that in China there could now be distinguished two great Quaternary periods, each having two principal aspects—an Upper Quaternary, with a loess form on the slopes and a sand form in the open basins, and a Lower Quaternary, with red clay (bearing limestone concretions) on the slopes, and with sands (bearing large *Unio* (*Quadrula*)) in the bottoms. Going beyond specialized research, Teilhard was turning towards the general philosophic problems raised in his field of study. He continued to speculate on the subject of evolution. We know that, during the winter 1925–6, he lectured on evolution on four different occasions. It was also about 1925 that he conceived the notion for which he coined the word "noosphere"[8] (the notion and

---

[7] Species of rat-moles. The establishment of their stratigraphic level enabled Teilhard to reveal a series of new stratigraphic boundaries between the Red and Yellow lands. It was through the rodents that he met J. Viret (now a professor at the University of Lyons) who describes the meeting in a letter to the author of 23 January 1927. "I was then teaching at the Lycée Ampère and working for my doctoral thesis in the geological laboratory at the University. Scattered on my table were the bones of little fossilized rodents I had collected in the Limagne (in the Bourbonnais). I can still see Teilhard's long thin form bending over my shoulder... 'It's most interesting', he said, without any preface, 'that you should be studying these. Exactly similar ones are to be found in China', and then introduced himself."

[8] "Noosphere" was coined by analogy with "biosphere"; it was first used in *L'hominisation* (6 May 1925).

3+

the word were then adopted by Édouard Le Roy and by Vernadsky, a Russian geologist). From 1920 to 1930 there was a close relationship between Teilhard and Édouard Le Roy, and their collaboration between 1925 and 1927 is quite clear. Teilhard used to visit Le Roy, who taught at the Collège de France, at his Wednesday evenings in the rue Cassette; and the two discussed in full agreement, ideas which were later passed on to Le Roy's students.

> I continue to see Le Roy regularly. These Wednesday evenings have really become, for me, one of the best weekly "spiritual exercises". I always leave feeling better and fresher. (10 January 1926.)

Édouard Le Roy, a thinker of great originality, had expressed a number of ideas which he came to share with Teilhard. In lectures at the Collège de France in 1925 and 1926 Le Roy frequently cited Teilhard, whose views on the philosophy of biology he had used in preparing the lectures. Similarly, when Teilhard's calculations for the future development of the biosphere seemed to go beyond anything that could be foreseen statistically, it was to Le Roy that he turned. The two worked together so closely that Le Roy wrote later, of his own *L'exigence idéaliste et le fait d'évolution* (1928), "I have so often and for so long talked over with Père Teilhard the views expressed here that neither of us can any longer pick out his own contribution."[9]

Teilhard's last letter to Le Roy seems to have been written on 28 January 1934, and after that date their interests seem to have diverged, Teilhard turning in a phenomenological, Le Roy in a metaphysical, direction. Even so, Le Roy was confessing, in 1940–1, "I have done little more than reproduce, sometimes almost literally, the results of our joint thinking."[10]

Upon learning of the death of his old friend, Teilhard wrote (1 December 1954):

> Yes, I was moved by the death of my dear friend, the great Édouard Le Roy.... There are few men whom I have so much

---

[9] See also Le Roy's *Les origines humaines et l'évolution de l'intelligence* (Paris, 1928): "We have discussed the views presented here so often and in such detail that we have come to arrange them in the same order, to express them in almost the same words, and to find it difficult to determine the limits of each one's contribution."

[10] *Essai d'une philosophie première* (Paris, 1956), vol. 1, p. 413.

admired and loved as I did him. So serene, so completely human
—and so deeply Christian.

And in a letter written two days later he sums up the relationship:

I loved him like a father, and owed him a very great debt. It
was not exactly that I owed any particular idea to him, but that,
particularly between 1920 and 1930, he gave me confidence,
enlarged my mind (and my feeling of loyalty to the Church), and
also served (at the Collège de France) as a spokesman for my ideas,
then taking shape, on "hominization" and the "noosphere". I
believe, so far as one can ever tell, that the word "noosphere" was
my invention; but it was he who launched it. After 1930, circumstances (namely, my stay in China) prevented close contact. But
we remained fond of each other. There are men who should be
recognized as saints for our times, Christians whose faith has impelled them to humanize themselves in every way and to the
highest degree.

Since to Teilhard intellectual and priestly activity were both one,
it was natural, in the early 1920's, for him to re-establish contact
with the Abbé Portal and his student groups. One of the students,
Gabriel Germain, recalls a talk by Teilhard (in December, 1924, or
January, 1925) on André Gide and his *Les nourritures terrestres*:

We used to meet in the Rue de Grenelle, at the Abbé Portal's,
Lazarist director of the group. I can still see clearly, around that
long green table, our fresh young faces—some of which disguised
merciless cynics, all ready to tear the speaker to bits as they walked
home between the Place Saint-Sulpice and the Rue d'Ulm.
Father Teilhard began to speak, and it soon became clear this
was no simple-minded priest but a bold thinker. From my place,
at one end of the table, near the door, I had almost a profile view
of his long face and imperious features. While talking, he kept his
eyes half shut, a clerical trick that I found distasteful in others
but which, on this occasion, was well suited to the meditative tone
of the address. He seemed to be speaking to himself, and we to be
overhearing; it was from this quality of soliloquy that his words
derived their force.
Though a scientist, he had chosen to speak, not of palaeontology, but of literature, and the most recent of that day, namely,
André Gide, and specifically of Gide's *Les nourritures terrestres*.
Teilhard's object was to show us that Christian spirituality might
benefit from this eulogy of the world of the flesh. Not that he was
seeking to Christianize the author by force; no, but through Gide,

and despite Gide, he sought—and found—in Gide's words, springs of clear water from which a Christian soul might drink.[11]

Germain's account is a reminder of Teilhard's interest in modern literature and of his characteristic "philosophy of acceptance", by which he sought to show that in love of the earth there is nothing incompatible with the Christian life properly understood.

From this same time in Paris dates the maturing in Teilhard's mind of what was to appear as *Le milieu divin*. Jacques Perret, now a professor at the Sorbonne, describes a three-day retreat at the beginning of Lent, 1925:

> Teilhard preached to us his *Le milieu divin*; the effect, on all of us, was enormous; here we found a brand of religious thought designed for Christians required professionally to live in the world, and to do their work there. Far from being a peripheral zone of Christian activity, far from having to be justified as a concession made by the Church to our weakness, activity on the human level—work in the world—was presented to us as the most immediate realization of God's will, the extension of his most central designs for the world. The dovetailing of all this with the most exacting spiritual ideals, and with the most deeply personal love of Jesus Christ, was for me, and for many of us, a great awakening.

[11] *Cahiers du Sud*, no. 335, pp. 96–7.

CHAPTER FOUR

Second Tientsin Period
(1926–7)

At the end of 1926, despite the protestations of Baudrillart, Teilhard's religious superiors pressed him to leave the Institut Catholique. For the story behind this, we must go back a few years. Whatever may have been the reception given to Teilhard's presentation of the theory of evolution, his presentation, to young seminarians, of his private speculations on the doctrine of original sin and his attempt to reconcile the traditional view with his concept of evolution seem to have been viewed as improper. It was decided—without any rancour, we note—that Teilhard was to confine himself to purely scientific publications, and that he was to leave Paris. Painful though this was to Teilhard, he was consoled by the sympathetic attitude of his superiors and of his friend Le Roy, and by his own realization that it was only through the Church and the Society that advance in the spiritual life could be found. On 16 August 1925 he wrote:

> I see now more clearly and concretely that nothing spiritual, nothing divine, can reach a Christian—or a religious—save through the intermediary of the Church—or of his religious community. And my deeper realization of this fundamental truth has certainly made me feel better.

And a week later:

> But to come to something still more, if possible, *"inside"*:[1] it seems that the spark kindled within me at St-Étienne not only continues to glow as it should but is penetrating my general atti-

[1] The italics within quotes indicate that Teilhard used the English word *"inside"*.

tude and my interior outlook. Now more explicitly and more concretely than before the "crisis" . . . I believe in, and love, the Church, as "mediatrix" between God and the world. And this, I feel, is giving me a good deal of peace.

A few months later, then (26 April 1926), we find him on board the *Angkor*, and on 10 June he was once more in Tientsin. His *Lettres de voyage* reveal his state of mind during the course of the voyage. He had matured: his first fundamental work, *Le milieu divin*, dates in fact from 1926–7. He was now much more aware, too, of the variety among races (he was never, as a biologist, to believe in the equality of races but, rather, their complementary relationship) and of the barriers between their mentalities. He was, on the other hand, less aware of the exotic quality of the Orient; the magic of his first encounter with the Far East had faded, though he could still appreciate and describe its beauty and interest:

> All morning we have been sailing along the coast of Sumatra—a pile of tall, partly wooded mountains, from which huge storm-clouds are forever rising. Seen from the strait here, under a wonderful blue sky, this accumulation of vapour is astonishing. What a pity that we cannot go ashore to visit this zoological Eden and to see, in their natural habitat, the orang-utans, the gibbons, and the tree-shrews. Still, I can pay my respects from afar to what may be the place where primates first left the trees.[2]

It was on this trip that Teilhard met Henry de Monfreid, who was returning to his estates in Ethiopia:

> I did make two real friends; but unfortunately they got off at Jibuti. They come from Neuilly, but during ten months of the year he plies the Red Sea, Arab-fashion, while his wife lives alone among the coastal Somalis. Both are unconventional, affable, and sensitive. We engaged in endless conversations on every conceivable subject, and parted with a promise to meet again in Paris. (15 May 1926.)

Henry de Monfreid, too, has given an account of the meeting that includes a portrait of Teilhard:

> I had noticed on the tourist deck, where there were a good many priests and nuns, one tall, thin priest who stood out if only

---

[2] The tree- or squirrel-shrew (*Tupaia*), by a curious association of characteristics, marks a kind of transition between insectivores and the lower primates. Common in the Eocene, it is now very rare, a sort of "living fossil".

because there was something virile and independent about him, quite different from the solemn, rather priggish air that priests normally pick up in the seminary. I had been attracted by his strong, narrow face, whose features, set off by early wrinkles, were as though carved in wood. There was a twinkle of laughter, though quite without irony, in his eyes, that indicated good humour and kindliness. . . .

When I walked by his deck chair he was reading, but, raising his eyes when I passed and catching my glance, he smiled and waved.[3]

Though Teilhard was what we call a good mixer, very few people really got to know him. To do so, one had to be both intelligent and original, as de Monfreid certainly was. Teilhard's meeting with "the Pirate"—Teilhard's nickname for him—was to prove valuable scientifically. Teilhard was working very hard during the voyage:

I have decided to put into shape, while aboard, the lecture on transformism which I gave several times last winter. I emphasize that to meddle with the basic concepts of transformism is to meddle fatally with the whole edifice of knowledge acquired through our senses; and I emphasize, too, that evolutionist concepts, when properly understood, lead necessarily to moral and religious attitudes which are both very lofty and perhaps indispensable in these times of ours. (15 May 1926.)

Teilhard had left for China before it had been finally decided that the severance of his connection with the Institut Catholique should be permanent. It was, accordingly, not until 16 January 1927 that he wrote to a friend:

. . . your letter of December 5 reached me only this morning, with its news that my connection with the Institut Catholique has been definitely severed. I am little affected by this news. When I left Paris in April it was with the impression that my future was wholly uncertain; and I have since lived in China with the growing feeling that in this country I have found a new home. So, you see, the break with my way of life from 1920 to 1926 was in some regards already complete.

Teilhard's adaptability enabled him, indeed, to make a new home in China, as he did later in America. Paris, however, was still the centre of his world:

[3] H. de Monfreid, *Chabas* (Paris, 1947), part 2, ch. V.

What I really want is to keep my roots in Paris, where I find the whole of my real life, my greatest capacity for activity, and the indispensable means for the completion of my researches (12 November 1926) ... I shall propose the following plan: that I be given time in Paris to publish what I have written and to resume contact with scientific circles (eighteen months), and that I leave again for China for a similar eighteen months (myself to find the money for travelling). (31 December 1926.)

... All I seek to save are my *roots* in Paris. As a scientist I find these necessary, for I can bring nothing to a final and publishable stage here; besides, my capacity for research is dependent upon contacts with geological circles in Europe. I am therefore going to propose that I alternate between Paris and Tientsin, with my formal residence (if a point is made of it) in Tientsin—to do, in other words, what I have been doing since 1923 anyway. (16 January 1927.)

Teilhard's plan was, in fact, adopted. He left for France on 27 August 1927 and continued to divide his time between China and Paris until 1929 almost uninterruptedly.

His life in China may be divided into field expeditions, association with scientific institutions, and contacts with Swedish and American colleagues, with Chinese scientists, and with the Museum in Paris and the Institut de France. These we may well consider in turn.

To come back, then, to mid-June of 1926: Teilhard spent his first days upon his return to Tientsin in cataloguing the considerable material which Licent, the year before, had picked up from the *Quadrula*-bearing deposits of the valley of the Sang-kan-ho, south of Kalgan and west of Peking. Both Licent and Teilhard were anxious to get back to field work. After Teilhard had spent a short time in Peking, they set out again: there were three main expeditions: one, uncompleted, towards Kansu, another into the valley of the Sang-kan-ho, and a fresh tour of eastern Mongolia.

Licent's plan was to proceed to southern Shensi, and then to go to Lanchow, in Kansu, at the gateway to Tibet, and to reach Tsinghai. There was more geographical than geological interest in this journey, and the route was probably to include ground not covered by the Swedes, just as the earlier Mongolian journey had avoided overlapping with the Americans.

Licent and Teilhard had not counted, however, upon running

3. Teilhard on the beach at Hastings, about 1910

Teilhard, L. Joleaud and L. Cottreau inspecting fortifications at La Fère (Aisne) in 1920

5. Teilhard, l'Abbé Breuil and Nelson at the entrance to the cave of Pasiega (Santander)

into a civil war, which had broken out between the Ou-Pai-Fou and the Communist Kuominchun from the west. In July, 1926, having set out from Tungkwan, they got to within three miles of Signan-Fou, right up to the line of fire, and were obliged to retrace their steps. Thus their exploration was limited to a study of central China, particularly of Shansi, and August 25 found them on their way back to Tientsin. Their geological, if not their palaeontological discoveries were considerable: Teilhard, in fact, learned enough to complete an important work on the Quaternary of China.

This journey gave Teilhard his first knowledge of central China, and enlarged his experience in the political and human field, for here he both discovered the China of older days, and obtained a first-hand view of the ravages of marauding soldiery:[4]

My trip—the first I have made into China proper—has taught me many things about the underlying masses of this country: hundreds of millions of peaceful peasants, as against the baleful military. Yet I do not think that these masses are the leaven of the future; they are at most the unrisen dough or (in the case of the soldiers) an obstacle. I have been moving about for whole weeks now among the pagodas and monuments of a country which is falling into dust: the real China is (despite the many dregs) in Europe, or in the big cities. From certain points of view I regret the defeat (for the time being?) of the Kuominchuns. They lean, for want of better support, on the Soviets; but undeniably their army is (a very curious phenomenon) a power for order, peace, and the spread of the Gospel. Their troops pray publicly, in common, to Christ; and I have seen some of the graves of their soldiers marked by crosses. China is still in complete disorder. The railways are disorganized. Three-quarters of the people are indifferent to what is going on. Despite all this I am convinced that within a generation something will succeed in coming to birth. (26 August 1926.)

The difference in tone between this letter and the one he wrote on 15 August 1923 is immediately evident. He continued to be struck by evidences of decay and by the passivity of the masses; but he felt the presence of a leaven which would bring this flat dough to rise.

In connection with the Sang-kan-ho valley, we should note that, through incorrect dating of documents, the discovery of the

---

[4] On this journey, see Letters from a Traveller, pp. 128–32.

3*

Nihowan deposit was attributed to Licent and Teilhard. In fact, the credit should go to Dr George Barbour. What happened was as follows.

Since 1922, Barbour, at the request of the geologists of the Central Asiatic Expedition, had been working on the map of the Kalgan district. In 1923, at the suggestion of a local farmer and Fr Vincent (a member of the apostolic mision to Kalgan) in the area, Barbour directed his attention to the valley of the Sang-kan-ho. Then in 1924 Fr Vincent also sent certain samples from the area to the Hwang-ho Pai-ho museum, which Licent subsequently showed Teilhard. It was on the strength of these that Teilhard agreed to accompany Professor W. W. Davis about 25 August to Kalgan, where he was taken by Barbour to the Great Gate near the city.

Here Teilhard discussed the puzzling aspects of the banks and the presence of *Unio* and of gypsum in the basin of the Sang-kanho, directed attention to the silicification of the bone deposits, and urged Barbour (because of the rumours of war) to hasten his excursion into the Sang-kan-ho valley.

Barbour, in the three days available, managed to determine the existence of two horizons, one above the other, the lower being that of Nihowan, containing large bivalves which resembled the *Quadrula* pointed out by V. K. Ting in the San Men rapids of the Yellow River. Lower Quaternary deposits of the San Men type, thitherto recognized in the Hwang-ho valley, were thus now found, elsewhere, accompanied by fossil vertebrates.

In view of the importance of these findings, Teilhard decided that this site should be revisited; this was done, during his absence; for in the autumn of 1924 Barbour and Licent made a preliminary examination of the valley. Then in September of 1925 they made a second trip to Nihowan, where they succeeded in gathering numerous fossils, which Teilhard, upon his return to Europe, was to identify as going back to the Lower Pleistocene period.

Teilhard and Licent left Tientsin again about 21 September 1926, to return about 11 October. Their trip was cut short for several reasons: the need to return a conveyance lent them by some missionaries, the setting in of cold weather, and, finally, the uncomfortable proximity of a gang of bandits, who had just exacted tribute from two villages in the vicinity. They were able, however, to gather seven cases of fossils. These included no human remains; but Teilhard had the opportunity of studying the basin at first hand, with the result that he was able to publish specific information on the geology and palaeontology of the site, a vast lacustrine formation containing the first Early Pleistocene fauna to be conclusively identified in China. Some months later, he was to become still more clearly aware of the importance of the findings at this site:

> Despite untoward circumstances (civic disorder, bandits) I succeeded in sizing up the geology of an important region; and the continuation of Licent's excavations yielded results which a subsequent study of the fossils has shown to be more important than I had hoped at the time. As I assemble the results of the work conducted in 1925, I find myself compiling a mass of information on a terrain hitherto hardly studied in China. So, even over and above the quantity and quality of the specimens I was able to bring back to Europe, the year was not a wasted one. (31 December 1926.)

Of the discovery of the Nihowan horizon we may therefore conclude:

First, Licent was not the pioneer though his published description of the Sang-kan-ho banks may make him seem to have been so. His "Terrasses du Sangkanho" in *Bull. Musée Hoangho-Paiho*, 1924, is dated before Barbour's "The Deposits of the San Kan-ho Valley", *Bull. Geol. Soc. China*, vol. IV, no. 1 (1925), but actually appeared later—the year 1924, above, being a pre-dating. That the discovery here must be credited to Barbour is beyond question. Licent's actual role was that of a travelling companion and collector of fossils.

Teilhard's role, too, was that of an assistant—a very valuable one, of course, for he intuitively foresaw discoveries at the site, he grasped the importance of the silicification of the fossil bones in relation to the lacustrine conditions obtaining, he hastened Barbour's first-hand examination of the valley in detail, and he assisted in getting the whole of the geology of the valley into focus.

Here, as elsewhere, Teilhard was sensitive to landscapes:

> As for Sang-kan-ho, our stay up there was not without its attractions. In that season, when the sparse fields of sorghum and millet have been harvested, the whole countryside is clay-coloured —grey, yellow, and red. But all this barrenness we saw bathed in a golden light of such quality that the eye never wearied of it. The height of the valley was but 2,500 feet; yet standing all

around, and stretching away, were chains of tall, jagged, barren peaks. To the south, a massif 10,000 feet high was white with snow; and to the north, through a few gaps, we could make out the high rim—sheer as a staircase step—of the great Mongolian Plateau. (12 October 1926.)

At the same time he was very conscious of the misery of China:

I have seen close up, for a second time this year, the wretchedness of China in time of war. Stripped first by one and then by the other army in the war, the Sang-kan-ho peasants are now pillaged by the occupying forces of the peace, who leave only to be promptly succeeded by bandits swooping down from the mountains. As a result, no one has any animals to work with, and everything has to be hidden away. Truly, China today, north and south, is the prey of the military. Raised by intensive recruitment, living off the country, the Chinese soldiers are in nine cases out of ten nothing but brutal and worthless bandits. They are to be found everywhere, and everywhere they provoke trouble and work havoc. From time to time the war-lords shoot them down in batches. But the trouble begins again at once.

Only the Kuominchuns from the west and the Cantonese from the south are disciplined; and they treat the poor civilians decently. On the other hand, however, they are Communistic, and implacably opposed to foreigners. If they win even a partial victory in the battle of arms, money, and diplomacy now being fought on the Yangtze, I feel that China will have order restored; but it will go hard for the missions, and only the native clergy will be able to fit in in the time to come. (12 October 1926.)

On 12 May 1927, after the appearance of the Sang-kan-ho article, Teilhard and Licent left Tientsin to visit the region south of the south-east limit of the Gobi, not far from Dalai Nor, and especially the Weichang area. The reason they chose to revisit eastern Mongolia was that they had to avoid areas devastated by civil war or infested by bandits. The decision, in any case, was primarily Licent's, who was a great deal more efficient than Teilhard in arranging practical details. When they returned on 7 August, Teilhard was thoroughly well satisfied with his latest expedition. Though he brought back few fossils, he had obtained information for an article giving a fuller and more accurate geological description of the hitherto little known formations of the Dalai Nor region, a terrain characterized by a deluge of Jurassic or Cretaceous rocks, andesites, granites, and rhyolites, followed by basalt of the close of the Tertiary division.

"At least three-quarters of my observations are new," he wrote. "Weichang has never been visited by geologists."

Of the Mongolian landscape he wrote:

> To look at, the country around where I now am is picturesque; and it would be good land too, if the Chinese did not crop it excessively, as they unwisely do, chopping down anything that will burn.
>
> ... Picture an immense, 1,700–1,900 metre-high platform, tipped gently eastward; it is a basaltic plateau, surmounted by rounded domes and by dikes (tabular bodies of igneous rock injected while molten into a fissure, often resisting erosion and standing in wall-like ridges), remains of an earlier 2,000-metre peneplain. The basalt covers a base of erupted Mesozoic rocks, which make their appearance as abrupt ridges at the bottom and on the sides of the valleys.
>
> Only the valleys are at all inhabited, the completely empty plateau itself being open pasture, with vestiges of a former fir, larch, and birch forest. We camped there for some days under the protection of some dozen armed and mounted Christians, who hunted deer, elk, and small grouse while Licent gathered plants, and I, rocks. The temperature used to fall to only a few degrees above freezing at night—and this at the end of June! But on the whole the weather was magnificent, and the place itself bewitching. I could almost have thought myself in Auvergne—but a bigger, more lonely Auvergne. At that season the prairies were in full flower: a carpet of red and amber lilies, scarlet primulas, white peonies, bright-leaved rhubarb. This was Europe, or at least Siberia, rather than China. Towards Ting-pang, of course, the landscape changes; white sands appear, filling the valleys and clinging like snow to the mountains—this being, already, the Gobi.

Between the two expeditions (to the Sang-kan-ho in 1926 and to eastern Mongolia in 1927) Teilhard was back at Tientsin; when he came to study the fossils he had collected, he began to think that there was something much more Upper Pliocene than Pleistocene in their appearance. Basing his calculations especially on the rodents, he began to identify in the whole of Northern China a distinct physiographical level—the San Men level—between the Pontian and the Loess. While he was thus revising his scientific conclusions, this winter was to him also a time of recollection and heightened spirituality. In a letter of 15 October 1926 he prays:

> May God preserve in me this deep relish, this lucid intoxication, as it were, which elates me with the joy of being, drunk as from an ever-flowing fountain. At times, when I am quite absorbed in rocks and fossils, I experience an ineffable happiness at the thought that I possess, in the form of a single, all-embracing, incorruptible, and loving element, the supreme Principle wherein everything subsists and is alive.

It was at this time, too, that he started on *Le milieu divin*:

> I am a little concerned about how to fill my time usefully during the winter here in China, for I foresee that before January I shall have got all I can out of the documents on hand, numerous though they are. Having finished some articles on geology which are to go to Peking, I have begun something which will amuse you: I am writing, in a form as simple, as orthodox, as devoid of philosophical system as possible, a little treatise on the interior life. I am calling it *Le milieu divin*, and am trying in it to confine myself to a practical, unquestionably Christian point of view.... My plan is to produce something easy, somewhat in the form of a prayer. (12 November 1926.)

A month earlier we find a first statement of a thesis that was to be developed in Teilhard's most important and characteristic work, the *Phenomenon of Man*:

> Intellectually, I have always been highly interested in technical researches in geology, a field where much remains to be discovered. Especially during the last two years, however, I have felt gradually drawn to the study, not of prehistoric, but of present-day humanity. I am developing an increasingly clear concept of man as the supreme terrestrial phenomenon, in which the great geological processes and the still greater life-stream reach their culmination. In other words, I am discovering geology in its human prolongation.... My first aim would be to make those who study general human problems—geography, economics, political science—realize that the beings whom they study are truly geological phenomena of a surpassingly high order, and biological —or rather hyper-biological—phenomena of a surpassingly high degree of organization.
>
> Without realizing it, we are living in our planet's most dramatic and most eventful age; yet geologists, I know not why, study all

the concentric spheres that make up the earth except one: that formed by the layer of thinking beings. To scholars specifically interested in man, geology is a closed book. What we have to do, therefore, is to unite the two points of view. (15 October 1926.)

To this anticipation of the *Phenomenon of Man* we may add another passage (from a letter of 16 January 1927):

I propose to undertake a study of Man, not just prehistoric Man, but Man as the greatest telluric and biological event on our planet. I am more and more convinced that we are as blind to the terrestrial layer of man as our forefathers were to the mountains and oceans. This conviction has come to dominate my attitude to science. To put it another way: geology extends into the human, and it is this prolongation that we have to bring out.

Teilhard's activities at this time are not fully clear unless we have some acquaintance with the scientific institutions then established at Peking. A note in the *Letters from a Traveller* enumerates them:

The International Research Organization at Peking included three centres: the Geological Survey (Chinese-American-Swedish), the Rockefeller Medical Institute (American-Chinese), and the Free Chinese University (an American foundation). The staffs, who were more or less shared in common by all three institutes, were grouped again in the Geological Society and the Natural History Society, to which had just been added the Institute for Prehistoric Studies (a Carnegie endowment). There were, in addition, visiting missions, such as the Andrews (American) and the Sven Hedin (Swedish).

The Geological Service had been created by V. K. Ting, a Chinese of outstanding intelligence, working on a foundation laid by the Swedish scientist J. Gunar Andersson, geological adviser to the Agricultural Service. Ting invited Dr A. W. Grabau to join him on the Geological Survey as chief palaeontologist, launched the review *Palaeontologia Sinica*, founded the Chinese Geological Society (a team of younger scientists), joined his colleague Wong Wen-hao in setting up laboratories, and undertook a topographical and geological atlas.[5]

Wong, Ting's colleague, had studied at Louvain (we have already

[5] "V. K. Ting: Biographical Note", *Bulletin of the Geological Society of China*, vol. 16 (1936-7).

mentioned his meeting with Teilhard in 1922 at Brussels). He was a distinguished man, a fine mineralogist, affable but discreet, a diplomat and not without ambition. He was to succeed to Ting's position in the survey when Ting resigned to devote his attention to the Peipiao mines.

A. W. Grabau, an American of German origin, had assisted Ting and Wong in founding the Chinese Geological Society and the Museum of Natural History at Peking. In addition, the Rockefeller Foundation had established, also at Peking, the Peiping Union Medical College, or Rockefeller Medical Institute, where Davidson Black,[6] a Canadian, started the anatomy department's Cenozoic Era laboratory. Many of Teilhard's letters are written on stationery with the heading "Department of Anatomy, Peiping Union Medical College, China".

There were three universities. The earliest, Yenching University, a dozen miles out of Peking near the Summer Palace, was established by an interdenominational Protestant association. This soon achieved a fine standing, thanks to an excellent staff, which included, for example, Barbour, who had taught there since 1920. The Pei-ta, or National University of Peking, where Grabau taught, was founded a little later. Thirdly, Fu-jen was a Catholic university founded somewhat later by the American Benedictines, who were succeeded by German and Austrian priests of the Society of the Divine Word.

Scientific research was organized chiefly by Swedes (from the University of Uppsala), and by Americans; the Americans, however, were educating Chinese destined to replace them. Other cities, too, had institutions of higher learning: Shanghai with its Université Aurore, Tientsin with its Hwang-ho Pai-ho Museum and its Peiyang University, and Nanking with its National Institute of Research and its Academia Sinica (of which Teilhard was to become, in 1929, a corresponding member).

Typical of Teilhard's relations with other scientists in China is his account of a lecture he gave (20 October 1926).

...I went to Peking on the occasion of a meeting held in honour of the Crown Prince of Sweden (himself an almost professional archaeologist) by the Peking scientific societies (at Peking the Swedish influence is very great). I was honoured by being

[6] See G. B. Barbour, "Memorial of Davidson Black", *Proceedings of the Geological Society of America* for 1934.

assigned one of the three lectures and spoke (in English!) between a Chinese and a Swedish lecturer. I delight in cosmopolitanism of this kind. The Prince, moreover, arrived this very day in Tientsin for the sole purpose of visiting our museum's prehistory series, which has given us considerable "face". But winter, setting in only last night with a sudden blizzard (presaged by flights of wild geese) has made access to the museum somewhat difficult. (2 November 1926.)

Though we know little about relationships between Teilhard and the Swedish scientist J. Gunar Andersson, we have a note about the great explorer Sven Hedin.[7] In a letter of 27 February 1927 Teilhard wrote:

This fortnight I have been spending at Peking for the meeting of the Geological Society and have made the cordial acquaintance of Sven Hedin, who is about to leave for two years in Turkestan. He has in fact sent four members of his expedition (two Swedes and two Chinese) to me to get some advice on looking for ancient worked stone pieces and fossil bones.

As for the Americans, one group was made up of members of the Andrews mission: Andrews himself, Matthew, Granger, and Nelson, all specialists in Mongolian studies.[8] Teilhard had his photograph taken with them, and later, 19 June 1926, Matthew, Granger, and Nelson visited Tientsin to examine and discuss Teilhard's findings. Andrews is frequently mentioned in Teilhard's letters; and Granger and Matthew were regular correspondents: we find references to arrangements for conferences and to exchanges of scientific information, of publications, of fossils, and of plaster impressions and casts. Their correspondence contained no philosophical or religious discussions and no exchange of confidential information.

Another important name, of course, is that of Henry Fairfield Osborn, founder of the Osborn Library and founder and director of the American Museum. Teilhard always treated him with great deference, though later there is an added tone of cordiality. Osborn (who died 6 November 1935, at the age of seventy-eight) was both a brilliant palaeontologist and a distinguished American gentleman,

[7] Sven Hedin appears to have been by no means over-modest. At a dinner in his honour in Peking, he spoke for two hours on end. Teilhard spent much of this time trying to make the Abbé Breuil laugh by imitating the speaker.

[8] This was known as the Third American Expedition. Matthew was a Canadian. Granger was the palaeontologist.

affable and unassuming but never forgetful of his dignity. It was he who wrote the first important work on Teilhard.[9]

Among notable scientists permanently employed at this time in China were the geologist A. W. Grabau and P. Davidson Black, chief palaeontologist of the Geological Survey of China.

Grabau, father of all the institutions for natural history in China, and frequent host to gatherings of scientists, was a former professor at Columbia University and a specialist in stratigraphic geology. Despite age and threatening infirmities, he was full of life, and an excellent conversationalist. Teilhard was very fond of him, and appreciated his intuitive mind and his sense of humour.

Black had in 1919 accepted the chair of neurology and embryology, and in 1921 that of anatomy, at the Peiping Union Medical College, that is, on the American medical faculty. An anthropologist, it was he who in 1927 persuaded the Geological Service of China to set up the Cenozoic Research Laboratory (supported by the Rockefeller commission) for exhaustive research of the Choukou-tien site, where the discovery of *Sinanthropus* was later made. He was active and nimble (the Indians in Canada had nicknamed him Little White Muskrat), of energetic mind, self-confident, with a passion for truth, modest, cordial both with his Chinese colleagues and with his subordinates, kindly towards children, and devoted to his work; he and Teilhard soon struck up a lively friendship, for the Canadian too, was fun-loving, and the two together could give free rein to boyish spirits. Teilhard was later to pay Black this tribute:

Davidson Black's extraordinary power to inspire was due not only to his charm and to the vitality of his personality, so completely human, but also to the combined universality and perfect co-ordination of his talents and interests. He was as methodical in administration as he was in bibliography, marvellously adroit in detaching fossils and in preparing castings, at once impulsive and self-controlled in research, and not only expert in his own science of anatomy but also extraordinarily well versed in geology, physics, and chemistry.

As he saw it, the discovery of human origins was but part of the single problem of the history of all life and of the continents themselves. . . . It seems that there is hardly anyone now alive who could control such a diversity of enterprises.

[9] *Explorations, Researches, and Publications of Pierre Teilhard de Chardin, 1911–31*, American Museum Novitates, 25 August 1931.

George B. Barbour, the Scot, was to begin his life's work as a geologist, at the University of Cincinnati in 1932. We have already noted his work at the Sang-kan-ho diggings in 1925. As a geologist he possessed an astonishing skill in analysing the successive stages of the geology of a region, at finding in it clues to the periods of erosion and of fills, and of connecting these with orogenic or climatic events. Partly as a result of his broad education, he was able to turn his attention from science to an understanding of religious problems; he was destined to become one of Teilhard's intimate friends, and to undertake a number of field expeditions with him. The two men—the one a Presbyterian and the other a Catholic priest— worked well together from every point of view.

This list of Teilhard's American and British friends is by no means exhaustive, but it brings out Teilhard's constant and friendly contact with Americans in China and with those connected with the American Museum in New York. These American friendships were to endure until the end of his life, when the United States had succeeded China as his adopted country.

Teilhard's relationships with the Chinese call for more explanation. Ting and Wong we have already introduced. Two other Chinese, Pei Wen-Chung and C. C. Young,[10] will make their appearance later, in what we shall call the first Peking period.

Teilhard, it should be remembered, was becoming "more and more a Chinese geologist". There were two reasons for this. First, the continued growth of Chinese nationalist feeling ("the whole country is riddled with nationalist propaganda", Teilhard wrote in 1927). Secondly, the West was no longer the only centre of scientific research. Thanks to assistance from the West, Peking was becoming increasingly important.

Gone are the days when you went to the Far East in order to haul back everything to the West as the only centre of scientific study. Peking, too, is rapidly becoming such a centre, one of specialized importance for geological studies. Personally, I am doing my work for this centre, at least as much as for Paris, where, to tell the truth, the real importance of a certain part of my work is being almost completely missed. (12 November 1926.)

[10] "Young" is an anglicized version of "Yang". He met Teilhard in Paris during the winter of 1927.

One result of rising nationalism was that scientific expeditions into any part of Chinese territory were meeting with increasing opposition from the Chinese authorities:

The Chinese have become so suspicious of research by foreigners that every non-Chinese *organization* (even though established in China, like the Licent museum) is looked at askance. *Individual* foreigners, on the other hand (like me), are welcome. (2 April 1929.)

Again, on 15 April 1929 he writes:

The past three or four years, ideas have changed very, very rapidly in China. A sort of "committee of public safety" has been set up, namely, the Commission for the Preservation of Chinese Antiquities (made up of writers!), and this organization, full of suspicions, obliges even the Survey to take rigorous precautions in dealing with foreign expeditions.

The Andrews mission found that this was so; and the Croisière Jaune (of which more will be said later) was to be forbidden by Nanking to undertake any scientific work whatsoever.

In connection with this growing feeling on the part of the Chinese, there is a highly interesting letter of Teilhard's, dated 13 April 1929, which indicates his ability to appreciate the mentality of a people:

The end of my stay in Peking has been interesting and busy. I have been to see Sven Hedin. We had three hours of friendly and even intimate conversation. Hedin is a *"most fascinating man"* who is obviously lavish with his charm. I had the impression that with me there was a more personal touch, and that for a reason I didn't then suspect. When he was getting ready to go to Turkestan in 1926,[11] Hedin came up against Chinese touchiness about rights in scientific material, and he was the first to accept the conditions they insisted on. . . . He was criticized at the time, I know, and disowned by even his best European friends, who accused him of going over to the Chinese. Just then I met him, and urged him to trust the Chinese and work in with them. He is still touchingly grateful to me, as though my words had kept him going during the long months that preceded his success, which is now complete. He now has the full confidence of even the most anti-foreign Chinese, and every single one of those he took with him is now his devoted friend.

[11] Teilhard has mistaken the date. They met in February, 1927.

The reaction of the Chinese to Teilhard's enlightened attitude to co-operation between East and West was to invite him to exercise general supervision over the Geological Society.

> The Geological Service at Peking has made me repeated offers. I am now to be practically in charge of the Survey, of all research and scientific work on fossil mammals (in other words, of geological studies of the Tertiary and Quaternary in China), and this by agreement among all the Chinese, Americans, and Swedes who are regular participants in the Geological Service. (27 February 1927.)

The importance of this position, it seemed to Teilhard, was twofold. From the scientific point of view, having become in a sense a Chinese official, he would have a wider circle of contacts, could train young Chinese scientists more easily, and would have greater authority, greater "face". From the human and religious viewpoint, the importance lay in Teilhard's being the first priest, and in fact the first Catholic, to gain such official acceptance in China in either a Protestant (Swedish or British) or agnostic (Chinese) institution. In this connection the Jesuit geophysicist Fr Lejay relates the following anecdote:

> I remember that, as I was leaving after one of the Service's meetings, I felt I should take the opportunity to congratulate an American scientist who had given a brilliant talk. "Nonsense," he replied, "of the four talks given just now, three were wholly Teilhard's. To make the sessions more lively, he simply chose not to appear himself. I was just a mouthpiece!"

The appointment meant that Teilhard was now in the field of fossil mammals what Grabau was in the field of stratigraphy, and he fully appreciated his new opportunity.

> I now regret even less that I am not returning permanently to Paris for I have a feeling that life is opening out for me in the Far East. If the Chinese revolution now going on does not force my friends in Peking to lay aside their projects at any minute, the official standing offered me on the Geological Survey is full of possibilities, both in the realm of science and in the realm of contact with and action upon the mass of humanity here. There is going on here, at this very moment, a human development of almost geological dimensions; to participate in it would be a rare chance indeed. (Easter, 1927.)

Thus we find Teilhard retracing the steps of those great Jesuits who in the seventeenth and eighteenth centuries introduced European science into China and communicated Western technical skills to the Chinese. Yet Teilhard was not by any means abandoning his activities in Paris, which still remained the centre of his apostolate. On the contrary, he believed that his post on the Survey, by enhancing his prestige as a scientist, would provide him with more solid footing.

One consequence of his taking root in China was an increasing attraction towards Peking. He explains, 15 April 1929:

> I am fond of Peking, which reminds me of Paris. . . . I like it here, because here I meet original thought and activity in all walks of life, and because here, where no one, comparatively, knows anyone else, people are likely to be more frank and candid. And then, the whole atmosphere suits me, with its almost indifferent serenity; the rest of China, nay, the whole world can be rocking from one end to the other: Peking remains motionless, under its blue sky, amid its white flowers, and in the midst of its enormous dust.

He was less charmed with Tientsin, that city of bankers and warehousemen, a sort of endless shopping centre in which any intellectual or spiritual contact was inconceivable. There he shut himself up as in a peaceful hermitage of thought, and prayer, and untroubled tenor of life. The result was that he came to be more and more often in the capital. He spent practically the whole of December, 1926, there with members of the Pan-Pacific Science Congress from Tokyo: Australians, New Zealanders, French (including, for a fortnight, Alfred Lacroix, permanent secretary of the Academy of Sciences), and Americans (including Barbour, Bailey Willis, and Nevin Fenneman).

It was on this same occasion, incidentally, that he finally paid a rather bored visit to Peking's art treasures and palaces; unlike Breuil, he had nothing of the art lover about him.[12] In China, Teilhard's aesthetic interest centred rather upon the geometry of the walls, the curve of the roofs, the storey upon storey of the towers, the poetry of the ancient, rook-ridden trees, and the lonesome profile

[12] There was nothing of the antiquarian in Teilhard. "It is a distortion of history", he wrote, "to see in it an attempt to gather up fragments of truth or beauty that have been abandoned or lost on the battlefields of life. Such things are no great loss to us." (*La vision du passé*, p. 267.)

of the mountains. Curios, enamels, porcelains, jades—these he shuddered at. He made no exception save for those four-thousand-year-old jades whose lines are as pure as those of the jewels of ancient Egypt.

Some time in February, 1927, he assisted at the meeting of the Geological Society, where he no doubt felt himself to be permanently representing France. We have already quoted him as saying that he delighted in cosmopolitanism of this kind; in these scientific meetings he was, therefore, in his element. As regards this meeting he wrote:

> Not that I love Paris any the less. But it strikes me that I breathe still more freely in the big, lively, international gatherings. Everyone is so free, so expansive, so cordial! (27 February 1927.)

Apart from enjoying the atmosphere of cordiality, Teilhard found in these meetings a direct intuition of human homogeneity:

> While I was spinning, I hope, more threads for my web (the web of possible influences), I felt myself becoming a more convinced internationalist, or, more exactly, "planetarian". (5 December 1926.)
>
> ... on that day, in that meeting, the last before many took their departure, in that Far East atmosphere, so heavy with hatred and passions, there certainly passed over the company some shadow of tragedy. The table was strewn with apple blossom, emblem of spring—and of storms. The speakers rose one after another to talk of friendship, of co-operation, of more or less high hopes. I am sure—for I feel it in myself, or find it in others, at every moment— that the world is full of vigour, yet it struggles and strangles, for there is no one, not even among Christians, to set an example and to pioneer a way of fully human action and life, a way passionately and actively open to every good, to every beauty, and to every truth. There is but one irresistible contact which draws and unites—the contact of whole man with whole man. (20 February 1927.)
>
> ... I contemplate in fancy a kind of "Book of Earth", wherein I should let myself speak, not as a Frenchman, or as belonging to any separate category, but as Man, or simply as "Planetarian". I should undertake to express the confidence, the ambitions, the fruition, and the disappointments too, the insecurities, and the feeling of dizziness, of one who has realized what destiny awaits the Earth (mankind) as one complete whole. I should not be concerned to reach agreement with any of the accepted currents of

thought, but only with expressing what I myself experience; I should try to communicate my faith in human endeavour and in human unity, and my impatience with all the petty barriers that divide and isolate minds whose true future lies in coming together; I should like, too, to picture the frustration we feel at finding ourselves imprisoned on one little sphere which will soon have nothing more to offer us, and our desolation when we realize that we are, all of us equally, alone in starry space.

Here, I believe, we have an immense psychological domain of thought and feeling that no one enters because it seems altogether too fanciful. In fact it is as rigorously objective as any concern with family or society. If I could get such a book written, it would be, in a way, the book of my life. (12 October 1926.)

This sense of Earth, in Teilhard's case, although congenital, was certainly developed by his experience as a research scholar. In fact, his idea of human convergence, his hope that mankind would find, through socialization, the self-realization which it seeks, was the fruit of a concrete experience, namely, his work on an international research team. For, whether Swedes, Americans, or Chinese, the men on the Survey became inseparable; moreover, this close-knit organization collaborated, in turn, with other such groups—not to mention the wider-embracing scientific societies and conventions which contributed to the creation of a sort of collective, unanimous consciousness. In the light of his experiences, Teilhard's cast of thought could hardly have tended towards individualism; yet we must remark that at the same time it was infinitely respectful of the individual personality. It reflected the interaction between his own astonishing personality and what he learnt in the course of a singularly rich career.

We mentioned earlier Teilhard's increasing attraction towards Peking. With this went a tendency towards a less close association with the Paris Museum and towards a closer association with the Institut de France, and especially with Alfred Lacroix, permanent secretary of the Academy of Sciences.

Teilhard had left France for China in 1923 as a student of Marcellin Boule's and with a commission from the French Museum, it being Boule's idea to associate Teilhard permanently with the latter and to make Teilhard his successor. These passages from Teilhard's correspondence define the relationship between the master and the disciple:

...my poor old teacher Boule, in the midst of his bereave-ment,[13] would so like me to return yet is so hesitant (as I learn from other sources) to ask me outright that I blush to ask him for any more money to finance my stay. I just don't know exactly what to do. Personally, I should look forward to a field trip in the spring—for the good it would do, and not just to please my-self. I ought to have something to show for my time spent here. (12 October 1926.)

Let me tell you that my preoccupation with swelling the fossil collections of France, though I keep in mind my obligations in justice in this matter (for after all I am being partly paid for that very purpose), has had to take a second place to my concern with and interest in co-operating with the Pan-Pacific's enormous pro-ject in geology. . . . In the past seven months I have succeeded in doubling the number of my acquaintances and my sphere of action in these circles. (31 December 1926.)

I now find myself (with several others, of course) heading the geological advance in China. In my own field I am succeeding in defining various formations spread over an area as big as half of Europe. This I cannot just let drop. Without me (that is to say, what I represent), the French Museum has no existence in the Far East—whatever Boule may think about it; with me, it is on an equal footing with Nagasaki and Uppsala. (20 February 1927.)

Another cloud has settled upon the Museum. Boule has lately written to tell me (though in a most affectionate letter) that he is cutting off my funds for this year. Let me add, in passing, that this does not require me to alter plans for my spring field trip. Well, I have learned from a reliable source at the Laboratory that Boule is dissatisfied: (1) because I left France against his advice (as if it were any of my doing!) and (2) I can now see that every-thing I have been telling him about my finds here (they are more valuable to Peking and geology in general than to his show-cases) has only served to annoy him. I feel a really filial affection for him as I always shall—so when I answered I did what I could to pacify him. But it will be plain to you that as far as I am con-cerned I am not going to change my methods one iota. Before everything else comes research in its widest perspective—the ser-vice of Truth. Afterwards, the Museum. It must be perfectly clear, surely, that the Museum can only gain from this? Lacroix certainly understod this; he saw it immediately. Anyway, I have written a formal apology to Paul Lemoine.[14] As for Boule, a

13 Boule had just lost his first wife.
14 Lemoine was director of the Museum, and professor of geology.

quarter of an hour's conversation with him would set everything right. (27 February 1927.)

In this "conflict", which remained entirely friendly, between Teilhard and Marcellin Boule, there was something to be said on both sides: Boule, like Licent, had had in mind somebody to work for his Museum; and Teilhard, in fact, did contribute to enriching the Museum. He sent his finds in the Ordos, and a letter of 12 October 1926 says that seven cases of fossils have been sent off. Yet it cannot be denied that on the whole Teilhard's expeditions (to Shansi in 1926, and eastern Mongolia in 1927) were of little profit to the Museum; he was turning his attention to the geology of China, and tending to rely on Sino-American organizations, with large funds at their disposal. Moreover, China was changing, and welcomed collaborators but not collectors. It was reasonable, in a sense, for Boule to suspend the subsidies from the Museum; but Teilhard's attitude seems no less reasonable. Whatever the Museum lost in immediate advantages it would regain, in the long run, in the form of French prestige in the Far East. If the National Centre of Scientific Research had existed at that time, it would have been the perfect solution to the dilemma.

In any case, relations between Teilhard and Alfred Lacroix became closer. Teilhard needed a firm link with the West, for his position (in the administrative sense of the word) in China appeared somewhat insecure. But the main consideration was that Lacroix (who, also, was a former teacher of Teilhard's, too) was a geologist,[15] and thus in a better position to understand Teilhard's work in China. Contact between the two men was continual. On 15 July 1924 we first learn that Teilhard was getting "not a few specimens for Lacroix". On 12 October 1926 Lacroix was having funds sent to Teilhard. In a letter of 16 January 1927 Teilhard wrote:

The whole month of December was spent at Peking in the company of the members of the Congress from Tokyo—Australians, Americans, and, to cut short the list, Lacroix, with whom I spent a fortnight. It was nice for me to see him again—so fine a man, and so human. We made quite an excursion to Kalgan together, in conditions of unbelievable discomfort. At least, how-

---

[15] Lacroix was a specialist in eruptive rocks. Teilhard continually sent him information on this subject, and his *Map of the younger eruptive rocks in China* attests Lacroix's influence. Lacroix died in 1948.

ever, he got a look at some of the principal eruptive rocks of China and was well satisfied with the experience.

These relations were to continue, and to become increasingly cordial. We know that at Easter, 1927, Lacroix wrote a friendly letter, promising to help Teilhard in every way he could. On 7 July 1927 Teilhard sent Lacroix over two hundred pounds of carefully selected specimens. In short, Teilhard had found ample compensation for the loss of Boule's support. He also received financial help[16] at a difficult moment when he was no longer able to dispose of Museum funds and was not yet getting the help of American money. He also had the moral support of the Institut de France— while waiting for the latter to open its doors to him. Finally he was recognized as filling practically the role of permanent representative of France in the domain of Pan-Pacific sciences.

Before the end of this second period in China, Teilhard was presented with a new and magnificent opportunity: the discovery of the celebrated site at Choukou-tien. His first reference to this is in a letter of 12 November 1926:

> The Chinese geological party has announced the finding of two human teeth in a very ancient Quaternary layer (approximately contemporaneous with the layer I worked in, south of Kalgan). This would be an event of importance; unfortunately, I am not wholly convinced that the teeth in question are human. I have seen only a photograph of them, the specimens themselves being in Uppsala.

A few months later we find a second allusion:

> For many reasons I suspect that the deposits in the Choukou-tien cavern are of the San Men period. Nevertheless, the two humanoid teeth presented by Zdansky would be extremely interesting. Unfortunately I must own that the photographs do not seem to me highly convincing. In any case, as you know, Dr Black has got some new diggings under way.

In *L'Apparition de l'homme* we find a succinct account of the diggings:

> Choukou-tien lies some thirty miles south-west of Peking, at the edge of the Si Shan (meaning Western Hills) that at this point

[16] From the Loutreuil foundation: cf. letter of 22 June 1926, acknowledging the receipt of 10,000 francs.

defines the great Cheli plain. All around the village the last foot-hills of the mountains come down in rounded ridges of very hard blue Ordovician limestone, which the natives since time im-memorial have used for making chalk. In this limestone, a net-work of fissures filled with red clay—and almost all bearing fossils—has been exposed by the quarrying. . . . A red window let into a rampart of hard, bluish rock: so it must have appeared to the discoverers a score of years ago in the abandoned quarries, of that fossil-crammed fissure, soon to become celebrated under the name of Choukou-tien's Site One.

It was Dr J. G. Andersson who, about 1921, saw it for the first time, without any idea that behind that red window was hidden, as Teilhard goes on to say:

. . . an almost inexhaustible deposit of sediments, nearly three hundred and fifty feet long, a hundred feet wide on the average, and well over a hundred and fifty feet deep.

In 1922 Andersson had it excavated by O. Zdansky, an Austrian palaeontologist attached to the University of Uppsala. Zdansky found here two isolated teeth (a third molar and an upper bicuspid) of the human type, which were at once a matter of lively contro-versy. Having gone around for a long time with these two teeth in his pocket, taking them out on occasion to show to specialists, he finally published his discovery in 1927, without, however, an appreciation of their exact import.[17] At this same time, Dr Andersson was leaving China. Andersson, however, found an enthusiastic suc-cessor in the person of Davidson Black. Thanks to the co-operation of the Geological Service of China and the Rockefeller Foundation, plans for extensive excavations were drawn up by Black and Dr Wong Wen-Hao, and with American funds put in hand immedi-ately. Work began in 1927, under the direction of Dr B. Bohlin and three hundred cubic metres of rock and fossil-bearing inlay were taken up from Site One; here a third tooth, of a type indisputably human, was found.

It is interesting to note that Teilhard, who was to be so promi-nently associated with the work at Choukou-tien and the defence of the hominid character of *Sinanthropus* and his cultural capa-

[17] "Preliminary notice on two teeth of a hominoid from a cave in Chihli (China)", *Bulletin of the Geological Society of China*, vol. 5, nos. 3–4 (Dec., 1927).

bilities, was at first sceptical of the human quality of the teeth. It is characteristic of his extreme prudence in the assessment and interpretation of facts. Equally interesting is his early presentiment of the importance, in the study of human origins, of the Far East. Fr Lejay, in his *Rapport sur les titres du Père Pierre Teilhard de Chardin*, recalls:

> ...a conversation I had with Teilhard aboard the ship we both happened to be in in 1926, when he was travelling to China for the second time. When I expressed my astonishment at his sacrificing so lightheartedly the brilliant career which would doubtless have been his in France, he replied: "But it's precisely there that the greatest progress is going to be made in the study of fossil man, whose traces will one day be followed from Java clear into Mongolia."

On 27 August 1927 Teilhard left again for France, arriving at Marseilles on 1 October. These fourteen months had been doubly fruitful. On the religious side he had produced *Le milieu divin*; scientifically he had done useful work in the field and had won a commanding position in the world of Chinese geology. The "smiling scientist", as the Chinese called him, had acquired incomparably greater "face", in China, in Paris, and internationally.

CHAPTER FIVE

Interlude: France and Ethiopia

E have little direct information about Teilhard's stay in
France (from 1 October 1927 to 7 November 1928). We
know, from his *Letters from a Traveller*, that he had been
longing to revisit the scenes of his childhood; and a note to Édouard
Le Roy shows that they continued an intimate exchange of ideas.
Teilhard writes:

> This strikes me as very good indeed. You have sharpened and
> systematized my thought (on the place of Man in the classifica-
> tion). I have put comments on pages 6, 7, 8, and 12. About these
> we can talk, as well as about Geoffroy-St-Hilaire's idea: Buffon
> on the "Kingdom of Man". I must be in Auvergne Wednesday,
> the twenty-sixth. I shall be coming to see you at eight-thirty in the
> evening on Monday, the twenty-fourth. Teilhard.[1]

His correspondence gives an idea of the atmosphere in which he
was living and working:

> Myself, I am caught up in the bustle of work resumed and
> contacts re-established.... I am again in touch with students at
> the École Normale, thanks to Hemmer, their chaplain, a friend
> of Portal's, and Parish Priest of La Trinité. I have a number of
> sidelines, too; I am hard at work on two articles—in fact three.
> I go the day after tomorrow to Brussels on geology business. I
> plan to spend twenty-four hours at Louvain, where Charles is
> expecting me. (11 November 1927.)

> My life goes on as usual, kept very busy at the Museum, with
> many odd jobs, and contacts in most circles, from extreme right
> to extreme left.... Outside the Lab., as I was saying, I see a

[1] 20 October 1927. The pages refer to the first three lectures on "Les origines
humaines et l'évolution de l'intelligence", which were first printed in the
Revue des cours et conférences, December, 1927.

certain number of people, among whom the students at the Normale are the most interesting. The Abbé Hemmer, who has charge of this group, can spare them little time and I, therefore, am free to go there often, upon request, which is to say as often as possible.... I am to give them their three-day retreat before Lent, at Gentilly. What with one thing and another, then, I don't have much time to think. Paris is demanding; so, thinking of Tientsin (where I fully plan to return in the autumn), I often tell myself, "*Haec nobis Deus otia fecit.*".... Saw Vialleton the other day. His heart is in the right place, I think, but his ideas grow more and more nebulous.... Here we have an excellent man, forced into philosophy by selfish admirers, who is going to end up by becoming dangerous. (14 February 1928.) Saw Valéry[2] again, a number of times. (9 June 1928.)

He continued to frequent the French Geological Society, and, in 1928, the Anthropological Society. He resumed his Belgian contacts. He contributed to various periodicals, including the *Comptes rendus sommaires de la Société de Bio-Géographie*, the *Palaeobiologica* (Vienna and Leipzig), the *Bulletin de l'Académie Royale de Belgique*, and the *Archives de l'Institut de Paléontologie Humaine*.

His priestly life was no less full. From Jacques Perret we learn:

When the death of the Abbé Portal, 19 June 1926, threw us into serious confusion, giving occasion to all sorts of uncertainties and disagreements—you know the Normale students' obstinate independence and contrariness—we were inclined to turn to Fr Teilhard, the only one who could restore harmony among us, so much did his intellectual superiority overwhelm us and at the same time give us confidence. We asked him to take charge of our group; this, of course, he was not free to do, but I note that from January to June of 1928 he was with us ten times, either for talks or for dinners ... to which we invited Normale students, alumni, and St-Cloud students.

A letter from a member of another group, G. Soulages, tells us how they, too, turned to Teilhard:

In about 1926 or 1927 the Rue d'Ulm group divided: on one side, a more conservative group, on the other, centred around Perret, Martel, and Légaut, those who were trying to take Christian teaching, the Gospel, holiness, not only seriously but as literally as possible. At the same time they wanted to remain in

[2] Teilhard met Paul Valéry through the Baron d'Huart, a classmate of Albéric's at the École Navale.

the world and work as students or scientists or technicians, with the same passion and devotion as you might find in the best of non-Christians.... It was this intensely religious group (something of an embarrassment to the ecclesiastical authorities) that Teilhard was particularly fond of. It was to them that he opened the best of his thought. And it was we who—with infinite precautions—ran off the first of his publications. You should read the *Lettres d'Antoine Martel*, published by R. Pons (*Revue des Jeunes*), to get an idea of the atmosphere surrounding this group.

During this year Teilhard gave a retreat, in the school at Gentilly, to the Rue d'Ulm group, treating such topics as "Life and Matter", and "The Religious Value of the World", and following the theme of *Le milieu divin*. This retreat had the effect of reuniting and re-inspiring the group. One ex-Normalien, then teaching at the University, borrowed Teilhard's manuscript for a few hours to read it and ended up by spending forty-eight hours recopying the whole by hand. The recollections of Étienne Borne give a vivid impression of this retreat:

> ...I shall always remember the retreat given in February of 1928 by Father Teilhard to the École Normale students of the Rue d'Ulm. At that time I was under the influence of Alain, and was impressed by his view of religion as a sort of wonderful poetry and mythology. To me, hesitating thus between Alain and religion properly speaking, Teilhard brought a conviction of the reality of the supernatural. Thanks to him I recognized in religion an authentic encounter, consisting not in the discovery of a system, a doctrine, but in contact with what is more real than the visible world. I discovered that the Mass is an action which changes the world, and felt the overpowering reality of Christian fact.

To Mme Jean Teilhard d'Eyry (*née* Odette Bacot) we are indebted for a copy of the address Teilhard gave at her wedding. *Pour Odette et pour Jean* illuminates his priestly mentality, and his approach to the supernatural through the natural. In the following passage he sums up the spiritual aspect of marriage, and stresses the attainment of the spiritual through the biological, constantly striving towards a common objective, "above" and "beyond", two key-words in his thought:

> If you wish, both of you, to respond to the call made to you (or, better, the grace offered you) today by a God-enlivened life, take

your stand, as you must, without fear or hesitation, upon tangible matter; but, through and above it, direct your belief towards the intangible spirit.

Believe in the spirit which lies behind you, that is, in the long series of unions like your own, which as age has succeeded age have accumulated, to transmit to you a treasure of health, wisdom, and freedom. This treasure is today placed in your hands. Keep in mind that you bear the responsibility for it before God and the universe.

Believe, next, in the spirit which lies beyond you. Creation never stops. Life strives to prolong itself through the two of you. Let your union, then, be not a closed embrace, but an activity— a thousand times more unifying than any repose—of common effort towards a common end, ever more grandly conceived, and passionately sought.

Believe, finally, in—and this word contains all the others—the spirit which you share. You have given yourselves to each other to provide infinite scope for understanding, for personal enrichment, and for the growth of sensitivity. It is, therefore, in an interpenetration and constant exchange of thoughts, affections, dreams, and prayer that you will discover each other above all. Only there, as you know, in the spirit beyond the flesh, lie no satiety, no disappointments, no limits. Only there, for your love, lies the free air, the royal road.

On 7 November 1928 Teilhard embarked at Marseilles, but not directly for the Far East. With Pierre Lamare, who was going on to the Yemen, he was a guest of Henry de Monfreid from about 20 November to the end of February in French Somaliland.

His visit included stays at Obok, and at Harar, in Ethiopia, and again at Obok, all described in the *Letters from a Traveller*. The Somaliland coast proved a disappointment, for the Governor, hostile to Henry de Monfreid, allowed him to visit only the edge of the eruptive massif of the Mabla. But on his return from Ethiopia Teilhard was to enjoy, from the scientific point of view, a good deal more liberty.

He spent a fortnight in a small boat on the Red Sea, leading a most primitive existence (they ground their corn to make bread), enjoying the scenery and the rock paintings on the coastal mountainside, watching the starry sky with De Monfreid, and teaching him to see Christ everywhere in creation, giving him the key to the mystery, helping him to understand that all elements, and all events,

4+

conspire to elevate us. De Monfreid made this comment on memories of those days:

> From that time on, Teilhard was my brother. . . . In humanity, in purity of soul, Teilhard was an extraordinary being. Not a shadow ever disturbed his calm. He had the limpidity of a diamond, flooded with divine light. The man himself was a light, surpassing measurement.

In an unavoidably technical letter of 4 December 1928 we find Teilhard hard at work in the tropical weather, and reporting:

> The history of the coral plateau here seems to me to have been as follows:
>
> 1. Emergence of the coralline beach (end of the Pliocene?).
> 2. Furrowing of a first network of torrents and littoral cuts.
> 3. Sinking, bringing in a return of the sea into the littoral cuts (some miles back in the clays). Simultaneously, a heavy fill of very large gravels, of the whole border zone of the Mabla (I believe I was able to make out the connection of the river banks and the marine banks). This phase, very important, doubtless corresponds to a European maximum glacial stage.
> 4. Re-emergence, bringing in the cutting of the torrents and present-day marine cliffs, up to a hundred feet below the fills that took place in the "glacial" phase.

At present, the Obok plateau forms a very level surface (where the coralline is on the surface, without any alluvial deposit), this surface being connected with the broken stones that cover the large gravels which came down from the Mabla. Now—and it was to lead up to this point that I set forth the preceding geological explanation—this plateau is strewn with pieces of carved stones (flint and rhyolites), which are highly polished.

I am not speaking only of such accidental fragments as the natives might produce when knocking open shells. Tools among these pieces are very rare, *but there are some of them.* Of these the commonest are Mousterian in style: discs, scrapers, and points (rare, but well defined). One single piece, rather small (about the size of one's little finger) is considerably and skilfully worked on both edges; but it is perhaps of a different age. All this is not very important; but I have gathered up as much as I could and shall send it to you soon. As for the age of the material, so far as can be seen the tools date after the final re-emergence (stage 4, above). I have in fact found some of these flakes on the eroded surfaces below the one-hundred-foot level, along the present-day wadis.

Men who fashioned these tools seem to have lived in a topographical situation closely like the present one. But there was at that time perhaps a modicum of topsoil, today carried away by wind. Nowadays no very dense population could be envisaged as living on this plateau. In Ethiopia I hope to do something to complete these partial observations. As for the chipping of the flints, I believe I have succeeded in establishing that the pieces left on the ground are liable to get further cutting from natural causes, when getting knocked slightly on the cutting edges; this is not, then, a result of further handling. You will see what I mean on the pieces that I send you.

In the above passage we see Teilhard at work, and can note his gift for observation, his critical spirit, and his general scientific method.

Teilhard was first of all a geologist, secondly a palaeontologist, specializing in mammals, and only thirdly a prehistorian and anthropologist. Of foremost interest in his palaeontological and anthropological discoveries, therefore, is the fact that they always had a solid, or in any case rarely questionable, geological basis. In the quotation above his method is clearly evident: first, to get a geological understanding of a region, and then to look for ancient traces of the presence there of human beings; he looks first, therefore, at the geographical situation, for it is this that gives, for the geographical context at least, a relative chronological scale permitting the fossils and artifacts in it to be dated.

Teilhard used to admire Barbour's talent for observation. Teilhard, we learn from those who knew him, was similarly talented. His quick eye would catch any chipped or chiselled stone that lay on the ground. Georges Le Fèvre, for example, noted in *La Croisière Jaune* that "His downcast eyes would spot the smallest bit of cut stone betraying itself by its redness on the bare greyness of the wind-swept soil."

The second thing we note is his critical mind and his extreme caution. He took steps to establish that certain further marks on the flints had been the work of nature. Palaeontologists are well aware of the troublesomeness of stones that have not remained *in situ* and have been subject to modifications not due to human industry.

There was considerable variety in Teilhard's letters, and often enough considerable variety in a single letter. Thus, after the technical passage cited, we read:

I did not deprive myself of the pleasure of inspecting the banks of living coral; they are something marvellous. Down in the water, transparent as crystal, there lie, rounding off or bushing out, the red, green, and veined madrepores; and in the midst of this forest of coral branches a swarm of fish swim in and out, bizarre, red, yellow, black, blue, violet, as shimmering with colour as hummingbirds.

On 8 December 1928 Teilhard and his companion Pierre Lamare boarded a train of the Franco-Ethiopian railway, a primitive conveyance that never exceeded 25 miles an hour and travelled only during the daytime. In the morning passengers were summoned from the company-built bungalows by blasts from the whistle.

Their route included the gorges of the Aouache, and Dire Dawa and the village of Araoiu (below the picturesque mud-hut city of Harar), in both of which De Monfreid had interests. Their finds in Ethiopia were important; Lamare was able to confirm definitely the identity of the geological make-up of Harar and the Yemen, and Teilhard, writing from Obok, 19 January 1929, said:

The end of my stay in Abyssinia was marked by two considerable successes. Quite apart from a fine store of rocks and observations collected for Lacroix, I found within a few days, around Dire Dawa (1) a cave with an important petrified deposit of fine tools (probably Palaeolithic) and several paintings; (2) a stratum rich in ammonites, so far unknown in this part of Abyssinia, and most valuable from the geologist's point of view. In each case, then, I have something completely new. I let Boule know at once, and I am hoping that a case of specimens will reach Paris speedily and safely. So I am now in a position to draw up at least two useful articles on Ethiopia and Somaliland.[3]

On one occasion, while exploring a cave pointed out to them by De Monfreid, they had to contend with an army of enraged mason wasps. De Monfreid describes the incident:

I remember a cave in which we had to battle against a formidable army of mason wasps, who hang their nests from the limestone roofs of caves. These large insects, with their black bodies and steel-blue wings, are generally harmless, but show great ferocity when defending their rock-clinging citadel.

Scarcely had we reached the narrow bank leading up to the rocky overhang of the cave opening when a swarm of them de-

---

[3] *Letters from a Traveller*, p. 150.

ployed themselves in a portentously buzzing curtain at the entrance. The African who accompanied us halted us just in time: one more step and all those enormous wasps would have attacked. Their sting is so painful that often the underlying muscle becomes paralysed. Moreover, the virulence of the poison is such that ten stings can cause death.

But explore we must, for Teilhard, judging from some stones lying outside the cave, had no doubt of the interest of what lay inside, and would have plunged in had the African and I not restrained him. So we had to resort to a regular siege to dislodge the winged garrison. Our procedure was to enter at night with enough brush to fire the whole opening, as if it had been a baker's oven. The African refused to help us, on, so to speak, religious grounds, for it seemed to him that we were trying to expel the formidable spirits guarded and defended by these giant wasps.

Finally, before sunrise the flames reached the larva-filled nests and their desperate defenders. We had to turn and run from their fury. When day broke, I could not recognize the fine and ascetic features of Teilhard in the enormous and swollen face that met my gaze. In the heat of battle, he had received a good many stings; and from the pain one sting was causing me I was able to measure the pain which he, without any complaint, was having to bear. Though it was impossible for that face to form a smile, I gathered that he was happy over our dearly-won victory.[4]

Teilhard worked on the spartan principle that: "It doesn't matter whether the water is cold or warm if you're going to have to wade through it anyway." (14 May 1922.) As usual, he was interested in the geography and the ethnology of his surroundings; and his observations on these subjects are precise and pertinent:

I find it a pleasant distraction from my work to look about me at natural scenes wholly different from those I have seen before. Once the strip of coastal desert is crossed, the traveller immediately encounters typical African bush, with its sparse mimosaceous growths, its giant candelabra-shaped, cactus-like spurges, its antelopes, its many-coloured birds, and its ant-heaps. Several times here at Araoui I have met our friends the monkeys: grey, arboreal varieties, and the terrestrial "dog-headed" monkeys, "down from the trees", seen in large bands (males, females, and youngsters of every age), moving at a great speed, in a squatting position.

[4] In *La table ronde*, June, 1955, pp. 68–9.

All this, combined with the warm sunshine (which even at this elevation of nearly 5,000 feet allows us to go in shirt-sleeves in the daytime), provides sparkling, colourful, and certainly invigorating surroundings. You would be in your element working here; a small hut would be built for you, all your own, and to refresh your spirits there would be toucans, hummingbirds, and, most tame of all the fauna, the little scarlet finches, so lacking in timidity here where nobody bothers them. If I were more of an anthropologist or ethnographer, I suppose the local aborigines would interest me a great deal. As it is, in the Dankalis, Somalis, Gallas, and others who live around us, I can see nothing but magnificent bronzed animals, who go around, even in the cultivated plains, at a short trot, Indian file, armed with long spears and broad knives. (30 December 1928.)

There were times when Teilhard's enthusiasm was almost too much for his companion. Pierre Lamare has an amusing story of their return by train to Dire Dawa:

After we had ridden a couple of hours, the train crossed a small viaduct over a gloomy, romantic chasm, at the bottom of which ran a tiny river, and which presented, moreover, a fine geological cross-section. As this tempting sight disappeared, my companion could not keep from crying out: "Oh, if only they could stop the train here! Isn't it too bad that we can't get out and take a look at that!"

Well, hardly was the rash wish out of his mouth when Clank! Clank!—and the train jarred and jerked to a sudden stop. The locomotive had gone off the track.... Teilhard and I profited by the resultant half-dozen hours of delay to examine the picturesque, shadow-filled gorge at our leisure....

The train, once more or less set to rights, limped off, willing, but not able, to make up the lost time. It didn't get into Dire Dawa till about midnight. But the whole rest of the journey I spent in moderating Teilhard's wishful enthusiasms. "Whatever you do, don't make any more wishes, because I don't know how you may stand with some of your superiors, but you certainly know the right people in heaven. If we're going to get any sleep before getting into Dire Dawa tonight, we don't want any more accidents, so please let's have no more petitions. We've had our miracle for the day."[5]

[5] Letter to the author, 1 August 1955.

CHAPTER SIX

Before the Croisière Jaune

AT the beginning of February, 1929, Teilhard embarked at
Jibuti. We know little about the voyage except that he read
Malraux's *Les Conquérants*. He found that in this

> The atmosphere, the noises, the feeling of China are evoked
> with extreme accuracy and intensity. But it is the general key of
> the book that I find so enchanting: tension and vigour in a work
> whose value may be debatable but which is conceived on a grand
> scale.[1]

On 15 March he arrived at Tientsin:

> So here I am at Tientsin, happy enough, and really feeling
> rather relieved at returning to a regular schedule of life (starting
> with morning visit and meditation). As a place China is always
> a tonic to me, I don't know why; and at the Higher Studies
> Institute I always experience a sort of mental reactivation, as if
> through the assimilation *in Deo* of all the raw energy I accumulate
> during the tense days I spend in Paris. (2 April 1929.)[2]

March, 1929, to May, 1931, was a singularly complex period for
Teilhard. In discussing it, we shall first examine Teilhard's situation in relation to the Geological Survey, then its consequences (his
role at Choukou-tien and the new form taken by expeditions), and
finally preparations for the Croisière Jaune and certain changes
entailed thereby.

We have already quoted part of a letter of 27 February 1927, in
which we learned that Americans, Swedes, and Chinese were all
asking Teilhard to take official charge, on the Survey, of everything
relating to fossil mammals. On 2 April 1929 his "delightful friends

---

[1] *Letters from a Traveller*, p. 151.
[2] *Letters from a Traveller*, p. 154.

on the Survey" were again urging him to accept this responsibility; but Teilhard found himself caught between two fires:

> ... I find myself in a delicate position between my friends on the Survey who, without Licent's blessing, are proffering me their hand, and Licent himself, whom neither friendship, nor gratitude, nor common decency, nor regard for the interests of the Jesuit Missions will allow me to drop. Right now I am attempting to thread my way in the business.... We shall come to some sort of understanding, I suppose.

But the Geological Service was becoming increasingly eager for him to join them; and his friend Wong, at Nanking, was devising the formal commission whereby Teilhard might be officially integrated into the organization as "Scientific Adviser to the Geological Survey". On 16 June 1929 the Service's invitations became pressing; and the very next day Teilhard, in the company of C. C. Young, a Chinese geologist, felt constrained to leave for western Shansi to assume duties as an Adviser of the Service. In Shansi, in accordance with arrangements earlier decided upon, he was charged mostly with work on the Tertiary and Quaternary formations. But on 7 October of the same year he wrote from Peking that he was henceforth to have an office at the Survey. Moreover, Nanking had appointed him a corresponding member of its National Research Institute. And Teilhard exclaimed:

> It is a real intellectual treat to be working (at the very centre of the development of Chinese geological science) on the gathering and co-ordination of the documents which come in here from all sides.

Teilhard was now increasingly taking over the direction, from the geological and palaeontological angle, of the work at Choukoutien. There the project was in full swing. In 1927 a thousand cubic feet of rock and fossil-bearing material was extracted; in 1928 thrice, and in 1929 ten times, that amount. By April, 1930, obstinate and painstaking work, which had nearly always to be carried on by blasting in that very hard terrain, was to yield fifteen hundred cases of fossils. The Americans, like the Chinese, did things on a big scale; they succeeded in sifting virtually the whole hill—the whole of the fossiliferous material, at least.

The result of this systematic work was the discovery of *Sinanthropus* (so named by Davidson Black). In 1928 two fragments of the jawbone had been found. On 28 December 1929 Teilhard and Black sent Boule a triumphant telegram (in English):

NEW YEAR GREETINGS. RECOVERED CHOU-KOU-TIEN UNCRUSHED ADULT SINANTHROPUS SKULL ENTIRE EXCEPT FACE. LETTER FOLLOWS.

The letter filled in details:

At Choukou-tien the largest part of the cerebral cranium of a *Sinanthropus* has just been unearthed, undamaged . . . the jaws are missing. Still, in its present condition the find is most exciting. The braincase is similar in its proportions to that of *Pithecan-thropus*, but with frontal and parietal protuberances distinct (somewhat as on the skullcap of Neanderthal men). Supraorbital ridges and postorbital constriction are more strongly marked than in the Neanderthals.

One could scarcely hope for a more typical morphological inter-mediary between man and prehuman types. Further discoveries fol-lowed (six skullcaps and a similar number of jawbones). On 31 July 1930 Teilhard reported:

Upon returning to Peking, I was agreeably surprised to see a second *Sinanthropus* skull, found during my absence. This second specimen is no more complete than the first (or only slightly, in some details), but is a highly satisfactory find all the same. Besides, both fossils are completely identical in shape. I have been lucky to be involved in this business. It's chances like these that have made me so singularly and fondly enamoured of the divine influence which controls the world.

It is important to appreciate the exact part played by Teilhard in the Choukou-tien discoveries. It was he who, with Licent, first found traces of prehistoric man, but the actual discovery of *Sinan-thropus* was not his. The first person to hold the skull in his hands was Pei Wen-Chung, but much of the credit should go to Teilhard's precursors in the work of excavation, Andersson, Zdansky, and Barbour, and a team that included Black, Teilhard, Young, and Pei. Teilhard was often to insist that all progress, including scien-tific progress, must depend on teamwork and co-operation, and it was these that bore fruit at Choukou-tien.

Teilhard's own role was an important and even, at times, a de-cisive one. He was, after all, the geologist at Choukou-tien,[3] and

[3] Cf. letter of 15 April 1929: "I am practically in charge of the stratigraphic and palaeontological study of the deposit."

4*

it was in the first instance due to him (and to the Chinese scientists in the second instance) that the stratigraphy was made clear, that the enormous cavity of Site One was identified as a cavern that had been filled in, and that the abundant deposit of animal fossils was dated as sub-loess—that is, connected with the Lower Quaternary (before the depositing of loess took place). Teilhard, then, by virtue of his geological knowledge, made his contribution to the demonstration of the extreme earliness of *Sinanthropus*. Nor should it be forgotten that if Site One was the only cavity that yielded remains of early man, it was far from being the only one that contained fossils, for a score of fossiliferous sites were finally located in the area.

Teilhard, as work at and near the *Sinanthropus* site continued, witnessed another important discovery, the nature of which we shall give as related by Fr Pierre Leroy, who, then a Jesuit scholastic, arrived as an assistant to Licent.

It was in April, 1931. Having arrived at Peking, young Leroy met Teilhard and was conducted by him to the Cenozoic laboratory, where Teilhard approached his friend Pei Wen-Chung, director of the excavations, to ask:

"Has anything new turned up in the diggings?"

"Nothing," Pei replied.

"Not a thing?" Teilhard insisted.

Pei hesitated, pulled open a drawer, and casually placed on his desk a piece of quartzite. Teilhard took it up, examined it, and exclaimed:

"This is very important. This is a worked piece." And he wanted to know exactly where the find had been made.

Further research at the site of the find turned up, in fact, several hundred pounds of fashioned stones—and traces of fire, as well. Samples were sent to Breuil, who affirmed that the stone pieces were artifacts. *Sinanthropus*, therefore, was *Homo faber*. Teilhard wrote of his excitement at this discovery:

> I was thrilled at being able to make out—thanks to the new diggings—several levels (in the *Sinanthropus* belt) which show characteristics of "human" habitation; in one of these levels, and in the underlying "ash", by an hour of grubbing we found a bison horn (blackened), the horn of an argali (the Asiatic bighorn), and some ostrich-egg shells, mixed up with numerous chips of white quartz. . . . We are going to start by having the

blackened objects analysed. Carbon, no doubt—but will this be shown to be charcoal, or, instead, some sort of peat? While awaiting the results of the analysis, I am congratulating myself on having made a tour of the diggings and directed the attention of the directors there (who, of course, have never seen archaeological levels in caverns) to what I found. The directors fully grasped what I pointed out. (3 May 1931.)

The discovery of cultural activities on the part of *Sinanthropus* now topped all the rest, save, of course, the discovery of the fossil bones themselves. *Sinanthropus* had, it was now clear, passed "the thought barrier", and, like Prometheus, had already "stolen" fire. He therefore occupied a position, along with Neanderthal and related types, in human genealogy, or rather in the various waves of human beings. His culture was already gathering the fruits of his ancestors' discoveries, and—as Antoine Meillet was to point out—he already possessed speech, howbeit of a quite simple and rudimentary kind.

Teilhard was far from spending all his time on the work connected with Choukou-tien. On 7 May 1929 he left with Licent for a month in Manchuria. He was back on 10 June and on the 16th he writes:

> I am just back after a month of travelling in Manchuria with Licent—one result being that our relationship at long last became cordial once more. . . . In Manchuria I mostly went by rail (but also, alas, by Chinese cart, through frightful mud). I pushed on beyond Hailar, beside the Trans-Siberian Railway, that is, within five versts of Siberia (nine days from Paris). . . . I brought back few specimens, but many observations, either made first hand or given me by the Russian geologist (Ahnert). There is a clear correspondence between the structure of these northern regions and that of the part of China I am familiar with. In one step, I have almost doubled my domain.

In another letter of the same date he adds:

> I can trace a clear connection between the Chinese Pleistocene and the immense mud plains of central Manchuria and the sands of the Noni and Argun basins. Also, and this will interest you more, I have verified that at the latitude of the Northern Jalainor the structure of the Great Khingan is exactly the same as that I found in 1924 near the Southern Dalai-nor.

Teilhard was now methodically annexing the broad empire of China. Already he was well acquainted with northern China and Inner Mongolia; now it was his plan to make further sallies, to undertake raids deep into surrounding territory, and so establish contact with other scientific campaigners and thus effect a general synthesis of the tectonics of the whole northern part of the area. This desire for synthesis was characteristic. After Manchuria, it was to be the Croisière Jaune, and the push towards Turkestan.

On 18 June 1929 Teilhard again left Tientsin for Shansi. Accompanying—at the request of Wong—the young Chinese geologist C. C. Young, he spent the months from 20 June to 10 September in the west and north of Shansi. The trip went off well, and took Teilhard into one of the strangest parts of China that he had yet seen:

> ...a land made up of one ravine after another, spectral under its shroud of grey loess, beneath the relentless glare of a waterless sky. (25 July 1929.)

A letter a fortnight later, on the Feast of St Lawrence, records his satisfaction:

> We had driven our little caravan (six mules and three boys) up to Tatung-fu; and for nearly two months we have been wandering around looking for fossils and geological phenomena, among the enormous limestone massifs and especially all over the extraordinary mantle of red clays (Pliocene) and yellow clays (loess) which characterize these forbidding regions. It appears to me that I have got some good work in, notably in forming a better conception of the red clays and palaeontological history of the Hwang-ho. I think I have also found some Palaeolithic traces (only a couple of miles or so from the deposits I located in 1923). I have some fine fossils, too (rodents especially: a group often neglected, but highly interesting). On the whole, I am satisfied. But this rain will have to stop if we are to move ahead and continue our work. This whole area (the basin of the Hwang-ho) has been suffering from an almost total drought, and consequent famine, these past two or three years. Now, in contrast, there is promise of too much water.

The sum total was more than satisfying:

> I have observed much and, especially in the Shansi-Shensi area, assembled much (documents on the great Mesozoic (Secondary)

flexures, and the history of the end of the Tertiary). I have material for more than a dozen articles of various lengths. Well, things are moving, as you see, and this with little merit on my part; it is just that chance made me the one man among Europeans (even among Chinese) who has seen most of northern China, right at the moment when our geological knowledge of this vast country is beginning to take shape. (7 October 1929.)[4]

It is interesting that nowhere in the letters written in the course of this trip do we find reference to the shocking diet which Teilhard for three months endured. Since he had not got used to Chinese food, one of the Tientsin Jesuits hired a cook for him; but at the first noonday stop out of Tatung (last stop on the Shansi North railway line) this cook was found to be unable either to get a Chinese camp stove going or even to boil eggs. Later, one of the boys helped him to get some eggs fried—three for each of the party. He was so delighted with what he had learned that everyone in the party got three eggs per meal three times a day for the whole three months! Teilhard was quite happy; when science was at stake, he seemed oblivious of everything else.

The important thing about this trip was that, for the first time Teilhard was travelling in an official capacity. Moreover, in Young, he had a Chinese companion ready to make all smooth before him, the more so that he and Teilhard were now fellow Chinese officials.

The two were well suited. Young admired Teilhard's scope: stratigraphy, general geology, vertebrate palaeontology, zoology, and botany. He declared himself an agnostic, remarking that with Europeans it is a case of having a single and inherited religion from cradle to grave, whereas among the Chinese a boy chooses his belief, changes to another when he is grown, and to perhaps still another later on.

Teilhard, however, with his unconditional respect for the individual conscience, forbade himself any proselytizing, and even refrained from saying grace at meals. Similarly, with other scientists, whether strangers or old friends, he confined his conversation to science. In this, his missionary spirit was perhaps guided by the gift of counsel; he was ready to talk Christianity to those who wished to hear, but not willing to spoil, by forcing consciences, the

[4] Cf. letter of 29 September 1929: "So you see things are moving. I have gradually, and through no merit of my own, come to be one of the geologists most familiar with the problems you meet in China."

impression he made simply by his example as a priest who was at home in the intellectual world of international science and at the same time was an admirable companion.

His next journey was far more comfortable. After having celebrated 22 February 1930 as Washington's Birthday with his friend Graham and the American colony, profiting by the occasion to discuss with Sven Hedin, at one in the morning, the meaning of life, Teilhard, at the beginning of March, made a two-week geological survey in the southern part of Shansi, taking Barbour as far as Tong-Kuan in south-west Shansi. The trip was a comfortable one on the motoring route—four hundred miles in forty-eight hours:

> I made my trip to Shansi . . . with Barbour, who was accompanying Nyström, who in turn had to go to the south of Shansi to settle a problem of supply routes for the Famine Relief. Knowing the region, I told myself that it would hamper our stratigraphic determination of the region if Barbour paid it only a hasty visit, without having seen it before, and without any guidance from me. So I made an abrupt decision to accompany him. It was a happy one, I think, for Barbour has completely accepted my views on the necessity of reassigning to the Lower Pleistocene or Upper Pliocene a very large part of what had been considered Middle Pleistocene or Upper Pleistocene (loess). We were received at Taiyuan in Nystrom's pretty and almost luxurious house. (22 March 1930.)

From 22 April (two days after Easter) to 21 May (date of the return to Tientsin) in the same year, he followed this trip to Shansi with a tour of the north-west, in Manchuria, accompanying Chinese geologists, among them Wong probably, and C. C. Young certainly. We know nothing of the scientific results of this trip, though one amusing incident is recorded: Teilhard wore whatever clothes he found most convenient to work in; generally khaki, and including puttees. His appearance was so military that one day when he called on a local general, the latter asked Young just who this Frenchman was, a Catholic priest or a military official.

In June and July of 1930 Teilhard took part in an American Central Asiatic expedition organized by Andrews. Two years before, in February, 1928, Osborn had cabled him from New York, asking him to join the expedition as prehistorian. They travelled by car. He reached Kalgan, and then the Gobi, and camped with his American companions (Granger among them) at Wolf Camp, at the

foot of a fossil-bearing cliff. On 30 July he was back in Tientsin.
The trip produced solid scientific results:

And now our eight blue tents are pitched here on the edge of
an immense plateau formed of red and white sedimentary layers.
Here, in large numbers, are the jaws of a quite extraordinary
kind of mastodon, whose lower mandible, flanked by two wide,
flat tusks, rounds out into the form of a gigantic spoon.

We are some two hundred miles north-west of Kalgan, well
into the Gobi, and exposed to the high Mongolian winds and
—even at this time of year—cold (two days ago all of us were in
furs). To make up for the icy blasts, we are able to see around us
a boundless solitude, unvaried as the sea, whose broad, flat, ter-
raced planes under the light of evening become something wonderful to see.

We live on gazelle killed for us by Andrews, quite as fine a
shot as he is a conversationalist. The members of the expedition
make up one big family, of which it is pleasant to feel oneself a
part. In short, I am enjoying a thoroughly agreeable and interesting time; and, during it, I am beginning to work out a connection
between the geological structure of China and that of Mongolia.
(25 June 1930.)[5]

Teilhard, in fact, had been taken up by the Americans. Supported
by American and Chinese money, he had become more independent
of French institutions, and particularly of Marcellin Boule. Yet the
situation had to be handled with delicacy. In a letter of 7 February
1930 we note:

But you say nothing of Lacroix. This may be a sign—I hope—
that his relapse, which Lamare told me about (25 December), was
not serious. But I continue to worry about it. That man is still
necessary to us—and I am very fond of him.

Behind Teilhard's concern for Lacroix lay his anxiety to continue
to alternate between Paris and Peking. At the back of his mind was
the thought that the time would come (he was now nearly fifty)
when the hazards and hardships of expeditionary work would be
too much for him. At the moment, Paris was not important to him
scientifically. Scientifically, he was now more at home in China.
The machinery of scholarship, thanks to American help, ran
smoothly in Peking, and there were sufficient specialists available
to make dependence on Paris no longer necessary. But Paris was his

[5] Cf. *Letters from a Traveller*, pp. 165-6.

religious home, and important to him spirtually. In China he found himself alone. He lived in a world that was either Protestant or positivist, or (in the case of the Chinese, except Wong) pragmatist or atheistic.

In contrast, Paris was the home of his confidants, his proselytes, and his student groups from the Normale, Polytechnique, and St Cloud; Paris was the real field of the religious activity he was never to give up. The solution to the dilemma, then, seemed to be to continue to divide his time between Peking and Paris, at least until he could see the future more clearly.

The only religious activity possible for Teilhard in China was to serve as spiritual director to his friends in Europe. He writes, for example, to Mme Haardt, widow of the explorer Georges-Marie Haardt (the Claude spoken of is their child):

I did indeed get your letter of 10 September, enclosing the snapshot of Claude.... Everything you have to say about him interests me a good deal. And I think you are right—there is no way in which he could more happily and more brilliantly take up where his father left off than by becoming a missionary. But, when it comes down to it, there are several different ways in which the courage and dedication of a missionary can be employed. So what you have to do is to find out gradually which side predominates in the child: the intellectual, the practical, or perhaps the mystical. Then you must foster this strong side, while at the same time inspiring in him a basic ambition of dedicating his life to the creation of something great. It is this atmosphere of dedication to something greater than oneself that you must tactfully create around Claude. In such an atmosphere he will instinctively seize upon and approve the form of service best suited to his own nature. Of course, the concept of, and the desire for, greatness of life is fostered by nothing so much as by tuition in the divine and in the love of God. But you must see to it that the divine is clearly revealed as a principle of the enlargement of one's scope—there must be no shamming, no such forcing as ends in distortion. And there must be nothing which dehumanizes, under pretext of superhumanizing.... Try gradually (and this in order to make of yourself the real Christian woman whom Claude needs in his life) to rise above the mass of complications and preoccupations which would disappear automatically if we saw things in a clearer perspective. All beings are to be loved passionately in so far as they are, or can be made, fine and help us to rise with them. As for the others, why bother with them? We must recognize a hopeless case for what it is and abandon it. Try to take the large, the clear-sighted, the simple view. And go right ahead, imperturbably, without bothering your head over what people say. "Only one thing is necessary"—finding God in the everyday walks of life. This you have known a long time in theory; try to put it into practice. (1 January 1934.)

At the present time, it seems clear, you are above all a victim of physical fatigue. You lack the physical strength to react against an invasion of the past—which, nevertheless, you absolutely must "exorcize" (in so far, I hasten to add, as the past debilitates and saddens you). Let me tell you once more: Do not keep trying to find Georges-Marie in the past—in Africa, in Asia, in the material traces of his life which are naturally so dear to you. He is no longer there. He no longer awaits you there. To speak as a Christian (and, when it comes down to it, all of us are that, even if in some latter-day fashion), Georges-Marie has now found the God for whom he was groping throughout his courageous odyssey. Of that I feel as sure as of what I hope for myself. It is therefore in God that you must seek him—ahead, that is, in the shaping of the life which you must begin anew.... That is where you must be faithful to him, and not in the backward-looking sentimentality which you must steel yourself to break away from. In a way, I feel as sorry as you do about the disappearance of certain concrete tokens of his activities. Still, it was not in these that the real mark of Georges-Marie is to be found; he would have been the first to smile at the loss of them, provided that the essentials of his thought and drive were preserved—and they are. In regard to your own feelings, I shall go so far as to say that the closing of the Citroën Museum, painful though you must find it, should liberate rather than depress you. Its closing is the physical symbol of the psychological turning of a new leaf which is going to be your salvation in your bereavement. I am not asking you to forget, but to look ahead. This will be the attitude towards Georges-Marie which, passed on to Claude, will invigorate and exalt him more than all the material mementoes of his father, in which he might become restrictively engrossed. (3 February 1936.)

And I suppose that, what with material difficulties on top of physical depression, your cup of sorrow these days is flowing over. No matter what has happened, I beg you, do not despair. A true view of life depends on a clear hope that the sun must eventually dispel all clouds. I must re-emphasize that despite whatever you may feel and whatever grounds you may have found for your belief, your life is decidedly not "over". I am convinced that it is, in fact, *beginning*. Simply make up your mind not to go on living any more in the past. No, this does not mean that you are to forget the past, but only that your way of being faithful to it—the right way—is to go on forging ahead, and thus to prove worthy of the past. So, do not isolate yourself. Do not turn in upon yourself. Instead, see your friends as much as you can. Live for others. It is the gift of yourself that will free and refresh you; I hope that you will find plenty of people and things to dedicate yourself to.

. . . yet what good does it do to say anything if what is said does not come from God as the inspiration of our sentiments and thoughts? Let me say, then, that the more forlorn you feel the more you must cast yourself upon God. Have you really tried to do so? (5 April 1936.)

What was Teilhard's method of spiritual direction? A complete exposition would require the sifting of the testimony of scores and perhaps of hundreds of souls that, privately, he converted, or directed, or simply helped. This would include the testimony of priests whom he brought back to the faith—testimony virtually unobtainable (though we do have some confidential documents at our disposal) and, in any case, too private to allow of publication. But the first thing that characterized Teilhard as a spiritual director was broad forbearance, an extraordinary capacity for sympathy. His first step was to put himself almost unreservedly in the place of the person who came to him, to attune himself to that person's feelings, and to share the weight on that person's mind. (What may be called Teilhard's tolerance was based on his attraction towards everything true; his first attention was given to whatever struck him as valid in the viewpoint whether of the unorthodox or of the sinner.)

As a result, the other always felt himself recognized and understood in his best self, a self, so to speak, greater than himself but struggling to come to light; and the rest—the imperfect, the evil —this seemed, astonishingly, to fade away, to pass into nothingness. Teilhard knew how to come right to the point, to sweep aside irrelevant complications, to inspire an unshakeable confidence in God, to turn souls away from morbid attachment to the past and constrain them always to look ahead, to live for others, for something bigger than themselves, realizing that the foundations of all true loyalties rest on the future. What was more, in the exercise of this skill Teilhard showed tireless patience. He stood squarely on the fundamental truths and the laws of the Church. A divorced friend who was thinking of remarrying has told us how clear-cut was Teilhard's response. If, in some letter, Teilhard seemed to be making a concession on some important point (not in a question of morals) this was simply because his correspondent was sound enough on other points, and was advancing by the right road; the point at issue would therefore be cleared up later, when he had attained a higher spiritual plane, and had seen the coherence and inter-dependence of all dogmas.

Teilhard had the gift of starting from scratch, and this not as a stratagem, but out of love of truth and through a need to reconstruct the truth, piece by piece, under the eye of God. He never dodged a difficulty, but faced it squarely; he was open, he never disguised what he really thought, and he shared his correspondent's quest. Even the quest alone had its value, and was consoling even in itself. "Be comforted," the Christ of Pascal had said long before, "for you would never be seeking me if you had not already found me." Yet spiritual value, in Teilhard's eyes, did not reside in the intention alone. To build the City of Man was already to be building the City of God. Action was no longer to be considered simply something thrown in for good measure, something non-essential, which could be dispensed with, if need be, so long as the intention was right. Indeed, action took on a Christianizing value, by uniting mankind and thus preparing the way for the Mystical Body—and this no matter what the nature of the activity, whether putting material things to spiritual use, or business activity (a whole theology of work and of business could be deduced from Teilhard's theories). And all this was proposed, not merely as consoling, but as exalting. He looked for:

> ...a religion made up not of ritual and obligations, and prohi-bitions alone, but a faith wherein all other faiths could find their haven and their flowering, under the light of life and of person-ality. (29 October 1935.)[6]

It was towards the end of 1929 that Père Teilhard received an offer that was to lead to one of his most important and interesting scientific missions. The firm of Citroën suggested that he should

[6] *Letters from a Traveller*, pp. 127–30, includes two letters of excellent spiritual advice addressed to Max Bégouën.

take part, as a geologist, in the Croisière Jaune.[7] Teilhard at first seemed not to attach very great importance to the invitation:

> The Citroën trans-Asia mission is insisting that I go along on the Chinese leg of the trip. . . . I do not feel much like accepting. And yet, if this trip could be combined with some useful and pleasant work for the Survey, I might agree. (29 September 1929.)

> I have been invited for the Chinese stage of the Citroën trans-Asia expedition. I do not know whether this can be managed. At best, the project means no more than making in a half-track the sort of trip I have been making ever since 1923. (7 October 1929.)

But he was then offered a larger share in the journey:

> After a meeting last week with the Citroën Croisière Jaune representative in China, Point, a naval lieutenant, just back from Paris, I have changed my mind about their expedition. My part in it is to be more extensive. I should have all the spring of 1931 to visit the west part of China by car, as a part of the caravan travelling from Peking to join the mission. Then the Croisière, whose geologist I should be as representative of the Geological Service of China, would take me from Peking as far as Hanoi. [My Jesuit provincial at] Lyons has given me full permission, and I have accordingly agreed to go. (7 February 1930.)

The expedition was not due to start, however, for another year; meanwhile, since it was difficult to make final arrangements from Peking, Teilhard, who was eager enough to visit France anyway, found it necessary to go to Paris and, a few months later, to the United States.

> I have scientific relationships to keep up, articles to see to press, fossils to be identified, contact to be established with the Citroën mission, and, perhaps above all, I need a breath of spiritual fresh air. (23 March 1930.)

He accordingly boarded a train on the Trans-Siberian line on 10 September 1930, planning to reach Paris a fortnight later, and to spend four months in France before leaving for America.

Although we are not fully informed about those months in France, a communication from Père Ganne, S.J., tells us that Teilhard spent some part of his time, at least, in Auvergne.

---

[7] The "Yellow Expedition", the Central Asian Expedition organized by the Citroën company and using their vehicles. In 1925 there had been a similar *Croisière Noire* in Africa.

I met Teilhard for the first time when I was a philosophy student, in 1930 ... at the Jesuits' in Clermont-Ferrand. The two of us were from the same part of France. He invited me to come for a chat in his room; the chairs, I remember, were so broken down that we sat on the bed. I shall never forget his concept of the "penetration of matter". "You know," he said to me, "what is going on today is very important. We are in the process of leaving the Neolithic period." I told him he would have to give me a moment or two to appreciate his meaning ... and when we finally parted it was between three and four in the morning. He had been as a free-flowing fountain, the purest that I have ever met. He it was who taught me that true humility is identical with the highest degree of boldness.

We know, too, that he had discussions with Lacroix, Cayeux, and Jacob in connection with scientific problems in the Gobi. And we also know that he was making arrangements for his participation in the Croisière Jaune; for instance, in November he and the two Bégouëns had dinner with Breuil's friend Field, grandson of the American millionaire founder of the Chicago Field Museum (Teilhard and young Field were to meet again in Chicago).

He also resumed relations with his students from the Normale, giving them a talk on "Humanization, Humanism and Divinization". A month later he also gave a series of four talks to the Marcel Légaut group at Chadefaud, in Auvergne.[8] Of these the general topic was "An Attempt to Integrate Man into the Universe". Copies of three of the talks are extant. In the last Teilhard summarized his theory:

> By considering man, not as something apart, but as one of the integral phenomena of the universe, we saw in the universe a progressive achievement of personality that is still going on. When we looked more closely at this personalization we recognized that it necessarily implies an attitude that one could call "action-effort". Then, in the third talk, we tried to discover the conditions which would permit this action-effort to continue to operate in the particular stratum of the universe which has freedom of choice. This led us to the conclusion that the essential

[8] These talks were given on 19 and 27 November and 3 and 10 December 1930. Légaut, a mathematician, had taught theoretical mechanics at Rennes. Dissatisfied with handling abstractions he took up farming in the Dauphiné. He got together a small Catholic group of students, university teachers and school teachers from the École Normale.

condition must be, in brief, that we keep before us some motive to lead us on, and that that is none other than the consciousness of achieving some durable work, in itself probably an addition to personality. Thus, we saw how the phenomenon of man gradually becomes enlarged in religion. Finally, tonight I should like ... to show you how, in the light of what we have learned in the previous talks, we can reach a clearer view both of the world around us and of the world within ourselves.

These talks constituted another step towards Teilhard's great synthesis, *The Phenomenon of Man*—in which he considered man:

no longer as an exception in, and something extrinsic to, the universe, but frankly integrated with, and intrinsic to it, and thus serving as an interpretation or a key.

The effect of Teilhard's lectures, and the discussions that followed them, might be judged from Marcel Légaut's account of some earlier lectures, given before the death of the Abbé Portal.

We were pleasantly surprised to find a priest who approached religious questions with intellectual vigour, with no attempt to conceal or avoid even the most thorny problems. As young believers of good will, we knew of course that such spiritual and intellectual honesty was possible. But the fact was that, despite the Abbé Portal's care to choose speakers from priests of such integrity, we often enough had occasion to spot the smile or joke which was really an evasion of an objection, to detect the lack of any real interest on the part of the speaker in the rigorous clarification of the questions treated, and to sense the desire to teach rather than to learn the truth, to solve the difficulties of others rather than one's own, and indeed to seek to forget the latter by busying oneself in the apostolate.

But with Father Teilhard the very opposite was true. When he spoke it was our turn to have the timidity of our pusillanimous faith unmasked, to recognize our own intellectual cowardice, our unconscious but unrelenting search for security and composure, in a word, the childishness of our faith, and—however disguised, the corroding dishonesty of our spiritual life.

Towards the end of January, 1937, Teilhard left France for New York, arriving about 8 February. His *Letters from a Traveller* refer to the main events of his stay in America. He addressed the Osborn Research Club (in English) on the principal results of his explorations in China, he gave a lecture at Columbia University, he interviewed specialists in Mongolian geology (for the Croisière Jaune was to proceed through Inner Mongolia), visited the French Ambassador (author of *La connaissance de l'Est*), Paul Claudel,[9] also to discuss that expedition, and paid a visit to the Field Museum in Chicago. In another letter he summed up his impressions thus:

> One way and another, I realize that I did well to return to Peking through the United States. . . . I have strengthened any number of half-formed contacts, and scores of possible new ones have come to light. If only I were still forty. . . . If for any reason Peking should fall through I could take my choice of the offers I'd certainly get from America. . . . Yes, I liked America, doubtless, of course, because I was made a fuss of (excessive admiration, in fact, which shows the rather "young" side of the country), but still more because everyone engaged in research gave me the impression of frankness and keenness without an eye on a Chair or some other academic advancement. I should only have to turn up in New York, or Chicago, or San Francisco, this very moment, and I'd immediately find work or an appointment. However, my future seems to be tied to China. (*Letters from a Traveller*, 23 February 1931.)

American modernity, which had so deeply shocked Georges Duhamel, offended Teilhard not at all. He found that in religious circles in the United States scientific theories which had long since gained free currency in all other countries were still causing difficulties. For example, evolution was still synonymous with materialistic monism. This was a notion that Teilhard was to spend his life in combating; "In Paris," he adds, "the attitude is less crude."

The concrete results of his visit were excellent. The National Geographic Society at Washington, with something like two million members, devoted to the spread of geographical science, granted to Georges-Marie Haardt, head of the Citroën Mission, a sum equal to that which it had granted Byrd for his expedition to the South Pole, and appointed as its representative with the Mission—something it had done for no other foreign enterprise since its foundation in 1888—one of its most eminent members, Maynard Owen Williams.

At the end of February, Teilhard embarked at San Francisco to return to China. During the fortnight which it took him to reach his destination, with stops at Hawaii (where he met the geologist William King Gregory) and at Kobe (with a side trip to Kyoto), he

---

[9] *Letters from a Traveller*, p. 167.

finished *L'esprit de la terre*, which is a reworking, from a new angle, of the material he had given in his talks to the Marcel Légaut group. He describes this himself as "an essay in the interpretation of the world, more particularly of the earth; taking as a starting point the spiritual forces working in man.[10]

> ... The day of "nations" is over. What we have to do now (if we are not to perish) is to shake off old-fashioned prejudices and set about building the planet Earth.

For this, Teilhard maintains, we must develop an "earth-sense", which he defines as follows:

> By "earth-sense" I mean a passionate feeling for the common destiny that is continually drawing the thinking portion of life still further forward. No feeling has firmer roots in nature and none, accordingly, is stronger. But, in fact, there is no feeling either that is so slow to make itself evident, since, if it is to become explicit, our consciousness must first rise above the widening (but still much too narrow) circle of family, country and race, and realize at last that the only truly natural and real human unity is *the spirit of the earth*.

First among the forces that make up this "earth-sense" is love:

> Love is the most universal, the most formidable, and the most mysterious of cosmic energies. . . . The most expressive, and at the same time the most profoundly true account of universal evolution would doubtless consist in telling the story of the evolution of love. . . . The progress towards Man, through Woman, is in fact the progress of the whole universe. The vital concern for Earth . . . is that these bearings be established.
>
> If man fails to recognize the real nature and the real object of his love, the result is deep-seated and irremediable disorder. Bent upon satisfying with too small a thing a passion which has as its real object the whole of things, he seeks perforce to remedy a fundamental disproportion by the ever-growing materialism or multiplication of his experiences. Vain attempts—and, in the eyes of one who can see the inestimable value of the human "spiritual quantum", a shocking waste! Put aside, I beg you, both any romantic attitude towards the matter and any righteous indignation, and coldly and detachedly, like a biologist or an engineer, look upon the red glow that suffuses our great cities as night

---

[10] *Letters from a Traveller*, p. 172.

comes on. There, and everywhere else, Earth goes on squandering prodigally—a total loss—its most precious power. Yes, Earth consumes itself profitlessly. How much energy, would you guess, is wasted thus in a single night at the expense of Earth's spiritual efficiency?

But let man, instead, discern the wholeness of reality shining spiritually through the flesh. Then his understanding will master what previously served only to frustrate and disappoint his power to love. Woman stands before man as the symbol of the whole world and the quintessence of all its charm. How shall he truly embrace her, then, save by assuming, himself, the dimensions of the world? But, since the world is continuously enlarging its dimensions, never reaching its full growth, yet always keeping ahead of our grasp, it is in a never-completed encompassing of the universe and of his potential self that man—to grasp the prize of his love—finds himself engaged. In these terms, man will never succeed in attaining woman short of the consummation of universal union. Love is a sacred fund of energy; it is the very blood of spiritual evolution. This is the first thing that earth-sense reveals to us.

After his arrival in China, Teilhard spent from March to May waiting for the departure of the Croisière Jaune; he made one trip to Choukou-tien, and spent some days finishing his *L'esprit de la terre*.

It was probably through him that the cultural activities of *Sinanthropus pekinensis* were brought to light; the hypothesis of the fossil bones being those of animal prey lured into the limestone cavern by still-unidentified men was thus ruled out. Teilhard had, moreover, the satisfaction of learning that new finds in the central basin of Shansi provided startling confirmation of his later conjectures concerning the Early Pleistocene in China. He also sent on an invitation to Breuil from Davidson Black, who was eager to have the great prehistorian come and see for himself the excavations at Choukou-tien. Teilhard also arranged the purchase of a fine collection of Neolithic objects from a Russian in Harbin:

We are dealing with a perfectly clear-cut deposit, including burials, at Tsitsihar. The objects are of the Linsi type, but with more characteristic tools, for bone-working. You will see all this on the spot, as well as in the drawings I am having made and think are good. I hope I haven't committed too many heresies; but we have no one here to consult on taxonomy. We have found a very fine graver, and harpoons with a row of barbs, of the customary bone kind. (3 May 1931.)

This period of waiting for the Croisière Jaune was for Teilhard a transition period leading to a new sort of life. Were it not for the sharp break introduced by the Croisière, we might consider his "first Peking period" to have already begun. Even before the just-completed trip to France and to the United States, his time had become divided, with a small part set aside for Tientsin (because Licent's museum was there, and the Jesuit Higher Studies institute, where Teilhard made his retreats), but the larger part reserved for Peking, city of the intelligentsia, the brain of China. Upon his return from America it was naturally at Peking that he awaited the departure of the Croisière. "Tientsin is virtually nothing more for me now than my legal residence, and all my time is spent at Peking, or with Peking people." (25 April 1931.)

Apart from the Manchurian journey, the once-frequent trips with Licent were practically at an end. Teilhard, having the official title of Scientific Adviser, had become a Chinese representative; he took part in Chinese expeditions, and was at the same time in request with the Americans, who looked on him as their scientific equal and treated him with affectionate admiration. Similarly, from the point of view of philosophy and spirituality we find Teilhard at a turning point, as will become apparent when we summarize what the years 1923–31 meant in Teilhard's system of thought.

CHAPTER SEVEN

The Noosphere: Christ All in All

IT is unfortunate that many of the documents necessary for a complete reconstruction of Père Teilhard's interior life have been lost or are not available. We can do no more than summarize what we know. In distinguishing and subdividing periods there is therefore some element of uncertainty.

In 1919, the period of *La puissance spirituelle de la matière*, and indeed in 1916, the date of the first of the tales (*Le Christ dans la matière*) in the style of Benson, Teilhard was already Teilhard. God in matter? The young soldier priest of 1914 already recognized this fact: the Holy Eucharist progressively assimilates mankind to itself, and, through mankind, the universe (a process indispensable for the achievement of the fullness of the Mystical Body of Christ). Human endeavour to conquer the earth, by developing *mind* in the material world, thus offers the Incarnate Word a wider domain. Already Teilhard had been re-reading St Paul (and St John) with new understanding, discovering for himself, and emphasizing in his thought, the Pauline *pleroma*: the winning back of all things to that maturity which is proportioned to the completed growth of Him who everywhere and in all things is complete.

To speak of periods is to imply exact dates. But when it comes to a system of thought as organic and as thoroughly unified as Teilhard's, such limits, with their air of exactness, may be misleading. We can only distinguish a fresh variation, during this time, on certain fundamental themes—a variation presented principally, as Teilhard himself attested, in *La messe sur le monde* (1923) and *Le milieu divin* (1926).

Paradoxically, too, in view of the power and assurance with which he now wrote, this was also a period of crisis. We can distinguish a number of factors that lay behind this.

The first debt that Teilhard owed to the Far East was its revelation of the immensity of the earth and of mankind. The result was a repetition, though on a scale far more vast, of his experience (already decisive, and liberating) in World War I, which showed him the multitude of men as somehow forming an entity, as a molecule combines its atoms into a entity. He was conscious of himself as being drawn into a fantastic mass of several hundreds of millions of human beings; he found himself existing in the very heart of paganism, amid a crowd living and breathing materialism and pragmatism; this contact, like a catalyst, activated his religious meditations and enlivened his response to the missionary vocation traditional with the Jesuits, and thus brought him to active reflection on the problem of mission work. It was now truly on a world-wide, a noospheric scale. He was seeing far, and he was seeing from a commanding vantage point. While he remained more than ever attached to his Jesuit confrères and to his fellow-members of the Church (from which he could never have detached himself), he still stood somewhat apart.

Furthermore, Teilhard, at once so deeply dedicated and so widely emancipated, found his position most uncertain. His stay in China had turned into an exile. First, until his definitive removal from the Institut Catholique, his case was hanging fire; then, after his severance from Paris, his position was still purely negative: he knew what he no longer was, but he did not know what he was going to be! He dared ask no precise questions. Of course, thanks to the understanding, admiration, and kindness of his immediate superiors, his exile was much mitigated. He was allowed to visit Paris in order to put his scientific articles into final shape, and, on occasion, to carry on his apostolic work. Of course, too, China attracted him more and more and became a sort of solid bastion for him, since he had become in a way a Chinese functionary and since Peking had grown to exert an especially powerful attraction upon him. Still, nothing in all this answered to his basic needs; and the future remained thoroughly uncertain. He still longed for Paris, for that was the laboratory where his ideas, through a sort of spiritual alchemy, developed and combined, and the place where he could carry on uninterruptedly the apostolate of which he dreamed and which he had begun so well.

The result, between 1926 and 1929, was an interior liberation which reached its peak in the winter of 1928 and the first two months of 1929, then moderated into a broader, calmer attitude and into a vast peace. What were completely changed were certain ways of feeling and judging, which were frankly left behind, faith and loyalty remaining intact. Teilhard allowed himself further scope, he rejoiced in the liberty of the children of God, yet remained convinced that God had willed him to be at such and such a precise place, at such and such a time, under such and such circumstances—and in the Jesuit community, and not elsewhere. Never for an instant was there any question of his leaving the Church.

Without rationalizing, I think that I have almost integrated, into a suitable Christian attitude, so many elements (as yet little Christianized) which bit by bit were revealed to me as the essential factors of my life. This is as much as to tell you that I am at peace, really, with the Church and with God. It seems to me that, always tending towards what is to come, yet admitting that that new thing cannot be born except of fidelity to what is, I now find myself quite beyond revolt. (29 September 1929.)[1]

Before the interior crisis it had been suggested to him that he leave the Jesuits and become a secular priest, like Bremond, since he could then pursue his scientific career much more freely. He refused, in that leaving the Society would mean leaving the *milieu divin* in which Providence had placed him.

I should feel as if I were betraying the world were I to shirk from the place assigned to me. . . . So I feel quite sure that even the idea of a single step towards leaving the Order has never entered my mind. I have perhaps never been so firmly attached to my Order as at this moment. (10 August 1929.)
The Society . . . it becomes more and more clear, is still *my*

[1] Well might the "Gentiles" be surprised at this loyalty. During the Yellow Expedition his companions put this question to him flatly. He answered them roughly as follows: "You cannot understand, yet you want to know. You, Reymond, have been a Young Communist and at the University. You, Point, were at Le Borda. As for me, I was at Jersey. Think of all that you owe to the teaching and friendship of your mentors, the friendship and comradeship of your fellow-students, think of the deep and intimate commitments which you took upon yourselves at twenty. Consider how all that holds you, and how morally difficult it would be for you to break away, even if you wanted to." And Teilhard, save out of consideration for his companions, would no doubt have added: "And besides, in the Society of Jesus there is Jesus, and Jesus is a leader one cannot desert." A quite probable addition, since Reymond, the first time he related Teilhard's words, finished them with that last sentence.

particular point of engagement and of activity in the universe. (29 September 1929.)[2]

We know that by April, 1929, his calm had returned; and on 10 August of that year he could speak with detachment of the "little crisis" that he had gone through. Finally, on 6 December 1929, he wrote:

I have the curious feeling of having lost the faculty of enjoying (or wishing) anything whatsoever in connection with myself; at the same time the supreme grandeur of the destiny of the universe, a business in which we are all engaged by the very fact of our existence, dominates me continually. This feeling is a sort of passionate indifference, in which all human frustrations or ambitions are, clearly, almost non-existent.

How profound was this sense of peace is shown by Teilhard's attitude in face of the delays to the printing of his *Le milieu divin* at the Museum Lessianum, delays which finally ended in the rejection of the book.

Incidentally, also from Louvain I have word that a little book of "piety", *Le milieu divin* (the Ms. of which, for lack of an extra copy, I never showed you), was to have gone to press. I still wonder about that, but from what I hear the censors "have all been very favourable" towards the work (in which I included much about the meaning of detachment and resignation, on the meaning of the Cross, etc.). (7 October 1929.)

On my return from the trip, I found a letter from Louvain (from Père Charles) telling me that my manuscript on *Le milieu divin* was to be printed without delay (about 5 July), "all the opinions having been favourable". Since then, no news. I am beginning to think that there may have been a hitch—and almost feel relieved (I put so much of my own self into those pages that I might prefer them to appear posthumously). (6 December 1929.)[3]

Oddest of all is the case of my *Le milieu divin*, which, according to what Charles told me, was supposed to go to the printer a whole year ago, but about which I have not heard a single word

---

[2] Two years before he had written (10 January 1927): "I shall come to the end, I hope, of crying 'Out of the depths...'. See also letter of 1 January 1930.

[3] This letter from Père Charles was dated 8 July 1929. The "hitch" was that mimeographed copies had been circulated, and some readers had brought them to the attention of Rome.

since. I am really not very much disturbed about it. It seems to me that I have never been so enthusiastic, and at the same time so firm, in my faith in the universe, nor more profoundly indifferent to what happens to me personally and to every other merely pettily human concern in that universe. (31 July 1930.)

It remains no less true that when the Jesuits at Beirut gave the book an informal and private printing Teilhard looked through his copy with emotion and declared that it was an immense joy for him to realize that one of his confrères had decided upon publishing this work—which he himself would never have had either the power or the right to publish.

Thus we find that Teilhard went through two fundamental experiences during this period. One was a new revelation of the human multitude; the other, an emancipation, critical to pass through, requiring an adjustment to new perspectives, but followed by a great peace. In this twofold experience we can distinguish two philosophic elements: the discovery of the noosphere and the emergence of a spirituality centred upon the notion of Christ as all in all.

In order to understand these two notions of Teilhard's we must recall that in the field of positive science, a desire to synthesize always played the major role in his thought. He wrote:

Science will have to find some way of tackling the study of the earth in a more radical and synthetic fashion, looking at it as *a whole*, endowed with *specifically global* mechanical, physical and chemical properties. (14 January 1929.)

But Teilhard did not stop short with sketching a unified science of the globe. He had a vivid intuition, while taking part in scientific teamwork in China, of the solidarity of scientific minds—of an international communion in *truth*; a network of spiritual stuff extending around the whole earth like a nervous system. This intuition was one of the starting points of his speculations on the noosphere.

Such speculations were characteristic of his bent for synthesis. Whereas physics is ordinarily accounted one thing, and biology another, Teilhard was struggling to create a generalized physics, one which would embrace such forces as are found in life—consciousness, spontaneity, even improbability. For life he saw as part of a universal process, terrestrial life being a function of the sidereal evolution of the globe (a function in turn of total cosmic evolution). As for biology, on the other hand, it is true that one of its branches is called anthropology; but this latter, as Teilhard knew it, was the study of the flesh and bone of man, excluding, as not relevant to positive science, the problem of reflective thought, man's incredible power to think, so that man, precisely in his most human aspect, remained a kind of monstrous and embarrassing left-over. Teilhard, in contrast, envisaged a generalized biology, insisting on the totality of human phenomena as an integral part of nature, of Earth, and of cosmic evolution. When, he argued, matter alone is taken as the starting point, man becomes an unknown in an insoluble function; but when life is considered as the expression of an impetus towards spontaneity and consciousness, then thought can be assigned its value.

In fact, if that complex mesh of qualities we know as man be taken as the starting point, then the cosmos reels off behind us and winds on ahead of us in accordance with a quite simple law. Thus Teilhard not only would create a generalized biology, in which the noosphere, the thinking envelope of the earth, is the natural crowning of the biosphere, but would also integrate such a biology with a generalized physics, in which the biosphere, as the legitimate issue of the hydrosphere, is the normal consequence (given favourable conditions) of cosmic evolution.

> ... I have gradually become aware that the direction of my scientific tastes and interests has shifted from the material and organic levels of the earth to the thinking layer which mankind constitutes on our plant. It is in this human belt, it seems to me, that geology and palaeontology have their natural extension; and it is there that I feel I am now discerning the essence of what it was that attracted me towards those sciences.
>
> Once a person has grasped—through a study of rocks and of ancient bones—the scale, and the degree of organicity, of the human milieu in which we are plunged, he discovers, I assure you, a magnificent object of study. We still pass this by with strange indifference, like that with which our ancestors used to look at mountains; but a century or two from now mankind will have become a classical subject of study—in a higher reach of what we call natural history.

We must be pardoned for anticipating, but it is indispensable to underline the consequences of this realization of the wealth of the cosmos as concentrated in the single phenomenon of man. In the first place, matter—"Sacred Matter"—is conceived of as the medium of spiritualization and appears, according to Teilhard's formulation, as the matrix of mind; spirit is born in the heart of matter, and as a function of matter. But this panmaterialism, from which emerges a spiritualization, has behind it a dialectical drive which in the end makes of it a panpsychism. The cosmos, in its inmost being, presented itself as spiritual in substance; and Teilhard, by a backward process, sought to reconsider the constitution of matter by taking spirit to be the primordial substance of things. What are the determinisms of matter? The result of the interaction of a mass of fundamental liberties in disorder, therefore subject to statistics.

This, of course, makes one think of Leibniz, whose term "monad" became one of Teilhard's favourite words. But Leibniz, not able to take evolution into account, much less convergent evolution, could not find a satisfactory solution for the problem of the communication of substances (a problem which the dualism of Descartes had rendered insoluble). Teilhard's effort to surmount this Cartesian dualism seems more successful because of the bearing of Teilhard's notion of *genesis*. At a time when science was already progressing towards a synthesis of the laws of matter and of life, Teilhard was going still further: he envisaged the unification of the laws of physical chemistry and the laws of physical psychology; as a part of the latter he was elaborating a human energetics; and spiritualized energy—that which forms the stuff of our intellections, affections and volitions, an energy imponderable but none the less quite real—seemed to him the flowering of cosmic energy. This human energetics is one of the most original points in Teilhard's thought and gives further testimony to his bent for synthesis—synthesis of matter, life, and reflective intelligence, and synthesis (leading to a panenergetics) of physical energy and psychic energy.

Teilhard's dialectic—in accordance with the claims of the real— mastered and synthesized concepts hitherto held to be contradictory. Such a dialectic was timely indeed in its elaboration of a concrete anthropology, which took as its subject matter a mind essentially human, submitted to conditions of time and space, and integrated in a body and in the cosmos. The discovery of the noosphere as the last of the scientific series (barysphere, pyrosphere, lithosphere, hydrosphere, biosphere)—but to which he was to add

5+

the Christosphere—was a step towards the integration of man with the cosmos, entailing, as well, a cosmic view of man's situation.

We have already emphasized the first of the revolutions introduced by Teilhard into the thought of his day: the definitive substitution of cosmogenesis for the notion of a static cosmos. Let us now emphasize, in turn, the second of those revolutions, directly connected with his notion of a noosphere. Teilhard rightly stressed this paradox, namely, that man, centre and creator of all science, was the one object which our science had not yet succeeded in embracing in a homogeneous representation of the universe. Teilhard understood that man alone could serve man in the deciphering of the world; for man and the world are unintelligible without each other, and man is truly the key to things, the ultimate harmony, the hub of the universe, around whom the elements of the world are distributed concentrically, in accordance with a definite structure.

Synthesis of the cosmic and the human—such is the profound meaning of the noosphere. But a further synthesis was taking form in Teilhard's mind, that of the cosmological and the Christological, a synthesis of which we have already traced the beginnings. Teilhard's premises are rigorously orthodox: first, the fact of the Incarnation, whereby Christ, the Son of God, really became, by virtue of his human nature, a part of the cosmos; secondly, the winning back of the entire cosmos, since the Son of Man shared all the activities of men, and blessed, by his passage, our brother fire and our sister earth; thirdly, the permanence of the Incarnation both in the Holy Eucharist and in the Mystical Body, since the Church, animated by the Spirit of Christ, is really the Body of the Saviour. Mankind, dominating and assimilating the universe, has transformed it into a human home. Christ, through the Eucharist, assimilates mankind, and, in the process, all the essentials of the universe.

The conclusion from Teilhard's premises is logical: since Christ before his death was an integral part of the cosmos, organically included in the stuff of the universe, then the risen Christ, who can have been nowise less than he had been before his death, became the organic centre of the cosmos. In all this Teilhard was following the inspired words of St Paul, who had already revealed the cosmic attributes of Christ, conqueror of death. By the resurrection, the body of Christ became coextensive with the cosmos, to which it had already been organically bound by the Incarnation; and the Pantocrator of the ancient Byzantine churches was revealed as the organic centre of the universe and the motive power of evolution. In the cosmic Christ, Christian realism found its logical conclusion.

The Sacred Heart of Jesus, having become a burning furnace, became immeasurably enlarged by virtue of the immensity of the universe; and history, through all its apparent chaos, was to resolve finally in the synthesis, in Jesus, of all the elements of the world, since through all the enormity of time and the bewildering multiplicity of individuals, one single operation was going on, namely, the annexation to Christ of his elect; and one single thing was being created—the Mystical Body of Christ, embracing all the scattered and inchoate spiritual powers in the world. Consequently, the greater man became, the more beautiful creation would be—and the more perfect adoration became, the more Christ would find, through his mystical continuations, a Body worthy of resurrection. It is this that we find well expressed in the following letter:

In the matter of "conversions" Christianity is obviously marking time. It is not by present-day methods, obviously, that the Kingdom of God will be established, but through some renaissance, some "revelation", which (once again in human history) will spread out in the human mass like water or like fire. It is this that we must desire and prepare for. It seems to me, myself . . . that the spark will spring up from the conjunction (which will take place, sooner, or later, in human hearts) of Our Lord and the world, the world becoming, in Christ, sacred and absolute, at the culmination of a long creative effort.

Thus we are brought to the spirituality of *Le milieu divin*, as summed up by the Canadian Jean Le Moyne in these words:

Here dogma begins to reveal its physical aspect. The spiritual affinities of matter—patient of the Incarnation, the Eucharist, and the Resurrection—become apparent. From every side man is receiving intimations of his cosmic relationship and is finding himself at home in the cosmos, allied to it all, and heir to it all; and he is assuming his full measure in time by identifying himself with a continuum that can be followed back into a past beyond those first discoverable divergences from instinctual pattern that signal the dawn of consciousness, and extending into the future beyond the era of full and dominant consciousness, even to the consummation of the Parousia.

One cannot over-emphasize the authentically religious character of this spirituality: a religious awareness of nature as the expression of the divine creative mind, as a divine design, and a religious awareness, therefore, extended to all human activities, even the most humble and—in appearance—the most profane. Similarly, it is difficult to over-emphasize the fact that this spirituality is not only religious, but authentically Christian, clearly centred upon the Incarnation—the historical coming of God upon earth, or coming of God, one might rather say, into the cosmos.

CHAPTER EIGHT

The Croisière Jaune

THE long period from 1931 until Teilhard's death *in Christo Iesu* (1955), despite certain definite breaks, is a unified one. Yet, for reasons we shall explain later, we may also consider the period 1931–8 as possessing a certain unity. It opened with the Croisière Jaune.

Of this adventure it would seem superfluous to speak at length, after the books of Georges Le Fèvre and Louis Audouin-Dubreuil and André Reymond's article,[1] besides Teilhard's own *Letters from a Traveller*.

First, let us summarize the facts. On 12 May 1931 Teilhard set out with the rest of the Chinese contingent of the Croisière Jaune, whom he had met at Kalgan, north-west of Peking. Their caravan proceeded due west along the Gobi towards Kashgar, in Chinese Turkestan, to join the other contingent in the interior of Asia. The principal stops were Suchow in the west of Kansu (from 11 June to 21 June), the oasis of Hami in the east of Sinkiang (28 June to 1 July), Turfan (5 July to 17 July), Urumchi, capital of Sinkiang (19 July to 6 September), and Aksu, not far from the Russian frontier (2 October), where the two parties joined. The return was by a somewhat different route, which followed the Yellow River for some distance. On 28 January 1932 they were attacked by bandits at the little village of Pa Tse Bolong, but two days later reached the Paotow railway terminal; and on 12 February Teilhard was back in Peking.

---

[1] Le Fèvre, *La croisière jaune* (new ed., Paris: Plon, 1952); Audouin-Dubreuil, *Sur la route de la soie* (Paris: Plon, 1935); Reymond, *Résultats scientifiques d'un voyage en Asie centrale* (Paris: *Revue de géographie physique*, 1938).

To the picturesque account given in the *Letters from a Traveller* we may add the following glimpses:

Turfan, Sinkiang
8 July 1931.

Over the rows of green poplars of this oasis (where we, a number of feet below sea level, are experiencing a temperature of 102 degrees), I can see, as I write to you, the high, snowy barrier of the Bogdo Ula, eastern extension of the Tien Shan. Ever since Suchow the skylines have been becoming really majestic.

After we left Kalgan our route led almost entirely through open desert, a scorched and bare wasteland more desert-like than any other I have seen. It is virtually lifeless, save for some sand gazelles and some large mountain sheep. The conditions are thus exceptional for the viewing of terrain.

Aksu
7 October, 1931.

...Sinkiang is a marvellous country, and the people are most friendly. I am writing to you in weather that stays clear and dry, in an orchard where grapes, peaches, and apples weigh down the boughs of the trees. Everywhere in this region we see bearded, turbaned men, veiled women, bazaars, and mosques, almost as if we had reached the Near East. Urumchi is more austere: it is almost Russia.

André Reymond sums up the whole expedition in the conclusion to his article:

Our route enabled us to survey the principal geological units of the interior of China, the closed basins with no outlet to the sea: Mongolia, the Gobi, Sinkiang, and the Celestial Mountains (Tien Shan chain), which we climbed on 3 August 1931. We were able to see the general structure of the countryside, the qualities of the vegetation, and the principal characteristics of the flora and fauna in a favourable season in each of the localities visited: June for the Gobi, July for Sinkiang, and August for the Tien Shan chain.

The return route...gave us an idea of the severity of the Chinese winter, destructive of flora and fauna, and the precarious life of the mammals, whether the thinly scattered gazelles in Sinkiang and Kansu, or the thousands of head of herbivores huddled together against the cold and the threat of wolves in the Mongolian grassland, in the steppes around Batkhalin, Pei Ling Miao, Bol Tai Miao, and Shara Muren.

It is this desperate quality of life in the winter and this long hibernation of the desert during the months from October to May that heighten by contrast the simultaneous riot of plants and insects in the Mongolian spring, before the furnace-like heat of July and August. This aggravatedly inland climate of the basins of Central Asia gives a residual character to their vegetation and their fauna. Here there survive, through very specific types of adaptation to the difficult conditions of drought, certain exceptional groups, in small numbers, out of the countless others that the desert has pushed back or exterminated.

Such, then, is life here: fleeting, ground-hugging, its beasts and plants alike specialized for existence in the steppes or the wastelands of these basins, on soils parsimonious or laden with salt and alkali from the evaporation basins—beasts and plants alike, then, limited to varieties and species capable of tolerating special, and in general, difficult conditions, yet privileged, too, by their very adaptation, which has assured them the exclusive right to populate these unkind regions. The narrow margin of existence coupled with the absence of competitors explains both the wide sowing of the vegetative species, which cover tens of thousands of square miles, and the extraordinary explosion of spring births and the swarming of biological populations in May, when every plant is in flower and the ground alive with scurrying insects, and when the purple of great fields of flags contrasts with the orange of basins of flowering *Zygophyllaceae* and *Sarcozygium*, with the blankets of pink blossoms of *Atraphaxis* on the hillsides, and with slopes mauve with the spreading petals of *Hedysarum*. Eight days of fleeting flower between two seasons of death—such is the burgeoning of the Mongolian Plateau and of the sunblasted gobis of the interior, such the royal progress of spring through these lands of fire and ice.

Taken as a whole, the Croisière Jaune has been very diversely judged. On one hand it has been praised to the skies (and in this acclaim André Sauvage's excellent film played no small part). It was a triumph of French engineering, an automobile record, a victory through tenacity over all obstacles, including the ill will of head-chopping, opium-smoking Marshal King, lord over Sinkiang, and was spiced by the gunshot of the bandits at Pa Tse Bolong.

On the other hand, some of the glory has faded, and the natural tendency is to exaggerate in the opposite direction. And, true enough, it takes no great critical gift to point out that, as a result of Russian malevolence (the Communists forbade the use of the one practicable route), the two automotive caravans never completely joined up. In the Chinese contingent deep disagreement reigned between the Nanking-imposed Chinese bloc and the European bloc (through the diplomacy of Teilhard, acting as a Chinese official, the friction was ended with an agreement signed—by Teilhard among others—20 June 1931). The captivity at Urumchi came close to turning out very badly. By an irony of fate it was the Soviets who, through their influence in Turkestan, saved the mission. Thanks to the sinister King (at odds with Nanking), and to mechanical difficulties arising out of a too tight schedule (happily somewhat relaxed as a result of the inevitable breakdowns), many observations that would have proved of value were out of the question. The return in the dead of winter was more like a retreat than anything else. As for the half-tracks themselves, the Chinese contingent from the moment they left Peking began to have trouble with the rubber for the tracks, which began to break. On top of everything the expedition cost a human life, that of Haardt, who died at Hong Kong of an infection.[2] Later, Teilhard paid a charming tribute to Haardt. Speaking of his various enterprises, he said:

> For all who had the honour of taking part in them, these expeditions were always, and in memory always will be, stairways to the stars.[3]

There was, perhaps, more glitter than gold in the expedition; even so, it was certainly more than a moderate success. It has been said that from the scientific point of view these nine months away were practically wasted time for Teilhard. But from his correspondence we can be sure that, on the whole, he was not dissatisfied:

> As regards the work, I am very well satisfied. Despite unfavourable conditions (haste, without adequate stops at points of interest), I succeeded in realizing my plan of combining the geology of China and that of Central Asia. The formations and structures show a greater coherence than I ever hoped to find. Without such prospecting I would have been greatly hampered in my future work. But no fossils, unfortunately—and nothing clearly very old in the way of prehistory. (7 July 1931.)

I shall not go into the whole story of my ten months of travelling, which ended so sadly in the death of Haardt. There was

---

[2] Victor Point's later suicide is not related to the expedition.
[3] Sermon for the wedding of Claude Haardt, 21 December 1948.

1. Tendances natives.

Aussi loin que je remonte dans mes souvenirs (dès avant l'âge de dix ans), je remarque en moi l'existence d'une passion nettement dominante : la passion de l'Absolu.

Évidemment, je ne donnais pas encore ce nom à l'inquiétude qui me pressait; — mais, aujourd'hui, je puis la reconnaître sans hésitation possible.

Le besoin de posséder, en tout, "quelque Absolu" était, dès mon enfance, l'axe de ma vie intérieure. Parmi les plaisirs de cet âge, je n'étais heureux (je m'en souviens en pleine lumière) que par rapport à une joie fondamentale, laquelle consistait, généralement, dans la possession (ou la pensée) de qq objet plus précieux, plus rare, plus consistant plus inaltérable. Tantôt, il s'agissait de qq. morceau de métal, Tantôt, par un saut à l'autre extrême, je me complaisais dans la pensée de Dieu-Esprit (la Chair de N.S. me paraissait, alors, quelque chose de trop fragile et de trop corruptible).

Cette préoccupation pourra sembler singulière. Je répète qu'il en était ainsi, sans arrêt. J'avais dès lors

6. P. 3 of the MS. of *Mon Univers*, 1918

le besoin invincible (et cependant vivifiant, calmant...)
me reposer sans cesse, en quelque chose de tangible et de
[final] ; — et je cherchais partout cet objet béatifiant.

L'histoire de ma vie intérieure est celle de
recherche, portant sur des réalités de plus en plus universelles
parfaites. — Dans le fond, ma tendance naturelle profonde (
"nisus" de mon âme) est demeurée absolument inflexible,
puis que je me connais.

Il est inutile de faire ici une revue de
[...] des différents autels que j'ai successivement dressé à
[...] mon cœur. Je dirai seulement qu'à mesure que [...]
forme individuelle d'existence se révélait à moi comme [...]
et caduque, je cherchais plus loin : dans la Matière élémentaire,
[...], dans les courants d'énergie physique, dans la Totalité
de l'Univers, — toujours, je l'avoue, avec cette prédilection
instinctive pour la matière (= considérée comme plus
solide que le reste) {que je n'ai corrigé} [dont] je ne me suis corrigé que beaucoup
plus tard (cf. l'Union créatrice & "La vraie Matière", et ci-
dessous p. 17).

Si, dès mon enfance, et depuis lors avec
plénitude et une conviction grandissante, j'ai toujours [...]
et scruté la Nature, je puis donc dire que ce n'est pas

little that was pleasant, much that was difficult, but finally, for me personally, there were results of prime importance (I think). I brought back few enough specimens, nor did I make major detailed discoveries; but I have hopes that I did bring back data for two or three fine syntheses of the antecedent and recent (Pleistocene) geology of Central Asia. Just think—I am probably the only geologist in the world who has ever seen with his own eyes all the country that stretches between Harbin and Kashgar. And I may draw important conclusions from what I saw when I combine my researches with those of my American friends in the Gobi and my Swedish friends at Sinkiang. I am working on this now. (26 March 1932.)

So I am back in good shape from that interminable trip to Sinkiang, which threatened to drag on almost a year. From many sides I shall be criticized for having lent myself to that pseudo-scientific adventure. This is because of their failure to see that I climbed into those Citroën half-tracks for the same reason I would have climbed onto a camel—I simply had to become acquainted with Central Asia. And now I am glad that I went. Over and above fine friendships formed (for example, with Hackin, director of the Musée Guimet), the trip, ill suited though it was to research needs, was for me nothing less than a revelation of the geology of Asia.

There were vexations at every turn. But stalled cars are sometimes the Providence of geologists! And there is this compensation, that I now understand a number of very important things about the structure of Asia: distribution of facies, eruptive series, etc. With the help of my friend Norin, of the Hedin Group, I think I am now in a position to prove (palaeontologically and stratigraphically) the contemporaneousness of the *flexed* cones of intrusion of the Tarim and of the Gobi with the upper Siwaliks on the one hand, and our San Men level (and of the Pliocene) in China on the other. Asia is beginning to present a coherent picture. It is all working out very well. My only regret about this trip is that on account of the political situation we were stopped a little short of Kashgar, so that I was prevented from seeing the connection between the inland and marine formations of the Cretaceous and of the Tertiary. (6 April 1932.)

Various incidents show that Teilhard, never without his geologist's hammer, his magnifying glass, and his notebook, was tirelessly active along the way. In the vicinity of Urumchi, for example, on 27 and 28 July, he was ranging the river valley above Bie Ango,

5*

returning with both geological notations and a quantity of mountain Compositae and such other alpines as the magnificent *Codonopsis ovata Benth*. From Urumchi to Aksu (6 September to 2 October), as a part of a four-vehicle detachment to meet the Pamir group, he was busy with very precise notations on both flora and fauna.

From Liang-chow at the foot of the Shan-Nan-Shau mountains, he went on horseback to the Shu Nin Keou coal-mines, a Carboniferous basin situated at an 8,500-foot altitude thirty miles to the south-east across river gorges banked with shales and granite. For a man of over fifty years, unused to horseback travel, a sixty miles round trip in the saddle between one midnight and the next was no small feat.

His scientific achievements—for geology—on this trip were, then, of considerable value. After synthesizing the geology of Northern China, and connecting it with that of Manchuria, he had now been able to draw in a considerable sector of China's Far West:

> As regards the Quaternary and the peak of the Tertiary, I have been able to unite the elements into a fine synthesis—that is, to show the extension of the Eastern China levels as far as Turfan. After Turfan, though, a curious change is to be seen: the San Men level becomes lost; and the loess, in contrast, remains clearly marked. (16 January 1932.)

Two of his fellow travellers have left us sketches of Teilhard on this expedition. Andé Reymond writes:

> Teilhard—you'd have to have seen him in those days! And I wish that you had seen him, or could see him standing before you as I do, in memory: vibrant as a flag fluttering under the Asian sky, energetic, lively, generous, tireless, greeting each day with a burst of joyous enthusiasm—one minute running like a youngster for a hammer to check something, sparing willing workers almost as little as himself.

Having little relish for being disturbed in his work, he refused to suffer ciné camera men gladly (not excluding the ubiquitous André Sauvage); and once on the return trip, at Turfan, when the photographers in the soft November light threatened to interrupt his work, he turned on them with—what was rare for him—language he had learned as a corporal in the trenches.

Sauvage has given us this portait:

> There was something very handsome about him. . . . He had

style, the matchless style of an unobtrusive yet irresistible distinction. His voice, his musical diction, his smile (which never degenerated into a laugh) will be recalled by anyone who ever observed him. There was nothing obtrusively clerical about him; in gesture and deportment he was as simple as could be. He was gracious and obliging, yet was as unyielding as a stone wall. You could be physically close to him yet realize that you were thereby no closer to his preoccupations, to his controlled thoughts. Most often we were stopped short by that rough-hewn face out of an El Greco canvas, and turned our attention instead to the endless day-to-day problems of the expedition.

Like the Jesuits generally, he knew when to dispense with formality.... And in this man, so courteous, so pleasant, so engaging—not to say fascinating—you could sense a kind of disarming loneness; he seemed to be interested in his companions only as a measure of good fellowship.

The fact of the matter was that the Croisière Jaune was a time of spiritual trial for him:

One of the disadvantages of this trip is the virtual impossibility of being recollected, in view of the numbers and the complexity of the group. They are a very agreeable lot (though the mechanics keep together in a different sort of gang of their own), but the trouble is you're never alone, either physically or morally. My life is identical with my work. Well, thought and reflection will come after it is all over, I suppose. This new plunge into pure unfiltered reality, free from all conventions, cannot be without its effect on me. I have a vague conviction that it will help to free me from many fetters, or from narrow and intemperate views. (7 July 1931.)

The members of the Croisière Jaune, though united in scientific endeavour, and when confronted by the Asiatics, were not, at least at first, so well disposed towards Teilhard, and rather held it against him that he was a priest and a Jesuit (in his letter of 13 March 1932 he said that there was not a single practising Catholic among them, except himself, of course). Sometimes their questions would be quite ridiculous. Thus Georges-Marie Haardt, in his sweeping way, once asked him.

"Father, what do you think of metempsychosis?"

"The Church," Teilhard answered, "of which I have the honour of being a member, has delivered a definitive opinion on that subject."

"Well," replied Haardt seriously, "you ought to get your Church to reconsider its position."

There was nothing really malicious in this kind of interrogation. With some of the mechanics, if we are to believe one witness, he had rather more trouble. Even so, he seems to have gained their good will and even their confidence, for, in spite of his aristocratic origins, he had a great feeling for the working man, and a lively sense of Christ as the son of a carpenter. Teilhard was always ready to lend a hand when trouble arose.

> From time to time the truck would sink into sand up to the axle. The driver would stay in his seat, and the rest of us, Teilhard included, would jump out, to go at it with spades and picks. And as we were ready for the last big shove, I'd see Teilhard's huge hand on the back of the truck, pushing it as you'd push a canoe into the water.

With a witty word, he could disarm maliciousness:

> At Urumchi, during a long and tedious wait, one member of the mission began to give an imitation of someone preaching (an activity not hard to parody), with plain reference to their Jesuit comrade, who despite the familiarities of the expedition still remained something of an oddity.
> "I get it," said Teilhard. "You're playing a Dominican!" From this opening—which tickled me, as he knew it would—he went on with an unlooked-for liveliness to explain about the saints, showing how in these Princes of Grace there was nothing of the Holy Joe.[4]

On another occasion, at Pei Ling Miao, in Mongolia (it was 25 May 1931)—while a slain kasarka, a golden duck, hung from the tent roof over their beds—Teilhard, upon hearing a doubt expressed about the existence of God, asserted, without changing his voice, and as if stating an algebraic theorem:

> God is a very simple choice, the choice between a Yes and a No, between a plus sign and a minus sign. This is a choice that none of us can escape. It is utterly impossible to get it wrong.

[4] Teilhard had, in fact, a great respect for the Friars Preachers. He wrote (3 February 1933) to a mother who had sent her son to school with them, "their humane and Christian influence is far-reaching and progressive. It's an order with breadth, tradition, and breeding. I am very happy about your choice."

If the expedition taught Teilhard something about the trials and tribulations of real life, at the same time he learnt how to build for his interior life an anchorite's cell, bounded by the distant horizon. His feelings are expressed in a letter written a few weeks before he had set out on the expedition (25 April 1931):

Adoration's real name, I am beginning to understand, is Research, qualified only by its passive counterpart, confident submission to obstacles that cannot be overcome: all this under the sign of faith in the future of the universe.

During the trip he meditated upon several prospective publications, at least two of which were realized. Nothing was allowed to interrupt his interior life or check his mental and mystical progress. At Urumchi, for example, he had a memorable conversation with the Mongolian princess Nirgidma of Torhout *"on the meaning of life and on God's part in the universe"*, and on another occasion, when laid up for four days with a raging fever and restricted to a liquid diet, he devoted his forced inactivity to meditation and prayer. A sentence from one letter seems to show us the result of this spiritual concentration:

Interiorly, I am on the whole peaceful, though more and more I am deliberately bent upon an objective which has always haunted me, the intellectual liberation of the world.

Not a single one of Teilhard's companions was a practising Catholic, and nevertheless not a single one of them was missing from the Mass which he celebrated on New Year's Day of 1932 at the Liang-chow mission.

Audouin-Dubreuil has kept a copy of Teilhard's brief address on that occasion.

My friends, we have met this morning, in this little church, in the heart of China, in order to come before God at the beginning of this new year. Of course, probably for not one of us here does God mean, or seem, the same thing as for any other of us. And yet, because we are all intelligent beings, not one of us can escape the feeling, or reflection, that above and beyond ourselves there exists some superior force, and that, since it is superior to ourselves, it must possess some superior form of our own intelligence and our own will.

It is in the consciousness of the presence of this transcendently thinking and willing force that we should recollect ourselves for a moment at the beginning of this new year. What we ask of that universal presence which envelops us all, is first to reunite us, as in a shared, living, centre with those whom we love, those who, so far away from us here, are themselves beginning this same new year.

Then, considering what must be the boundless power of this force, we beseech it to take a favourable hand for us and for our friends and families in the tangled and seemingly uncontrollable web of events that await us in the months ahead. So may success crown our enterprises. So may joy dwell in our hearts and all around us. So may what sorrow cannot be spared us be transfigured into a finer joy, the joy of knowing that we have occupied each his own station in the universe, and that, in that station, we have done as we ought.

Around us and in us, God, through his deep-reaching power, can bring all this about. And it is in order that he may indeed do so that, for all of you, I am about to offer him this Mass, the highest form of Christian prayer.[5]

[5] *Sur la route de la soie*, p. 225.

CHAPTER NINE

First Peking Period (1932-8)
—Contacts with France

AFTER the Croisière Jaune Teilhard's life entered a new stage, his first long association with Peking (1932–8). The return to Peking inaugurated a series of trials and sorrows. He was greatly moved by the death of Haardt, as he says in the *Letters from a Traveller*:

> ... the desert would have been a nobler tomb for him, not that Hong Kong hasn't its own beauty. To me, personally, the sudden loss of a man whose generosity and warmth of heart had captivated me is a real grief, deepened by my regret at not having been able to be with him in his last moments. From what I knew of him, he would have turned to me for support, and I am sure that I could have eased his passing. It is a real sorrow to me. (p. 192.)

In these few lines priesthood and friendship go hand in hand; we see quite another side from the "stone wall" to which André Sauvage compared his resistance, and from the aloofness he noted.

But Teilhard suffered even crueller losses. A note to the same letter reminds us that:

> On getting back to Peking Père Teilhard learnt also of his father's death. He was deeply moved by a series of family bereavements during his exile in China, two of his brothers, his mother, and a sister. He was never able to get home, even though he knew the end was near. (*Letters from a Traveller*, p. 192.)

In a letter of 15 September 1936 he speaks of the death of his sister Marguerite:

> Towards the middle of August I lost my younger sister (the last surviving). I was only too well prepared to learn of it. She and I

understood each other particularly well, and her death leaves me with a great emptiness (as Black's did, though in another way). There are now only we three brothers out of the ten in 1900.[1]

It is profoundly sad that Marguerite saw fit to destroy almost all her brother's letters to her. But what she was to him we may divine from the preface to his *L'énergie spirituelle de la souffrance*, and particularly from his *Témoignage fraternel*. Marguerite gave him an example of suffering transformed into an expression of love and a principle of union. Teilhard ends his *Témoignage fraternel* thus:

> ... Marked by sickness from her youth, and surrounded later by an immense family of the sick, Marguerite had as her special function to seek out and to find God in the heart of human infirmity.
>
> There was nothing pessimistic, nothing passive, nothing morbid in this predilection for the more sombre side of existence. On the contrary, by virtue of her own quite realistic (and quite Christian) notion of perfection, Marguerite succeeded in setting an example in her obstinate fight for health, and in her tireless use of such energies as had not been affected by her sickness. The Christian's aim must be not only to master suffering and sickness but to transfigure them in their very essence. Like many before her and during her time, Marguerite sought to prove by her example that such a transfiguration is possible. Was it not enough to know her to perceive that hidden in the depth of suffering lies a power that can dissipate egoism, bring tenderness to the heart, clarify the understanding, and reveal God?
>
> Illuminated by the invisible light, Marguerite lived so as to be led and to lead others towards that centre of creative power which shines upon us through the shadows of death.

Fortunately, sustaining him in these trials, correspondence with France continued to be regular and abundant. Among his principal correspondents, besides the faithful Abbé Gaudefroy, there was always the Abbé Breuil, to whom Teilhard sent particularly detailed reports. Twice—in 1931 and in 1935—the Abbé Breuil came to China to see his "pupil" and to examine the diggings at Choukou-tien. The first time, unfortunately, Teilhard was absent, the return of the Croisière Jaune having been delayed. On the second occasion the

---

[1] Marguerite died on 17 August. Cf. also the letter of 5 September 1936 in *Letters from a Traveller*.

two scientists had the happiness of being together in Peking. It was then that there took place what we may call "The Adventure of the Jade Buddha". In Peking, north-west of the Imperial Palace, lies a small tree-clad hill. Here, hidden by the trees, stands a minute Buddhist temple which Teilhard used to love because it contains a rather more than life-size statue of Buddha, carved in concentrically veined grey marble and improperly named by Europeans "The Jade Buddha". This statue, as Breuil described it, is lovely because of the beauty of the face, on which hover tranquil joy, buoyant calm, and the trace of a smile. One day Teilhard took Breuil there and whispered: "I am very fond of this head, because it says something to me. It tells me that here is something which Christianity ought to adopt."

This brief whisper echoes a thought recorded in a letter of 27 May 1923:

> ...I feel, more strongly than ever, the need of freeing our religion from everything about it that is specifically Mediterranean. I do not believe—note well—that the majority of oriental thought-patterns are anything but outmoded and obsolescent, fated to disappear along with the human type to which they are native. But I do say that by taking these forms, decayed though they be, into account, we discover such a wealth of potentialities in philosophy, in mysticism, and in the study of human conduct that it becomes scarcely possible to be satisfied with an image of a mankind entirely and definitely enveloped in the narrow network of precepts...in which some people think they have displayed the whole amplitude of Christianity.

Teilhard's pleasure in seeing Breuil again was enhanced by their return together at the beginning of May 1935, via the Trans-Siberian railway, to France.

Another source of joy was the news of Breuil's election to the Institut de France.

> Now I must tell you how happy I am over your success at the Institut. You are indeed right; prehistory must be represented there. ... I am glad too that you find you like Helmut de Terra, as he does you, according to a letter I had from him. We can't complain about our circle of friends, which is expanding but growing more cohesive at the same time. Today M told me that the Movius family visited the Institut while on their tour. I should

be interested to know what you think of the Irrawaddy industry. (22 June 1938.)

Teilhard, if he was an excellent practical psychologist, was no long-range schemer. At the same time, without his suspecting it, the representation for prehistory now gained at the Institut paved the way for his own future election.

Still other stars had risen on the horizon: Vaufrey, professor of human palaeontology at the Institut and director of the periodical *L'anthropologie*,[2] the Jesuit geophysician Lejay, and Jean Piveteau, professor at the Paris Faculté des Sciences, who from 1932 was publishing in collaboration with Teilhard,[3] to name but a few. Paul Rivet, founder of the Musée de l'Homme, was already a friend of long standing.

Teilhard's esteem for the Musée de l'Homme was returned with interest. There was even a plan afoot to have him posted to Hanoi,[4] though nothing came of it:

The project in question (to the author of which I feel infinitely obliged) would seem difficult of accomplishment. I do not think that my Order would agree to my accepting so isolated a post, in a country where we have no house to which I could be, even if only nominally, attached. Besides, I do not know what I should have to gain by exchanging Peking for Hanoi.

So the only practical thing that I could envisage would be to make one, two, or three visits there to get some researches under way, in connection with Yunnan. The latest *Javanthropus* find convinces me that the proper research procedure is, just as I thought, to follow the vein of deposits and to institute diggings methodically from north to south, from Peking down to Malaya. (5 June 1932).

Another enduring bond was with Édouard Le Roy. True, Teilhard wrote to him only infrequently (though his letters covered a wide range of scientific and spiritual questions) and Le Roy—

---

[2] It was at the repeated suggestion of Teilhard that Vaufrey presented himself to Marcellin Boule, who immediately brought him into his Laboratory and offered him a subject for a thesis. Regular correspondence began in 1928.
[3] When Piveteau was still just a student at the Sorbonne, Teilhard had sponsored his membership of the Société géologique de France, 23 January 1922.
[4] According to a letter of 16 January 1927, he had already been approached by the Institut national d'Ethnographie (Lévy-Bruhl, etc.) with a view to undertaking excavations in Indo-China.

prohibitively busy—made no answer to these. Even so, there was no cooling of relations, no weakening or slackening of the bonds of friendship; and Gaudefroy, a regular correspondent, served as intermediary. The central event, in 1931, was the placing of Édouard Le Roy on the Index of Forbidden Books.

But no amount of friendly correspondence was a substitute for Paris. Despite his increasing absorption with China, he still insisted on the desirability of moving back and forth between Peking and Paris. Yet it seems that, in 1936, he finally gave up the idea of teaching at the Museum in Paris:

> I have had no official advice of the plan of which you speak [Museum]. I confess that it does not tempt me very much. I have the impression that the wise thing for me to do is to follow my present line until it either ends or changes by itself into something else; and I do not feel that I have reached the end of all that awaits me here. (11 February 1936.)

The first of his visits to Paris was from the end of September, 1932, to the end of January, 1933. As usual, we know little about how he spent his time. In a letter of 28 April 1933, to the geologist and archaeologist Joseph Hackin, with whom he had made friends during the Croisière Jaune, he says:

> What can I say about myself? My stay in Paris was one grand rush. I was able, however, to leave there, practically ready for the press, a short article and a rather fine geological map in colours of the Kalgan-Hami stretch....

We know, too, that he was studying the Choukou-tien fauna, that in October he saw Breuil, completely gay and enthusiastic, and that before Christmas he went to London, where he met Black. Of his English connections we know little. He had some friends at the British Museum and doubtless at Oxford—old friends perhaps from his Hastings days, and new friends, assuredly, on account of his growing reputation, now, as a specialist in Far Eastern geology and palaeontology.

At Paris, around the New Year, in the chapel of the Franciscan Missionaries of Mary, he gave a talk to the members of the Catholic Union of the Sick on the meaning and constructive value of suffering.[5] He was at the presbytery of Saint-Séverin for a meeting of the

---

[5] Published in *Le trait d'union*, no. 45 (1 April 1933), pp. 6–11.

Society for Religious Studies, the guiding light of which had been Father Laberthonnière, who had recently died (in October 1932). About the same time he again saw his friends the Normale students. This was my own first meeting with Father Teilhard, when I sat at the other end of the long green-covered table, scratching away furiously at my notes. And here is an exact transcription of what I wrote:

Orient and Occident
Mystical Views on Personality
(Teilhard de Chardin)

The opposition between a contemplative Orient and an Occident immersed in life is a questionable one; we are attributing our own qualities to the Orient.

(1) *Oriental mysticism.* Mysticism does not exist save when the mind seeks to resolve the opposition between unity and multiplicity (no mysticism of pluralism). For the oriental mystic, the resolution of the many into the one is brought about through suppression of the many; the one has nothing in common with this many, from which it must be separated (Maya). The state of nirvana is an ecstasy of emptiness. Now this is an attitude that is true (a) neither for the past: The whole past is an effort towards accentuation of the realities which constitute the multiple, (b) nor for the future: It gives no grounds for efforts for a future, (c) nor for our interior life. The religious aspiration is for a unification which will not be a dissolution of being. For things to be united, there must be two.

(2) *Occidental mysticism.* It starts with the idea that the multiple is by nature convergent, with elements capable of a gradual unity leading to unities of a higher order. Unity is reached through the most thorough realization of things in themselves. Consequently, to make one's goal the bringing of the world to its fullness is the only means of living present-day life. The Orientals, in contrast, are interested in positive things.

(3) *Its connections with Christian mysticism.* Occidental mysticism is the legitimate extension of a Christian attitude. One finds an oriental component in Christianity (cf. the flight to the desert), but there is the belief in the resurrection of the body (perfection and purification of the elements). In the idea of mysticism through convergence, there is an element of ascesis. Convergence is different from repose. Renouncement consists in continually transcending things. The extreme limit of the affections leads to unity. For St Paul, the form of the world is a great movement of attrac-

tion of creatures towards God. God descends, through Christ, into the many, in order to draw the many to himself. Difference between the unity of abstraction and the unity of richness (of concentration), where the elements find unity through all they possess of perfection.

There is no Christian philosophy, as if there were two opposed entities. Faith is born only from faith; there is not reason on one side, and faith on the other. More and more elevated acts of faith. The world has a sense—this sense is spirit—this sense is achieved through unification—adherence to Christianity. Philosophy is pre-Christian, but it has the attitude of a faith.

These notes (presented in the rough form in which they were taken down) are a summary of a very fine essay, *La route de l'Ouest, vers une mystique nouvelle*, dated at Penang, 8 September 1932, the germ of which is to be found in a letter of 22 May 1932:

> These last few months I have been led to make a sort of sketch of the main ways in which mysticism has attempted to solve the fundamental intellectual and spiritual problem: How explain, and then surmount, the multiple, and arrive at unity?
>
> It strikes me that there are two theoretical solutions (both of them attempted): the oriental (that we arrive at unity by dissipating—through evasion or suppression—the illusion of the multiple) and the occidental—scarcely formulated yet, I should say—(that we arrive at unity through the effort of extending, in their proper direction, the potentialities—convergent by nature—of the multiple). Mysticism of detachment from things, or mysticism of passage via things? I think (it is my whole life) that present-day Christianity is tending towards the latter, in which the salvation of humanity consists.

This criticism of Eastern thought did not arise from any belief that radically the Westerner is superior to the Oriental.

On 29 June 1954 Teilhard was still protesting: "They say I am a racist, but I am not a racist. It is a fact that at the present time the West is the place where ideas are to be found. But later on that may change." But if there was no racism in Teilhard's thought, it is equally true that at that time he considered himself a convinced Occidental, though recognizing that India was to remain for a long time the religious pole of the earth, and wondering to what refinements of culture or of thought the mystical "cyclone" on the Ganges plains could have corresponded. *La route de l'Ouest* was the subject of sympathetic discussions between Teilhard and one of his most faithful and fair-minded friends, who lived in India.[6] His friend's initial objection was this: Is there not a Christian detachment, and can it be maintained that Buddhistic renunciation is void of all moral validity? Teilhard's reply was:

> I was most interested in your friendly criticisms of *La route de l'Ouest*. But, if I am not mistaken, they prove precisely the importance of what I tried to show. . . . . I fully allow the alternation of detachment and attachment (cf. *Le milieu divin*). But I believe that it is in the particular, *specific* nature of the Buddhist detachment that there lies the weakness and the (at least logical) danger of oriental religions. The Buddhist denies himself in order to kill desire (he does not believe in the value of being). The authentic Christian, also, denies himself, but by *excess of desire* and of faith in the value of being.
>
> This is one of those cases where the same appearances cover contrary realities. It seems to me to be supremely desirable to unmask the ambiguity here. This is not to say, of course, that, vitally speaking, Buddhist renunciation has no moral validity. But it is expressed in a false theory (as in the case of so many other pantheisms). (8 October 1933.)

His correspondent did not surrender: Are the religions of India in fact as negative as Teilhard believed? A new reply came from Teilhard:

> Basically, if the religions of India are less negative than I said, that fact does not essentially affect my thesis, the purpose of which is above all to distinguish the two possible essential types of mysticism. It would be quite extraordinary, I confess, for either of these types to be met anywhere in the pure state. I therefore took oriental mysticism as an example, as close as possible, of negativism. Such reservations, or concessions, once made, I still believe that oriental religions and oriental contemplation mean death to action. I fail to see that the Far East affords an exception. In China, Buddhism is dead. And was it not a Japanese Neo-Buddhist who was telling Grousset that his religion culminated in "the intoxication of emptiness"? I know that fully-achieved being can be called non-being. But I do not believe that there is, in the case in question, no more than a question of words. (29 April 1934.)

[6] The Abbé Monchanin. This very cultured priest, impelled by an overwhelming vocation, went to India, to the diocese of Trichinopoly, in order to live an ascetic life, centred on the contemplation of God and the Trinity. Teilhard and Monchanin had met once or twice and had got on well.

We know, finally, that this stay in Paris ended with a dinner with the members of the Croisière Jaune, the only shadow over which was the absence of Haardt and of Point.

We know rather more about his journey back to China (in February and March, 1933), in company with Breuil and Lejay, and including a talk to the Saigonese on 10 March. Here is a brief account, dated 26 February 1933, of the crossing:

> *"Outside"*, we have been gliding for a week over the glittering blue waters of the Indian Ocean. My friend Breuil was taken off at Jibuti in that "pirate" Monfreid's boat. *"Inside"*, I am trying to pull myself together and do a little thinking. To remain faithful to my habits, I am writing a few pages (for personal study), *La structure de l'esprit*, in which I am trying to express more exactly a kind of metaphysics of spirit-matter, or more exactly of matter-spirit (the juxtaposition is not so troublesome as one might think), with corollaries on the creation and on evil. . . .
>
> I am exploring this road as a possible line of approach towards one of the facets of truth. I am spending quite a little time, too, in talks with various sorts of people. And each time I discover a mind or a heart bound by the same chains as those I have taken twenty years to break. Let me tell you that these encounters, one after another, on top of the latest checks suffered by my writings, have awakened in me one passion (hitherto unknown): to liberate. Until now I have led a speculative life above all; I feel that life is about to push me more and more towards action. Nor do I really see what could keep me from acting. I leave it to Heaven! There are vocations which one does not resist. The only thing that would frighten me would be what the Epistle for today speaks of as being "a tinkling cymbal".

The latest checks suffered by his writings, which he refers to here, were two in number. The first was the shelving of *L'esprit de la terre*, the second a hold-up for the *Le miliu divin*:

> Saw Father —— here, who brought me the two final censorship reports on *Le milieu divin*. Both are very favourable—except (in one) a request for precision on the "Sense of the Cross", which I can easily satisfy, I think. Pity that the whole thing must be held up. (Christmas, 1932.)

The second trip to France was made in early May of 1935. Teilhard travelled by the Trans-Siberian, with Breuil, for a stay of several months, not re-embarking—for Bombay—until 6 September.

Of this second stay again we have no detailed knowledge. Teilhard stopped at Harbin, where he saw Ahnert and the few Russians remaining at the museum. In Paris he met a large number of people —Dr George Barbour among others—but did little scientific work. At the Museum, however, he admired Jean Piveteau's work on the Triassic fish from Madagascar. In the church of Saint-Louis des Invalides on 15 June he delivered a beautiful address on the occasion of the nuptial blessing of M. and Mme de la Goublaye de Ménorval.[7]

He made one visit to London, no doubt in July, inspected the remains of Palestine Man (over three skeletons), and saw, on his friend Hopwood's desk, Zdansky's article in which his own and the Chinese scientists' ideas on the San Men level were rather severely criticized.

A good deal of the atmosphere of this stay in Paris, however, is available to us in the letters. We know that he was "no sooner ashore than swamped", and that, despite the rush, he had "a chance to see a good many people in the busy square of the Rue de Grenelle.... And so many contacts with men of all ages filled me with hope". (18 January 1936.)[8]

Besides joining a brief family reunion, he renewed his ecclesiastical contacts, entering into closer relations with his religious Order and with the Church. Was not Christianity

> ... around us, the sole collective current of living thought, sustaining and furthering the idea of a personal whole in the world? (4 June 1935.)

He was greatly touched by the attitude of his Jesuit friends:

> I feel ashamed when I consider how much they count on me.... What reassures me is the thought that, while I really have no worth in myself, the influence that I exercise radiates from the *truth* of what I am convinced I *see*. And there lies the greatest success that I can hope for in my life—to have published a new vision of the world. (8 September 1935.)

[7] Happily, this has been preserved. Éliane Basse de Ménorval, geologist, palaeontologist and naturalist, is today research director at the National Centre for Scientific Research. She worked with Piveteau in Boule's Laboratory.

[8] 42, rue de Grenelle, was Teilhard's third Parisian address. The first two were 13, rue du Vieux-Colombier and 5, rue du Regard. Later he was to live at 15, rue Monsieur (*Études*).

He gave valuable advice to a friend in religion:

> In your talks on human origins, do not fail (you give thought to it, I am sure) to give minor emphasis to the flimsy and provisional hypotheses such as we are able to form at the moment from the ever-changing data of science, and to give major emphasis to the general changes in point of view, which amount to the establishment of man in the *universe*, and to the evident recapitulation in him of all antecedent life, on a new and higher level. (23 June 1935.)

Another friend, a religious, seemed disposed to publish *Comment je crois* (written October, 1934, Peking), prefacing it with *Les fondements et le fond de l'idée d'évolution* (Gulf of Bengal, Ascension Day, 1926), and *L'esprit de la terre* (Pacific Ocean, 9 March 1931).

> That, of course, would be simply ideal. But I dare not hope for so much. (29 July 1935.)

It seemed always the old story of Teilhard's repeated efforts to get his key works published, and the repeated dashing of his hopes. There was a charged atmosphere, it seemed, during this Paris stay, clear portent of the years 1938–9:

> Everything seems to be an impossible muddle at present in the world. And yet every day brings me new evidence that we are playing our part in the birth of some great thing. I think that at no other time has the vital tension been so strong. (30 June 1935.)
>
> Everywhere in the country little groups are beginning to spring up, each with its own message (mind, the new earth, the new mankind, etc.), but each distinctly the same in the orientation of ideas, which are all directed towards a spiritual rejuvenation of the world. This plainly heralds the coming of something. (16 June 1935.)

Teilhard was to become increasingly certain of his own position:

> I wonder whether today mankind is not really in the process of cleavage between those who believe and those who disbelieve in the future of the universe. And I feel more decidedly than ever that I must line up with the former, for the conquest of the world. (4 June 1935.)

His ideas were taking shape and coherence:

> Apart from a small number of contributions in the world of science, my greatest personal accomplishment to date has been the

attainment of a clearer insight into the further possibilities still undeveloped in my "philosophy". A "philosophy of union", based on an analysis of the personal structure of the universe, seems to me both what modern thought has most need of and the work which I am best able to do. This conclusion becomes increasingly clear to me as I talk with my friends and gauge their highly favourable reaction to my *Comment je crois*. (16 June 1935.)

As a continuation, then, of what he had already sketched out on the subject of the "person" in that work, Teilhard was meditating one of his key works, *Esquisse d'un univers personnel* (1936). What effected the profound unity between science and thought, in Teilhard, was much less the (evident) convergence of the two than their common characteristic of a perpetual moving ahead to new positions. Closed thought, or open-ended thought? Teilhard constantly chose the latter.

On 6 September, then, Teilhard embarked for Bombay, where he went ashore a fortnight later. While in the Red Sea schools of dolphins "showed their backs above the water or sported in a row in the wake of the ship", Teilhard was busy meditating. The past had revealed to him the shape of things to come, and finally he concluded:

> . . . that there is only one real road to discovery (as we learn if we study history); it is to build the future. It's perfectly simple, but there are still so many people who behave as though the past were interesting in itself, and treat it as only the future deserves to be treated. (*Letters from a Traveller*, p. 209.)

There had never been anything of the devotee of the past about Teilhard; never had he been sensible to the charm of old things; until now, he had been a geologist and a palaeontologist. Now, his attitude and interests were beginning to change. As a scientist, he would go on producing abundantly; but already the last phase of his life was heralded, the Franco-American period, in which preoccupations with the future of man were to become dominant.

As for his third Paris visit, we do, alas, know how Teilhard spent most of his time. Coming from the United States, he was in France from 19 April to 6 August 1937. Amid the social bitterness of the period, and after a brief meeting with friends, including Wong and Pei, he was in for months of sickness:

> First of all my stay in France was not so successful as my stay in America. Scarcely had I set foot in Paris when I came down

with an attack of some weird, recurrent fever (malaria, maybe; but then again, maybe not! the doctors have located no pathogenes in my system), a fever which kept me from doing any serious work whatsoever while I was in Europe. I had to cancel talks, and a trip to England, and, finally, the convention at Moscow. In the end, I was so disgusted that I resolved to go back to China, and that's what I did, via the Suez, at the beginning of August. (9 October 1937.)

He was sent as a patient to the Pasteur hospital. But only in 1949 were chest X-rays to show scars of healed lesions. His English trip was to have taken him to Cambridge. In July, when the Moscow convention was scheduled to be held, he was recuperating in Auvergne before his return to Asia.

There were few external checks to Teilhard's life: we have noted or will note, among others, the ill-fated trip to Kansu in 1926, this sickness in 1937, a graver sickness in 1947, still another in 1949, his being forbidden to enter his candidacy to the Collège de France in 1948, and his inability, for reasons of health, to visit Kenya in 1951. The year 1937, in the matter of his health, constituted the first warning, and some after-effects were to remain. Like every other deeply thoughtful man, Teilhard had calculated the slowing down which age and sickness generally bring about. As early as the time of *Le milieu divin* he had called upon all the unifying force of these powers of suffering, but this Christian acceptance was not to take from him his normal part in the agony of the Master, like whom, though essentially courageous, he feared "this chalice".[9] He forced the negative to change its sign, to become positive, to the profit of his interior life.

Teilhard's reaction to his sickness was characteristic. On 27 June he wrote from Puy-de-Dôme:

> I am in my native Auvergne, amid the deep green of the trees on my brother's little place here. . . . In this soothing atmosphere I feel as if I were expanding interiorly, and I am becoming more conscious of a kind of new light which has not ceased to brighten within me these several (on the face of it disappointing) weeks of this stay in France.

[9] Perhaps he had been moved by his sister Marguerite-Marie's painful illness; in *Le milieu divin* she was doubtless the inspiration for three beautiful meditations on the "helplessness" of diminishment, and the Christian way of diminishing *in Christo*.

Never before, perhaps, have I so clearly perceived the possible meaning of the evolution of my interior life.... I was forced to miss many, many opportunities these past weeks; yet nevertheless, as a final outcome, I feel more than ever *myself*. Is it possible that I needed to be somewhat cut off from science and from the past if I was to perceive more distinctly the highest ramparts of the universe of the future?

Already, in a letter of 13 June 1937, he had written of this new light:

Through better realizing (in a vivid and personal experience) how much we depend upon the divine harmonization of life, I have formed the impression that my familiar views of the world were growing deeper, and above all were passing a little more from the theoretical to the practical plane. (The best test, after all, for any theory!) Crowning my convictions about, and my growing admiration of, human energy, I am at this moment discovering the astounding value, and function, of the "love of God" (properly understood, of course) in the building up of the human world. "Love of God", which until now has been studied principally as an individual relationship between man and the pinnacle of existence, must now be understood as the highest and most universal form of activity.

About the return trip, from Marseilles to Shanghai (6 August to 8 September 1937), we are well informed. The effect of the splendour of the Indian Ocean was somewhat spoilt by anxiety aboard over the Sino-Japanese War:

The Red Sea was hot, but not excessively; and now we are in the breezes of the Indian Ocean. You would love its blue waters, where the flying fishes play.... We are somewhat anxiously following on the ship's radio the confusing events in China. I imagine the situation in Shanghai will be straightened up by the time we get there. (21 August 1937.)

It was during this passage that he wrote one of his basic works, *L'énergie humaine*, in which he aimed at completing human science with a science of man, and therefore set out the main lines of a human energetics:

No object ... can claim the total of human energy, at least if that object does not possess a soul—is not *somebody*. Therefore, left in a state of impersonal collectivities, earth and mankind are positively incapable of supporting and maintaining the spiritual impulse residing in the world. . . .

On the one hand, the risen Christ of the Gospels cannot succeed in maintaining himself (in the consciousness of the faithful) at the summit of the universe which he must by definition consummate, except by incorporating within himself the very evolution which people are saying is opposed to him. On the other hand, this same evolution, in order to succeed in meeting the requirements of the conscious activity born of its own processes, is painfully seeking, in the depths of each of us, a universal focus of thought and volition. On the one side, a sphere which calls for a centre; on the other, a centre which awaits a sphere. . . .

The principle which can claim the total of human energy is love:

The very persons who receive with the greatest scepticism any suggestion tending to promote a general co-ordination of thought on this globe are the first to recognize and deplore the present state of division in which human resources are being wasted: a Brownian movement of little activities in the individual, a Brownian movement of little individuals in society. Of course, they say, an immense power is neutralized and lost in this aimless agitation. But then, they say, how are you ever going to crystallize these colloidal particles? Naturally divided among themselves, these human fragments continue to repel one another. You could, perhaps, force them together mechanically; but to infuse a common soul into this artificial unity would be physically beyond realization.

The strength and at the same time the weakness of all the objections raised against any ultimate unification of the world seem to me to rest on the fact that the objectors insidiously inflate all too-real surface appearances but overlook certain new factors already perceptible in humanity. Pluralists always argue as if there existed, or tended to exist, in nature no linking principle outside such vague or superficial relationships as are available to everyday observation and to sociology. Those who argue thus are at bottom mere pettifogging conservatives who cannot even imagine anything beyond what seems to them to have existed always.

But let us see what will take place in our souls, if only there emerges in them—in the fullness of evolution's time—the perception of an animate centre of universal convergence. Let us just imagine (yet this is no fiction, as we shall declare in a moment) a man who has become conscious of his personal relationships with a supreme *personal*, to which he is drawn to attach himself by the entire play of cosmic activities. In and beginning with such a man, it is inevitable that a process of unification will already have begun, a process which will go on to exhibit the following stages: totalization of each operation in respect to the individual; totalization of the individual in respect to himself; totalization . . . of individuals in respect to the human collective . . . totalization, in a total act, of total human energy. . . . But where, you will protest, in nature today, is there any preliminary appearance, any first approach to the total act which we allowed ourselves to envisage? Nowhere more distinctly, it seems to me, than in the act of Christian charity such as is possible for a modern believer for whom creation has become expressible in terms of evolution. In his view, the history of the world is the history of a vast cosmogenesis, in the course of which all the fibres of reality converge, without losing their identity, in a Christ at once personal and universal. Strictly speaking, and not metaphorically, the Christian who grasps at once the essence of his Creator and the spatial-temporal interconnections of nature is in the happy situation of being able, throughout the whole variety of his activities, and in union with the multitude of other men, to pass into a single act of communion. In short, exactly like the omega point which our theory has foreshadowed, Christ (provided he be discerned in the full reality of his Incarnation) tends to produce exactly the spiritual totalization to which we have been looking forward.

It is remarkable that this could have been written at the singularly trying end of the trip, as described in this paragraph written 9 October 1937, in English:

> The journey back was relatively easy. We escaped by two days a bad typhoon in Hong Kong, spent a day at Woosung, got another typhoon in approaching Kobe. Anyhow, I found the next day, in Kobe, a nice little Maru which landed me peacefully in Tangku. I was back to my Peking office at the end of September.

A few lines from a letter of 15 October 1937 add some details:

> I could tell you of my trip, but it's ancient history now. It went very well, despite a cholera epidemic in Hong Kong, the blockade of the coasts, and a typhoon in the anchorage outside Kobe.

A final assessment of Teilhard's three vists to France probably reveals that not much of importance occurred as a result of them.

No doubt he was under orders to stay for only a few months there on each visit, and had just enough time to see his family and friends, make a brief trip to England, avail himself of sources of scientific information, and report to his religious superiors. His visits were to be periods of spiritual refreshment above all.[10] The last visit, especially, yielded on the concrete plane purely negative results. We can, however, pick out two things: his moving Breuil to take a hand in the discoveries at Choukou-tien, and his patient struggle—producing tangible results in 1938—to obtain a regular post of some kind in Paris which would enable him to continue moving back and forth between Peking and Paris, and would offer him some sort of refuge later on.

[10] Before the Yellow Expedition he wrote (2 April 1929): "Here [in China] I always feel a kind of spiritual renewal—the assimilation of God of the huge supply of raw strength which I amass during my stays, so tense, in Paris."

CHAPTER TEN

First Peking Period (1932–8): International Ties

Nₒₜ only did Teilhard remain closely bound to France, but his international ties also became increasingly strong and far-reaching. His relationship with the Swedes, for instance, continued to be cordial, even if no more extensive. His last meeting with Gunar Andersson took place on a Hong Kong–Sweden steamer in late April of 1938, when Andersson, increasingly absorbed in archaeology, was returning to his homeland. During the Croisière Jaune, at Urumchi, he had a meeting with Erik Norin:

> We are mixing more with local society and getting to know it better: Russians, Danes, and also the curious "Princess Palta", a Mongolian who has become Parisian to her finger-tips and with whom some of the expedition had danced in Paris and Peking. Parties make a gay interlude in the preparation of furs and over-hauling of equipment and stores for the journey back to Peking. The other day it was one given by the Swedish expedition (which is just off), at which I thought the Russian dances charming. It has been a real joy to meet Norin again, Sven Hedin's geologist, who has been working in the country for the last four years. The two of us spent hours on end building up the geology of Central Asia, and had the rare pleasure of discussing the vast expanses we both know and love. Norin's leaving for Kashgar and India. I should very much like to follow him, but my future is obviously tied up with M. Haardt for some months still. (*Letters from a Traveller*, p. 187.[1])

On 5 November 1933 Teilhard writes that Sven Hedin was preparing to draw up plans, on behalf of Nanking, for an automobile

[1] A note to Norin is extant, dated 16 November 1964. It ends: "Cheerio!"

route between Kweihwa and Hami (almost following the itinerary of the Citroën expedition). It appears that Hedin, besides being an explorer and scientist, was ready to put his talents as a topographer at the service of China and of the resistance against Japan. In the course of World War II, in 1941, there was a brief exchange of letters between Teilhard and Hedin, frankly affectionate in tone. The Jesuit wrote to the Swede in English:

> I am glad to have found this opportunity to assure you of my everlasting affection. To have had several years of friendly contact with you in Peking is one of the lucks of my life. (10 February 1941.)

But the great explorer—no Francophile, either—took the trouble to send an answer in French, dated 22 May 1941, Stockholm:

> Reverend and dear Father Teilhard de Chardin: I thank you sincerely for your pleasant and friendly letter of 10 February, delayed in the Siberian posts. It was really touching of you to have taken such pains to help us and to facilitate our efforts to save Dr Norin's collections. . . . All friends of China suffer from this war, which has gone on four years without benefiting anybody. . . . You, in contrast, dear Father Teilhard, spend your days in the service of science and for the welfare of mankind. I wish you the best of success, of health—and of great scientific discoveries.
>   Best regards to all our friends in Peking.
>   Devotedly yours,
>   Sven Hedin.

Before we leave Sven Hedin, it may be interesting to glance at Father Lejay's contrast of the scales on which Hedin and Teilhard undertook their travels:

> Sometimes Teilhard was called upon to exhibit an unusual tenacity. For a long period he had only very slender means: at the same time Sven Hedin was fitting out his famous expeditions into Chinese Turkestan (it was my privilege to be present at one of these imposing departures of the Swedish traveller, with caravans bearing de luxe supplies—and machine-guns, not to speak of dozens of technicians). Teilhard, in contrast, set out with *one* travelling companion [Licent], two Chinese servants, and—a few mules. (9 October 1937.)

The Swedes and the Americans each took roughly half of the Chinese dependencies as a field of research; the former, Sinkiang

6+

and Tibet; the latter, the Gobi. Relations with the Americans were therefore as important as relations with the Swedes, or more so, since the Americans were the greater power in Peking. We shall attempt to give an account of Teilhard's American contacts, though it can only, unfortunately, be incomplete.

Members of the Third American Expedition turn up again, though without C. D. Matthew, whose place was largely taken by Walter Granger. Correspondence from Teilhard preserved by the American Museum begins with a telegram dated Peking, 24 April 1933, and concludes with a letter dated Peking, 12 December 1940. The tone of this correspondence is not very different from Teilhard's letters to Matthew. These are letters from one scientist to another, a very friendly exchange of news, information, scientific data. They contain no lofty theoretical discussion either of science or of philosophy or religion; yet they are more than business letters, remaining personal in form, with sometimes a touch of humour. They were more than mere communication; they were a friendship carried on in the scientific field. It is quite probable that the weeks spent together on the Gobi and with the Andrews Mission, in 1930, created a solid affection, and that these bonds grew closer especially in the spring of 1937, when Teilhard was going to the United States. He says in a letter, in English:

> Now I must tell you (very late) how much I have appreciated last spring, your friendship, and the kindness of everybody in your department.

Next to the Andrews group were the other members of the American Museum and those who gravitated around that institution. The great philanthropist Osborn is alluded to once in the correspondence; but Osborn, when Teilhard was going to New York in February, 1931, spoke of him as "the adopted son of our household". George Gaylord Simpson, too, makes an appearance. Already in April, 1934, Teilhard was sending him a telegram. He went on to inquire what the American scientist was doing, and on 12 July 1938 sent to him, by Granger, congratulations on his brilliant promotion. On the whole Teilhard's tone was changing: he found himself on equal footing with the best men in his field.

There were several changes in the American Museum team. New names included, among others, those of Colbert, from Granger's department, and of Rachel H. Nichols, scientific assistant. The correspondence speaks of all these people affectionately and cordially, and of Colbert admiringly. Among those moving in the orbit of the American Museum was Childs Frick, of Long Island, a very rich amateur palaeontologist. With him Teilhard was on close enough terms to co-operate with him in making the rather delicate choice of the forms—in the interests of Chinese stratigraphy—to describe first among the materials assembled in Shansi. Without at all assuming the role of a dictator, Teilhard was by now directing or discreetly overseeing such work in Chinese geology and palaeontology as fell within his competence.

Among American names, however, that of William King Gregory deserves a special place here; it appears in a letter of 16 March 1931, in which Teilhard is telling of a stopover at Honolulu:

> To initiate me into these wonders, a geologist named Dr Gregory, director of the Pacific Services, placed at my disposal both his car and the society of himself and his wife, thus contributing to making my experience here a delightful one.

Gregory's name appears again only at the close of a letter dated 12 December 1940. But he was one of the members of the Pan-Pacific organization set up by the Americans, and a sort of relay in the intellectual network linking California to Peking, and China, with lines to Japan, the Indies, and Australia.

Dr George B. Barbour is only first among a number of the scientists of many nationalities who deserve further attention here as friends of Teilhard's. Not only did Barbour and Teilhard work side by side in geology, and share a number of views, but Barbour was willing and able to follow Teilhard's philosophical and religious speculations; he later referred to Teilhard as "our dear saint"; they talked together without reserve, using Christian names and, in French, the familiar *tu*. The following short account by Barbour gives an interesting picture of Teilhard.

> Père Teilhard was always the most patient and the most ingenuous of men—always ready to put the kindest interpretation on any action, never questioning any man's motives. In a country where it is thought impolite to meet requests with blunt refusals, and where a plausible excuse is a normal courtesy, *laissez-passers* were sometimes denied on obviously fictitious grounds. But Pierre always accepted the alleged reason as if it were the truth, seemed troubled that the authorities should have any reason for with-

holding the needed sanction, never pausing to wonder whether these authorities might not have been urged by other persons for political or personal reasons to deny the request. On one occasion we sat for two weeks in Shanghai waiting for a clearance which was refused repeatedly, each time on different specious grounds. Finally we abandoned the trip for which I had crossed the Pacific Ocean, and changed our plan for the summer, which was just what was wanted by some of his former Chinese colleagues, who had hoped that his activities might be curtailed.

... In the field he seemed tireless, and stood long days without confessing fatigue. He always wore a suit of khaki drill that seemed indestructible. He had a characteristic stride, and always turned his right foot out a little more than his left, as if some slight malformation of a joint led to a faint asymmetry of gait.[2] He seemed tireless when on horseback, and at all times was gifted with very sharp sight. He could spot a single Palaeolithic implement in a bed of gravel three metres away without dismounting, and his field notes—usually on the quadrille pages of a shiny black notebook—revealed again and again the accuracy of his observations and the brilliance of his power of deduction and interpretation. His quick grasp of the meaning of some new structural detail was never seen to better advantage than in his unravelling of the problems of Pliocene and Pleistocene geology recorded in the superficial deposits along the Mongolian border.

And in a letter of 6 May 1958, to the author, Barbour added:

Everything I had was his, always. Any discovery I made I came so to share with him that I considered it as much his as my own —as for example the Nihowan locality—and thereto was added a personal affection and closeness that never seemed to call for explanations or apologies.... Teilhard treated me as a younger brother, and somehow the work of each complemented the contribution of the other as we grew in our understanding of Chinese geology. He was the noblest man I ever lived with.

While Barbour was of the young guard, Grabau was of the old guard. From time to time, Grabau appears in the correspondence, as in these three letters, in English:

Dr Grabau is going all right, more and more absorbed by the endless developments of his "pulsation" theory (of which it would be difficult for me to give a clear appreciation: too far away from

[2] Teilhard habitually turned out his toes as he walked: "The hill-man's stride", he used to say.

the direct contact with the facts in the field, I am afraid).
(8 November 1936.)

Grabau keeps incredibly young, more and more wrapped up in developments of the "pulsation" theory. I do not think that his views will be accepted under their present complication. But one must admit that on several points he brings suggestive solutions and rejuvenates the traditional representations of things. He works very hard, day *and* night, and hates to leave his house. (12 July 1938.)

Grabau is O.K. and "pulsating". Now he can walk with only a stick, without crutches, and he goes again to parties, up to 2 a.m. We celebrated in a grand way his 70th birthday, last 9 January.

It is interesting to note in these letters the kinship between Grabau's preoccupation and Teilhard's notion of the basically uni-directional development of the earth. We have already spoken of his dream of a total science of the planet Earth. The aspect of this projected science that is of importance in the present connection is the concept of the geological evolution of the globe. We know that in the Tertiary and Quaternary divisions of the Cenozoic era the upper half, roughly, of the northern hemisphere underwent a number of glaciations—a series of very slow pulsations, so to speak, made up of the advance, and then the retreat, of the great glaciers. Both this fact and others suggest that the history of the globe is not fundamentally irreversible, but rather dominated above all by certain rhythms, all of which seems to justify, on the scientific plane, a cyclic conception of time.

Teilhard did not deny these rhythms but they seemed to him only surface ripples, which did not affect the underlying drift in the history of our globe, namely, the progressive building up of the con-tinents by granitization. In other words, time, even geological time, was in his view irreversible—a theme which dominates his whole philosophy, and is one of the points where one may observe the unitary quality of his thinking.

Another very good friend of Teilhard's, Davidson Black, died in 1934:

I wrote to you only a few days ago, but I must begin again in order to give you some details about a misfortune you will have read about in the papers. Davidson Black died suddenly in the evening of the day before yesterday (heart failure). His heart had been giving trouble for some time, and five weeks ago we had a warning of what might happen. We were hoping that he was pulling round, but then the end came suddenly. Black was feeling better (or seemed to be); he had just been talking briskly with some friends and was full of plans, as usual. A moment later he was found dead, in his Lab. you know so well, between the *Sinanthropus* and the skull from the Upper Cave. A fine death, in the full force of activity. But he leaves a great gap. We shall have to close our ranks to get on with the work. (*Letters from a Traveller*, pp. 201–2.)

Today I am deeply aware of the call to rescue the world from the blackness of its materialism. You already know that Dr Black has died. The apparent absurdity of that untimely end, the noble but blind acceptance of this tragedy by his friends here, the complete absence of "light" on the poor body lying in that cold room at the Peiping Union Medical College—all these lent a leaden quality to my sadness, and revolted my spirit.

Either there is an escape from death—somewhere—for an individual's thought, for his self-consciousness, or else the world is a hideous mistake. And if it is, then there is no use in our going on. But, since the uselessness of going on is an idea intolerable to everyone, the alternative must be to *believe*. To awaken this belief shall be, now more than ever, my task. I swear it. I have sworn it on the mortal remains of Davy, that more than brother of mine. (A second letter of 18 March 1934.)

I miss Black very much. Missing him is like a shadow, or an emptiness that I carry with me wherever I go. (25 June 1934.)

Black was certainly one of those whom Teilhard, apart from his own family, loved the most. For the two men were like each other. This friendship of the two scientists, though it was lacking, of course, in a common philosophical and religious background, was most brotherly. Communion in science was not, for Teilhard, an empty expression.

Dr George G. Barbour has recently supplied us with a letter, dated Peking, 6 December 1933, which he received from Davidson Black:

I have delayed writing this until I could assemble the gang, viz., V. K. Ting, Wong Wen Hao, J. S. Lee, and Teilhard, for a chat on the problems of the Cenozoic. Tonight we have had such a chat, and I think I am correct in saying that our opinions were unanimous that we need and would welcome your help. J. S. Lee is of course the one to whom we must look for aid in extending our Cenozoic studies into the Yangstze basin, because that area is his special field in view of the present distribution of "research spheres".

...I enclose Teilhard's letter (Wong has written separately) outlining the chief problems in which he wishes to have your aid.... The more I think of these things, the most strongly I favour the idea that the Yangstze valley holds the key to many of the peculiar Cenozoic problems which confront us here in the North.

We must add the sequel that, for Black and Teilhard's sake, Barbour resigned from his position at the Geological Society of America, and gave the year at his own expense (except for the field and travelling expenses).

So far, most of the names mentioned will already be familiar to the reader. But Teilhard saw also many new faces. From the large number of his new acquaintances we are selecting, somewhat arbitrarily, three of particular importance: Weidenreich, De Terra, and von Koenigswald.

Dr Franz Weidenreich (1873–1948), visiting professor at the University of Chicago, after his scientific career had been twice interrupted in Europe by political interference, was selected by the Rockefeller Foundation to succeed to Black's post. He was characterized by quietness, scholarliness, scientific precision, and thoroughness, and proceeded to establish the human nature of *Sinanthropus* solidly on anatomical grounds. After Weidenreich's death in New York (the Asiatic wars had brought a third interruption to his scientific career), Teilhard wrote a memorial tribute to him, as he had done for Black. In *L'anthropologie*, 1949, pp. 329–30:

Dr Weidenreich arrived in China when the diggings at Choukou-tien were in full swing.... Without haste, but with a method learned through long experience as an anthropologist, he succeeded in pushing on the fourfold work of preparation, casting, measurement, and description with such speed and such precision that the complete disappearance of this precious material at the close of 1941 (the time of Pearl Harbour) does not, scientifically speaking, constitute anything especially disastrous (the New York Museum, for example, has a collection of Weidenreich's casts).... To Weidenreich, after Black (who must never be forgotten) we owe a second debt for Peking Man. Even at that time, the activities of "Dr Wei" were not limited to Choukou-tien ...

close relations having been established between the two centres of Peking and Bandung (Java). From this there soon arose the close association of Weidenreich and Ralph von Koenigswald, so that the inseparably linked researches on *Pithecanthropus* and *Sinanthropus* could be co-ordinated. As a man, Dr Weidenreich did not exercise the same attraction, did not have the same power of inspiring, as Davidson Black. Yet perhaps it was well that Weidenreich came in his turn, with his charming and natural good nature, and his impressive scientific solidity, to complete the work launched by his brilliant predecessor.

If Teilhard was not bound to Weidenreich with the ties of old friendship that had united him to Black, he and Weidenreich, with Grabau, were united as the final line of defence, under the Japanese military rule in 1937 and 1938, of the scientific collections at Peking; and the three put their heads together to consider the grave problems raised by the Japanese invasion. It is to Weidenreich, too, that we owe the anatomical reconstruction of "Nelly", the *Sinanthropus* female, the face being modelled, at the instance of and under the direction of Weidenreich, by the American artist Lucile Swan.

Another American scientist who had come from Germany was Helmut de Terra, whom Teilhard had already met at the international convention of geologists at Washington in 1933, to which he travelled from Peking with Graham, Barbour, and Black. Teilhard accompanied De Terra on the latter's field trips to the East Indies (1935), Burma (1937–8),[3] and Java (1938), which De Terra was examining for the second time. Dr Terra, whom Teilhard was able to brief on the geology of China, was a keen observer and a geologist of experience and vision, and Teilhard believed him destined to play a key part in the vast field of research that promised to open in Asia. He was a pleasant and congenial companion, and he and Teilhard got along well together. A letter of the latter's of 8 October 1935 ends with the postscript: "Greetings from De Terra (*un chic type!*)." Another letter, of 20 January 1938, declares: "De Terra and I understand each other like a couple of brothers." De Terra in turn, in a letter to the author, speaks of Teilhard in similarly warm terms: "Father Teilhard was my friend, the most cherished and revered human being I ever met." It is remarkable

---

[3] It was in Burma that Teilhard met Hallam L. Movius, Jr., "a charming and very knowledgeable young man" (letter of 30 January 1938). They developed a warm and lasting friendship.

8. Shara-Osso-Gol. Pleistocene rock formations, photographed by Teilhard

9. Gobi Desert. Pliocene rock formation, photographed by Teilhard.   On the back of the print is a note in his handwriting that "these high outcrops of red earth tell the story of the erosion of the plateau dating back over a million years".

10. Pleistocene terraces at Bäzäklik, Turfan,
photographed by Teilhard

that, despite their variety of temperaments and backgrounds, Teilhard's acquaintances formed the same estimates of his character.

As usual, Teilhard arranged for Breuil to become acquainted with these new friends, since he always wanted to seal his friendships through his master.

> I am very happy that you liked De Terra. After his last letter I can say that the feeling was mutual. It is fortunate that our circle of friends expands and contracts at the same time. I learned today that the Moviuses visited the Museum. I would like to know what you think about the Irrawaddy industry. (22 June 1938.)

Another friendship sealed through the master was that with von Koenigswald:

> Marthe (Vaufrey) writes that von Koenigswald visited Paris. I hope you were pleased with him and that you looked after him. I like him very much, and he may do some great things in Java. He, in my mind, is with Pei, De Terra, and Collings (Singapore) one of the pillars of the organization of whose existence I dream. (7 January 1937.)

The German-born scientist, in the employ of the Dutch government in Java, was closely associated with Teilhard's later trips in the Dutch East Indies, and will be discussed more fully later. But from the first day in Java, Teilhard was thoroughly impressed with him (and his words remind us that at that time the great von Koenigswald was only thirty-three):[4] "... von Koenigswald—a delightful, enthusiastic, and very intelligent youngster". (19 January 1936.) Starting in February, 1936, there is a fine scientific correspondence between the two men, the affectionateness of Teilhard's tone being attested in the following letter, in English:

> I arrived in Peiping only a few days ago. No time so far for sending you a few lines in order to thank you for the marvellous days I have so deeply enjoyed with you. Now, I am sure, we are friends for ever. On my arrival, I immediately sent a long letter to Merriam (Carnegie Institute) in order to recommend you and

[4] Ralph von Koenigswald was born in Berlin in 1902, of a German father and a Dutch mother. He was brought up in Germany, and for three years worked at the Museum in Munich. In 1930 the Dutch Government offered him the position of palaeontologist in the geological service of the Dutch East Indies, where he lived and worked until 1946. From then until 1948 he was at the American Museum in New York. In 1948 he became professor of palaeontology at Utrecht.

6*

your work warmly to the attention of the Carnegie Institute. (11 February 1938.)

Teilhard worked hard on von Koenigswald's behalf. He used all his influence with the Carnegie Institute, broadcast in every quarter the news of von Koenigswald's fine discoveries, got him to distribute offprints of his articles and to exchange castings with the Paris Museum, arranged to have Weidenreich come, in September, 1938, to see him, and, finally, rejoiced to learn that von Koenigswald had chosen Hallam L. Movius, Jr., as his collaborator (Movius was an American, and associated with Harvard).

But the greatest service Teilhard rendered von Koenigswald was one of criticism and counsel, as in the following letter (11 February 1936), in English:

> Thinking more on the things which we have seen together, I feel more and more convinced that, in your publications (for instance, in Sweden), you must refrain from giving too definite views on the evolution of the Palaeolithic industries of Java. You need more stratigraphical evidence for your Chellean. Suggest what you like *in your conclusions*. But insist primarily on the *material facts*. They are most interesting. And scientists want to know the facts more than your personal interpretation.

In another letter, again in English, 2 April 1936, on the important discovery of a very early fossil cranium of a child, he writes:

> My own impression is that you have to be careful before deciding that you have to deal with a young *Pithecanthropus*. The first point, as you have surely realized immediately, is to ascertain carefully the conditions of the find. Tell me, when you write me next, whether the specimen has been collected *in situ*, or at least in conditions of mineralization making its level more sure. Are other fossils known from the spot? How do you know that it is Djetis? Make these points *extremely clear* when you will make your first announcement: they are fundamental.

In short, Teilhard was acquainted with practically the whole English-speaking scientific world. He had contacts in England (Oxford in particular), some secondary contacts in the United States, and a first-class contact in New York. With the latter he kept in close connection, as with France. He kept up relationships not only with his immediate collaborators in Peking, Tientsin (notably M. Trassaert), and Choukou-tien, but also with all other European scientists stationed or travelling in the Indies and China.

These relationships were friendly, cordial, and sometimes brotherly. One has the impression of a vast web, of which Teilhard held in part the threads, where he served as liaison agent, or, better still, as chief of staff, able, like a magician, to make American money flow, or at least to channel it for the greatest good of palaeontology.

It is certain that this world of scientists, a few exceptions apart, did not, however, satisfy his deep spiritual needs. These Anglo-Saxons proved themselves remarkable scientists; but, embedded in their scientism, their positivism, their empiricism, their neo-Darwinism, all but Barbour and a very few others were incapable of following his philosophical thought. Later, only in Julian Huxley was he to find a satisfactory interlocutor.

He nevertheless anglicized himself in certain regards. He continued his progress in English; even his letters in French and his own notes bear witness to this, for English words are frequent in them, and English technical terms almost constant.

Teilhard was now definitely adopted by the Americans. His 1931 trip had been a triumph. The two following trips (1933 and 1937), which took place during this first Peking period, were no less successful. The *Letters from a Traveller*, and another unpublished letter, tell us something of the 1939 trip. Teilhard had no diplomatic goal, but was merely to attend, with Graham, Barbour, Black, Grabau, and V. K. Ting, the international convention of geologists from 20 to 30 July in Washington (after a few hours in San Francisco and again in Chicago—the Field Museum—and a few days in New York—the American Museum). Teilhard left China with some reluctance:

> This new journey doesn't thrill me particularly, for it seems to me to be so much time taken from my own researches (which time, with increasing age, I grudge the more), but it may open up new horizons and lead to unforeseen contacts, so that I can't let the opportunity slip by. (*Letters from a Traveller*, p. 199.)

The convention was, however, far from profitless.

> It was a highly successful meeting, despite the heat (which we fought off with beer, this, as everyone knows, having begun to flow again now in America). I signed up for the G-2 Excursion and went with it as far as Oregon.... From John Day Basin in Oregon I accompanied two students from Berkeley down to San Francisco on the route of the Sequoias (Redwood Highway), which borders the Pacific, in an admirable setting, too little

known. Then I spent three weeks studying the Sierra Nevada range and the coastal ranges, in order to determine their analogies —which are impressive—with the corresponding ranges in Asia. This was in fact my principal objective in coming to America. I hope to derive from this first-hand study of the Pacific coast a number of insights (which are not purely imaginary, either). (21 September 1933.)

We note that, though a specialist in China and the Far East, to Teilhard even more important—for he did not forget his function as a priest—were his religious contacts, in New York and Washington. The question most often put to him in these circles was:

... whether the universe is really millions of years old. One feels very clearly that they regard these figures as simply fancies, which will be forgotten tomorrow. How to shift this monumental scientific and philosophical incomprehension! First, this generation will have to pass away, of course. (25 July 1935.)

But he made some pleasant discoveries as well:

And I am very happily surprised to meet here and there among the better minds, a current of ideas exactly parallel to that with which we ourselves are familiar. This discovery is valuable for it shows, once and for all, the spontaneity and the universal quality of the movement. Moreover, it permits us to hope that through mutual control or correction on so wide a base it will be possible for us to extract the really orthodox elements and formulas from the rather dazzling complex. (Ibid.)

The 1937 trip took place in "a burdensome and complicated year" in the course of the "endless pilgrimage" which was Teilhard's life. The purpose of this trip, as given in the invitation from Helmut de Terra, was a Symposium on Early Man, to take place 25 March 1937, in Philadelphia, under the sponsorship of the Carnegie Institute.[5] This was not a large general conference, but a meeting of a select few; it included De Terra, von Koenigswald from Java, Dorothy Garrod from Oxford, but not, unfortunately, Breuil, who was unable to come. The actual purpose of the meeting was to form an executive committee to act for the Carnegie Foundation in matters of prehistorical research and to set up a systematic and

---

[5] Teilhard sailed from Shanghai, probably on 25 February 1937, in the *Empress of Japan*. He went through Tokyo, where he visited the American ambassador. On 13 March he landed at Seattle and, travelling by train, spent three days in Chicago; then to Philadelphia, where he stayed with the De Terras at Bryn Mawr.

financially sound plan for the scientific exploration of China, India, and the East Indies.

Although no record of the meeting is available to us, there is no reason to suppose that Teilhard was a mere observer; it was he who had had von Koenigswald included in the symposium; and that a plan for concerted attention to Eastern and Southern Asia was not new to him is clear from his letter of the previous 26 August to von Koenigswald (in English):

> De Terra seems now very interested in the Phillippines and Java. He, you, Collings, myself and the Chinese: what a fine converging attack we can make on S.E. Asia, if we get the funds!

While in Philadelphia he was presented with the Mendel Medal by the Very Rev. Edward V. Stranford, President of Villanova University. From Philadelphia he visited New York, and here made the acquaintance of Alexis Carrel, to whom he outlined the possibility of a new science of human energetics. He later crossed to France in the same boat as Carrel and seems to have owed in part to conversations with him the inspiration for *L'énergie humaine*.

While in New York he visited members of the American Museum, as indicated in a letter already quoted, of 9 October 1937, in English:

> Tell my best regards to all of them (Colbert, Thompson) and to the Pinkleys. And "my love" to Mrs Nichols! I should have written to her, and she must be cross with me. What are Nelson and Simpson doing? My *"fidèle souvenir"* to Roy [Roy Chapman Andrews evidently].

As suggested there, he was cordially received, especially by Granger, who later saw him off on the *Normandie*. It was probably about this time that Teilhard was named corresponding member for Asia by the American Museum, for in 1938 this honorary title was renewed by Andrews.

These three American trips in the thirties seem to present some sort of gradation. The first, which was to fulfil an official mission, also resulted in Teilhard's being made at home at the American Museum and at the Field Museum. The second presents Teilhard as included among the number of the world's significant geologists. But in the third he is included in a carefully chosen small group, less than a dozen, engaged in making decisions affecting geological work over a large part of the world.

CHAPTER ELEVEN

First Peking Period (1932–8):
Choukou-tien

WE may recall that on 20 June 1931 Teilhard put his signature to the agreement between the Chinese and the European contingents of the Croisière Jaune. As a Chinese official and yet a European he had logically been chosen as mediator. Now it is time to speak further of his relationships with the Chinese. V. K. Ting and Wong Wen-hao have already been mentioned. Ting, unfortunately taken by death in 1936, was a commanding figure:

> To our further delight, V. K. Ting has just accepted the general directorship of the Academia Sinica. This is an influential position, in which he can be of much help to us. However, the appointment moves him to Nanking, just when we have need of him here. (12 March 1934.)

Ting reigned officially over the Geological Survey, and he had a word to say in the management of the funds of the Cenozoic Research Laboratory, that is, about the use of money allotted for the Choukou-tien diggings. Teilhard seems to have been on good terms, though not necessarily intimate, with him, since in 1934 he successfully interceded with him for the continuance of the credits allotted to Black for Breuil's trip to the Far East.

He was on much closer terms with Wong (Teilhard's rampart against schemers), as passages from two letters attest:

> There is little news about my external life, except this, which could involve serious consequences. The director of the Geological Survey, our very good friend Wong, was in a very serious automobile smash-up the day before yesterday near Shanghai. They

believe he may have a skull fracture. I refuse to think of the consequences that this mishap (if it proves as grave as feared) may have on geological work in China. The Survey is the soul of research in this country today, and Wong in turn is the soul, and the armour, of the Survey.

Well, it's to be another case of triumphing over events by trusting in them. I'll strive to do so. The catastrophe occurred just when the work was reaching full development. We shall try to manage so that there will be no slowing down. (18 February 1934.)

We are going through a worrying period; in fact in that respect February has set a record. First (and worst), Wong had a very bad car accident near Shanghai, fracturing his frontal sinus. The cuts are healing up, but there seems to be a fragment of bone lodged in his brain, and this will call for surgery. Meanwhile, too, his mental state is not too good, with periods of excitability and delirium. There are signs of improvement, but you can imagine how worried we are, both for him and for the Survey. Of the latter, as you are aware, Wong is the moving spirit and the guardian. (12 March 1934.)

Here we see not only Wong's decisive role in the Survey, but also the deep affection which united the two men—each, in his way, profoundly spiritual. 1934 was certainly a grim year, for Black's death was to follow this accident of Wong's. Fortunately after a long convalescence Wong was on his feet again, for in January of 1935, as Teilhard tells us: "We all three left together—Wong the inseparable, and Pei, official excavator of Choukou-tien."

Not a shadow ever came between Teilhard and Wong. But the Japanese invasion posed a formidable problem. An intransigent patriot, refusing any compromise with the invader, Wong, in 1936, wished the Choukou-tien diggings to be hastened so that the site would be emptied before the Japanese came. Teilhard opposed the plan on technical grounds. On 11 February 1936 he wrote:

At any rate, the Choukou-tien diggings are to go on. . . . You can count on us neither to neglect nor to spoil the deposit. Of course Wong would like the diggings to be through as soon as possible, so as to leave nothing for the Japanese later on. But science above all.

As the Japanese penetration continued, the members of the Survey withdrew to the Yangtze valley; and Wong, naturally, wished to concentrate scientific research efforts on the south, which was the free zone.

All the Chinese members of the Survey are now in the Yangtze valley. And I am left practically alone here (with Weidenreich and Grabau), wondering what is going to happen. I think it might be perfectly possible to assure the continuation of the work at Choukou-tien (without any really troublesome interference) if only Pei were sent to me. And I still hope to get him. But Nan-king feels very strongly on this subject. Do you suppose I, too, shall be asked to emigrate to the south? I wonder. Meanwhile, I'm hanging on here. Of course, I'll never do anything against the wishes of Wong and the others. But, with a number of Japanese scientists already in the city (just to inspect), my position is morally delicate. . . . Wong's plan is to concentrate efforts on the south; and it accords pretty well, after all, with my own plans. Even so, we need connections with the north. (9 October 1937.)

It was a difficult time. On one hand, there were urgent reasons why Teilhard should stay in the north. The exploitation of the Choukou-tien deposits was not finished, and a return to work would be possible only through a tacit agreement with the Japanese in-vaders. Scientific endeavour here, besides the digs themselves, had been financed by the Rockefeller Foundation, whose interests ought to be protected. Secondarily, how were the collections at Peking to be kept from the Japanese scientists if there was no one there to guard them?

On the other hand, there was the patriotism of the Chinese, rejecting any compromise, and their scorched earth tactics in the face of the enemy (for collaboration with the Japanese could only further the latter's propaganda purposes), and there was Teilhard's clear desire not to offend Chinese patriotic feelings nor to disappoint his friend Wong.

Teilhard's decision was to stay unless he got strict orders to the contrary. His prestige must have been very great indeed, for he won leave to stay and even succeeded, around the middle of 1938, in getting back two of the Chinese—Chia and Pei, intransigent patriots though they were.

Both Young and this Pei clearly belonged to the younger genera-tion. Young Chung-Chien, with his high forehead and his glasses, a student of the Munich scientist Schlosser, and totally devoted to Wong, was primarily a laboratory man. He had been one of the

Choukou-tien specialists since 1928. In 1929 he published a *Rapport préliminaire sur les dépots fossilifères de Chou Kou Tien* with Teilhard's collaboration. In 1929 he and Teilhard went to Shansi and Shensi together, in 1930 to Manchuria, and in 1930 to Shensi. These trips, to which should be added, at least in 1936, diggings with Charles Camp in Eastern Shansi and in Szechwan, did not keep him from continuing to work at Peking and at Choukou-tien in company with Pei and Teilhard at least until 1937, after which he parted with Teilhard, whom he never saw again, and went south. When he came back to Peking, in 1947, Teilhard was no longer there. During the few months preceding Teilhard's death, the two scientists reopened their correspondence, for Young (like Pei and Chia) had survived the Communist revolution and continued to work at Peking.

Young (whose correspondence with Teilhard extends from 1930 to 1953) wrote a six-page *Memories of Père P. Teilhard de Chardin*, which should be read in the light of the testimony of M. N. Bien and of Dr Barbour. Naturally, he knew nothing about Teilhard as a priest, or of his religious position:

> Although he was a Catholic [*sic*] he had an unusually wide knowledge of the natural sciences, to my surprise. He had come to China as a sort of punishment by the Cardinal [*sic*], for something he had written against the idea of religion [*sic*].

At the same time: "I liked him very much, as one of my dear friends and teachers." He found the day of their final separation a painful one:

> Soon after the Japanese invasion I had to leave Peking for the south. It was a sad moment, still fresh in my memory, when he and Dr Weidenreich saw my train off at the Peking station in the morning of an early winter day.

And after the war he had the disappointment of finding that Teilhard had left:

> After the end of the war I had no opportunity to come to Peking and see him at once, as I had hoped. Even now I cannot understand why he left Peking almost immediately after the war ended, and did not wait for me.... In 1947, when I returned to Peking, I had a chance to visit his desk in the Institute of Geobiology. There I saw his pen, his books, and his offprints and other things still intact, but he himself was gone.

If Young collaborated with Teilhard, Teilhard in turn was a useful and kindly mentor to Young.

My work on the archaeological section and the implements of Choukou-tien is ready for the press, as well as Young's article (extensively recast by me) on the Artiodactyla.

And in a letter of 5 November 1933:

Since returning to China I have been rather busy, principally with Choukou-tien. Two long articles (the Carnivora of Choukou-tien by Pei, and the Microfauna of Choukou-tien by Young) are almost in the press (the illustrations are ready), and I have had to revise—and sometimes to recast—them with care.

This work of revising others' articles had begun, in fact, immediately after the return of the Croisière Jaune, for he speaks of the same kind of thing in a letter of 6 April 1932. And Father Charvet, in a letter to us (16 December 1957), says:

He was for several years the tactful educator of the young Chinese, whom he gladly took along on his explorations, and whose scientific articles he corrected or recast. His name used never to figure in connection with those articles; when I expressed my surprise at this, he answered: "It doesn't make any difference to me."

Mentioned with Young in Teilhard's letter above we meet again the name of Pei Wen-chung. Since 1928 he had been one of the official excavators of the famous site discovered by Andersson. It was he who, developing observations made by Teilhard, demonstrated the cultural activities of *Sinanthropus*.

In January, 1935, he undertook a trip southward into Kwangsi. Then, still in 1935, his government authorized him to go to Europe, where in Paris he studied for and received his doctorate from the University. He returned in 1937 to Southern China, and in 1938, despite his feelings about the Japanese invasion, he yielded to the insistence of Teilhard and took up work again in Peking. At the moment he was happy at having recovered, after eight months of effort, a number of cases of Ordos Desert and Choukou-tien specimens, which had been sent by mistake to Shanghai.

Pei is still living. Among those who approved the fall of Chiang Kai-shek, he occupies an honourable place in Communist China, where he continues to pursue fruitful research.

Pei was profoundly affected by Teilhard's death. And Teilhard, indeed, had reserved for the young Chinese an affection and esteem of which there can be no doubt. In 1932 he spoke of him politely as "the illustrious Pei", and in 1935 characterized the discoverer of the first *Sinanthropus* skull as "Pei, a charming and very enthusiastic youngster".

On 21 June 1937 he wrote from Paris, in English:

> ... I have much enjoyed, all the time, the society of Pei. Pei will be a "doctor of the University of Paris" tomorrow by this time. His thesis is well printed, and interesting. On the whole I have the feeling that during the two past years he has much improved his scientific personality. And still just as nice a boy as before.

In 1938 he noted: "Meanwhile, Pei is busy, and is running the laboratory very well."

It seems likely that Teilhard played the role of mentor to Pei as well as to Young. In discussing Choukou-tien he wrote: "I keep on at Pei to be more scrupulously exact in his stratigraphy." (8 May 1932.)

Pei was not sufficiently solid in geology. On the other hand, he was a good typologist, could make sense of cut stone pieces, and could excavate methodically. When Pei was with Breuil in Paris to complete and defend his thesis, Teilhard, marvelling at how much the great prehistorian was able to show the young Chinese, warmly thanked his former teacher for this kindness. Teilhard took an almost paternal interest in Pei.

> I don't understand exactly why he has embarked on his work on Quaternary stratigraphy instead of concentrating on the correction of his thesis. At any rate it forces him to learn. (15 October 1936.)

> I hope Pei is getting on with his thesis. . . . (28 November 1936.)

> Yesterday I saw a letter from Pei to Mrs Hempel, speaking of difficulties that have come up regarding his thesis. What's the trouble? Try to give him a hand. (8 December 1936.)

While discussing Black and the Chinese scientists, we broached the subject of the vicissitudes of the Choukou-tien project and of the Survey. It lies beyond our scope to detail the results obtained at the site after 1932, that is, after the conclusion of the Croisière Jaune, but it may be useful to summarize them.

We have already mentioned Teilhard's and Pei's finds of stone implements at this site. Among the facts revealed by a study of Choukou-tien was that the ash levels were structurally part of the original sedimentary formation, so that stratigraphy and palaeontology forbade the separation, in the deposits, of the material of the fissure (as earlier) and the ash (as more recent). Again, at first sight, the artifacts discovered at Site One seemed as homogeneous as the fauna there; but later, in 1936, the artifacts of the lower complex were revealed as clearly different from those of the upper complex. In any case, *Sinanthropus* was *Homo faber*, a maker of tools, so that it is scarcely probable that he had been the prey of unknown men whose own fossil remains have disappeared.

The number of fossil-bearing and implement-bearing pockets found was increasing. And each furnished an important contribution to the knowledge of the Choukou-tien complex. The number of animal remains—carnivores and their prey—was remarkable. One such pocket, for example, revealed dog-faced baboons, predecessors of *Sinanthropus* as tenants of the caves; another, Pliocene sandstone; another, fossils characteristic of an important Shansi formation. In 1938 Pei was working on Site Fifteen—probably a branch of Site One—which yielded a number of very remarkable implements; but Site One remained the most important, the only one to yield teeth, skull fragments, and jaws of *Sinanthropus*. The year 1936 is outstanding because on 28 November Teilhard informed a correspondent of the discovery of three skulls under the lowest cultural bed. On 6 January 1937 another important event occurred, the discovery of an upper jaw with six teeth, which allowed Weidenreich and Lucile Swan to reconstruct the entire face and cranium. On 30 May 1938 Teilhard wrote that he had seen in the laboratory fragments of skeletal bones of Peking Man (scientists had expressed surprise that only skulls had been found).

There was a final surprise in store. Teilhard had advised the drilling of a horizontal gully and a vertical shaft. To facilitate the digging of the shaft the workmen cut into the top of the hill. To their surprise, in 1933, they discovered at the top a separate cavern (designated Upper Cave), about fifty by thirty-five feet in area and thirty-five feet high, containing numerous animal bones, three fine Neolithic skulls, some tools, a bone needle, and a necklace of twenty-six pierced fox teeth! Here, then, the soil displayed, at the very bottom, brute animals, and, at the top, *Homo sapiens* (more recent than the remains in the Ordos desert), but, midway, pre-hominoids or parahominoids, already masters of fire and tool-makers and therefore within the margin of reflective consciousness, speakers no doubt of some rudimentary language, with brains of perhaps 1,200 cubic centimetres. Dog-faced baboons, *Sinanthropus,* and *Homo sapiens*—no wonder Teilhard exclaimed ironically: "What a menagerie—or what an hotel!"[1]

It should be remembered that this work, of such tremendous importance to palaeontology and prehistory, was often hampered by setbacks and anxieties, some of them financial. The first black year was 1934, when V. K. Ting left for the Academia Sinica, which absorbed the best part of his time and intellectual energy. That was the year, too, of the accident to Wong, soul of the Survey, on which the Choukou-tien project depended: the year, too, of the death of Black. In accordance with the desire of Roger Greene, director of Peiping Union Medical College, and with the formal approbation of V. K. Ting, Teilhard had to take the interim appointment of Acting Director and was thus immobilized in this work. To all this was added the menace of a lack of money. It was to Davidson Black personally that the Rockefeller Foundation had granted funds, to be extended, in fact, only to 1936. Roger Greene went to America for the purpose of ensuring the continuance of Black's work; and the Rockefeller Foundation gave its assurances; but, as already noted, they deliberated for some time before naming Black's successor.

Finally these troubles were eased: Wong recovered from his skull fracture. Weidenreich was appointed Black's successor, and not only resolved to see the Choukou-tien exploration completed but also did capital work as an anthropology specialist—work perhaps even finer than Black's. Financially the Cenozoic Laboratory was back on a sound footing. Ever since 1933, however, there had been the Japanese threat. In April–June of that year Peking was first alerted to the approach of Japan. The Geological Survey packed up a part of its books and collections and deposited them with Black at the Rockefeller Foundation. But the excitement died down, and the digging at Choukou-tien went on as before. But by February of

[1] Teilhard summarized it: "the *Sinanthropus* (Lower Pleistocene) fits in precisely between the cynocephalics (end of Pliocene) and a higher Palaeolithic man (end of Pleistocene)". (Letter of 10 December 1933.)

1936 Teilhard, returning to China, found the situation dark and difficult. From Peking he wrote:

> Most of the Geological Service has already moved into fine buildings in Nanking, but there is a "Northern Branch" of the Service maintained here, and here I have dug in, almost without books or specimens for comparison. The Choukou-tien diggings are to proceed in the spring. . . . I shall not forget to send you specimens from Choukou-tien: [extinct forms of] deer, bear, hyenas. The trouble lies in our specimens' being partly in Peking and partly in Nanking. (11 February 1936.)

On the Feast of the Assumption, 1936, he declared:

> My own life goes on as usual. In our unpeopled surroundings, we go on working at Peking, our undertakings and our discoveries even tending to increase. . . . And we look for still better things in the autumn.

The digging went on until 6 July 1937. By 20 September Teilhard was wondering sadly: "But now when are we going to take up the work again?"

Actually, Choukou-tien was in a no-man's-land, the plain being held by the Japanese and the mountain by the Reds. Resumption of the excavations depended on Japanese–Chinese agreement, but of this the Chinese, in accordance with their resistance policy, would not hear.

This situation would not have been too intolerable, for at the Cenozoic Laboratory there were many things to be sifted, sorted, prepared, studied. The Survey, however, shared the political troubles of the time. The Nipponese had set up a puppet government in Peking, with which the native government at Nanking would have nothing to do, so that the Northern Branch of the Survey was threatened with isolation. Practically, work went on at the Cenozoic Laboratory as usual; but the scientists there were cut off from Nanking. We have noted Teilhard's complaint that he, Weidenreich, and Grabau were left alone, wondering what would happen. In a letter a fortnight later (24 October 1937) he wrote:

> Here conditions continue to be most tricky. The time is coming when we shall have to bring our laboratories into line with the new political situation. And up to this point it continues to be hard to guess just when some or all of our Chinese friends will have to leave here and move south. In any case, we shall do our

best to keep a skeleton crew of workers in the security of the Peiping Union Medical College.

How this problem was solved, and Teilhard's part in the solution, we have already seen.

There was, of course, much controversy among anthropologists concerning *Sinanthropus*.

> Boule, Abel, and others make him out to be a *Pithecanthropus*. Dubois and Herdlikča wish to see in him a simple Neanderthal (Dubois, so that nothing can supervene to eclipse *Pithecanthropus*; Herdlikča, because nothing important can be discovered without him, or outside his native Central Europe). Between these two extremes, Black is keeping to his initial position. (28 January 1934.)

This position was that *Sinanthropus* was closely related to, but not the same as, *Pithecanthropus*. And Teilhard tells us that, after Black's death:

> Weidenreich is more and more convinced of the identity of *Sinanthropus* and *Pithecanthropus*, and of the complete difference between this type and the Neanderthal men properly speaking. And I think he is completely right. (15 October 1936.)[2]

In other words, Peking Man was becoming increasingly thought of as a stage of humanity preceding Neanderthal Man. Teilhard, of course, was anything but an unthinking observer. In the course of his reflections on Weidenreich's studies, the notion of stages tended to supersede, in his mind, the notion of *phyla*.

> Weidenreich's researches point to the conclusion that, down to the detail of the teeth, *Sinanthropus* is the most primitive Hominid that we know. We see appearing, and overmastering the notion of *phyla,* the notion of stages[3] : the *Sinanthropus-Pithecanthropus* stage, the Neanderthaloid stage, and the *Homo sapiens* stage. For example, the *Homo solonensis* of Java seems to be the Neanderthaloid stage of *Sinanthropus-Pithecanthropus*. Now one more stage should be recognizable—and discoverable—between the *Sinanthropus* stage and the anthropoid (Prehominid) stage. But where should it be sought?

[2] In 1937 the discovery of a half-mandible of *Pithecanthropus* caused Teilhard to return to Black's view.
[3] Teilhard used the English word "stages".

What Teilhard meant was that living beings and species show distinct lines of descent. Theoretically, then, one ought to be able to draw up a complete genealogical tree. This tree is given the name *phylum*. But prehistory—and more generally palaeontology—can discover only a fraction of the species that have disappeared, especially since mutant individuals are few in number and generally atypical. Origins thus tend automatically to be obliterated. Therefore, the actual point of a species' introduction in the *phylum* is almost impossible to detect, apart from exceptional cases, so that in fact, instead of the more exact and more detailed *schema* of the *phylum*—with trunk and with branches that go on dividing—we can only produce a far more crude approximation, some *schema* of specific waves succeeding one another, of apparently connected stages whose actual points of contact cannot—at least at the present time—be discovered. In what Neanderthaloid form did the ancestor *Homo sapiens* lead his undetected existence? Perhaps we shall never know; and it is to this state of affairs that we owe the conception (false, absolutely speaking) of successive stages rather than of filiation.

Teilhard's bibliography from 1932 to 1938 shows that while he kept up his other work he published both semi-popular articles in the *Revue des questions scientifiques* and in *Études*, tending to spread the fame of Peking Man and to stimulate interest in anthropology generally, and scholarly articles (with which his revisions of Young's and Pei's work should perhaps be included), bearing for the most part on the stone implements discovered and on the fossil mammals of the place—all, of course, with a solid and recondite substructure of geological learning. These included exhaustive studies of Site Nine and Site Twelve. We find such articles—embracing geology, palaeontology, and archaeology—continuing into 1939 and later.

Teilhard's most important role at Choukou-tien was not, however, observation, or reflection, or even publication. His chief contribution there was as a geologist and co-ordinator of operations and publications. That is what justified the enthusiasm of his letter of 23 May 1932:

I should never have dared hope for such a scientific career as this one. Think of the honour, for a geologist or for a palaeontologist, to be employed in first-hand work on *Sinanthropus Pekinensis*.

In his quality as Field Director, it was he who urged the others to be more minutely careful in stratigraphy; he who determined to what geological ages the different fissures belonged; he who drew up the plan for the excavations; and it was he who succeeded in elucidating the mystery of the enormous cavity at Site One:

> My impression ... is that the site developed as the result of a gradual internal caving in of a mass of limestone that originally contained a complex system of subterranean passages (we know positively from the quarrying that such conditions are met at Choukou-tien). Following this process, the cavern moved gradually from the base to the summit of the hill, until the final caving in of a thin residual roof. It is exactly the way in which the Upper Cave filled up and finally caved in. (20 September 1937.)

And it was Teilhard, finally, who, thanks to constantly accumulating data and to his bent for synthesis, was able to place the very complex geology of Choukou-tien in the vast geological framework of Far Eastern Asia. As previously noted, he felt that the proper method of research was methodical progress from the north down into Malaya. On 28 January 1934 he was able to say:

> Briefly, in six months our ideas on the stratigraphy and physiography of Choukou-tien (and hence of Northern China) have— while remaining fundamentally unchanged—become far more precise.

Already by 1935 his synthesis was taking shape:

> My work at Peking is increasingly absorbing and interesting. In the course of the last ten months I hope I have succeeded in finding the connection between the geologies of Northern and Southern China for the Tertiary and Quaternary divisions. I have a mass of plans and projects on hand. (14 February 1935.)

Letters to Breuil illustrate the central position Teilhard held in co-ordinating the work of the Survey:

> Upon my return to Peking I first took care to go and see Black, Pei, and company. Your coming here has been wonderfully helpful, and has left an atmosphere of good feeling. I have read your paper (being printed), have found your letters, got our friends talking, and looked at the number of new specimens found since my departure. Finally, my impressions—at the moment—are as follows:

(a) Concerning the making of stone implements: I feel, basically, in full agreement with you. Yet I am not (that is to say, without feeling myself "keen on" this rather than on that, you know, and all with full freedom of mind) as forcibly struck as you are by the *perfection* of this manufacture of stone pieces. The rock crystal points, as it seems to me, owe their apparent perfection only to the properties of their material. Neither in this nor in other regards, therefore, am I able to see in them any kind of definite tool. It strikes me, in other words, that Peking Man used stones by taking advantage of their shapes and of their edges as he found them, without imposing upon them any forms of his own.... Time may prove you right, but for the moment I feel a little undecided about the degree of Peking Man's culture.

(b) Concerning the making of bone implements: In this material (probably because I have less experience than you) I find myself quite hesitant. We have found obviously broken and scored bones. Yet I am not convinced of the existence of any definite implement-making, for I believe I have met, in fossil-bearing deposits of every geological age, certain pieces showing the characteristics which struck you at Choukou-tien. . . . One dare not be too hasty in these matters, therefore, I think, especially when it comes to the Men-toukou site; we are being closely watched, and the first opportunity that presented itself we should be attacked. But these criticisms or objections are only matters of detail. The really big thing, for both Black and me, is that having come here you have in a way become one of us, acquainted with the country, the people, and the material. It would be ideal (and perhaps not impossible) for you to return here for a few months, with a view to definitive publication. (21 February 1932.)

To come back to the manufacture of bone implements, we on the Survey (cf. in your talk, the note at the bottom of the page) have decided not to commit ourselves on what seem to us uncertain grounds. A few months or years hence, time may have proved you right; but, here, we are obliged to advance nothing but what is certain, or as certain as can be, in order not to risk the reputation of the undertaking. (You, of course, in contrast, are an independent scholar, who would be committing only yourself, and hence you can afford to go ahead much more boldly.) . . . It remains, of course, none the less true that the Survey is still enjoying the glow and the excitement of your visit, and that all we want in addition is for you to return here. (25 March 1932.)

We may sum up the Choukou-tien question in a few brief statements: Teilhard neither discovered the Choukou-tien fissure nor discovered the Peking Man skulls. Nor did he describe them. But he was the soul and animator of the research, and when the Japanese invaded China it was thanks to him that the work was not abandoned and the site neglected. Choukou-tien was one of Teilhard's greatest strokes of luck. On 22 May 1932 he wrote to a correspondent:

You envy me in some way my having had the chance to reveal material so interesting "to general thought" as the discovery of *Sinanthropus*. I recognize the value of it without being particularly proud of it.

CHAPTER TWELVE

First Peking Period:
China and Elsewhere

TEILHARD had hardly returned from the Croisière Jaune when he had to leave for Shansi:

> So, off on another trip tomorrow—with no great enthusiasm. After all my gypsying during these past years, the prospect of a journey on muleback, with stops at dirty inns, through rather dull country, hardly sets my blood tingling. But I am not denying that it will one day serve me in good stead; and so out of a sense of duty I am packing my bag. (3 July 1932.)

He made his way with Young into south-eastern Shansi, to study the Pliocene and Pleistocene deposits there in a wide region ravaged by erosion, and practically unknown. He had in mind to go down to the Hwang-ho and to rejoin the Peking railway. By September, 1932, he was back, after a month of primitive travel, on which he commented understandably:

> I have an idea, too, that this is the last time I shall be off on this sort of expedition. I can see new vistas opening before me, probably of a different sort, more suited to my age and the sort of work I can now contribute. In any event, I feel I am reaching a turning point in my life, and it is precisely in order not to miss the turning that I have accepted the present journey. (*Letters from a Traveller*, pp. 193–4.)

South-eastern Shansi, whose extensive badlands offered both fossils and an easy study of the Upper Cenozoic, played an important part in Teilhard's geological and palaeontological studies, as his bibliography shows. In early June of 1933 (*Letters from a Traveller*,

p. 199) he returned to Shansi with Barbour, making a Protestant industrial school south of Taiyuan his base for a short tour. Here is how Barbour describes the arrival, at evening, in a Chinese village:

Arriving at a village just before dusk, we used to find quarters either on the *k'ang* or mud platform on which guests of the local caravanserai slept in rows, or the stone stage of an open theatre platform beside the village temple. While we set up our canvas camp-bed, the cook lit a fire, boiled water, and bought eggs and noodles in preparation for the evening meal. When dark fell we had only the feeble light of a candle or storm lamp. After writing up our field notes, we would discuss the day's observations, before crawling into bed and extinguishing the light to avoid attracting mosquitoes. It was then that Pierre talked most freely, relaxed and content, about the ideas close to his heart. Many times since, I have wished that I had recorded some of the conversations of those nights, for in them lay the germ of many ideas which he later developed more fully in *Comment je crois* and *Le phénomène humain*.

These two, and perhaps other, trips to Shansi allowed Teilhard to accumulate valuable data, the source of numerous publications in 1933, 1936, and 1937, either his own or in collaboration with Young or M. Trassaert, a physicist of remarkable brilliance of mind and of rare adaptability, who was attached to the Tientsin laboratories and had been "converted" to palaeontology by Teilhard.[1]

Shansi gave Teilhard what every scientist must have, a solid field of specialization. But his synthetic bent remained. Thanks to the systematic exploration of the north of the Chinese Empire, and to the countless problems raised by Choukou-tien (reconciliation of the geology of the fissures and that of the basins and banks), the Tertiary and Quaternary structure in Northern China were on their way to definitive scientific clarification. The next step was to connect this with Southern China and thence with Malaya, Burma, and the Indies, following the line of fissure and cave deposits from north

[1] Cf. letter to Stehlin, 28 May 1938: "I expect you have had my article (with Trassaert) on the Cervids of Shansi; you must read it with indulgence. We lack so many books here, and specimens to compare with Europe. At the same time it is impossible to get the fossils to Paris or elsewhere. So I do the best I can. It seems to me more important to publish (even in incomplete form) than to 'bury' facts that are important for palaeontology; in fact, if I had not done so, many things would have disappeared to Nanking for good. However, I count on you, Schaub, Helbing, and others to correct me."

to south. Already in 1932 one of the Survey members returned from Yunnan with specimens proving that there were fossil-bearing caves there of about the same age as Choukou-tien. This explains why Teilhard's interest (apart from interludes in Honan in 1934 and Shantung in 1936, provinces watered by the Hwang-ho (shifted to Southern China, and especially the Yangtze valley.

His exploration of the Yangtze was in two parts. In April, 1934, Barbour persuaded Teilhard, Norin, C. C. Young and J. S. Lee to join him on a trip up the middle Yangtze. Teilhard met Barbour at Shanghai and went up the river to Hankow, with a side trip to Lushan; by 25 April he was back in Peking. After spending three days (8, 9, and 10 May) with Barbour, and attending a special meeting of the Geological Society of China, 11 May, to honour the memory of Dr Black, Teilhard took the train on 13 May for Hankow in order to finish, with Barbour and C. C. Young, the ascent of the Yangtze into Szechwan, with stops at Ichang, Wanhsien, and Chungking, before pushing on to a point near Chengtu and heading west to the limits of the basin, on the road to Chinese Tibet. By late June Teilhard was back at Tientsin.

Teilhard's primary concern was with Quaternary formations; in the letter in which he described how, following a plan drawn up with Black, he studied the Yangtze from Nanking to the first foothills of Tibet, he continued:

> Very interesting geologically, but none too "*promising*" for prehistory. There is very little Upper Pleistocene exposed. The banks (probably just a little too old for man) have decayed to laterite to quite a depth and thus evidently offer no hope for fossil bones (which would be dissolved). The best areas were the fossil-bearing fissures of Wanhsien (in Szechwan), which I was able to visit (fauna of the Choukou-tien period, it seems). Unfortunately, though, here we find not the habitat of the fauna, but simply dissolution pits which acted as natural traps, a fact which lessens the chances.... It was a splendid trip, however, quite enthralling. The Province of Szechwan, especially, is marvellous country.

In fact, this discovery of Southern China, on foot, in palanquin, by sampan, and by aeroplane, was a wonderful revelation:

> We arrived here yesterday, after a splendid journey through the gorges: they have certainly not been overrated, especially from

the geologist's point of view. For over sixty miles the powerful waters force their way between high walls of cliff, with frequent rapids, where you can read almost the whole geological story of China. Once through the gorges, you enter Szechwan, a rich green country in which every moment showed me a China more Chinese than the north. The pagodas are more brilliant and more mannered, hats are wider and more pointed, the whole country-side more like the China we know in books. (*Letters from a Traveller*, pp. 203-4.)

It was on Teilhard's visit to the fossil-bearing fissures of Wanhsien that there occurred a pleasant incident recorded by C. C. Young:

As we toured, we sometimes took advantage of opportunities to stay in Catholic missions, in order to get better food and more comfortable quarters for the night. Usually there was no difficulty in making such arrangements, but in Wanhsien, eastern Szech-wan, we found quite a different situation. When we reached it, the city was so crowded that we were unable to find rooms in an inn.

Père Teilhard knew that there was a large Catholic mission there and suggested that we stay there for a few days. When we reached the mission, a Chinese in a long black gown appeared, and looked at us very strangely as if he suspected we were criminals. He asked the profession of Père Teilhard, who was in field dress as usual. We told him the truth, that he was a Catholic priest, but of course he did not believe it, and began to speak to Père Teilhard in Latin. Although Teilhard knew Latin very well, he had not had practice in speaking it for years, so could not talk fluently with the Chinese Catholic Father, whose suspicions were thus confirmed. He considered Père Teilhard a bad man, re-garded all of us with suspicion, and refused to receive us in a friendly fashion. He allowed us to stay, but gave us a very poor room.

Two days later the same Chinese Catholic Father visited us very politely, moved us to a much better, lavishly decorated room, and gave us very good food. He apologized to us with good grace for his unfriendly manner when he first received us. From his change of manner, we knew that he had telegraphed to the mission centre of Chengtu.

In midsummer of 1934 Teilhard, Barbour, and the Chinese scientist M. N. Bien travelled in western Honan (which had been cleared of bandits); leaving the train at Loyang they crossed the Tsinling range, their purpose being purely geological, to tie up their studies on the relationship of the Tertiary and Quaternary formations of Northern and of Southern China. "Our hopes have been surpassed," Teilhard exclaimed with joy.

It was not enough, of course, to study the two ends of the chain, the north and the south; the intermediate links had to be examined, including necessarily delicate analysis of the regions where the geological transitions occurred. Barbour has preserved for us some episodes of this Honan trip:

According to my dilapidated field notebook, on Tuesday, 29 July 1934, we pulled into the courtyard of the Yamen or magistrate's palace at Lu-shih on the Lo-Ho River in west Honan. We had left the railway at Loyang two days earlier. From the excitement and curiosity that greeted our arrival in the villages along the way, we were evidently the first *Yang-kwei-tze*, or "foreign devils", to enter the district, which for several years had been bandit-ridden and was still regarded as a hornet's nest. The Nanking government under Chiang Kai-shek had just cleared the area and appointed new district military officers to restore order, and these had not yet taken over their new duties. The pass across the Tsinling range ahead was still not considered safe for travellers, and we had been directed to the military headquarters, to present our credentials and be granted access and safe-conduct. The new command had arrived so recently that we were their first official visitors and had appeared even before the buildings had been swept out. The keen new district commandant felt obliged by the laws of courtesy to offer us hospitality, and kept us in the outer court while he made the place presentable and prepared a meal to welcome us. Only thereafter would our business be discussed.

We had been on the move since leaving Ku-hsien before 8 a.m. and had wasted at least an hour getting our cart and beasts across a ferry. It had rained and we had covered only some fifteen miles of thoroughly bad going. Pierre sat down on the stone steps of the *Yamen* to rest and await developments, and watched the efforts of some soldiers trying to unload their gear from the back of a balky mule. One of the men shouted in Chinese that the brute had a nasty temper. But the remark was lost on Pierre, who was still commenting on the applicability of a comment by Li T'ai-fo (which C. C. Young had translated from an inscription in the Red Basin, earlier in the summer): "It is as hard to travel in Szechwan as to go to heaven."

Just at that moment, the men dropped their load as the mule struck out with a hind leg and struck poor Pierre on the temple. The blow broke a blood vessel, and within a few minutes he had a blister the size of a bantam's egg right over the temporal artery. Within five minutes we had commandeered the nearest room in the *Yamen* and set up his camp cot. Through the night I kept his temple cool with constantly changed compresses. Ice simply does not exist in a Chinese village in July, and the medical orderly of the post had no supplies of any kind except a little ether. I read to Pierre from the little breviary he had been using in the cart earlier in the afternoon, and waited in fear for the dawn. But his one concern was for *"ces pauvres gens"*, our poor hosts, who had prepared the meal with such care with no guests to partake of it.

By morning the swelling was distinctly reduced, and he tried to insist on going ahead. But I pointed out that the mule had prevented my writing up the conclusions of the previous day's survey, and that the chief of police had said we might not proceed until word came back from a messenger who had been sent ahead to warn the outposts of our coming.

Two days later he was in fit condition to travel. The path had become so narrow that the cart was paid off and we put our baggage on mules, the muleteer in Chinese fashion counterpoising the weight of Pierre's metal box by three heavy stones, to keep the load in balance. Pierre always preferred to travel with this long metal military kit-box, in the bottom of which were stowed some two hundred Chinese dollars—the only currency that was always accepted in face of the inevitable sudden changes in value of unlimited paper money.

Two days later we threaded the pass over the summit of the Tsinling range. On the southern face the descent was by a winding gorge, so narrow that the footpath had to cross and recross the stream at every bend. The fourth day started with a four-kilometre stretch during which we had to ford the current waist-high thirteen times before 8 a.m. The number 13 must have struck the mule as unlucky, and the ill-balanced load began to slip. As the beast neared the bank, it tried to lie down and roll, but managed first to drop the trunk in two feet of water. The next hour we sat on the bank with clothing spread on the bushes until the sun dried out the box's soaking contents, from which Pierre had surreptitiously removed the hoard of silver dollars.

I have preserved a precious memento of the occasion. The river was so deep that we had had to cross the water half-naked with our clothes and shoes in a bundle over our shoulders. I had a

7+

rucksack, which made for easier crossings, and had reached the shore ahead of Pierre in time to use the last unexposed twenty feet of cine film to perpetuate the memory of that eventful morning. I had to leave China before the film could be processed, and it lay unseen in the Cenozoic Laboratory for two years before reaching me in New York. When I showed it to Pierre fifteen years later, he remarked: "If *le chef de mon Ordre* had seen this, would he not have considered me to have been unfrocked prematurely? Tell me, George, did you ever find colder water anywhere than in that wretched river?"

Szechwan straddles the Yangtze. But Teilhard had to go farther south. As he remarked on the Nanking to Chengtu tour:

A magnificent trip, which revealed a whole new third of China to me. But I still have the final third to do—the southern one— and then I think we shall begin to see the Tertiary and Quaternary of China in its proper light. (13 July 1934.)

In early January of 1935, another departure, with Wong and Pei, was prepared for. Kwangsi and Kwangtung (the province Canton is in) were completely new to Teilhard, and he looked forward to seeing and learning a good deal there. Here is his summary of the results:

. . . the succession of Pliocene and Pleistocene deposits is beginning to take shape, south of the Tsinling Mountains, as follows:

1. At the base, a massive series of gravels and silts (Piedmont deposits) would seem to correspond with the Villafranchian.
2. Above, an irregularly developed system of altered laterites and of grey silts would seem to represent the ensemble of the Quaternary properly so called.

So far, no vestige of human beings has been found in the Pleistocene formation of these slopes and basins. In contrast, the exploration of the caves which are so numerous in the extensive karsts of Southern China, from Kwangsi and Yunnan to Szechwan, should provide prehistory—for the same period—with certain definite and interesting data.

On the one hand, these caves contain (throughout Kwangsi and doubtless elsewhere) important deposits where implements of the Mesolithic type . . . are found in an accumulation of consolidated ash and fresh-water shells. . . . On the other hand, in these same caves are to be recognized vestiges of a much more ancient, yellow, clay formation, containing a quite characteristic fauna:

Stegodon ... and orang. No certain human vestiges have been announced yet for these earlier clays, but one may expect such an announcement at any time. In any case, various considerations move us to think that the *Stegodon* and orang deposits in Southern China are the exact equivalent both of the *Sinanthropus* beds in Northern China (where fauna of the northern type predominates) and of the *Pithecanthropus* beds in Java. . . .[2]

Writing from Nanking, 18 January 1935, in English, he regrets the cold weather:

People look frozen, and go along the roads under blankets or with small baskets with burning charcoal on their belly. It's a pity to see the country without sun, everything is so tropical: the huge green trees, the fruits, the red soil, the ferns, and the bright birds.

Near Kweilin he finds nature surprising:

From the picturesque point of view we are in one of the most famous and strange places of China. All around Kweilin, and far south, the country is a forest of high pillars or needles of limestone (about eighty or ninety metres high), forming a most extraordinary landscape. These are the remains of a highly dissected limestone plateau. Amongst the maze of fantastic rocks, emerging from a brick-red soil, the river runs, its waters a transparent jade-green. The pity is only that the country is so much deforested. Here the vegetation is not so tropical as in Nanning. No more palms nor *Cycas* in the rocks. But we are still in a country of oranges, mandarines and pomelos. The weather is cloudy and almost cold. The houses are mostly open, and there is no fire except for fire-bowls. (28 January 1935, again in English.)

Teilhard's *"Drang nach Süden"* was now to lead him beyond the Chinese border. We have several times mentioned Helmut de Terra, whom Teilhard met in Washington in 1935. A short time later De Terra received a letter from Davidson Black, asking him, should he plan to return to Northern India, to co-operate in researches on fossil man. In answer, De Terra asked whether a member of the Peking Institute might accompany him in 1935 to

[2] This was confirmed in *1955*, when the Chinese found in Kwangsi teeth of *Gigantopithecus* and *Stegodon*; similarly, in *1958*, in the same province, they found two mandibles of *Gigantopithecus*, close in appearance to the human (*L'anthropologie*, 1935, p. 740).

help him and his group. As director of the Yale North India Expedition, he had it in mind to study the stratigraphy of the Siwalik Hills (west of Nepal and south of Kashmir) to collect fossils of primates, and to pursue his investigations into the Pleistocene and the associated Palaeolithic civilizations in the Salt Range and Kashmir. Thereupon De Terra heard from Teilhard, who expressed his interest in the project and his readiness to co-operate.

The trip is recorded in *Letters from a Traveller*.[3] Their object was to resume the question of the Pleistocene of India by connecting the alluvial sheets of Northern India (the Punjab, the Salt Range) to the Himalayan moraines, and so determine the three principal Himalayan glaciations, which resulted in three quite distinct formations. Conclusions reached here could be extended to other regions of India, for example, to the southern Punjab; a probable equivalent of the sub-Himalayan Pleistocene formations is found in the beds of the Narbada river in Central India.

The next aim was to establish a connection between the Punjab and Sinkiang, and thus to knit together the geology of India and that of China.

Teilhard's geological investigations naturally led to investigations in prehistory. Both in the neighbourhood of Rawalpindi (small worked quartzites), at Sukkur, near the Baluchistan border, and in the valley of the Narbada river, Palaeolithic finds abounded. At Sukkur:

> Above the immense alluvial plain emerges a platform of nummulitic limestones rich in flints. The whole platform is nothing but a fabulous workshop . . . millions of points and implements. (27 November 1935.)

> The Narbada ranks as the classic Pleistocene of India—and only a single Palaeolithic implement had yet been found *in situ* (about 1850). Nothing else has been done there during the subsequent eight decades! De Terra and I resolved to go and have a look at the place. Great was our surprise to find there vastly rich deposits of ancient industry—as rich perhaps as Madras, and with fauna. (18 December 1935.)

[3] Teilhard arrived at Bombay from Marseilles on 20 September 1935; thence by rail to Rawalpindi, where he met the Englishman, Patterson; he then joined De Terra at Srinagar, and spent a week in Kashmir; then back to the Punjab for a fortnight in the Salt Range, with a detour to Mohenjo-Daro, leaving on 30 November for Central India. After a fortnight in the Narbada valley they left Calcutta for Batavia on 22 December.

On some enormous boulders in the region of the Indus, which were brought from elsewhere by natural forces, the party found drawings graven on the surface, but probably of a late period; and they went to look at the famous pictures in red and black on the quartzite walls near the town of Hoshangabad in the region of the Narbada. Teilhard thought the pictures had been quite badly analysed and that they were done in two distinct periods, the older, in red, being naturalistic depictions of animals, the more recent showing war scenes, with people of three nationalities represented.

We have some material on Teilhard's Indian expedition which supplements the *Letters from a Traveller*. There are some sociological comments: the rise of anti-English sentiment, the shortcomings of Moslem civilization (with hopeless inferiority of women), and of the Hindu (with its sacred cows encumbering the roads and its sacred monkeys ruining the crops). Here are three decriptions, the second (for November) being in Teilhard's English:

1 October 1935: I needn't describe for you this Vale of Kashmir, the appearance of which is familiar to you: a bed of greenery between two rows of snowy peaks. The weather is magnificent. The paddies are amber, and the enormous sycamores, at the first touch of fall, beginning to turn red. This side of the pinewoods, turbaned peasants are gathering nuts near orchards red with apples.

November, 1935: Here the conditions are simply exquisite. Two days ago in the badlands I had the most beautiful evenings of my time in India. The sun was gold over the yellow and pink clays of the desiccated desert, over the dry grass and the thorny trees of the bush. Just like firm white clouds in the blue sky of the east, the snowy, lofty Pir Panjal (the last-borne [*sic*] Himalayan range) were floating above the landscape. And troops of green parrots were passing, too.

16 December 1935: A golden light lay over a charming countryside (Central India) thickly dotted with enormous trees which are always green—mangoes, banyans, and so forth. Here on both sides of the valley are the tabular masses of the peninsular Indian ranges, covered with dense jungle—a tiger jungle—and here can be seen peacocks flapping in the woods, a few crocodiles in the river, and numbers of black-faced, white-ringed monkeys everywhere in the brush and all along the roads. The natives are pleasant and scrupulously clean, the men with white clothing and turbans, the women all enveloped in veils of scarlet or pink; they

have a more agreeable look than people in the Punjab. Geologically, the place was a feast.

Helmut de Terra supplies a picture of Teilhard in the field:

I can well remember the day (in October, 1935) when our guest stepped out of the train at Rawalpindi, his face smiling with that eager expression, that very special light that he radiated when he perceived the prospects for some important studies. We spent several weeks together, searching for fossil bones, for artifacts, and all the geologic features.

I marvelled at his endurance; he would walk in tennis shoes over the rough ground, touching it lightly as if dancing; and at noontime, with the sun beating down in a merciless heat, we took a cold meal, and after that he lay down in the shade of a bush, sleeping at once, for some ten or fifteen minutes, then to awake completely relaxed and refreshed.

He never asked for privileges, which he well might have done, being my senior. While in the field his dedication for the work was so great that it seemed to irritate him at times to hear my complaints when something had gone wrong with my arrangements in camp or for transportation. He lived in his own tent, sharing with me a native servant, whom he treated with greater consideration than appeared justified considering the annoying shortcomings of our native helpers.

He was the first among us to discover the tooth of a fossil anthropoid, a tiny speck of white on the bright red wall of a canyon, and recognized Palaeolithic artifacts with an uncanny sort of instinct. Often he would pick one of these from the ground, look at it briefly from all sides, and hand it to me, saying: "It is suspicious; we must find more to be absolutely sure."

Later in that same autumn we went for two weeks to the Valley of Kashmir, where Dr T. T. Patterson and I had studied the Pleistocene; and after that Father Teilhard and I went to the Narbada Valley in Central India. Here we found a vertebrate fauna in the Middle Pleistocene in association with Early Palaeolithic industries. We had been hoping for some human bones, my friend expecting them any day, but when we finally left this place, I turned in disappointment to him. "Never mind," he said. "We have found some important clues; there will be others to follow up our work."

I also recall how on one occasion when we walked through thick, jungle-like vegetation, Father Teilhard stopped abruptly, as if listening. The forest was silent. "The forest is like the ocean, so full of hidden life." He stood there quite still, enjoying the silence, and seemed to breathe in something of the hidden life which he loved so much.

On 22 December 1935 Teilhard left Calcutta for Singapore, where he spent three days with the prehistorian Collings, director of the Raffles Museum. From Singapore he took the *Ophir* for Batavia, where he landed about 4 January.

Teilhard interrupted his return to Peking for a ten-day stay in Java at the invitation of Ralph von Koenigswald. Research in human palaeontology on the island had been conducted along a line passing approximately north and south through Solo (east of the centre of the island), a place situated on a river of the same name. Along this section are found two Pleistocene (Quaternary) series, both of significance for prehistory. To the north, the Solo series includes, from higher to lower, the following horizons: Ngandong, Trinil, Jetis. The Ngandong beds are found in horizontal banks the length of the Solo river. The Jetis-Trinil series forms a long band extending from Solo eastward to Surabaja. One good section appears in the Sangiran dome, near Solo. In the southern part of the island, a karst series, in the Patjitan region, is found, south of the Solo basin, not here in a depressed basin, but on an elevated region where the Miocene limestone (descending towards the south) has developed a region of karst formations.

Teilhard remembered the discovery of *Pithecanthropus* as a comparatively old story, going back to 1890. During the subsequent forty-five years there had been much controversy over the famous skull found, through the efforts of Dr Dubois, beside the Solo river at Trinil. After long discussions, most scientists had finished by agreeing that *Pithecanthropus* was probably a member of some vanished group of large simians: a giant gibbon of some kind, Marcellin Boule thought.

Then in 1932, in the most recent Ngandong beds, von Koenigswald and his collaborators had discovered eleven skulls, or large fragments of skulls, of *Homo soloensis*, Neanderthaloid in the wide sense of the term, along with cultural remains. In 1935 there had been further discoveries; at Sangiran, in the Trinil beds, a microlithic industry; and, in the Patjitan region, an abundant industry of Chelleo-Acheulean flints (Madras type), both found by von Koenigswald.

But the real ray of light had appeared when in that same year, and thus not long after the discovery of *Sinanthropus* in China, there had been found, at Sangiran, a second *Pithecanthropus* skull, much more complete and in a much more satisfactory stratigraphic situation. A decision had been easily reached: *Pithecanthropus* was not simian, but a Hominid; and, among the Hominids, he was assigned an evolutionary stage approximately the same as that assigned to *Sinanthropus*. *Pithecanthropus* was certainly a man of the very early Pleistocene and perhaps even somewhat older geologically than *Sinanthropus*.

In short, Java, because of its geographical position, seemed to present a crossroads where two Palaeolithic currents met: one, a north-western current probably derived from India (Chellean, with hippopotamus); the other, a north-eastern current rising from China (with *Pithecanthropus-Sinanthropus*, orang, and buffalo). From these facts the point of Teilhard's trip is clear. Java seemed to be a hinge between India and China; some capital discoveries, thanks to von Koenigswald's keenness, had just taken place there; and, finally, it was of importance to attempt to establish a satisfactory connection between *Pithecanthropus* and *Sinanthropus*.

Teilhard spent ten days on the island from 4 or 5 to 15 January. From Batavia he was taken to Bandung, where he devoted most of his time to excursions in the southern and central parts of the island. First he studied the stratigraphy of the island, examined at first hand the *Homo soloensis* skulls, confirmed the identification of the microlithic industry found in the famous highly fossil-bearing Sangiran dome, cast doubt on the pre-Trinil (that is to say, Jetis) dating of the Chellean artifacts found in the southern karst formations, clarified for von Koenigswald the Patjitan (southern karst) site (which von Koenigswald had seen but once and had incompletely understood), and insisted on establishing for this site a much more certain stratigraphy.

To crown these efforts, just above the valley in the limestone of this southern part of the island he and von Koenigswald discovered a cavern floor with an abundance of isolated teeth—orang, large gibbon, bear, and so forth—"absurdly" similar to the fossil-bearing deposits of Kwangsi. For the first time, orang, gibbon, and bear were found in Java. A correlation was thus established with Southern China. He summed up these journeys:

In brief, both in India with De Terra and in Java with von Koenigswald, I pitched most opportunely on two of the hottest sectors on the prehistory front—and just at the moment to take part in decisive offensives. This proving a great addition to my experience and another valuable plank in my platform. (*Letters from a Traveller*, p. 218.)

Teilhard came to the conclusion, too, that he had been made for a life in the tropics.

I lived in the Javanese kampongs among the gentle and graceful natives, and I fairly revelled in the exoticism of this marvellous country. Java is over-populated; apart from the high peaks and some remnants of jungle, it is nothing but one immense village; but the huts are so small, so scattered and lost in a sea of green, that all you see is a forest of palms enclosing rice-fields, the whole dominated by a series of volcanoes, each as big as Etna. (*Letters from a Traveller*, p. 222.)

CHAPTER THIRTEEN

First Peking Period:
Last Field Expeditions

ENCHANTED by his trip through Southern Asia, Teilhard spent
the latter part of January aboard the *Tjinagara*, crossing
from Batavia to Shanghai, whence he went on to visit the
Survey at Nanking, and to arrive by 11 February at Peking. It was
during this solitary crossing, spent entirely in thought and prayer,
that he undertook one of his most characteristic works, *Esquisse
d'un univers personnel*. He saw the direction his thinking must
take; it must include not simply Christ as coming into the world,
but the world, in fact the universe, as receiving a new polarization
thereby. These thoughts grew out of his reflections on the capital
status of personality, and on the universe as reaching its culmination
in personality:

> Really, I think there is no better, even no other, natural centre
> of total coherence of things than the human person. Starting from
> the complex mesh wherein the soul is bound to the body, the
> cosmos reels off behind and knits up before us in accordance with
> a simple law, which both satisfies the understanding and meets
> the requirements of action. Herein, too, the false oppositions
> between spirit and matter, universality and personality, and
> psychological and physical forces all vanish. . . . Christianity is pre-
> eminently a person-centred religion. . . .
> The essence of Christianity is nothing more nor less than belief
> in the unification of the world in God through the Incarnation. . . .
> Thence it would follow that so long as society had not passed the
> "Neolithic", familial, stage of its development (that is to say, until
> the dawn of the modern, scientific-industrial stage), the Incarna-
> tion obviously could find, for its expression, only symbols of a

juridical kind. But since the modern discovery of great cosmic unities and vast cosmic energies, a new and more satisfactory meaning is beginning to be found for the old words. In order to be Alpha and Omega, Christ must, without losing his human determination, become coextensive with the physical immensities of time and space. To reign upon earth, he must extend his quickening power through the world.

By all the logic of Christianity, then, in Christ the personal expands (or rather reaches a commanding centre) to the point of becoming universal.

In Teilhard's mind, the Omega, that is, the Personal-Universal keystone of the world and motive power of cosmogenesis, had now taken on substantiality. In the same book are found his reflections on the sexual sense, the human sense, and the cosmic sense:

> What name, in harmony with our system, is to be given to that psycho-physical energy of personalization to which all the activities manifested by the stuff of the universe are to be ultimately reduced? One name only (provided we give it the generality and force it must have when given cosmic extension): love. It is a love that builds the universe physically. Let us trace in ourselves, in order to recognize them and direct them, the manifestations of that fundamental force out of which our life is woven. I find three degrees wherein this force is successively manifested to our consciousness: in the opposite sex; in society; and in the whole.
>
> (a) *The sexual sense.* Through woman, and only through woman, can man escape the isolation in which his very perfection may too easily imprison him. In the light of this experience it is no longer quite exact to say that the nexus-element in the universe is the thinking monad, for we find that the complete human molecule is something more complex, and hence more spiritual, than the individual person: it is a duality, comprising the masculine and the feminine.
>
> ... By virtue of the same principle which requires the "simple" person to find completion in the complexity of the couple, the couple must in turn seek outside itself the completion which its growth demands ... the very centre towards which the two lovers converge in their union must manifest its personality in the very centre of the circle in which that union seeks to isolate itself. The two will find internal equilibrium only in a third who lies ahead. ...
>
> (b) *The human sense.* The energy of personalization manifested in that first degree must ... be completed by an attraction which

draws the totality of human molecules towards one another. It is this particular force of cohesion, diffused through the whole of the noosphere, which we are here calling "the human sense".... Today, for the first time in the history of the world, the possibility of *conscious masses* is revealed. Already the human phenomenon has left the scale of the individual to extend into the immense.... The human sense, if it is not to be inhuman, must be a species of love. And this means that society will inevitably become mechanical if its successive stages of development do not culminate in *someone*. Mankind, if it is not to be oppressive, must take on a transcendent human form....

(c) *The cosmic sense.* I call the cosmic sense that more or less conscious affinity which binds us psychologically to the whole in which we are enveloped.... In the cosmos as I have described it here, it becomes possible for us, however surprising the expression may be, *to love the universe.* And it is in fact in that act alone that love can develop with unlimited clarity and power.

We rightly mistrust an overgeneralized affection. "He who loves everything loves nothing," the saying goes. But no such danger exists, at least in theory, for anyone who has grasped what a personalized "everything" is, namely, a definite central figure appearing as the term of elementary figures, themselves increasingly better defined. Directed towards such an object, the heart is in no danger of trickling away into the dry sands of impersonal and diffuse yearnings. Instead, without losing contact with the concrete reality of the human beings who are its immediate world, the heart discovers the means of embracing them all together in a sentiment which preserves, despite its boundless extension, the warmth of human affection.

Once Teilhard was back at home (so to describe the Tientsin-Peking-Choukou-tien triangle) tasks were not wanting. The first of these was to join his colleagues in sending scientists to gather fossils from the Szechwan fissures and in the red-earth beds of the Yangstze valley. While in Tientsin, he spent time examining fossil fauna from southern Shansi; and while in Peking he did a good deal of work on Pliocene and Pleistocene material from central Shansi. He also worked on his long-planned map of the eruptive rocks of China. Now he found, however, that he lacked information on Shantung, and decided to spend three weeks there in July and August. The following letter offers a good summary of the trip:

Geographically, the Shantung Peninsula is to China what Brittany is to France. I have now covered the peninsula from Tsingtao to the easternmost point. Road conditions made the trip difficult and forced me to renew acquaintance with the most primitive forms of locomotion. But what I saw interested me a great deal; moreover, the weather was cool and the scenery extraordinarily picturesque: jagged peaks rising from a plain lush with the green of millet and sorghum.

I went there to see the structural geology and the eruptive rocks, matters of little interest to you. But I noted incidentally that the south of the Shantung Peninsula is as poor a place for prehistory as you could think of, with no trace of marine terraces (everything drops sheer as we had feared), no stone suitable for implements, no loess or clays. The mountains, all granite, are thickly covered and fringed with arkose, probably Quaternary in many points, but offering no chance of anything being found. (21 August 1936.)

Despite other interruptions (trips to the United States and France) that year, on 6 December 1937 Teilhard left Peking to arrive at Rangoon, in Burma, on 28 December. From one of the succession of cargo steamers he used for the trip he wrote, in English:

I have decided to use the first part of my journey for making my "*retraite*". I somewhat miss my notes and familiar surroundings. And yet to be practically alone on the sea, and bound for action, is a favourable atmosphere for perceiving the best of God. Many points seem to appear more simply and more distinctly in my mind. (10 December 1937.)

The preceding March, in Philadelphia, Teilhard had met his two friends De Terra and von Koenigswald. In June Helmut de Terra, with the Carnegie Foundation behind him, had made definite overtures on the subject of a three-month Burma tour, to begin in December; and Teilhard had decided, health permitting, to join him.

The trip appeared all the more inviting since in Yunnan, next door to Burma, the Chinese scientist M. N. Bien, besides his orang-fossil fissures, had found a series of Eocene and Upper Oligocene basins analogous to the formations in Mongolia and thus establishing a geological bridge to Burma. He had also discovered some consolidated deposits with clearly human traces.

It had therefore become possible to repeat in the western part of the Indo-Chinese Peninsula the fortunate discoveries in India. Just as the connection of Sinkiang, Kashmir, and the Punjab had been

successfully established, so was there hope of establishing a connection between Burma and Yunnan, and thus with Southern China.
The result would be a gigantic geological edifice, having as its
pillars Manchuria, Mongolia, Sinkiang, Kashmir, the Punjab, the
Narbada valley, Northern China, Southern China, Burma, Malaya,
Java, and even Annam. There were therefore excellent reasons for
going to the Indo-Chinese Peninsula, where Fromaget, director of
the geological survey of Indo-China, was already at work.

The *Letters from a Traveller*, and other letters, again record the
trip:[1]

> As for stratigraphy, I think we are making the connection for
> Indo-China all right. At Mogok, in the ruby pits, De Terra has
> found *Stegodon, Elephans namadicus*, and rhinoceros—the same
> fauna as for Szechwan, Yunnan, and Kwangsi.... Sixty miles
> west of Mogok, on the Irrawaddy, with banks roughly like those
> on the Narbada, we are geologically already in "India"....
>
> As for archaeology, after having despaired of finding any Early
> Palaeolithic in the high bank with hippopotamus and *namadicus*,
> I think we have at last hit on something.... There exists here,
> besides the quartzites, a fossil-wood industry that is going to take
> special study but seems to me fairly sure. (20 January 1938.)

He wrote of the Shan Plateau:

> A covering of forests and of laterites closes this to archaeology,
> and no fossil-bearing fissures appear [later in March he was to
> announce such fissures, with familiar South Asian fauna]. But
> study of the banks and of the slope conglomerates is not without
> interest, especially in relationship with China. Since my letter of
> 13 February, gathering of specimens on the Irrawaddy has pro-
> gressed, with literally about a thousand Palaeolithic pieces already
> picked up. Movius is completely dedicated to the task, and seems
> now to have caught on to the technique of the silicified wood. I
> hope he'll show you a series of specimens when he goes to Paris

[1] On 31 December 1937 Teilhard joined de Terra at Mogok on the Shan
Plateau near the borders of Yunnan. In January, descent to the plain where
the geologists, with the prehistorian Movius, worked on the terraces of the
Irrawaddy, a little to the south of Mandalay, or on the slopes of the Arakan
Yoma (the chain that separates the Irrawaddy from the Bay of Bengal). In
the second half of February, Teilhard and de Terra, leaving Movius on the
Irrawaddy, went to Lashio (on the high Shan Plateau) to the west of the
Salween, whence they moved along what was later to become the Burma
Road as far as Salween, a few miles from Yunnan. On 24 March 1938, Teil-
hard, de Terra and Movius left Rangoon for Batavia.

in the spring. The industry seems well defined now (half of it quartzite, half of it silicified wood). (5 March 1938.)[2]

A letter of 2 July 1938 sums up:

You know we have finally been rewarded by the discovery of an Early Palaeolithic industry in the bank a hundred feet above the Irrawaddy. It strikes me we have pretty well analysed the Pleistocene in the Mandalay zone, and succeeded in connecting the phases of the lowlands of that region with those of the Shan Plateau and consequently of Yunnan and Southern China.[3]

Apart from his scientific work, Teilhard was delighted by life in Burma:

A bewitching life ... in an unusually colourful and picturesque country, only with too many pagodas and too many Burmese monks. It's frightful, this parasitism. ... Despite the dry season, which has put an end to the flowers and the insects, the jungle is fascinating, especially the great jungle of the Shan Plateau. This country, it seems, is still full of elephants. In fact everywhere you look, you see monkeys, muntjacs, and wild chickens (just like small barnyard fowl, but more alert).

With our Burmese domestics ... we lead a quite pleasant life. The nights are still cool; and the sky a changeless blue. (20 January 1938.)

The jungle fascinated Teilhard. For the first time he saw gibbons swinging among the trees, the first close contact he had ever had with living anthropoid apes in their natural environment. He supplies further details in a letter in English:

After a few days spent near a very majestic volcano in the plain (Mt Popa) we have migrated to the Shan Plateau. Very cool weather, and such magnificent scenery; huge green forests, on which spring spreads touches of cream and pink, and sometimes with patches of flame-red.

Two days ago we motored on a precipitous road, to the deep

[2] A later letter of 16 March 1938 speaks differently of the fossil-bearing qualities of the Shan Plateau: "Demonstration of the existence, on the Shan Plateau, of fossiliferous fissures parallel to those of Southern China"; cf. the letter of 28 May 1938: "Fissures with *Stegodon* are found on the Shan Plateau as in Southern China, Indochina (and Java)."

[3] Cf. the letter of 16 March 1938: "We now have, I believe, the necessary elements roughly to knit together the Plio-Pleistocene of Southern China and Northern India (and perhaps Malaya) which was, in my thinking, the principal goal of this little expedition."

valley where the Salween river runs parallel with the Mekong. A few miles farther were the first slopes of Yunnan. Chinese everywhere in their blue clothes and their mules, just like Peking! You would enjoy to observe the people of the hills: black-turbaned Shans; Ketchim women in low-necked bodices, with a coloured kilt; wild Wans, almost naked and as shy as jungle creatures; a complete ethnological collection. (7 March 1938.)

Teilhard brought back from this trip a fine collection of slides, illustrating both physical and human geography, landscapes, culture, local industry, mines (e.g. the ruby and sapphire mines worked by native processes).

This Burmese interlude lasted until March, 1938. On 24 March Teilhard, Dr and Mrs Movius, and Dr and Mrs De Terra set off for Java. There von Koenigswald had been hard at work. In the karst lands of Patjitan, south of the Solo basin, he had found *Stegodon* in the limestone fissures, thus establishing a connection between the Solo basin and the Kwangsi fissures. Teilhard had almost had a presentiment of this discovery when, on 14 January 1936, speaking of these karst formations, he wrote:

> *Stegodon* or hippopotamus will have to be found here for a connection to be made with the Solo basin. Let's hope that some will be found. Deposits of this kind ought to abound in the karsts.

He was still more excited when on 2 April von Koenigswald wrote to him that in the Modjokerto region in Surabaja, he had just found a skull which had come from a lacustro-volcanic horizon (Jetis) underlying that of Trinil and Ngandong and, therefore, considered to be geologically older. Unfortunately, this was only the braincase of a child of a year or less (preventing comparison with other fossil material), so that it is difficult to say whether it is a young *Pithecanthropus* or other early type; nor, apparently, was the Jetis age clearly established. (Von Koenigswald named the find *Homo modjokertensis*, and it was nicknamed the Baby Skull.)

The Sangiran dome, too, was yielding new treasures. On 20 September, Teilhard tells of his excitement on learning of new finds by von Koenigswald: new *Gigantopithecus* teeth, and above all a massive *Pithecanthropus* half-mandible, in the Sangiran dome. Teilhard's letters of 15 and 24 October show further excitement over von Koenigswald's discovery of a new *Pithecanthropus* brainpan.

From the evidence it appeared that the Sangiran bed was much richer than the Trinil, and that in any case the Java beds were remarkably rewarding. Apparently, too, in the face of the complex of similar yet mutually contrasting forms that turned up, it was impossible to identify Peking Man and Java Man with each other purely and simply, and to call *Sinanthropus* merely another *Pithecanthropus*. Teilhard suspected that the two, in any case, formed a marginal branch, highly individualized, which had proliferated independently in the Early Quaternary of China and Malaya, alongside more central human groups.

In any case, he felt he should go and see for himself, and try to determine the exact levels where there had been found, respectively, *Homo modjokertensis* and the *Pithecanthropus* brainpan. Moreover, it was Teilhard's ambition to get von Koenigswald assisted by the Carnegie Foundation. It was therefore necessary to attract American scientists to Java.

A letter of 26 April 1938, confirmed by one of 28 May, supplies useful technical information on this trip, and the *Letters from a Traveller* some further details.[4] The stay in Java was not long; Teilhard, feeling himself now overdue in Peking, left the trip before its completion, and did not see the site, near Surabaja, of the Baby Skull; both coming and going he stopped at Singapore, not only because this was the only route but also because it afforded contact with Collings, a part of the Teilhard "network". In fact, in a letter from Hong Kong, 26 April, Teilhard wrote:

> While we were in Java, Collings (of Singapore) went to inspect the Pleistocene sands on the Perak river, south of Penang; these sands had been brought to his attention by the Geological Service. And here he at once came on (*in situ*, in the diggings) an abundant industry of remarkable qualities. ... This seems to be the first Palaeolithic find in Malaya. At last!

While in Java Teilhard visited the Ngandong region (not easily accessible), and saw again the Sangiran dome (site of the new *Pithecanthropus*) and the karst lands in the south (Patjitan), with their substantial industry. Movius and von Koenigswald were going ahead with a summary classification of the enormous material gathered in the karst region: it seemed to have a close relationship with that found on the Irrawaddy; but the problem of the original

[4] Teilhard left Rangoon on 24 March 1938; arrived at Singapore 30 March; left Singapore on 1 April in the *Ophir*; arrived at Batavia 3 April; left Batavia for Singapore 16 April; arrived at Singapore 18 April; and left 20 April for China in *Felix-Roussel*, arriving in China in May.

site of the large Palaeolithic instruments yielded by the banks here (volcanic eruption, mud streams, and heavy rains throughout the earlier Quaternary had shifted the soil and its contents) could not always be settled. In contrast, the new *Pithecanthropus*, a fine specimen, had been found in a clear and certain stratigraphic situation, in the base of the fluvio-lacustrine beds of the Trinil horizon.[5]

De Terra has given a glimpse of Teilhard in Java:

> From Burma we went via Singapore to Java, where Dr von Koenigswald expected us for a joint excursion to the Solo river, to Trinil and Sangiran. It was in April, 1938, that we made a memorable trip along the Solo river. Von Koenigswald had arranged for us to stay overnight in a native hut, where we slept on the ground watched by a lot of villagers.
>
> The day following we walked through forest along the river and got frequently mired on the muddy path. Drenched from perspiration, we used to joke about Father Teilhard's tennis shoes and the way he retrieved them now and then from a muddy patch of the road. Our noon meal, coconut milk and bananas, was taken under a cluster of palm trees. A native seeing us in our muddy clothes took us for some escaped convicts, but when he learned that we were collectors of old bones he fled in haste as if he had seen ghosts. When we arrived in late afternoon on a highway where we expected to meet our car, my friend looked pale and exhausted. It was the first time that I felt seriously worried about him, but when he recovered on the following day we found out how eager he was to join us on a trip to a Palaeolithic site in eastern Java.

APPENDIX

A brief chronological table may be useful before treating the last months of Teilhard's first Peking period.

1932

4 July	Departure for Shansi
September	Departure from China for France
late September–January 1933	Stay in France

---

[5] Cf. the letter of 28 May 1938: "In Java I saw with von Koenigswald the new *Pithecanthropus* skull and its bed: clear stratigraphic position, entirely within the Trinil layers, so magnificently exposed at Sangiran near Solo. The skull is as well preserved as the first *Sinanthropus* skull described by Black. The vexing thing is that it is not yet possible to correlate the magnificent industries of the South and the Northern Man beds."

1933

February–March	Return trip, Marseilles–China
late June	Departure for Shansi
late July	Departure from China for U.S.A.
July–September	Stay in U.S.A.
later September	Departure from U.S.A. for China

1934

11 April	Departure for middle Yangtze
13 May	New departure for the Yangtze as far as Szechwan
17 July	Departure for Honan

1935

January	Departure for Southern China (Kwangsi and Kwangtung)
May	Return to France via the Trans-Siberian railway
6 September	Departure from France for Bombay
20 September	Arrival at Bombay
22 December	Departure from Calcutta for Batavia

1936

15 January	Departure from Batavia for China
late July	Departure for Shantung

1937

25 February	Departure from China for U.S.A.
April	Departure from U.S.A. for France
19 April–5 August	Stay in France
6 August–8 September	Return trip to China
6 December	Departure from China to Burma

1938

24 March	Departure from Burma for Java
16 April	Departure from Java for China via Singapore
mid-September	Departure from China for U.S.A.

This part of Teilhard's life was marked by a triangle of limited extension. The apex is Peking, where Teilhard frequented the Cenozoic Laboratory and the office furnished him by the Survey. From Peking he went to Choukou-tien, to supervise the excavations, and to Tientsin, both for his retreats and for work in his other laboratory (the Hwang-ho-Pai-ho Museum), where Trassaert, for example, was working. From the triangle he branched out to the United States (on which he depended, for half his friends were there and Chinese science was supported by American foundations) and France (where he wanted to establish a solid position for himself, where he counted other very dear friends, where he had left the better half of his soul, and where he might resume the contact he needed with the spiritual movement of his times).

The movement towards Southern China, with the bifurcations towards India and Burma, and Java, was dictated by purely scientific reasons.

At the beginning of this period Teilhard already "held" Northern China and its Manchurian and Mongolian dependencies, and he had penetrated Sinkiang. In the course of this first Peking period, while consolidating his hold upon Szechwan, his favourite domain, he progressively "annexed" Southern China, Szechwan, then Kwangsi (and Yunnan). His knowledge of Sinkiang permitted liaison with Kashmir and the Punjab; his knowledge of Yunnan, a connection with Burma and Java.

CHAPTER FOURTEEN

First Peking Period:
Last Months

WHATEVER troubles Teilhard had had with his religious superiors, he seemed now to have settled down to a peaceful acceptance of his position. Nine-tenths of what he wrote could not be published, but he himself could still work as a leaven in the world in which he found himself. On 25 May 1933 he wrote:

Rome has told me . . . that I must refuse any situation or official appointment that might be offered me in Paris.

A year later, however, he says, "My relations with the authorities are peaceable."

But the day was passing when he would be strong enough for strenuous field trips. A month later he wrote:

Nevertheless the years go by, and often I think I note the lengthening shadows that mark the journey's end. The only thing that keeps me youthful and active is the growing belief that there is something immense, something beautiful about to take place throughout the world, and that we must abandon ourselves to the mighty current of this development.

In 1937 he was ill. His reserves enabled him to recover, but he was left weaker than he had been. By 1938 he was quite worn out and apprehensive. It was therefore time for him to leave behind some permanent mark in France. This was the motive behind his *Rapport en vue d'obtenir un laboratoire des Hautes Études pour des recherches de "géologie continentale" (considerée dans ses rapports avec la paléontologie humaine)*, a plea for a continental geology related to human palaeontology, addressed, 1 October 1937, to the

Director of the Third Section of Higher Studies and strongly supported by Marcellin Boule (Director of the Institute of Human Palaeontology), Breuil (teacher at the Collège de France and at the Institute of Human Palaeontology), and by Charles Jacob (geology professor at the Faculty of Sciences and Member of the Institut de France).

The aim of this laboratory was to be to connect Pleistocene geology with the earliest appearance of man, and to combine the study of continental geology with that of the evolution of pre-human primates. We know that on 26 April 1938 Rome agreed to Teilhard's taking this Higher Studies laboratory. A month later Jean Zay set up for Teilhard a laboratory for geology as applied to human origins (a laboratory later permanently attached to the Institute of Human Palaeontology).

Teilhard thus once more acquired a plaform in France itself (his natural field of the apostolate), and he could at last return there regularly. His reaction, however, to the news was curiously luke-warm. On 22 June 1938 he wrote:

> In my heart, I am not very enthusiastic about the Higher Studies laboratory; but I thought it was clearly enough the right step to take. Left to my own inclinations, I should prefer not to stir from here. That would have been the easiest choice. In any case, I have decided, as I must have told you, to return to China for some months in the summer of 1939.

While waiting to embark, towards mid-September, for France via the United States, Teilhard remained in Peking. Things were coming to a standstill in the old capital, now increasingly under the influence of its invaders. The number of Europeans diminished. It was impossible to work at Choukou-tien, for any resumption of the digging would have been construed as collaboration with Japan. Happily, Pei was still around, and it was still possible to work at least at half-pressure in the laboratories, and to publish, both on the various Choukou-tien sites and on Shansi.[1]

Scientific life, along with Free China and the Kuomintang, had taken refuge in Southern China, where Young and Bien were at work (one result was increase in knowledge of the southern part of the country). It was in this depressed and half-hearted atmosphere

[1] There was bad news on 30 May 1938: "We have to hand over to a new Minister of Industry the southern buildings of Ping Ma Ssu (Pei's ex-lab, etc.). So far, we are left in possession of the northern buildings."

of the beginning of the end for Peking that Teilhard's preliminary sketches were done for his great work on man, which was to become *The Phenomenon of Man.* These final months constituted in fact a transition period which clearly prefigured his second Peking period—the time of the Japanese "captivity", and the time, too, of Teilhard's great intellectual syntheses.

Two events worth noting occurred during the summer of 1938: the election of Breuil to the Institut de France, and Licent's departure from China:

> Since Licent, you know, left Tientsin for France, you will surely be seeing him in Paris. He seemed very doubtful about returning, though he has not ruled out that possibility. To tell the truth, the Hwang-ho-Pai-ho Museum is taking on a new look, and I have hopes of seeing it soon turned into a continental research institute, with a youthful staff. In a sense, Licent made it all possible—while making himself impossible. It's odd how in some ways he and Boule are so much alike; perhaps that's why they could never hit it off. (22 June 1938.)

Indeed, what had been Licent's museum was already styling itself: "The Institute of Geobiology". Licent had been interested only in the basin of the Yellow River (a vast field, to be sure). Teilhard was envisaging research on a continental scale, in a spirit quite different from that of a collector and curator.

Poor Father Licent! In 1937 his buildings had been at last completed, his laboratories had been organized, and young Jesuit collaborators had been sent to him. But then came the Sino-Japanese war, and sickness; and Licent, who had travelled tens of thousands of miles through difficult country, using primitive means of transport, and had accumulated so great a mass of data was now obliged to give it all up. Father Pierre Leroy, his historian, concludes:

> Henceforth he was to live in Paris; his kingdom was to be no longer a continent, but the little room of a religious; the itinerary of his travels was to be the monotonous little trip from the Rue de Grenelle to the Museum (exceptionally, Montpellier or the woods of Versailles and Chantilly). This great explorer, built for prying into a world, was now to poke about in a cardboard box, where he kept a few collections of insects. It was in such straitened circumstances that he spent the last years of his life.[2]

[2] *Jésuites de l'Assistance de France,* no. 4 (1956), pp. 15–16. Licent died in 1952. At the news of his death, Teilhard wrote: "I was not aware of Licent's death. A true 'void', despite all." (Letter of 6 March 1952.)

Although Licent and Teilhard were temperamentally incompatible, their names must ever be associated for the work they did in China. It was Licent who, before ever the Americans came, launched scientific research in China; and it was Teilhard who was responsible for its rapid development, gave it continental extension, created a vast network of scholarship, and so solidly educated Chinese scientists that geology and palaeontology flourish today in Communist China. In any case, the successor to Licent was well chosen: the Jesuit Pierre Leroy, who had finished his theological studies and was to be, during Teilhard's second Peking period, the latter's faithful and affectionate companion.

Before telling of Teilhard's return to France, we should consider his not strictly scientific activities. Up to this point it has been possible to fit the development of Teilhard's scientific life (and of his life in general) to his philosophical speculations. As a matter of fact, the vicissitudes of Teilhard's external life produced impacts which had a marked resonance in his interior life, providentially deepening and widening it. Such were the impact of World War I, and its disclosure of the collective soul, and the impact of Asia, which, he found: "revealed the greatness and the beauty of the earth and its phenomena".

We can, we believe, continue to avoid any artificially imposed symmetry in treating the period under consideration. Of course, the Ethiopian interlude and the Croisière Jaune were merely episodes, and we must not overemphasize their importance. Yet that same period, around 1930, was recognized by Teilhard himself as a turning point in his thought: the moment when a superior structural organization of matter, with its vast psychogenic envelope, gave a closer binding force to the energy of the Incarnation.

We may consider the years 1931–8 roughly as years of preparation. Teilhard proceeded characteristically: a series of relatively short, compact, systematic and closely knit essays,[3] whereby he pushed ahead, as streams of lava move ahead through brush, or as reconnaissance units of an army explore the contours of the enemy's lines, forcing him to reveal himself, and seeking to infiltrate the gaps. These essays embodied always the same profound intuitions; yet Teilhard seldom repeated himself.

[3] 1931, L'esprit de la Terre; 1934, Comment je crois; 1936, Esquisse d'un univers personnel; 1937, L'énergie humaine.

In contrast, from 1938 to the end, his great syntheses succeeded one another; and among these one, *The Phenomenon of Man*, was highly developed. *Le milieu divin* was to remain permanently the profound expression of his spirituality. The fundamental themes of *The Phenomenon of Man*, however, had been in gestation for a long time; and by September, 1937, this great synthesis existed consciously in the form of a project at which Teilhard worked from October. On 23 May 1938, Teilhard presented the preliminary sketches for it, and on 5 August 1938 he stated that the first chapter had been begun and was advancing slowly, but surely.[4]

Some years earlier (23 September 1934) he had described the direction of his thoughts:

> I am studying the successive developments of an adherence which, from faith to faith, joins the Christian current (or phylum), by convergence: faith in the world, faith in the spiritual in the world, faith in the immortality of the spiritual in the world, and faith in the expanding personality of the world. It seems to me that I have a better grasp than a year ago of ideas that allow me to believe in it seriously.

In fact, as he explained on 14 February 1935, his spiritual edifice was "built on the basis of a complete adherence to the supreme value of what is developing around us, and in us, in the universe." Christianity was seen as the spearhead of evolution and Christ as the only term for a universe struggling towards unity.[5]

A further realization:

> As I recently wrote to Fessard, my present great discovery (?!) is: 1. that the whole human problem comes down to the question of the love of God; but also, 2. that the legitimacy, the psychological possibility (everywhere questioned, to my great surprise), and the triumph of this love depend upon the compatibility (or, better, the essential association) of the two terms *universal* and *personal*. . . . By and large, our world denies both the personal and God, on the grounds that it believes in the whole! Everything tends to show on the contrary, that it must believe in the

---

[4] For these dates, see *Letters from a Traveller*, pp. 232, 241, 243.

[5] Cf. letter of 4 February 1934: "I often think that if our humanity is really to become more adult today than it was two thousand years ago it somehow needs a 'rebirth' of Christ—Christ reincarnating himself for our intelligence and heart in the dimensions newly discovered for experimental reality. Our Christ must be able to overspread and illuminate these almost boundless advances."

personal precisely because it believes in the whole. (15 August 1936.)

To "baptize" progress and human faith in final unity meant seeking to reveal the convergent character of the universe and the existence of a personal centre of that universe, a guarantee of the conservation of the personal, without which the world would cease to be a place where human, conscious activity is possible, instead of surrendering to the *taedium vitae*, the "what's the use?" so dolorously symbolized by Dürer's "Melancholia". To "Christify" the humanitarian pantheisms entirely oriented towards the universal meant showing them the marvellous and necessary association "... of the universality of the personality which is the God whom we need if we are to be totally human". (End of August 1937.) It meant bringing out the metaphysical, ethical, and mystical riches contained in the formula: "Union differentiates (that is, personalizes)."[6]

His final discovery was the need for a human energetics. As early as 8 October 1933 he disclosed his first presentiments of this need. It was no longer enough, he said, to supply "... oil to the gearbox of the world. Fuel is what is needed now that the universe is seen to be moving forward." In 1936 his energetics began to take shape:

Another concrete line of thought occupying me at the moment (and gradually taking shape) is this: The practical science of man (morality, economics, political science, and so forth) seems to have been conceived until now chiefly as a problem of balance, giving to each his rights, his daily bread, his territory, and so forth. Now, instead, we find a problem of energy—of giving to mankind its full of spiritual energies. I imagine it is here that men in the future will increasingly seek the rule for determining wherein consists the good. (22 November 1936.)

The connection between this human energetics and Teilhard's notion of the personal universal is clear:

... the proper function of Christianity in the world ... in my opinion comes down to this: animating (superanimating) human effort: 1, by presenting it with a limitless outlet, beyond the narrow circle of present cosmic dimensions; and, 2, by presenting

[6] Cf. the letter written as early as 15 July 1929: "After the idea of the Spiritual, that of 'Person' immediately assumes, in my view of the World, an extraordinarily increasing importance."

this outlet as a superior personal centre, one not only theoretical, but from now on partly perceptible in the domain of facts ("Revelation," Incarnation). In this twofold way Christianity seems to me the supreme motive force of human progress, the crown of the universe's culmination in man. (15 December 1936.)

Pascal, too, devoted himself to a sort of existential analysis of man. Pascal was continually emphasizing that the intolerable discrepancy between man's greatness and man's wretchedness could be explained, not on purely logical grounds, but only through reference to the mystery of original sin, a mystery which provides an approach to all the other mysteries.

But Pascal, great as was his genius, lived in a pre-evolutionist and pre-Marxist universe. Teilhard, in contrast, had broken right away from the Neolithic age, and felt himself plunged into space-time, that is, that tremendous cosmic evolution whose momentum terminates in mankind as the culmination of the universe, a mankind become conscious of itself and submitted to the acceleration of history constituted by progress.

The contradictory make-up of man, insoluble in a static universe, even though it does not disappear, in Teilhardian thought, ceases to be the main problem; for in evolutionist perspective man, by all the evidence, is an unfinished being. Even though the problem of evil (including original sin) had to be fitted into Teilhard's synthesis, his apologetics had a wholly different scope from Pascal's: Teilhard's interest was to determine under what conditions an evolution become conscious of itself might continue its task, and to show that Christianity, rightly understood, and broadened to the dimensions of our new cosmos, answers those requirements.

A still more decisive passage in one of his letters, written 27 June 1937, in English, brings out the conscious progress of Teilhard's thought:

> Never before, perhaps, did I perceive so clearly the possible meaning of the deep evolution of my internal life: the dark purple of the universal matter, first passing for me into the gold of Spirit, then into the white incandescence of Personality, then finally (and this is the present stage) into the immaterial (or rather supermaterial) ardour of Love.

Meanwhile Teilhard was feeling that as a scientist by the beginning of his second Peking period the midday of his scientific career had long passed:

I have the impression that I am, during the time that the Lord spares me, in the prime of my scientific performance. Yet I feel that I must hurry. I keep having the strong feeling that my sun is hastening towards its setting. It is four o'clock in the afternoon for me, so to speak. . . . (26 March 1932.)

Thus we find a paradox. On the one hand, the joy of learning seemed to him all the more pure as research appealed to him more and more as "the burgeoning higher form of adoration". (26 March 1932.) On the other hand, though his publications in the field of science did not decrease, from 1935 to 1937 he was disengaging himself from geology and the whole science of the past. As someone rightly said of him, "Paradoxically, here is a scientist whose speciality is the past, but who is interested only in the future."

But all this must not be allowed to obscure a thoroughgoing coherence of thought. When Teilhard wrote: "What is past is dead, and does not interest me any more" (18 January 1936), he was expressing no weariness, no senescence, no fall in creative power, but an attitude resulting both from his closer mystical contact with Christ, the radiant vision of whom increasingly occupied his attention, and above all from the fact that the object of his activities, fruitful though these were, was withering in his grasp. In the past Teilhard had already read its essential message: "that we are borne on an advance wave of consciousness" (8 September 1935). Apparently he had already perceived what would be the basic principle of his phenomenology, that is, that the coming into being of anything must be understood in terms of its culmination, and that nothing is intelligible save in terms of the totality of its future.

But so little did Teilhard actually abandon the pursuit of the positive sciences that, as he indicated in 1932, he felt it his special vocation to conduct his philosophical inquiries on the margin of, or within the radius of, science.[7] Already he was conceiving a generalized physics, which would not be a metaphysics, for "it is the human phenomenon *here and now* which is the clearest, the most illuminating, and the most 'fruitfully' paradoxical for modern physics." (11 October 1936.) Without rejecting, for all that, the transcendental principles of classical metaphysics, he dreamed of a

[7] Cf. letter of 23 May 1932: "To sum up: I pursue with all my might, and I will pursue so long as I have the power . . . my scientific line. But behind it lies a whole religious attitude to the World and to research that has developed in my life . . . and it is this above all that I wish to spread, through such reputation as I may have as a scientist."

phenomenology which would satisfy the craving for totality which, underneath all the compartmentalizing and all the differences in techniques, is the hidden impulse of the scientific spirit:

What I should like is to construct a continuous series of *phenomena* extending, under the action of a fundamentally unique evolutionary process, from the spiritual to the material pole of experience. As you know, my "*hobby*" is showing that science is marking time, and turns its back on religion, simply because scientists have never attempted to integrate *thought* into their systems. It is towards *history*, then, that I am tending, rather than towards metaphysics. (13 October 1933.)

It strikes me, at the moment, that there are two kinds of knowledge: an abstract, geometric, extra-durational, pseudo-absolute knowledge (the world of ideas and of principles)—and this kind I *mistrust*, instinctively—and a "real" knowledge, which consists in the *conscious actuation* (that is, in the extended creation) of the universe around us. The first of these two kinds of knowledge changes neither the world nor the knowing subject. The second coincides with both a perfecting of the world and an ontological growth in the knowing subject (this is especially the case with mystical knowledge). . . . I mistrust metaphysics (in the customary sense of the term) because I feel it is a sort of geometry. But I am ready to recognize another kind of metaphysics, which would really be a hyper-physics—or a hyper-biology. (29 April 1934.)

. . . I should be happy to see you do what I am trying to do, that is, penetrate still further into spiritual and human questions by the use of the methods of science, substituting for the metaphysics of which we are dying an ultraphysics (the real *phusike* of the Greeks, I imagine) where matter and spirit would be embraced in one single coherent and homogeneous explanation of the world. (11 October 1936.)

We spoke, at the end of the preceding period of Teilhard's life, of a powerful experience of spiritual liberation.[8] There is no such thing as "pure" religion, still less is there any esoteric Catholicism. It remains none the less true that we must distinguish between the essential and the secondary, the latter often being due to mere historical accidents, tending to obscure the essential, and to certain interpretative ritual and moral constructions built up in the course of the centuries. Now Teilhard, from the period spoken of, made

[8] Cf. letter of 3 July 1933: "I have the obscure feeling that something stirs and grows within me; as if, during his period of complete liberty, the true 'me' continues to free itself of the world of conventions."

a sharp distinction between the primary and the secondary category, a definite advance.

Sure of his adherence to the essentials, he went ahead with his exploratory thinking, and paid little attention to the fate of the accidentals or to the activities of those who cherished them. But he was surprised when people did not try harder to see what there was of the constructive, and even of the conservative, in his own endeavour.

Earlier he would have loved to see his influence freely working, and clearly exhibited; but now he discovered real happiness in the consciousness that he was working obscurely, and in a supreme gesture of adoration. Never for an instant did the idea cross his mind of turning his back on his Order, to pursue an independent career. To do so would have stifled his confidence that he was in the hands of God. He succeeded, in short, by the grace of God, in reconciling an irrepressible originality and an iron fidelity to the Church and to the Jesuits. Nor was he long in receiving his reward:

> ... since perceiving more distinctly than I did two years ago what is priceless, and irreplaceable, and cosmically necessary in Christianity, I have become much more filial in my attitude. When people love what they criticize, they can criticize without danger. (11 October 1936.)

Ama et fac quod vis. Teilhard intimately loved Christ both in the Church and in the Society of Jesus, and humbly and simply accepted the function of an invisible leaven. He learned from his somewhat trying relationships with the representatives of authority to meditate more profoundly on Christ, to feel more deeply his membership in the Mystical Body, and to appreciate more keenly his missionary vocation of turning modern unbelief back to Christ.

In the course of the Croisière Jaune, in fact, Teilhard was surrounded by non-believers, not to say militant anticlericals. His Chinese companions, apart from the Buddhist Wong, lived in a complete agnosticism to which Christianity made no sense. About his American and English associates it is more difficult to judge, except in the case of such clearly religious persons as Dr Barbour and Mrs Swan.

On 7 January 1934 Teilhard was writing:

> In replying to Mgr Bruno de Solages, I told him again how much everyone in the Far East is looking for a book on the essence of Christianity—or on the Christian point of view as contrasted with the Confucianist or Buddhist—that would appear in all their

languages. Such a book, however, would have to have something of the breadth and serenity of Bergson's latest—a book with a natural development, and made up of ideas. The origin of faith in Christ, starting with a simple faith in being ... a passion for the truth. Who will give us this *Summa ad Gentiles*?

The missionary zeal of Teilhard apparent in *Comment je crois* is now clear. It was to satisfy it that he elaborated a whole hierarchy of acts of faith, the first being faith in the world, in the hope of finding a common ground with non-believers. As he expressed it, the problem was this: "If one is to influence by contact, one must first be reborn, in such a way as to have a living conception of the world to contribute."

We may justly say that Teilhard's career developed amid critical circumstances. He made his Jesuit juniorate during the height of twentieth-century French restrictions on clerics and religious. He completed his seminary studies at the height of the Modernist crisis. From 1923 he was a first-hand witness of the anarchic conditions prevailing in China. From the time of Japan's virtual annexation of Manchuria (1931–4) he was caught up in the Sino-Japanese struggle. Japanese immorality and brutality were unspeakable.

Nor was tragedy confined to the Far East during Teilhard's day; mankind itself was in crisis. Tension among the powers of Fascism, Communism and democracy increased, and in 1936 the Spanish Civil War began a series of ideological wars. Teilhard was grieved at having to be absent from Europe during these times, first because he never liked to feel that he was shirking active service, and secondly because the turn in human affairs taking place at that moment bore immediately upon his own preoccupations. He objected to the various brands of Fascism as lacking the spirit of progress, and was alarmed to see rallying to them all the defeatist, conservative elements in the world. His own attitude towards the whole imbroglio was the combative optimism of a citizen of the world seeking to use his bent for synthesis to rally all progressives to a common programme:

> What you tell me about political conditions has been pre-occupying me deeply, even from the theoretical point of view of the future of mankind. ... My concept would be a new movement, rallying the progressive energies of the world to the following programme: universalism, futurism (that is, faith in a renewal of the world), and personalism. This may not have the appeal of the

old "liberty, equality, fraternity", but it is a programme for reconciling kindred forces which, at the present time, are divided among the old, already outmoded categories of democracy (confusing universalism and individualism), Communism (confusing universalism and equalitarianism), and Fascism (confusing the past and the future). Once agreement is reached on the general course to be pursued, there would remain to be found the politico-economic forms which, *technically*, would be the best (the American, the Italian, or the Russian type—it would be all the same to me). My chief concern is that the new spirit be freed for action. . . . I am alarmed at the attraction that various kinds of Fascism exert on intelligent (?) people who can see in them nothing but the hope of returning to the Neolithic. (15 October 1936.)

The outcome of this was Teilhard's short *Sauvons l'humanité, réflexions sur la crise présente* (1936 and 1940).[9] Teilhard's universalism had about it nothing of the utopia (so contrary to the facts of biology) of the equality of races. But the most interesting thing to note is that Teilhard's political theory not only was in harmony with his general conceptions but also faithfully reflected his synthetic bent. A few pages earlier we remarked on how much the science of this specialist in the past was oriented towards the future; here we note that the programme he proposes is a resolute rejection of all that is reactionary, and a refusal to be frozen in outmoded political categories. His association of universalism and personalism re-echoes his religious theory of a personalist universe, with the love of God as the inexhaustible source of human energy, since love is the only force which makes things one without destroying them; love alone, then, might harmonize the totalitarian tendencies of human society on the one hand, and the realization of personality on the other. All of Teilhard's thinking was coherent: his political theory, his working out of synthetic categories, his mystical discovery that union differentiates, and, finally, his energetics.

On 28 September 1933 Teilhard wrote a sort of profession of faith, which he was to stand by until his death, and which sums up his intellectual and religious position at that time. He wrote it in English:

We cannot be fundamentally, and inexhaustively, happy, but in a personal unification with something personal in the Whole (that

---

[9] In a shortened form it appeared in *Études* (1937).

is, with the Personality of the Whole). This is the ultimate appeal of what is named Love.

Hence the substantial joy of life is found in the consciousness, or feeling, that by *everything* we enjoy, create, overcome, discover, or suffer, in ourselves or in the others, in any possible line of life or death (organic, biological, social, artistic, scientific, etc.) we are gradually increasing (and we are gradually incorporated into) the growing Soul or Spirit of the world.

This feeling presupposes only that we have a passionate human heart, and that we admit, in addition, the following three points, namely:

1. The evolution or birth of the universe is of a *convergent, not* of a divergent, nature—towards a final unity.
2. This unity (gradually built by the work of the World) is of a *spiritual* nature (spirit being understood, not as an exclusion, but as the transformation or a sublimation, or a climax of the matter).
3. The centre of this spiritualized Matter, spiritual whole, therefore, has to be supremely *conscious and personal*. The Ocean collecting all the spiritual streams of the universe is, not only something but somebody. He has got Itself, a face and a heart.

If one admits those three points, the entire life (including the death) becomes for each of us a continuous discovery and conquest of a divine and overwhelming Presence.

This Presence enlightens the deepest secret zones of everything and everybody around us. We can reach it *in the achievement* (*not* in the mere enjoyment!) of everything and everybody. And we cannot be deprived of it by anything, nor by anybody.[10]

---

[10] Another statement complements the passage quoted: "You ask yourself: 'Is scientific research a derivation or a deviation?'—I think that it is one form (one of the most perfect, of the most direct) of what we call being, or life, or Evolution. I cannot define the World otherwise than by a gradual awakening of consciousness: research is precisely the frontier in the spreading of this universal consciousness. Thus, the question of the value of our efforts is solved. Our efforts have the same value as the Universe which atomically develops itself in each of us. It all comes back to accepting the hypothesis that the Universe is neither a negligible nor an absurd thing—and that as a consequence it is satisfying (or even beatifying) to be entrusted to that which develops itself in one's depths. This hypothesis seems to me infinitely more probable than the other. Logically, we are caught between only two possible attitudes: we mistrust things so deeply that we go on strike against them, or we trust them so fully that we accept them with passion."

(Letter of 10 December 1933.)

CHAPTER FIFTEEN

Franco-American Interlude:
Second Peking Period:
Scientific Activities

TEILHARD's life from 1938 until his death in 1955 began with a Franco-American interlude, and then fell into three parts: the second Peking period, the second Paris period (the first was from 1919 to 1923) and the final American period. Intellectually there was a constant progress, but these years were also a time of final synthesis, and brought Teilhard to full realization of spiritual unity.

Towards mid-September of 1938 Teilhard, exhausted and worried, left China. But he did not go at once to France. He took Father Pierre Leroy to Japan to see what could be done to protect the position of French scientists in Northern China. Leaving Leroy in Japan, on 21 September he boarded the *Empress of Japan* at Kobe, on 4 October reached Vancouver, and a week or so later had established his headquarters with Granger in New York. After a weekend in Worcester with his Peking friends, the Merells, a visit to the Moviuses at Harvard, and a staff meeting at the American Museum, he left again for France, arriving in November.

We know more about his half-year stay in France. During this time he visited London[1] and several parts of France, giving

---

[1] Teilhard belonged to the Zoological Society of London and was an Honorary Life Member of the Society of Vertebrate Palaeontology; in 1937 he was made Honorary Fellow of the Royal Anthropological Institute. This trip had a special purpose: to meet Patterson at Cambridge and persuade him to serve as De Terra's substitute on the American Museum's projected expedition to the basin of the Indus and the Sutlej.

some talks at Toulouse upon the invitation of Mgr Bruno de Solages.[2]

Although Teilhard wrote (15 April 1939) that he "had accomplished little scientific work during this period", his bibliography, which is reasonably copious for 1938–9, shows that he was a little severe on himself.[3] At the same time he was busy planning a more methodical investigation of continental geology, visited Cambridge while in England, kept in close touch with the Far East, wrote as usual to Young, and wrote to Granger in the United States, asking him to send Young and Bien some books on the palaeontology of the Vertebrates, since the Geological Survey of China, in its retreat at Kunming, found itself terribly short of such works just at the moment when the Chinese were making gratifying discoveries.

Another example of the kindness which always prompted Teilhard to help others. Similarly, on 6 February 1939, he undertook to place his finest Tientsin collaborator, M. Trassaert, with Gaudefroy at the Institut Catholique, to be initiated into the study of mineralogy.

Needless to say, Teilhard kept up with the latest developments in science. For example, on 13 March he noted the fine Neanderthal skull that had been discovered in February by the Italian scientist Alberto Carlo Blanc, who after World War II was to become his devoted friend.

[2] "Before his return to the Far East, R.P. Teilhard de Chardin, at the invitation of the Most Reverend Rector, agreed to devote some days to Toulouse.... On 26 February he spoke to the Philosophy Society on 'La place de l'homme dans la nature et la structure qui en résulte pour l'Évolution'. On the 27th he gave a lecture to the Faculté des Lettres on the excavations at Choukou-tien and the *Sinanthropus*. On the 28th he gave another at the Institut Catholique on the geology of the Quaternary of China and the Far East. Finally, on the 29th, he spoke in the great hall of the Institut, before a very large audience, on prehistoric research in Burma. His Grace the Archbishop presided at this session." (*Bulletin de littérature ecclésiastique*, no. 2 (April–June 1939): "Chronique de l'Institut", p. lxv; cf. in the *Bulletin* the résumé of the lectures by Fr F. M. Bergounioux, O.F.M., pp. 92–3).

[3] Cf. also the letter of 5 January 1939: "I am settling in in my lab (just beginning) at the Institut de Paléontologie Humaine in the room next door to Breuil's. Boule still comes in twice a week; and then the afternoons are spent listening to the old but always interesting stories of the Golden Age of Prehistory. The old man's mind is still terribly sharp, and so full of good sense in scientific matters. In fact, I have not furthered my scientific work very much since my arrival here.... Nevertheless, I am beginning to do something about organizing a 'collaboration' in Europe and North Africa for the systematic study of the continental deposits of the recent Cenozoic."

Several letters give us the key to Teilhard's activities during this time. The following three were written in English:

Something deep and broad is obviously moving in the world, and in France especially (far behind the ridiculous political stage). Since a fortnight, I have been spending hours, almost every day, with the most extraordinary variety of people, ranging from the boundary of the working class up to the most refined, agnostic or sophisticated parts of the society. Everywhere I find the birth, or at least the expectation, of the new creed of man in a spiritual evolution of the world. (7 December 1938.)

Indeed poor France, in some ways so weakened in her external energies, seems to be tremendously alive inside, much more so perhaps than any other country in the world. I had the most unexpected meetings with the most influential—and sometimes, you might say, the most incredulous—people in Paris. And each time, I realized I could give them, at some extent, the thing they are craving for....

I am deeply interested in your impressions of Washington. The need of a change in the heart of politics, an "ideal" for democracy: you are absolutely right. I am just having a series of talks on this subject with a group of influential young men in Paris.... If we succeed, something new will come in the world. This is the very fight of my life. Art and idea. I have met the problem already three times since I have been in Paris. This great question we shall discuss, because I need an answer. (Christmas, 1938.)

I had an especially interesting talk, which will amuse you, to some sixty artists (sculptors, painters, writers, musicians) forming a new section in the group for the study and improvement of Man, organized by the French *ingénieur* [Jean] Coutrot in association with Aldous Huxley. I had to address this select gathering at the end of lunch and my subject was, "How to understand and use art in the line of human energy." I expressed the idea that art was the expression of the "exuberance" of human energy, so that its function is to give a kind of consistency, an intuitive and almost instinctive shape, and a *personal* character to this ever growing supply and excess of spiritual forces gradually freed from material ties: like science and philosophy, but in a much more spontaneous and personalistic way. (29 March 1939.)

Later, after addressing some Catholic clubs for young people, he wrote:

I am convinced that unwittingly we are taking part in one of the most revolutionary movements in man's history, a movement taking place with *not a trace* of any sort of bitterness or hate: simply love—but love founded on the conviction that the world is converging towards *someone*, someone equally loving and well defined. And this is the point where my poor intellectual efforts come in: to these young workers, girls and boys (as to other classes of people) my "views" furnish a prospect where past, present, and future meet in an atmosphere of material progress and progressive love. Once again, probably, a new life is spreading from the masses below. (7 April 1939.)

From these and similar letters we gather that Teilhard was extremely active, and not in propaganda, but in priestly action. Not only did he often see people of importance, like Lecomte du Noüy,[4] but he expended himself in every direction, in every sort of company—believers or non-believers, workers or *bourgeois*.[5]

The time was auspicious. In France, where forebodings of war and catastrophe reigned, intellectual activity was more vigorous than ever, and there was a premonition that the world was approaching a decisive crisis, and was entering a period of profound change. Teilhard, whose ideas were now fully matured, felt himself especially fitted to meet the anxieties of the time. Through the darkness of the storm he could discern the ever brightening rays of the Omega, and the rapturous dawn of the ultra-human. His optimism was not blind; he was well aware that the masses had need of enlightenment; but his sanguine spirit was aggressive and contagious, because founded on absolute hope, and justified by the synthesis of Christian faith and faith in progress.

He extended his priestly activity. He began to reach the working classes. Yet he never meddled in politics. Though he had wished

---

[4] "Who was at that time passing through a hypercritical or even sceptical phase with regard to the spiritualizing and hominizing value of Science." (Letter of 25 August 1947.) Lecomte du Noüy had been disappointed by the elementary materialism of certain scientists in his group, and by pessimism about Man and Science. The first meetings took place aboard the liner *Ile-de-France* during the New York–Le Havre crossing: "We immediately developed a mutual sympathy." (Letters of 7 November 1938.)

[5] It is not easy to identify the groups whom Teilhard addressed. The only one we can be certain of is the Légaut group. Their organ was a stencilled monthly, *Le Moncelet*, edited and run off by the Abbé Gaudefroy. In this we find, February, 1939, "Observations on the significance and biological conditions of research" (a lecture by Teilhard); 30 April 1939, an essay on Teilhard's *L'énergie humaine*, by Pierre V.; 21 May 1939, "The place of man in nature" (a lecture by Teilhard). Teilhard's influence was, in fact, counterbalanced by that of Gabriel Marcel.

to avoid seeming to shirk active duty, he now felt himself above the dust and smoke of battle, in the best meaning of the expression. He had never been a progressive in the narrow sense of the term, nor a Christian democrat, and still less a demagogue. At the same time he succeeded admirably in speaking to workers, manual or otherwise, and was later to be a warm partisan of the worker-priest movement. His spirituality, in fact, had a spontaneous turn towards work and a natural attraction towards Christ the Worker.

It was not surprising that, with his eyes so directed towards the future of mankind, Teilhard shared in the activities of technicians interested in human problems. What may seem more surprising is that he was to be found delivering a talk on aesthetics, the problems of which had hardly interested him before.

Teilhard was never an aesthete, nor an antiquary, nor a collector. He scarcely went out of his way to visit museums, and it was some time before he went to see the curios of the Peking Imperial Palace, whose errors in proportion had shocked him. Though talented as few writers have been, he took no care with his style. Yet it would be wrong to argue that art was a closed book to him. Like his sister Françoise, he had a passion for all beauty, but only in its connection with the Eternal. A great city was more to him than a museum of natural history.[6]

True, Rome failed to enchant him, but that was because he went there after having contemplated too many finer beauties; in contrast, one witness tells of seeing him stop to admire the scenes of Paris. Admittedly, he wrote (3 April 1930):

> The greatest happiness that a gothic cathedral provides me with is the triumphant consciousness that our minds have now escaped from its vaulted aisles for ever!

But he qualified his sentence with a parenthesis: "I find such a building marvellous, of course."

He in no wise disdained the company of artists. In China he knew the American sculptress Lucile Swan. When he used to watch her work he used sometimes to say in his blunt way: "This is wrong." And, Mrs Swan tells us, he was always right. He met Mrs Swan, by the way, in late 1929. "Almost at once," she recalled, "we were engaged in serious conversation. Speaking as a scientist he said

[6] In this connection, see an important letter (2 February 1953) in *Letters from a Traveller*, pp. 336–7.

that the deeper he went in science the more sure he was that there was a God ... it was a light to me."

In 1939, in the United States, he met another sculptress, Miss Malvina Hoffman, who later did a bust of him, as Lucile Swan had done two or three years earlier. In Peking, he became a friend of the painter Mond, who painted in the Chinese manner; on seeing one of Mond's pictures, Teilhard exclaimed: "My dear Mond, how I regret never having studied art!" About 1945 he was a member of the Society of the Friends of Music, founded by Mme Arsène-Henri, wife of the French ambassador to Japan, and an excellent musician, whom Teilhard used to ask, for example, to play Beethoven sonatas, to which he listened attentively, though otherwise, aside from Wagner, he had little taste for music.

Later, in Paris, he knew Jean Cassou and the painter André Marchand. He used to go, moreover, to concerts and to the big art shows, and was interested in sacred art. Love of beauty, with him, was as if unconscious and spontaneous. He saw it, and expressed it, as if instinctively, without artifice; for he was a man of truth, and beauty sprang out before his eyes like the splendour and the halo of truth.

This visit to Paris opened Teilhard's second long Paris period (1946–51), a period of activity and struggle. But on 23 June 1939 he boarded the *Champlain* for the United States. About his stay here we know little more than is found in the *Letters from a Traveller*, two unpublished letters, and an unpublished note. In New York, he was busy during most of July at the American Museum, where he again met Weidenreich, who was to spend the year there. At the end of July he visited George Gaylord Simpson on the day when the first copy of the latter's *Quantitative Zoology* had reached its author.

Next he went to Chicago, where he visited his friend Field, and proceeded to the San Francisco area, where he took part in a convention of geologists at the University of California in Berkeley:

> ... I concluded my stay there by attending the San Francisco convention, where I gave two talks. Probably the most interesting conversation I had was with Bailey Willis, who in youthfulness of mind might be compared only to you. He is working with youthful vigour on a vast theory of the formation of the continents (the Asian especially) as resulting from successive deposits of granite; and I must say that this line of thought, which already had some vague shape in my own mind, immediately fascinated me.

After leaving the Bay area by train for the Pacific Northwest, Teilhard reached Vancouver and embarked once more on an indigo sea where he watched the flying fishes play (though his mind was elsewhere—especially on the European powder-keg) until, in late August, he arrived in China. As things turned out, he was to remain a virtual prisoner in Peking from 1939 to 1946.

We know more about this second Peking period, thanks both to the correspondence (particularly in *Letters from a Traveller*) and to an unpublished talk given by one of Teilhard's closest friends on 3 January 1957 (of which we shall be making extensive use here).[7] During the winter of 1939, he had hopes of being able to go south, to Yunnan, but finally gave up the idea on account of the responsibility of the Cenozoic Laboratory. Towards mid-June he was forced to go to Tientsin to try to set to rights the Hwang-ho-Pai-ho Museum, which had suffered from the floods of that year.

I recently spent a week at Tientsin. The flood had been terrible: over two feet of water in the halls of the Museum, and people were going from one building to another by boat. And this was nothing to other parts of town, where there had been water over a storey high in some of the streets. It will never be known how many hundreds (I hear speak of thousands) of Chinese were drowned. . . .

At the Museum, many large fossils (Proboscidia) suffered grave damage; and many Cervidia antlers will have to be pieced together again, having split in the damp atmosphere. I have an interesting plan for rearranging the geology and palaeontology room. The upshot of the flood at Tientsin was extensive damage to a number of pieces (Proboscidia jaws and Cervidia antlers). We hope to salvage what is important, but have not yet done so. And, from the lack of coal, the large rooms are too icy cold to stay in. As regards the Museum we have plans for extensive alterations in mind (even for the essential nature of the institution). But I cannot tell you of these till later. No point in your making any mention of this to Licent, you understand, if perchance you should run into him.

By mid-October of 1940 he found himself picnicking almost every Sunday in the Western Hills close to Peking. Towards the close of November he made a trip to Choukou-tien. All this autumn he

[7] See also articles by Georges Magloire in *Synthèses* (May, July, October, November, December, 1957), later published together by Grasset (1958).

had been hoping that in another year he would be able to go to the United States and, with the help of the fine Frick collection there, do some work on his Shansi Pliocene Carnivora. But this plan was brought to a sudden end by Pearl Harbour (7 December 1941). The summer following, he spent some time by the sea, in Manchuria, and in the autumn went to Shanghai and gave an address at the Université Aurore. After his return from Shanghai he had not, he wrote over a year later (13 November, 1943), stirred from Peking.

> ... save for an excellent four-day stay in the Hills with an old friend, Dr Bussière ... who here in the heart of China has succeeded in re-creating a corner of Auvergne (situated on granite, too, like Auvergne).[8]

Nor did Teilhard foresee any travelling to speak of until the war should be over; the good old days (however tiring sometimes) of fruitful explorations seemed now over and done with. And of course scientific activity was curtailed:

> Of course, what is tedious is not having the stimulus and illumination of new material any more. We have just the old things to work on.

His contacts with the outer world were sporadic, apart from the brief correspondence with Sven Hedin quoted earlier in these pages. Since December of 1940, in fact, Teilhard had complained of being out of any useful touch with field research. As for his trip to Choukou-tien, with an impressive escort of influential Japanese (and an amusing and quite pointless deployment of military forces),[9] this was simply to inspect the condition of the beds, where any work was out of the question. The site, of course, was intact, though the workings had been thoroughly rifled. In 1940 there was some hope that diggings might be resumed in the spring, but this had flickered out. Fortunately there remained the laboratories.[10] The Cenozoic

---

[8] At the end of August, 1944, he returned there for three weeks with Fr Leroy.

[9] Cf. Magloire's charming description of the expedition in *Synthèses* (October, 1957), pp. 82–3.

[10] The *Sinanthropus* skulls were originally in strong boxes at the Peiping Union Medical College. Weidenreich had written to Chiang Kai-shek to persuade him to send them to America for safe keeping. Finally he consented. The skulls were packed and given to American soldiers who, at Taku, had agreed to take the chest with them. But after Pearl Harbour the Japanese ordered the confiscation of all American goods and the chest disappeared. Neither the local constabulary nor the Japanese military police who had been

8*

Laboratory[11] was still open; Weidenreich, after his year in New York, was again active there; and Teilhard (with Pei, his sole support) worked there regularly, for in the drawers was an enormous amount of material that had to be catalogued and described, locality by locality. All these odds and ends of description seemed extremely tedious, but Teilhard had resolved, once they were finished, to distil them into a kind of "zoology of China", wherein the various groups would be presented along with their history from the Lower Pliocene onwards. He felt the product would be enlightening on account of the abundance of precise data, covering a large number of separate beds. On 18 February 1941 he wrote:

> ... we are concentrating on laboratory work (there is still a pile of things to be studied and described); and I am also trying to synthesize, in several ways, data scattered over the past twenty years in too many fragmentary publications. This kind of work turns out to be much more interesting—absorbing, in fact—than I thought when I began.

Actually, the project did not turn out exactly as planned, and became Number 8 in the Publications of the Institute of Geobiology: *Chinese Fossil Mammals, A Complete Bibliography* (1942, in collaboration with Pierre Leroy). This was something less ambitious, perhaps, but it lay more within Teilhard's competence as a specialist in mammals; it was a complete and handy reference work; and it demonstrated the brilliant outcome of the collaboration (dating from 1920) of the Licent Museum, the Uppsala palaeontologists, the Central Asiatic Expedition, and the Cenozoic Laboratory.

Speaking of Licent's Museum, we must recall that its buildings were part of the complex of the business college founded by the Jesuits. It so happened that a number of students here, from Southern China, found themselves caught in Tientsin by the troubles of the time, with no possibility of the Jesuits' building

---

called in were able to find it. It is possible that the Japanese N.C.O. in charge of making an inventory of the American crates at Taku had simply thrown the skulls into the water. According to another source, the chest containing the *Sinanthropus* had been put down on the shore in a little cove off Tangshan. There they disappeared. See the testimony of Colonel Ashurst in the *New York Times* for 5 January 1952. See also Magloire's amusing story of Japanese discomfiture at Peiping Union Medical College.

[11] The Cenozoic Research Laboratory still belongs to the National Geological Survey of China. Of course, Peiping Union Medical College was emptied of its foreign and Chinese personnel by the Japanese after Pearl Harbour.

dormitories to house them. The Rector decided to take over the Museum, and the new director, Fr Pierre Leroy, was told to gather up all his treasures—everything from the thousands of embalmed frogs and fish to fossil elephants—and find them a new home in Peking.

In Peking, the French ambassador, Henry Cosme, made room for them in the embassy guard-barracks. Teilhard, though grudging the amount of time wasted, set out for Tientsin to undertake the task of dismantling, sorting, and airing. This staggering undertaking kept him busy during all May and June of 1941. Teilhard and Leroy had had an idea of changing what had been Licent's Museum into a kind of institute of continental research. But this was to remain partly only an idea, for to realize it they would have had to find a good petrologist (principally for research on sedimentary formations) and a good palaeobotanist (especially for the Mesozoic and the Cenozoic), both uncommonly difficult to find in the France of those sad days.

Furthermore the projected name for the institute had to be abandoned, for the "Eastern Ocean Island People" took "continental" to mean "mainland" and to bear political overtones.[12] Nevertheless, the two Jesuits got the organization going under the title of Institute of Geobiology, a name more ambitious than their first choice —Teilhardian, too, since Teilhard was accustomed to seeing everything in world-embracing dimensions.[13] Its purpose remained the same: to study the combined evolution of soil and life on the Asiatic continent, this being considered as a semi-autonomous unit of the earth's crust; and to treat only of such geological and biological facts as had continental relevance.

Teilhard, Leroy, and others wrote articles in connection with this work, and these, despite the difficulties of the time, were published with the help of Henri Vetch, French publisher at Peking, the Ambassador Cosme, and the Alliance Française de Shanghaï. Among the most important of Teilhard's contributions, we may note "New Rodents of the Pliocene and Lower Pleistocene of North China", the importance of which he indicated in these few lines:

That year [1942] I published an article that seems to me one

[12] After Pearl Harbour a Japanese palaeontologist was attached to the Institute of Geobiology.
[13] Teilhard dedicated the Institute to Christ the King. Inside there was an inscription taken from St Paul: "*Ut sit Deus omnia in omnibus.*"

of my better ones, on a group of fossil mole-rats which permits the drawing of certain general conclusions on the living groups.[14]

We have twice pointed out the great importance attributed by Teilhard to the Siphneida. In this article he was able to recast completely the phylogenesis of that group. The same letter adds that "Another article on the prehistory of China, published earlier, also merits attention." The reference is to "Early Man in China" (1941), an original synthesis of all information on formations of the recent Cenozoic and the distribution in China and of human traces in the Pleistocene.

The Institute of Geobiology, despite the difficulties of the time, did more than inspire a series of articles, each devoted to a well-developed analytic or synthetic study of one question concerning the geological or biological structure of Asia. In September of 1943 the two Jesuits launched a review, *Geobiologia*, which appeared for two issues, the second in 1945. It was advertised as being, not a miscellany, but a careful selection of information and ideas, for the benefit of geologists and naturalists of the Far East. Its purpose was not to embrace as much information as possible, but to select such published material as seemed to provide an interesting and important contribution to an over-all understanding of the biosphere. In a brilliant introduction (pp. 5–6), Teilhard defines the term "geobiology":

> ... it should first be remembered that from year to year a double line of evidence has been growing up around us, contributed by scientists of all disciplines, showing that:
>
> First, the world of life, taken as a whole, forms a single system bound to the surface of the earth; a system whose elements, in whatever order of association they may be considered, are not simply thrown together and moulded upon one another like grains of sand, but are organically interdependent like the pipe-lines of a hydrodynamic system, or like molecules caught in a capillary surface.
>
> Secondly, this organic sheet, which is spread over the whole surface of what is often called the "crust" but is in fact chemically the most active "sphere" of our planet, is not, either in its genesis or in its duration, physically separable from the general mass of the earth it covers. The earth is not merely a spatial support for, but the very matrix of, this living envelope. Hence the growing im-

[14] Letter of 13 November 1943. The report was published in 1942.

portance science attaches to the notion of the *biosphere*, considering it not as a mere metaphoric entity but as a physical reality, as objective and as essential to the earth as the various other "spheres" (mineral, liquid, gaseous) whose concentric structure constitutes our planet.

The notion that the inorganic matter of the earth constitutes a natural whole whose elements, far from forming an accidental aggregate, manifest in their proportions and arrangement a definite structure and composition bound up with the atomic and sidereal architecture of the universe, is one long since accepted by chemists and physicists. Hence the remarkable individualization of a chemistry and physics of the earth.

And now the same current of thought manifests itself in the domain of *life*, leading to the same results.

On the one hand, taking shape and gaining momentum (as I have just said), is the movement which tends to bring the biosphere within the range of the greatest scientific realities known to us.

And, simultaneously on the other, the need is becoming felt for a specific discipline consecrated to the investigation of this biosphere.

We already have geophysics and geochemistry.

Now, completing the triad, appears geobiology.

Defined as the "science of the biosphere", geobiology stands on its own, distinct from such other disciplines, such as palaeontology, ecology, or biogeography, whose subjects of study are likewise life in its relations to the past or to the whole extent of the earth. In fact, it is not simply a branch of biology, as those sciences are, and of rank co-ordinate with those sciences, but it stands above the whole group as their dominating principle out-ranking, directing them and binding them into a single whole, with a dual object, inalienably its own, namely:

The study first of all of the organic links of every description that are recognizable between living beings considered *in their totality as a single closed system.*

And, secondly, the study of the physico-chemical links by which the birth and development of this living envelope are bound up with the history of the planet.

Here assuredly is a most characteristic aspect of Teilhard's science. Though Teilhard had constantly shown himself a first-class analyst, he had always envisaged, as an ideal, a global and synthetic science. In his view, there are organic connections among all living things, with the result that the sum total of living things constitutes a whole, this whole, in turn, being bound up with the global physico-chemical evolution of the earth (itself a function of sidereal evolution).

The Institute of Geobiology by no means undertook to cover the enormous field of inquiry described above; as the review specified (pp. 6–7):

> Beginning with the auxiliary postulate (plausible, indeed, but still to be tested by experiment) that the continents are not accidental fragments but natural units of the earth's crust, whose nature permits an approach to the problem of the biosphere on a reduced scale without distortion, the Institute has set itself the following threefold goal:
>
> 1. To study, in every possible way, the formation of the Asiatic continent.
> 2. To reconstruct, at the same time, the gradual establishment and differentiation of the flora and fauna of that continent; and
> 3. To make clear, if possible, the synchronism and reciprocal action of these two developments.
>
> Restricted thus to this preliminary subject of the genesis and genetic interdependence of the continents and their flora and fauna as represented by Asia, geobiology represents in reality a "mental attitude", a method, an avenue of approach rather than a fully individualized science.

The positive, practical sense in Teilhard's thought is immediately apparent; despite his passion for synthesis, he kept his feet on the ground and never lost his sense of the real. Being in Asia, and particularly familiar with the Far East,[15] he limited himself to it as a typical case.

In the geological sphere, Teilhard gave preference to problems of a more specifically continental nature, the recording and analysis of recurring phenomena, and the investigation into coherent and continuous processes underlying recurrences of various kinds. For this reason the first publication of the Institute of Geobiology, signed by

---

[15] North China is a wonderful "laboratory" for the palaeontologist, for the fauna developed there continuously without having been hunted or destroyed by cataclysms. Already Teilhard had for a long time sought to reform palaeontological methods by making it more "biological", that is, by placing the fossils dug up into the biological context of the area studied: "one of the first attempts, never before tried, if I do not deceive myself, to build up a Zoology wherein no difference would be made between living and extinct forms in the same region". (*Titres et travaux*, p. 7.)

Teilhard, was entitled *The Granitization of China* (1940); in it he suggested the formation of continents as due to granitization, by a sort of positive and irreversible growth—the ultimate explanation of flexurations having to be sought in the pressure of subcontinental magma. It is for the same reason that in the first volume of *Geobiologia* there appeared (p. 43) his well-known article "The Genesis of the Western Hills", a tectonic and geological synthesis on the heights close by Peking. In this he says:

> The exceptional interest of the Western Hills for geology, therefore, is that their formation exhibits, on an elementary scale, and in remarkably pure conditions of simplicity, a tectonic mechanism ("flexuration") whose study should clarify our views on the building of the continents.

In short, the genesis of the Western Hills constitutes a case exceptionally illuminating in its simplicity; and the phenomena noted there find a surprising parallel in the Japanese Cordilleran mountain chain. Thus the whole of Teilhard's scientific production, happy accidents apart, followed a sort of logic, a sort of intellectual prearrangement. Even exterior constraints and limitations were made to contribute to the interests of science; for example, had Teilhard not been a virtual prisoner in Peking, would he have had time to devote himself to so deep a study of the Western Hills?

If we have here devoted some time to the Institute of Geobiology,[16] we have done so in order to emphasize once again one of the characteristics of Teilhard's science—its synthetic tendency—and to show that it did not stagnate through deprivation of contact with the field (the Western Hills excepted). Yet beginning with the latter part of 1943, though he continued to publish, he was beginning to feel that he had run out of original material and could now do no more than resift older material. Time passes quickly; and it was precisely the years on which he had counted so much that ran on, he thought (though he was hardly fair to himself in so saying), "with nothing accomplished" (a letter of 13 November 1943). As

---

[16] The Institute was in fact the heir of Yenching University, the Cenozoic Laboratory, and the Fan Memorial Institute; this last was founded thanks to the liberality of a Chinese Maecenas named Fan, whose purpose was to assemble in laboratory-museums collections relating to the natural history of North China and to allow specialists to analyse them in a series of publications pertaining to the different disciplines (zoology, botany, general biology, palaeontolgy).

for the fields of philosophy and religion, these were profitable and fertile years; his philosophical and religious thought, too, found a solid basis in science:

> ... gradually, through a slowly effected *rapprochement*, through exposure to the facts, between the two connected notions of the genetic structure of fauna and the genetic structure of the continents, a third notion, that of the genetic structure of mankind (considered as a biological unity *sui generis*, of planetary dimensions) has finally established itself in the mind of the geologist.

CHAPTER SIXTEEN

Second Peking Period (1939-46)

IN the letter of 13 November 1943 quoted above, Teilhard added:

> To make up, I am extending the list of my scientifico-philo-sophico-religious manuscripts—still on the same themes, but going deeper and simplifying my views.

His unpublished works were, in fact, piling up, from *The Pheno-menon of Man*, the bulk of which was finished in June, 1940, to *Vie et planètes* (June, 1945). Among these (13 December 1934) was his very important *La centrologie*, which attempted to present,

> ... under the form of a sorites, an essay of universal explanation: not an *a priori* synthesis, not a kind of geometry taking some definition of "being" as its point of departure—but an experiential law of recurrence, verifiable in the field of phenomena, and correspondingly capable of being extrapolated into the totality of space and time. Not an abstract metaphysics—but a realistic ultra-physics of union.

In the second Peking period he evolved two themes: complexity "engenders" consciousness; and reflection grows. These maxims contain the essence of what is called in Teilhard's phenomenology the law of direct proportion of complexity and consciousness, and what is viewed in Teilhard's eschatology as the appearance of the ultra-human, made possible by the progress of reflection.[1]

Pascal saw man as lost between two infinites, the infinity of greatness (as we should say today, the macroscopic), and the infinity

---

[1] Cf. letter of 30 April 1952: "... under the influence of the facts and of the development of my thought (particularly in China) during the war, I have become convinced that the right thing *for me* to do ... is to express and defend my conviction that we are progressing (because of socio-technico-mental convergence) towards an ultra-human, and towards a higher centre of that ultra-human."

of littleness (the microscopic). Teilhard was aware of a third infinite, corresponding in his mind to the actual drift of the universe, the infinity of complexity. Complexity he saw as the extraordinary capacity of matter, in the framework of space-time (that is, of evolution), to produce more and more complex structures so long as the physico-chemical conditions are favourable.

From the well-known progressive series: crystallization, formation of macromolecules, appearance of viruses, appearance of living cells, combination of cells in colonies, and then in organisms, upward thrust of life towards a more and more complicated nervous system —from these Teilhard abstracted the law of complexity-consciousness.[2] Matter tends naturally towards life, which appears when the structure is sufficiently complex. Life then creates, around the earth, a sort of envelope whose reactions are increasingly adaptable and free—the biosphere.

But when the nervous system, and particularly the brain, attains sufficient development, the more or less elementary psychic quality of life is transformed in turn into consciousness, which means that life, in man, acquires the singular property of reflective thinking about the world around it and about itself, and becomes conscious of itself. There thus supervenes upon the envelope of life a new envelope, the noosphere, the sphere of thinking humanity; and this then tends to assume mastery over the evolutionary process.

Another novelty in Teilhard's thinking was the priority of the collective over the individual,[3] the collective being understood as a biological super-organization, allowing mutual consciousness of elementary individual consciousness. This is consciousness to the second power, a super-consciousness; for once the human threshold is crossed, consciousness continues to progress and to grow.

Nietzsche's idea that man is an uncompleted being is well known. Nietzsche, however, envisaged an individual superman; human activity now appears more and more to be a type of teamwork, especially in the scientific sphere. Mankind, under whatever political régime, is tending towards collectivization. Teilhard's idea, in har-

---

[2] Cf. the letter written as early as 28 July 1939: "... the great problem of the hour (in mysticism and religion as well as in morals, in history, biology, physics, in metaphysics and in sociology) is to set up a new conception of Spirit, no longer in opposition to, but in transformation and sublimation of, Matter."

[3] Teilhard put it strikingly: "The isolated man no longer thinks and no longer progresses."

mony with his law of complexity-consciousness, was that if mankind really succeeded in becoming organized collectively, the make-up of the collective organism would be matched by a higher consciousness. In short, human socialization is not an epiphenomenon, but an authentic extension of hominization, and thus of human evolution. Human socialization, in fact, is man's hope of achieving that ultra-human condition which will allow him to mirror the Divine with greater fidelity, until the day when humankind, in an extreme tension, will slide into ecstasy by its most spiritualized (Christianized) part.

These ideas were now being developed both in his writings and in the lectures he was often asked to deliver. In November and December of 1940, Teilhard gave three talks to very different audiences (a college women's association, a Protestant theological group, and a Yenching University audience). The French embassy asked him to talk, on 3 March 1941, on the future of man as seen by a palaeontologist. In 1942 at the Université Aurore at Shanghai he delivered a talk so successful that some listeners, dismayed at the force and originality of his ideas, asked him not to come back.

Sometimes, too, he rather shocked his audience, when it contained a certain number of "gentiles" (as he called non-believers), for then, to avoid irritating them, he avoided the use of the word "God" entirely, and spoke only of "Logos", or "Omega", to the great scandal of those who were expecting traditional homilies in the style of the nineteenth century.

We hasten to add that he used the name God in every other case, for God was to his mind a self-evident fact. On 26 March 1943 Teilhard spoke on human fossils at the Catholic University of Peking. On 28 December of the same year he lectured on his own ideas on happiness. Several of his shorter works were developments of lectures he gave. So it was with *Vie et planètes*, also given as a lecture at the French Embassy in Peking, 10 March 1945, but in this instance before an audience of admiring, and generous, Americans. That it originated as a lecture is clear from the text:

Today we are unquestionably living and experiencing events bound up with the general evolution of earthly life, events of planetary dimensions. It is therefore in a planetary perspective that you ought to place yourselves—and I invite you to place yourselves for some minutes, with me—so that you may be better able to understand, better able to support, and better able—if I may say so—to love what is going on around us, is greater than ourselves, and draws us along with it. How, in the light of the vastest, newest, surest conceptions of astronomy, geology, and botany (conceptions interpreted both objectively and optimistically)—how does the world-wide adventure in which we are all involved appear? That is what I am going to try to establish during this evening with you.

Later, we personally heard some of the talks given by Father Teilhard. We noted that his natural shyness was not apparent, and that he seemed to possess great poise. The plan of his discourses was always clear, didactic, in the best sense of the word. His nicely modulated voice served a vigorous mind, and he used neither a manuscript nor many notes. His manner was simple, distinguished, and restrained. On the platform he indulged in few pleasantries; his thought had too much gravity to allow any frivolity or even to spare his audience—it was grave, heavy with meaning, but never inflated, much less oracular, despite the immense perspectives that it opened up.

During these years, Teilhard profited from his enforced leisure by reading a great deal, and making notes and comments on what he read. Since books in English were easier for him to obtain in China than books in French, English titles predominated.

Among literary classics and works of at least more than ephemeral interest we note several with a religious theme. He read, for instance, Dostoievski's *The Possessed*, Gide's *Lectures on Dostoievski*, Tolstoi's *The Kreutzer Sonata* and *War and Peace*, Graham Greene's *The Power and the Glory*, Camus' *The Plague*, Sartre's *Nausea*, Sinclair Lewis's *Elmer Gantry*, Santayana's *The Last Puritan*, and Koestler's *Darkness at Noon*.

Non-fiction works with a religious theme included the following: Sir Arthur Evans, *The Earlier Religions of Greece in the Light of Cretan Discoveries*; J. L. Myres, *Who Were the Greeks?*; De Labriolle, *The Pagan Reaction*; Rougier, *Celsius*; E. Troeltsch, *Christian Thought*; Barth, *God in Action*; F. Foerster, *Christ and Human Life*; Maréchal, *Studies in the Phychology of the Mystics*; Roger Bastide, *Problems of the Mystical Life*; Aldous Huxley, *The Perennial Philosophy*; Johans, *To Christ through Vedanta*.

Philosophical works included Novalis, *Fragments*; some works of Nietzsche; Bachelard, *The New Scientific Spirit*; Condorcet, *Pros-*

pectus of an Historical Table of the Progress of the Human Mind;
Cournot, *On the Progress of Ideas and Events in Modern Times*;
Gobineau's *Renaissance*; Gide, *The Future of Europe*; Gerald
Heard, *The Ascent of Humanity*; Toynbee, *A Study of History*. He
also read with interest Draper's *History of the Conflict Between
Religion and Science*.

As indicated in part earlier, besides Nietzsche, he had read
Spinoza, Leibniz, Karl Marx, Bergson, and Maurice Blondel. An
interest in the philosophy of science was not surprising in a naturalist
who kept up with the latest development in physics and had studied
Whitehead's *Science and the Modern World* and Juvet's *The Structure of the New Physical Theories*.

Of more importance was Teilhard's interest in the philosophy of
history. He was familiar with Spengler and Toynbee, of course, and
expressed the greatest admiration for them, but, faithful to his bent
for synthesis, may be said to have come out the same door that
he went in. He felt that, while treating human social evolution in
terms of biology, they still kept history outside of and apart from
biology, separating the domain of zoology from that of culture.
Teilhard, in fact, maintained that human collective unities are psychological species, groups just as natural as any variety of ruminant
or carnivore, with the difference that in human collectivities the
psychic element has become preponderant, and that chromosomatic
heredity, graven in the germ cells, is matched by a kind of extra-
individual educational heredity, which ensures both the retention
and the expansion of what has been won.

At the same time Teilhard was reading works of general biology,
sociology, and ethnology. Among these were Darwin's *Descent of
Man*, Jean Rostand's *Thoughts of a Biologist*, J. Murphy's *Primitive
Man; His Essential Quest*, Gerald Heard's *The Ascent of Humanity*,
Oswald Spengler's *Man and Technics*, Marcel Blanchard's *Saint-
Simon and the Saint-Simonians*, John Dewey's *Can Science be
Humanized?*, James Burnham's *The Managerial Revolution* (to
which he devoted long meditation), B. Malinowski's *The Argonauts
of the Western Pacific*, E. Nordenskjoeld's *Origin of the Indian
Civilization in South America*, and P. A. Means's *The Ancient
Civilization of the Andes*.

The list is an instructive one, for, though Teilhard always had an
interest in ethnology, we are struck by his readings in sociology.
Life, as he noted, has a social aspect; living beings have a tendency

to associate; indeed, among the insects life has become the captive of socialized instincts. For man, collective activity alone holds forth the promise of self-transcendence, according to the law of complexity-consciousness, by which every heightening of complexity is proportionate to a higher consciousness. The development of an increasingly complex social life, as necessitated by the demands of scientific research and an advancing technology, and by the drawing together of populations through advances in transportation and communication—this whole development opens to the noosphere immense vistas of progress. Teilhard did not fear a technological civilization. On the contrary, he abstracted from it its deep-lying spirituality, and so restored it to Christ.

With this went an interest in economics, which was not due simply to curiosity. Capitalism is directed above all towards production and profit, and leads to unemployment; Teilhard believed that there is a biological coincidence between the appearance of unemployment in production (unemployment which sets free a part of human energy) and human endeavour to advance evolution through research, by promoting discovery. Why not use this freed energy for the vital ends of the human evolutionary future? The whole problem consists in transforming raw energy (the greater part of the unemployed do not belong to the working or the intellectual *élite*) into creative energy, a transformation which would allow the era of profit to be changed into the era of discovery. Teilhard's sociology is one of the most important chapters in his human energetics. It mattered little to him what form of government was used to achieve the end; the important thing was to prevent the waste of human potential, and to speed up, through rational organization of research, the supreme development of mankind (always with a view to giving Christianity new possibilities of self-transcendence).

It was particularly fortunate for Teilhard that he could find an intellectual stimulus in such books at a time when he was very much cut off from the world outside Peking. Thus he wrote:

Despite everything, on the whole we here are cut off from every main current of life (many such a current brushes by us, but without catching us up or moving us). The result is a kind of creeping torpor. Here, then, I feel, despite the suffering and tragedy spared us, we are in a bad place to pass through the present crisis. (13 November 1943.)

At the same time, however, he was heartened by the feeling that the world was in the process of a thoroughgoing renewal:

I wonder whether you, in France, feel today something of that change of perspective or of scale as regards human values which was our experience during World War I. I refer to certain things which now count less, or count not at all, compared with certain others. My hope—and up to a certain point my conviction—is that we are coming into world conditions which will forbid us any hope of patching up the old wine skins (Matt. 9.17), and that we are due for a change of diameter in the sphere which will burst the old envelopes.

In short, Teilhard managed in difficult and even depressing conditions to carry on. When he arrived in Peking at the end of August, 1939, his reception was not an encouraging one. He was received by the Jesuit superior, a man nicknamed (from his real name) the Great Navigator. This superior was not an especially tolerant and broad-minded man, and at the first opportunity he said to Teilhard: "Father, as an evolutionist and a Communist, you are undesirable here, and will have to return to France as soon as possible."

"A Communist? I'm not a Communist!"

"You are an evolutionist, and that is sufficient to show that you are a Communist."

Until 1937 Teilhard had lived at Pet'ang, with Peking's Lazarist bishop, Bishop Montaigne; here he was subject to a little teasing, but allowed to go his own way. On 6 November 1937, however, he wrote that he had just moved:

Much against my will, I have had to leave Pet'ang. The Jesuits have just founded a house here for young recruits who are to learn Chinese. So, I can't very well live elsewhere. In fact, there are certain advantages in my new situation; when all is said and done, I am more permanent here, and, in a sense, at home. But there are plenty of drawbacks: The house is in an out-of-the-way location (north of Fu Jen! a half-hour by rickshaw from the Peiping Union Medical College and a quarter of an hour from the Survey); the building has as yet only the bare essentials; there is a miscellaneous group of nationals (predominantly Spanish and Canadian, which is to say exclusive), whose preoccupations and occupations have nothing in common with mine. But all that is a trifling matter. They are as kind as possible to me, and I shall make out all right here as elsewhere. The only thing is that I don't feel at ease. Tientsin would be far preferable.

Chabanel Hall, named after a Jesuit martyred in the seventeenth century in Canada, was a disagreeable place, where a very strict discipline was enforced; it consisted of a collection of barrack-like buildings, with rows of rooms occupied by priests and scholastics busy studying Chinese and leading a highly austere student life; (moreover, one could hear everything from one room to another). Here Teilhard spent as little time as possible, leaving every morning and evening for the Peiping Union Medical College, which he reached by a pleasant walk through the imperial park, a springtime view of which appears in a letter of 2 April 1940:

Yesterday I strolled through the imperial park on the way back to my "monastery". All the cherry trees showed pink against the grey earth, under a dust-dimmed blue sky. A real Chinese spring, unconscious of the troubles of the war.

Happily, after the Hoang-ho-Pai-ho Museum's conversion into the Institute of Geobiology, Teilhard was able to leave Chabanel Hall. The Institute was located among the embassies, so far away from the building piloted by the Great Navigator that commuting was impractical, and the only solution was for Teilhard to stay at the Institute with Father Leroy.[4]

Here Teilhard's schedule was a very regular one. At seven in the morning he said Mass. About eight he and Leroy smoked a cigarette and talked together for twenty or twenty-five minutes; then, saying, "Well, to work!" he took up a notebook which served as a kind of philosophical daybook, in which he wrote down ideas which had germinated during the night. Indeed, Teilhard had this peculiarity, that his power of thinking doubled when he was lying down. Sometimes, in the afternoon, he was found lying on his bed, his head on both hands; and following this postprandial thinking he would scribble indecipherable notes on odds and ends of paper, to be thought over again the next day and committed to his notebooks.

His morning notebook work lasted till nine, when he would go to the Cenozoic Laboratory and work on some scientific article until noon. In the early afternoon, at two o'clock, he would be back at the Cenozoic, busy with the Choukou-tien fossils, emptying and inventorying thousands of cases. There was still some activity in Lockhart Hall at the Peiping Union Medical College (where the

[4] A pleasant place, run by a Fr Minister, or procurator, with a little court-yard, fruit trees and chickens.

fossils were stored), since Pei was still there, and Weidenreich as busy as ever.

At five Teilhard used to go out visiting—for three hours only, for at the last stroke of eight the door of the Institute of Biology was locked by the Jesuit in charge.

Sundays, when the weather was fine, were a break in the week's monotony. As already related, Teilhard, towards mid-October of 1940, took to going to the Western Hills; and there was always a place reserved for him in the big wagon which the French colony used for picnics.

On arrival at the picnic grounds, Teilhard always asked, "What time shall we be eating?" Then he would set off, in his khaki trousers and felt hat, his geologist's hammer in his hand (and later, wearing the red armband issued by the Japanese to "enemy aliens"), to return at lunch-time with fine specimens of rock and even of fossil plants.

In December of 1940 life in Peking, the good old life of former days, was not yet extinct despite the departure of many of Teilhard's American friends. Grabau was still there, and Grabau's home, with a woman's touch now to lend it grace, had regained its former liveliness and even a touch of gaiety. People loved to gather there on a Sunday afternoon, reviving an atmosphere almost like that of old times. As the Japanese power extended, however, the life became more constricted; people to talk with became fewer, more and more Americans were packing up, and the French colony, though the embassy remained, continued to thin out.[5]

Teilhard, given to thought as he was, loved to provoke discussion on ideas. Generally, too, his ideas emerged clarified and strengthened by this treatment. Every evening he would broach some wide subject: love, union, personalization; and on every occasion he displayed his gift for phrase-making. Though it has sometimes been said that, while optimistic on the theoretical level, he was never sure of himself, and needed conversation for reassurance, the truth of the matter was that, while he felt a need for conversation, this was not because he doubted his profound vision. Basically, this vision remained unshakeable. One credible witness relates that he never

---

[5] "The embassy with the visitors it attracts from Japan and Shanghai is still the great social resource." (Letter of 13 November 1943.) France had already surrendered by the time Japan entered the war, so technically there were no hostilities between the two countries. Teilhard reserved his Tuesdays for the French embassy.

knew Teilhard to change his opinion after a conversation. Without any conceit, Teilhard dominated all the others, and was never dominated by anyone.

Many different people have testified to the general esteem in which Teilhard was held. His doctor, for example, a Protestant who sometimes discussed with his patient what Teilhard used to call "our little differences of jurisdiction":

Father Teilhard was a patient who edified by the simplicity with which he accepted the little ills that flesh is heir too. It took a good deal of persuasion to get him to take to his bed even when it was quite necessary (as was only rarely the case, by the way).

Mme Arsène-Henry, wife of the French ambassador in Tokyo, speaks of his solid, religious, and priestly mind. In emphasizing his sanctity, she adds this striking declaration: "Whoever has not seen Teilhard say Mass has seen nothing." And here is a part of a letter from Mme Henry Cosme, widow of the ambassador to Peking:

Everyone can make a masterpiece of his life; more have done so than one might think; but few have succeeded so well as Father Teilhard de Chardin. Every person of good will consciously or unconsciously strives to reproduce the example of Christ the God-man. I have never met anyone more earnestly devoted to this effort than Father Teilhard. . . .

Hard on himself, he had the make-up of a real soldier, God's soldier, as a genuine son of the Order he had chosen and to which he was to remain always strongly attached. But more striking still was his unfailing kindness to all, good or bad—a distinction, by the way, which he would scarcely admit, with the result that it was impossible when he was present to make any uncharitable remark. He refused to listen to any accusation, and in each man chose to see only the good qualities, deliberately leaving the rest in the shadow. When with him, therefore, one felt a better person.

But this extraordinarily kind man was also brave. He had devoted his life to combat, to combat against false ideas and against every form of ugliness, fighting courageously, without even taking account of whom he might be addressing or of what might be made of his words, speaking at such times from the fullness of his heart, as an apostle. . . .

French *seigneur* he was and always remained, with a certain detachment that enhanced his magnetism. When he referred to his researches in palaeontology, it was always with diffidence, though fascinatingly interesting.

The testimony of his superiors in China is unanimous. Here are two exactly parallel declarations, by Bishop Montaigne and Fr Charvet, S.J.:

> He lived our life and customarily took his meals with us. His life among us was that of any good religious living in community: daily Mass, spiritual exercises, work.... He was always very affable, very good to everyone, and to us non-initiates always ready to give explanations of his own work that we could understand. His kindness and obligingness made him very attractive to us—in fact, made him one of us.[6]
>
> In his conversations his modesty was always striking. He employed suggestion rather than dogmatic assertion, often interrupting himself with "What do you think?" and "So it seems to me."
>
> ... His personal charm, upon which all were agreed, sprang not only from his simple and natural distinction, but above all from an affectionate spontaneity which put him immediately at home in any company. He was thoroughly human....
>
> Of course, I knew him mostly as a member of our house. Here he made himself just another religious, like everybody else, with no allowances having to be made, nor special schedule. He recognized his obligations simply and honestly. "Don't hesitate to give me orders," he said to me on one of my visits to Peking, "I'm a Jesuit, and I'll obey." Personally, I as a superior never had a bit of trouble with him, but on the contrary very pleasant and friendly relations.
>
> In the privacy of our houses in Tientsin and Peking, he proved an enjoyable companion, given to joking about himself as founder of the "Congregation of the Divine Fantasy". In all his contacts with the Scheldt Mission Fathers when he was on explorations or outings between the Pei-Chang river and Peking he was always simple and friendly.[7]

All this, however, has to do with Teilhard's exterior life. If it is difficult to write of the interior life of a priest, it is all the more so of a priest who possessed two juxtaposed and harmonious spiritual orientations, one, what he called the "cephalic sacramental operation" (meaning the consecration of the eucharistic host); the other, what he called the "Christification" of human activity in all its forms, aiming at a new type of sanctity (to spread through factories and laboratories), culminating in the "universalization" (in the

---

[6] Letter of Bishop Montaigne to the author, 29 October 1957.
[7] Letter of Father Charvet, S.J., to the author, 16 December 1957.

sense of what he called "immensification") of Christ, and in the adoration of a universal, evolving Christ.

It is certain that Teilhard's mind was constantly turned towards the presence of God. He strongly insisted on this divine presence, and never ceased to repeat: "We must think of God." When Father Leroy used to tease him about his neologism "the Omega point," Teilhard would reply, "God is a person, God is a person. We must think of him as we do of a person. A God not a person would not be God."

Petty devotions could have little attraction for a man like Teilhard whose religion had a deep philosophical basis; but he always carried, and used, his rosary. His breviary was full of bits of paper on which he had jotted points from his meditations on the various offices of the day. One day he was invited to Chabanel Hall because the Apostolic Delegate, Archbishop Zanin, was making a visit there. When Zanin found that he had left his breviary behind, the superior of the house lent him the first one that came to hand. Zanin, having said his office, handed it back with the remark: "This book belongs certainly to a man of high spirituality." The owner of the volume was Teilhard.

Teilhard was, in fact, deeply spiritual and burned with the desire to draw closer to God. On 15 February 1940, in the midst of writing his long-planned work *The Phenomenon of Man*, he declared:

> I should like to feel myself already free to forget nature's scientific aspects for a while, and to turn more directly to the consideration of its mystic overtones.

Another aspect of Teilhard's spirituality was his docility to Providence:

> ... the more the years pass, the more I begin to think that my function is probably simply that—on a much reduced scale—of John the Baptist, that is, of one who presages what is to come. Or perhaps what I am called on to do is simply to help in the birth of a new soul in that which already is. In saying this, I do not think that I am trying to get out of any duty. But I think that when Our Lord wishes to bring about some great thing, he produces it out of our simplest and least elaborately calculated activities, without our suspecting what he is about. Such is the story of all the great religious movements, and all the discoveries. . . .

And when it comes to taking an objective view of things, and of my particular capacities, I always come to this conclusion: what is required of me is, while following my individual line, to be at the same time ever more thoroughgoingly a Jesuit. If the great Christ is indeed what we think, and if he really wishes to use me to preach him, it is in the ranks of the thoroughgoingly faithful that he will seek to find me. (13 April 1940.)

Moreover, the second Peking period was one of exterior and interior crosses.[8] Life was harassing for him in the Chinese capital. Cut off from so much, he felt he was growing stale; moreover he experienced a series of physical and psychological torments during these war years,[9] and to these were added probably stages of mystical purification.

Teilhard suffered greatly during his life. The one great trial, indeed, was always spared him. Never did the light of his faith flicker out, or even grow dim. It may even be said that in his case faith and hope (the one drawing the other in its train) went on ceaselessly growing, becoming more and more heroic in the measure that religious obedience deprived him of the human means of realizing the apostolate which was his basic reason for existence. He was as much convinced of this as in 1934: one can act only by

[8] He sometimes suffered from hunger and cold. Naturally, he felt the fall of France deeply as well as his own helplessness in the matter. He was greatly disturbed even before the disaster: "I ask myself sometimes if I am right in not returning to the country [France]. If you have an idea don't hesitate to tell me what you think or feel." (Letter of 20 December 1939.) And after the catastrophe: "The collapse of France has been a hard blow, but perhaps necessary. What makes me more anxious in the matter is that I have not felt so far, from where I am, the rebirth of a true constructive spirit. A new formula must be found and will eventually be found in order to achieve Man, and the Vichy people seem (from afar) the least able to discover it." (Letter of 5 September 1940.) He never felt the Lucretian detachment of "Suave mari magno ..." Cf. letter of 5 July 1940: "It is time for the French to have much courage, faith in the future and imagination. It is now that I really regret not being in France."

[9] On this point the witnesses are definite and unanimous. Teilhard suffered cruelly from the contrast between his own vision of God and views that are still too frequently accepted.

A letter (Letters from a Traveller, 5 April 1946) summarizes the effects of these years. "These seven years have made me quite gray, but they have toughened me—not hardened me, I hope—interiorly. The first war started me on the ladder. This one has cut clean across my life, but I have a better grasp of certain distinct central points, and to those I wish to devote all that is left to me of life."

believing in one's liberty and in the existence of God, and one cannot act *as if* one believed, that is, continue to act despite a serious doubt of the reality of liberty and of God. To imagine for an instant that Teilhard could ever dissociate action and faith would be to misunderstand him utterly. Complex and full of qualifications as was his thinking, still he was monolithic, incapable of simulating a faith that had ceased to be his. And it was precisely for this reason that he was able to bring back priests to the Church, or to clear up their doubts on this or that essential point of faith.

But, if Teilhard never experienced the pain of feeling himself drifting far from the true Church, he experienced frequent contradictions and frequent opposition; and he suffered deeply from not seeing his major books published. In April, 1944, *The Phenomenon of Man* reached Rome. An early answer could hardly be expected in those difficult times. But on 6 August 1944 Teilhard learned that ecclesiastical permission to publish the work had been refused; he would have to present the manuscript for consideration again, in a revised and more acceptable form. His disappointment was profound; it was sad to think that because this or that point grated a little, his views, constructive, and of high contemporary interest, could not be published, and might even be lost for ever.

And Teilhard exclaimed: "*To worry, to worry* [in English] . . . Life, the more conscious it is, is so painful that it is explicable neither as *état-en-soi* nor *pour-soi*!"

If the Cross seemed to him a symbol of progress, of achievement, of return through the effort of centration, of super-centration (and of course by redemption), he recalled that Christ, too, came as an ex-centrant, that unavoidable suffering (and such alone) is a reserve, an energy of excentration, infinitely precious, and that it constitutes an energy of decentration of the element in God, directly. Teilhard even wondered, with characteristic conscientiousness, whether he had perhaps not overlooked this point since *Le milieu divin* (in which he accorded it its due place). At the same time, his warm nature allowed him to recover his gaiety and liveliness. As he says somewhere: "It is absolutely necessary to keep smiling. The essential, and doubtless most fruitful, gesture is to smile, with something of love in the smile."

One evening when he was feeling more than usually depressed by a feeling of his own uselessness, a sudden relaxation was granted him. He heard a clandestine BBC broadcast on the radio; the announcer's voice came in, weighted with an accent of regret: "We have just learned today of the death of Father Teilhard, who was assassinated by brigands in Tibet." This cheered him immensely.

When, on 25 June 1947, at the instance of the Foreign Affairs Ministry, he was promoted to the grade of officer of the Legion of Honour, the citation summarized all that France owed to Teilhard the scientist:

> Outstanding service rendered in the propagation of French intellectual and scientific influence, through a body of writings, written and published for the most part in China, which have won the highest standing for him in international scientific circles, American and British in particular. He may be properly ranked today, in the field of palaeontology and geology, as one of the glories of French science, the international prestige of which he has done so much, through his personal relations with scientists of other lands, to develop and maintain.[10]

[10] This is confirmed in a letter from Movius to Professor Le Corbeiller at Harvard: "It is simple justice to point out that no part of the Ancient World (in which researches into the origins of man have been undertaken and are presently going on) owes so much to the direction and individual organizational capacities of a single man as does China." (21 May 1952.) This chapter had been completed when Max-H. Bégouën produced, at the tenth reunion in honour of Teilhard de Chardin at Cerisy-la-Salle (24 July–4 August 1958), an unpublished essay entitled: *L'heure de choisir—un sens possible de la guerre* (Peking, Christmas, 1939), in which Teilhard offers us an admirable lesson in hope: "At the roots of the great troubles in which the nations find themselves engaged, I think I can see the signs of a new age for Humanity. . . . Whether we wish it or not, the era of tepid pluralisms has definitely come to an end. Either a single people will succeed in destroying and absorbing all others, or all people will come together in a common soul in order to be more human. This, if I make no mistake, is the dilemma posed by the current crisis. . . . If only, under the shock of events, the passion for unity could be kindled among us and burn more fiercely than the passion to destroy. Perhaps the other side may come to see that, though we fight them, we respect them and need them more than they imagine they hate us. Then they would see that we resist them only to bring them what they want. Cut off at its source, the conflict would thus die of itself, and for ever."

CHAPTER SEVENTEEN

Second Paris Period (1946–51)

O N 8 May 1945 the bells of Peking announced the armistice in Europe and moved Teilhard to write:

V-Day Relief, but not "joy"; for, in itself, at least here and now, this brutal victory of Man over Man is not a victory on the part of Humanity.

On 17 August of the same year the Japanese troops, after the two-fold lesson of Hiroshima and Nagasaki, ceased fire in China. The road to France was thus open to Teilhard. The British consul-general at Chungking granted him a visa, and an aeroplane was put at his disposal—through the influence of his American friends—by an American general, which deposited him, bag and baggage, the following 26 March at Shanghai, where he could take a ship, the *Strathmore*. On 1 April they touched at Hong Kong; by 30 April he was in England, embarking three days later at Newhaven for France. He had unfortunately had to abandon almost all his books and papers at Peking, as well as the bronze bust of himself done by Lucile Swan—another copy being fortunately preserved. As for the papers, among them some philosophical notebooks, they were left at the Institute of Geobiology, then moved to Chabanel Hall. What became of them after the Communist seizure of China nobody knows.

In attempting to describe this second Paris period of 1946–51 (the first was 1919–23), we meet some serious difficulties. First, it is evident that the first trip to South Africa in 1951 meant no break in the development of Teilhard's thought. We do not know the date of his last suggestive work, *La convergence de l'univers, l'évolution converge*, though it was some time before 25 July 1952. After 1951 no new planet appeared in Teilhard's intellectual sky, even though it was bright with the synthesis foreshadowed in *La Terre Promise,* a title he gave to the final chapter of his last essay, *Le Christique.* The break in 1951, then, appears purely exterior, leaving his inner life unaffected; it seems all the more artificial in that he had heard the call of South Africa as early as 1946.

A second difficulty is that these years in Paris were astonishingly complicated. As Teilhard remarked, in letters of 7 October, 4 December 1947, and 12 May 1950:

> I count on the Lord to show me the way, step by step. At the moment I am not able to see very clearly. I advance only one step at a time, into the fog ahead. I live from day to day, following the thread of ideas which goes on being spun out even after I thought there was no more left.

Teilhard had many friends and contacts in Paris, but it is impossible to determine which were of real significance. At first we get the impression of a scattering of forces, we might even say, of a worldly life. Teilhard was not a society priest, yet with his aristocratic background he found himself at home in drawing rooms, for instance, that of Marianne de Goldschmidt-Rothschild, or that of the Duchesse Edmée de la Rochefoucauld, where he met Paul Valéry, Maurice de Broglie, Leprince-Ringuet and Paul Rivet (we note a passage of a letter from Paul Valéry to R. Jouve: "I did not get to see Teilhard, missing my always charming discussions with him"). He was also at home in the world of diplomacy, renewing the friendships he had made in Peking. New contacts and new invitations followed in a sort of chain reaction. Unfortunately he was now a famous man, and hostesses figured ways of capturing this brilliant conversationalist who, with his critics (so necessary for discussion), provided lively entertainment. Teilhard, we may say, was conversationally at home with much of the *élite.* He corresponded with Emmanuel Mounier, personalist philosopher and founder of the well-known review *Esprit.* He was in contact with Roger Lévy, professor at the École Nationale d'Administration and a specialist in Pacific affairs. Levy went to see him at the *Études* office, questioning him at length on Chinese politics and on Chinese Communism. He invited Teilhard and Gabriel Marcel to visit his home together. Teilhard was also often in scientific circles. After the liberation, Paul Rivet, the founder of the Museum of Man, had started to arrange for a group to dine regularly, every

9+

three weeks or so, at the Museum's restaurant; it included Inspector-General Dayras, Detœuf, an engineer, Guillaume de Tarde, Francis Perrin, Henri Boucher, Sauvy, Isambert and Parodi. They were men of every political and social point of view, bound together by a friendship and desire to understand one another. After a first invitation, Teilhard expressed a desire to join this group, and naturally was immediately admitted. He was at first very regular in attending the meetings, but later came less frequently because of his failing health, until towards the end of 1950 he stopped altogether, to the great regret of all the members.

Teilhard was touchingly loyal to his Far East friends now in Paris, and he worked hard to keep up their morale and find work for some of them. As suggested in *Le Prêtre*, however, this "social life" sprang much less from a desire to cultivate his popularity than from a fidelity to his vocation. His influence operated both on individuals and on groups. In the mornings, Père Teilhard welcomed many friends at *Études*. The afternoons were reserved for his works and his own calls. Among others, he received intellectuals, young or middle-aged, who were enthusiastic about his thought, who argued with him, questioned him, collected his writings and even sketched out works along his lines. He was never vain about this, but encouraged them, seeking to clarify issues, to orient and set them on the right path, with great patience and occasionally with forbearance. These relationships, moreover, were not purely intellectual. It was through the exchange of ideas that the Teilhardian spirituality operated, and as the young people entered into his confidence, he shared in their lives: one asked him to witness his betrothal (we have already noted that Teilhard spoke at the wedding of Claude Haardt, the son of the explorer, in 1948); another, already married, asked him to baptize his daughter.

His later departure for America did not break these attachments and was, in fact, the occasion for valuable correspondence. It was evidently Teilhard who gave the most in these relationships, but the others supplied him with intellectual fodder: news, newspaper clippings, articles from reviews; while, with their questions and objections, they provided a helpful stimulus.

Upon his return to Paris in June, 1946, Teilhard wrote enthusiastically:

I am very excited and absorbed by everything I see in France. Could it be that France is truly the cradle where, after two thousand years, Christ is pleased to be reborn "universally"? In any case, a light is certainly rising on the horizon.

The following year he was more precise, in a letter dated 7 October:

> Since my return, all my time has been taken up with work, mostly para-scientific—conversations and all sorts of lectures—oriented in the direction which has always been and is now becoming even more essential: a re-thinking of Christianity on the scale and dimensions of the Universe as it is revealed ever more clearly to us.

He made endless contacts in order to bring himself up to date. In May or June of 1946 there was a meeting between Teilhard and Berdiaeff at Abbé Pierre's home. They discussed the subject of "Marxists and Existentialists". (The "convergence" of these two great minds would make a valuable study.) Teilhard's dialogue with Communists dates a long way back to years spent with Ida Treat in Marcellin Boule's laboratory. She was the first wife of Vaillant-Couturier, whom Teilhard knew. On 15 December 1945 Teilhard had a discussion on historical materialism with the Russian Vinogradoff. It is also worth noting that Teilhard was interested in Eastern Christianity because it had preserved intact the cosmic sense. At a meeting on "Science and Consciousness", 21 January 1947, a debate took place between Teilhard and Gabriel Marcel in the presence of Père Dubarle, O.P. Teilhard prefaced the debate with some remarks on the question: "To what degree does the material organization of humanity lead man to the point of spiritual maturation?" It was a fine subject for two great, but very different, minds to discuss, as the following brief extract illustrates.

Marcel: "My personal answer is very sceptical. I am perfectly aware of your insistence on the collective nature of this integrating consciousness, but I ask myself why such a consciousness should necessarily produce a spiritual value. By 'spiritual' I understand a reference to certain values which are very precise. Let me take the example of the doctors at Dachau. On this level, can one be optimistic? What is the integrating consciousness of these scientists worth? I see nothing hominizing there."

Teilhard: "Man, to be man, must have, as a man, tried everything to the very end. This seems essential. To have an integrating vision is very spiritual and to begin to know a thing in its entirety is to move from material to the spiritual." (If the shorthand text is accurate, it seems that Teilhard meant that the collective effort to penetrate the secrets of matter is a spiritual act. And the more spiritual an action is the more thoroughly it can be Christianized if supernatural charity completes it.)

Marcel: "An anti-Christian concept which leads us back to Promethean man!"

Teilhard: "No! Man, if he reflects on what he does, finds himself forced to realize that he must rise above himself to attain his summit. What makes a man Promethean is his refusal to transcend his deeds. The Promethean man is confronted with total death."

Here we see clearly two opposing views of Christianity. For Gabriel Marcel, the universe is a "broken" world. Like Teilhard, he has an intense awareness of man's condition as an incarnate being. But granting this deep rift that evil has introduced into the human condition, granting that man, in a very personal drama, wavers between invocation and refusal, Marcel is particularly sensitive to what collectivization and the development of technique (linked phenomena) mean as far as dehumanization is concerned. He sees in the triumph of collectivism and technique a new manifestation of the Promethean spirit which is pride and a refusal of God, the will to snatch from God his good in order to become God oneself. Teilhard does not deny evil, but for him technique is an effort to spiritualize matter in order to assimilate the cosmos to man, and so to enrich the pleroma. On the other hand, collectivization, by creating a new complexity, clearly entails a higher consciousness, clearer, more reflective and more susceptible of reflecting the Divine; and, since the ultra-human exists already in the germinal state and can only grow, collectivization can only bring about the maturation of mankind; that is, it brings a state of superior tension, and level of consciousness by which "the face of God", in its richness and unity, can be reflected in a more adequate manner. The integration of humanity is the necessary, but not in itself the sufficient, condition for the achievement of the pleroma. Insufficient, because there must be, in addition, a sort of release of the spirit, from matter, its matrix, in order to fall finally within the divine orbit. Marcel's reference to the doctors at Dachau is characteristic. Do not these men—with their "sadistic" and generally absurdly useless experiments, camouflaged tortures—betray the existence in

Man of an inexplicable devilish perversion, if we make of evil no more than a by-product of evolution? The existence of concentration camps is one of the commonest arguments against Teilhardian optimism. To this, Teilhard replies that he has never denied the existence of men at once intelligent and perverse, and that the concentration camps only illustrate with more intensity the very essence of evil, which is the refusal of unity, integration and the love of God. The opposition between Teilhard and Marcel seems irreducible. Soon, it appears, the two men had little in common, but "all that rises converges" and the paths, at first divergent, now approach each other. Gabriel Marcel has evolved very much in Teilhard's sense of the word, while remaining himself one of our most original contemporary thinkers.

The meetings with Berdiaeff and Marcel were not the only ones. In May of 1947, before an audience of some two hundred and fifty at the Catholic Centre of French Intellectuals, Louis Lavelle gave a paper on the theme, "What use is the world?" He maintained the following thesis: "This world presents aspects with which man is not in agreement. Man is dependent upon the world; but, in proportion as spiritual life becomes deeper, man separates himself from exterior realities in order to attach himself to those that are interior. He begins to feel that only the soul offers any profound interest, and that the real problem lies beyond the society of bodies, in assuring stricter relationships between spirits." This is the typical statement of French university idealism. The world, this vast "appearance", is marked by our limitation. Yet in fact this limitation helps to awaken in each man a multiplicity of powers, for Man, by contact with the world, is enriched and becomes more himself. For Man the world is a fruitful "experience". Moreover, the universe plays the role of intermediator between our consciousnesses. On the other hand, it is proper to the world that one day it will have to be abandoned. Against this view Teilhard rises up in protest. He asks that we act in such a way that what we ascribe to God will not necessarily have to be removed from this world. Is there not an "isotope" of being? In its first form, a being possesses its perfect unity directly; it is God. Under a second form, this unity of a being has to be accomplished and is reached only through a long process of unification. *Esse est uniri.* "To be is to be united." The whole meaning of cosmic evolution lies in this statement. In thought such as Teilhard's, which is dominated by the idea of union (which is better explained than in the old metaphysics of being) the cosmos becomes a masterpiece and is no longer considered either as an appearance or a simple obstacle. From his viewpoint, Teilhard was right to conclude: "One cannot help finding in Lavelle a lack of interest in the world, which is considered too much as a means, in spite of the great breadth of view in his explanation." This disagreement never led to any breach of friendship. On 15 November 1949 Louis Lavelle wrote:

> I shall be most happy to associate myself with every undertaking whose object is to allow Fr Teilhard de Chardin to realize the great enterprise towards which he labours with such admirable zeal. Everyone who is concerned with the spiritual destiny of humanity can only desire to collaborate with him. I shall be glad of every opportunity of joining with him in an endeavour to promote the spiritual future of humanity.

In 1951 Lavelle welcomed the idea of a Teilhard de Chardin Foundation, suggested by one of Père Teilhard's loyal friends.

A meeting with J. Hyppolite, a student of Heidegger, "that charming professor of philosophy at the Sorbonne", as Teilhard spoke of him in a letter of 28 March 1951, marked a contact with another aspect of university philosophy, phenomenology and existentialism. The two men, apparently, experienced the greatest sympathy for each other. This friendship began, after the liberation, with a gathering at Mme Romain Rolland's home on 24 June 1948. Teilhard, Hyppolite and three Marxist professors were present, and a discussion on the subject of Mankind's future followed. Hyppolite wrote to me, 24 April 1957, that "Père Teilhard was far removed from political questions, but his openness and his generosity struck me the first time we met." Teilhard himself noted the subject of this discussion:

> Two important points:
> 1. *Zeal*. Non-Christians psychologically do not know what we are talking about, just as often happens among Christians themselves on the point of faith in Matter. The notion, the *experience* of love, escapes them.
> 2. *Irreversibility*. For me the important thing is to establish a *point of planetary maturation*: "circumflexion". Following in the steps of Haldane, the neo-Marxist tends to escape into the perspectives of a vital *expansion*, in other words, into a *vitalization* of the *Totality* of stellar *Space*. Let me stress this second point a

little. From his own viewpoint, the Marxist will approach willingly and with an open mind the idea of an eschatology for a classless society in which the Omega point is conceived as the point of natural convergence for humanity. But suppose we remind him that our Earth, because of the implacable laws of entropy, is destined to die; suppose we ask him what will be the outcome allowed humanity in such a world. Then he replies—in terms that H. G. Wells has already used—by offering perspectives of interplanetary and intergalactic colonization. This is one way to dodge the mystical notion of a Parousia, and the gradual movement of humanity towards an ecstatic union with God.

Several such meetings, one in March, 1951, took place at Mme Delhomme's home. Hyppolite wrote (24 April 1957):

> We discussed existentialism a great deal at that time. From the first, I was struck by Teilhard's *optimism*—in this sense he was more Hegelian than I:[1] I felt more reserves than he on the crisis in the consciousness of Humanity. I insisted on the total risk; he recognized the threat, but answered me with comments about "the light years" and the general curve in the future of Man—a philosophical and also Christian confidence. I think that Père Teilhard clearly went beyond existentialism in that poetic and prophetic vision of the future which he supported with his science. He agreed with me that the present crisis in consciousness was tragic, but this was for him only momentary. He was moving toward the future with a Bergsonian confidence, with the certitude of a prophet and scientist. Certainly, there was between us a direct sympathy.

Here also, in this encounter with another form of philosophy, Teilhard's reactions are negative. Elsewhere we have already quoted a fragment which has become a classic, from a letter written to the author on 11 April 1953 (somewhat later than the period under discussion, but pertinent nevertheless):

> I recognize that my "phenomenology" is not that of Husserl and Merleau-Ponty. But where can I find another word to define

[1] This is true only in this sense. In other respects Teilhard had no sympathy with a metaphysic in which the historical and the real (cosmogenesis) are forced to accommodate themselves to a line of reasoning. One of the master theses of Hegel was, in fact, the rationality of history, the identity of logical movement with the real. In other words, history is the living illustration of a dialectic. For Teilhard—and here he approaches Marxism—the dialectic is purely and simply one with the movement of the real, whose articulations are brought out by science. For science is a continual oscillation between hypothesis and experiment, each providing information for the other.

a *Weltanschauung* based on the study of the development of the Phenomenon? We are forced to use the word "evolution" for theories which are very much different from one another. In fact, if I understand them properly, the "phenomenologists" rather usurp their title in so far as they appear to ignore one of the most essential dimensions of the Phenomenon; this consists not only in being perceived by an individual consciousness, but also in making it clear to that consciousness, at the same time, that it is included in a universal process of "noogenesis". I do not understand how anyone can call himself a "phenomenologist" and write whole books without ever mentioning or touching on cosmogenesis and evolution.

Teilhard adds that certain philosophers "still move in a pre-Galilean universe". He is also, it goes without saying, very hostile to philosophical atheism. How could evolution, having become conscious and its own master, pursue its *élan*, if it did not take full cognizance of the cause and end of this *élan*, of a personal centre, both infinitely loving and lovable? The certainty of the existence of God is the fundamental postulate behind Human Energetics, the only hope of re-launching evolution.

Generally, Teilhard felt himself to be a "free-lance thinker", a solitary. In a letter of 7 April 1950 he remarked:

You see, if some change is taking place in me, it is only the outcome of an internal evolution, beyond any influence of persons, an evolution which began when I first knew myself and which now, for various reasons of a greater consciousness, of different struggles, etc., tends to accelerate.

The collection of his *bêtes noires* is now complete: those who seemed to share his vision, but without accepting its full message and import. Among these were the existentialists: how can the Other, working in the same team and animated by the same scientific ideal, be a hidden enemy?; the millenarists who, like latter-day Joachims of Fiore, imagine that after the reign of the first two persons of the Trinity the Holy Spirit must appear, the golden age in which truth will no longer need symbols in order to manifest itself; the Hinduizers, led by swamis who elaborate doctrines in which Christian and Vedantic ideas are muddled together; and finally, the modern apocalyptics:

In their short-term anticipations I see only an outbreak of "illuminism" which turns them from the great work which, in

11. Teilhard with Haardt and other members of the Croisière Jaune group

12. Choukou-tien, North Face, Locality 1, photographed by Teilhard, showing a group of diggers at the base of a rock formation marked out in squares

13. The Upper Narbada River, showing excavated terraces, photographed by Teilhard

14. Karst of Patjitan, Java, photographed by Teilhard

my eyes, *alone counts now*; to work in every heart the living synthesis between the evangelical, ascensional movement (faith in God) towards the above, and the modern, progressive movement (faith in Man) towards the future. (From a letter of 17 November 1947).

Animated by a profound faith in the future of man, Père Teilhard rejected forebodings of catastrophe, and this brought him into conflict with some of his immediate circle. His rejection of apocalyptic eschatology—not specifically Christian in nature—in no way excludes a very living sense of the Parousia, which reminds one of the ancient faith of the primitive Church. Even more, we can see in the thought of Teilhard a Catholicism (a Christianity) which is a return, and which, once more master of its permanent values, should embrace the whole modern world. This is because Teilhard was able to recapture the true meaning of tradition, that is, the sense of spiritual continuity in the Church, to which he remained faithful till his death.

On the whole, apart from Marxism and the humanist pantheisms of the nineteenth century, which were always a stimulus to Teilhard, his attitude is rather one of rejection. This is not an *Einseitigkeit*, a disdain for someone else's thought; it is simply that he instinctively possessed the gift of rejecting all useless or harmful nourishment. Moreover, after his return from Peking, his thought was practically completed.

Teilhard alternated intimate private conversations with the wider activity of semi-public discussion. He had been forbidden to give large public addresses, and even refused them on his own accord. At the meeting with Lavelle, when he saw how many were present, he at once refused to mount the platform. He attended, of course, Jesuit or Jesuit-sponsored meetings, or at any rate followed them with interest. Thus, on 19 January 1947, he went with Fr Dubarle to the monthly meeting held at Fr Lejay's. Fr Dubarle spoke on cosmology and theology. One of those present has preserved the substance of this discussion:

... Père Teilhard declared that if there is evil in nature, that is, if God permits evil, it is because a price has to be paid for order. Pain is the price of being. As for the role of chance in the development and appearance of life, we must see in this a seeming impossibility on God's part to attain being as he wishes, that he comes up against some resistant. God then plays with chance and

9*

uses the chances that occur to assure the insertion of life in the world. (In creating the multiple, God faces resistance. He uses the possibilities offered by the universe and by beings to produce and bring forth life.)

God cannot fully and efficaciously intervene, notes Père Dubarle, unless he finds a power worthy of himself. Thus man is necessary that the world may be supernaturalized. "That is exactly what I think," Teilhard said, "when I ask Gabriel Marcel to admit the necessity of a parousia-point so that, in some way, Christ may rest there."

Concerning evil, Abbé Semat distinguishes evil in nature from evil as sin. "The evil of sin is", according to Père Teilhard, "the form of disorder corresponding to the conscious state of the multiple." Teilhard recognizes that this type of evil becomes more and more serious. This leaves in suspense the success of the universe. Yet, by the statistical infallibility of free decisions, nothing can prevent a truth from emerging.

Dubarle: "A comet could destroy the earth."

Teilhard: "That will never happen."

Dubarle: "That is the answer of a theologian, not of a philosopher."

Teilhard: "Our life should be only a life of believing."

This brief summary of a discussion brings out a number of fundamental points in Teilhardian philosophy. (1) For the Incarnation of Christ to be possible, it was necessary to have reached a certain point of maturation in human and religious evolution. For the parousia to become possible, it is necessary for humanity to reach a certain point of unanimization. (2) God acts globally on the whole of evolution and consequently utilizes, in selective fashion, all the possibilities offered by secondary causes. (3) Evil is a by-product of evolution, for there is no evolution without groping, without the intervention of chance; consequently, checks and mistakes are always possible. Sin is the reflective, conscious form of evil. (This comes very close to what Teilhard meant by the formula that "evil is a by-product of evolution": evil becomes possible through the appearance of the multiple (creation). The multiple evolves towards unification, and evil is the lack of unification (physical evil) or the voluntary opposition to unification (moral evil).) (4) Teilhardian philosophy is an ascendant series of acts of faith which represent the series of certitudes acquired during a lifetime. As for the hypothesis of an abrupt destruction of humanity by a cosmic catastrophe, Père

Teilhard rejects this as an extreme improbability; and astronomers would hardly contradict him.

These meetings of priest-scientists had only a semi-official standing. They began in 1946. In a different category was the international meeting of the Society of Jesus at which Teilhard gave a fine discourse on the capital role of research and its importance for the Jesuit Order. This was on 20 August 1947. Priests and laymen gathered in other organizations of an official nature. There are, for instance, a number of Catholic intellectuals in France who each year organize a week of discussion centred around one theme. There is also the Catholic Union of French Scientists (the U.C.S.F.). In these Teilhard took part. On one such occasion, he intervened in a debate organized by the U.C.S.F. (in February, 1950) on the theme of religious thought and the fact of evolution. He spoke after Piveteau, Tinant and Dubarle. Here is a brief résumé of what he said, in a letter of 19 February 1950:

> I intend, since the meeting is on evolution, to point out to them that for a century there has been a profound development in the idea of evolution—this idea being both "universalized" to the point where it has become in every domain a mode of knowledge, and "humanized", centred around Man, with the result that we are now forced to a physics much more complex than that of the relativists and Einsteinians.[2]

There is no doubt that Teilhard would have attended more such meetings, and taken a more active part in them, had he not feared that his thought might be too strongly original for his audience. He was only too sadly aware of the unintelligent resistance still aroused by views that he knew to be true. "What is specially serious", he wrote on 23 March 1930, "in this transformism-evolution quarrel is the frightening inertia of official Christian thought in accepting or, better, furthering the advances of human consciousness and knowledge."

Twenty years later (2 June 1952) he wrote:

> As far as I can judge, this year's Week will have shown once more that there are two opposed Christianities at this moment: a Christianity of disdain or evasion of the world, and a Christianity of development, or Evolution. No subject could be more crucial than the one chosen.

[2] The text is published in *La vision du passé* (Paris: Éditions du Seuil, 1957).

"Human hopes" have been discussed without any attempt to look at the question that must be answered first: what is man justified in hoping for, *objectively*, leaving aside any emotional, philosophical, or mystical considerations? Taking man as he is, here and now, experimentally, are we dealing with an infant, a youth, an adult—or an old man? In other words, what, in evolutionary terms, now, in 1951, is the *probable* human potential? I shall protest until my dying breath against all the stupidities of pseudo-existentialism and a pseudo-Christianity: that's where the whole trouble lies.

Teilhard was a brilliant lecturer, but between 1946 and 1951 he confined himself, in deference to his orders, to limited audiences. The author is indebted chiefly to L. Roinet for the following list.

May or June, 1946, meeting of Teilhard and Berdiaeff at Abbé Pierre's residence. Subject: "Marxists and Existentialists".

19 June 1946, conversation with young priests at Rue du Regard on "Towards a New Mysticism? The Love of Evolution".

26 June, lecture at Professor J. B. Barrière's, with Dubarle, Mounier and others present. Subject: "The Psychic Repercussions of the Atomic Bomb". This was published in *Études*, 1948.

14 August, lecture at the congress of the Union Française Universitaire in Besançon on "Man and Palaeontology".

19 January 1947, meeting of priest-scientists at Père Lejay's. Dubarle spoke on "Cosmology and Theology" with Teilhard joining in the discussion.

Two days later, the "Science and Consciousness" group presented a discussion between Teilhard and Gabriel Marcel at a meeting with the Catholic Intellectuals and Père Dubarle. The subject was the "Law of Complexity and Consciousness".

20 August 1947, a paper to the Jesuit International Colloquium at Versailles.

18 January 1948, lecture at Mme Borgé-Lagarde's home. Theme: "The Two Faiths". (See *"Agitation ou genèse?"* in the Bibliography.)

4 July, lecture at the Devêche gallery, rue Brey, on "Mysticism in the Orient and the West".

21 September 1948, talk at the École Sainte-Geneviève in Versailles, during a meeting of the chaplains for the Catholic Action Workers, then being formed. Subject: "Modern Neo-humanism and its Reactions on Christianity".

29 January 1949, talk at the Comtesse de Saint-Martin's, on the "Existentialist Fear". (See *"La peur de l'existence"* in the Bibliography.)

16 October, a lecture to the Catholic Intellectuals at rue Madame, on "The Ultra-human". (See *"Le cœur du problème"* in the Bibliography.)

21 January 1950, talk at the Comtesse d'Hauteville's. The exact topic of this discussion is not known. (See *"L'unanimisation humaine"* in the Bibliography.)

17 February 1950, talk at the offices of *L'âge nouveau* on "Socialization and Human Unanimization". Teilhard referred to this in his letter of 19 February 1950. "The day before yesterday, at a fairly mixed gathering (almost a little trap) to which I was invited at the offices of *L'âge nouveau*, I was forced to take a strong line on the new 'Galileo case'—reaffirming that certain sceptical and conservative positions were by now biologically untenable."

25 February, a communication for the debate organized by the U.C.S.F. (mentioned above).

18 March, talk at the Cité Universitaire on "The Phases of a Living Planet". (See *"Réflexions sur l'ultra humain, ou les phases d'une planète vivante"* in the Bibliography.)

30 April, lecture at the Devêche gallery on "A Look at the Future of Man".

23 October 1950, lecture at Liège, at the request of the Jesuit Fathers, on "The Future of Humanity as Seen by a Biologist".

The next day he gave the same lecture in Brussels.

8 April 1951, talk on "Cosmos and Cosmogenesis" at Mlle Mortier's home. (See Bibliography under the same title; I was present at this talk and took notes.)

Finally, in July of the same year, a talk arranged by the review *Psyche* on the "Evolution of Responsibility in the World". This was later published in the review.

This list is doubtless very incomplete; a letter of 11 December 1950, for instance, refers to a discussion on 9 December. Another meeting took place some time in 1948, at Marcel Mare's, where Berdiaeff, Gabriel Marcel and Vladimir Lossky met Teilhard. It also excludes the activities of the World Congress of Faiths, courses at the Sorbonne and lectures in America. Even so, the total number was comparatively small, for, in spite of many invitations, Teilhard generally kept his own counsel; he confined himself to his own basic interests and often spoke first on subjects of which he would write later. His thought centred around a few major themes: the vision in cosmogenesis; the laws and ethic-mystical consequences of evolution; the future of mankind; socialization and appearance of the ultra-human.

These Parisian contacts helped Teilhard to feel that he was being saved from the intellectual rustiness he feared in China. Another source of vigour and refreshment was the land of Auvergne and his family. He needed both to restore his worn-out health and to feel at home again in the Auvergne he always carried in his heart and found in distant corners of China—the more so that at this time, 1947, he was deeply distressed by the death, by drowning, of a nephew.[3]

Teilhard had for long been under great strain, and the evening of 1 June 1947 sounded a warning. At Mme Solange Lemaître's home he had spoken very movingly on the mystery of the Ascension, saying that it was the most beautiful feast of the year and that we did not celebrate it with enough solemnity, since it is the anticipated consummation of the Universe returning to the Father in the heart of the glorified Christ. The next day he had to baptize an adult, a person of high society, who had confided to him his desire to become a Catholic and whose religious instruction he had directed. During the night, following a myocardial infraction, brought on perhaps by injections against yellow fever, he began to choke. One of the Fathers at *Études* sent him to the hospital of the Frères de Saint-Jean-de-Dieu in rue Oudinot. He had a syncope during the trip to the clinic, and for fifteen days he was between life and death with a high fever.

Père Teilhard was obliged to remain sitting up, supported by two pillows. He felt brushed by the wings of death. "Tell me what keeps me alive?" he asked a friend who had come to see him. At times he could scarcely talk. When his friend Roger Lévy came to visit him, Teilhard was content to put his finger on his mouth, and, at his departure, with two fingers on his lips, he gave him the kiss of peace. Fortunately, his native robustness and joy of living got the

[3] Cf. letter from Les Moulins (Puy-de-Dôme), 14 September 1946: "This fortnight, coming after a rather hectic time at le Doubs and Lyons, has been a real rest. Perhaps, as you get older, you become more conscious of the need to get back to your own home. Those long years in China had made me feel as though I no longer belonged to Auvergne: now I see that was an illusion."

upper hand. One day a fellow-Jesuit surprised him in the act of playing like a child with an adding machine. Still, at the end of July, he had to spend some months in the clinic of the Augustinian Nuns of the Immaculate Conception, on the edge of the Saint-Germain forest, where he walked each afternoon, profoundly admiring the beauty of the large trees with friends who came to visit him. A letter tells us that he was still there on 2 September 1947, hoping to return to Paris towards the end of the month. He continued his convalescence there until 1 December, which prevented him from joining in the conferences of 1 and 2 November at Chatenay, organized by Emmanuel Mounier on the theme "Christianity and the Modern World". This severe trial was surmounted, but his health remained precarious. No coffee or tobacco. Plane flights were forbidden, and in some barely accessible areas of South Africa he had to be carried in a litter.

His illness inspired some reflections dated 20 July, from which we quote:

> In the early hours of 1 June, a heart attack which could have sent me to Jesus. Then a stay in the hospital (rue Oudinot). A turning point in my life: forced to renounce a grand life in the field. Today, at this very moment, I ought to be on an aeroplane for Johannesburg. What does it all mean? What will come of these restrictions? Essentially, I am determined to and can see only one meaning: *an uprooting of the Cosmic for a more intimate and more real insertion in the Christic*, the only ultimately Necessary in the Universe.

He benefited greatly from staying at Les Moulins, his brother Joseph's property, in Puy-de-Dôme:

> Your letter . . . found me in the extraordinarily peaceful setting of Les Moulins, in beautifully gentle weather. From my window, while writing to you, I can see behind a frothing of wooded hills (we are 400 m. high or a little more), the bottom of the Limagne, then, forming the *"skyline"*, the whole chain of the volcanoes, from Mont Doré to the Puys, the Puy de Dôme opposite in the west, it is or it ought to be very *"relaxing"*. Since my arrival here (it will soon be a fortnight) I have written letters, not many—some supplementary notes to my "Comment je vois" (now in the process of "re-typing" and being mimeographed by a friend), and, finally, I have written about a dozen pages to accompany my bibliography (up-to-date), in view of a possible candidacy at the

Collège de France. Between times, I walk with my brother who is showing me his plantations.[4]

My two other sisters-in-law came to see us. These visits, and the permanent presence of the young people ... cheer up the old house, which often has need of it.... (28 August 1948.)

I have just spent a week of great calm at my brother's place ... an old family house of the seventeenth century, full of old tapestries and pretentious arms, but perfumed with age, full of old noises and surrounded everywhere by tall oaks with an admirable view. Above the rolling lacustrine hills, the entire volcanic chain on the horizon from Mont Doré up to the last peaks and even beyond towards the north (the Puy de Dôme is exactly in the centre of the line, and on 14 September, the sun sets directly behind it).... (17 September 1948.)

I have been here at my brother's, since the eleventh—and I expect to remain here until 15 September. Everything is so calm here—and such a beautiful view of the Puys chain, behind which the sun sets splendidly each evening. Because of the heat, one hardly moves. Last Saturday, however, we went to see some friends in the Haute-Loire direction, in a delightful château of the seventeenth century, entirely of that period—everything, even to the bed-covers. The château is lost in the middle of the woods, in one of the most remote corners of Auvergne. Green and almost damp, in spite of the season. You would love this place.[5] Otherwise, I remain in my room facing the view. And very slowly I progress in the final writing of my conferences on Man. More than a chapter and a half (already written) to be set right. (17 August 1949.)

Your letter of the twelfth reached me here, where I usually take my vacations, at my brother's, in the vague capacity of a "chaplain"—facing the Puys mountains, far from every railway and in the midst of oak trees. I arrived here a week ago, and I expect to stay here until the middle of September.... Here, there is nothing new. I am jotting down a first outline (definitive?) of an essay about which I have been thinking for a long time: "Le cœur de la matière" (not at all in the sense of Graham Greene!) It is an essay on the reconstruction of the psychological genesis which

---

[4] With natural reserve, Teilhard did not mention his short solitary walks, when he raised his soul to God, nor his evening recitation of the Rosary. He often made his retreat at Les Moulins (30 August–7 September 1948, 25 August–2 September 1949, 27 September–4 October 1950).
[5] The Château de l'Ibertie.

historically has brought me (since my childhood) to pass from a vague and general cosmic sense to what I now call "the Christic sense". (18 August 1950.)

Père Teilhard had enough resources in himself to draw from it all the riches that he needed, but, just as *La messe sur le monde* was born in the solitudes of Mongolia, so it is probable that the majestic and smiling form of Auvergne inspired this autobiographical masterpiece.

CHAPTER EIGHTEEN

Second Paris Period
Relations with Rome: Scientific
Activities

O NE of the most important aspects of these six years in Paris was Teilhard's relations with his superiors in Rome. Many years earlier (about September, 1934) he had written:

> At present, it does not matter to me what I cannot publish. What I see is infinitely greater than any inactivity or obstacle.

Teilhard still took this prohibition calmly. All he wanted, in his own words, was to be a stone dropped into the foundations. On the other hand he had such faith in the truth that he refused to believe that important works or ideas could be lost. On 6 June 1951 he tells us: "We must have very great confidence that no effort will be completely lost." It remains no less true that with the stubbornness of an Auvergnat, and still more as part of his priestly vocation to attract souls to Christ, he did all he could to obtain publication. He was anxious to see *Le phénomène humain* appear, and after his return he asked permission again; on 26 June 1946, a letter tells us that he is waiting for two reports. A friend has been "kind enough to re-type the manuscript with three copies".

In September, 1947, however, he was told to write no more philosophy. This news reached him at Saint-Germain a little after the news of his nephew's death, and some of his friends feared that he might take it terribly to heart. In fact, this restriction was not a personal attack on Teilhard. A theologian, well thought of in Rome, had written a paper on "The Defence of Theology", in which he urged that the writings of five religious should be placed on the *Index*. Teilhard was asked to leave theological subjects alone, in case the Holy Office might step in and condemn his work.

Mgr Bruno de Solages, in a very strong article, boldly entered the controversy, and emphasized the important point in contemporary thought; it is

> ... generalized evolution; I mean the substitution in every field of an evolutive time for the cyclic time of Aristotle and, as a consequence, the invasion by history of all the human disciplines, since, from now on, all creation and all human thought is immersed in this evolutive time. Science gives only the history of life; geology gives the history of the earth; astrophysics gives the history of stars; atomic physics gives the history of atoms. The entire universe is carried along in this current of time instead of turning on itself like Aristotle's eternal clock. But this is still nothing. If everything in the universe evolves, if the Universe itself has a genesis, a development, a history, the thought of men is also carried along in this current; we write the history of cultures, the history of philosophies, the history of religions, the history of theology, the history of dogmas. But does that mean that everything changes and that there is no immutable truth, no stable and transcendent values? Well, yes—there you have the real problem for Christian thought, how to maintain, in the midst of this general evolution, transcendent values and realities. *Hic labor, his opus.* ("Pour l'honneur de la théologie", *Bulletin de littérature ecclésiastique*, no. 2 (April–June), 1947, pp. 81–2.)

He then goes on to a reasoned eulogy of Teilhard.

> Biological evolution was mechanistic and materialistic. It is the deep Christian significance of this great scientist's work—of world-wide fame—of this powerful thinker, of this enchanting writer, and, I add—for he would not use private papers in a public controversy—of this *"gentleman"*, Teilhard de Chardin, to have succeeded in showing, more than any other man, that evolution itself can only be finalistic, that it is advancing towards the spirit, that it can be explained only by the spirit, and that it postulates at the beginning because it postulates at the end, a transcendent God. Père Teilhard is not a professional theologian and we must not ask him for a solution, on his own and immediately, for all the theological problems. It is for theologians to work on them. But theologians are indebted to him for this great service: first of revealing to them the dimensions of the

world of science in which, henceforth, they must think, if they wish to practise their trade in the twentieth century, following the example given in the thirteenth cenurty by St Thomas; and second, of presenting to them a conception of evolution rectified from within, and which, instead of opposing itself by its materialistic and mechanistic nature to a Christian view of the world, opens itself to it very naturally.

This defence of Teilhard is all the more remarkable in that Mgr de Solages, though friendly to Teilhard, was in no sense a "disciple". He was, philosophically, a strong traditionalist, but, like Père de Sertillanges, he combined loyalty to scholasticism with a readiness to accept the demands of modern thought. However, the prohibition remained and Teilhard sometimes found himself in an embarrassing position. For example, the article "The human resurgence of evolution and its consequences" written in the summer of 1947 and published in the *Revue des questions scientifiques*, 20 April 1949: was it, as Teilhard maintained, scientific, or was it philosophical?

In 1948 one of the finest opportunities in his career was offered to him. The Abbé Breuil, professor at the Collège de France, was about to retire. At Francis Perrin's request, Paul Rivet presented the candidacy of Père Teilhard, and officially let him know that the Collège de France would unanimously vote for him if he should stand. As early as 18 September, Père Teilhard told a correspondent that, in all probability, he was going to leave for Rome at the beginning of October.

> By the beginning of November I must be able to say yes or no to the Collège de France, and, if possible, get back here in time to make some visits before 15 or 20 November.

Teilhard arrived in Rome on 5 October. His letters give a vivid account of his impressions:

> It is already nearly a fortnight since I arrived in holy places which I never thought I should visit, and where I have been most kindly received, by the way. It is time to send you some news and some impressions. Rome has not given me nor will it give me, I feel, any shock, either aesthetic or spiritual. I was expecting this. So far as the past is concerned, I am immunized; and as for the picturesque, there is nothing more to surprise me—after the great East. On the other hand, I felt immediately at ease in this colour-

ful, southern atmosphere. And then, a much more important thing, I have realized (at St Peter's, and only there) how Christianity is a phenomenon apart ("the Christian phenomenon"—I was right) with its paradoxical but irrefutable and active claim to represent the terrestrial extremity of an "arc" stretching between man and what lies beyond man. . . . After St Peter's—on a smaller scale—it's the Gesù that so far I have liked best—yes, the Gesù, in spite of its orgy of statues and mouldings, and its extraordinary paintings or frescoes that overflow, as though they were cut out of pasteboard (sometimes it's a leg, sometimes an angel's wing) onto the cornices and columns. I confess I was moved at the altar of our father Ignatius—and still more in the little chapel of the Madonna della Strada. All the great names that have prayed before that picture . . . family memories . . . impressions of a religious childhood . . . and, there too most of all, a feeling that the Order is something very great . . . the Curia is an imposing modern building, flanked by pretty gardens (palms, orange trees, mimosa) clinging to the rock. A heterogeneous community (I am with the "writers", i.e. the archive rats, next to the Vatican Radio), a little too much (in fact far too much) like Chabanel Hall . . . mostly Spaniards, but Germans, too, Swiss, Hungarians, an Irishman, and an American. They are all, as I was telling you, very cordial and kind. Saw the General once and he immediately won me: honest, direct and human. (15 October 1948.)

I contine to see Rome from end to end and, gradually, quite a few people. Day before yesterday, at a meeting, I was introduced to Garrigou-Lagrange: we smiled and spoke of Auvergne.[1] (30 October 1948.)

On 19 October he seems to have made an excursion with Baron Alberto Carlo Blanc to Monte Circeo, some ten miles from Terracina, in the extreme south of the Pontine Marshes. They had already met in 1938 and had planned an excursion to northern Italy. At Monte Circeo Baron Blanc had found his famous Neanderthal head in 1938, lying, among remains of hippopotamus and hyena, on the floor of a cave. This Roman sojourn, however, which ended on 7 November, was not a happy time. When Teilhard compares the Curia to Chabanel Hall, he shows how much he felt the loss of his freedom, for, in China, he had been accustomed to great independence (which he never abused). He felt his isolation too, the more so that he was not an archivist (he used to destroy his own papers,

---

[1] The point behind this is that Père Garrigou-Lagrange was one of his most vigorous critics.

including letters he received) nor a historian, and that the society of the "Writers", occupied with the study of the history of the Jesuits, was not congenial to him. His greatest trouble, of course, was the attitude of some circles in Rome to evolution.

On the practical level the visit was a failure. On his last day he received a negative answer to the Collège de France proposal. The proposed chair involved too controversial a subject. The Society of Jesus could not be mixed up in it—although it was not so much the subject that concerned them as that Teilhard would then be in a position to expound his ideas openly. About *Le phénomène humain*, nothing was decided. A first report had been critical and pernickety. A second was much more intelligent and practical, and recommended publication. Teilhard had also asked for permission to publish *Le milieu divin*. The text of his request read: "Examined officially at Louvain, in view of publication in *Lessiana*, the manuscript had been accepted—the examiners not only accepted the possibility of publication, but favoured an early printing. I still have a copy of the reports."

Back in Paris, Teilhard gave the impression that he was happy about this trip. Nevertheless, he was not unduly upset about the Collège de France, where he could have taught only for two years. In September he still felt too tired to undertake a busy year. At Rome they had shown him great sympathy and confidence, particularly the Father General. If the Society did not support him, on the other hand it made it clear that it recognized him as a true son of the Society—which it will always do. On the whole, this trip reinforced and clarified Père Teilhard in his sympathies and in his oppositions. More than ever he felt deeply bound to the Society and to the Church. But for that very reason he felt more bound than ever to his vocation of preaching a Christ fully "humanizing", and a Christianity, consequently, fully sensitizing the human soul by all the developments still awaited from Creation. *Sentire cum Ecclesia*, but in such a way that *Ecclesia sentiat cum mundo*. It is almost certain that "Le cœur du problème" (sent to the assistant in charge of French affairs in Rome) was in large part inspired by his Roman experiences. The fundamental theme is:

> The urgent necessity for Christian faith in the "Above" to incorporate the human neo-faith in a "still to come". This latter is born (and this is something that has happened and nothing

can change) of the objective emergence of the ultra-human (releasing a neo-humanism, and automatically entailing a neo-Christianity).[2]

The reaction was characteristic:

> At Rome they see neither the timeliness nor the reliability of an apologetics based on faith in man. For the Church, the only thing that makes an assured future worth while is eternal life.

To this Teilhard replied:

> The synthesis of the two forms of faith in *Christo Jesu* is not an arbitrarily chosen tactical move *ad usum infidelium*. It represents *hic et nunc* a condition of survival for an increasing number of Christians. We have to choose right now between the Christianizing of neo-humanism and its condemnation. The problem is with us now, and time is short. (29 October 1949.)

In October, 1949, the prospect for *Le phénomène humain* seemed more hopeful; but Teilhard was still urged to wait, and it was not until after his death that publication became possible. In February, 1950, a manuscript of the *Groupe Zoologique Humain* was sent to the authorities, supported by a very strong letter from a friend. At the beginning of March there was a non-committal acknowledgement. At the end of the month there was good news. It had been well received in Rome, the only criticism being on some points of detail. Teilhard dealt with these, but there was still an uneasy atmosphere in Rome. Vague threats were made against certain French theologians; there was talk of a *Syllabus*. During April and May there was no word from the authorities; in June the silence became more ominous in view of more definite threats against the "new theology" represented by the Jesuit theologians of Fourvière, in Lyons.[3] There were rumours that five professors were to be replaced, with consequent unrest and letters of protest from various quarters. Finally, on 28 June, the answer came: No. No particular proposition was singled out as objectionable, but Teilhard was told that he had gone outside the purely scientific sphere. His answer was courteous but firm; and he allowed his friends to mimeograph the text.

[2] By neo-Christianity should be understood a transcending of Christianity.
[3] There was, in fact, no such thing as a "new theology". It was simply a useful, if unintelligent, label to attach to a number of victims whose views met with little sympathy in certain Roman circles.

An anonymous author took the opportunity to attack Teilhard in a pamphlet entitled *L'évolution rédemptrice du P. Teilhard de Chardin*.[4] Teilhard ignored this silly and incompetent attack:

The title is sufficient in itself to show how hopelessly he has misunderstood me. He implies that, in my view, the cosmic future will have some sort of immanent, saving, virtue, whereas, in everything I have written, I have always insisted that the "redeeming" properties of evolution must flow from a Christic (a personal and transcendent) centre . . . he could hardly miss the point more completely. (15 July 1950.)

With fine ecumenical spirit, Catholics and Protestants alike rose to Teilhard's defence, among the latter Théodore Monod, Professor at the Museum, and Director of the French North African Institute. On the Catholic side he was supported by the *Esprit* group. At the same time, Teilhard sometimes suffered from his friends: there was one, for example, who spoke of Teilhard's "clandestine" publications almost as though they contained the germ of a new religion. There was, in fact, nothing clandestine or secret in the circulation of his writings. Ever since 1935 various friends of his used to mimeograph his essays: he felt it was his duty to let any friend who needed it have a copy of what he wrote, and this means of reproduction saved constant re-typing. That this was a real duty he said quite clearly, in a letter of 18 August 1950:

How can I stop without failing in my most urgent duty to God and man? . . . I have decided to continue as before, trusting to the good fortune, or rather, the legitimacy of my cause. I know that that is what all the heretics said. But, for the most part, they did not take up their position solely to exalt Christ above all things: and, basically, that is the only charge that can be brought against me.

There is always tension between the hierarchy and the pioneer, a tension that is healthy and fruitful. At first the pioneer appears dangerous and a threat to the Church's established ways; later he is accepted as orthodox. Some conflict is inevitable, for life involves conflict, and the Church is a living being. Teilhard's personal letters are undoubtedly bolder than his writings revised by professional theologians, but it would be a mistake to conclude that there was an exoteric and an esoteric Teilhardianism.

---

[4] Ridiculously enough, this was attributed to Teilhard himself by a hasty bibliographer of Jesuit works. Teilhard declined the ascription in *Études*.

In the Church, Teilhard was not a reformer, but an evolver. Teilhard's Christ is none other than the risen Christ, but instead of being Lord and Master of the Cosmos, he is seen henceforth as the living mover of the cosmogenesis. For Teilhard, it is traditional Catholicism plus evolution; it is simply, with all its consequences, one more dimension given to the mystery of the Incarnation, that of space-time: i.e., the duration of the world. In a letter of 1 January 1951 Teilhard remarked:

> Recently, the whole "nucleus" of my interior perspective has again come to appear to my mind as entirely dependent on, and "deducible" from, nothing but the transposition into cosmogenic dimensions of the traditional view expressed in cosmic terms: Creation, Spirit, Evil, God (and, more specifically, original sin, the Cross, the Resurrection, the Parousia, Charity . . .)—all these notions, once they are transposed to a "genesis" dimension, become amazingly clear and coherent.

Even during these difficult times Teilhard continued to act as a director of souls, with endless tact and infinite charity. A priest-scientist submits a philosophical-religious essay to him. Teilhard answers him:

> Your pages are full of interesting perceptions, often new; correct aspirations; frank admissions, comforting to the reader. All in all, I thoroughly understand you. But I do not see how an essay of this type could have the "imprimatur"—not only because of the freedom of its criticisms, but because of certain ambiguities or possible confusion in the expression. (21 December 1949.)

There is nothing more touching than his correspondence with Lucien Cuénot, a great, unbelieving, biologist who knew his days were numbered and for a year struggled intrepidly against death to finish his last book. Lucien Cuénot was too intelligent to be completely positivist; he was conscious of metaphysical uncertainties, pantheistically religious but still, because of his positivist training, incapable of understanding the thought and spirituality of Teilhard. On 12 May 1950 he wrote to Cuénot:

> There is no need to tell you how, for the last six months, I have kept informed about you . . . I do not think that there is any better (nor in fact any other) form of adoration. I know that you are working on your "testament" as a man and scientist. If the Lord gives me the time, I should like to do that. You know how much all your friends wait for this word from you.

And his correspondent wrote him a half-joking, half-sad letter, but very moving, in a shaking handwriting, which ended with this postscript: "Just the same, think of me in your prayers". Teilhard answered on 5 May 1950 in these admirable words:

Dear Master and Friend:

I was extremely moved and touched by your letter. That you took the trouble to answer me! And then, everything that you tell me so clearly and calmly about yourself! I like to believe that you will have the time and the strength to leave us, even if it be only a few pages, your testament as a man who has observed the world a great deal, and has seen it in broad perspectives. And with more than common emotion, yes, I pray for you in the conviction that, however hesitant these efforts of good will may be, they will find the right road, gain strength and pierce beyond the "phenomenon", when they unite.

And so I pray for you, as I do for myself, that we may be given the vision (as keenly reasoned and yet as warmly felt as possible) of a universe fundamentally loving and lovable, and that after working so long for it we may at last close our eyes and abandon ourselves to it. That is how I, too, before very long, shall try to end.

God bless you,
Very affectionately,
Teilhard.

What is so beautiful in this letter is the sensibility it evinces, and its deep humility. It is impossible not to love the man who wrote those lines. Only Père Teilhard was capable of inspiring this wish in an unbeliever: "Just the same, think of me in your prayers." Only Teilhard could bring to him, in his capacity as an intercessor, the first ray of the great Christ, were it only for an instant.

One of the reasons for devoting some attention to Teilhard's relations with the authorities in Rome is that these to some extent determined his scientific activities. Thus, behind his trips to the United States and South Africa in 1951, lay the desire to ease the situation by retiring from the scene.

It may be convenient here to summarize his scientific position, his official appointments and his own individual activities. From 1938 Teilhard had been a director of the Geological Laboratory for the study of human origins (1, rue René Panhard), in the Institute of Human Palaeontology, a section of the École pratique des Hautes

Études—an unpaid appointment. In 1947 he became director of research at the National Centre for Scientific Research and was promoted to the rank of officer in the Légion d'Honneur. In the same year he was elected a corresponding member of the Académie des Sciences (mineralogical section), a recognition of the valuable work he had done in the Far East. In 1948, as we have seen, he was unable to take up the offer made to him by the Collège de France. This is the more to be regretted in that his "Observations on the teaching of Prehistory" (23 September 1948) indicates the line he would have taken:

> Even abroad, in the best-equipped universities, the teaching of prehistory still tends to study human problems in a fragmentary fashion, breaking it up too much into a series of disconnected details (stratigraphical, osteological, archaeological, ethnographic, etc.), so that the main lines of the phenomenon lose their definition. . . . Nowhere, so far as I know, do you find courses in which the setting, the structure and the expansion (then the compression on itself) of the human zoological group, taken as a whole, is presented technically—beginning, no doubt, with precise facts, but studying them also in the broad lines of their order and development. It is in this direction, still unexplored, that I would like to see the Collège de France organize an experiment I would be happy to share: to start from human palaeontology and palaeosociology, and using these as the necessary roots or foundation, try to draft the first outlines of a science of anthropogenesis—a higher reach of biology that has still not been sufficiently studied in its own right.

In 1950, however, some compensation came. At the beginning of May Teilhard was invited to stand as a candidate for the Institut de France.

> At the unexpected suggestion of Jacob, I have been, since a fortnight ago, a candidate for the Institute (non-resident member, mineralogical section, to replace the botanist Maire, from Algiers): a candidacy *in extremis*, in which I find myself (much against my will) in competition with Guyénot, from Geneva (for whom I have a great esteem). The latter is backed by Caullery, who normally would be definitely on my side. The election is in ten days time. There are plenty for me, but Guyénot has many supporters, too. If I fail this time, it should be a certainty in three months time for the place vacated by one of the Cottons. I didn't want to stand . . . but my friends made up my mind for me. I rather feel

that I've been weak. Membership of the Institute, you know, interests me only in so far as it will shield me from some attacks, or, to change the metaphor, give an armour-piercing skin to my "projectiles".

Teilhard was elected a non-resident member on 22 May. His scientific standing, his prestige and popularity were in themselves sufficient to ensure him a majority, but we are probably justified in concluding that the Academy, though not necessarily sharing his ideas, wished to pay tribute, too, to his integrity and independence as a thinker. Teilhard himself recognized some such intention. "Behind the election", he wrote, "lay an unspoken further motive: a gesture of approval for freer 'religious' thought, and perhaps some small compensation for the earlier history of the Collège de France" (26 October 1950). Teilhard, of course, had little worldly ambition or interest in titles. In his scientific career he embraced every opportunity offered to him in his "God-given environment", but this was always in order to pursue his researches, research being to him a form of adoration.

Among the Jesuits and Teilhard's other friends there was great rejoicing. Teilhard went from reception to reception. On 3 June there was a party for him at the Vaufreys. On the 12th:

Champagne at Études, with the Academicians: more than forty were there, without counting those who were prevented from coming, and who sent their regrets. Evidently, I was nominated less for my "science" than for my ideas—which is infinitely more interesting. June 24th, "a large cold buffet", in his honour, at the home of a convert lady: "Very amusing: Caullery was there, and Gouhier. (Letter of 20 June 1950.)

Election to the Institute may not have eased Teilhard's relations with some of the authorities in Rome, nor proved as effective a shield as he hoped, but it was certainly a great compliment to the Society. It was followed by invitations to lecture for the Jesuits in Liège and Brussels, in London by election to the Linnean Society, and in Paris by the award (in 1952) of the Prix Gaundry.

His scientific work during this period is best reflected in his bibliography. This shows that on the strictly technical level he produced little—notes and jottings in China and Central Asia, a trip to Siam and another to the Harar (1951), an article, "Remarks on the Continental folds of China" in the Bulletin de la Société Géologique *de France* (1946) summing up his conclusions on the presence of granite in the old Chinese shelf. Teilhard notes himself the "complete official inactivity" of his Geological Laboratory for the study of man. This is very different from the days that produced the mass of publications inspired by the Institute of Geobiology, and illustrates the price he paid for losing contact with work in the field. Teilhard had commented on this lack shortly after his return from China (21 November 1946):

> My life has been and still is in something of a turmoil. Certain philosophico-scientific ideas, whose growth during the past twenty years has never flagged, remain an object of constant enquiries, so that the better part of my time is absorbed in private or public discussions, in writing articles, etc., yet with some profit still for my own thought. All this is very interesting, and even exciting, but then very little time remains for technical science. As a matter of fact, I have practically no material left to study. During the war in China I was able to write and publish practically everything I had to say in geology and prehistory, so that now I must wait for new opportunities.

This period of waiting and transition was, in fact, less empty than appears. From 17 to 23 April 1946 Teilhard took part in the International Palaeontological and Genetic Conference in Paris: meetings and receptions at the Faculty of Sciences, a conference in the geological theatre, a visit to the Institute of Human Palaeontology, with a group photograph in the grounds. Many important problems of orthogenesis and the purposeful development of species were discussed. More than once the question was asked, "What does Teilhard think?" The company included many famous specialists: Mlle Alimen, Lucien Cuénot, Grassé, Guillaume, Haldane, Menchikov, Jean Pivetau, Simpson, Viret, Watson, etc.; they were meeting with World War II only just come to an end—an attempt—as Teilhard might have put it, to repair the ravages inflicted on the noosphere.

Teilhard was anxious to extend the network of research he had initiated in the East:

> I should like to discuss with you a closer co-operation among students of prehistory. My plans, still rather vague, envisage a symposium in South Africa on the *Australopithecus* fissures. . . . During the war I published in China all that I still had to say or describe, drawing on my memory, my notebooks and files: so

that I really must get back into the field somewhere. In a year's time will China be sufficiently reorganized for work to be resumed (either at Choukou-tien or in the *Gigantopithecus* clefts in the South)? It's impossible to say. (18 July 1946.)[5]

The interesting part of this letter is the reappearance of South Africa as a possible field of research. As long ago as 1934 he had written (18 February):

The discovery in Kenya of a *sapiens* type would (if confirmed) be a new proof that the Neanderthaloids did not survive."

And on 15 September he wrote to the same correspondent that among recent interesting prehistorical finds has been

...the jaw (fragment) of Kannan at the end of 1932 (Kenya) which Dr Leakey is making a great fuss about in England.[6]... The bed is apparently very ancient Quaternary (fauna in large part extinct, including *Dinotherium*, an elephant different from the African elephant, etc....); but the jawbone recalls *Homo sapiens*. The hypothesis is that *Homo sapiens* appeared in Africa, and at the moment when, moreover, a neanderthaloid or pre-neanderthaloid type still prevailed. I think that it is necessary to wait for more complete osteological data. In any case, the Kenya beds are of first importance. Many tools, predominantly Acheulean.

Teilhard first mentions *Australopithecus* in a letter of 16 December 1930:

Von Koenigswald has just written me. In the deepest strata of Trinil, near Sangiran, he has just found a major mandibular fragment belonging to a large anthropoid (the anterior premolar has two roots but a small head)—which tends to approach the Australopithecine group.[7]

And again in a letter of 2 April 1940:

In the January issue of *Natural History*, Weidenreich has published, with excellent illustrations, a reconstruction, recently com-

---

[5] Cf. letter of 21 November 1946: "my idea is to see how effective would be a working party of specialists concentrating on a clearly defined and carefully selected problem."

[6] A fossilized mandible, probably found not *in situ* but on the surface: small teeth, markedly prominent chin. In a much later letter (14 December 1953) Teilhard showed some scepticism as to the authenticty of the fragment.

[7] It should be noted that Man belongs to a branch separate from the anthropoids properly so-called, i.e. the Hominids, which broke off from the anthropoids as a distinct branch some time during the Oligocene.

pleted with the aid of technicians at the New York Museum, of the latest *Pithecanthropus* cranium with the upper jaw included. ... The resemblance of *Australopithecus* is remarkable. In this connection, I would like to pass on to you a letter to Weidenreich from South Africa in which it is mentioned that Dart and the others have begun to suspect that *Paranthropus* might well be a true Hominid.

In 1924 Dr R. Dart discovered (at Taung, north of Kimberley) the first *Australopithecus* skull.[8] But it was only at the beginning of 1946, that is, after the systematic diggings carried out by Broom and Dart in the fossil-bearing breccia of Sterkfontein, near Johannesburg, and Makapan, north of Pretoria, that the accidental find at Taung, after much opposition, began to assume its full value in the eyes of anthropologists. Teilhard was *au courant* with this campaign of systematic diggings, thanks to the Abbé Breuil, the great authority on South Africa. Breuil had made three trips to South Africa, the last during World War II. It was at his suggestion that his friend General Smuts brought Barbour and invited Teilhard to visit Africa and make an appraisal of the collections of fossils recently found in his country. In any case, the idea of a voyage into the southern hemisphere had already taken shape in Teilhard's mind at the beginning of March, 1947; he planned it for the month of July, very much hoping that Barbour would be there. Teilhard counted on joining the expedition directed by Camp, the palaeontologist at Berkeley. On 25 August 1947 he writes from Saint-Germain-en-Laye, where he was convalescing:

I am not yet consoled for having missed my trip into South Africa which I counted on for getting back to scientific work. But this is the occasion to remember Léon Bloy's very profound words which Termier liked to repeat in his misfortunes: "Everything that happens is adorable" (provided, we should add, that we allow God to give a meaning to events, even seemingly absurd, through our confidence and our faith).

Consolation came, however, in the form of an invitation from America, "practically my second fatherland", as Teilhard once

[8] A primate not at present recognized as homidian (the cerebral capacity is too small, the muzzle too elongated, he did not use fire). Osteologically, however, he is much closer to man than any other known Hominid. Whether *Australopithecus* used stone implements is a matter of controversy. His gait, as shown by the shape of the pelvis, was upright.

described it. Simpson wrote urging him to come to the American Museum in New York. On 5 December 1947 Teilhard sent a grateful answer:

> I am very pleased and touched by your charming letter inviting me to come and work, for a while, in your department at the American Museum. How far this dream will materialize I am not yet absolutely sure. However, I feel that nothing could do more to rejuvenate me, heart and mind, than to find myself, once more, at work with you.

In fact, at the end of February Teilhard was able to embark for New York. Here are some impressions of the trip and his arrival:

> An uneventful voyage. Embarkation at night at Cherbourg, in snow squalls. . . . Cold weather, but seasonable, except for one day of huge waves, with dishes breaking and everything on board shooting off at a tangent (including my bed which, with me on it, slid right across the cabin). [Teilhard was never bothered by seasickness.] Very comfortable, of course, and very fast (600 miles a day). Five days is too short to make an acquaintance, if you don't know anyone on board. . . . Succeeded in establishing the first connections with the American Museum and some of the Fathers here. . . . A warm reception at the American Museum. But I feel the gap left by Granger. Von Koenigswald has been away for a few days (he is going to teach at Utrecht). Weidenreich has not changed appreciably. He is very active and is going to publish a remarkable report on *Homo soloensis*. Have not seen Frick yet. Shall I admit to you that on finding myself in this palaeontological society I felt very vividly (as I foresaw) that except in what concerns human origins (and, curious thing, the formation of continents—why? undoubtedly, because it is "planetary"), I experience a new sort of nausea for the study of the Past. . . . This does not clarify my immediate future. What am I going to do here, technically, during these weeks? Very little, without doubt. On the other hand, I would like to multiply my contacts with Humanity here. Very vaguely I feel or anticipate that Providence awaits me, perhaps, to engage me in something, though I cannot say what. Let us wait . . . I am still far from having made, even in New York, my first tour of the horizon. (1 March 1948.)

"A sort of nausea for the study of the Past"—this concentration on the future had already manifested itself before World War II. It became more intense with the passage of time. A few days after the letter quoted above, 20 April, Teilhard noted again that:

This idea of a super-evolution of humanity, now going on, is becoming more and more my scientific platform. . . . Meanwhile, I have definitely decided that fossil work has no interest for me any longer, apart from fieldwork, which I can hardly foresee for myself.

Teilhard was writing less at this time. Except for a few articles, he gave little attention to technical geology.[9] Man, his origins and his outlook for the future alone interested him. Even before the Institute of Geobiology, his scientific thought was satisfied with nothing less than the entire globe. If he continued to meditate on the formation of continents, it was because this presented a planetary aspect. It was also because under the rhythm of the cycles, continentalization conceals an irreversible current similar to the evolution of living beings. There is a hidden parallel between the formation and granitization of the continental masses, and the increasing complexification of life. Life has attained higher consciousness only because it freed itself from the sea; and that was made possible only by the formation and spread of the continents.

Teilhard took advantage of this visit to learn more about postwar America, and particularly American science:

Here I follow the same rather aimless existence, with no definite work, and still without any decision for the future, though I have many different contacts. But, obscurely, I feel that beneath (because of?) this agitation, I continue to polarize my ideas—in the direction of that still nameless science whose object is the biological analysis of the most general conditions of ultra-anthropogenesis. I have told you that I am to give a talk, 9 April, on that subject at the Viking Fund. This evening, I am meeting Höppeli at Weidenreich's. . . . When you have a chance give me some idea of the political temper of the country: here, it is hysterical anti-Communism. But one hears too much propaganda. (20 March 1948).

I visited Washington. A pleasant stay, in a ravishing springtime setting: the still sombre woods of Virginia were iridescent with pellucid greens, pinks and reds. Saw many friends from China again. . . . You should see family reunions here! Established (or re-established) two good contacts at the Catholic University: F.

[9] "The Chloritoids of the Western Hills of Peking" (1949): "On the Nature and Significance of the Pre-Cambrian Collenia" (1952). He was most interested, too, in the stratigraphy of South Africa (1951 and 1953).

Connolly (a brain specialist, very unreserved)—and F. Coopers
(an ethnologist), a very kind reception. . . . Aside from this,
I have spoken twice since last week. Yesterday, at the American
Museum on the genesis of Eastern Asia; and last Friday (to a
group of anthropologists) at the Viking Foundation, "On the
Trend and Significance of Human Socialization". I was surprised
to find I could express myself so easily in English, and even so
forcibly. . . . I think that this made an impression. Perhaps I
won't do so well at Harvard, about 10 May. I am thinking, too,
of a series of six lectures, next year, at Columbia or Harvard. . . .
Provided the authorities don't put a spanner in the works. With
all this, I expect to put off my return to France until the end of
June, the more so that I'm expecting some useful Jesuit contacts.
Last Sunday, four "Nathaniels" came to see me, in the evening.
I spoke to them for two hours on end (very much as a Christian
should, I think) on subjects of real importance. What I told you
about my recent impressions of the clergy here remains true: but
things are much more hopeful than I thought. Many of the young
and not so young only need to re-form their ideas somewhat. Saw
Barbour at Washington and here. (15 April 1948.)

The six proposed lectures at Columbia or Harvard fell through.
About this same time Teilhard was invited to the Century Club as
guest of honour by Fr Gannon, the president of Fordham University, and some of the staff.

As the example of the four "Nathaniels" shows, Père Teilhard
would never separate the intellectual from the spiritual. The two
lecture themes mentioned symbolize his preoccupations: the genesis
of the continents and the future of humanity. The two meetings
with Barbour could have been important and might have dealt with
South Africa, for at least since 1947 Barbour had been extremely
interested in that country. Professor J. C. van der Horst, president
of the "Bernard Price Foundation for Palaeontological Research" at
the University of Witwatersrand, had invited Barbour, as a geologist,
to visit the caves of Makapan—about one hundred and fifty miles
north of Pretoria, along the dolomite slopes of the Makapan Valley.
Barbour had accepted this invitation as eagerly as he had a similar
invitation in 1947, when Dr van Riet Lowe had recognized, in the
course of preliminary soundings in the "Cave of the Hearths" a deep
series (early Palaeolithic) of breccia and ashes, rich in bifaced artifacts. On 13 and 14 August 1947 Barbour, guided by van Riet Lowe,
had visited the valley of Makapan, examined the Cave of the Hearths

and drawn up a memorandum on it; a copy of this was in Père Teilhard's hands, who had marked it on the back "Barbour, Cave of the Hearths 1947". It is not unreasonable to suppose that Barbour and Teilhard discussed South Africa and its potentialities when they met.

The important point, in the letter quoted, is the talk to the Viking Fund on the goal and significance of human socialization; for it was here that Teilhard found an organization from which he might hope for great assistance. The lecture, as summarized in a report, concludes:

> ... A fresh and new stage of general Evolution is at this moment beginning with Man. For not only in Man is Evolution becoming conscious of itself (J. Huxley), but in Man (in so far as Man is discovering socially the scientific way of super-arranging himself towards ultra-reflection) Life is taking a forward leap under an already considerable and ever-growing power of *self-transformation*.

> If we accept this view, obviously a new era is beginning for Anthropology. So far Anthropology has been regarded in the main as no more than the description of past and present individual or social Man. Henceforth, its chief function should be to guide, to promote and to operate the *forward evolution* of Man. Non-biologists often forget that underlying the various laws of Ethics, Economics and Politics there are written into the structure of our Universe certain general and absolute conditions of organic growth. To determine in Man's case these basic conditions of biological progress should be the specific field of the new anthropology, the science of Anthropogenesis, the science of the further development of Man.

This lecture to the Viking Fund was the highlight of his American stay. He felt himself more and more drawn to dedicating the rest of his life to analysing and demonstrating the biological value of the social phenomenon and the reality of a "super-humanization", already in progress (letter of 8 November 1948). By the end of May Teilhard considers that he has achieved his purpose:

> Nothing more to do. People are going away now. Everything is emptying. Was at Boston (Harvard) last week, but saw very few people outside of Anthropologists (Movius, Hooton ...).

Teilhard drew from the United States all that it could then give him. The results were considerable, for he met again his friends from the American Museum, in addition to Weidenreich, Barbour and Movius; and at the Viking Foundation they had learnt to appreciate his quality. The United States would pave the road for him to South Africa; the contacts with American Catholicism were equally valuable; but most important of all was the opportunity to regain his spiritual bearings and intensify his interior life:

> Finally, this new contact with America will above all have helped me to know my own soul more profoundly: a growing lack of interest in the past—and an almost "blinding" perception of the two poles of my thought and of my action: (1) Man is still in full zoological growth; and (2) consequently Christian faith in God must develop a new component which will keep pace with human progress—this, incidentally, is the sufficient and necessary condition for 'tuning' Christian faith to the right frequency, and so enabling it to make the world vibrate with a new resonance. In future, everything, so far as I am concerned, comes down to this, and to getting this view across. (17 May 1948.)

Teilhard's return from America in June, 1948, was the beginning of a rather barren period. He was tired and depressed. He went for a rest in the Seine-et-Oise, and finished his holiday at Les Moulins (August–September). The question of the Collège de France was still unsettled, and this meant going to Rome in October. From the scientific point of view, we find only "Geo-Biological Observations" on the determination, structure and possible ultra-development of Humanity, a draft for a treatise or course in Anthropogenesis, December, 1948. This essay is an outline of the *Groupe zoologique humain*. At the beginning of February, 1949, he was back in Paris and began a series of lectures at the Sorbonne on the same subject.

One day when Mme Lauffrey, Professor Jacob's daughter, was to take him to dine at her father's home, Père Teilhard had a chill, and it was necessary to take him in a taxi to *Études*. From there, they took him to hospital, where he remained until 18 April, suffering from pleurisy. On Tuesday of Easter Week, 19 March, he went to Saint-Germain-en-Laye in order to stay there until 6 June, and to convalesce at the clinic of the Immaculate Conception Nuns. A brief paper of four pages, "The meaning of species in mankind", is dated "3 May, Saint-Germain-en-Laye". As in 1937 this attack testified to his overwork and exhaustion. Again his robustness enabled him to recover, and he profited from his enforced leisure to complete his *Groupe zoologique humain* (a more coldly scientific version of *The Phenomenon of Man*, whose last page is dated from Paris, 4 August 1949.

The end of 1949 brought a renewal of scientific activity. Between 16 and 22 October he gave a paper at the International Congress on the Philosophy of Science, on "The Vision of the Past". In 1950 and 1951, with improved health, Teilhard was still more active. There was some return of his old joy in living, and he welcomed the Parisian spring:

> Here spring is quietly asserting itself: the chestnuts are growing green again, and in the Champs-Élysées the pink of the fruit trees is coming back, just as in Peking. (31 March 1950.)

He gave a course of five lectures at the Sorbonne, on the Pleistocene of the Far East, for a diploma in anthropology; and he was asked by the students (18 March) to speak at the Cité Universitaire. From 19 to 25 March he participated in a symposium:

> Last week, at Grassé's, an international symposium on the Sociology of Animals; two professors from Chicago, Emerson and Allee, were there. A real success. . . . On the other hand, the literary sociologists of the Sorbonne were conspicuous by their absence! Why are they so obstinate in treating Man as a cosmos independent of the other . . . ? (31 March 1950.)

Since his last American visit, Teilhard's preoccupations had been concentrated on the problem of human socialization, the biological phenomenon whose roots go back to animal socialization. His distrust of the "littérateurs" was to increase as he grew older. By "littérateurs" he meant those who see man as a Kingdom within a Kingdom, and are blind to his roots in the cosmos and to the fact that socialization is by nature biological.

In May he attended the biology day at the Catholic Intellectuals Study Week; and after his election to the Institute Teilhard received a new invitation from his friend Jean Piveteau:

> Now there is a question of a course "For Advanced Students" in Palaeontology at the Sorbonne—and Piveteau asks me to collaborate. My plan is to finish for this a third version of my views on the Human (biological structure and physical nature), and to publish it, without revision, or censorship, as I am entitled to do, in the *Annales de paléontologie*, which Piveteau wishes to extend to subjects not strictly technical. (6 July 1950.)

The subject was defined more exactly as "the human zoological group". As Teilhard got to grips with his theme it shaped itself more clearly in his mind:

> I am definitely to give a series of "seminars" at the Sorbonne in December–January, on "the phylogenic structure of the human group", a second re-hash of *The Phenomenon of Man*,[10] but better *"focused"* I hope. I expect to send it as an article to the *Annales de paléontologie*.[11] (11 November 1950.)

On Friday I begin my free course at the Sorbonne on the phyletic structure of the Human Group: five days, one a week—my text is three-fourths written. I would have liked a very small group of *"Advanced Students"*. Piveteau (who opened the series) tells me there will be about eighty present. So much the worse. (1 January 1951.)

Towards the end of the series, which closed on 2 February, Teilhard commented:

> Next Friday I end my series of "seminars" at the Sorbonne on the phyletic structure of the human group. When it's over, I shall have greatly enjoyed giving them. And the final version, which I am writing as I go along, with a view to an article in the *Annales de paléontologie*, is noticeably different from the draft I made at Rome six months ago. In any case, this keeps me busy. (28 January 1951.)

The *Human Zoological Group* was even more important to Teilhard than the *Phenomenon of Man*. The theme was the same but, as so often happened when he repeated himself, he had the gift of presenting new aspects of his subject, of enriching it, focusing it more exactly, and expressing it more concisely. How dear to him was his view of the phenomenon of man we can judge from his constant efforts to make it better understood, and to remove from the various versions he produced anything that might justify the censors in refusing permission to publish.

This course was Teilhard's last major scientific activity during the second Paris period, before his visit to South Africa. On 15 July 1950 he writes that he is "seriously thinking of South Africa in

---

[10] "Re-hash" expresses Teilhard's modesty rather than his real opinion of *The Human Zoological Group*, which he regarded as even more important than *The Phenomenon of Man*.

[11] The article appeared in February, 1951.

1951". Théodore Monod had been urging that it was Teilhard's duty to see the *Australopithecus* finds for himself. At the end of August Teilhard wrote, "I am carrying on as though I were to leave for Johannesburg at the end of July," and (an interesting light on his interior state) he adds, "this gives me an interest, a reason for living, and, incidentally, serves as a welcome distraction and *'screen'* ". (19 October 1950.) [12]

Various preparations had to be made before Teilhard could leave France. The matter had to be raised with the authorities in Rome, and finance had to be arranged. Moreover, he had to brush up his geological knowledge of South Africa:

> Here, the days go by, and bring me, imperceptibly, closer to my departure for South Africa.... It is becoming increasingly clear to me that this plunging back into geology is *the* gesture for me to make—but it's just the gesture, too, that calls for a real effort. Well, we must leave it in the hands of God. (9 May 1951.)

It seemed that matters could be arranged. Teilhard had hopes, later realized, for a subsidy from the Viking Fund (later the Wenner Gren Foundation of Anthropological Research):

> Received an answer from Fejos: [13] nothing decided concerning my subsidies before the meeting of the Board (in March?); but the situation seems favourable. I have already reserved a place provisionally in a Union-Castle ship for 15 July.

Meanwhile, the trip somewhat changed its character. Not only was the subsidy granted but Teilhard was invited to draw up an entire research plan. Moreover, he hoped to start something at New York, which might involve prolonging his American sojourn:

> For you, as for me, there is a need for a *"shelter out of France"*. I am just off, please God. I have my ticket for London, 5 July. Departure from Southampton, 12 July. I must meet Barbour in London: and he will rejoin me in Johannesburg ... everything has turned out providentially. It seems that I can be of real service to the South Africans by helping them as *"adviser"* in devising a plan of research, which I would send on to New York in the autumn. This immediately puts a new complexion on my journey:

[12] "Screen": Teilhard sometimes uses an English word or phrase rather inexactly. He may have meant that the trip would shelter him from the annoyances involved in his attempts to express his views. Cf. beginning of letter dated 19 June 1951.

[13] The director of research at the Wenner Gren.

collaboration and assistance, instead of just a semi-tourist visit. It's providential, too, that I can escape the limelight of Paris. . . . In fact, my activity is becoming more and more concentrated on the problem of revealing (on indisputable evidence) and bringing out as "scientifically" as possible the significance of the human phenomenon seen as an effect of the universe's "convergence on itself by arrangement": I want to show that this effect is not slowing down (as is so often said, especially in America) but is in full acceleration—just like the astrophysicists' expanding universe. That, I feel, is the capital phenomenon to distinguish, and we must follow it until we see that the biological and the "spiritual" are in fact one. I rather hope, too, that I may be able to bring about the birth of an organization specially built up and equipped to study and express this phenomenon (a sort of small Palomar,[14] but of a different sort), when I fix things with Fejos in New York, this autumn. . . . I wonder whether all this will mean a *much* longer stay in New York, in November. (19 June 1951.)

If we try to sum up what Teilhard achieved scientifically during these years in Paris we first realize, what hardly needs saying, that his contacts with the world of learning were of the utmost value. In particular is this true of the world of Anglo-American science, as it is of the various congresses and conferences he attended; for here, too, it was not so much the subjects discussed that mattered, as the incidental contacts, the conversations in corridors and the informal meetings with people who shared his interests.

Technically, the period was rather barren. Teilhard was no armchair scientist. He could work profitably only in the field; and for that reason South Africa was a godsend. Most important of all, however, was that his scientific work had taken on a new character. Like so many scientists who are approaching the end of their career (Teilhard was sixty-five in 1946), he had accumulated the facts he needed; now he handles those facts in such a way as to synthesize them in a valid philosophical system. His chief interest is now anthropological, but he sees anthropology as the study, too, of man's approach to the spiritual:

It is still the subject of the human zoological group that enthrals me (structure, expansion, compression, and convergence); and, of course, the religious (or mystical) extensions of the problem fascinate me still more. (9 May 1950.)

[14] i.e. the Mount Palomar Observatory in California.

15. Teilhard with Lucien Cuénot, the author's father, at
the International Convention of Palaeontology, 1947

16. Teilhard in 1952

Photograph taken by George G. Simpson when Teilhard was staying
with him in the summer of 1952

It was to anthropology that he now devoted his efforts, as shown by *The Human Zoological Group* (1949), *The Phyletic Structure of the Human Group* (1951) and articles, for example in the *Revue des questions scientifiques*, on the same lines. His anthropological views were now so mature that he could anticipate expounding them in America and winning recognition for them in the concrete form of a vast research institute.

CHAPTER NINETEEN

Second Paris Period: Philosophical Activities

IN November 1946 Père Teilhard sent a communication to the International Congress of Philosophy at Rome, entitled: "The Degrees of Scientific Certainty on the Concept of Evolution". In October, 1949, he presented (at the 21st International Congress on the Philosophy of Science) "The Vision of the Past, What it Contributes to and Takes from Science". These two papers are symbolic, for in this second Parisian period science and philosophy come together. A scientist must be a thinker, too, and this was particularly true of Teilhard. It may be well, then, first to consider the general tenor of his philosophical development, and then to look at two special manifestations of it, his relations with the World Congress of Faiths, and his association with Julian Huxley.

There was no weakening of Teilhard's creative powers. There were no substantially new ideas, but he was continually throwing new light on concepts that he had long been developing. He was like a man who has reached the summit of a lofty peak; he does not simply retrace his steps over the route he has followed, but can now see it in new contexts, appreciate its progress to the top, and from his commanding position dominate the whole panorama.

Teilhard's correspondence was still rich in fruitful ideas, and gives evidence of a continued inward tension. New interests match this mental activity; he devoted much thought, for example, to cybernetics, to the notion of "feed-back", and the relation between information and the principle of entropy. An article in *Études* (March, 1950) on "Computers and super-brains" illustrates his great interest in such machines. Teilhard was impressed by the analogy with the human brain; he saw in them a sort of super-brain ready to serve collective humanity, and they were to him a symbol of what collective thought might be in a single-minded, unanimously thinking noosphere. Between 1949 and 1952 his reading (though mostly confined to articles and newspaper cuttings) was still basically the same: anthropology, sociology, cultural and racial problems. Unlike a thinker who believes he has found the truth and, clinging intransigently to his own view, is in fact a prisoner of his own system, Teilhard was constantly searching for a clearer vision and a more concise expression of the truth. Sometimes, indeed, he was impatient, for his own intuition was so dazzling and overpowering that to be misunderstood seemed to him quite inexplicable.

Teilhard lived with his philosophy; it was part and parcel of his daily life; it was not an ingenious intellectual system, self-contained and expressed in a definitive statement, but a living thing, unfolding gradually, and filling his whole life. Rhythms of thought and the rhythm of life coincided in Teilhard. These years were marked, too, by a progress towards simplicity. "My ideas", he wrote on 9 May 1950, "seem to have reached a stage where they become more simple, less numerous, more comprehensive, less ramifying."

The basic themes of the second Parisian period are summarized in a letter of 19 March 1948:

> I am focusing more and more on a twofold conviction (1) that the heart of the present spiritual problem lies in the synthesis of an "Above" with a "still-to-come", and (2) that the principle on which the solution of this problem of two Faiths depends is the distinguishing, above us, of a critical point in the maturing of mankind, the experiential face and point of impact of the Parousia. This idea of super-evolution of man stretching ahead of us (through the social effect of totalization) is one that has been oddly neglected by the greatest minds of our time. (19 March 1948.)

This notion is clarified in *From Cosmos to Cosmogenesis* (March, 1951). Here Teilhard emphasizes that, in spite of setbacks, man has just crossed a new threshold, an intellectual step forward from seeing things in the context of a cosmos (an immobile world, with a cyclic time) to seeing things as a cosmogenesis. (19 March 1948.) The concept of cosmogenesis is well defined in Teilhard's own words: "An organic universe in which no element and no event can appear except by birth, i.e. in association with the development of the whole. . . . Since the days of St Thomas the Universe has taken on a new dimension: *organicity*." (28 September 1950.)

Evolution, then, must be seen in the light of Teilhard's two basic principles:

> As we look around us we cannot help being dismayed to see how tenacious is the really infantile idea that the word "evolution" covers no more than a mere "local" dispute between biologists, divided on the subject of the origin of living species. We still hear evolutionism called Darwinism! . . . as though during the last half-century the rapid crystallization of the various individual currents of thought developed, more or less independently, by all groups of scientists without exception, was not daily making it more apparent that the ontogenesis of the microcosm (which we all are) has no meaning and no possible physical place, unless we see it not simply within the phylogenesis of some particular zoo-logical branch but within the cosmogenesis of a whole universe: and it has become equally apparent that the "idea of evolution" consists in realizing this fundamental dynamic unity. So we must realize once and for all that from now on times and psychological dimensions are completely changed for us and our descendants.

From this dynamic unity of the universe there follow religious consequences. The God of the Bible is also the God of the still-to-come, the God of evolution (as the "days" of Genesis seem to suggest), but men could not see him as such until the universe was seen as a cosmogenesis. In such a concept, while God still remains essentially transcendent, the relation between creator and created world cannot still be simply external, as with work and worker. Cosmogenesis is not simply divergence and change, but primarily a movement of convergence, synthesis, and union. And how could God unite without immersing himself in the world, and so participating in the world's suffering, which is the fruit of unrealized union? Thus Creation and Incarnation are not simply isolated, revolutionary, events in the history of the world. Creation is still going on all around us; as a phenomenon, it is a daily experience. On the other hand, while the Incarnation is still, in the human-divine "cell" of Jesus, an isolated event, it is clear that when God immerses himself in the world he cannot but Christify himself. The foreshadowing of Christ runs through the Old Testament; and, through the Church, Christ's activity still continues in the Eucharist, which extends the effects of the Incarnation. *From Cosmos to Cosmogenesis* states this theme as follows:

At all costs (and from cosmic necessity) we must, of course—and this must come before everything else—maintain the primordial transcendence of this new evolutive God, who emerges from the heart of the old Worker-God. For, had he not pre-emerged from the world, how could he serve it as Issue and Consummation still to come? Equally, and even more, we should feel more deeply, wonder at, and savour his immanent character, for it is in that that the renewal we await consists. In the context of convergent cosmogenesis, to create is, for God, to *unite*: and to unite with something is to become immersed in it. But to be immersed (in Plurality) is to "corpusculize" oneself: and this, in a world whose organization statistically entails disorder (and, mechanically, effort) means plunging (in order to overcome them) into imperfection and pain.

And thus, step by step, we find a remarkable and fruitful connection between Theo- and Christology. In spite of the spirit, and even the letter, of St Paul and St John, we may say that until recent times the saving figure and function of Christ retain, in their usual dogmatic expression, something of the conventional, the juridical, and the accidental. Why the Incarnation? Why the Cross? Emotionally, and pastorally, the Christian economy seemed perfectly viable and effective. But, intellectually speaking, it appeared more as an arbitrary series of fortuitous events than as an organically bound process. And mysticism suffered from this....

Well, it is this lack of ontological coherence (and so of spiritual grip) that is rectified by the discovery of a type of universe in which, as we have seen, God cannot appear as the Prime Mover towards the future without becoming Incarnate and without redeeming, that is without *Christifying Himself* for us.

This view of God in an evolving universe had been adumbrated some ten years before, in *Possible Foundations of a Common Human Credo* (1941):

The sense of the earth, as it unfolds and bursts open, upwards in the direction of God; and the sense of God, as he thrusts his roots downward in the direction of the earth, and nourishes himself from below: God, the transcendent personal, and the universe in evolution forming no longer two antagonistic centres of attraction, but entering into a hierarchical union to raise the human mass on the crest of a single tide. Such is the astounding transformation that the idea of a spiritual evolution of the universe entitles us to expect.

The synthesis between the Above and the still-to-come operates, *essentially*, at the moment of the Incarnation. It continues through the Eucharist. It will be consummated in the Parousia. But this Parousia, like Creation, must have an experimental aspect. There must be a maturation of cosmic noogenesis through a social effect of totalization, through a super-evolution, that is, by a sort of super-creation constituting a decisive progress in union.

And at the Parousia the Omega point, the centre of human convergence, and Christ the Omega (that is, the eternal Word) will coincide and be seen to be one and the same. The perfect synthesis of the two faiths will be realized:

It seems to me both vital for our mystical sense and evident to our reason that, however more than gratuitous be the depth to which the heart of God now lies open for us, this God must, on the other hand, satisfy the condition of being the summit of a universe which we now see to be monocephalic and evolutively incomplete. Accordingly, if Christ is, in St Paul's words, to gather up all things in himself and return to the bosom of the Father, "with the world within him", it is no longer enough for him to sanctify supernaturally a harvest of souls; he must, in addition, carry cosmic noogenesis creatively, in the same movement, to the natural term of its maturity.

If noogenesis is to reach that term it is vitally urgent to foster and nourish man's "appetite for life", the evolutive pressure that is without any doubt the most fundamental of cosmic energies. Mankind is, at the moment, passing through a formidable crisis. Evolution has become conscious in man. Instinct and the hidden life-forces are no longer sufficient to keep it moving. Man asks himself the meaning of his existence in the world, and is plagued by *taedium vitae*, with its eternal "what's the good?". Conscious evolution can escape this only if it is irreversible, that is, immortal: and that is not a matter of emotion, or logic, but simply of energetics.

. . . The universe from physical or psychological necessity—here they amount to the same thing—must possess certain properties corresponding to the functional exigencies of reflective activity: without this the mass of mankind will succumb to a torpidity, a nausea even, which will neutralize or even reverse all propulsive vigour at the heart of life.

The first of these properties or conditions ... is that Conscience, having flowered in Complexity, shall escape, in one way or another, the decomposition from which nothing can ultimately preserve the corporal or planetary stem which bears it. From the moment when it *reflects* on itself, Evolution can no more accept itself, nor prolong itself unless it recognizes itself as *irreversible*, that is immortal. And the second condition—a simple corollary of the first—is that irreversibility, thus revealed and recognized, shall affect not just any individual part, but the very innermost centre, the most precious and the most incommunicable of our conscience. ...

An *irreversible* ascent in the *Personal*: if it fails to satisfy either one of these two related attributes, the universe can only stifle, and that rapidly, all reflective activity; in other words, it would be radically unfit for any resurgence of Evolution. ("The human resurgence of evolution and its consequences", *Revue des questions scientifiques* (20 April 1948), pp. 177-9.)

Thus we see how Père Teilhard's thought progresses. Faced by the urgent problems of the time, he chose two crucial points, and pursued them with vigour. If there is a rupture between Christianity and science, we must reconcile, or rather synthesize them. If a part of the *élite* has lost the appetite for life, and is afraid of our growing socialization, we must restore its courage and make it understand the meaning of this evolution. There remains the practical task of proving convergence experimentally. Teilhard saw this as his most urgent duty:

My internal and external activity is becoming more and more centred on the problem of revealing with incontestable evidence and of showing as scientifically as possible the meaning of the Human Phenomenon seen as an effect "of convergence by arrangement" of the universe upon itself. (19 June 1951.)

For this, a scientific research organization was necessary, and Teilhard hoped to create it in New York. In such enterprises he was eminently practical, knowing where to look for support, how best to direct his friends' initiative, and where his spiritual influence could most fruitfully be applied.

One useful field was the World Congress of Faiths for Peace. Teilhard was only too glad to give what help he could to Jacques

Bacot, the Orientalist, president of the French branch. Although he could not actively and officially co-operate, he was anxious to encourage the movement for unity. At the request of the Congress, he wrote an inaugural address ("Faith in Man", February, 1947) which was read by René Grousset, and edited papers presented by foreign delegates unskilled in French. Mme Solange Lemaître, one of the two general secretaries, has recorded how valuable an influence he radiated:

> Marked with the sign of genius—if by this we mean not only the rare gift implied in the word, but also a sense of fullness, of clarity, of inspiration, this true Christian had something of solar illumination in him, something radiant and vitalizing. He was a man of great generosity of mind ... Père Teilhard could forgive immediately, with a smile, some gross betrayal of which he had just learnt, while those who had witnessed it were deeply incensed. It was no effort for him to excuse the guilty and overlook some unjust imputation. The truth is that he expected nothing from men, because he received everything from God. He really knew how to love his neighbour in the sense of the Gospel precept. Pessimism in an individual was as objectionable to him as inferior seed to a gardener. It was always a shock to him to note the perversity of those who laid too much stress on evil, on the sombre, on the ugly, instead of turning their eyes towards beauty and the world's sure progress towards its term. At a single penetrating glance, he could discern in a questioner something of positive value, destined to bear fruit, but if good soil was lacking he was always ready to kindle and foster the least glimmer of enlightenment. He was diametrically opposed to anything negative. Knowing how eager men are for hope and how they long for the human warmth of intelligent sympathy, he was always ready to encourage others. Père Teilhard de Chardin must have made many minds fruitful, enriched much "poor land" and strengthened the faith of many that wavered.

Among the founder members of the World Congress was René Grousset, the great historian of the Crusades and the Orient. The friendship between Teilhard and Grousset was an important event in this period, and Teilhard was greatly moved by his death:

> I felt very much for you the other day when I heard of our dear Grousset's death ... it will take us some time to get accustomed no more to look for, and meet, his smile ... there was one man, at any rate, who throughout his whole life followed, and

marked out for us, the true road of a believer. Once again, I hope you have not suffered too deeply—and that this loss may rather help you (and us) to walk straighter and look higher.

Conversationally, the two men were well matched. One evening, late in January, 1949, Teilhard was dining with Grousset:

At the time, Grousset, who had been reading of some new discovery, was particularly interested in astronomy. He said that if astronomical calculation had not involved such masses of figures, he would have studied the subject more deeply, for it fascinated him more than any other. "For most people", he went on, "to think about the heavens, the sun, the moon, the stars, the planets, and the fundamental problems they raise, leads to great metaphysical distress." He then briefly attempted a definition of the "existential fear" that seemed to him to be one aspect of human biology. Attributing to the words a much wider and deeper meaning, he used them to denote a cosmic anguish from which every man who is wise enough or thoughtful enough may suffer when he tries to apprehend and measure the abysses of the world in which he lives.

The next day Teilhard lent Mme Solange Lemaître a copy of *A Phenomenon of Counter-evolution in Biology, or, Fear of Existence.*

His *The Spiritual Contribution of the Far East* (February, 1947) was similarly the fruit of a conversation with Grousset.[1] In this he produced a brief but vigorous defence of Western civilization, whose apparent materialism disguises the first indications of a new mysticism, which, through scientific conquest of the real, strives to master the earth in order to offer it to God. He looks at Asia and distinguishes three cultural blocs: Japan, China, and India. While recognizing their value, he sets against them the originality he finds in the West. "The heroic sense of the collective in Japan" leads to a closed morality, that of the clan or race; "the practical naturalistic sense of the human in China" leads to a sort of stagnant peace in which man, deprived of the Promethean sense of action, seeks under a closed heaven an immobile cosmic equilibrium. He devotes more space to the "metaphysical sense of the divine in India", but objects

[1] At this time Teilhard was less tied by scientific commitments and could indulge his interest in comparative mysticism. He spent some time studying Far Eastern art and philosophy at the Musée Guimet; and in 1948 he attended the Orientalists' Congress.

that it achieves the reconciliation of the one and the many by suppressing the many, since, for the Hindu, unity has nothing in common with, and must be divorced from, multiplicity. Western mysticism, on the other hand, "starts from the idea that the multiple is by nature convergent", that it "is made up of the potential elements of a progressive unity, leading to unities of a higher order", and, in brief, that "unity is achieved by developing things to the full extent of their potentialities"; and this means, first of all, that we bring the world to its full development. India, in short, offers the ideal of a "unity from abstraction" or "release"; the Western ideal is "unity from concentration", in which all the elements come together through the perfection of each. There was genius in Teilhard's intuitive realization that true mysticism and science's forward march, which will end by spiritualizing the earth, coincide and are one and the same.

Talking with Grousset helped Teilhard to see more clearly the implications of the religious currents he had become familiar with in the East. He was too broad-minded not to sympathize with Eastern thought, but he wished to see it break out of its barriers, and, since "everything that rises, converges", he saw that there must be a peak at which unity is achieved; and it was through this liberation that, in Teilhard's eyes, reconciliation between East and West would be achieved.

Unexpectedly, "The spiritual contribution" first appeared in the *Revue de la pensée juive*. Robert Aron, the editor, was visiting Teilhard, who said to him, half ruefully, half in joke, "What do you think they've done to me? they've turned down my article!" Aron offered to publish it, and it appeared, over the initials T.C., in his review.[2]

Teilhard's interest in a dialogue between East and West was exemplified in a lecture he gave at the Devêche gallery (4 July 1948) on mysticism in the East and the West. It may be summarized as follows:[3]

1. Sense of species

The expansion of human consciousness favours forces that tend towards disintegration. This is countered by a planetary impulse towards solidarity. We must work to build up a common mind.

---

[2] It was later published with the author's name, in *Monumenta Nipponica*.
[3] For this summary the author is indebted to L. Roinet.

2. *A Western mysticism*

In the Eastern view, spirit is always seen as antagonistic to matter. In Western mysticism, spirit is reached through arrangement of matter; this stems from our view of the species as something that is still in process of growing. This mystical principle, still insufficiently explicit, needs to be developed.

3. *Renewal of the Christian spirit*

Christian doctrine took shape in a time when the world was regarded as static. The human species, however, is in movement, and so progresses towards its spiritual culmination. Looked at in this way, Christianity incorporates all the aspiring tendencies of man, and can give life to the whole reaction upon itself of humanity.

An ecumenical view of humanity emerged clearly in Teilhard's mind during this time. He was most anxious to integrate Eastern thought into this concept, but a sentence in a letter of 21 December 1949 shows how far he was from any desire to Hinduize the Christian view of the relation between God and man: "If you only knew how much I mistrust Hindu mysticism—it is based not on union, which generates love, but on identification, which excludes love."

Another organization in which Teilhard's influence was felt was Unesco, with whose first director-general, Julian Huxley, he formed a close friendship. Teilhard had been introduced to Torrès-Bodet, who had expressed a desire to meet him. At that time, of course, great things were expected from Unesco, and Teilhard was, naturally enough, ready to co-operate.[4] In March, 1947, he wrote "Some Reflections on the Rights of Man" (published in 1949). The main theme was as follows:

> The objective of a new definition of the rights of man can no longer be, as formerly, to ensure the most complete independence for each element in society; it is to determine under what conditions the inevitable totalization of mankind can be achieved, not only without destroying, but in such a way as to enhance the incommunicable individuality of being (a very different thing from autonomy) that each one of us possesses.

[4] Later, though still sympathetic, Teilhard expressed some disappointment. "In my opinion, the curse of Unesco is that it started with a staff chosen for their social position, without a critical appraisement of their human capacity for vision. I'm not talking of Huxley, of course, who is a striking exception." (Letter of 28 March 1951.)

In February, 1949, in answer to a Unesco questionnaire on democracy, which sought to ease the tension between East and West, between liberal and socialist democracies, Teilhard wrote "The Essence of the Democratic Idea: a Biological Approach to the Problem", in which he sought to reconcile the two by looking at democracy from a biological angle:

There is a strange and persistent cleavage at the heart of all the movements we call democratic. It continually produces the two contradictory notions of liberalism and directionism, in other words, individualism and totalitarianism. There is only one explanation for this, that these two apparently contradictory forms of the social ideal simply correspond to the two natural components (personalization and totalization) whose combination determines biologically the essence and progress of anthropogenesis. On the one hand we have a centring of the system on the elements; on the other hand, we have the opposite, a centring on the group. Sometimes it is the first of these two vectors that releases itself and masters the other, to the point where it seeks to absorb the whole system. We have a step to the right, a step to the left—in this, there is no fundamental contradiction: simply a displacement, a biological hypertely, even (why not?) an inevitable and necessary alteration. Biologically, I repeat, there is no true democracy without a balanced combination of the two complementary factors, that, in their pure state, are expressed, the one in individualist, the other in totalitarian, régimes.

Here Teilhard uses his principle that "union differentiates" to neutralize the opposition between the two democratic ideals. His solution is based on biological grounds. On one hand life shows us the vital impulse leading to the elaboration of the monad, the human person, the cell in which, for the first time, the universe becomes conscious of itself; on the other hand, since the animal stage, we find socialization playing an essential part; and, for man, it is on socialization that our hope of progressing to the ultra-human must depend. The contradiction is resolved once the problem is seen in its true light, as biological. To heal the cleavage, the collective must be personalized, and individual democracies must become more collective-minded.

More important still were Teilhard's letters to Torrès-Bodet on Unesco's attitude to racial problems:

The various "races" of man (in so far as we can still distinguish between them in spite of their convergence) are *not* biologically equal but different and complementary (like children of the same family). And there is no doubt that it is even to this very genetic diversity that we must attribute the extreme biological richness of mankind. Nature makes nothing with "the same as before". Is it not precisely because there are so many human "isotopes" (and because still more are being produced every day) that mankind has such great inventive and constructive potentialities? Just as, to produce a beautiful picture, you must have a wide range of different colours on your palette.

To recognize not the equality of races but their complementariness through convergence is the only way of explaining the historically evident fact that, before the modern tendency to compression that forces them into combination, the different human ethnic groups followed cycles of development that were to some degree independent of one another: so much so, in fact, that some of them would no doubt have become definitively fixed (or would shortly sink back into immobility) if they had not been revivified (and if they did not continue to be stimulated) by younger and more progressive groups. There is nothing in this, I think, to hurt anyone's pride: provided, of course, that each one of us understands (like each member of a family) that the only thing that ultimately matters is the general triumph of all mankind— by which I mean that globally it shall attain the higher term whatever it may be) of its planetary evolution.

Further, even if some minds, insufficiently "humanized", found themselves shocked by the fact that, in mankind's common advance, there are not only "better endowed" individuals but also "better endowed" groups, "leader-groups"—need that disturb us? ... In sociology, as in physics, there are laws we cannot trifle with.

It is important that Teilhard's views on racial problems should not be misunderstood. "They accuse me", he said, "of being a racialist. I am not." For the racialist, mankind is divided into higher and lower races, any fusion of the two being immoral and degrading. The biologically inferior races have, for him, only one useful purpose, to perform the meaner tasks; and humanity will never attain unity. For Teilhard, there are some races that act as the spearhead of evolution, and others that have reached a dead end. All mixtures, in his view, are not equally good; certain proportions constitute the optimum. The analogies, however, cannot be carried beyond that. The dominant factor in the whole racial problem is that the human zoological racial group is still biologically incomplete; before it there still lie vast potentialities of ultra-human development. Mankind is evolving towards a form of totalization, and this process necessarily entails a particular role for every race; for the various races are not equal, but complementary, and capable of coming together in synthesis. Teilhard therefore insists that they must share

> ...an attitude of sympathetic collaboration in a unanimous effort towards "ultra-humanization", for which every shade of humanity needs the others in order to attain maturity.

Teilhard's views were not too well received at Unesco, but his relationship with Julian Huxley, the director-general, was to prove far more fruitful. They had been in correspondence since about October, 1944, after Teilhard had read Huxley's *What I Dare Think*,[5] and first met in November or December, 1946, at a luncheon given by Baron Guillaume, the Belgian Ambassador, whom Teilhard had known in Peking. They took to one another immediately, and a close friendship, both personal and intellectual, soon resulted. They saw one another from time to time in 1947 and 1948 when Huxley was serving as director-general of Unesco (he had been appointed in 1946). In September, 1950, Huxley wrote to Teilhard from America, sending him his *Evolutionary Humanism*. Teilhard answered (17 October):

> I have read your essay with eager delight—for in it you express with great clarity (and with your unique experience of Unesco) the exact essence of what I have been dreaming of for such a long time. Surely such a coincidence of thought directed to the facts we know must be the best proof that something is now on the move in human consciousness and beginning to become explicit.

In December of the same year, Teilhard and Huxley met as the latter passed through Paris. Teilhard wrote on the 29th, expressing his joy:

> Just a line to tell you how happy I was to see you as you passed through Paris—and to send you (and Mrs Huxley) my best wishes

[5] Before this, Teilhard wrote (12 July 1941): "At the same time, I am still trying to arrive at a clearer and more concise statement of my ideas on the place of man in the Universe. Julian Huxley has just brought out a book, or rather a collection of essays, *The Uniqueness of Man*, which takes a line so close to my own (though without integrating God at the term of the series) that I feel greatly heartened."

for 1951—and to thank you for sending me your new book (*New Bottles for New Wine*), which I found fascinating reading.

They met again towards the end of March, 1951, when Huxley asked Teilhard to contribute to a collective work to be published in England under the title *Evolution as a Process*. This sort of relationship continued right up to 1955, with exchange of letters and papers, and later, meetings at the Wenner Gren Foundation, where Teilhard was delighted to find that Huxley became more and more at home. With such different backgrounds and origins it is indeed surprising that there should have been such sympathy between the two men. After Teilhard's death Huxley wrote an impressive tribute (*Encounter*, April, 1956):

> From the moment of my first meeting with Père Teilhard in 1946, soon after I had gone to Paris as head of UNESCO, I realized that I had found not only a friend, but a partner in the intellectual and spiritual adventure. Though he had approached the problem of human destiny from the standpoint of a Christian and a Jesuit Father, and I from that of an agnostic and zoologist, we had been thinking along the same lines and had come to astonishingly similar conclusions. This was because we had both been determined to look at human destiny (that is to say man, his cosmic background and home, and the relation between them) as a phenomenon, not as a metaphysical, an ethical, or theological problem. In such an approach, man is seen not as a creation alien or separate from nature, but as a part (and a very essential part) of the phenomenon of evolution. And mind and spirit appear not as an irrelevant epiphenomenon nor as a supernatural injection, but as highly important natural phenomena.

There was a real meeting of the two minds, but this did not entail a complete coincidence of opinion. Teilhard was more inclined to stress the importance of applying scientific method to history and sociology (in which qualitative differences and the notion of value are involved) and of seeking to reconcile subjectivity and objectivity. Above all, too, the final goal of evolution was not, according to Teilhard, only the production of more fully developed personalities. That the purpose of society was to develop personality, in the individualist sense of the word, was in his eyes a complete mistake. A letter of his to Huxley, written somewhat later than the period we are discussing, illustrates the high level of their correspondence:

Thank you for sending me *Evolution in Action*. I read it with such interest and eagerness that the pages are now covered with pencil marks. It is remarkable how closely your thought, and mine (and even, in spite of its pessimism, C. Galton-Darwin's in his *Next Million Years*) approach one another when we consider the place and critical significance in the Universe of the phenomenon of man.

All three of us are impressed by the revolutionary gathering in on itself of mankind, and by the development, within this totalized whole, of a ramified network of cultures and "creeds", which oddly reproduces, in the context of thought, the various "patterns" of zoological phylogenesis. Where we still differ (you, G. Darwin and I) is when we come to estimate the biological importance of socialization. For you (and for Darwin) there is, in the phenomenon of human totalization, no more than a sort of cumulative process that leads ultimately to equilibrium—or so it would seem (?). Could we not, however, go a step further, and recognize (scientifically) that the "pool" you describe so well is not simply confluence but also convergence (an irresistible and irreversible convergence) of thought upon itself? Such a convergence (provided that there is no lack en route of either physical energy or psychological "drive") would define a critical point of speciation in the future (or, if you prefer, of reflection or unanimization), which is just what would give your *Evolutionary Humanism* full energetic value....

Another thing. I am completely with you in admitting that the prolonged effect, statistically, of large numbers is capable of starting a drift of some part of the universe towards the impossible. But how are we to explain the property we find in natural selection of "*persistantly*" [*sic*] causing to increase in the world that particular form of the Improbable that leads to the most organically centred (and hence most conscious) arrangements? Is it by chance (as Bergson said in his *Creative Evolution*) that the *Weltstoff* presents itself to us, scientifically, as endowed with a special sort of "gravity" that makes it take advantage of every chance always to fall (or rather rise) through greater complexity to greater consciousness?—in other words, if the *Weltstoff* were not originally "*loaded*" with a certain bias, do you believe it would offer any purchase to natural selection? (27 February 1953.)

Julian Huxley is a man of action. In March, 1951, he showed Teilhard two reports on a scheme for a "brains-trust" to examine human ideology. This brought from Teilhard a memorandum of which the first part ran as follows:

Strategically, I believe, it would be better, at least provisionally, to reduce the terms of reference, and to break the operation up into several stages: the first should be the establishment of an *"Institute for human studies"*, or, more explicitly:
a research institute for the study and control of human forces of self (ultra-evolution), or, more simply:
"an institute for the study of human self-evolution".
Broadly speaking, I see such an institute as divided into two branches, one theoretical, and one applied; the latter being divided into three sections.

Theoretical Branch

This would have two functions:

(a) to establish on increasingly irrefutable evidence, the existence of and

(b) to determine with increasing clarity the axes of a progress (continually more reflective, inventive and planned) of the human towards some form of ultra-human.

Examples of points to be studied:

Evidence for a planetary "rise in psychic temperature".
Effects on human arrangement of planetary compression.
Totalization and personalization.

General conditions, either physical (the question of resources) or psychic (the problem of maintaining the appetite for evolution) necessary for self ultra-hominization.

Applied Branch
Energetics section
Eugenics section
Steering section

The idea of an institute for human studies reappeared in a report of Huxley's dated 9 April 1951. Behind it lay three main ideas:

(a) The unity of experience, and the present need to integrate and study different aspects of experience.

(b) The broad principles of evolution, in particular the fact that the most significant characteristic of the evolutionary process is auto-transformation; and with this, the progressive but gradual realization of new potentialities.

(c) The value of scientific method in every field of study, with, as a corollary, the danger of a dogmatic or purely subjective approach.

The similarity of the two schemes is immediately apparent: the importance of the socialization of man; the need for synthesis; evolutionism; the appearance of new thresholds of progress, not due to purely external and mechanical actions; the application of scientific method to the study of phenomena, in the widest sense of the word, in such a way as to subordinate considerations of value (which means qualitative and subjective considerations) to objective considerations; the rejection of a metaphysic that deduces the world from *a priori* principles, and the insistence that our view of it should be relational and not deductive. On the other hand, while Huxley, without rejecting Christianity or theology, believes that science can replace the older mystical concepts, Teilhard believes that science can be used to strengthen them. In spite of this difference, the two thinkers had, from very different starting points, reached conclusions that had much in common.[6] Thus, Huxley wrote in *Encounter* (April, 1956):

It is, I think, of interest to mention that all those points had also been stressed by me quite independently. (I first formulated the idea of a critical point between biological and human evolution in 1919); it is of interest as showing how two thinkers, one as a palaeontologist starting from Christian premises, the other a general biologist starting from rationalist premises, are almost bound to pick out the same phenomena as significant and to draw the same general conclusions from the facts.

[6] There is an excellent study by M. Gex, of the similarities between Teilhard and Huxley, in the *Revue de théologie et de philosophie* ("Vers un humanisme cosmologique", 1957, no. 3).

CHAPTER TWENTY

The American Period (1951–5): Life in New York: First Visit to South Africa

IN July, 1951, Teilhard was to leave for South Africa. Always bearing in mind the risen Christ who placed him in what he called his "divine milieu", he had just made the necessary arrangements for ensuring that, after his death, his writings should continue the apostolic mission to which he had vowed himself, and for which he was ready to accept exile and end his days as, in his own words, "a child of obedience". A week before he left, Père Jouve, the editor of *Études*, had told him that he would never be able to publish his work for him, and urged him to take steps to see that it was not lost. Some of Teilhard's friends were anxious for him to leave the Society and benefit from the greater freedom of a secular priest. This he refused to do. "It would mean", he said, "cutting myself off from my 'divine milieu'; I should be breaking the thread that binds me to the will of God, and I should no longer be able to entrust myself to its guidance." In following Père Jouve's advice, however, he was quite certain that he was doing his duty. Moreover, his vow of poverty was no bar to his ownership of his own manuscripts, and, though canonists are not at all in agreement on this point, canon law does not formally prohibit their being disposed of by gift or testament.

On 5 July 1951 Teilhard left France for London, where he met Barbour. On the 12th he sailed from Southampton, and was in Johannesburg by the end of the month. He had, as usual, taken advantage of the voyage to get on with his writing, and had completed *The Convergence of the Universe*.

Although this visit to South Africa preceded Teilhard's period in America, it may be well to look first at his life in New York, since his work in Africa is more easily understood in the light of the American background. We have a great mass of documentary material covering these years, mostly in the form of correspondence. This was partly because Teilhard was cut off from some of his friends, and kept in touch with them by writing, and partly because, in New York, he was very much in demand and acquired many new correspondents. Moreover, his thought seemed to find expression more easily in letter form:

> I find that my thought emerges more vigorously and readily than in formal essays, if I write just as chance dictates or when I have the stimulus of a letter that I must answer.

His correspondents, in fact, supplied him with endless material for thought, for he received a constant stream of inquiries, of problems to advise upon, of articles and cuttings to read.

In treating of this period, the logical order conflicts with the chronological order; and it is necessary, if the picture is to be coherent, to sacrifice the latter to the former. Writing from New York (on 10 December 1951) Teilhard spoke of the work he was taking up:

> I envisage my work here as on three levels (each progressively more personal): Collaboration in the organization of world-wide research into human origins. (My "grant" is earmarked "research associate for palaeoanthropology".)[1] An attempt to deal scientifically with the problem of extending (and under what form?) the biological forces of evolution and speciation in contemporary man. And finally (and this concerns me alone) a continuation of my effort to synthesize the "above" with the "still-to-come", within a context of religious thought (a Christology) adjusted to the new dimensions of the Universe.

Thus, we shall have to distinguish three essential aspects: Teilhard's technical work, his attempt to re-shape anthropological studies, and his religious thought—these three being preceded by an acount of his daily life in New York.

---

[1] The Viking Fund, founded by Wenner Gren, an American of Swedish origin, covered scientific, educational and charitable projects. When it was renamed "The Wenner Gren Foundation" it was reorganized with a more explicit emphasis on anthropological research.

Normally, his time was spent between the Wenner Gren, the American Museum, and Loyola House on Park Avenue (where he lived) and in meetings with friends. The Rector of Loyola House, Fr Robert I. Gannon, S.J., writing to the author, recorded his impressions of Teilhard:

> ...at evening recreation he was always entertaining, sometimes in a deep discussion, sometimes in a light-hearted conversation. He could be merry and had a fine sense of humour. He was popular with all the American Fathers, who regarded him as a model of humility and charity. Every month he came to my room for an hour's conference and would discuss his work, his problems and troubles with the simplicity of a young scholastic. His death brought us all a sense of personal loss.[2]

The Fathers still point out the corners of the garden where, after celebrating Mass in the chapel of the Sacred Heart, Teilhard liked to meditate or say his Rosary, sometimes at the foot of a massive crucifix set in the wall, in a corner formed by two buildings, or sometimes before a niche in which stood a statue of the Virgin, hidden by an enclosure and looking out over bushy flowering shrubs.

Though he remained a member of this community until his death, at the end of two years he had to find somewhere else to live:

> These last weeks have been rather eventful for me: first because I went to spend a few days in Washington, and then because last week I had to look for accommodation outside St Ignatius's. A complication of demolition and difficult tenants has forced the charming Father Gannon to put seven Fathers out of the house for three months, in a week's time. Thanks to the broadmindedness of Fr McMahon, the Provincial, and to Mr Roger Strauss ... I have been able to find a relatively economical asylum in a very smart and very quiet men's Club (strict enclosure!), the Lotus Club at 5 East 66th Street, two steps from the Wenner Gren Foundation, and only five minutes, too, from a Dominican parish church. All is well that ends well. But all this does not facilitate work. . . . Patience. Even so, I ought to be able to establish myself a little better in the "divine milieu". (7 March 1954.)

Teilhard's adaptability enabled him to lead a well-balanced life, and to be as happy as an exile from his native land can hope to be.

---

[2] All the staff regretted his death. The lift-boy and the coloured woman who looked after his room were in tears. "He was so good a man", they said. Cf. *Synthèses*, December, 1957, p. 454.

It was during these years, however, that he learnt of the death of a number of friends, Jouve (1952), Auguste Valensin, to whom he was particularly devoted, Emmanuel de Margerie, the geographer and geologist (1953), and Pierre Charles (1954). Jouve's death left "a great gap" in his life, and of Charles's loss he wrote that he now felt "terribly lonely".

At the Wenner Gren Teilhard had an office to himself, and his position enabled him to meet many of the most interesting people in the United States. The appointment worked out most successfully. He was reaching more precise conclusions, and was able through "gentle pressure" to influence the Foundation's policy. Although he maintained that his English was still, in spite of help from his American friends, "terribly French", he understood the language perfectly and could use it readily to express not only technical matters (which he had long been able to do) but also abstract ideas and his own philosophical concepts. Paul Fejos was greatly overworked and could seldom be seen, but Teilhard enjoyed his confidence and affection. "He has become a great friend," Teilhard wrote in July, 1954. As time went on he became more and more attached to the Foundation and to his work. "I feel very happy here," he wrote in his last year, "a warm and easy atmosphere."

In short, Teilhard liked New York. He had acquired a circle of chosen friends, with whom or in whose houses he divided his leisure, and so did not have to dissipate his energies in too many directions. As ever, he was no proselytizer, but more than one confirmed materialist gradually, through his influence, found his way towards faith and trust in God and sometimes decided in the end to accompany Teilhard into a church.

From time to time the regularity of his life was interrupted by the arrival of some eminent visitor from Europe, by a party or a short trip. Thus on 17 February 1954 he wrote:

I am just back from Washington (Georgetown University) where I had a charming reception, in particular from the Rector, who once lived in the rue Reynouard while working on a thesis for the Sorbonne. At the Catholic University, the Anthropology Department gave a cocktail party for me at which I met many people, notably two brilliant scholastics, one studying physics and the other biology, in whom I slyly sought to inject the "demon" of research. I saw the people at the Smithsonian, too (palaeontology and anthropology). Dined tête à tête with my friends the

Grews (the former ambassador to Japan). There was a very blue sky over woods that were still black; soon they will be pink. This outing on the Potomac did me a lot of good.

A few months later, 24 March 1952, he wrote again:

This morning I leave for Boston (Harvard) for three days. Last week-end I was at Yale, which I had not visited before. Then to finish my New Haven tour I went to spend a day in the "deep" of Connecticut.... The countryside, a granite platform ravined by glaciers, surprised me with its wildness, once you leave the scattered islets of over-population. Everywhere there were woods, as far as the eye could see. Everything is so lovely in its tender foliage, with apple orchards and dazzling "dogwoods".

About the middle of November, 1952, he went to Boston for the annual meetings of the Geological Society and the Society of Vertebrate Palaeontology. Teilhard knew a number of artists, too, in New York. At times, of course, he had to take part in official ceremonies. More important to him, however, were the visits he received from eminent scientists and men of letters when they arrived in New York. There was Pierre Chouard, for example, professor of plant physiology at the Sorbonne; Père Bergounioux, professor of geology at the Institut Catholique in Toulouse; Alberto Carlo Blanc, the Italian geologist and palaeontologist; the Arabic scholar, Massignon; André Malraux; Denis de Rougemont; Roger Lévy; Jacques Rueff; the biologist Henri Prat, with his sons. A letter from the Dutch parapsychologist, Dr Michel Pobers, records the impression made on him by Teilhard's conversation:

I am delighted to answer your questions about my meeting with Père Teilhard de Chardin in New York. It was at dinner at the house of Monsieur Hervé, attaché at the French Consulate-general.

I knew little of Père Teilhard's work. I had read his article on "The Future: Its Aims and Conditions", but I was not familiar with his writings.

During dinner, someone mentioned the research expedition I had just made in Jamaica and Haiti, and the curious physical and psychological phenomena I had been able to observe during certain ceremonies of "Obeah" and "Voodoo". After dinner, Père Teilhard took me aside, and for about two hours we discussed scientific methods of studying "paranormal" phenomena. I was surprised to find that Père Teilhard was familiar not only with all the literature on such phenomena and on paranormal faculties to be found among primitive people, but also with the laboratory work and the statistical computations of Professor J. B. Rhine at Durham, North Carolina, and Dr S. G. Soal in London. He made some very just critical remarks on the application of statistical evaluation and probability-calculation to psychology and to human sciences in general. I told him about new experiments that I was trying to organize in collaboration with Professor Jung and his Institute at Zürich. Here again I was greatly impressed by his wide knowledge and appreciation of Jung's theories, in particular the true concepts of the Archetype and the Collective Subconscious. Although Teilhard was very non-committal about psychoanalysis in general, he nevertheless made a sharp distinction between the theories of Freud, Adler, and Horney, and the ideas of Jung, with which his own thought had something in common.

We soon agreed about the impossibility of analysing the particular aspects of the individual's psychology or psychopathology without first facing the problem of "the whole of Man", perhaps even without first integrating a still wider whole, the "human universe". It was in this connection that Père Teilhard gave me a brief sketch of his theory of "man's biological success".

Teilhard's lack of sympathy with Freudian psychoanalysis is understandable, for he was a well-balanced personality, without repression or complex. He was far too open-minded, however, to reject all psychoanalytical theories, since he realized that psychoanalysis demonstrates that the human mind has a history, and can thus be of use in constructing an energetics of man. All man's faculties, he believed, entered into this energetics, since love is, both in God and man, the supreme energy.

That Teilhard should have studied parapsychology is interesting. He detested any woolliness of thought or emotional belief in phenomena impatient of scientific investigation. On the other hand he by no means rejected the possibility that, through unanimization, man's faculties might develop to a higher level. He wrote (20 January 1955) of his mistrust:

of anything resembling occultism, "secrets" handed down from the wisdom of long ago, communications with the beyond that cannot be checked. . . . I by no means entirely exclude scientific exploration of extra-sensorial phenomena—i.e. of some sort of "interpsychic" field possibly allied (cosmically) to the physicists' electromagnetic field.

One institution in New York for which Teilhard had long retained a special affection was the American Museum of Natural History, which he used constantly for research in connection with the Wenner Gren. A member of the staff, Mrs Rachel H. Nichols, in a letter to the author, recalls his charm and gaiety:

He used to come into the Osborn Library and sit where he could look at my magnificent view of the 59th Street skyline, across Central Park, admire the view, and catch up on all the news, etc. He seemed to really enjoy being invited to the departmental parties which we occasionally have, and we always asked him to the Christmas parties, and any others if there were guests he might enjoy.... And he always insisted on helping me with the dishes! Two or three of us would take all the glasses into our laboratory and he would gaily wipe, while I washed them. It was, of course, this warmth of personality which made him loved by everyone who knew him. He used to come to dinner occasionally, and once, afterwards, I took him up through Times Square, having learned that in all his years in New York, he had never seen the bright lights of Broadway! He was as delighted as a child with all the fabulous advertising signs....

With his passion for human unanimity there was, for Teilhard, something special about Christmas and the Christmas spirit in a large city, though his appreciation was sometimes tempered by amusement:

At the moment we are in the full fever of "*Christmas*". It is very odd and touching to see how this time is characterized by a spirit of good will and inter-human sympathy (even though it is too divorced from religion): the "*Christmas spirit*", in fact, something specially real. (23 December 1952.) New York is rapidly blossoming out in trees and the Christmas spirit. Santa Claus is everywhere, in a red cloak and white beard, and the shops scintillate with lights. It's very nice and, basically, very innocent even though very commercialized. (5 December 1954.)

The enchantment faded with the New Year:

Yesterday, for the first of January, I went into the country to "eat turkey", in magnificent dry-cold weather. The woods, which cover the whole countryside as soon as you leave the towns, were wonderfully beautiful. So now "Christmas" is over: the shops are empty and the discarded Christmas trees litter the doorways. (2 January 1955.)

11+

No news here. The Christmas trees and Santa Clauses have gone (Valentines are beginning to appear)...but I like New York...you know the sort of weather: heavy falls of snow, followed immediately by fine, bright, "*crisp*" days as in Peking. It's gayer than Paris. (13 January 1952.) — go to p. 362

These largely happy and profitable years in New York were preceded by the visit to South Africa, to which we referred earlier. Teilhard himself summarized the situation he found when he arrived in Johannesburg:

My first impressions of the possibilities of work in South Africa, in relation to the discovery of skeletal remains of Early Man, are good. In my opinion, there are at present three main lines of research open to immediate attack.

A. Most important of all, it seems to me, is the further investigation of the Sterkfontein *Australopithecus* sites (combined with laboratory preparation of the non-primate fossils excavated by the late Dr Broom). My main effort will be devoted to reconnoitring, with Robinson's assistance, the most promising aspects of this area.

B. Next in importance, unquestionably, would be to complete Dr van Riet Lowe's excavation of the remarkable Makapan site. In this small South African "Choukou-tien" (where typical hand-axes are found in a hard breccia associated with a rich fauna) there should be a good chance of finding bones of the Early Pleistocene Man of South Africa. I am planning to visit the site this month. Apparently the work of excavation could be completed in a fairly short time at relatively moderate expense.

C. Quite recently an open site (consolidated sand-dunes) has been found by the sea, some 100 miles north of Capetown. Here heavily fossilized remains of elephant, rhino, horse and ruminants are associated with hand-axes (and also with Upper Palaeolithic implements: probably from two horizons). This locality might provide us with a surface equivalent of the Makapan cave deposits and should therefore be studied closely. But the place (which is difficult to reach by car because of the sand) has not yet been examined by competent stratigraphers.

Project A should be carried out under the Geological Survey of Pretoria (Dr Robinson).

Project B would come under the jurisdiction of the Archaeological Survey of Johannesburg (Dr van Riet Lowe).

Project C belongs to the Capetown field (Dr Goodwin). But as all three of these are friends and share a common enthusiasm for research, there should be no difficulty in securing intelligent co-operation.

In fact, the network of scientific organizations in South Africa was somewhat complicated. The chief institutions were:

In Transvaal: The Archaeological Service of Johannesburg, headed by Dr van Riet Lowe;[3] the Price Institute of Palaeontology of Johannesburg (J. Kitching); the School of Medicine at the University of Witwatersrand, Johannesburg (Dr R. Dart); and the Transvaal Museum and the Geological Service of Pretoria (Dr J. T. Robinson).

In the Orange Free State, the Museum of Bloemfontein.

In Cape Province, the University of Capetown (Dr Goodwin).

Research was directed to three points:

1. The Australopithecine fissures, one of the most important being the *Paranthropus* and *Telanthropus* fissure at Swartkrans, near Sterkfontein in the Transvaal.

2. The Cave of the Hearths:

About 250 kilometres north of Pretoria, along the dolomite slopes of the Makapan valley, a string of caves, or fissures, stretches at various levels: the lowest (downstream) completely filled and densely stalagmitized (Australopithecan fissures); the highest still partially covered and containing (generally above a considerable stalagmite base) unequally consolidated deposits. (*L'anthropologie*, 1954, p. 75.)

In the middle section of this system lies an almost completely filled-up cave known as the "Cave of the Hearths". A sketch by van Riet Lowe (1951) shows, from bottom to top, a stalagmite bed; a bed of younger red sand (about three metres thick, Acheulean in period) with abundant traces of hearths (whence the name); a thick layer of red sand, highly cemented by a first roof collapse; a cultural bed of the Pietersburg (Middle Palaeolithic) culture, with hand-axes, etc., covered by a second roof collapse; a third roof collapse; and finally a Bantu cultural bed. Van Riet Lowe had made pre-

---

[3] Formerly a civil engineer, he took up prehistory and became a student of John Goodwin. He was a man of untiring and skilfully directed energy, and became one of the chief organizers of South African prehistory. At the instance of the Abbé Breuil, he founded the Archaeological Survey. Originally a materialist, he became, partly through Breuil's influence, interested in the things of the spirit, a believer in God and, in fact, a very liberal Christian.

liminary borings in 1947, and had found an anterior portion of a mandible, belonging to a neanderthaloid child of about twelve years of age.

3. Teilhard describes the Hopefield deposits as follows:

> About 120 kilometres to the north of Capetown, and about a dozen kilometres to the east of Saldanha Bay (on the Elandsfontein farm, near the little town of Hopefield), a partially consolidated dune formation appears here and there under a covering of recent dunes. By corrugated erosion, this relatively soft system of calcified or iron-bearing deposits is furrowed into numerous basins. In these basins are numerous heaps of completely fossilized bones and implements separated by the wind, but often caked again by their matrix of "calcrite" or "ferricrete". The fauna is not particularly archaic but there are a number of extinct types . . . biface tool industry: Final Acheulean (Stellenbosch) according to the specialists. (*L'anthropologie*, 1954, p. 74.)

Père Teilhard's mission required a certain tact, not so much because the Transvaal Museum is much more dependent on local politics than the University of Witwatersrand, as because of the situation created by Broom's death.[4] An exceptionally vigorous and colourful personality, supported by public opinion, boasting publicly of defying established authority, Broom had confined himself to "hunting" the Australopithecans, and to an anatomical comparison between the different members of this group. Anything else interested him only in a very general way, and then only in relation to *Australopithecus*. He had neglected an exhaustive study of the fauna and its relations with the geologic and climatic conditions. In particular he had failed to carry out a careful study of the stratigraphy and make comparisons with similar deposits, on the ground that it was a dispersion of effort. As a result he had not gathered all the fruits of his discoveries, had aroused much criticism and had differences with Dr Dart. What made replacing Broom particularly difficult was the departure, in 1950, of the brilliant geologist, S. H. Haughton, who had left the direction of the Geological Service in order to become head of the Atomic Energy Committee of Pretoria. The new man responsible for the Australopithecine sites at Sterk-

---

[4] Broom enjoyed the protection of General Smuts. He was a Scottish doctor who had devoted himself to the study of Triassic reptiles while in Australia. Boule considered him one of the greatest experts on these. In South Africa Broom had begun with an anthropological study of the Bantu races. He was an idealist and a warm advocate of evolution.

fontein, Dr Robinson, was much younger than Broom. He found it
difficult to succeed Broom, the more so that the Geological Service
was much less interested in the Quatenary era after the departure of
Dr Haughton and after the excitement of Broom's first discoveries
had died down. The main difficulty, however, lay in the recent
resurgence of Afrikaner nationalism. (From this point of view the
situation in Southern Rhodesia was much better.) Finally, the
presence of a Jesuit evolutionist in the midst of South African, anti-
evolutionist (except for the scientists) Protestants, could be highly
disturbing—and this in spite of the good impression left by the
Abbé Breuil.

Teilhard, however, was in no way dismayed. Barbour gave him
some valuable advice, and he had sufficient tact and intelligence
himself to steer a careful course. The general plan of his activities
included, first, a headquarters at Johannesburg-Pretoria (with an
excursion to Kimberley); secondly a journey through Durban to
Capetown; and finally, with Capetown as headquarters, visits to all
the important museums with palaeontological collections.[5] Although
Teilhard regretted that he was no longer to travel rough as he had
been used to do, he enjoyed motoring on good roads and wrote that
he had managed to see most of what he regarded as essential, and
that he felt better than at any time in the last three years. His letters
again record his impressions:

It is spring here—a Peking springtime without the sandy winds.
Cool nights (we are almost 2,000 metres high); but the sky is

[5] In more detail the tour included: a stay in Johannesburg and Pretoria with
a visit to Sterkfontein with Van Riet Lowe and Barbour and a visit to the
caves of Makapan; a stay at Kimberley in the Orange Free State with excursions into the environs and a visit to the quarries of Taung; a second visit to
Johannesburg with excursions to Vereeniging, south of Johannesburg; another
visit to Sterkfontein and Swartkrans with Robinson; a brief trip to Pretoria to
see Robinson and his collection of Australopithecine material; then a departure from Johannesburg in the last days of September to return to Capetown
via the following route: Durban (a visit to the Museum and the gorges of
the Umgeni River with Dr Chubb); embarkation at Durban for Capetown,
with a call at East London to visit the Museum; then to Port Elizabeth; and
finally a stay in Capetown (a walk with Goodwin to Sea Point, an excursion
to Stellenbosch, and another to Hopefield-Elandsfontein with Drennan and
Goodwin). During this time Teilhard met and talked with many scholars
interested in South African prehistory; they included Van Riet Lowe,
Haughton, Dart, Basil Cooke of the University of Johannesburg, Jackson,
Malan, Read, Robinson, Schönland, Dr A. Chubb, Miss Latimer, Goodwin,
Drennan, etc.

imperturbably blue, with fruit trees covered with pink in the gardens. Johannesburg is a sort of Detroit (with *"skyscrapers"*) situated between a zone of white slagheaps to the south (the *"dumping"* from the gold-mines), and a residential zone of suburban homes with shady eucalyptus trees and mimosas to the north. The town is still full of the pioneer spirit; but by no means disagreeable. It is much less pleasant after one leaves the city, for, to the south, you fall into vast stretches of the *"veld"*, very similar to the Chinese steppes—once you leave Pretoria you are immediately in the midst of the African bush. (16 August 1951.)

Here is a more technical account of an excursion to Kimberley:

I think that my last letter was written before my visit at the end of August to the Kimberley region—the diamond city. A less picturesque excursion than that to Makapan—but still very interesting. In the old gravel of the Vaal, constantly and everywhere moved by the diamond-searchers, ancient Palaeolithic man abounds *"in an amazing way"*. An astonishingly flat country (in fact, it is the old continental surface, abraded by the Carboniferous moraine and denuded), covered, as far as the eye can see, with large thorn bushes among which one is surprised at (and regrets) no longer seeing giraffes and rhinos wandering. To end our trip, we went to see the Taung quarries, where the first *Australopithecus* was found in 1925. A true Choukoutien, on the edge of the Kalahari. (7 September 1951.)

China was constantly in Teilhard's mind when he looked at South Africa. "An extremely interesting tour for me," he remarked in a letter of 11 September 1951, "in so far as it allows me to compare and 'contrast' another continent with Asia." Near Johannesburg he still speaks of "an unchangeable Peking sky", and notes that the fruit trees are very red as in March in the Western Hills. South Africa, toward the end of his stay, could still surprise him. He writes of Capetown:

As you see, I have now left (not without regret) the grand horizons and the magnificent Transvaal sun, to find a magnificent spring here also (at least as far as the vegetation and the flowers are concerned), but much more unsettled weather. Splendidly clear days are suddenly interrupted by ugly Southern storms, covering with clouds the famous Table Mountain which rises straight up, right in front of my window. We came here by way of Durban in a coastal steamer. The voyage was long and rather boring because of loading or unloading cargo—and a spell of bad weather: three whole days of rain at Port Elizabeth! All the same, I do not regret the experience. In return, I was able to see several geologically interesting things on the edge of the continent, not to mention the famous Crossopterygian (*Latimeria*) caught in East London in 1937 (Miss Latimer herself did me the honours): an extraordinary sight, certainly, this enormous ganoid almost two metres long, with lobed fins, the most amazing living fossil that I have ever seen. Our ship for Buenos Aires is expected here about the 15th. Meanwhile, I am making some side-trips, interesting and picturesque. The day before yesterday, under a magnificent sky, the countryside sparkled with unexpected flowers: a carpet of large white arums, anemones, multicoloured composites, heather of such intense redness as to fatigue the eye. (8 October 1951.)

At first, the fascination of South Africa was its palaeontological and geological interest; later Teilhard's interest was aroused

by the elementary forms, schematic and extreme, that clothe (as in an enclosed laboratory) the "human phenomenon": that extraordinary psychic ferment started by gold and the diamond. ...(4 September 1951.)

At the same time it strengthened his vision of man's development, for he continues:

All this has finally strengthened my passionate conviction, as I look at and beyond the Australopithecans and the foundation of the continents, that man is in some obscure way discovering (or seeing as it manifests itself) a new face of God: the evolutive God of cosmogenesis.

Another aspect of the problem of human origins was profitably studied in South Africa: the position and age of the "pebble industry" (the working of chipped pebbles, the oldest known human industry). In South Africa the development of this can be studied from its earliest origins. In a report to the Wenner Gren, Teilhard gave a forceful summary of his new point of view:

a. *The Australopithecid problem*

After inspecting the entire material collected so far in the Taung, Sterkfontein and Makapan areas, it is my conviction that the zoological significance of the Australopithecids, far from being exaggerated, is still rather underestimated. Because of their

wide geographical extension and the high density of their population (about twenty-five individuals recorded in the small Swartkrans fissure alone!), because of their high polymorphism, because
of their definitely humanoid features and in spite of a most
peculiar type of dentition (extraordinarily expanded crowns of
the molariform teeth associated with extremely reduced canines
and incisors) the Australopithecids, possibly culminating in
"*Telanthropus*" *Capensis*, represent a most illuminating group
which is as close, if not closer, to man from *below*, as the Pithe-
canthropids are from *above*.[6]

b. *The Early Pebble Industry*

In the Transvaal, as well as in East Africa, unquestionable
artifacts of the most elementary type (chipped pebbles) occur
in situ, in old gravels before the appearance of the most primitive
type of hand-axes. In fact these are possibly the earliest traces of
human activity recorded so far anywhere in the world. To trace
more and more carefully the distribution of these earliest tools
and to try and decide their chronological position in relation to
the Australopithecidae is without doubt one of the most fascinating and useful lines of research open today for a general Science
of Man.

c. *The Evolution of the Lithic Industry*

Probably in no other country (with the exception of Kenya) is
the gradual development of the lithic industry (from roughly
chipped pebbles to hand-axes and finally to flakes) as clearly and
completely represented (by well-separated and dated steps) as in
South Africa. Although only of secondary interest compared with
problems concerning human origins, this remarkable process of
technical evolution is well worth an increasingly accurate study:
the more so that it apparently reveals a perfectly uniform and
universal trend of human culture, curiously independent of the
various zoological types of Man successively or simultaneously
responsible for its development.

[6] This expression is somewhat elliptical and obscure. Teilhard had in mind
the well-known schema of the overlapping human waves. *Homo sapiens* is
separated from *Pithecanthropus* by the Neanderthaloids. In the same way,
between the Australopithecines and the Pithecanthropoids there existed an
intermediary, hypothetical at present (though perhaps *Zinjanthropus* branch
may fill this gap), which would mark the dawn of true Man. *Pithecanthropus
Pekinensis* (*Sinanthropus*) is already too advanced to have just emerged from
animality. Teilhard seems to have meant that "the Australopithecines are as
morphologically near to the first Hominid (for example, *Sinanthropus*) as the
Pithecanthropus is to *Homo sapiens*."

On the whole, although somewhat peripheral to the presumable centre of human origins (and in spite of having been submitted since the Tertiary to a dominantly erosional régime), South Africa, perhaps because it forms a blind alley at the end of the continent, seems to have registered and preserved in a most vivid manner the main phases or pulsations of early hominization. And consequently it represents, strategically, a most appropriate domain of attack for anthropological research.

Teilhard therefore proposed two main lines of action:

a. *Short Term Research*. First to subsidize the diggings at Swartkrans, under the direction of Robinson, and the Cave of the Hearths, directed by van Riet Lowe. Then to assist the Hopefield geological prospecting.

b. *Long Term Research*. For the moment, considering their spirit of close collaboration, there is no need to centralize the various institutions into a single "Institute of Man" or "Laboratory of the Cenozoic"; Robinson would be capable of submitting a long-range programme.[7]

What Père Teilhard did not say in this report was that he was maturing a complete theory in his mind. On 15 September 1951 he notes:

Conversation at dinner with Cooke

3. . . . Idea: the Australopithecans pushed back by Man (with the help of the climate?) as the *Bushmen by the Bantus* (cul-de-sac . . .).

And on 23 September, more precisely:

In Acheulean 4, Human Anticyclone in Uganda-Kenya.[8]
In the Upper Palaeolithic, the Mediterranean Anticyclone.
In the Mesolithic Anticyclone: two centres: North Africa—Northern Europe?
In the Upper Neolithic Anticyclone the arc Egypt-Mesopotamia.
The *"shifting"* of the anticyclones of hominization . . .

These very elliptical notes indicate that it is probably in the regions of Uganda and Kenya that humanity developed. In the second

---

[7] After a conversation with Haughton on 8 September 1951, Teilhard had thought at least for a moment of a "comité d'Afrique sud-saharienne" with Haughton, Th. Monod (director of the I.F.A.N.) and Millot from Madagascar as directors.

[8] By a "human anticyclone" Teilhard means a zone of very strong human pressure in the sense of an evolutionary tendency to expand, radiate and change.

11*

period, the human task would have been extended, and would have scattered the Australopithecans towards the south, who, in spite of their humanoid characteristics (upright posture) were still only animals.[9] After which the anticyclone, the zone of strong

[9] It is confirmed today (1963) that at least the Zinjanthropine type of Australopithecine was "human"; a tool-user; "the oldest kind of creature yet found that the geologists and anthropologists will allow in the human race". (*Science News Letter*, 83, p. 154, 9 March 1963.)

Édouard Boné in "Les industries humaines au Transvaal", *Études*, July–August, 1955, pp. 111–13, refused "to separate the Australopithecines from the problem of primitive industries" on the basis of recent evidence. On the other hand, J. Piveteau remains very negative in the excellent seventh volume of his *Traité de paléontologie*. But in "L'Australopithèque et le problème des origines de l'homme", *Nouvelles littéraires*, 15 October 1959, Piveteau admits that "we cannot reject a priori the hypothesis that the Australopithecines may be the makers of the stone industry associated with their remains."

The discoveries of Dr and Mrs L. S. B. Leakey (17 July 1959) seem to make this conclusion more certain. The *Zinjanthropus* skull discovered in the Oldoway gorge, Tanganyika, presents essentially the same characteristics as the Australopithecines and is now considered one of this group. The pebble tool culture found with the *Zinjanthropus*, technically known as the Oldowan industry, lasted for some half a million years, beginning 1,750,000 years ago. This culture was then replaced by the Chellean which persisted down to about 450,000–400,000 years ago. Before the *Zinjanthropus* tool culture was the Kafuan culture which "lasted for a comparable length of time. Tool-making Hominids thus are given an antiquity well beyond two million years". (*Science News Letter*, 83, p. 154, 9 March 1963.)

The dating of *Zinjanthropus* at 1,750,000 years and his inclusion in the Australopithecine group posed some confusing problems. The Pleistocene (the Age of Man) had previous been dated as beginning anywhere from a million years to 300,000 years ago. Now, the advent of Man, the glacial ages and the Pleistocene are set around three million years ago (*Scientific American*, 208, no. 2 (February, 1963), pp. 69–70; and *Science News Letter, loc. cit.*). Yet, despite the agreement at the December, 1962, meeting of the American Association for the Advancement of Science, at Philadelphia, other factors make our dating and conclusions uncertain for the moment. Particular reference is made to the work of Columbia University's Lamont Geological Observatory, whose findings on Pleistocene sediment cores taken from the ocean bottom place the start of this era at "not less than 800,000 years ago". (*Scientific American*, 208, no. 3 (March, 1963), pp. 76–8.)

Reports of the discoveries of L. S. B. Leakey can be found in several journals: "A New Fossil Skull from Olduvai", *Nature*, no. 4685, 15 August 1959, pp. 491–1; "The Newly-discovered Skull from Olduvai: First Photographs of the Complete Skull", *Illustrated London News*, 18 September 1959, pp. 288–9; "Finding the World's Earliest Man", *National Geographic Magazine*, 118, no. 3 (September, 1960), pp. 420–35; "Exploring 1,750,000 Years into Man's Past. Clock for the Ages: Potassium Argon", *National Geographic Magazine*, 120, no. 4 (October, 1961), pp. 564–92; "Adventures in the Search for Man", *National Geographic Magazine*, 123, no. 1 (January, 1963), pp. 132–

human pressure, would be displaced towards the north, reaching the Mediterranean, crossing over Europe and Asia.

On 12 October Teilhard noted again:

> Idea: the *Australopithecus*: more than an African shell? A covering thrown over all the ends and fringes of the continent (this explaining *Meganthropus*?)—who would not be a *"true"* *Pithecantropus?*

Teilhard meant that the equivalent of the Australopithecine stage could have existed in Asia, and that the drama in which the Australopithecines were the victims in Africa, retreating before Man, could also have had its counterpart elsewhere.

In all this, we find Teilhard's skill in immediately picking out the crucial points and distinguishing the essential from the non-essential. Evidently, he was guided by Barbour and the South African scientists, but it was he who grasped the importance of the Australopithecine phenomenon.[10] Secondly, we see his gift for generalization. In less than two months and a half, he outlines a whole conception of African prehistory. In less than three-and-a-half months, he begins to include Africa and Asia in one synthetic view. About the middle of October he gave an important lecture to the

---

52; see also the *Scientific American* and *Science News Letter* articles mentioned above.

In the process of hominization, as Piveteau notes, the first acquisition was bipedal posture. Then the first psychic progress entailed the use of tools which, in turn, provoked a development of the hand, from which flowed a new development of the brain—the three terms are correlative. Reflection is not detached from action, nor does it seize on an object as a good, later on.

Returning to Teilhard, it seems that his views are confirmed and that Africa may be the only country in the world to possess all the links in the evolutive chain of Humanity leading to modern Man. But it is evident that Teilhard could not know that *Australopithecus* had passed the animal stage when the proof was not yet available.

[10] Teilhard was the first to underline the special character of the Saldanha–Hopefield site and its value for prehistory and human palaeontology. The Saldanha site is Upper Pleistocene, the same age as that of the Rhodesian Man of Broken Hill. When first discovered, in 1921, the skull of the Rhodesian Man was a puzzle and many considered it an isolated freak. Then, some seventy miles north of Capetown, on the Atlantic coast, Keith Jolly collected twenty-four fragments of a skull from the dunes in 1953. This was two years after Teilhard pointed out the specific potentials of the site. The Saldanha skull indicates that the Rhodesian-type man occupied South Africa for a long time, at least during the two periods in which first the Old Stone Age and then the Middle Stone Age developed. It provides us with the first fossil man belonging to the Old Stone Age.

South African Geological Society, of which the following is a rough summary:

> Turning now to the origin of Man, Father Teilhard said that after having been told, first that Man had originated in Europe from a Neanderthal stock, and later on that he was born in Central Asia along a Sinanthropian line, he had come to believe since 1933 that the Far Eastern fossil men (*Pithecanthropus*) and allied forms were nothing but a somewhat lateral branch of Hominians, probably developed in South-eastern Asia, quite peripheral to the main centre of hominization. And he was therefore much pleased when visiting this country to realize that Man, from all the evidence, was decidedly older and deeper-rooted in Africa than in Asia: palaeontologically speaking first (presence of numerous Tertiary apes, and Lower Pleistocene spread of Australopithecinae), but also culturally. For while in Asia lithic industries are scattered irregularly and discontinuously from south to north, as if it had taken the entire Pleistocene for Man (coming first from the south, then from the west, and finally from the north) to gain a definitive foothold on the continent, in South and East Africa there is an astonishing continuity and wealth of stone implements, ranging from a very old pebble industry and culminating in an incredibly perfect Acheulean culture.
>
> In Europe and in Asia, Early Man seems like a newcomer, but in this country he appears to be autochthonous. For an Asiatic geologist and palaeontologist this is the great lesson taught by a visit to South Africa.

There is no doubt that this first South African visit was a success, materially, for Père Teilhard. An eyewitness wrote from Buenos Aires to a mutual friend:

> He is, I know, much too modest to tell you that he has been offered jobs and contracts both here and in South Africa. In spite of his laughing it all off, I think he is pleased (as he should be) at his renown!

It is very important, too, to emphasize that this trip was, above all, an interior success. In a letter of 16 September 1951 he writes: "... This contact with the terrain has stimulated me and rejuvenated me intellectually." And fresh contact with the past helped him to see the future more clearly:

> In short, I have learned a great deal here on the problem of human origins (however, I missed Kenya! ...). But at the same

time (as much by reaction to the pre-Cambrian as to the Pleistocene) I shall leave even more convinced that knowledge of the
past is empty if it does not lead to movements or processes which
are at this moment prolonging themselves in and around us, and
which we must both espouse and control. From this new period
of isolation and contact with the Real, I shall emerge, I feel, more
and more irrevocably devoted and decide to affirm and to preach
the physico-biological reality of an irresistible human movement
in the direction of increasing Reflection. An impulse as inflexible
as that of Matter in the bosom of the Atoms or of the galaxies (I
am working on a new essay... on "The reflection of energy",
in the same way as we speak of the "conservation" or "dissipation" of Energy... I don't know where all this will lead me....
But I know one thing perfectly well: it is that henceforth
absolutely nothing save sickness or death, of course, will be able
to stop me. (7 September 1951.)

Teilhard was in excellent form, when in the last ten days of
October he embarked for New York, travelling the long way round,
via Buenos Aires, Rio de Janeiro, Trinidad; he explains the reason
for this route:

It will be very useful to me to have seen Argentina on my way
back from South Africa, for I shall immediately be able to
appreciate, *"both from the geological and the anthropological
point of view"* the analogies and contrasts between the two continents.[11] It's quite a shock to find here Permian glaciation and
Devonian sandstone similar to those I have just left at Durban
and the Cape (a point for Wegener). And as for Man, it's quite
a shock, too, after leaving the "explosive" centre of Palaeolithic
industry, to meet the wave at its furthest extension, on the very
circumference of its radiation, after crossing the whole breadth of
Asia and length of North America. Unfortunately, I have been
able to experience this only in collections and museums. Even so,
I've been lucky, because of the presence here of a fine German
prehistorian, well known (Dr Oswald Menghin, retired here
since the war). He is engaged in a complete reappraisal of all that
is known of the country's prehistory (in particular, Patagonia).
With him I saw a great deal that no one outside of here yet knows

[11] In another letter (15 October 1951) Teilhard writes: "As I pass through,
it will be entertaining to check a number of recent statements about the age
of some of the lithic industries of this region—statements which seem to me
to be pure guesses or based on no more than analogies of form. Too many
even well-known prehistorians, in fact, have too little geological training."

about. It's immensely interesting, not only because of the contrast but because you can complete the curve of the first "planetary" expansion of man. Interesting, too, for anyone who wishes to measure and delineate in its broad movements the "phenomenon of man". Apart from that Buenos Aires is a huge Marseilles, or a vast "concession" from which anything exotic seems to have disappeared (except in the waters—the strange fishes—of the Rio de la Plata). (8 November 1951.)

Another interesting note runs:

"South America" = the antipodes of "South Africa"!
"atomized" industries, multiple, "*dissipated*".

South America thus helped to complete the pattern, in Teilhard's mind, of human expansion. He would dearly have loved to have "annexed" all the continents; and it must always be a matter of regret that Australia eluded him.

CHAPTER TWENTY-ONE

The American Period:
Second African Visit

TEILHARD was back in the United States during the second half of 1951. While travelling he had been turning over in his mind an essay for Julian Huxley, which he had finished by February of the next year, on "The Transformation and Prolongation in Man of the Process of Evolution". His position in New York was now a little uncertain; there was always a place for him at the Wenner Gren, but at the same time there was no suggestion that he was to settle permanently in America. On 7 December 1951 he wrote: "As for myself, I am temporarily stranded or perched here—the perch being the Wenner Gren Foundation, where I am invited to stay as long as I wish."

What had happened twenty-eight years earlier was now repeating itself: to leave Europe for a distant continent, at first for a limited stay which later was prolonged indefinitely. Teilhard was, accordingly, again feeling distressed by his long absence from France.

I can't help feeling rather depressed at being cut off from Paris. However, there are compensations. I'll get over it, and the important thing is that I can do some good here. (10 December 1951.)

Meanwhile, there was a good deal to keep him busy. He worked at his South African notes, and produced a series of short memoranda and papers. In March, 1952, for example, he gave two lectures: one at the National Academy of Sciences (of which he was an honorary member) on "The Zoological Position and Evolutionary Significance of the Australopithecines"; the other at the Wenner Gren on "New Advances made by Prehistory in South

Africa". In June the Wenner Gren arranged a short symposium of its own members on anthropology. To this Teilhard made a more important contribution on "The Birth, Growth, and Present Status of our Idea of Fossil Man". With his South African experience behind him, he was hoping to direct the Foundation's effort towards that field of study. The June symposium seemed to promise the results he hoped for:

> Here at the Foundation, it seems that an indirect result of the June symposium has been the decision that the Foundation should concentrate its efforts in support of research on the origins of man in Africa. So far, the project is only being examined, but it can develop and yield something quite fascinating. (2 October 1952.)

On 7 November he wrote again:

> ... the latest is that the Wenner Gren Foundation has just decided to concentrate its efforts on research into human origins in Africa. The first drafts of the project concern Southern Africa and the region around the Great Lakes.... The Wenner Gren Foundation does not wish to interfere with the local researches— but only to assist researches into points systematically chosen— the choice being left to those already concerned.

A further and more important result for Teilhard was that he himself was chosen to return to South Africa.[1] On 13 January 1953 the Board of Directors gave him a subsidy of $5,000. The programme, in his own words, included:

> 1. The examination of human bones and tools recently found at Hopefield (near Capetown) in view of an eventual intensification of work in that locality.
> 2. A more intensive inspection of the "Cave of Hearths", at Makapan (the earliest Palaeolithic), where Dr van Riet Lowe will begin comprehensive diggings next summer with the support of the Wenner Gren Foundation.
> 3. A recapitulation of the fossil-bearing fissures recently discovered or explored in Transvaal and Rhodesia; at the same time, a better "planification" for research of such fissures in the area under consideration. (12 March 1953.)

---

[1] In January, 1952, Teilhard, in a report to Paul Fejos, had been in favour of sending Dr Oakley, of the Natural History Museum (London), to South Africa, to apply the fluorine-dating technique to the Australopithecines. At the same time he stressed the primary importance of excavation.

We know that the diggings at Makapan had begun by 30 April 1953:

> Backed by the Wenner Gren Foundation, van Riet Lowe has just begun the diggings in the cemented ashes (hearths rich in bifaced tools) of the Cave of Hearths at Makapan. I would have liked to go into Kenya, but I could not because of the Mau-Mau and also because of a possible cardiac allergy to yellow fever inoculation.

It was indispensable for Teilhard to revisit this "small Choukou-tien"—probably younger than its Asiatic counterpart and the only excavation of this type yet located south of the Sahara. There was hope of finding a skull. Paradoxically we are ignorant of the cephalic characteristics of Man at the dawn of the African Palaeolithic, while his tools abound *in situ*. Yet, at the beginning of 1953, new data became available:

> In January, the cranial dome of a man similar to *"Homo Rhodesiensis"* was found north of Capetown (in consolidated sand dunes which I visited two years ago): but its age is relatively recent. It seems to be from around the extreme end of the Lower Palaeolithic (?). The geology of the site has not yet been worked out in a satisfactory manner. Likewise, at the beginning of this year, other interesting early breccia have been explored in Rhodesia, which contain an industry of very primitive aspect, a pebble industry associated with a large baboon.[2] More and more it seems that the Australopithecines are never found in association with Man, or with any industry whatsoever, and that, consequently, they ought to be considered both as "ante-human" chronologically and "para-human" zoologically and psychologically. (18 June 1953.)

It was, however, something of an effort for Teilhard to undertake the travelling involved. In September, 1952, he refers to his success in persuading the Wenner Gren to turn its attention to South Africa and says that Fejos has asked him to act as his "chief lieutenant". "But," he adds, "what a pity I'm not ten years younger!" Later, in June, he writes:

[2] The brainpan had been found by Keith Jolly. The breccias were at Lusaka, Northern Rhodesia. *Homo rhodesiensis*, representing an earlier Palaeolithic culture (of the last Pleistocene) and belonging to a para-*sapiens* fringe of some very ancient *sapiens* (or pre-*sapiens*) stock, had been discovered before Teilhard's first trip to South Africa.

I am not particularly excited by this voyage into places I already know and by a type of work which appears to me less and less "vital". Even so, I understand that I can, at this precise moment, give a useful impetus down there, either to the research itself or to its organization. Then, as I was telling you, I need this humble platform to make myself heard. . . . I count on these months at large to give myself a new start in life and ideas: on Man, the continents, and also (if not above all) on the present and future state of hominization.

There is a characteristic reference in the passage quoted to work which appears less "vital" and to the primacy in Teilhard's mind of the present and future state of man's development. What matters for him is not the science of the past but the study of processes that are still in operation, and the past interested him only in so far as it elucidates the present and the future. He was, however, wanted in South Africa, and when he arrived he recognized that he had done well to accept the assignment:

All in all, everything that I have seen and heard in the fortnight I have been here confirms me in the conviction that I have done well to come. I have coincided with a complete reorganization of research into human origins, with a new drive behind it—and this in a critically important part of the world. In organizing and inspiring, I believe that I can really be of use. In any case, I am learning a great deal—and ideas are beginning to come. It is simply a matter of trusting oneself more and more to the guiding influence of the "divine milieu". (30 July 1953.)

On 1 July 1953, accordingly, Teilhard sailed from New York in the *African Endeavour*. During an uneventful voyage he was working on "The Stuff of the Universe", which is dated 14 July 1953, "in sight of St Helena, on passage from New York to the Cape". In this he tried once again "to grasp and express rather more thoroughly the real heart—which always seems to elude me—of what I feel, of what I see, of what I live."

Teilhard's movements in South Africa were determined by his wish to visit three important centres, Hopefield (for which he stayed at Capetown on arriving and before he left), Makapan (from Johannesburg and Pretoria), and Lusaka (in Northern Rhodesia).[3] It was

[3] Teilhard's movements were as follows: 18 July, land at Capetown and stay for five days; 23 or 24 July, arrive at Johannesburg and examine the Hopefield material; 29 July, at Pretoria, with Robinson and Haughton; 2–4

not possible, unfortunately, to visit Kenya. The work begun by Broom at Swartkrans had been completed in 1952 by Dr Robinson, and *Australopithecus* was now being studied chiefly in the laboratory in "blocks of fossil-bearing breccia obtained either from excavations in the old lime-kilns at Makapan or from various fissures in the Sterkfontein area". These laboratories were at the Johannesburg School of Medicine (Dr Dart) and at the Transvaal Museum in Pretoria, under Dr Robinson, who had developed a remarkable method of dissolving the breccia with acetic acid.

Writing on 5 August 1953, Teilhard gave a summary of the first part of his visit:

> ...our comfortable little ship (10,000) arrived at Capetown in spring-like weather just a week before a cold spell, which might have been unpleasant and is now over. I remained five days at Capetown, time enough to see the pronouncedly neanderthaloid cranium found this year in the consolidated, fossil-bearing, sand-dunes of Hopefield, and to discuss the course of operations at Hopefield. Then we went up to Johannesburg, where I have done quite a lot: a visit to Pretoria, to see Robinson and the new australopithecine material, and these last days, a visit to the large excavations at Makapan (300 kilometres north of here, on the asphalt highway from the Cape to Cairo), where my friend, van Riet Lowe (financed by the Wenner Gren) is in the process of emptying a "little Choukou-tien".

August at Makapan (on the road to which he passed a clump of big trees where Livingstone once camped); a series of conferences with Cooke, van Riet Lowe, Dr Jeffreys and Dart, followed towards the end of August by a flight from Johannesburg to Livingstone in Northern Rhodesia (in spite of the doctors' orders not to travel by air); 26 August, at Lusaka, with visits to the Cave of the Bees, Grand Cave, the Kafue Gorge, and up the Zambezi river (of this visit to Lusaka he wrote in November to Oakley), "Near Lusaka Desmond Clark showed me Freeman's Hole, where we found several more broken pebbles *in situ*, and the Twin River fissure (where we, or rather Clark, extracted the other half of the tool that you and he had found and broken some months before)"; 31 August, back at Livingstone, where he visited the Museum, of which Desmond Clark was director, and from which he made a trip to Victoria Falls; beginning of September, back to Johannesburg, second visit to Pretoria and Makapan (15 September); 20 September, from Johannesburg to Capetown, where he examined the most recent finds from Hopefield in the University Medical School (a new site had been found near Elandsfontein); there was also a visit to the museum at Bloemfontein in the Orange Free State, where he saw Hofman and T. F. Dreyer, who in 1932 had found an important fragment of fossilized skull twenty-five miles north of Bloemfontein.

On the whole, I am extremely interested by all that I see: both from the general viewpoint of human origins, and from the particular point of view of the strategy to follow in order to mount a general attack on Africa south of the Sahara. With a good "five-year plan" (to which I hope to convert Fejos) it should be possible to establish at Makapan an ascending series of super-imposed deposits running from the Australopithecine layers (Lower Pleistocene) to the higher Palaeolithic. With two or three similar points (of which we have Hopefield, near Capetown, and Olduway in Tanganyika) we shall have, I repeat, a first triangulation south of the Sahara. To complete the network I hope, towards the beginning of September, to go to Northern Rhodesia (Lusaka), where they have just found breccia containing remains of an industry that appears to be "pre-Chellean". All this work of organization is the more interesting in that (thanks to the friendli-ness of Fejos) I feel that the sinews of war are in reach of my hand, and that, in addition, they're building up a team of energetic and attractive young people. In fact, I can see the development (but this time in Africa) of the same sort of inter-national *"team"* as that which, just before 1939, made our research into *"early man"* in the Far East so exciting.

Besides this, I am deeply interested by the economic and social situation of the country: the uranium industry developing, with an irresistibly accelerating rhythm, in a country still populated by cattle-breeders. Again, and this time from a completely opposite point of view, I greatly enjoy this countryside: the large animals have unfortunately (and inevitably) disappeared in the last seventy years (apparently elephants and giraffes still used to walk around Pretoria when I was born), but its main features are still the same. Everything is more or less grey or yellow, this month; but at the same time, to brighten up the view, at the moment we have the aloes in flower; you can see their stems everywhere, red, pink, or yellow, among the weeping acacias and the candelabra of the euphorbias. I'm speaking of the bush to the north of Pretoria, which looks just the same all the way to Abyssinia. Around Johannesburg, on the high plateau, the appearance of the country is more austere. But at this time of year the quality of the light is magnificent. An unruffled blue sky, and the air dry and "crisp". Just like Peking towards the end of autumn. There's a little frost in the morning.

So, everything is going as well as could be.

We have a similar picture of Teilhard's "raid" into Rhodesia. On 25 or 26 August he was going through bush country, very dry, often burnt, and terrifyingly vast and monotonous, but at Lusaka he found the golden-flowered *Quassia*. On the 30th he went up the Zambezi with Clark; and though he thought of Livingstone covering the same ground, he had no time for anything that was not still in evolution.[4] The Zambezi, with its reeds and clumps of papyrus, its crocodiles and hippopotamuses, belonged to the past, and the energy held in its waters now waited for man to direct it towards a new beauty. Teilhard was untouched by nostalgia for the past.

Northern Rhodesia, as his correspondence shows, made a deep impression:

The core of this visit has been a trip into Northern Rhodesia around the end of August. There, near Lusaka, I was able to see a series of fissures containing fossiliferous breccia with implements that may perhaps establish a bridge between the Australopithecine beds and the first African lithic industries (the pebble industry). I hope to persuade the Wenner Gren Foundation to subsidize a digging there which will possibly fix a new and important point in the "triangulation" of human origins in Africa, south of the Sahara. In the course of this excursion I have learnt a great deal, but I also saw a very impressive country whose appearance has not changed since Livingstone traversed it. Immense undulating surfaces, covered with deep bush, in which, towards the end of the dry season, a certain number of trees begin to show green against the background of tall yellowing grasses. Above the Victoria Falls, where I spent two days, you can often see hippopotamuses bathing quietly in the Zambezi. From Johannesburg to Livingstone and back we travelled by Jet Comet (less than two hours, instead of three days by train or car); we went up to about 12,000 metres, which did not permit us to see much. Returning, however, the visibility was such that I could make out the great saltpan of Kalahari.

And now I am spending my last days in Johannesburg. To-morrow I must go back to Pretoria (the Geological Service and Robinson); and the week after that I expect to visit the main diggings at Makapan, which should be resumed next year. As I told you, it is a question of establishing a complete typical series, connecting the Australopithecine with the biface layers. No human bone remains found yet, which is a little disappointing.

[4] In this same month (August) Teilhard was present when Desmond Clark found some undoubtedly authentic implements.

(It may be, however, that the greater part of the deposits has not yet been touched.) On the whole, I shall leave well satisfied, and completely convinced now that the movement is well under way, and that all we have now to do is to "feed" it, at seven or eight useful points, spaced out between the Cape and Tanganyika. What I most lack (and I don't see what I can do about it, because of yellow fever and inoculation against it) is a knowledge of the magnificent lacustrine series in the Great Lakes area. (9 September 1953.)

Teilhard contributed an excellent account of research in South Africa to *L'anthropologie* (1954) under the title "Research Directed to the Discovery of Human Origins in Africa South of the Sahara", in which he described how "palaeo-anthropological research, in this area peculiarly well situated for the study of human origins, had improved in organization, accuracy, and intensity".

The first question was to define the position of the Australopithecines. After a conversation (on 29 July) with Robinson, at Pretoria, Teilhard noted:

1. The two lines   *Australopithecus-Plesianthropus*
                      (skull more humanoid)
                      (dentition less humanoid)

                      Paranthropus
                      (skull less humanoid)
                      (teeth more humanoid)

2. *Telanthropus* separate (3rd line)

As a first step it was necessary to establish a complete stratigraphical scheme, with the corresponding palaeontological and archaeological characteristics: Australopithecine layers, pebble-industry (*in situ*) layers, hand-axe layers, with their five different types of industry. From such a synthesis, Teilhard believed, it would emerge that *Australopithecus* and Man are mutually exclusive.[5]

---

[5] The question of what determines the human nature of a fossilized creature is a problem. It has generally been accepted that the making of tools in a definite pattern and the use of fire are characteristics of a rational creature. A "tool culture" involves speech as a means of handing on the tradition of tool-making technique; hence speech also enters the discussion. Yet it is certain now that Leakey's *Zinjanthropus*, one of the Australopithecines, was found in association with a tool industry. Whether *Zinjanthropus* made these tools is another question, but it would seem that *Zinjanthropus* was a rational creature and hence human. This contradicts Teilhard's conclusion.

Allowing for the different circumstances, Africa played the same part in Teilhard's life as Asia. Writing on 23 December 1952 he says, "in 1925 Peking was the chance of my life: perhaps New York will be my second Peking". "But", he added ruefully, "I'm no longer forty years old." As in Asia, his eye ranged far afield, embracing the whole continent south of the Sahara, with side-glances at Mozambique, Angola, and French West Africa. A letter to Théodore Monod, director of the French North African Institute, is characteristic:

Your "tips" about the Tananarive meeting were confirmed for me by a nice letter from Mouta (a Portuguese geologist), to which I have replied (at his suggestion) in a letter which he will be able to show to the Minister for "Oltramare" in Lisbon, in order to convince him that it is to Portugal's interest not to stand apart from the movement, now well under way, for research into human origins in Africa south of the Sahara. We certainly need, and that without delay, a good foothold (by which I mean a good examination of a carefully selected fossiliferous fissure) in Angola—and also an exact study of the Mozambique seaboard terraces. . . . Haven't you calcareous massifs (either crystalline or not) in your territory? If you have, examine the breccia in the fissures. Wherever I've seen them, the karsts of the African platform contain Man or pre-Man.[6]

The letter to which Teilhard referred was the following:

I was very glad to see your letter for I am now convinced that a very flexible and active organization is now being spontaneously developed "for the study of human origins south of the Sahara", and that, in this organization (or organism), Portugal is called on to take a leading place by reason of its position and the extent of its dominions in Africa. Already contact has been established between members of a brilliant group: Leakey in Kenya, D. Clark in Rhodesia, Robinson at Pretoria, van Riet Lowe, Dart, Cooke, etc., at Johannesburg. . . . Everyone here awaits closer collaboration with Angola and Mozambique.

[6] Cf. a letter to Théodore Monod of 30 July 1953: "It is becoming evident that within the next five years the history of human origins in Africa will be traced through a network of fossiliferous fissures (Plio-Pleistocene karst) "providentially" furnished by the pre-Cambrian dolomites almost everywhere south of the Sahara. Robinson and Cooke agree in thinking that we must begin immediately a methodical inspection of these fissures, beginning at selected points: Sterkfontein, Makapan, Lusaka, Angola. . . . I believe it will be easy to convince Dr Fejos of this."

... Without wanting to interfere in any way with your work of research and description ... the Wenner Gren Foundation is willing, I know, to help you make the necessary diggings at important sites.

Teilhard's suggestions came near to bearing fruit, for a letter of 26 March 1954 tells us that Mouta is proposing to introduce Clark to the fossiliferous deposits in Angola.[7]

Africa enabled Teilhard to focus his ideas on human origins in relation to geological development. Writing on 15 November 1953, he again records his satisfaction with this visit; not only did he feel that he had learnt a great deal himself, but he had the additional pleasure of knowing that he had been largely responsible for initiating ("with the Foundation's dollars") a comprehensive research network. Practical examples of the financial assistance he was able to call upon were the Wenner Gren's decision to subsidize the excavations at Twin River in Rhodesia, and at Makapan. Thus van Riet Lowe, writing to Fejos, acknowledges the sum of $8,400, and Teilhard assures him that the remaining $1,600 will be available, because "in African research Makapan has, and will continue to have, priority".

The very metaphors that Teilhard used indicate his strategical approach to the problem. He speaks of an "attack", a "line of attack", a "raid" and refuses to be diverted from the main objective. Thus, he constantly insists on the central point, "to clear up the question of pre-Chellean man (Kafuan)[8] and the Australopithecines" and deprecates too much attention to the hand-axe cultures, even though they are "more spectacular, easier, and more entertaining".

On the personal level, too, Teilhard was equally successful. Everyone he met and worked with in South Africa spoke of him with esteem and affection. Desmond Clark's tribute (in a letter to Paul Fejos) is typical:

Father Teilhard's death has removed one of the most brilliant and the most successful palaeontologists from our midst, and the gap that his passing leaves will be felt for many a year to come.

---

[7] Unfortunately, the Portuguese authorities did not allow Mouta's far-reaching plans to be carried out.

[8] Kafuan is another name for the pebble industry; the name comes from a tributary of the Zambezi, the Kafue River in Rhodesia, which passes near Lusaka.

His charm, his courtesy and interest we shall never forget, and the memory of his personality and his visit to us is as vivid today as if it had taken place only yesterday. Though he himself is no longer with us, we shall long remember his vitality and kindness and we feel with very many others that we have lost a true friend and master.

Teilhard's conclusions were excellently presented in an article ("Africa and Human Origins") he contributed to the *Revue des questions scientifiques* (1955); but what is particularly interesting to us about this period is to follow the development of his ideas from their conception. According to Teilhard, anthropogenesis is bi-polar, and includes two centres, each with concentric rings (pongoid, australopithecoid, pithecanthropoid, neanderthaloid). One centre was in Asia (Indo-Malayan), and proved abortive, for it did not lead to *Homo sapiens* (who is an invader in Asia); the other was in Africa and this is the more important and more interesting, for there hominization was complete. Teilhard, however, did not believe in polyphyletism, but in the segmentation of an evolutionary front, a splitting of the human phylum in the immediate vicinity of its origin. This "law of segmentation of evolutionary fronts" is seen also, for example, in the strepsicerotine antelopes.

Geographically and anthropologically the African "reservoir centre" had, for Teilhard, two functions. Equatorially, Africa is a melting-pot; the south has drawn off the fluid, and, being a cul-de-sac, retains in a dispersed state a more or less complete spectrum of the successive waves of speciation. We thus find three historical periods in Africa. First, a period of elaboration. Man, and with him *Homo sapiens*, is born somewhere in Kenya-Uganda, the active mutation-zone. Secondly, a period of expansion. Man is drawn up to the north, and so we have an intermediate period in which we find scattered traces of Man (Bushmen?). Thirdly, a re-invasion of this void by the true negroes, the Bantu, with mutation on the spot of *Homo sapiens*, who takes advantage of this unoccupied territory to expand again (somewhat as the American Indians).

There is, of course, an overlapping at times of the successive waves. Thus we read (29 January 1953):

> Hopefield man would seem to indicate that the African man who used bifaced tools himself formed a fissile complex in which conjectured proto-*sapiens* types were surrounded by marginal

"neanderthaloid" types.[9] We have not fully realized yet to what degree the genesis of a new zoological type (in speciation) is a phenomenon at once exact and complicated, obeying completely determined mechanics (or following a "*pattern*").

Africa, in short, forced Teilhard to evolve a much more flexible definition of monophyletism, and so better to understand or perceive "speciation patterns". These led him to a new science of orthogenesis and enabled him to distinguish a central orthogenetic axis with a series of divergent branches.[9]

The picture he arrived at is like a tree growing taller and taller. As it rises, branches leave the trunk. The main stem, crowned by the terminal bud, is woody and fibrous; lateral shoots are continually produced but the tree has its own direction of growth.

For Teilhard the study of human origins was not simply a discovery of the past; it was to be integrated with a picture of man's future. "What", he asked, "is our position—not our static but our dynamic position—in the universe?"[10] Africa thus led him towards an "anthropodynamics" which leads to God; and this involved the determination of an axial continuity between hominization and the evolutionary current, a task that calls for the geologist, the palaeontologist and even the physicist; of Teilhard's thought it may truly be said that it was above all unitary.

Towards the end of September, 1953, Teilhard embarked at Capetown to return to New York. It was not until 2 November that he arrived, for he took the opportunity to pay a quick visit to South America.

> I feel that I must get a clear idea of (by which I mean see for myself) the Pampas lands, and of the structure of the Andes, where they end: this because I want to try and verify some ideas, very important to me, on the genesis of continents. (8 September 1953.)

---

[9] Of the monophyletism of *Homo sapiens*, Teilhard had no doubts. The question he leaves open is whether certain races such as the Bushmen are marginal survivors to one side of the monophylic *Homo sapiens* group or whether they are marginal forms of this same phylum. On the other hand, he is convinced of the extreme antiquity of *Homo sapiens* whose pre-*sapiens* forms (still unknown) would be contemporaries of the pithecanthropoid and neanderthaloid forms.

[10] Speaking of Africa, Teilhard said that he had appreciated contact with the past, "but only in so far as it enables us better to estimate our 'trajectory'."

In fact, though he had useful conversations with Dr Menghin in Valparaiso, he was unable to fulfil his plan. The railway line between Buenos Aires and Valparaiso was blocked by a broken bridge, and a strike made it necessary to sail for New York earlier than Teilhard had intended. However:

> At Dr Menghin's in Buenos Aires I saw the latest results of researches into early man in Patagonia: a collection at once disappointing and interesting—it illustrates what you might call the fading out at the end of its journey, six thousand years ago, towards Cape Horn of the great Palaeolithic wave that arose in South Africa several hundred thousand years before. (21 October 1953.)

Back in New York, and until his death, Teilhard retained his interest in South Africa. In February, 1955, he wrote an interesting note on the pebble industry:

> Interest in the recently found pebble industry continues to grow:
>
> 1. It confirms the fact that there was in fact a pre-Chellean level of "chipped pebbles" in Africa, Kenya and the Transvaal.
>
> 2. There are indications that, at least in the Transvaal, the first human industries are: (a) contemporary with, (b) later than the Australopithecines (or at least, as we now know, than some Australopithecines): Robinson, like Oakley, believes that some Australopithecines lived a long time after the advent of Man: this I strongly doubt.
>
> 3. Makapan is gradually establishing a stratigraphic series covering *all* human history: the "Chellean" has not yet been found in the caves of Makapan but it must be there, for in 1953 some "Chellean" deposits rolled at the base of the lateral embankment which is "Acheulean", at the entrance to the valley—it is almost "too beautiful" and "regular" to be *true*.... (6 February 1955.)

In the same letter Teilhard refers to his "cherished ideas on the origin of continents". These never appeared in any complete essay, but we have the notes he made for a lecture in Capetown to the South African Archaeological Society.

1. *The Origin of Continents*

When I took my degree in geology (Haug, Termier) the classical theory was the "sinking of the continents" (Atlantic, even the Pacific! ...).

Then came Wegener, "The drift"....

Both theories assuming an original *quantum* (partially consolidated or even cracked).

Now, as a result of my personal observation, a *third* idea (factor) "the *growth* of continents based on two phenomena:

(a) *gradual uplift* of the continental shelf (more or less oscillatory, but positive in direction) = *continentalization*;

(b) *still more gradual expansion* by marginal addition of granitized flexures....

This theory had already been conceived in China, and Teilhard seeks to apply it to Africa. On 14 September 1951 he writes to Théodore Monod:

The fact remains that, by analogies and contrasts with Eastern Asia, your Africa fascinates me. And I am becoming increasingly convinced that there is, much more than a drift—a genesis of the continents. The silicified and "Collenia-ized" dolomites of the Transvaal are *identical*, to an extreme and almost ludicrous degree, with the Sinian of China: this is much more than a superficial coincidence—I mean a continental "season", a "phase"....[11]

And in the lecture quoted above reappears the same expression with regard to his ideas on the growth of continents:

It was a great pleasure for me to feel this conception *reinforced* in my mind—through a whole collection of facts: particularly by the study of your pre-Cambrian—and by the consideration of the *dolomitic phase* of your Transvaal system—"Amazing analogy of the silicified Collenia."—More than a simple appearance (unmistakable evidence . . .). But a *season*, a stage, a *phase* in the building of the continents: cf. a line of growth on the section of a tree....

This general theory of continentalization explains Teilhard's interest in the Collenia, one of the few technical points of geology

[11] It took some time for Teilhard to abandon Wegener's theory. On 16 September, he spoke of a "corrected Wegenerianism". And a letter of 8 November 1851, dated from Buenos Aires, declared: "It was a shock to find here a Permian glacier and Devonian sandstone parallel to those I saw before leaving Durban and the Cape, a point for Wegener...." On 29 July 1953 he spoke of a "neo-Wegenerianism", but he abandoned his belief in the continental drift.

The Collenia mentioned here are in the group of blue-green algae, Schizophyta (Schizophyceae in the older manuals or Myxophyceae in newer works, phylum Schizophyta). They are almost as simple in organization as the bacteria with which they are grouped in the phylum Schizophyta: no cellular nucleus; chlorophyll diffused. Secretions of these plants formed the primordial limestone of the pre-Cambrian period.

which still interested him towards the end of his life. It also testifies to his effort to separate himself from his "quaternarism". It is one of the reasons that urged him, in 1952, to tour the American West for his vacation: [12]

> I am thinking of leaving New York on 3 July, to spend a day with Simpson in New Mexico, and to arrive in Berkeley by 10 July. My plan is still to return to New York 1 September, through Glacier Park (Montana), where I would like to see the pre-Cambrian Collenia, in order to complete what China and South Africa have taught me in this line (which I think interesting for the genesis of the continents). (Letter of 27 June 1952.)
>
> The stop at the Simpsons [George Gaylord, the palaeontologist] was very congenial and picturesque. They live 8,000 feet up, on the edge of a national forest, three hours by car from Albuquerque, in full view of the Bad Lands of the San Juan basin (this winter the wild turkeys came to scratch for food along the house). I lodged in a tent.... In a few hours I learned a great deal of geology, and solidly established my friendship with the two Simpsons (which could have some consequences for the birth of the "neo-anthropology" of which I dream). (12 July 1952.)

Of Berkeley he wrote:

> From my windows, I see in beautiful sunshine the Gulf of San Francisco, the Golden Gate (and its bridge): the first time that this Golden Gate will not open to allow me to enter the Pacific. (12 July 1952.)

Teilhard met many friends again during this holiday, and made some new and interesting contacts; among them was the musician Darius Milhaud, who told him that he was "really getting down to what will be the work of his life, a lyrical composition, commissioned by Israel, for the three thousandth (?) anniversary of David and the foundation of Jerusalem".

The Chinese restaurants in San Francisco took him "straight back to the atmosphere of Peking or Shanghai". Invitations multiplied, but although Teilhard was on holiday, he took the opportunity to

---

[12] His time was spent as follows: left New York on 3 July for Berkeley, stopping on the way at Chicago for a few hours; then to Santa Fé, Albuquerque (3 days); Los Angeles (a day and a night). Arrived at Berkeley on 10 July. On 8 August, left Berkeley for a week in Glacier Park in the Rockies. 17 to 19 August were spent in crossing to the east. From the 21st (or perhaps earlier) until the 28th he was at Bar Harbour in Maine, and on 5 September was back in New York.

refresh his knowledge on many points at the university, and to study new aspects of subjects that interested him. Berkeley was the finest centre in the world for stratigraphic study; there, too, he experienced a new thrill when he saw the great cyclotrons:

> Yesterday, I was admitted to visit Berkeley's great cyclotrons, the old one, and the new betatron under construction. You ought to see that! Naturally, I did not understand everything. But what impressed me strongly is the sense of contemplating an absolutely new type of manifestation (or organ) of man: something in which we find speculation, industry, politics, war, medicine, and, even to a certain point, what we called philosophy (every verified and effective concept of Matter). A sort of bud of a new state of Humanity, all the more vigorous that it emerges from a natural convergence of irresistible causes. And, in this bud, what a complexity of theories and of different associated techniques, not to mention the extraordinary unanimity created at this particular point, among a good hundred "brains" bent on the realization of a work from which we can expect almost anything.... A cell (neuron) such as we had never yet seen. (24 July 1952.)

> Another humanity which is born from the natural force of things.... Looking at these extraordinary products of the "noosphere", I could not refrain from thinking that tomorrow, without doubt, it will be tools of this order that will be used by the new biology to control life. And it is, without doubt, as an extension of this same movement of recasting and generally re-thinking the world basically that there will arise a science of man, less absurd than that we now hear so much of. (20 July 1952.)

This visit produced Teilhard's essay "On Visiting the Cyclotron: Reflections on the Infolding on Itself of Human Energy" (published in *Recherches et débats*, 1953):

> As I penetrated further into the monster's interior, it was as though, by a gradual change of plan, another group of images took the place, in my mind, of the atomic accelerator I was looking at. My guide went on talking to me about interlocking fields. Meanwhile, I could not help feeling and perceiving, beyond and around this electromagnetic whirlwind, the concentric afflux of another and no less formidable radiation: that of the Human sucked in on me, in a vast wind from the four corners of space....
> Before my distraught eyes, the Berkeley cyclotron had completely disappeared. And in its place, my imagination saw the entire noosphere, which, coiled in upon itself by the breath of

research, formed a single enormous cyclone, whose property it was to produce, not nuclear energy, but psychic energy in a continually more reflective state, in other words the ultra-human itself.

And what was remarkable was that, faced by this colossal reality that should have made my mind reel, I experienced, on the contrary a calm and joy, a *deep-seated* calm and joy. . . .

Thus, the more I tried to extend and extrapolate into the future the progress of the vast physico-psychic spiral in which history has caught me up, the more it seemed to me, that what we (altogether too simply, I think) call research, began to be charged with— coloured by, warmed by—certain forces (faith, adoration) that have hitherto been regarded as foreign to science. . . .

The closer I looked at research, the more I saw that an interior necessity forced it ultimately to direct its efforts and its hopes towards some divine centre.

Glacier Park and Maine were similarly rewarding:

At Glacier Park [Montana, on the Canadian border] I was able to see all the Collenia that I wished, thanks to the kindness of the Chief Naturalist and to the fortunate presence of a young geologist from the National Survey whose particular work is on the Collenia. I am going to send some observations on them (in comparison with China and the Transvaal) to the Geological Society of France and to the Institute.[13] Magnificent weather, luckily— and a landscape of great mountains and forests: we spent a week in the chalets of Lake Macdonald. A flood of tourists, of course. Finally, I went to spend ten days in northern Maine, near Mount Desert Island . . . in a "cabin" deep in the woods, at the edge of a fjord. . . . An impressive country with its stretches of forests, of lakes, of fjords, quite levelled and rounded by moraines. It was most interesting to be able, in a few days, to compare the western and eastern coasts of the United States; geologically speaking, night and day. (9 September 1952.)

During the last part of this journey it was the moraines and granite intrusions that particularly interested Teilhard:

The vastness of the glacial phenomenon! . . . Have not left moraines since Oregon . . . I must get to the root of it; critical effect of epeirogenesis? of change of climate? . . . Maine. Cf. a "Carboniferous" (instead of pre-Cambrian) Canada or Finland

---

[13] After this visit, Teilhard wrote a very technical note (*Compte rendu de l'Académie des Sciences, 1952*) on the nature and significance of pre-Cambrian Collenia, which led to a friendly exchange of views with Théodore Monod.

(Palaeozoic granites?...enflexures...). No one has yet written "the granitization of America".

Thus he returns to the ideas that lay behind the geo-biological institute in China:

> Replace Wegenerism by the (bio-geophysical) parallelism of the genesis of continents.
> Combine with the desiccation of continents the appearance of glaciation.
> Pleistocene (different from Palaeozoic glaciation??)
> Distinguish *"tide"* —epeirogenesis, climate
>   *"waves"*—climate
>   —cultural
> (transformation of pluvial *"into"* glacial...)

The megatectonics of the future, according to Teilhard, will be a vast synthesis both geophysical and biological, initiating the parallel and comparative study of the continents, trying to connect the glacial periods with more general phenomena:

> It's interesting that I'm not at all concerned with the glacial, unless it's related to some pan-geological process, and is no longer presented as a Quaternary anomaly. (Man himself has deep roots!) I know very well that there are all the Carboniferous and pre-Cambrian glaciations, and I have seen them in Africa (not the pre-Cambrian, about which I am not absolutely convinced...). But those are quite separate blocks. Very often the "Quaternarists" seem to me like the "anthropologists": parachuted into a small self-sufficient sphere, where they install themselves as in an absolute. Of course, the Quaternarists work in an order of grandeur different from the other geologists. But it is necessary to try to relate the phenomena (or distinguish for ourselves their law of disappearance) when we change from one order to another. (14 December 1953.)

Someone has said that future thinkers will have to reintegrate the notion of cycles into the Teilhardian vision of irreversible and oriented time. In fact, this is not so, for Teilhard had taken up and gone beyond this notion of cycles in an evolutionary scheme which can be pictured graphically as an ascending spiral drawing ever closer to its centre. Every effort of Teilhardian science and philosophy is a reaction against the Aristotelian conception of cyclic time, strictly subordinating the waves to the tide, and the oscillations to the orthogenetic drift. On the geological level, this effort is already evident:

> In these conditions, I ask myself more and more if the Quaternary glacier was not really, at least in its intensity, an absolutely new type of phenomenon in the history of the Earth: associated directly with a critical value reached, at the end of the Tertiary, by planetary continentalization. ... From this point of view, the Permo-Carboniferous "Gondwanian" and pre-Cambrian glaciations ought to be interpreted as due to "premonitory" tremors in continentalization; but they would not have had, by any means, the intensity nor the character of "established régime" that the Quaternary glaciers possessed. And there would not have been in fact any glacial periods between the Permian and the Quaternary. (11 November 1954.)

This "anticyclism" of Teilhard appears also in his idea of history:

> All the same I was unable to refrain from a brief protest against the barren *cyclism* in which not only the geologists but also the theorists of human history from Spengler to Toynbee try to enclose us. In the universe, it is the *drifts* which are important, not the *rhythms*. Only, the drifts are much slower than the rhythms, and so much more difficult to separate. (31 January 1953.)

An interesting note on Rachel Carson's *The Sea Around Us* introduced a concept of Teilhard's that illustrates his integration of biology and geology.

> Impression: sea = immense melting-pot (immense holocaust) ... = enormous biological mass, with low *"conscience-average"*.[14]
> CONTINENTALIZATION AND CONSCIOUSIZATION. (Man: a function of continents, of granitization ...)

Here the interest lies in the bond he suggests between the growth of the continents and the progressive development of consciousness, with man "a function of granitization".[15]

[14] Teilhard uses the English words to represent "level of consciousness".

[15] *La vision du passé* (Éditions du Seuil) contains some extracts from the important correspondence with Henri Termier, at that time professor of geology at the Faculty of Sciences in Algiers. These texts effectively summarize the final thought of Teilhard. There is a certain kinship between Teilhard's thought and that of the Viennese scholar Eduard Suess. The term "biosphere", for example, appears in Suess's *The Face of the Earth* (1909), where he uses it to express the solidarity of all life. Teilhard added depth to the term, using it to describe a structural layer of the globe.

12+

Although, in a technical context, Teilhard uses the word "instinctively" or speaks of an "intuition", it would be a mistake to conclude that his geo-biological ideas were divorced from facts and determined either by preconceived notions or by a particular mental attitude. It was contact with facts (as, for example, when studying the structure of the Western Hills near Peking) that made Teilhard conscious of certain principles that presented themselves as logical necessities. The data he collected later, in India, Africa, and America, served only to confirm this necessity; and it is for this reason that study of his thought must be based on his geological and palaeontological work. The fundamental theme of Teilhard's thought is the existence of an evolution, of an irreversible time in the universe, an oriented time which constantly brings something new.

CHAPTER TWENTY-TWO

The American Period: From Anthropology to Anthropogenesis

IN speaking of his visit to Simpson near Albuquerque, Père Teilhard alluded to a "neo-anthropology" which was the fruit of more profound reflection on the problems of general biology and, especially, of orthogenesis. What exactly is the problem? Teilhard's rejection of contemporary anthropology explains it. In 1929 he had written, "We must learn to look at humanity with the eye of a geologist and palaentologist." In 1952 (11 February) he was more explicit:

> ... what strikes me more and more is the evident necessity of conceiving and of building a new anthropology. Since the time of Darwin, evolution has passed beyond the narrow limits of zoology and become a general process covering the atom as well as the cell. And, during the same period, while successfully attacking the roots of nuclear and cellular evolution, Man has at the same time learnt that he is both the maker and the subject of some sort of ultra-evolution.
>
> For these two main reasons, the science of Man can no longer be left in the hands of the "writers" or "humanists" for whom Humanity is only a type of isolated and self-sufficient microcosm in the universe—nor in the hands of pure anatomists, whose only interest is to search for osteological differences between Man and the anthropoids, without ever being aware of the frightening power, which suddenly emerged in a Pliocene primate, to change the whole face of the earth in the course of a million years. ...
> One way or the other, anthropology cannot fail to become a pro-

longation of physics, and not just a department of medicine or of philosophy.

Elsewhere we find the same criticisms:

> And it is ridiculous to see the leaders and pontiffs of a certain cultural, social, or psychological "anthropology", to say nothing of the "phenomenologist" or "existentialist" philosophers now in vogue, still treating Man as a world apart from the rest of the great world; if not starting from *a priori* ethical, aesthetical, or ontological postulates, at any rate in such a way as to square with them. In our scientific age, we have not yet succeeded in defining a science of Man. . . . (18 April 1953.)

In fact, anthropology is in the hands of two very different categories of men. On the one hand, we have the philosophers, psychologists, and sociologists. For them, the knowledge of Man is a deductive science, starting with *a priori* principles. (In attempting to summarize Teilhard's thought on this point, we cannot pass over the fact that, in conversations, he was not blind to the existence of experimental psychology and sociology.) These form a heritage of the old humanism which makes Man an empire within an empire. Existentialism is a good example of this attitude: Man, who is free, who alone has the power to be "objective", is a "for himself" being, a creature who is conscious of himself, and precisely because of that opposed to the "in-themselves" beings, the mass of things whose essence is simply to "be there" and nothing more. On the other hand, we have the doctors, or rather the anatomists, who are concerned only with anatomy and comparative osteology. Treating of analogies and differences only, their narrow specialization prevents them from seeing an essential fact, that Humanity, whose coming has changed the face of the earth, constitutes a new realm which prolongs and crowns the preceding stages.

Teilhard's synthetic spirit refused all compartmentalization—the separation of physics and anthropology, the splitting of anthropology into various disciplines. Moreover, one of the persistent themes of his thought is that the idea of evolution, originally a biological theory, has invaded all the sciences. There is a genesis of the atom just as there is a genesis of Man. The various anthropological disciplines must, therefore, be assembled into a single science of anthropogenesis.

One basic intuition came to Teilhard as early as December, 1919.

It was the notion of convergence. Humanity presents a double character which constitutes its originality. On one side, since it is a young species, it continues to form new species which in the noosphere assume a cultural aspect. On the other hand, it has the strange peculiarity of not only being fertile between "species" but also of converging on itself, of being compressed and elaborating a common civilization whose foundation and features are already apparent. (An example, scientifically, was the 1957 international geophysical year.)

In other words, the cultural totalization of Humanity is biological in nature, since Humanity is only a breakthrough of life into the realm of reflection. This is one of the characteristic traits of Teilhard's philosophy of history: not only does it reject the pessimistic conception of cyclic evolution but it affirms energetically the biological character of the history of civilizations.

For Teilhard this convergence is the essential point to be clarified. After his arrival at Capetown he wrote:

> From all the evidence, we find ourselves irrevocably engaged at the moment, as everyone can see, in a rapidly accelerated process of human totalization. By the combined effect of multiplication (in number) and of expansion (in radius of action) of human individuals on the surface of the globe, the noosphere has begun to compress itself sharply and to compenetrate itself organically, for almost a century now. This, without doubt, is the most enormous and central of modern events on the earth. (*The Convergence of the Universe*, 1951.)

Other letters confirm this position:

> ...It is still vital at this time to fix some points *at the origin* of the curve of "Hominization". But it is in fact only the *present* course of this trajectory in and around us that our generation must determine. A dead end? Or a rebound? The whole problem rests on the answer. (10 September 1951.)
>
> Man: a species that has broken through into the Reflective, and whom this new condition forces to converge on itself. By dint of hammering in this point, I am convinced that one can explode the whole system. (10 January 1953.)
>
> It is on this fundamental question (which still needs to be formulated more explicitly)—and not on the reality of a general evolution of the universe, nor on the reality of a secondary or

partial cosmic flow towards greater complexity and greater consciousness—it is, I repeat, on the fundamental question of the
convergence on itself (in a reflective form) of this consciousness-
current that the great battle will soon, I believe, be fought: and
from it there can emerge for those who come after us the vision
of a universe structurally unified in its main lines and energies,
from the atomic to the human (inclusively): not a "resolved" and
completed universe, of course, but one sufficiently coherent to
afford a solid base for thought and action. (13 February 1953.)

Teilhard is explicit in insisting that the convergence of which he
speaks is a biological, and therefore a physical, phenomenon: he
takes his stand on:

the physical nature of the irresistible, incontestable and uncon-
tested, phenomenon of human "racio-socio-economical-mental"
convergence whose acceleration we are now witnessing. Yes or no,
is this phenomenon eu-biological or epi-biological? (6 April 1952.)

And even more forcibly:

At the moment, and for the year, I am in New York—pre-
occupied with the urgency of bringing about a reform of anthropology, separating it finally from "letters" or "philosophy" in
order to make of it, by its essence (which is an analysis and study
of the Human), an authentic extension of physics and biology.
(21 September 1952.)

This involves a radical change in method:

Man can be understood only by *ascending* from physics,
chemistry, biology, and geology. In other words he is *first of all*
a cosmic problem.

This is a point to which Teilhard constantly returns: we must
recognize the "biological prolongations of 'speciation' in the 'social
and cultural'"; "at all costs we must study Man as 'a natural
force', studying the 'reflective' exactly as one studies the 'nuclear'".
He complains that too little attention has been given to the "comparative study of physical and psychic energy". So far no one has
gone beyond the level of "verbal analogies", and what is now
wanted is some sort of generalized "energetics covering both". We
speak of moral and spiritual, as well as of physical energy, and an
attempt should be made to connect the two. Thus Teilhard concludes his "Reflections of Energy" (*Revue des questions scientifiques*, October, 1952):

In substance, the different considerations mentioned above can be reduced to the following points:

1. Taken at its origin, in each human element, Reflection (or the passage of a single being *from the conscious state to the self-conscious state*) corresponds to a critical point separating the two species of life from each other.

2. Once begun elementarily in the interior of individuals, reflective life continues to diversify and intensify itself following a collective process closely bound up with the technico-cultural convergence of mankind, prolonging and transposing into a new domain the movement of non-reflective life.

3. At the end of this process of ultra-reflection, operating on a limited planetary "quantum" a pole of maximum convergence appears, which, as a result of the exigencies of irreversibility inherent in the reflective state, cannot be considered as a transitory or "flash" state, but rather as a critical higher point of reflection beyond which, for us, the evolutive curve of complexity-consciousness rises from time and space.

4. Finally, from the energetic viewpoint, everything happens as if the universe were propagating itself not along a single axis but rather along two *joined* axes; one (entropy) the axis of greatest probability and the other (life) of the greatest complexity—consciousness developing all along as a function of entropy in keeping with the exigencies of thermodynamics, but finally avoiding "disorganization" by a specific effect of reflection, either as a separate energy "of the second species", or as an interiorized fraction of a common energy.

5. All of which amounts to this: that, in order to cover entirely the evolutive economy of the universe including life, a third principle, that of the reflection of energy, must be added and associated to those of the conservation and dissipation of energy already admitted.

In physics, matter moves irresistibly along the line of least effort towards the most probable distributions; a phenomenon called entropy. In biology, this same matter moves toward more and more improbable arrangements because they are more and more complicated, which creates an antinomy between physical entropy and biological "orthogenesis", with life appearing to develop counter to the enormous wave of entropy. A generalized energetics must necessarily be constructed not along the single axis of entropy, but along the joined axes of greater probability and great complexity. Entropy appears to succeed in recovering its advantage since the complex edifices of life die and decompose. But once become reflective, evolution is incompatible with the hypothesis of total death, whose prospect, if certain, would paralyse the revolutionary drive. Complexification, then, is not a simple, momentary sub-effect of the general decline of the world. There is, in fact, a divergence: on one side, a fall back into entropy, on the other side, an escape from it. As a result of reflection, the interiorized fraction of common energy finds a new consistency, not in the infrastructure of the organism, but on the real point of the convergence of reflective humanity, which means that it floats away into eternity.

It is impossible to describe in detail Teilhard's speculations and to show why he went beyond the classic distinction, explained in *The Phenomenon of Man*, between tangential energy (the measurable energy of the physicists in the domain of material reactions), and radial or centric energy (the domain of the imponderable actions of arrangement and union—psychic energy which is released in proportion to the complexity of matter and which, grafting itself on the first, purely mechanical, "arrangements", directs animated matter towards higher and higher syntheses). It would be interesting, too, to know more exactly why Teilhard hoped to find in cybernetics, those machines endowed with "memory" which imitate with prodigious speed certain proceses of the human brain, "some light on the nature and the mechanism of the 'forces of arrangement' in the world around us".[1] It is a great pity that Teilhard died before he could put these views in order. We do, however, know in what direction he was leaning, to seeing, by a bold stroke of intuition, measurable energy as a sub-product or rather as a particular case of psychic energy, somewhat as Newtonian gravity or Euclidean space are only approximations of Einsteinian gravity and curved space.

---

[1] "What really interests me in cybernetics is the transformation of materialism it suggests to us. A machine is not (or is no longer) an affair primarily of energy set in motion, but of the information put together and transmitted." (Letter of 15 May 1953.) As L. de Broglie has written (in *Nouvelles en microphysique*, Paris, 1956, p. 78), "The theory of calculating machines, that of the transmission of signals, and more generally all those which together make up modern cybernetics, must, it seems, give us a great deal of information about normal or pathological functioning of the nervous system, and in particular about reflex mechanism." Calculating, and all similar, machines have this in common with the nervous system that a given number of signals can, with small loss of energy, originate and transmit information that can stimulate or modify energetic phenomena of infinitely greater magnitude.

It is tempting to make a comparison between Teilhard and Leibniz. For Leibniz, the material points of energy studied by the physicist are only the exterior of the monads which, seen from within, are thinking spiritual substances; and, like Teilhard (who also favoured the word "monad") the universe of physical forces is only an exterior whose interior is psychic. Leibniz, however, was ignorant of evolution and still more of the law of complexity-consciousness and solidarity in space-time. What is more important to emphasize is the significance of this anthropogenesis and of the generalized energetics for the interior evolution of Père Teilhard. The concept of anthropogenesis testifies to a new progress in the synthesis of the Human and of the Cosmic, the Human participating by becoming cosmic and rooting itself in it. On the other hand, this effort to subordinate physical energy to psychic energy, this extraordinary dialectical reversal by which the spirit, after having slowly separated from matter, is seen to be the hidden web of the *Weltstoff* and the true consistency of things; all this expresses intellectually a corresponding emergence of Teilhard's soul, which is progressively released from the attraction of its body, to come under the ever more powerful influence of God.

This Teilhardian anthropogenesis expands into a generalized energetics capable of integrating in itself an anthropodynamics.[2] This in turn unfolds into a philosophy of action and an eschatology; the two aspects being closely allied:[3]

It seems more and more evident to me (and this has nothing to do with my personal predilections or religious background) that once evolution becomes reflective, it can no longer function biologically except in a universe offering to human organic convergence an *irreversible* centre of super- or ultra-personalization, that is, in a universe generally definable as of a "lovable and loving" nature. (Just think this over a little and you will see that there isn't any "sentiment" here but pure energetics.) (8 September 1952.)

[2] An American enterprise, under John Stewart and P. Bridgman, is seeking to establish a "Sociometry" by mathematical research into the statistical regularities in the human phenomenon. According to Teilhard, this attempt ought to be completed by "an effort to establish a socio-dynamics which will investigate the conditions of functioning and activation of human energies". (*Le phénomène humain*, note for J. Rueff, 1954.)
[3] Cf. letter of 8 February 1955: "An energetics remarkably close to the Blondelian metaphysics of action."

12*

I am more and more convinced that, if it is to found a neo-humanism, evolution must not only be of a converging nature (as co-reflection proves), but that it must converge in the direction of a *real* focus (i.e. not simply "virtual"). This, I repeat, is not for philosophical reasons, but on pure grounds of "psychological energetics". There must be, in the future, some integration on itself of the evolutive whole, under some superconscious form (an integration in which I may be, in some way, integrated myself). Otherwise, I feel, I lack the stimulus, I *would* lack the stimulus is what I mean to say—to go further. (31 January 1955.)

In other words, Man is evolution become reflective and tending more and more to take possession of its own forces. Evolution has become capable of questioning itself about itself and about its end. What would happen, then, if it lost its faith in itself? It needs, besides its biological impulses, a supplementary incentive[4] to continue to "evolve" and to "self-evolve", to urge it, through organization, towards some supra-human state of reflection. Man needs a faith and must build on the eternal—an eternal which guarantees the survival of his work and especially of his person, which is more precious than his work. It is necessary then, not on the basis of sentiment but purely on the basis of energetics, that the point of convergence of humanity be not virtual but already existing.

Since, under the effect of socialization and of reflection, humanity must clear a new critical threshold, the perspectives which Teilhard reveals to it are naturally eschatological. And there, like Jean le Bon at the battle of Poitiers, he has to watch both flanks. On the right are the apocalypticists who dream only catastrophic dreams, while on the left are the millenarists or Marxists whose nostalgia looks to a golden age:

I am thinking of writing . . . a few pages also on "The end of the species" (human): a disguised criticism of the apocalyptics and an open attack on the myths (Marxist, etc.) of a golden age in the future. A critical point of ultra-speciation: that is what the scientific probability for the end of humanity appears to be for me, provided that we decide to make a bridge between physics and the psychic. (26 November 1952.)[5]

He sees the end of humanity as an extreme state of psychic tension, preceding a critical point in which the pleroma must be consum-

---

[4] Teilhard often used the English word "incentive" in such contexts.
[5] The article appeared in *Psyche*, 1953.

mated in Christ. Nothing is more striking in this period than this extrapolation from considerations of a scientific, or at least, of a phenomenological order.

For Teilhard, then, the task was to initiate a true science of Man and of human energy, and to establish scientifically the reality of a converging type of evolution; and for this he needed to multiply contacts and exchanges of views. Paul Fejos was interested.

> The Director of Research at the Foundation, Dr Fejos, is interested in my idea, and has decided to start all the necessary meetings with all the men that count. We are going to see what comes of this. (7 December 1951.)

Teilhard used every means at his disposal. He continued to correspond with Julian Huxley and with a wide circle of scholars and scientists, in the United States and elsewhere, concerned with Man, e.g., Birks, Dodds, Hirschfeld, Needham, Northrop, Redfield, Stewart:

> ... Meanwhile I am beginning to make contact with men interested in Man under non-humanist, non-anthropological aspects, for example, John Stuart, Director of the Princeton Observatory, and a Professor Roger Williams, Director of the Institute of Biochemistry in Austin, Texas. I do not yet know what this will bring, but it is a change from the tedious atmosphere of the "Machabees" and of ethnology. (6 March 1952.)

Private meetings continued and it is not necessarily Teilhard who sought them, for his name was becoming familiar in wider and wider circles. We know, for example, that between 26 and 29 September 1952, Gerhard Hirschfeld, Director of the Research Council for Economic Security in Chicago, took advantage of a stay in New York to visit him, having sent him previously a note on the concept of humanity. Teilhard also sought contact with groups interested in the problem of Man:

> Yesterday I met a group that included a Harvard astronomy professor and Margaret Mead, the ethnographer: they seem to approach the problem of Man somewhat in the way I want to, in the same way as one studies physical energy. (19 January 1952.)

Lectures helped to spread his ideas:

> At Harvard, ten days ago, I tried out my batteries (the relation between sociology and biology) before a select group of about

fifteen lecturers. I think this one way of making some progress. (5 June 1952.)[6]

Finally, he attended or organized conferences. The first, however, was a disappointment:

> Around 20 March, there was a three-day "meeting" on physical anthropology at the New York Academy of Sciences. Charming people—but a stifling intellectual atmosphere in the conference room. Interminable discussion on deformations of the vertebral column, etc. Anthropology or orthopaedics? We must at any price open up a real science of the human phenomenon. (6 April 1952.)

In a letter to Huxley (1 April 1952), Teilhard had described what he had in mind:

> What I dream of is a "symposium"—*"informal"* and limited, in which about a dozen suitably selected people (you, Needham, Grassé, with some chemists, doctors, and astrophysicists, but no one "literary" or "philosophical") would meet to find out in what terms the physical problem of the human can be expressed, and how to approach it. And I think that Fejos is favourable to the idea. Tell me what you think.

From 9 to 20 June 1952 there was a large anthropological congress at the Wenner Gren. In a report issued in September, Teilhard records some satisfaction:

> Such as it was (i.e. however hazy the atmosphere in which the discussions took place) last June's "test" was, I believe, valuable and revealing, since it made it apparent that, for the majority of those present, humanity still unfortunately represents a sort of self-sufficient, enclosed, island within the universe—a sort of neo-plasm—and that it is still legitimate and possible to study it in itself, with no particular reference to the general processes of cosmic evolution as at present being brought to light by physicists and biologists.
>
> Most of the anthropologists who met last summer at the Wenner Gren Foundation spoke as Americans or archaeologists, as logicians or jurists, but not as humanists, not as scientists: and this *because, for them the social was not really part of the general evolution of matter and life!*

[6] The lecture, suggested by Movius, was on "The Biological Meaning of Human Socialization". It was given on 26 May 1952.

From this Teilhard concluded:

> The natural sequel to the June symposium should be the setting up of a small committee whose task would be to investigate, broadly speaking, how to determine the objective reality of anthropogenesis and approach its scientific study—treated at last not as something simply parallel with, but as an extension of, biogenesis.

It was on this point that he continued to insist. Thus in December he wrote: "As a start, we should issue a manifesto (we are biologists . . .) affirming the ultra- (not para-, nor epi-) biological nature of the human phenomenon (including socialization, culture, technique)"; and a manuscript note on a copy of the report on the June symposium runs: "Urgency of a reform of anthropology—reform based on recognition of the fact that man (in spite of special properties derived from psychic emergence into the reflective) cannot be understood or studied except through an extension of the general laws of speciation." Huxley's help was sought, and on 6 October 1962 he wrote to Teilhard proposing a "committee for evolutionist humanism", to be sponsored by the Wenner Gren, and expressing his appreciation of the importance of the problem.

No progress was made, however, in 1953, though it was during this year that Teilhard, tired of professional blindness to the true dimensions of the human problem, wrote "The Special Properties of the Human Species". In 1954 he was told by a friend of a plan for a symposium in Paris, suggested in conversation with Robert Courrier (professor at the Collège de France, and permanent secretary of the Académie des Sciences). Teilhard's reaction repeated his earlier arguments:

> 1. I imagine that what is planned is a symposium with a *limited* number of participants. My (convinced) opinion is that *only* biologists, physicists and geologists should be admitted to it (i.e. the same sort of people as are admitted to the Académie des Sciences). *Not* historians, nor sociologists, nor "cultural" anthropologists. Only men capable of studying man in his *ascent* from the atom, the protein, the cell, the species . . . you can see what I mean. This seems essential to me.
>
> 2. Next, we should limit the problem of the "human phenomenon" to some central point: we shall then be able to "state the problem", and, so far as possible, initiate various concrete studies; or, at any rate, define what practical approach those who take part should adopt.

It is immediately apparent that as things are now, this vital point lies somewhere within the question "What is, or is not, the *biological* value of the evident totalization (planetization) of man?" What I mean is this: has the technico-mental totalization of humanity, in which we are now participating, a biological value, or has it not? That is to say, does it, or does it not, extend the process of organization which, as all the evidence shows, runs from the hydrogen atom to the individual human organism, through all the "zigzags" and across all the frontiers we are all familiar with? If we agree that this question *"makes sense"* and that it must be answered in the affirmative, then we have a series of subsidiary problems, for example:

(a) Socialization and speciation. Does humanity continue (at least potentially) to ramify within its global totalization?
(b) Socialization and cerebration. The mechanism and progress of "co-reflection" (new mental dimensions, "cybernetic" acceleration of thought, the possibility of man being able, through self-transformation, to make himself evolve cerebrally).
(c) The maintenance and development in man of evolutionary "drive" (the whole question—which is growing as rapidly as that of totalization—of the "activation" of human energy?).

All this, of course, will have to be straightened out (and I forgot to mention the question of the formation, real or apparent, of a certain new human acquirement—an additive *not* a *residue*, but an active nucleus, a germ!), which is both technical and psychic, and is transmitted and increased by education, *at any rate, irreversibly* (the problem of what I have already called "noospherical heredity").

3. Of course, a symposium devoted to such a subject would have to be regarded as mainly "preparatory", to clear the ground and define the problems rather than solve them: a very first attempt to evaluate scientifically the human (the reflective) in the world of matter and life. For a start, that would be sufficient. (15 January 1954.)

Two other meetings are referred to in the same letter, one suggested by Professor Jean Piveteau, the other to be organized by Jacques Rueff, of the Institute. The latter had been discussed with Teilhard when Rueff was in New York. Teilhard drew up some notes (marked in pencil, "prepared for Rueff, June, 1954") under the heading, "The human phenomenon (how we are, going beyond philosophico-juridico-literary anthropology, to arrive at a real science of man, i.e. anthropo-dynamics or anthropogenesis?)"

In June, 1954, Teilhard was able to pay a visit to France. Here again he did what he could to forward his plan. Writing to Edmond Faral, who held an important position in university life, he outlined his idea:

> With M. Jacques Rueff (of the Institute), Auger (Unesco), Piveteau (Sorbonne), and Théodore Monod (Museum, Dakar) we have for several months been thinking how interesting would be a congress to examine, from the atom to man, the phenomenon or process known as "integration" which gives birth to organized systems, in physics, in biology, and in sociology; the only way, it seems to us, of bringing out scientifically, the decisive significance, in the universe, of the human phenomenon.
>
> With Grassé's support I have recently discussed with Courrier the best way of realizing this ambitious plan. Courrier's suggestion was that the Singer-Polignac Foundation might be interested in the idea—and take it up. (21 July 1954.)

Writing to the author, Jacques Rueff confirmed the subject for discussion, "Integration in physics, biology and sociology" and added, "The purpose was to discuss processes that give rise to absolute objects; in other words, in brief, association-mechanisms." The congress took place, in fact, in March 1955, but Teilhard was unable to attend.

Before that, however, Teilhard attended, and made considerable impression at, a conference organized to mark the bicentenary of Columbia University. It took place in October, 1954, at Arden House, in the foothills of the Catskills, a magnificent property given to the university by the Harriman family. The place, the people and the subject all interested Teilhard:

> ... a wonderful countryside about two hours from New York ... covered just now with a fantastic gold and purple mantling of sycamores. There were about seventy of us, ranging from physicists like Niels Bohr to poets like MacLeish, via naturalist-philosophers like Julian Huxley and theologians like Van Dusen (leader, with Niebuhr, of the new American Protestant movement).
>
> The subject was the unity of human knowledge. In my section a deep "cleavage plane" became apparent between humanists and

scientists, which turned ultimately on the new Galileo question: Is man still moving biologically upon himself? With Huxley and the majority of the scientists, I, of course, vigorously attacked the immobilist position taken up, alas, by the more Christian-thinking members of the section, such as Gilson, Malik (Lebanese representative at the U.N.), Battaglia (lay rector of the University of Bologna), and even Van Dusen. (*Letters from a Traveller*, pp. 353–5.)

Earlier, anticipating the congress, Teilhard had indicated the line he wished to take:

I hope to take advantage of the congress to insist on the "energetic and scientific" necessity of envisaging the existence of some point of emergence into the "super-conscious" at the natural term of human co-reflection. (22 September 1954.)

After the congress, again, he noted with dismay the "immobilist" attitude of too many Christians:

Meanwhile, what seems to me more and more important is that there is developing and spreading in contemporary man, the feeling of planetary biological convergence: the feeling that is, that in Man (through convergence) the species is still in movement ... in the course of animated discussions, I was struck by the realization that those who were most vigorous in rejecting the existence in the future of a global ultra-human were in fact the Christians (of all denominations).

Teilhard was looking forward, also, to another meeting, organized by the Wenner Gren, which was not held, unfortunately, until after his death. Here, again, he had hoped to introduce his own approach:

In spite of the lesson of 1952, we have started, at the Foundation, to organize a new symposium (June, 1955). Subject: the modification of the earth under the influence of Man. I don't know yet who is responsible for the subject and the programme; in my opinion, the faults are the same as those of two years ago: too many people (over fifty)—an imprecise programme (because of too many "humanists" and literary people)—even so, I shall try to take the best advantage I can of the situation. (28 August 1954.)

A later letter (22 September) is more explicit:

In June I hope to attend another conference, organized this time by the Wenner Gren, to study the changes introduced by Man on the face of the earth. Among the preparatory papers I should like to include one (not yet planned) on the noosphere, for which, strangely, no provision has been made in the list of over fifty subjects. Toynbee will be there. The noosphere leading me, of course, to raise the question of the Omega point.[7]

A final project is referred to on 5 December 1954:

In addition Fejos has just asked me to become a member of the Council of a new Wenner Gren Foundation (even better supported financially than the present one) aimed (though in terms that I find still too vague) at interrelation of the sciences. I have accepted. With more experience, the scheme will take shape. Once it is concerned directly with "convergence" and co-reflection I feel I shall be really interested.

It would be premature to attempt a final judgement of Teilhard's views on anthropogenesis. Although he was untiring in urging the necessity of studying man as a phenomenon still in process of evolution, he died before he could win wide acceptance for his belief. We know, however, that no historian of the science of man can afford to overlook Teilhard, and that his influence will always survive in a global, organico-synthetic approach to problems that he showed to be fundamentally interconnected.

[7] The paper referred to was "The Antiquity and Planetary Significance of Human Culture" (October, 1954). The conference was held at Princeton in June, 1955.

CHAPTER TWENTY-THREE

The American Period : Mystical Testament

THE close connection between Teilhard's anthropological and Christological thought is evident. A letter of 28 April 1954 emphasizes this:

We have been forced to abandon the static Aristotelian cosmos and introduced (through the whole modern physico-chemico-biological system) into a universe still in a state of cosmogenesis. In future, therefore, we have to rethink our Christology in terms of Christogenesis (at the same time as we rethink our anthropology in terms of anthropogenesis). And such an operation is not simply a matter of slight readjustment of certain aspects. As a result of the introduction of a new dimension, the whole thing has to be recast (just as when you move from plane to spherical geometry) —a tremendous effort: and from it, I assure you, Christ will emerge in triumph, the saviour of anthropogenesis.

Co-reflection among men, Teilhard had pointed out earlier (16 September 1951), must imply a universal centre of convergence and consciousness:

not as something engendered by energy as it reflects upon itself— but a centre that constitutes the generative principle (the mover) of that reflection. The phenomenon, in fact, of the third reflection —by which "Omega" reflects itself upon (reveals itself to) a universe that has become (through reflection 1 and 2) capable of reflecting it in turn.[1]

Omega is not a potential centre, but something real and already in existence: and only a sufficiently high degree of socialization can

[1] By "reflection 1 and 2" is meant first individual and second collective reflection.

enable man to reflect it. Its reality is not asserted for emotional reasons, nor to satisfy intellectual requirements, but because energetics demand it:

> You know, too, that I attribute an essential place in the rise of this third reflection to what I call the demands (as a matter of energetics) of irreversibility: the absence of the divine (i.e. total death) seeming to me necessarily to "deflate" (if I may use the word) evolution that has reached the reflective stage. (17 September 1952.)

Moreover, if our evolutive drive is to be maintained, the centre must not only be apprehended intellectually; it must be "lovable and loving". Thus Teilhard's desire to "recast" anthropology leads to his Christology.

This development, and his whole attitude towards Man's place and future in the cosmos, should be seen against the background of his reaction to contemporary religious feeling and of his relations with his superiors in Rome.

Teilhard was distressed by some aspects of Catholicism in America:

> How is it that Catholicism finds it so difficult to rise above the sectarian and make the faithful the most active agents in the hominization that must precede any Christification? In other words, why is it that nine times out of ten a believing Christian is, as regards Man, a "sceptic". That is the great stumbling-block for the Gentiles. (10 January 1953.)

As an example of immaturity in thought Teilhard quoted a letter from a Redemptorist, printed in *Time* (15 August 1952), commenting on stories of flying saucers:

> If these rational beings [travelling in flying saucers] escaped original sin, if, that is, they possessed the physical immortality originally enjoyed by Adam and Eve, it would be ridiculous for our pilots to try to kill them: they would be unkillable.

Although Teilhard felt more at home with his French friends, and more in sympathy with French Catholics (who often represented the most advanced element in religious thought) he gradually arrived at a better understanding with Catholics in America. In January, 1952, he was tending to keep to himself:

> I still have few at all personal contacts with the Fathers here. That will come later, perhaps. In any case, people are agreeable,

and I try to be the same ... and above all, not to be a nuisance. (As in the army: never attract attention.)

He had already begun, however, to make friends in such circles. In December, 1951, he had dined with the Jesuits of *America* (which corresponded to the French *Études*) and had had a "very kind reception from the new team". "They made an excellent impression on me."

Later, about the end of February, 1953, Fordham University invited him to take part in an officially organized discussion on the present position in science of the concept of evolution. Some months before this (September, 1952) he had written a little ironically about a similar discussion at Laval University in Quebec:

> Tomorrow (I believe) the leading lights of Laval University meet to decide whether the earth rotates (i.e. whether there is such a thing as evolution). Whether it's flirtatiousness or bluff, they've invited some well-known non-Catholics—among them Simpson (who has accepted, smiling into his pointed beard, "to see the dope").

It is only fair to add that the first official congress devoted to the study of Teilhard's thought was held at Montreal in November, 1956.

Teilhard found sympathetic understanding in his immediate superior, the Rector at Park Avenue. With Rome, too, his relations were becoming easier. One of the reasons, it may be remembered, that had originally induced him to visit South Africa was the desire to remove himself from the limelight of Paris and so escape unwanted and possibly unsympathetic attention. In August, 1952, however, he speaks of receiving an "extremely kind and understanding letter from N.":

> The first time a superior has invited me to think freely and constructively with him ... such gestures do more than any orders to bind me more closely to the Society.

Paris, however, was still barred to him. Next year saw a further relaxation of tension, for in August he wrote, "I am on the most friendly terms with my Order (even in Rome)"; finally, in 1954, he received permission to visit Paris.

Teilhard left New York on 3 June 1954, arriving in Paris on the 9th. On the 21st he had an interesting conversation with Jean

Guitton on the probability of other planets being inhabited. Guitton has recorded Teilhard's view:

> The more we expand the world and the potentialities of the biosphere, the more out of character and even unworthy of God it seems that all the energy of matter and its combinations should be dispersed over an immense universe for just one single living human kind.[2]

On 28 June Teilhard lectured at the Hôtel des Sociétés savantes "On Africa and Human Origins", to a large audience that included many of his fellow-Jesuits. It was noted that physically he had lost ground. His diction, indeed, was clear (as it remained till the day of his death) and his thought skilfully arranged and presented; but his comments on the slides shown were not as interesting as they might have been, and he seemed to be under considerable strain. At the end, though his friends hurried to congratulate him, there was little applause. There had, in fact, been some criticism of his presence in France, and he was greatly hurt by this campaign against him. Moreover, he was very tired, after too heavy a round of visits and meetings.

Teilhard spent some weeks in France, returning on 5 August to New York through London. It was a busy time, with a lecture on instinct in animals at the beginning of July, an examination, with Arambourg at the Museum, of a fossilized baboon skull found in the Angola breccia, and a long series of conversations with many different types of people. The two bright spots (or "white spots", as Teilhard, whose English was fluent but idiomatically erratic, called them), were his visits to Lyons and Lascaux, to which his old friend Leroy drove him. The Lascaux caves had been discovered in 1940 and Teilhard had never, apparently, seen them. At Lyons he met his Provincial, and found him comforting and full of understanding. He was lodged in the scholasticate at Montée de Fourvière, where the friendly atmosphere of the whole house, Rector, professors, and scholastics, brought him joy and peace. He was loved and respected by all, and some of the scholastics came to see him to learn more of the Teilhardian philosophy.

From Lyons Teilhard paid a visit to his old home of Sarcenat. He insisted on entering the house alone; then he walked through the park, to the old church at Orcines where all the family had been

[2] Jean Guitton, *Journal* (London: Collins, and Baltimore: Helicon, 1963).

buried. Coming back, very tired, he confided to Fr Leroy, "I shall never see Sarcenat again." It was after this that he went to Lascaux, so that his last contact with his own country was to the cradle that holds the first evidence of man's peculiar genius.

Teilhard was in London from 6 to 10 August. He was disappointed to miss Desmond Clark, but had the pleasure of meeting Oakley. Dr René Loriot, treasurer of the World Congress of Faiths, was able to enliven what was a sad interlude, for these few days were the last step towards what Teilhard felt to be a final exile. In a letter to the author, Dr Loriot says:

> I was among those to whom Père Teilhard gave a great deal of affection, and, incidentally, perhaps the last Frenchman whom he saw before his final departure for the United States. In London, my wife and I shared his last dinner in Europe. Seeing his sadness at the order to return to the United States, I wished to give him a mark of friendship and to make him feel how dear he was to me. I can still see myself on the pavement in the Strand in August, 1954, shaking his hand for the last time; his sadness was painful to see and we separated quickly.

Teilhard summarized his feelings on leaving France:

> I am still rather bewildered by those restless weeks in Paris—by the accumulation of too-rapid contacts—by the *"hectic"* rhythm of meeting and parting. And yet *"on the whole"* I feel satisfied (clarified and heartened) by this renewal of contact with France. (24 August 1954.)

> From this too rapid visit to Paris, I retain only a mass of rather chaotic impressions, from which, however, a certain number of clear, or clarified, points emerge, such as:

> 1. I feel, in my inmost self, more and more dedicated to my vocation, which is to devote my life (what remains of it) to the finding of Christ and to his service—and this in absolute loyalty to the Church.

> 2. That, for the immediate future, at any rate, I shall certainly have to work in darkness and exile. (22 September 1954.)

Back in New York, Teilhard had some periods of terrible desolation, when he longed to see France once more, if only for a moment, but when Fr Leroy saw him at Christmas he was more relaxed and tranquil and busy with plans for the next Wenner Gren symposium. He had been invited by Jean Piveteau to attend the palaeontology congress planned for April, 1955, but he was unable to accept. An "extremely friendly" letter from Père X. advised him to refrain. Moreover, permission was refused for a proposed German translation of his articles in *Études*. Some of Teilhard's friends in Paris felt that it was hypocritical to allow him to go to New York, on the pretext that this would best forward his scientific work, and at the same time refuse him the opportunity to make known the fruits of that work. Teilhard's reaction was, as ever, magnanimous. Faced with the same situation, he had written before (September, 1952):

> What distresses me is not that I am shackled by Christianity, but that Christianity should at the moment be shackled by those who are its official guardians: the same problem that Jesus had to face two thousand years ago.

No one who reads Teilhard's correspondence at this time can fail to be both edified and moved by his loyalty. Over the years, he repeats the same constancy and optimism:

> I always feel that the Church is phyletically essential to the fulfilment of the Human. (16 August 1951.) As you know this situation produces no bitterness in me, only a firm optimism, founded specifically on the vast and unique potentialities of the God of the Gospel. (16 August 1951.) Properly understood, Christianity (and Christianity alone) will be found capable of stimulating human energy, thoroughly and in its entirety. (15 November 1953.) Don't picture me as an underground worker or as persecuted. The most you can say is that I am a man trying to express frankly what lies at the heart of our generation: and that is the necessity, that will take no denial, to preserve and intensify in one another the warmth of an ultra-personal God, and the vast organicity of the astounding cosmogenesis we are now witnessing. In fact, the closer I come to the end of my life, the more indissolubly I feel myself caught up in a Christian current outside which I can see no complete fulfilment of potential value (and even more, no possible progress towards love) in what we call evolution. (25 January 1955.) Meanwhile, all one can do is to follow the line of that which has been vindicated a thousand times: continue the struggle, without bitterness but with immense confidence from within. Nothing can stand up against an ever-growing love of "the Christic phylum". (14 March 1954.)

"If the Church fall", he wrote once to Père Bergounioux, "all is lost." It was thus that Teilhard reached an ultimate peace: for "nothing can prevent Man from adoring to the maximum of his powers ... knowing this makes it easy for me to retain a sense of peace, and even to find a deep-seated joy".

How difficult it must have been for Teilhard to retain this serenity is apparent in what Père Bergounioux wrote of him:[3]

His most agonizing trial was not being understood, seeing himself disclaimed, even practically abandoned. There was sometimes a great sadness in his look, generally so transparent and confiding. I shall never forget the last words he spoke to me. I had met him in New York and we had spent a long time discussing nothing but his own problem. He had been delightfully gay. As we parted, he placed his hands on my shoulders, leaned over me, and (a thing he had never done before) kissed me and said, "Pray for me, that I may not die embittered". I was quite overcome as I left him, and in the aircraft that was taking me to Montreal all sorts of confidences came back to my mind, always unobtrusive, but infinitely moving.

It was in this atmosphere of tension and yet of peace that Teilhard formulated the final expression of his religious thought. It stemmed from two premisses. The first that we are no longer dealing with the problems of a cosmos, but with a cosmogenesis, and that it is the priest's duty to "Christify" evolution:

The line of attack has been pushed much further forward: it is no longer the existence of evolution but what I call the "Christification" of evolution (i.e. cosmogenesis). (1 February 1954.)

Whatever may be said, our century is religious—probably more religious than any other (how could it fail to be with such vast horizons opening before it and with such problems to be solved?). The only thing is that it has not yet the God it can adore. (10 December 1952.)

The tragedy is that this need to adore a God should be met by a new faith, Marxism, offered as the religion of Man in evolution, and accusing Christianity of paralysing faith in Man:

The only way to overcome Communism is to present Christ in his true light: not an opiate (or distraction) but the essential driving force behind a hominization that can never reach its full development of energy except in a world whose peak is open to love—is "amorized". (14 October 1952.)

[3] *L'âme sacerdotale du Père Teilhard de Chardin*, p. 11.

What constitutes the contagious strength of Marxism is its (illegitimate) monopolizing of the *sense of evolution* (the human sense of the species). (25 April 1954.)

In consequence, Teilhard urges that we must first abandon traditional ontology, the metaphysics that deals with essences:

You are, quite rightly, concerned with the question of "essences". But you must realize that since we have now to advance from a "metaphysic of the cosmos" to a "metaphysic of cosmogenesis", the question is not exactly how to preserve but how to transpose (into an additional dimension) the notion of the *fixity* of essences.

In cosmogenesis, essence becomes genesis: so that what is fixed is direction—this constant direction being accompanied by an accentuation of certain characteristics—and operating through certain steps or thresholds (separating domains that are essentially different: for example, the pre-living and the living, the simply living and the reflectively living—physics in full of such "steps"). (18 May 1954.)

Here we have a revolution in philosophy as far-reaching as the existentialist emphasis on existence at the expense of essence. Teilhard went further: the next step was to synthesize the transcendent God of traditional theology with the immanent (hidden) God of evolutionary religious thought:

The only God we can now adore "in spirit and in truth" is, in a phrase that appeals to me, the synthesis of the (Christian) God of "above", with the (Marxist) God of "ahead". (May–June, 1952.)

How this synthesis is arrived at, Teilhard explains:

1. If it is true (and it seems to me indisputable) that we are no longer in a cosmic régime but in one of cosmogenesis, then the Christian God must necessarily be a God of cosmogenesis, i.e. a God of evolution.

2. From another angle, if we admit (and experience, I maintain, proves this) that cosmogenesis is essentially a "noogenesis" (we know this from study of the phenomenon of Man), then there is only one way in which the God of evolution can animate evolution to the very end (which, by definition he must be able to do): he must be (and so appear to reflective consciousness) super-personal, which means supremely loving and lovable. And so we come back to the Christian God. (28 January 1954.)

Teilhard's pursuit of this line of thought culminated in his last great essay (March, 1955), *Le Christique*. This had been preceded in 1953 by *The God of Evolution*, which concludes:

Prediction, of course, and extrapolation are always dangerous.

Nevertheless, it must in the present circumstances be apparent that the gradual rise of Christ in human consciousness cannot continue much longer without being followed by a complete change in our interior climate: by this I mean the coincidence of Christ with the Centre (which we can now foresee) of a global co-reflection, and, more widely, with what we must presume to be the focal point of all reflection within the universe.

Continually forced more closely together by the advance of hominization, and continually more drawn to one another by their basic identity, the two Omegas (the Omega of experience and the Omega of faith) are without any doubt, I repeat, preparing to react upon one another in human consciousness, and ultimately to be synthesized: for the cosmic is on the point of magnifying the Christic to an astonishing degree, and the Christic is on the point (incredible though it may seem) of "amorizing", i.e. of energizing to its maximum, the entire cosmic.

This is indeed an inevitable "implosive" conjunction; its probable effect will be very shortly to weld together science and mysticism in a flux of liberated evolutive power—with, as a centre, a Christ who two thousand years after Peter's acknowledgement will have been identified at last, after centuries of toil, as the final summit (i.e. as the only possible God) of an evolution now definitively recognized as a movement of convergence.

That is what I foresee. And that is what I look forward to.

Teilhard insists on this: there are two focal points, the Christ known to the mystic and described with such passion by St Paul, and the cosmic pole disclosed by modern science, which our new knowledge of the world must postulate as the ultimate goal of evolution. In these two Teilhard sees first, correspondence, then parity, and finally identity. Reacting upon one another, Christ assumes a cosmic or cosmogenetic dimension, and the cosmos or cosmogenesis becomes Christified, "amorized" or transferred into the dimension of love.

Le Christique was in fact Teilhard's final testament:

It is a long time since in *Mass on the Altar of the World* and *Le milieu divin* I tried, in the light of my still half-formed vision of the world, to find exact expression for my wonder and amazement.

Today, after forty years of continual reflection, it is still the same fundamental view that I feel I must put forward, and share with others, but in its mature form—just once more.

I must do so, I fear, with less freshness and exuberance of expression than I could command when I first came to it.

But I still retain the same sense of wonder and the same passion.

Cosmic convergence, and Christic emergence: this twofold hope inspired Teilhard's final optimism:

On the one hand, there is the irresistible confluence of my own individual thought with everything else upon the earth that thinks—and so, closer and closer, with everything that is in process of "arrangement", wherever it may be, and to whatever degree, in the immensity of time and space.

On the other hand, the continual individualization at the very centre of my own little ego, of an ultra-centre of thought and action; the irresistible rise, in the depths of my consciousness, of some sort of Other, more me than I am myself.

Teilhard continues to drive home the point that convergence must be irreversible:

Observed experimentally at its extreme extension, towards the Improbable, the universe converges upon itself. . . .

To my mind, it is impossible to be fully and correctly an evolutionist without seeing and admitting this "psychogenic" gathering-in upon itself of the world.

It is impossible too, I may add, to have one's ego opened to such a "centripetal" form of cosmogenesis without being obliged to recognize and conclude (for many reasons, drawn as much from physics as from psychology) that it must be in the direction it coils in upon itself (and not in the reverse direction) that the universe takes on at the same time both consistence and value.

Thus we discover and must acknowledge—transfiguring the world that it illuminates, gives warmth and solidity to—a universal flux, bringing unity and irreversibility, in which we are immersed.

When Teilhard spoke of "Christic emergence" he was echoing his own personal growth of union with Christ. Théodore Monod spoke of him as one of those rare believers who had really "tested" Christianity. It was this that gave such depth to his view of the faith:

In fact, no religious faith releases (or has ever, at any moment of history, released) a higher degree of heat, a more intense dynamic drive towards unification, than—the more Catholic it is —Christianity at the present moment. And, logically, it is perfectly natural that this should be so; for in no other creed, ancient or modern, do you find so "miraculously" and effectively associated to attract us and hold us, the three following characteristics of the incarnate Christian God:

(a) Tangibility, experimental in order, the result of the historical entry (by his birth) of Christ into the very process of evolution.

(b) Expansibility, universal in order, conferred on the Christic centre in virtue of "resurrection".

(c) Finally, assimilative power, organic in order, potentially integrating in the unity of a single "body" the totality of human kind....

What, when all is said and done, constitutes the invincible superiority of Christianity over every other type of faith is that it is becoming more and more conscious of being identified with a *Christogenesis*, i.e. with the rise, collectively recognized, of a certain universal Presence, at once immortalizing and unifying.

The phenomenon of man, in fact, and the Christic complement one another:

On one side (in the case of the Christian) a centre in process of expansion, which seeks a sphere for itself.

And on the other (in the human) a sphere looking deeper into itself, which seeks a centre.

Between the two, as between anode and cathode, a spark must leap to bridge the gap:

For, in the end, however convinced we may be that a higher pole of completion and consolidation (which we may call the Omega) awaits us at the higher term of hominization, this Omega pole can never be decisively attained except by extrapolation; it will always be by its nature a conjecture and a postulate.

And this without taking into account the fact that, even if we admit that it is "guaranteed in its future existence", our anticipation of it can see only a vague, misty picture of it, in which the collective and the potential are perilously confused with the personal and the real.

On the other hand, what happens when our minds awake first to a suspicion and then to clear evidence that the *Christ of Revelation* is one and the same as the *Omega of evolution*?

Then, in one flash, we both see and feel in our hearts that the experimental universe attains its fulfilment and is finally energized.

On the one hand, we see above us the positive glimmer of an *opening* at the highest point in the future. In a world that quite certainly opens out at its peak into Christ Jesus, we no longer need fear to die, stifled in our prison.

And on the other hand, from the heights above us, it is not only air to breathe that flows down upon us, but the radiance of love. For life that has once awoken to this vision of the future, the world is no longer simply a place in which one can breathe: we realize that, by virtue of its evolutive peak, it is entrancingly desirable.

Teilhard was overwhelmed by this vision of a promised land:

> Energy taking on Presence. And so the possibility appears, opens out, for man not only of believing and hoping but (what is much more surprising and much more worth while) of loving, co-extensively and co-organically with all the past, the present and the future of a universe in process of concentrating around itself. . . .
>
> It would seem that a single ray of such a light falling at random on the noosphere like a spark, must have produced an explosion powerful enough to re-fuse and re-cast the whole face of the world in one instant.
>
> How is it, then, that as I look around me, still dazzled by this revelation, I find that I am almost the only one of my species, the only one to have seen it? . . . And so it is that, when I am asked, I cannot quote a single writer, a single book in which one can find a clear expression of this "diaphany" that has transmuted all things for me. . . .
>
> Evidence, first, of the coherence that this ineffable Element (or Milieu) introduces into the depths of my thought and of my heart.
>
> Evidence, too, of the contagious power of a form of Charity in which it becomes possible to love God not only "with all one's heart, and all one's soul" but with the universe-in-evolution. . . .
>
> Evidence, finally, of the *superiority* (and at the same time of the *identity*) of what I see, in relation to what I had been taught.
>
> A new proof that for truth it is enough to appear once, in one single mind, for nothing to be able to prevent it from encompassing all things and setting them aflame.

In this we find expressed the deepest and most intimate belief that possessed Teilhard, a formulation of a mystical experience that coloured the whole of his existence as a priest living entirely for Christ:

> *Domine, fac ut videam, ut te videam, ut te omni-praesentem et omni-animantem videam et sentiam.*[4] . . . Jesus, help me to perfect the perception and expression of my vision—of my vision of your hidden and universal essence, O *"golden glow"*. Help me to the right action, the right word, help me to give the example that will reveal you best—without scandalizing, without rupture—through convergence.

There was a practical side to this mystical attitude, for it led Teilhard to a spirituality that included scientific work and research. His last essay, in fact, was on "Research, Work, and Adoration" (March, 1955). Here his theme is that science and technology have an irreplaceable spiritualizing function, and, in a convergent world, they constitute a higher form of adoration. Faith in God cannot lead Man into passivity: and to set a true value on research is to exalt work:

> A Christian appraisal of work can only be possible, I think, if we start from an outlook (*Weltanschauung*) that stresses the relation between Arrangement of Matter and Christification: or, if you prefer, from establishing a certain relation between cosmogenesis, anthropogenesis, and Christogenesis.

Work, in fact, is an "arrangement" or organization of nature: hence a spiritualizing, and so a Christifying of the earth. But this cannot be done unless the Christian is fired by a human ardour, too. As Teilhard said in connection with the worker-priest movement, referring to suggestions that some had been infected by Marxism:

> There are increasingly large sections of humanity (the most progressive, too) on which Christianity can no longer make any impression, because humanly it has become *lukewarm*.

Urere aut uri: burn or be burned. It was so that Teilhard saw the choice that faces the Church today.

---

[4] "Lord, grant that I may see, that I may see you, that I may see you and feel you present in all things and animating all things." *Golden glow* (he uses the English words): for Teilhard the Epiphany was the feast of the "golden glow", since it was the first physical manifestation of the divinity of Christ. Cf. his use of "diaphany" for the blaze of illumination that came to him.

CHAPTER TWENTY-FOUR

Omega : The Final Synthesis

T EILHARD's last four years, in America, were in fact only the final stage of a longer period in his intellectual and spiritual development, that had started about 1932. Looking back, he recognized himself the first important step:

> Today, when I re-read the pages of *Le milieu divin*, I am astonished to note how much, even then, the essential features of my Christo-cosmic vision were already fixed. On the other hand, I am surprised to see how vague and undecided my picture of the universe still remained. . . . It was to be the work, and the constant joy, of the next twenty years to see, step by step and keeping pace with one another, two convictions build up around me, each gaining strength from the other: Christic "density" and the cosmic "density" of a world whose "communicative power" I could constantly see increasing with the increase in its "power of convergence". . . . The heart of the universalized Christ coinciding with a heart of "amorized" matter, of matter impregnated with love.

Teilhard's great discovery, in the thirties, was the recognition of a cosmic focus in evolution, with all the consequences implied in the notion of cosmic convergence: the law of complexity-consciousness; the confluence of human branches, the existence at the summit of noogenesis of an Omega point, the rebound of evolution through the energy released by the conjunction of cosmic and Christic. One fruit of his genius, then, was to indicate an apologetic for biologists and anthropologists.

Even if, as with Teilhard, an apologetic proposes a series of progressively ascending acts of faith, which is necessary to a conscious evolution's continual forward progress, it must still employ the method of immanence; it must, that is, endeavour to show God as already present in the universe, positive reality, suitably interpreted, being already pre-Christian or peri-Christian. In other words, the sculptor has left the mark of his thumb on the clay of reality, so that the modelling of the universe bears the imprint of its God. *Caeli enarrant gloriam Dei*. Teilhard's task, then, was not to construct a metaphysic but a sort of ultra-physics that would bring together in harmony all the fruit of scientific experience. In crossing this bridge he could not lean too heavily on any philosophical system; he had to confine himself to scientific facts and so discover the significance and direction, if such existed, of evolution. He developed, therefore, a phenomenology—which has practically nothing in common with that of Husserl and still less with that of Hegel. Unlike the former, so far from turning his back on science in order to discover a pre-reflective *cogito*, it is on science that he relies. Again, in his view, an essential feature of the phenomenon is not that it is perceived by an individual consciousness, but that it forms part of a noogenesis. According to Teilhard, phenomenologists of Husserl's school forget that science is a common act of perception, the manifestation of a collective consciousness, and that one of the essential marks of the phenomenon is to be convergent. With a keen awareness of universal interdependence, he sees the world as one whole, and, rising above the close-knit totality of beings and phenomena, he perceives a global reality that must be much more essentially necessary than any of the individual things it embraces, just as the organ is less real than the organism which is the only justification of its existence.[1]

Within this phenomenology we still find the three main components of Teilhard's thought, the cosmic, the Human, and the Christic, the three completed by his energetics. Now, however, they live in symbiosis, reducible one to another, or deducible one from another; we may, too, pass freely from one to another. The notion of the Universal Christ—the Christ of the Universe, Christ the King,

---

[1] Père Malevez has written in *Theology Digest* (Autumn, 1960): "*The Phenomenon of Man* seems a little out of step with contemporary thought and curiously uncontemporary. I am thinking particularly of phenomenology and the various forms of existentialism that spring from it." However, as another writer has pointed out to Père Malevez, this criticism overlooks the fact that one of the great shortcomings in contemporary philosophy is that it fails to integrate science. The argument, moreover, is somewhat specious: existentialist phenomenology is contemporary; Teilhard rejects their methodology; therefore he is not contemporary.

Pantocrator—achieves the synthesis between the cosmic and the Christic, and so, by a stroke of genius, what might have been pantheistic becomes a pan-Christicism—God in all of us—that preserves human personality while drawing all to converge upon a "Universal-Person", Christ-Omega. This synthesis between the "God above" (the classical transcendent God) and the "God of the future" (the immanent God whose face has been revealed in evolution) is not simply a synthesis on paper. Even though Teilhard first disclosed the cosmic function of Christ, this explanation, grand though it might be as a concept of the concrete reality of the Incarnation, would have seemed barren to an unbeliever had he not, by studying evolution as a phenomenologist, gone on to disclose, too, the Christic function of the universe—the ascent of the world towards Christ the King with the irresistible surge of the ocean tides under the pull of moon and sun. The Human, the third component, falls similarly into place as the first reflective mirror in which God can be reflected over the universe. Thus the Human is the necessary unit between the cosmic and the Christic, for the noosphere is an essential stage between the biosphere and ultra-human. And so cosmogenesis, proceeding through anthropogenesis, culminates in a Christogenesis.

In one of his last letters (30 March 1955) Teilhard wrote:

> At the moment, following on some articles on my great friend Auguste Valensin, I have been turning over in my mind something on *"Humanism and Humanism"*. Even Père Blanchet in a remarkable article in *Études* still seems to see humanism only *à la Grecque* (Plato, the Renaissance), as an aesthetic flowering, while, in fact, we are already involved in an evolutive neo-humanism dominated by (defined as) the conviction that there is an "ultra-human". Cosmic humanism is out of date, a thing of the past—and is being replaced now by cosmogenetic humanism (of which, I fear, Valensin was unaware).

To this he had added a note: "not simply the full flowering of man (the Greeks) but man fully evolved (us)." Another note, of about the same date, repeats the point:

Man. 1. In full flower (cosmic Humanism)
2. Fully evolved (= the phyleto-planetary or the human planetary)

If we seek to discover what Teilhard regarded as the central and fundamental problem, we have some indication from his own state-

13+

ments that the starting point of his thought was the same as that treated by Plato in the *Parmenides*, the relation between the one and the many. In his "Sketch of a Personal Universe" (1937) he wrote:

Plurality and unity: the one problem to which in the end all physics, all philosophy, and all religion, come back.

Fourteen years before (1923) he was saying the same thing:

I find that the one great problem of the one and the manifold is rapidly beginning to emerge from the over-metaphysical context in which I used to state it and look for its solution. I can now see more clearly that its urgency and its difficulties must be expressed in terms of real men and women. (*Letters from a Traveller*, pp. 66–7.)

The more I look at it, the more I think that the only knowledge—the one that can be acquired even in all our weakness and ignorance—is the vision of unity in becoming under and through the incoherent multiplicity of things. (27 May 1923.)

Similarly in 1932:

For some months now I have been trying to make some sort of attempt to describe the main lines along which mysticism has sought to solve the fundamental intellectual and spiritual problem: how to explain, then surmount the multiple, and so attain to unity? (22 May 1932.)

He returned to the point, in a different context, during a wedding address:[2]

Unity: an abstract expression, maybe, that philosophers delight in. But it is essentially a very concrete quality, with which we all seek to endow all that we do and all the world around us. . . . Happiness, power, riches, wisdom, sanctity; all these are synonymous with victory over the multiple. At the heart of every being, creation dreams of the principle that will one day organize its scattered treasures. God is unity. Then by what significant act can one pursue and attain this divine unity? . . . You have chosen the unity of union. . . . True union differentiates in just the same measure as it brings together. It is an unceasing discovery and a continual conquest.

Teilhard, characteristically, approached the problem as a mystic: in his case we might more correctly say, a cosmo-mystic. "Natural"

[2] The occasion was the wedding of Monsieur and Madame de la Goublaye de Ménorval (15 June 1935).

as opposed to religious mysticism consists essentially in freeing one-self from the multiple so that one can see and breathe nothing outside the ambience in which everything is one. Teilhard, quite correctly, distinguishes two types of mind, the pluralists, who never go beyond nor even feel the need to go beyond perception of multi-plicity, and the monists, for whom the perception of multiplicity must necessarily be completed in some unity. He ranges himself with the latter, and has no patience with the former, saying that their attitude is like a refusal to see or explain the universe. During World War I, Teilhard, as though appalled by the immense multitude of beings whom he was witnessing in such turmoil, wrote an essay under the title "The Struggle against the Multitude". In his eyes, multiplicity means dispersion and so annihilation, for things do not grow by multiplication. "Fragmentation" of beings brings perpetual disappointment, for until now the monads have been distressingly separable, standing apart from and indifferent to one another. Teilhard even confesses an instinctive hostility to the generality of mankind that our Lord tells us to love. "Multitude is in fact the fundamental obstacle to Charity."[3] Plurality is the thinker's un-known quantity: as Pascal was terrified by the eternal silence of space, so Teilhard felt looming over him the essential agony of the atom lost in the universe, lost, that is, in the terrible multiplicity of atoms. It was not unnatural accordingly that he was attracted, though never seduced by, the religious thought of the East.

Christ will be victorious over the initial multitude of bodies and souls, for it is he who has inspired in us the longing that makes us pray, "Lord, make us one!" Christ in his glory, as we have seen, appeared to Teilhard as the dazzling centre in which the countless fibres of the many are knit together, vivified by his omnipresence. Then we see that the many that so oppressed us takes on a singular validity, for it is through the many that the divine beleaguers us, that the Spirit of God makes its way into and works in every sphere. Without the multiplication of humble roots how could the great tree of God draw nourishment from the earth?

This relation between the one and the many was, with Teilhard, the subject of continual deep reflection. He saw that it was through convergence, which makes all things cohere, that the two were reconciled, the one being born of the concentration of the many. It is

---

[3] "Les fondements et le fond de l'idée d'évolution" in *La vision du passé*, p. 192.

here that his study of anthropogenesis supplies the key; for evolution shows us that the real progresses through a series of syntheses, in the course of which the many appears in continually more complex and highly organized forms, passing through successive stages of consciousness: a new plurality thus coming into being to allow a higher synthesis. The synthesis, however, sublimates, without annihilating the elements. We meet here another principle that Teilhard continually insisted on—as in the address quoted above—that union differentiates. Thus Christianity safeguards the essential aim of all true mysticism, to find unity (to become, that is, one with the other) without losing one's own personality, and we can lose ourselves in God only by carrying to a still higher pitch those qualities that most determine our individualities.

Convergence synthesizes the one and the many. More than this, however (and this is a particularly valuable Teilhardian principle), love, in unifying, ultra-personalizes. Thus Teilhard's cosmo-mysticism falls into line with the demands of orthodox Christian mysticism. This was the core of his spiritual life, the life of a man who could with justification speak of it as "a great and splendid adventure".

CHAPTER TWENTY-FIVE

"I go to meet him who comes"

As I come to the brief story of Teilhard's last days, the picture of the man I knew and loved comes back to my mind.

I can remember so clearly making my way towards the Jesuit headquarters in which Teilhard was living: a tall white house, the walls newly roughcast, in a quiet and elegant part of the city. It was always such an excitement to see him that my heart was beating as I went past the little glass box, rather like an aquarium, in which the old porter with a black skull-cap used to potter about except when the telephone galvanized him into activity. Then, up the staircase smelling of beeswax, along the passage—impersonal, spotlessly clean as only religious houses are—and past a series of doors, each with a name-card attached. On one of these I would knock and enter a room as impersonal as the rest of the house, so spick and span that it made up for the sombre furniture and faded curtains. A prie-dieu with a cushion, a crucifix. A little radio playing softly an extract from *Parsifal*. Scattered about are various books and papers, among them a number of paper-backed novels which I recognized from their coloured covers as English Penguins. A typewriter has managed to find room for itself on the desk. Teilhard, I can see, still has the same working habits: scribbled notes (scraps of sentences), then a first draft in pencil, with many erasures and corrections (resting the paper on a sheet of glass), then a typed copy, with manuscript additions, and illustrated with the geometrical diagrams in which Teilhard, who always saw things as a visual pattern, used to express even the most abstract ideas.[1]

[1] Teilhard seldom kept his rough drafts. In conversation, he would often jot down notes on a scrap of paper. His first typescript was often followed by a second, with many fewer alterations.

Looking through my notes, I find some jottings that I give just as I put them down: "great height,[2] thin, hair white and rather sparse, eyes light grey, parting on the left, aquiline nose." I retain a very clear picture of his face, an elongated oval, deeply lined, with three furrows running across his forehead and others in a sharp V cut into the curve of the cheek; three small brown patches of keratosis, one on the left cheek, the others above and below the left eye; the thinness of his lips made up for by the look of kindness and intelligence in his eyes, as he looked at you quizzically over the top of his spectacles. His voice was aristocratic, warm and well modulated, expressive (still to be heard only on American recordings).[3] He wore a leather jacket over his gown and Roman collar.[4] Physically, there was little sign of weakness, though the two alarms of 1947 and 1949 had left him with a certain nervous tension or anxiety, cardiac in origin.[5] (This was one reason why he could not face any violence in discussion.) In these days Teilhard had changed a great deal from the man who sailed with Henry de Monfreid in the Gulf of Aden. His smile was less broad, even (though I fear he would turn in his grave to hear me say so) more disciplined. In fact, valiant fighter and independent thinker though he still was, there was now something more conventionally "clerical" about him. There was still the same bright glance and the same kindliness that distinguished him from the less sympathetic clergy, but it was now the fruit of a triumphant resignation which gave Teilhard a personal quality so precious that I can describe it only as a state of pre-beatitude.

No one is a great man to his own household, but in spite of his simplicity that was not true of Teilhard; even those who lived on the closest and most intimate terms with him recognized that there was something outstanding in his character and genius. He had, moreover, a great sense of humour. An old friend of his was vastly

[2] His last passport gave his height as 1.81 m. (just under six feet) and the colour of his eyes as blue-grey. One who knew him well, however, says that he had brown eyes, with great depth of expression; his military service certificate (1919) gives brown for both hair and eyes. Quite possibly the apparent colour of his eyes varied with the light at different times of the year.

[3] "There was nothing unctuous in his speech; his voice was deep and vibrant, with the softly muted tone you hear in the Italian of Lombardy." (*Synthèses*, May–June, 1955, p. 30.)

[4] As a child, he could not bear the black of a priest's *soutane*. Meeting one in the street, he would cross over to the other pavement.

[5] Teilhard, on his doctor's advice, had given up smoking. He was always sparing in the use of alcohol.

amused once to find an early number of a periodical to which Teilhard had contributed a violent attack on evolution: Teilhard was the first to laugh when confronted with this error of his youth.

He combined aristocratic breeding and ease of manner with a complete lack of worldliness; he was a wonderful host, and a wonderful guest, too, though never seduced by the pleasures of social intercourse.

All who met Teilhard were immediately impressed by his creative intelligence. In these last months his synthesis was completed and he had come to understand exactly where he stood. He lived his own ideas, deeply and intimately, though still open to the world around him and to what the future might bring. His judgements were sure, expressed with brevity and force. He always went straight to the essential point, and had the gift of finding the right word and the right image. He never wasted his time in useless reading, but always managed to keep up to date. His modesty was such that he never seemed to realize the genius he possessed, thinking that he was no better, or more important, than anybody else. All he felt was that, for a number of quite accidental reasons, a happy combination of heredity, education and environment, his own was a particularly significant case and for that reason he should leave some record of it. He felt that he had a prophetic gift. In short, he had had the good fortune to be a man who lived passionately with his own time.

Teilhard was vividly aware of contemporary spiritual needs, and yet he found that he stood almost alone, the only one to have seen and clearly expressed the wonderful "diaphany" that, for him, transfigured all things. Thus, as he once said, he knew that for the immediate future, at any rate, he was obliged to work in the shadow of exile. No man could have had less pride in himself. "I know my faults and shortcomings", he said; and when he said that all he wanted was to be "a stone cast into the foundations" he was completely sincere. He was impervious to flattery: fine words meant nothing to him. Moreover, his simplicity was such, and he seemed so naturally superior to other men, that even justified praise seemed beside the point.

Above all, Teilhard was an apostle devoted to the discovery and service of Christ. He continually re-dedicated himself to the task of serving as the apostle of evolution, to incorporating cosmogenesis in Christ, to Christifying evolution. Sharing intensely in the hopes of his time, his ambition was to give the world to Christ, for the modern world could be saved only through Christ. By his boldness, by the contagious strength of his faith, he was a power that gave testimony to the victory of Christ; for men could see that here was a soul that had found salvation in Christ and was living evidence of a presence that made him the spokesman of one greater than he. His piety, based on the transfigured Christ and in particular on the risen Christ of Easter, was an adult piety, with no trace of immaturity, the piety of a son of God, a man who stands erect and strong.

His unvarying kindness was equalled only by his forgetfulness of self.

This, indeed, was his rule of life:

The rule that guides me is this: there can be no serious error to fear if my interior attitude results in my becoming more faithful, more attentive, more passionately interested in men and man's work—less concerned, at the same time, in a selfish way, with my own self. (28 July 1939.)

Nothing can stand up against affection and kindness—particularly when it is humbly sought for at its divine source. (8 August 1944.)

Another's suffering caused him terrible distress. All that he had was at the other's disposal. Similarly, there was never any anger or hatred in him. He never complained, never attacked another. He never sought to avoid souls, but was ready to spend his time freely in their service; even the too-loquacious, the importunate and the cadgers were not turned away. Sometimes, not realizing how underhand some people can be, he would be taken in by lies. With the unconquerable optimism of a man whose own life is without stain, he despaired of no man, looked for what was best in anybody, and helped him to advance along the line that best suited him.[6] Teilhard never tried to impose his own personality on or dominate another person. What made his intellectual direction so successful was that, having achieved his own synthesis, he was able to attune himself to most types of minds and philosophical or religious attitudes, to face every difficulty squarely, to start back at the beginning with the man who needed help, to share his doubts, search with him, and so ease for him the road to faith.

[6] The Abbé Breuil, who was long a familiar friend, testifies that he never heard Teilhard speak uncharitably of anyone. Père Leroy once said to Teilhard, "If you met the devil, I expect you'd say, 'You know, he's not as bad as all that.' "

Teilhard was in the front rank of spiritual directors. He could always find the right words to cure distress (I know, from personal experience, that he was the only man who could, effortlessly, dispel the pride and sense of revolt in the soul of one well known to me). And this gift came from his great charity. He knew that the greatest joy was to give oneself to one greater than oneself, without taking too much account of one's own feelings. Loving all men in God, he dedicated himself to all, for, being a passionate lover of Christ he saw Christ through each person and had an infinite tenderness, worthy of St Francis, for every created being.

"You'd almost believe", said another priest of him with a smile, "that there was no original sin in Teilhard."

To the very core of his being, Teilhard was a priest. In him the three theological virtues, faith, hope and charity, often attained the heroic. In virtue of his humility, and his absolute devotion to souls, in his dedication of the universe to God, in his witness to a presence greater than himself, he bore the mark of a man of whom we rightly say, *"Tu es sacerdos in aeternum"*—a channel through which grace pours into the mystical body.

More, Teilhard was a Jesuit, and of the high Jesuit aristocracy. In him you find all the qualities that mark the wide-ranging Jesuit spirit: scientific skill and intelligence, the aristocratic temperament, the missionary passion and zeal for education, the love of the youth of Europe, intellectual intransigence allied with absolute loyalty to the Church and the Holy See.

In 1955 Teilhard was an old man whose eyes still saw the true light. He feared death no more than he did under the shrapnel and shell-fire of the Great War. He realized its grim power to decompose and dissolve, but he knew, too, that this physical relapse into the multiple can become, for each human existence, the fullness of unity in God. Death, this passage into the one, seemed to him no more than a sleep to be followed by a glorious dawn. He wrote:

With God's help, we make for ourselves, here below, the eyes and the heart that, by a final transfiguration, will become the organs of a power to adore and of a capacity for beatification that will be peculiar to each one of us.

And when a friend died, he said of him, "Now he can see."

That he might share in the Cross, Teilhard set himself to meditate on decline, on growing old, on death. For death he had no fear,

13*

but old age he dreaded. So, he made himself love the decline of life, and love life still in spite of its decline. While praying, *"usque ad senectam, ne me derelinquas, Domine"*,[7] he made himself accept and love the frailty of increasing years, the longer shadows falling behind, and the shorter days still to come. He sought to find, in Christ, the source of youth, gaiety, enthusiasm, initiative, not allowing himself to equate melancholy or indifference or disillusionment with true wisdom. While he hoped for the grace of a rapid end, he prepared himself to accept death in whatever form it might come, *in Christo.* As he recited, *"Appropinquat hora, appropinquat Christus"*,[8] he strove to analyse and examine more deeply the conditions of fullest "communicability" (his own word was *communiance*), he sought to share in the agony of the world through the "excentration" that comes with old age and death. To discover, spread, and make real the mystery of Christ is summed up in his two words, to Christify and *Christifieri*—to be Christified. To Christify, on the intellectual and affective plane, is to advance the Christification of evolution. *Christifieri*, to allow onself to be assimilated by Christ, is to commune with, become at one with all that happens, including, when it becomes inevitable, physical decay; for all the forces of diminution allow one to abandon oneself to Christ.

On the tomb of a Cardinal Archbishop of Toledo, primate of Spain, is inscribed: *Ingenio praestans, caritate praestantior homo tamen: orate pro eo.*[9] We could speak of Teilhard in similar terms. Scientist, thinker, poet, prophet, mystic, he was all these. And to these he added sanctity. Yet his real grandeur lay in having taken on, for Christ, the fullness of the human.

"I go to meet him who comes."

A little before 10 April 1955, Easter Sunday, the day on which Teilhard was given the grace to die suddenly (from a rupture of the coronary artery), he had said, "I go to meet him who comes."[10] According to André George, the last words that Teilhard wrote were a meditation on St Paul and an act of faith in Christ.[11]

---

[7] "Even unto old age, abandon me not, Lord."

[8] "The hour draws near, Christ draws near."

[9] "Eminent in his natural gifts, in his charity still more eminent: and yet a man. Pray for him."

[10] A month earlier (15 March) he had expressed the wish that he might die "on the day of the Resurrection".

[11] He stated this as a fact in the course of a lecture on Teilhard.

A note he left runs thus:

7 April
Holy Thursday. *What I believe*
Syntheses
(a theological confirmation.
Satisfying Revelation).

1. St Paul . . . three verses:
2. Cosmos — Cosmogenesis — Biogenesis — Noogenesis — Christogenesis — the still-to-come.
3. The Universe is centred evolutively on the still-to-come. Christ is the centre of it (the Christian phenomenon) Noogenesis—Christogenesis.

These final words of Teilhard's may well be pondered on in the light of the remarkable apologia (addressed from Capetown, 12 October 1951) he sent to Fr Janssens, his General, in which he sums up his religious attitude.[12]

Appropriately, then, he ended with a gesture of adherence to the "phylum", as he might have said, of the Church. A week before he returned to God he had seen Fr Gannon, Rector of St Ignatius's. Fr Gannon found that he "opened his mind to me with such spontaneity and charm that it was like being with a child". On the eve of his death, he had made his confession to Père de Breuvery, a fellow-Jesuit. One of his oldest friends, Père Leroy, has left an account of Teilhard's last moments:

He was in good form. On the morning of Easter Sunday he had been to High Mass at St Patrick's Cathedral.[13] In the afternoon he had been to a concert. Going back to some friends, he was congratulating himself on this "magnificent day" and was in excellent spirits. He was about to take a cup of tea and had just put down a paper on the window-sill when he suddenly fell full length on the floor, toppling over like a stricken tree. Seeing that he was unconscious, it was thought at first that he had fainted, and a cushion was placed under his head. After a few minutes he opened his eyes and said, "Where am I? What's happened?" "You're with us, don't you recognize me?" said his hostess. "Yes, but what's happened?" "You've had a heart attack", he was told. "I can't remember anything," said Teilhard, "this time I feel it's terrible," by which I think he meant that it was a really serious

[12] An English translation is included in *Letters from a Traveller* (pp. 41–4).
[13] He had said his own Mass earlier.

or even mortal attack. His doctor was telephoned, but was out. A few minutes later another doctor arrived, and seeing how serious his condition was, advised them to send for a priest. Père de Breuvery was also out and in his place an American Father came from St Ignatius's.[14] When he arrived Teilhard had just died, but he nevertheless gave him absolution and Extreme Unction.

So, on the feast of the Resurrection, died the witness of the risen Christ.

Père Teilhard's body lay in the chapel of Park Avenue, in a coffin lined with white satin, on a violet pall. He was in his priestly vestments, with a crucifix and a rosary in his hands. When the body had been (as is customary in the U.S.A.) embalmed, his face bore a striking resemblance to that of his compatriot from Clermont, Pascal: the smooth forehead, the sunken cheeks, the prominent nose and cheek-bones, the tightly drawn lips. The funeral was on Tuesday, 12 April, with Père Breuvery officiating. There were few present, for many of his friends were away for the week-end and could not be told in time. Among the dozen or so who attended the Requiem Mass were the French Ambassador to the United Nations, Monsieur Hoppenot, and Paul Fejos. It was a very quiet and simple ceremony, even poor: Low Mass, with no singing, not even *In Paradisum*. It was raining. One of those present wrote later, "My heart was so heavy that I could hardly pay attention. It seemed too incredible and too sudden to be real." Only Père Leroy and the Fr Minister from St Ignatius's accompanied Père Teilhard to the Jesuit novitiate at St Andrews on the Hudson, some sixty miles from New York, where the coffin was laid in a temporary vault, awaiting the final interment, the only flowers being a floral cross sent by Malvina Hoffman. Still in exile, Teilhard lies under a simple stone inscribed with his name. His own words may well console us for his loss:

Lord, since with every instinct of my being and through all the changing fortunes of my life, it is you whom I have ever sought, you whom I have set at the heart of universal matter, it will be in a resplendence which shines through all things and in which all things are ablaze, that I shall have the felicity of closing my eyes.

[14] Fr Martin Geraghty, S.J.

CHAPTER TWENTY-SIX

General Conclusion

TEILHARD's whole life may be summarized in this brief epitome of *The Heart of Matter*.

1. A search for unchangeable matter—from childhood this is an irresistible lure; a vocation to science; a progressive discovery of the universe in which he finds unity through convergence (which involves the transition from cosmos to cosmogenesis); with this the discovery of irreversibility (which involves centring on an incarnate God).

2. The meeting of his science and his faith in the Pauline pleroma, which he sees in the dimensions of our twentieth-century universe: the word embracing in his power, his sanctity and his infinity the whole creation that, through the Incarnation, he has incorporated with himself even to the remotest galaxies.

3. To enable this universe to evolve to its culmination, there must be a single energy, the love of God, manifested in and working through the heart of Christ, which is also the heart of the world, the cause and animator of the universe's energy (from the simple forces of attraction, through biological tactism and instinct, up to human love).

Any final judgement, or even any attempt at such a judgement, of Teilhard would be both presumptuous and premature. But some personal reflections may not be inappropriate, and may even win some measure of agreement. In any case, Teilhard loved discussion: he even thrived on contradiction, so long as it was not the result of obstinate and invincible misunderstanding; in such a case he would simply let the matter drop. To try, then, to map out the broad lines of his thought is an act of loyalty to the Teilhardian spirit, which was always first and foremost the spirit of truth—*credo quia verum*.

The mere "fact" of Teilhard de Chardin is one whose importance cannot be exaggerated. He stands at a key-point in the spiritual history of France, of the Catholic Church, and of the world. A master of prose and a magnificent poet—though he never deliberately strove to be such—a scientist inspired by love of science and by devotion to Christ, a thinker, a mystic, his great figure dominates a singularly rich but disturbed age.[1]

Many contemporary problems were illuminated by Teilhard's intelligence. On the racial question, for example, the source of so much muddled thinking and partisan views, his calm approach is reassuring. Races are not, and never will be, biologically equal. To believe that they are is to shut one's eyes to biological fact. Are all the children of one family equally strong or equally intelligent? A Chinaman is not a Frenchman. Yet the eye cannot look down on the hand, nor can the hand operate without the eye. Races are not equal but complementary, and therein lies their true dignity, for each contributes its own individual note which will be included in the final harmony of a humanity that has at last become conscious of its unity and is converging on the same focus of love and adoration. While Teilhard granted the West its pride and its sense of mission, he held out to a world increasingly torn asunder, a real hope of ecumenicity. "Everything", he said, "that ascends must converge."[2]

His optimism, it may be urged, has not been justified by events. In spite of an increasingly close and elaborate network of communications, in spite of the spread of Western techniques, and of the general economic and political interrelation between everything that happens anywhere in the world, there has been no easing of tension between nations, no real convergence: in fact, men are still more sharply divided into hostile camps. Teilhard, however, was

[1] As early as 1957 Teilhard already had a place in books dealing with the history of philosophy. Cf. Weber and Huisman's *Tableau de la philosophie contemporaine*; Maurice Merleau-Ponty's *Les philosophes célèbres*; Roger Garaudy's *Perspectives de l'homme: Existentialisme, pensée catholique, Marxisme*; E. Callot's *Philosophie biologique*; J. Carles, *Le transformisme*, etc.

[2] This accounts for the high regard in which Teilhard was held in various Moslem and Marxist circles in Morocco and French West Africa, and for the remark made by some negroes recently to a friend of Teilhard's: "Monsieur, you are the first white man to tell us that Negroes can contribute to building the world of tomorrow."

fully aware of the nature of the present crisis, and there was nothing naïve in his optimism. A friend of his has written, very justly:

> For my part, I would qualify his "fundamental optimism", not to minimize it, but to bring out that it should not be confused with the starry-eyed optimism you so often meet, shallow, and without any human or spiritual experience behind it. Teilhard's optimism was the fruit of a victory, the victory, in the first place, of his magnificent temperament as a man, but also of his thought, and still more, ultimately, of his faith. It was not a matter of an uncritical acceptance of appearances, still less of a naïve belief in "progress". He sought to penetrate beneath appearances,[3] and knew very well that the whole universe, like Man, must die, to be reborn transfigured, in God. This he never ceased to insist upon. From this, which is the really essential point of view, he might well, with his deep sense of tradition, serve as an antidote to the "temporalist" malady so rife today, even among us.

Renouvier used to say, very justly, "this world will end in the way it makes up its mind to." Teilhard well knew that man is what he wants to be, and it was for that reason that he offered man the grand ideal of convergence, so that he might be forced to rise, and rise above himself.

Of the power and extent of Teilhard's continuing influence there can be no doubt. To him we may well apply his own words:

> The spiritual value of a man, the range of his influence, depends on the degree of reality that God has assumed for him: not on the degree of speculative or even affective perfection, but, I repeat, on the degree of reality. To have transposed God, in his life, from the plane of the imagined (or imaginary) to the plane of the real—in that lies a fortifying power and a proof of truth for all who seek to believe—but for whom the world of the divine is hopelessly unreal—imaginary.

Teilhard, therefore, was also a great "catcher of souls", intellectuals, businessmen, workers, or the poor. Intellectuals could not fail

[3] Cf. some word of Teilhard's recorded in *Synthèses* (October, 1957, pp. 78 and 80): "To exist in joy, to find that joy which is always the most divine of duties! An unconditional joy in the context of all terrestrial realities.... Joy! This alone uplifts and nourishes, urges on and brings into bloom, creates undaunted optimism, shares truly in human action.... For me, this is the only way to live: to gain altitude and climb so high that, under the superficial chaos of details—however distressful they may be—there is revealed the meaningful order of some grand destiny for man."

to be attracted by him, for he had an enquiring, exact mind, never satisfied if it could not justify any action he took; moreover, in his interior life they saw the virtues of a man who could attain his own fulfilment only through a unitary conception of the world.[4] Businessmen he attracted, because the only sin to which, in spite of his general indulgence, he was merciless was fear of effort, lack of confidence in human effectiveness.

Simple souls were drawn to Teilhard by his kindness, by his faith in the universal value of creation, by his innate spiritual attitude to work, an attitude that allowed even the humblest contribution to share in the collective value of Christianity. Every worker, he maintained, at whatever level, has a responsibility for the whole. "A radiant soul, that knew no frontiers", someone once said of Teilhard.

With the great advantage of being both a priest and scientist, and with his rare insight that enabled him to see where his contemporaries were, without realizing it, in agreement with Christianity and where they instinctively rejected it, he was able to re-orientate many different types of mind, especially the young. Marxists, jealous of their intellectual independence, yet found in Teilhard a keener sense of totality and of the future, and realized that in this lay the source of dynamic drive.[5] Freemasons, while fully aware of his priestly character, respected his sense of the universal which brings together all men of good will. In Teilhard there was a basic humanity in which the high-minded unbeliever could find a common point of departure. One of the finest of contemporary French philosophers, Maurice Merleau-Ponty, speaking at the Collège de France (in March, 1957) said of him:

> In Père Teilhard we meet a sensitiveness to truth that is extremely rare in (and outside) the Church, which always gives the

[4] Père Boné has emphasized this. "He did much to help a whole generation infected by scientism to listen to the message of faith." (*Revue des questions scientifiques*, 20 January 1956, p. 102.) Through his influence at the Museum and in scientific circles, he spiritualized, and we might even say, baptized evolutionary thought by purging it of all ambiguity and putting an end to the traditional confusion between evolution and transformist theories with a mechanistic or materialistic flavour. On the more positive plane, scholars of note, such as Jean Piveteau, introduce certain Teilhardian concepts into their own purely technical writings, concepts such as the disappearance of peduncles and the notion of convergence. After Teilhard, palaeontology became an "open" science.

[5] Teilhard, of course, was above all party politics, for he loved all progress. He never, however, made any spiritual concessions to Marxism.

impression of considering, before making any statement, whether it will be expedient, or prudent, or whether it may give offence. Teilhard has a remarkable confidence in truth, and remarkable intrepidity.[6]

Jews, again, could see in him a prophet of Israel and recognize the prophetic inspiration of an Isaiah. (The Grand Rabbi of France, for example, declared that not for hundreds of years had there been so fine a book as *Le milieu divin*.)

Many French Protestants, fundamentalist and Augustinian, are apt to resist outside influences, yet it was one of them who wrote:

> Basically, we are completely illogical. "Positivist" science, after striving desperately to dethrone man from the position accorded to him by orthodox thought, and after forcing him back among the "other animals", has never, in this sphere, gone beyond this purely material, anatomical, plane. All the rest still remains, therefore, *sui generis*—which makes things much easier, of course, for juridico-literary anthropology, even if unbelieving. We needed a *homo duplex*, at once a "son of the earth", and a "child of heaven" to make us realize that "the rest", too, depends on the laws of cosmic evolution. I well know that many children of Heaven will be dismayed and think that this is to drive the divine from its last redoubt. But you feel, as I do, that it is, on the contrary, to give back to it . . . the totality of the real.

It was a Protestant pastor, too (B. Château), who wrote to me:

> It seems to me that the great originality on the religious plane of Teilhard de Chardin . . . is to have brought Christianity back to the vision of the universal Christ, of the cosmic Christ. This spiritual advance is contained in an extension of the highest flights of Johannine and Pauline thought. At such a level the doctrine of the Redemption finally takes on its true religious dimension; it is no longer expressed in juridical terms, which are far too human and limited, but in a love that embraces the totality of men and the totality of worlds. It is that love, a love on the scale of God, that illuminates with its clarity, at once magnificent and comforting, a truly eschatological vision of the meaning of being and of life.

[6] Cf. Teilhard's letter of 20 October 1932: "We are dying because we have no one who can lay down his life for the truth." It should be emphasized that there was no contradiction between his spiritual submission and the boldness of his thought.

The best Catholic thought in France, Belgium, and Canada—and in Spain, too,[7] was deeply impressed by Teilhard's contribution. Evidence such as the following could be multiplied:

There is a debt that I have never paid in full. It is all that I owe to the thought of Père Teilhard de Chardin. It was his manuscripts that opened my eyes to new truths, that kindled a fire in a soul darkened by sorrow and gave life to almost exhausted spiritual powers. A four-line footnote is a very poor acknowledgement of the spiritual benefit I received from those manuscripts, so unassuming in appearance and yet so full, so triumphant in spiritual riches. As I read them, it seemed to me that everything in my own thought that was still vague and disjointed began to take on form and coherence. I felt a thrill of joy. Taking up again my earlier attempt, it seemed to me that I was brought right back to the Creed of my childhood. Science, pushed to its logical extreme, took on meaning and life in this Christian creed. The Incarnation, the Redemption, the Resurrection, Communion, embraced the whole world. This was the new spirit that breathed from the thumbed pages. As I read, I began to loathe the complacency with which I, as a writer, believed in my own imperfect work. I shall never, I expect, have the honour and joy of meeting Père Teilhard de Chardin, but I should be happy if someone would tell him what moral assistance he has been to me, and that I am now his faithful disciple. (Gaston Roupnel, January, 1946.)

Thus, too, Étienne Borne wrote in *Le Monde* (13 April 1955) shortly after Teilhard's death:

A man of this time and a man of the Parousia, Père Teilhard lived with prodigious intensity the coincidence of the human and divine history of the world. Genius is reluctant to divide greatness. Such was the genius of Père Teilhard, who from positive knowledge and prophetic impatience formed one indivisible greatness.

H. I. Marrou's tribute in *Témoignage Chrétien* (22 April 1955) deserves to be quoted in full, and might well be published as a booklet. From it the following may suffice for now:

The historian knows ... to what an extent the feeling for the cosmic scope of Christian salvation has been progressively blurred and atrophied in Western theology. This we must blame (and I am in a good position to know this) on the influence of St

[7] For example, the distinguished palaeontologist Miguel Crusafont Pairó has worked tirelessly to advance Teilhardian thought.

Augustine, whose psychological depth and richness is given full play, to the detriment of his interest in the world.

And, paradoxically, this atrophy became more pronounced at the very time when the development of modern civilization was turning more and more on knowing and mastering the forces of nature. From this arose the ever-widening gap between modern civilization and the Christian message; the latter seemed to dissociate itself from the former, to have nothing to say to it and nothing to contribute to it, when, in fact, our civilization had a most urgent need to be animated, taken in hand, exorcized, baptized, confirmed.... All of us, therefore, immediately appreciated, as year by year we have come to appreciate even more, the extraordinarily wide significance of the lesson to be learnt from Pierre Teilhard de Chardin.

Many others have expressed, as in the quotation from Roupnel, the wonderful sense of discovery they gained from Teilhard's writings. A Canadian novelist, Jean Simard, writing to a fellow-Canadian essayist, J. Le Moyne, speaks of the tremendous impact of the *Phenomenon of Man*:

> I've been devouring this shattering book. I've read it, and re-read it, and it's been a complete revelation: a great breath of fresh air blowing away the accumulations of dust and anachronisms; a great light suddenly illuminating the dark nave of a sleepy church.

Teilhard, in short, gave back to Christians the true sense of the earth, a sense of virile constructive effort. This was the spiritual mission to which he devoted himself, to "manifest and exalt the divino-Christic power contained in the unitary development of the tangible world."

There are, of course, difficulties in Teilhardian philosophy. Many objections, however, are answered when his thought is fully understood, and such understanding is best reached by careful study of his own words, and a painstaking attempt to share his synthesizing vision and his cosmic sense. He has been accused, for example, of opening the road to a general "concordism". Such a charge will not stand up against Teilhard's letter of 14 April 1953:

> Avoid like the plague any form of "concordism" that seeks to effect a mutual reconciliation and justification between what is quite possibly an ephemeral form of dogma and what is possibly also an ephemeral stage of the scientific view ... on the other hand, strive ... to bring out and develop the basic coherence of

what can already be regarded as the definitive axes of science and faith, *"respectively"*. And here I am thinking particularly (though not exclusively) of the problem now raised by the appearance (through science) in human consciousness of the general notion of organic-time (a real new dimension)... that is, the notion of evolution in the widest sense of the word. No "scientist" sees the universe any longer except as a cosmogenesis (it would be impossible for him to work or think otherwise). Now, in fact, dogma is still expressed (I don't say lived!) in terms of a cosmos. There we meet a fundamental and grave "dis-coherence".... Yet, (a) the universe of science (that is to say, a world in a state of cosmobiogenesis) is an exceptionally favourable setting (far more so than the Greek cosmos) for Christian vision and adoration; (b) while Christianity, on its side, by providing an exact and extraordinarily living expression of the higher pole of cosmogenesis that science postulates (i.e. by "amorizing" evolution) is seen to be the form of "religion" most amazingly adapted to becoming "the religion of evolution"—which alone can survive in the man of tomorrow.

It has been said many times that Teilhard was a pioneer. He hacked his way through unexplored forests, and to reach his destination had to clear, axe in hand, the trees and undergrowth that stood in his way, leaving it to others to make the roads. Or we may see him as the leader of a Commando, sent to seize a position and hold it until the main force can be disembarked. It must always be borne in mind that he was also a builder and organizer of ideas and that it took many years of thought and study to lay the foundations and go far to complete the magnificent structure he left us.

For this, there can be no doubt, he paid a heavy price. We know, from the absolute frankness with which he spoke to his friends, that the only rule of conduct in his own life was the will and interest of Christ, and that he was a stranger to any willed evil. We know, also, that he was alive to the problem of evil. He noted (29 November 1947):

A mortal flaw: "to be obtuse to evil" (and absorbed in one's own part), "to underestimate the forces of evil" (= dangers of miscarriage for terrestrial evolution),

and on 2 January 1952 he speaks of "the very great importance that the explicit consideration of evil is assuming in my thought". He was aware of the demoniacal which, though it left no bitterness in his soul, he met in the obstinate and seemingly motiveless enmity from some quarters that continued to pursue him. That, and what he referred to as the "fundamental tragedy of uncertainty", was part of the price he paid for his work as a precursor. Fortunately, Teilhard seemed armoured against such attacks. The family motto from Vergil was indeed appropriate to him: *Igneus est ollis vigor.*[8] Étienne Borne, whom we quoted earlier, summed up Teilhard's philosophical position in a lecture later printed in *Recherches et débats* (August, 1955, pp. 159-64), which includes the following striking passage:

> ... there are, as it were, two poles in Christian thought, between which a tension reigns and a dialogue unfolds. One of them is Jansenism, the Pascalian vision of a personal and direct relation between the soul and the divine absolute, of the presentation of an individual soul to a personal God—a vision allied with a certain pessimism and initiating a dramatically personal colloquium. In this view, history matters little. The cosmic dimension is neglected because the world and history are something unessential, or rather an obstacle, an absolutely opaque reality wherein reigns the silence that terrified Pascal. Père Teilhard's thought is a very conscious negation of Jansenistic thought. What is fundamental in his eyes is this perspective of evolution because, for Père Teilhard, so profoundly enamoured of unity, evolution is always more than positive scientific evolution. It is an upward surge, a growth, an ascent, and there must be a divine meaning in this evolution.[9] Teilhardian cosmology is fundamentally optimistic about this ever-ascending world, with complete confidence in the future of life and the universe. Briefly, in order to find the divine, we must not by-pass the cosmos but pass through it.[10] And in this, Teilhard stands at

---

[8] *Aeneid* VI. 730: "Fiery is their vigour".

[9] Universal evolution is bound up with the growth of the mystical body and the preparation of the Parousia.

[10] We might say, more exactly, "we must not turn away from the cosmos". In an important letter (12 December 1919) Teilhard worte: "Fundamentally, I admit that the fulfilment of the World will not be consummated except through a death, a 'night', a turning back, an excentration, and a quasi-depersonalization of the monads. The integration of a monad with Christ presupposes in it some sort of internal disintegration, that is to say a re-shaping of its whole being, without which it cannot be re-created and integrated in the Pleroma. In my view, the whole Christian effort consists in three things:

"1. To collaborate ardently with the human effort, in the knowledge that not only by loyalty in obedience but also by work done we are contributing to the fulfilment of Christ, because we are preparing the more or less proximate matter of the Pleroma.

the end of a long tradition which has left witnesses throughout all Christian thought. Have we not already seen St Thomas standing up against Augustinianism, affirming that the world has its own consistency, interpreting it with pagan concepts and with full confidence in the goodness of the universe?[11] An essential dialogue reigns then in Christian thought, and under pain of interrupting it, we cannot exclude Père Teilhard's thought.

As a matter of fact, these two poles do not exercise the same attraction; Jansenism represents a sort of refuge, a rock to which one clings desperately in the storm. It can give lofty lessons of austerity but it can conquer little or nothing. In the progress of Catholicism, it is Père Teilhard who plays the principal role and is the master, for his influence is widespread within and outside the Church. One of the fundamental reasons for this power of expansion is very clear. It is expressed in a fine essay by the Protestant Georges Gusdorf:[12]

> The discovery of new skies and new lands, a triumph of Western genius, has had as a necessary consequence a reconversion of man himself. For man and his earthly setting do not exist independently of each other. . . . The cosmos of the ancients, adapted for its use by a mediaeval Christianity, is henceforth nothing more than an empty shell. . . . With the sixteenth century, modern man gradually comes to see himself like Adam after his fall, driven from a marvellous garden where everything seemed so well organized for his use. Henceforth, he no longer lives in a privileged place. No longer can he think of himself as the centre of the cosmic world, nor even as the centre of the human world. More and more he finds himself in a strange world, like a displaced person in search of a new home impossible to find. . . . He finds himself alone and without a centre in an immeasurably enlarged domain, wherein the reassuring presence of God can no longer be felt as before. Hence the famous words of Pascal, that

---

"2. In this arduous task and in the pursuit of a progressively wider ideal, to achieve a first renunciation of and victory over narrow and lazy selfishness.

"3. To love, equally with its "fullnesses", the emptiness of life—the passivities and the diminishments sent by providence, through which Christ eminently and directly transforms into himself, the elements, the personality, that we have tried to develop for him."

[11] It might be added that St Thomas already looked forward to evolution, for he said that he would have preferred it had God created man *ex limo jam informato*.

[12] "Science et foi au milieu du XXe siècle", *La revue d'évangélisation*, September–October, 1956, pp. 352–5.

first testimony to the contemporary anguish: "the eternal silence of these infinite spaces terrifies me . . .".

The mediaeval scheme of divine creation has been destroyed, but man cannot attain the same control of totality in the sphere of knowledge as he has in that of technology. So far, after losing his bearings, he has not yet succeeded in finding his own place by putting everything else in its correct place.

Teilhard's greatness lay in this, that in a world ravaged by neurosis he provided an answer to our modern anguish and reconciled man with the cosmos and with himself by offering him an "ideal of humanity that, through a higher and consciously willed synthesis, would restore the instinctive equilibrium enjoyed in ages of primitive simplicity". To put it more exactly, what he did was to replace man at the head, not of a cosmos but of a cosmogenesis, and thus to present in its true dimensions a Christogenesis, identified, in the light of the risen Christ, with cosmic evolution. No longer do we have geocentrism, or monogeism (Teilhard's speculation, quoted earlier, on the other inhabited planets may be remembered), or an immobile hierarchically arranged cosmos, or anthropocentrism. All these have gone, but man is still left as the spearhead of evolution and has recovered his true place in the universe. Man ceases to be an enigma, between the two infinities of the great and the small, for he constitutes a third infinity, that of complexity. No doubt the cosmos, being unconscious, or rather pre-conscious, does not know him, but Christ the Evolver, who lies at the heart of cosmogenesis, knows him, as the still incomplete species progressing, through countless trials and troubles, towards a transcendent future. By a master stroke Teilhard, by reconciling twentieth-century man with himself, reconciles Christianity with evolutionist science, substitutes progressive optimism for static pessimism, and finds again a treasure buried since the days of St Paul and St Irenaeus, "the meaning of the cosmic component of salvation", of Christ, in whom all things are taken up.

Writing (in a letter to the author) of Teilhard's place in philosophy, Georges Gusdorf suggested that though he stood alone in his own day, he has links with the natural philosophy that began to be formulated at the Renaissance. But Renaissance philosophy is exclusively pagan, while Teilhard's love of Nature and the natural world is Christian in origin. It was by sharing in the love of the creator that Teilhard loved the universe. Between Teilhard and the

Renaissance there is, in fact, a radical opposition. In his cosmic love, there is a much closer kinship with St Francis of Assisi. We should, then, look farther back in history, to Thomistic scholasticism, to Duns Scotus,[13] St Irenaeus, and, beyond the early Fathers, to the Neoplatonists and even the Ionian philosophers. Teilhard's cosmological optimism recalls certain mediaeval and patristic traditions, while his substitution of a hyper-physics for metaphysics echoes the speculation of the Ionians, in whose scheme of thought science and philosophy were one. And yet, even if he harked back to a physics of the Greek type, Teilhard realized that his aim was to answer the questions that his contemporaries were asking:

> Of course, in all this I am conscious (and it is important that I should continue to be so) of being, for what you have to say, an example, rather than a model or an explorer. I can see quite clearly that my strength (or, if you prefer, the source of such influence as I may have) derives in no way from my having "invented" anything—but simply from the fact that I have found myself "resounding" in tune with a certain vibration, a certain human and religious note which at the moment is all around us, and in which people have recognized and rediscovered one another. (10 December 1952.) In all my work I am conscious of being no more than a sort of sound-box, amplifying what people around me are thinking. Take from me what suits you and build your own structure. (1 January 1954.)

Teilhard's modesty minimized his own contribution. It was he who pointed the way, and one reason why he could do this so effectively was that he was in tune with the modern mind. This again was why, though he never sought for disciples, a book like *Le milieu divin*, for example, could deeply effect so many thousands of readers. Père de Lubac has an illuminating comment on this point:

> It was because a person found that someone, quite unknown to him, had searched for him, had striven to express for himself, with the utmost rigour and sincerity, what he thought and believed— it was for this reason that Teilhard, without aiming at it, found so wide an audience. He put himself into his work, with all his faith as a Christian, with all his mystical soul, with all his culture as a scientist, with all the demands of an unsatisfied intellect. He

---

[13] The comparison with Duns Scotus was first suggested by Père Wildiers, one of the greatest authorities on Teilhard's thought.

lived and so he reached the living. More, he stimulated life. Along the road he had found he led minds that still stood at the cross-roads. And because he first won over a handful of his con-temporaries whose minds, though they did not know it, were already in harmony with his own, then, and very soon, the echo of his voice reverberated in the depths of the great mass of people. He found what he had never looked for. And that does not mean that apostolic ardour was not of great importance as a source of his effort in thought. The Christian who seeks, even in his inward effort, is seeking for all.[14]

On a much higher plane, and without any trace of egotism, Teil-hard might have said, as Victor Hugo did, "When I speak to you about myself, I speak about you. Fool, to think that I am not you!" Teilhard never made any display of his ego; he never sought for a public and still less to please one. He remained himself, in con-formity with the noblest virtues, in silence and humility, and that was why he was able to touch the hearts of men. He was isolated because he rejected all philosophical fashions and schools, even when they carried the prestige of a Hegel, a Nietzsche, a Husserl, or a Heidegger. Teilhard always lived in direct contact with the cosmos and God, and this is what gives the singular character of authenticity to his testimony—which is that of a man who speaks of what he has seen and touched. He is both contemporary and non-contemporary, strangely and curiously an innovator and traditionalist at the same time, for every defence and explanation of Christianity must have two sides to it, a return to the sources, and an awareness of the categorical demands of the most up-to-date science and philosophy. This is possible with a faith whose values are eternal and can there-fore inform the future of man; with a gospel whose Church will exhaust its riches only at the end of time.

Among the thinkers who despise Christianity, there are only three we can take seriously, Spinoza, Marx, and Nietzsche, for only they have penetrated to the root of things and touched the quick. By some indefinable gift, Teilhard, in the whole sweep of his thought, went beyond all three, and so released the Christian intel-lectual from their bewitching power. No doubt can remain about the radically and authentically Christian character of the Teilhardian *Weltanschauung*. For many reasons—an unfailing love of Christ, a participation in the mystery of the Cross, mystical trials, condemna-

[14] *Paradoxes* (1949), pp. 98-9.

tion to silence, a life often ascetic and exhausting, the memory of the sacrifice of his sister Françoise, the sight of his sister Marguerite-Marie's long martyrdom—few men have had so keen a sense of human suffering and the Cross.

What a vast ocean of human suffering is represented by the whole of the suffering earth at any moment! But what makes up that mass? Blackness, deficiency, waste? No, we repeat, but rather potential energy. In suffering is concealed, with extreme intensity, the world's power of ascension. The whole problem is to liberate it by making it conscious of what it means and of what it can achieve. What a leap forward the world would make towards God if all sick people at the same time converted their pain into a common desire that the reign of God should rapidly mature through the conquest and organization of the earth. All the sufferers on earth uniting their sufferings so that the world's pain became a great and unique act of conscience—would that not be one of the highest forms which the mysterious work of creation could take in our eyes?

And is it not exactly for that reason that creation, in the eyes of the Christian, is consummated in the Passion of Jesus? We are perhaps apt to see nothing more on the Cross than individual suffering and expiation. The creative force of that death eludes us. If we took a wider view we would see that the Cross is the symbol and the focus of an action whose intensity is inexpressible. Even from an earthly point of view, fully understood, Jesus crucified is not an outcast or defeated. He is, on the contrary, the one who bears the weight and leads always higher towards God the progress of the universal advance. Let us do likewise, that we may be united with him all the days of our life.[15]

Without doubt, he experienced the fullness of the Ascesis, mysticism and contemplation, but it was by clinging firmly to the Catholic axis:

There can be no doubt that Christianity, by its belief, boldly maintained (and boldly modernized) in a totalization of the universe on and in the Personal (through forces of love), is the only morality and mysticism we can see that is capable of animating the phenomenon (as we foresee it) of super-hominization. But there is still a great deal of thinking to be done about this, and, even more important, a great deal to be experienced and

[15] "The Meaning and Constructive Value of Suffering", translated from the French in *The Wind and the Rain*, edited by Neville Braybrooke, 1926.

lived. I often get the impression that men are now vegetating, waiting for the appearance of a new "saint" to give them the lived formula, show them a practical example of a form of adoration and perfection that they can vaguely conceive but cannot formulate for themselves. (25 August 1947.)

The same appeal is made in a letter written over twenty-five years earlier (21 June 1921):

I am convinced that all around us there is accumulating a vast religious potentiality that is not being realized. For one reason or another—and for the first time in the Christian era—a civilized humanity has grown up outside the consciousness of Christ. What is needed is a sort of "reincarnation" to animate this great body; and this reincarnation is called for primarily by all the truth and beauty that we have built up during the centuries. How will this movement be initiated? I dream of a new St Francis or a new St Ignatius to show us the new type of Christian life (at once more involved in, and more detached from, the world) I pray that our longing may at least be the dust from which such a man will be formed.

Teilhard, in his humility, saw himself only as a forerunner who announced the coming of such a saint. Many who knew him well would agree that in fact it was in him that were to be found the very qualities for which he was looking. "The saint", he wrote, "is the man who Christianizes in himself all the human of his own time." That definition might well, indeed, be applied to Teilhard himself.

Even before World War I he had made up his mind both to serve God and to play his part in the world around him: to follow the Cross and at the same time share in the building of the universe. In this there was no contradiction. *Le milieu divin* brings out the union of contemplation and action in Christ. He held firmly to his belief in the universal value of all creation: he knew the stages through which the "human group" must pass and its growth in the spiritual order, and it was for those reasons that he strove to advance the material development of the world:

Note this well: I attribute no definitive and absolute value to the various constructions of man. I believe that they will disappear, re-cast in a new whole that we cannot yet conceive. At the same time I admit that they have an essential provisional role—that they are necessary, inevitable, phases through which we (we or the race) must pass in the course of our metamorphosis. What I love in them is not their particular form, but their function, which is to build up, in some mysterious way, first something divinizable —and then, through the grace of Christ alighting on our effort, something divine. (12 December 1919.)

Full spirituality was for Teilhard, as true philosophy was for Marx, a practical mode of life. Work (associated with research) is, in the full sense of the word, a prayer, if it is directed towards Christ, dwelling in the heart of matter. Teilhard once said, "The return to the Father—everything is summed up in that." That return, however, can be made only if humanity takes on as fully as possible the "form" of Christ, and allows itself to be assimilated by him. As we read Teilhard, we are continually amazed by the acuteness with which he searched for the most effective ascesis, the truest mysticism. The new ascesis, leading us through and beyond the cosmos, allows technological man to feel that henceforth he is on the road (planned by God) to Christianity, and not simply the servant of a de-humanized, accursed world: thus the modern world of technology acquires positive value from the invisible world.

Of Teilhard's spirituality we may add that it was both specifically Catholic and specifically Jesuit. His clearly Eucharistic piety, his idea that the Incarnation is still continuing and that Revelation is made explicit in and through the Church, his fear of seeing dogma evaporate in symbolism, his attachment to Mary, his constant devotion to the Sacred Heart, all these are straightforwardly Catholic. With astonishing boldness of thought he combined a sort of ingenuousness, even a *naïveté*, in his faith that preserved in him the spirit of childhood our Lord called for in those who sought to enter the Kingdom of Heaven. There was never any question of a breach between Teilhard and the Church. It is true that he defended his right to follow the vocation to which he felt himself called and that he said and wrote what he believed to be true, but he was never lacking in respect or obedience. He was no reformer in the sense of the sixteenth-century reformers. The really great Catholic thinkers —Augustine, Albert the Great, Aquinas, Dominic, Ignatius, Teresa, Bérulle—are never in danger of straying from the Church, for they share (as any man of good will may) in the inspiration of the Holy Spirit that guides the Church. So it was with Teilhard.

When Teilhard celebrated his golden jubilee in the Society, he said that if he had to go back fifty years, he would do exactly the same; and the strictly Jesuit characteristics in his spirituality are clearly recognizable. As a correspondent, a man of real perception, wrote to me:

You have realized that Père Teilhard was a Jesuit through and through, in spite of all the trials you know he underwent (and which, for that reason, he felt all the more deeply). His Jesuitness explains his loyalty. The essential part about him can be expressed very simply. He was an apostle: his spirituality was essentially apostolic. He was human: his humanism was completely real. He passionately loved his own time: he had a genius for adaptation. He had learnt to love Jesus Christ absolutely unconditionally, to put into that love all the yearning for the absolute that is in man, and all the absoluteness with which man gives himself. These are all distinguishing characteristics of the spirit of the Society of Jesus.

One only has to look through the *Constitutions of the Jesuit Order* to find in it the framework of Teilhard's spirituality. The primacy of God (*major Dei gloria, majus Dei obsequium*)—Teilhard lived only for Christ; the apostolic goal—Teilhard, with his Christological vision of evolution, centred upon it his apostolic zeal; subordination of natural to supernatural means, but respect for and use of the natural—for Teilhard the whole of cosmogenesis was an aspiration (divine in origin) for super-nature, but the spirit of God acts normally through the medium of cosmogenesis; the ideal of a theocentric culture and humanism—all Teilhard's efforts were devoted to the creation of a new humanism of which Christ the Evolver is the centre:[16] heroic and discreet charity (*discreta caritas*), that is to say charity that can distinguish, a provident charity, love that can keep within the appropriate bounds—Teilhard's heroism needs no emphasis, for he made it his own special task to carry the Gospel into the most inaccessible places; his *discreta caritas* may not be apparent to so many, though he possessed it in abundance. He had always an anxious care for souls and could win them without deliberately seeking to do so, but he was fundamentally reserved. He never said anything without a purpose, and in spite of the boldness of his words and letters, he retained the prudence and the intransigence in essentials that characterize the Jesuit; in such

[16] The development of a Christian humanism is one of the great merits of the Society of Jesus. The Jesuit way of life is not to spend long hours in prayer but to see God in all things, even in the most mundane occupations.

matters he would have no deviation nor dangerous concession. The mobility and flexibility in obedience that makes a Jesuit ready to set off anywhere at any time—Teilhard was always on the move, and always in accordance with the orders of his superiors. "One day," he wrote, "I expect I shall end up by the roadside, like the wandering Jew; but there's nothing I'd like better." Few men, indeed, have been more obedient or have had a stronger sense of discipline. "*Agere contra*"—Teilhard would never let his own inclinations dictate his action. Finally, the sense of community—Teilhard's development of the idea of the necessity for the socialization of man and of the widening of consciousness that it entails was based partly on his experience of working in a scientific team, and partly on community life in the Society. The solidarity of the Jesuits, in spite of the diversity of their interests, is impregnable and, with their long training, their high cultural standards and their apostolic sense, is one of the secrets of their strength.

Teilhard the priest will never pass away. When the philosopher has led man across the threshold of a new era and into the age of synthesis, when the author of *The Phenomenon of Man* has become a classic, piety will still be nourished by the priest who wrote *Mass on the Altar of the World*, by the consecrator of the Pleroma, in which the sacramental touch of the Incarnation will be seen to reach to the ultimate particles, by the animator of the Catholic concept of an evolution that in readiness for the final return of its Head is progressively assimilating the vast spiritual effort, the awful material labour of the universe advancing to its consummation in Christ.

Now, Lord, in the consecration of the world, the shimmer and fragrance floating over the universe take on for me, in you, form and feature. What my hesitant thought could only glimpse and my heart longed for with a yearning that seemed beyond all reason, your lordly munificence now grants me: that all creatures may be not only so one with another that none can exist without all the others to encircle it, but that they may all so depend from one and the same real centre that a true life, lived in common, gives them for ever their consistence and their unity.

Through the boldness of your revelation, my God, shatter the timidity of an infantile thought that dares conceive nothing more vast, nothing more living in the world than the wretched perfection of our human organization! Day by day the children of this world, advancing towards a more daring understanding of the universe, outstrip the masters of Israel. Do you, Lord Jesus, "in whom all things find their consistence", manifest yourself at last to those who love you, as the higher soul and physical focus of creation. For us, see you not, this spells life or death. If I could not believe that your real presence animates, gives warmth and suppleness to even the least of the forces that run through me or impinge upon me, then a mortal cold would penetrate the very marrow of my being. . . .

At this moment, when your life has just, with a new burst of vigour, passed into the sacrament of the world, I shall savour, with a more vivid consciousness, the strong and calm intoxication of a vision whose coherence and harmonies I can never exhaust.[17]

We have tried to determine Père Teilhard's position on the philosophical and religious plane. The essential still remains. In an essay dated 1919, "The Spiritual Power of Matter", Teilhard attempted to bring out, in a poetic form of rare beauty, the philosophical and mystical significance of matter. He compares man's struggle with matter to Jacob wrestling with the angel, for matter is ambivalent, ambiguous, and to release its spiritual power we have first to battle obstinately with it. This dates back to an early stage in his thought, when he first perceived "the glow of matter". But at the end of the piece, the Man—that is, Teilhard himself—feels himself swept away by matter as though in a whirlwind, as Elias was carried up to heaven; and he describes his feelings:

Then the heat of battle gave way, in his heart, to an irresistible yearning to experience: in a flash he saw, all around him, the one thing that is necessary. . . .[18]
He felt pity for those who tremble at the thought of a century of time, and whose love cannot extend further than to one country.

So many things that had formerly disturbed or disgusted him, the discourses and pronouncements of learned men, their affirmations and prohibitions and their refusal to allow the universe to move . . .—all these now seemed absurd, non-existent, compared with the majestic, down-flooding reality of energy that was now revealed to him, universal in its presence, immutable in its truth, irreplaceable in its development, unchangeable in its serenity, maternal and sure in its protection.

[17] From *La messe sur le monde.*
[18] The *unum necessarium (l'unique nécessaire).* Teilhard was fond of using this phrase from St Luke (10. 42): "But only one thing is necessary, and Mary has chosen the best part of all."

At last, then, he had found a foothold and a haven outside society!

A heavy mantle fell from his shoulders and slipped to the ground behind him; the weight of all that is false, narrow, tyrannical, artificial, human, in humanity.

A wave of triumph liberated his soul.

And he felt that now nothing in the world could detach his heart from the higher reality that manifested itself to him—nothing, neither men with their intrusiveness and individuality (so little account did he take of them), nor heaven and earth in their height, their width, their depth, their power (since it was precisely to them that he dedicated himself for ever).

A profound renewal had just taken place within him, such that he could now be man only on another plane.

Now, when he should step down again to common earth, even were it to be by the side of the faithful companion he had left below, stretched out on the desert sand, he would be for ever a stranger.

Of all this he was conscious: even for his brothers in God, better men than he, he would inevitably be speaking now a language they could not understand, for the Lord had chosen him to follow the road of fire. Even to those he loved best, his affection would be a burden, for they would feel that he was irrevocably searching for something behind them.

There, in his own words, we reach the essence of Père Teilhard's personality.

He will have all the appearance of sharing the same footing as his companions: sharing their joys and sorrows, their anxieties, their studies; but, in the midst of a conversation on the most animated and spiritual level, or at a level best suited to the average person, he will remain the man of vision, the man of the heart of Christ, which he can see through the whole of the universe. No influence will be able to touch him, for his vision will fill him completely. He knows it to be a true vision. He sees it and he possesses it.

As men looked at him, he seemed to be an eagle poised for a moment within reach of one's hand. With one beat of his wings he soared up to the heights where not one of his friends could follow him.

The real Teilhard was left alone with the risen Christ: borne off in the chariot of fire.

BIBLIOGRAPHIE DES ŒUVRES DE TEILHARD DE CHARDIN

Bibliography of the Works of Teilhard de Chardin

AUTHOR'S NOTE

It might seem strange for the English translation of this biography to be rounded off with a French bibliography of the works of Teilhard de Chardin. But to translate it into English would have served no purpose. The titles of his articles—with the exception of notes written originally in English—are only known and recognizable in their French form. (Messrs. Collins even kept the French title for *Le milieu divin*.) The same holds for the French language periodicals in which they appeared.

The straightforward solution is then to leave the bibliography in French, particularly since, while the biography is addressed to a wide public, this unique bibliography is primarily of value to specialists, who cannot undertake a serious study of the works of Teilhard without a working knowledge of French.

We have therefore confined translation to the List of Abbreviations and Table of Contents.

LISTE DES ABRÉVIATIONS

LIST OF ABBREVIATIONS

M.	manuscrit—manuscript
D.	dactylographie—typescript
R.	ronéotypie—stencil duplication
d.i.	double interligne—double spaced
s.i.	simple interligne—single spaced
s.l.	sans indication de lieu—no indication of place
s.d.	sans indication de date—undated
s.l.n.d.	sans lieu ni date—no indication of place or date
h.t.	hors texte—interpolation
T.	purement technique—purely technical
Sc	scientifique (au sens le plus large)—scientific (in the most general sense)
Ph	philosophique—philosophic
R	religieux—religious
B	biographique—biographical
Pal. Sin.	*Palaeontologia Sinica*
Œ.	*Œuvres de Pierre Teilhard de Chardin* (éd. du Seuil)—The collected works of Pierre Teilhard de Chardin, published by Éditions du Seuil:

t. I: *Le phénomène humain* (1955)
t. II: *L'apparition de l'homme* (1956)
t. III: *La vision du passé* (1957)
t. IV: *Le milieu divin* (1957)
t. V: *L'avenir de l'homme* (1959)
t. VI: *L'énergie humaine* (1962)
t. VII: *L'activation de l'énergie* (1963)
t. VIII: *La place de l'homme dans la nature* (1963)
t. IX: *Science et Christ* (1965)
t. X: *Le cœur de la matière*
t. XI: *Christianisme et évolution*

Écrits 16–19=*Écrits du temps de la guerre 1916–1919*
TC explique=*Teilhard de Chardin explique sa pensée*

OBSERVATIONS GÉNÉRALES

1. Les chiffres arabes [entre crochets droits] qui apparaissent à la fin de la plupart des références rappellent les numéros de la bibliographie française (Plon, éditeur), que nous avons refondue, révisée et complétée.

2. Sont marqués d'un astérisque (*) les textes demeurés inédits (ou édités hors commerce) du vivant du Père.

3. La confection systématique de ronéos n'a guère commencé qu'en 1935. Celles-ci ne sont donc pas forcément de la même année que les œuvres originales. De plus, les mêmes stencils ont pu servir à plusieurs tirages éloignés dans le temps.

4. La présente bibliographie annule et remplace celle que nous avons fait paraître dans "Essais sur Teilhard de Chardin", *Recherches et Débats du Centre Catholique des Intellectuels Français*, Paris, Arthème Fayard, oct. 1962, cahier 40, pp. 99–139, et que nous considérons comme périmée.

GENERAL OBSERVATIONS

1. Arabic figures [in square brackets] at the end of most of the entries refer to the numbering of the bibliography in the French edition (Librairie Plon), which has here been recast, revised and completed.

2. Asterisks (*) indicate texts unprinted (or privately printed) at the time of Teilhard's death.

3. Systematic stencil duplication of Teilhard's works hardly started till 1935. These do not necessarily, therefore, date from the same year as the original. The same stencils may also have been used to produce several impressions with considerable time intervals between each.

4. This bibliography cancels and replaces that published by the author in "Essais sur Teilhard de Chardin", *Recherches et Débats du Centre Catholique des Intellectuels Français*, Paris, Arthème Fayard, Oct. 1962, volume 40, pp. 99–139, which can now be considered outdated.

ŒUVRES DE TEILHARD DE CHARDIN

WORKS OF TEILHARD DE CHARDIN

I—NOTES, MÉMOIRES ET OPUSCULES BIEN DATÉS

*1905   "De l'arbitraire dans les lois, théories et principes de la physique", *Quodlibeta* (revue jésuite manuscrite), juin, no. 2, pp. 247–274 (Sc Ph) [1].

1907   "Huit jours au Fayoum", *Relations d'Orient*, Bruxelles, déc., pp. 274–281.—Œ., t. X (T B) [2].

1909   "L'éocène des environs de Minieh", *Bull. de l'Institut égyptien*, Alexandrie, 1909 (séance du 18 mai 1908), 5ᵉ sér., t. II, fasc. 1, pp. 116–121, 2 fig. (T) [3].

1909   "Les miracles de Lourdes et les enquêtes canoniques", *Études*, 20 janv., t. CXVIII, pp. 161–183 (analyse et extraits *in*: *La nation française*, 9 avril 1958) (R) [4].

1909–   "Homme: IV: L'homme devant les enseignements de
1912   l'Église et devant la philosophie spiritualiste", *Dict. apolog. de la foi cathol.*, Paris, Beauchesne (imprimatur 11 janv. 1909, copyright 1911, date de public. 1912), t. II, fasc. 8, col. 510–514 (Ph R) [5].

1910   "Belle défense d'un Acridien", *Bull. Soc. Entom. d'Égypte*, avril–juin, 2ᵉ fasc., pp. 56–57 (communication) (T) [6].

1910   "Notes complémentaires sur les roches éruptives de l'île de Jersey", *in*: F. Pelletier, "Notes minéralogiques et géologiques sur l'île de Jersey", *Soc. Jersiaise, Bull. annuel*, Jersey, Labey et fils imprim., vol. VII, bull. 25, pp. 108–111 (T) [7].

1912   "Pour fixer les traits d'un monde qui s'efface—La semaine d'ethnologie religieuse de Louvain", *Le Correspondant*, 10 nov., t. CCXIII de la nouv. sér., CCXLIX de la collect., pp. 553–560 (Sc R) [8].

1913   "La préhistoire et ses progrès", *Études*, 5 janv., t. CXXXIV, pp. 40–53, Œ., t. II, pp. 23–38 (T Sc) [9].

1913   "Sur une formation de carbono-phosphate de chaux d'âge paléolithique", *C. R. Acad. Sc.*, 1ᵉʳ déc., t. CLVII, pp. 1077–1079 (T) [10].

1914   "Présentation d'échantillons de quercyte (phospho-carbonate de chaux)", *Bull. Soc. Géol. France*, t. XIV, pp. 9–10 (T) [11].

1914–   "Les Carnassiers des phosphorites du Quercy", *Ann. de Pal.*,
1915   t. IX, fasc. 3 et 4, pp. 103–192, 13 fig., 9 pl., 8 tableaux (T) [12].

1916–   "Sur quelques primates des phosphorites du Quercy", *Ann.*
1921   *de Pal.*, t. X, pp. 1–20, 6 fig., 2 pl. (T) [13].

1916   "La vie cosmique". M., 40 pp. (cahier écolier, mais écrit dans
les lignes et interlignes)—D.d.i., 64 pp., s.i. 38 pp.—Intr.
datée de Nieuport, 24 mars 1916, à la fin le manuscrit est
daté de Fort-Mardik (Dunkerque) 24 avril 1916, lundi de
Pâques (rédaction commencée le 15 mars), fragm. impr. *in*:
Œ., t. V, pp. 396–397; *Cahiers Sainte Jeanne*, nov. 1959, p. 258;
Ernest Kahane *Teilhard de Chardin*, Paris, Publications de
l'Union rationaliste, 1960, p. 116; *Hymne de l'univers*, 1961:
"Pensées choisies par Fernande Tardivel", I, LVIII, LXXXI;
C. Cuénot *Teilhard de Chardin*, Paris, Éd. du Seuil, coll.
"Écrivains de toujours", 1962, p. 18; C. Tresmontant "Le
Père Teilhard de Chardin et la théologie", *Lettre*, Paris,
sept.–oct. 1962, nos. 49–50, p. 12; J. Madaule "La saisie de
l'univers chez Teilhard de Chardin et Claudel", *Cahiers de vie
franciscaine*, Paris, 1963, 4e trim., no. 40, p. 56; *Foi vivante*,
Paris et Bruxelles, avril–juin 1964, 5e année, no. 19, pp. 73–77;
brèves cit. *in*: H. de Lubac, *La prière du Père Teilhard de Chardin*,
Paris, Fayard, 1964, pp. 2, 74 (n. 2), 117 (n. 4); *Écrits 16–19*
(Ph R) [14].

*1916   "La maîtrise du monde et le règne de Dieu". M., 13 pp. D.s.i.,
12 pp., s.l., 15–20 sept.; brève cit. *in*: *L'homme devant Dieu.
Mélanges offerts au Père de Lubac*, Paris, Aubier, Éd. Montaigne,
1964, T. III, p. 125; *Écrits 16–19* (R) [15].

*1916   "Le Christ dans la matière. Trois histoires comme Benson".
M., 12 pp., D.d.i., 17 pp. Nant-le-Grand, 14 oct. (l'idée du
conte "La custode" remonte au 16 juillet; conception générale
des 3 contes le 9 oct.); début reproduit *in*: "Le cœur de la
matière", 1950; impr. *in*: *Hymne de l'univers*, 1961, pp. 39–58;
réimpr. *in*: *Écrits 16–19* (R) [16].

*1917   "La lutte contre la multitude". M., 27 pp. D.s.i., 14 pp. s.l.,
26 févr.–22 mars (en projet le 6 févr. 1917 sous le titre pro-
visoire "La peine de l'isolement"; le 12 mars 1917 rédaction
commencée sous le titre "Le mal de la multitude"); extr. *in*:
Hymne de l'univers, 1961: "Pensées choisies par Fernande
Tardivel", XLVI, XLIX, LXXIV; *in*: C. Tresmontant, "Le
Père Teilhard de Chardin et la Théologie", *Lettre*, Paris,
sept.–oct. 1962, nos. 49–50, pp. 13–14; *in*: H. de Lubac, *La
Prière du Père Teilhard de Chardin*, Paris, Fayard, 1964, pp.
76–77; *Écrits 16–19* (R) [17].

*1917   "Le milieu mystique". M., 43 pp. D.d.i., 30 pp. Beaulieu-les-
Fontaines, Oise, 13 août (en projet le 10 juin, non terminé le
5 août); extr. *in*: *Hymne de l'univers*, 1961: "Pensées choisies

par Fernande Tardivel", IV, V, XI, XVIII, XXII, XXV, XXXVI, XLIII, XLV, LXXX; *in*: H. de Lubac, *La pensée religieuse du Père Teilhard de Chardin*, Paris, Aubier, Éd. Montaigne, 1962, pp. 355-358; *in*: "Essais sur Teilhard de Chardin", *Recherches et débats du centre catholique des intellectuels français*, Paris, Fayard, oct. 1962, cahier no. 40, pp. 68-69; *in*: *TC explique*; *Écrits 16-19* (R) [18].

*1917   "L'union créatrice". M., 38 pp. D.s.i., 16 pp. s.l.n.d. (Champigneul, Marne, 10 nov. 1917, d'après "L'âme du monde", 1918, et Mlle M. Teillard-Chambon citée par Madeleine Barthélemy-Madaule *in*: "Introduction à un rapprochement entre Henri Bergson et Pierre Teilhard de Chardin"; en projet le 4 oct. 1917); extr. *in*: C. Tresmontant, "Le Père Teilhard de Chardin et la théologie", *Lettre*, Paris, sept.-oct. 1962, nos. 49-50, pp. 14-15, 15-16; *Écrits 16-19* (Ph R) [19].

1917   "La nostalgie du front", *Études*, 20 nov., t. CLIII, pp. 458-467, en projet dès le 25 sept., terminé à la fin du mois, fragm. *in*: *La Table ronde*, juin 1955, no. 90, pp. 64-67, dern. § inédit reproduit *in*: "Le cœur de la matière", 1950, p. 14, no. 3, et publié *in*: *Cahiers Pierre Teilhard de Chardin*, 2, Paris, Éd. du Seuil, 1960, pp. 39-40, et P. Grenet, *Teilhard de Chardin*, Paris, Seghers, 1961, pp. 161-162; *Écrits 16-19*; Œ., t. X (B) [20].

*1918   "L'âme du monde". M., 20 pp. D.s.i., 9 pp. Mourmelon-le-Grand, Épiphanie; au texte sont adjointes une note de 3 pp. du 21 déc. 1917, et une note d'une p., s.d. "La considération d'astres habités, autres que la terre, confirme grandement l'hypothèse qu'il y a une âme du monde . . ." (inachevée); extr. *in*: Henri Duquaire, *Si les astres sont habités*, Paris–Genève, La Palatine, 1963, pp. 127-128; *Écrits 16-19* (Ph R) [21].

*1918   "La grande monade". M., 14 pp. D.s.i., 7 pp. 15 févr. (et non janv.), impr. *in*: *Cahiers Pierre Teilhard de Chardin*, 2, Paris, Éd. du Seuil, 1960, pp. 39-48; *Écrits 16-19* (Ph R) [22].

*1918   "L'éternel féminin". M., 15 pp. (cahier écolier, mais écrit seulement sur les lignes). Verzy, commencé le 19, terminé le 25 mars; *Écrits 16-19* (Ph R).

*1918   "Mon univers". M., 20 pp. en 2 fasc. ou 22 pp. en 1 cahier. D.d.i., 13 pp. s.l., 14 avril. Photocopie des pp. 3 et 4 (manuscrit Marcel Légaut) *in*: C. Cuénot, *Pierre Teilhard de Chardin*, Paris, Plon, 1958, entre la p. 74 et la p. 75; brève cit. *in*: "Le cœur de la matière", 1950, p. 3, extr. *in*: C. Cuénot, *Teilhard de Chardin*, Paris, Éd. du Seuil, coll. "Écrivains de toujours", 1962, pp. 25-26; brève cit. *in*: *L'homme devant Dieu. Mélanges offerts au Père de Lubac*, Paris, Aubier, Éd. Montaigne, 1964,

t. III pp. 338–339 (différent de "Mon univers," 25 mars 1924); *Écrits 16–19* (Ph R) [23].

*1918   "Le prêtre". M., 20 pp. D.s.i., 11 pp. s.l., 1918 (conçu vers le 26 mai, daté des "grands vœux" prononcés à Sainte-Foy-lès-Lyon, rédigé vers le 4 juill., sûrement achevé le 8 juill.; fragm. *in*: Œ., t. IV, 1957, p. 120; *Hymne de l'univers*, 1961: "Pensées choisies par Fernande Tardivel", XLI, XLVIII, LII, LX, LXI, LXXIII, LXXIX; *Le Père Teilhard de Chardin, Apôtre du Christ dans l'univers*, plaquette (cf. Progr. vendu le 11 mai 1962 au concert de gala européen à Bruxelles), pp. 1–2; brève cit. *in*: *Cahiers Pierre Teilhard de Chardin*, 4, Paris, Éd. du Seuil, 1963, p. 39; extr. *in*: P. Smulders, *La vision de Teilhard de Chardin*, Paris, Desclée, 1964, pp. 254–255 et *in*: *TC explique*; 2ᵉ version abrégée et récrite sous le titre "Le Christ et l'univers", D.d.i., 10 pp., s.i., 6 pp., dont la frappe remonterait aux années 1933–34 ou 1934–36, la 2ᵉ version datant elle-même des années 1920–23 (?), publiée *in*: *Christus*, Paris, 1964, T. XI, pp. 393–401, avec note critique de M. de Certeau, S.J., pp. 402–403; cf. lettre du P. Christian d'Armagnac, S.J., à Claude Cuénot (Chantilly, 24.x.64): "Puisque vous remettez au point votre Bibliographie, j'ajoute ceci: je viens de trouver un troisième exemplaire dactylographié [D.s.i., 6 pp.] du texte intitulé *Le Christ dans l'univers* extrait un peu remanié de *Le Prêtre*, texte que *Christus* a publié en juillet (. . .). Le 1ᵉʳ exemplaire était dans les papiers du Père Bidard, mort à Franklin, le second était avec les autres inédits du fond de la Bibliothèque venant d'Enghien qui est maintenant ici; et le troisième appartenait au Père Desqueyrat, qui m'a légué ses inédits avant de mourir. Il est donc prouvé que ce texte circulait comme étant de Teilhard et avec les autres textes de Teilhard, parmi les Jésuites, vers 1934. De plus, je suis moralement sûr que c'est Teilhard qui l'a ainsi extrait du *Prêtre*, et légèrement remanié, car les remaniements sont d'un style absolument teilhardien, parfois plus que le texte original du *Prêtre*. Puisque j'en ai un autre ici, je vous communique ci-joint l'exemplaire qui me venait du P. Desqueyrat. C'est lui qui a mis en tête une date [1933–34] avec ? (. . .). J'ajoute que la dactylographie de cet exemplaire ci-joint est identique à celle des autres textes de T., que possédait le P. Desqueyrat. Les 3 dactylographies que j'en ai vues sont de frappes différentes". 1ʳᵉ version impr. *in*: *Écrits 16–19* (R) [24].

*1918   "La foi qui opère". M., 37 pp. D.s.i., 14 pp. s.l., oct., peut-être en projet dès le 17 août, brouillon achevé le 27 sept.; extr. *in*: *Hymne de l'univers*, 1961: "Pensées choisies par Fernande

Tardivel", XXIII, LVI, LXIV, LXX; cit. *in*: Maryse Choisy, *Teilhard et l'Inde*, Paris, Éd. universitaires, Carnets Teilhard, 11, pp. 5–6; brève cit. *in*: *L'homme devant Dieu. Mélanges offerts au Père de Lubac*, Paris, Aubier, Éd. Montaigne, 1964, T. III, p. 127, no. 11; *Écrits 16–19* (R) [26].

*1918   "Forma Christi". M., 25 pp. D.s.i., 17 pp. comportant: I. l'essai proprement dit, daté du 9 déc. (peut-être en projet dès le 17 août, plan construit le 4 nov., en voie de rédaction le 8 déc.); II. un appendice de 4 pp. "Note sur l' 'élément universel' du monde" daté du 22 déc.; III. une note d'une page: "ce paragraphe est sans doute trop simpliste et systématique . . .", datée du 23 déc., s.l.; extraits *in*: H. de Lubac *La pensée religieuse du Père Pierre Teilhard de Chardin*, Paris, Aubier, Éd. Montaigne, 1962, pp. 358–359; cit. *in*: L. Barjon, "Fidélité du Père Teilhard de Chardin", *Foi vivante*, Paris, juin 1963, 4ᵉ année, no. 15, pp. 74–75; *in*: H. de Lubac, *La prière du Père Teilhard de Chardin*, Paris, Fayard, 1964, pp. 7 et 173; *Écrits 16–19* (R) [26].

*1918   "Note sur l' 'élément universel' du monde," cf. *supra*: "Forma Christi"; *Écrits 16–19* (R) [26].

*1919   "Note pour servir à l'évangélisation des temps nouveaux." M., 15 pp. D.d.i., 19 pp., R.s.i., 8 pp. Strasbourg, Épiphanie (en voie de rédaction le 5 janv., presque fini le 8 janv.; texte revu en 1920); *Écrits 16–19*. Œ., t. XI (R) [28].

*1919   "Terre promise". M., 14 pp. D.s.i., 7 pp. Goldscheuer, Bade, févr.; *Écrits 16–19* (Ph R B) [29].

*1919   "L'élément universel". M., 15 pp. D.d.i., 17 pp. Goldscheuer, Bade, 21 févr. (en voie de rédaction le 19 janv.) brève cit *in*: H. de Lubac, *La prière du Père Teilhard de Chardin*, Paris, Fayard, p. 198, n. 1; *Écrits 16–19* (Ph R) [30].

*1919   "Les noms de la matière". M., 17 pp. D.s.i., 10 pp. Paris, Pâques (en voie de rédaction le 20 avril); *Écrits 16–19* (Ph) [31].

*1919   "La puissance spirituelle de la matière". M., 19 pp. D.d.i., 12 pp. s.i., 6 pp. Jersey, 8 août (en projet le 14 avril, en voie de rédaction le 2 août, terminé le 8 août); reproduit *in*: "Le cœur de la matière", 1950; citat. par: A. Billy, "Le Père Teilhard de Chardin", *Le Figaro littéraire*, 16 avril 1955, p. 4; M. Gex, "Vers un humanisme cosmologique", *Rev. de théol. et de phil.*, Lausanne, 1957, fasc. 3, pp. 198–199; citat. *in extenso* ou partielle de "L'hymne à la matière": I. avec trad. all. par L. Boros *in*: *Wort und Wahrheit*, Vienne, janv. 1958, pp. 25–26; II. *in*: *Lettre*, Paris, mai 1959, pp. 18–19, revue ronéotypée; III. *in*: *Morale chrétienne et morale marxiste*, La Palatine, 1960, pp. 121–122; IV. *in*: *Points et contrepoints*, Paris, no. 55, déc.

1960, pp. 3–4; imprimé *in*: *Hymne de l'univers*, 1960, pp. 59–75; réimpr. *in*: *Écrits 16–19* (R) [32].

*1919 et   "Maurice Blondel et le P. Teilhard de Chardin, mémoires
1961 échangés en décembre 1919", présentés par H. de Lubac, *Archives de philosophie*, janv.–mars 1961, t. XXIV, pp. 123–156 (Ph R).

1920 "Sur la structure de l'île de Jersey", *Bull. Soc. Géol. France*, 4ᵉ sér., t. XIX, pp. 273–278, 1 coupe géol. et 1 carte géol. et tect., note présentée à la séance du 17 nov. 1919 et publiée en 1920 (cf. "Note sur la structure de l'île de Jersey", *C. R. somm. Soc. Géol. France*, pp. 130–131) (T) [27].

1920 "Sur la succession des faunes de Mammifères dans l'Éocène inférieur européen", *C. R. Acad. Sc.*, 6 déc., t. CLXXI, pp. 1161–1162 (T) [33].

1920 "Le cas de l'Homme de Piltdown", *Revue quest. scientif.*, t. LXXVII, pp. 149–155 (T) [34].

*1920 "Note sur le Christ Universel". D.s.i., 3 ou 4 pp. sel. les cop.; d.i., 7 pp.; ex. impr., 4 pp. in-4°; s.l.n.d. (daté de janv. 1920 dans l'exempl. du R. P. Henri de Lubac); Œ., t. IX (R) [35].

*1920 "Note sur les modes de l'action divine dans l'univers". M., 9 pp. D.d.i., 14 pp. s.l., janv.; Œ., t. XI (R) [36].

*1920 "Chute, rédemption et géocentrie". M., 12 pp. D.s.i., 6 pp. s.l., 20 juillet; Œ., t. XI (R) [37].

*1920 "Note sur le progrès". 1ʳᵉ vers., D.d.i., 13 pp. 2ᵉ vers., D.d.i., 19 pp. s.l., 10 août.; Œ., t. V, pp. 23–37 (Ph) [38].

1921 "Sur la présence d'un tarsier dans les phosphorites du Quercy et sur l'origine tarsienne de l'homme", *L'anthrop.*, 16 mars, t. XXXI, pp. 329–330 (T) [40].

1921 "Note sur la présence dans le Tertiaire inférieur de Belgique d'un Condylarthré appartenant au groupe des Hyopsodus", en collab. avec Ch. Fraipont, *Bull. Ac. Royale de Belgique*, classe des Sc., séance du 4 juin 1921, 5ᵉ série, vol. VII, pp. 357–360, 3 fig. (T) [39].

1921 "Comment se pose aujourd'hui la question du transformisme", *Études*, 5–20 juin, t. CLXVII, pp. 524–544; Œ., t. III, pp. 17–40; extraits *in*: R. de Sinéty, "La vie de la biosphère", *Archives de Phil.*, Paris, Beauchesne, 1936, vol. VI, cahier I; cit. *in*: E. le Roy, *L'exigence idéaliste et le fait de l'évolution*, Paris, Boivin, 1927, pp. 128–129, 149, 155–156, et *Essai d'une philosophie première*, Paris, P.U.F., t. I, 1956, pp. 339, 343, 354, 373 (Sc Ph) [41].

1921 "Bulletin scientifique. La face de la terre", *Études*, déc., t. CLXIX, pp. 585–602; Œ., t. III, pp. 43–74 (Sc) [42].

*1921 "Science et Christ (ou analyse et synthèse). Remarques sur la manière dont l'étude scientifique de la matière peut et doit servir à remonter jusqu'au centre divin". D.d.i., 15 pp., s.i., 11 pp. s.l., 27 févr. (conférence); Œ., t. IX (Ph R) [43].

*1921 "Sur le progrès". M., 14+1 pp. s.l., 24 avril (Ph) [44].

1921– "Les Mammifères de l'Éocène inférieur français et leurs
1922 gisements", *Ann. de Pal.*, t. X, fasc. 3 et 4, pp. 171–176, 2 fig., et t. XI, fasc. 1 et 2, pp. 9–116, 40 fig., 8 pl. (thèse de doctorat) (T) [45].

1922 "Sur une faune de Mammifères pontiens provenant de la Chine septentrionale", *C. R. Acad. Sc.*, 20 nov., t. CLXXV, pp. 979–981 (T) [46].

1922 "Observations sur le calcaire pisolithique de Vertus et du Mont Aimé (Marne)", en collab. avec P. Jodot, L. Joleaud et P. Lemoine, *Bull. Soc. Géol. France*, note présentée à la séance du 8 mai, 4ᵉ sér., t. XXII, pp. 164–176, 6 fig. (discuss. avec observat. du P. Teilhard, pp. 174–175) (T) [47].

*1922 "Note sur quelques représentations historiques possibles du péché originel". D.d.i., 11 pp., s.i., 7 pp. s.l. (Paris) n.d. (correspond à l'écrit dont parle Teilhard à Auguste Valensin dans la lettre du 14 mai 1922); à la suite de cet écrit Teilhard fut invité, le 2 nov. 1924, à signer un "Engagement sur le péché originel", dont il existe une copie D.d.i., 1 p., s.l.; brève cit. *in*: C. Tresmontant, "Le Père Teilhard de Chardin et la théologie", *Lettre*, Paris, sept.–oct. 1962, nos. 49–50, p. 50; Œ., t. XI (R) [452].

1923 "Cenozoic Vertebrate Fossils of E. Kansu and Inner Mongolia", *Bull. Geol. Soc. China*, vol. II, pp. 1–3, avec abstract (T) [49].

1923 "Les gros blocs Quaternaires du port de Bonneuil", en collab. avec P. Lemoine, *La Nature*, no. 2560, 28 avril, p. 272, 2 fig. (T).

1923 "La loi d'irréversibilité en évolution", *L'anthrop.*, communicat. du 21 mars, t. XXXIII, pp. 183–184; Œ., t. III, pp. 73–74 (Sc Ph) [50].

1923 "La paléontologie et l'apparition de l'homme", *Rev. de philosophie*, Paris, Marcel Rivière, mars–avril, t. XXX, pp. 144–173 (tiré à part, paginé de 3 à 31); Œ., t. II, pp. 53–81 (larges cit. par R. de Sinéty, art. "Transformisme" du *Dict. apolog. de la foi cathol.*, 4ᵉ édit., fasc. 24, Paris, Beauchesne, 1928, col. 1838–1841; cit. *in*: É. Le Roy, *Les origines humaines et l'évolution de l'intelligence*, Paris, Boivin, 1928, pp. 84, 152–153, 161, 176, 177, 178, 219, 220) (Sc Ph) [51].

*1923 "Panthéisme et Christianisme". D.s.i., 13 pp. s.l., 17 janv.; Œ., t. XI (Ph R) [52].

*1923 "La Messe sur le monde". R.s.i., 10 pp. (rééd. 1957); la première conception remonte à juin 1918 sous le titre "Messe sur toutes choses", cf. lettre du 28 août 1918; œuvre attestée par la lettre du 7 août 1923 et présentée comme une œuvre déjà connue du correspondant; rédigée à Tientsin en déc., cf. lettre à H. Breuil du 30 déc. 1923; extr. impr. *in*: I. *La messe sur le monde d'après le R.P. Teilhard de Chardin*, plaquette d'une p., ornée d'un bois, exécutée en Chine à la demande de Madame Cosme; II. *Textes mystiques d'Orient et d'Occident*, choisis et présentés par Solange Lemaître, Paris, Plon, 1955, t. III, pp. 295-300 (les lignes d'introd. sont du P. Teilhard); III. *La Table ronde*, juin 1955, no. 90, pp. 29-30; IV. *L'étudiant catholique*, Aix-en-Provence, 2ᵉ année, no. 3, 1955, p. 1; V. *Jésuites de l'Assistance de France*, 1956, no. 4, p. 17; VI. P. Chauchard, *La science détruit-elle la religion?*, Paris, Fayard, 1958, p. 121; VII. Jean Peyrade, *Jeunes hommes*, Paris, Spes, 1959, sous le titre: *Tout espérer pour le Christ!*, pp. 365-367; VIII. *Mission de l'Église*, t. XV, no. 5, déc. 1959, pp. 199-200, sous le titre: *La Messe sur le monde, l'offrande*; IX. 12 lignes traduites par Claire Bishop, *in*: "Pierre Teilhard de Chardin (1881-1955)", *The Third Hour*, New York, issue VII, 1956, p. 51; impr. *in extenso* A. sur les presses de la Légion étrangère, Algérie, Sidi-Bel-Abbès, entre oct.–nov. 1960 et le début 1961 (avant le 21 avril 1961), gr. in-4° broché, couverture grise, 11 pp., s.l.n.d.; B. *in*: *La Messe sur le monde*, Pierre Teilhard de Chardin, *Messa della domenica* Girolamo Frescobaldi, église Saint-Jacques, Anvers, 12 mai 1961 (festival organisé par la Société Pierre Teilhard de Chardin, programme pp. 15-26); C. *in*: *Hymne de l'univers*, 1961, pp. 17-37; D. *in*: *La Messe sur le monde*, Bruges, Desclée de Brouwer, 39 pp., coll. "Les carnets D D B"; E. *in*: *La Messe sur le monde*, éd. de poche, par les Éd. du Seuil; F. Œ., t. X (R) [53].

*1923 et "Choses mongoles". D.s.i., 7 pp. s.l., juin–oct. 1923, impr. *in*:
1956 *Lettres de voyage*, Paris, Grasset, 1956, pp. 52-62, et P. Grenet, *Teilhard de Chardin*, 1956, Seghers, 1961, pp. 167-177 (B) [55].

1924 "Note sur la structure des montagnes à l'ouest de Linnming-kwan (Chihli méridional)", *Bull. Geol. Soc. China*, vol. III, nos. 3-4, pp. 393-397, 2 fig. (T) [56].

1924 "On the Geology of the Northern, Western and Southern Borders of the Ordos, China", en collab. avec É. Licent, *Bull. Geol. Soc. China*, vol. III, no. 1, pp. 37-44, 5 coupes (T) [57].

1924 "On the Discovery of a Palaeolithic Industry in Northern China", en collab. avec É. Licent, *Bull. Geol. Soc. China*, vol. III, no. 1, pp. 45-50, 2 coupes (T) [58].

1924   "Geology of Northern Chihli and Eastern Mongolia", *Bull. Geol. Soc. China,* vol. III, nos. 3–4, pp. 399–407, 1 fig., 1 pl., 1 carte géol. (T) [59].

1924   "Observations géologiques sur la bordure occidentale et méridionale de l'Ordos", en collab. avec É. Licent, *Bull. Soc. Géol. France,* 4ᵉ sér., t. XXIV, pp. 49–91, 2 croquis et 14 coupes géol. (cf. *Comptes-rendus sommaires,* p. 20) (T) [60].

1924   "Observations complémentaires sur la géologie de l'Ordos", en collab. avec É. Licent, *Bull. Soc. Géol. France,* 4ᵉ sér., t. XXIV, pp. 462–464, 2 pl. h.t. comportant 16 photogravures en tout (T) [61].

1924   "Communication relative à des observations complémentaires sur la géologie de l'Ordos (Chine)", *C. R. somm. Soc. Géol. France,* séance du 17 nov., pp. 162–163 (T) [62].

1924   "Les gisements de Mammifères paléocènes de la Belgique", en collab. avec L. Dollo, *Quarterly Journ. Geol. Soc. of London,* 17 mars, vol. LXXX, 1ᵉʳᵉ partie, no. 317, pp. 12–16; cf. 1923, "The Deposits of Paleocene Mammalia in Belgium", en collab. avec L. Dollo, *Proc. Geol. Soc. of London,* p. 103, abstract (T) [63].

1924 et "Conférence" (Titre fictif). *L'Écho de Tientsin,* 5 avril 1924; 1926   extr. *in:* Henri Bernard, S.J., Hautes-Études de Tientsin, "Dix années de séjour et d'exploration dans le bassin du fleuve Jaune, du Pai-ho, du Loan-ho et des autres tributaires du golfe du Pe-tche-ly", *Rev. quest. scientif.,* Bruxelles, 20 janv. 1926, 4ᵉ série, t. IX, 1ᵉʳ fasc. (45ᵉ année, t. LXXXIX de la collection), pp. 118–119 et 121–123 (Conférence donnée au Cercle d'escrime, à Tientsin, le 4 avril 1924, lors de l'ouverture du Musée Hoang-ho-Pai-ho et portant sur l'expédition des Ordos 1923); brève analyse *in:* Augustin Bernard, S.J., "L'ouverture du Musée Hoang-ho-Pai-ho à Tientsin", *Chine-Ceylan-Madagascar,* Lille, sept. 1924, no 65, pp. 163–165 (T).

*1924   "Mon univers". D.d.i., 58 pp., s.i., 34 pp. Tientsin, 25 mars (différent de "Mon univers", 14 avril 1918), fragm. *in:* Œ., t. V, pp. 401–403, et *Hymne de l'univers,* 1961: "Pensées choisies par Fernande Tardivel", II; extrait *in:* Le *Père Teilhard de Chardin, apôtre du Christ dans l'univers,* plaquette (cf. le Progr. vendu le 11 mai 1962 au concert de gala européen à Bruxelles), pp. 4–5; cit. *in:* L. Barjon, "Fidélité du Père Teilhard", *Foi vivante,* Paris et Bruxelles, juin 1963, 4ᵉ année, no. 15, p. 73; C. Cuénot, "Situation de Teilhard de Chardin", *Bull. Soc. industr. Mulhouse,* 1963, no. 3, p. 16; L. Barjon, "L'appel de Pâques", *Revue Teilhard de Chardin,* Bruxelles, déc. 1963, 4ᵉ année, no. 17, p. 15; H. de Lubac, *La prière du Père*

Teilhard de Chardin, Paris, Fayard, 1964, p. 69; *TC explique*;
Œ., t. IX (Ph R) [64].

1925   "Le paradoxe transformiste. À propos de la dernière critique
du transformisme par M. Vialleton", *Rev. quest. scientif.*, janv.,
4ᵉ sér., t. VII, fasc. 1, pp. 53–80; Œ., t. III, pp. 115–142 (cit.
in: É. Le Roy, *L'exigence idéaliste et le fait de l'évolution*, Paris,
Boivin, 1927, pp. 120–121 et 122, et *Essai d'une philosophie
première*, Paris, P.U.F., t. I, 1956, pp. 357–358 et 359; R. de
Sinéty, art. "Transformisme" du *Dict. apolog. de la foi cathol.*,
4ᵉ éd., fasc. 24, Paris, Beauchesne, 1928, col. 1835) extraits *in*:
R. de Sinéty, "La vie de la biosphère", *Archives de Phil.*, Paris,
Beauchesne, 1936, vol. VI, cahier I (Sc Ph) [65].

1925   "L'histoire naturelle du monde. Réflexions sur la valeur et
l'avenir de la systématique", *Scientia*, janv., pp. 15–24; Œ.,
t. III, pp. 145–157; extraits *in*: R. de Sinéty, "La vie de la
biosphère", *Archives de Phil.*, Paris, Beauchesne, 1936, vol. VI,
cahier I (Sc Ph) [66].

1925   "Observations nouvelles sur les Mammifères du Tertiaire
inférieur de Belgique", *Bull. Ac. Royale de Belgique*, classe des
Sc., séance du 7 février, 5ᵉ sér., vol. XI, no. 3, pp. 48–50 (T)
[67].

1925   "Note sur deux instruments agricoles du Néolithique de
Chine", en collab. avec É. Licent, *L'anthrop.*, t. XXXV, no. 1,
pp. 62–74, 3 fig. (photos d'outils) (T) [68].

1925   "Le Paléolithique de la Chine", en collab. avec É. Licent,
L'anthrop., t. XXXV, nos. 3–4, pp. 201–234, 16 fig. (1 carte,
4 coupes, 11 pl.: 10 de photos, 1 de dessins d'outils) (T) [69].

1925   "Le massif volcanique du Dalaï-Noor (Gobi oriental)", *Bull.
volcanologique*, Naples, 1ᵉʳ et 2ᵉ trim., nos. 3–4, pp. 100–108,
1 carte (T) [70].

1925   "Note sur quelques grès Mézozoïques à plantes de la Chine
septentrionale", en collab. avec P. H. Fritel, *Bull. Soc. Géol.
France*, 4ᵉ sér., t. XXV, fasc. 6, pp. 523–540, 7 fig., 2 pl.—
"Les observations géologiques", pp. 523–528, 1 carte, sont
du P. Teilhard—Note présentée à la séance du 8 juin (T)
[72].

1925   "M. Teilhard de Chardin présente une communication sur
l'ancienneté de certains éléments des faunes continentales",
C. R. somm. Soc. de Biogéographie, séance du 20 nov., 2ᵉ année,
no. 15, pp. 111–113 (T) [71].

*1925   "L'hominisation. Introduction à une étude scientifique du
phénomène humain". D.d.i., 46 pp. s.i., 22 pp. Paris, 6 mai
1925 (la date proposée dans l'éd. Plon est erronée; la conclusion présente 2 vers. diff.; "l'opuscule" "Les propriétés

expérimentales de l'humanité" constitue simplement le noyau de "L'hominisation"); extr. et adapt. *in*: É. Le Roy, *Les origines humaines et l'évolution de l'intelligence*, Paris, Boivin, 1928, pp. 9, (24), 35, 39–40, 54–55, 118, 119, 134, et *Essai d'une philosophie première*, Paris, P.U.F., t. I, 1956, pp. 346–347, 407; Œ., t. III, pp. 77–111 (Sc Ph) [54].

1926   "Étude géologique sur la région du Dalaï-Noor", *Mém. Soc. Géol. France*, nouv. sér., t. III, fasc. 3, mém. no. 7, pp. 1–56, 2 pl. (24 fig.), 3 cartes géol. en couleurs (T) [73].

1926   "Le massif volcanique du Dalaï-Noor (Gobi oriental)", *C. R. du Congrès des Soc. Sav. et des départements tenu à Paris en 1925*, sect. des Sc., Paris, pp. 460–463 (T) [74].

1926   "Description de Mammifères tertiaires de Chine et de Mongolie", *Ann. de Pal.*, t. XV, fasc. I, pp. 3–52, 25 fig., 5 pl. (T) [75].

1926   "Sur quelques Mammifères nouveaux du Tertiaire de la Belgique", *Bull. Ac. royale de Belgique*, classe des Sc., 5ᵉ sér., t. XII, nos. 4–5, pp. 210–215, 2 fig. (T) [76].

1926   "Palaeontological Notes", *Bull. Geol. Soc. China*, vol. V, no. 1, pp. 57–59 (T) [77].

1926   "How and Where to Search [for] the Oldest Man in China", *Bull. Geol. Soc. China*, vol. V, nos. 3–4, pp. 201–206 (T) [78].

1926   "Geological Study of the Deposits of the Sang-kan-ho Basin", en collab. avec G. B. Barbour et É. Licent, *Bull. Geol. Soc. China*, vol. V, nos. 3–4, pp. 263–280, 1 carte, 3 coupes, paru réellement en 1927; cf. lettre de Barbour à C. Cuénot du 4 mai 1958: "I wrote the introductory section (I recognize my own use of words and the style on pages 263–265) and also sections 3 and 4. Teilhard wrote sections 2 and 5 with the determination and description of the fauna. Then we wrote section 6 together and at Teilhard's request I added a statement as a Note on the Correlation. I also drew all the illustrations and diagrams. Licent did not contribute a word, as far as I know!!"—Textes de Teilhard traduits par Barbour; originaux perdus (T) [79].

1926   "On a Presumably Pleistocene Human Tooth from the Sjara-Osso-Gol (South-eastern Ordos) Deposits", en collab. avec É. Licent et P. Davidson Black, *Bull. Geol. Soc. China*, vol. V, nos. 3–4, pp. 285–290, 1 fig., 1 pl. formant la p. 291 (T) [80].

1926   "Le Néolithique de la Chine d'après les découvertes du Dr. Andersson", *L'anthrop.*, t. XXXVI, nos. 1–2, pp. 117–124 (T) [81].

1926   "Sur l'apparence nécessairement discontinue de toute série évolutive", *L'anthrop.*, séance du 17 mars, t. XXXVI, pp. 320–321; Œ., t. III, pp. 161–162 (Sc Ph) [82].

1926   "Fossil Man in China and Mongolia", *Natural History*, New York, vol. XXVI, no. 3, pp. 238–245, 10 fig. (trad. C. D. Matthew, texte original fr. perdu) (T) [83].

*1926   Les fondements et le fond de l'idée d'évolution. 2 éd. avec var. 1° D.d.i., 36 pp. 2° D.s.i., 23 pp. Golfe du Bengale, Ascension 1926; Œ., t. III, pp. 165–197 (Sc Ph) [84].

*1926–   *Le milieu divin*, Tientsin, nov. 1926–mars 1927. Nombreuses
1927 et   éd.—Citons entres autres: I. 1re vers. (a) sans l'Avertisse-
1957   ment, R.s.i., 74 pp. (b) avec l'Avertissement, R.d.i., 152 pp., s.i., 65 pp.; II. 2e vers. D.d.i., 128 pp. + 1 p. non numérotée contenant l'épigraphe et la dédicace et 1 p. non numérotée en fin de vol. contenant le sommaire, vers. dont il ne subsiste que 2 ex.; environ 150 variantes, mais peu de changements profonds sauf quelques remaniements de § et des notes supplémentaires apportant des précisions théologiques, cf. lettre de Péking, 20 mars 1932: "Je vais, pour commencer, chercher à faire les retouches qu'on me demande d'apporter au 'Milieu Divin', pour une publication éventuelle (?)"; III. Copies et réimpr. de la 1re vers., p. ex. (a) Pékin, 1942 (b) par un groupe de la S.N.C.F. après 1955 (?); IV. éd. de luxe in-fol. de 56 pp. sur la 1re vers. sans lieu ni date ni nom d'éditeur (tirage privé à l'imprim. Cathol. de Beyrouth par le R. P. Coron, S.J., vers 1935–36; V. Œ., t. IV, Paris, Éd. du Seuil, 203 pp., photos h.t., brèves citat. de lettres à A. Valensin et M. Teillard-Chambon, et d'opuscules: *Le prêtre*, 1918, *La Messe sur le monde*, 1923, *Le cœur de la matière*, 1950, *Le christique*, 1950. Cette édition représente la 2e version, prêtée par Mgr Bruno de Solages et préparée pour l'impression, d'où les différences avec le texte courant; VI. 5 prières extraites du *Milieu divin* *in*: Pierre Bernard, *Devant Dieu*, Le Puy, éd. Xavier Mappus, 1er trim. 1948, pp. 213–219; extr. *in*: *La Table ronde*, juin 1955, no. 90, pp. 74–75, et *Jeune Ingénieur* USIC-MICIAC, Liaison no. 51, sept. 1957, pp. 25–30 (R) [85].

1927   "Les Mammifères de l'Éocène inférieur de la Belgique", *Mém. du Mus. royal d'hist. nat. de Belgique*, no. 36, pp. 1–33, 31 fig., 6 pl. (T) [86].

1927   "On the Basal Beds of the Sedimentary Series in South-Western Shansi", en collab. avec É. Licent, *Bull. Geol. Soc. China*, vol. VI, no. 1, pp. 61–65, 1 croquis et 3 coupes (T) [87].

1927   "On the Recent Marine Beds, and the Underlying Fresh-Water Deposits in Tientsin", en collab. avec É. Licent, *Bull.*

Geol. Soc. China, vol. VI, no. 2, pp. 127–128, pas de fig. (T)
[88].

1927   "Observations sur les formations quaternaires et tertiaires
        supérieures du Honan septentrional et du Chansi méridional",
        en collab. avec É. Licent, *Bull. Geol. Soc. China*, vol. VI, no. 2,
        pp. 129–148, 1 carte et 8 coupes (résumé chinois p. 149) (T)
        [89].

1928   "Quelques données nouvelles sur la mise en place de la
        faune moderne (Mammifères) en Chine septentrionale",
        C. R. somm. Soc. de Biogéographie, 20 janv., 5ᵉ année, no. 34,
        pp. 1–3 (T) [90].

1928   Communication sur: "Les couches de passage entre le Ter-
        tiaire et le Quaternaire en Chine septentrionale", *C. R. somm.
        Soc. Géol. France*, 23 janv., pp. 12–14 (T) [91].

1928   "Observations sur la lenteur d'évolution des faunes de
        Mammifères continentales", *Palaeobiologica*, Vienne et Leip-
        zig, vol. I, pp. 55–60, 1 fig. (T) [92].

1928   "La nature et la succession des éruptions post-paléozoïques
        en Chine septentrionale", *C. R. Acad. Sc.*, séance du 2 avril,
        t. CLXXXVI, pp. 960–961 (T) [93].

1928   "Note complémentaire sur la faune de Mammifères du Ter-
        tiaire inférieur d'Orsmael", *Bull. Ac. royale de Belgique*, classe
        des Sc., 5ᵉ sér., t. XIV, no. 6, pp. 471–474, 2 fig. (T) [94].

1928   "Les roches éruptives post-paléozoïques du nord de la
        Chine", *Bull. Geol. Soc. China*, vol. VII, no. 1, pp. 1–11, 1 fig.
        (T) [95].

1928   "Le Paléolithique de la Chine," en collab. avec M. Boule, H.
        Breuil et É. Licent, *Arch. de l'Inst. de Pal. Hum.*, Paris,
        juillet, Mém. 4, VIII et 139 pp., 53 fig., 30 pl. h.t. (cf. 1ʳᵉ
        partie "Stratigraphie", par Teilhard de Chardin et Licent,
        pp. 1–26) (T) [96].

1928   "Les tendances intellectuelles de la Chine moderne", *Dossiers
        de la Commission synodale*, Péking, juillet, vol. I, no. 2, pp.
        127–130.—Anonyme, mais extraits sous le nom de Teilhard
        de Chardin, *in*: H. Bernard, *Sagesse chinoise et philosophie
        chrétienne*, Tientsin, 1935, pp. 228–229 (Sc).

*1928   "Le phénomène humain". D.d.i., 15 pp., s.i., 8 pp.
        Montesquieu-Avantès, Ariège, début sept. (différent du
        "Phénomène humain", *Rev. quest. scient.*, nov. 1930); Œ., t.
        IX (Sc Ph) [97].

*1928   "Les mouvements de la vie". D.d.i., 13 pp., s.i., 7 pp. s.l.,
        avril 1928; Œ., t. III, pp. 201–210 (Sc Ph) [98].

1929   "On Some Traces of Vertebrate Life in the Jurassic and
        Triassic Beds of Shansi and Shensi", en collab. avec C. C.

Young, *Bull. Geol. Soc. China*, vol. VIII, no. 2, pp. 131–133, 1 fig., 1 pl. (T) [99].

1929 "Preliminary Report on the Chou-kou-tien Fossiliferous Deposits", en collab. avec C. C. Young, *Bull. Geol. Soc. China*, vol. VIII, no. 3, pp. 173–202, 10 fig., 1 pl. (T) [100].

1929 "The Times of the Loess and Early Man in China", *in*: "Some Problems of Earth History", *Contributions of the Department of Geography and Geology*, Yenching University, Peiping, no. 27, pp. 14–16 (English version by George B. Barbour, texte fr. perdu) (T) [101].

1929 "The Early Man in China. Key to his Appearance and Disappearance is Found in Loess", *Dossiers de la Commission synodale*, Peiping, déc., vol. II, no. 12, pp. 904–906 (T).

*1929 "Le sens humain". D.d.i., pp. 1–22, s.i., p. 23. Ceylan, 12 fév.; Œ., t. XI (Ph R) [102].

1929 et "Que faut-il penser du transformisme?", *Dossiers de la Com-*
1930 *mission synodale*, Peiping, juin–juill. 1929, vol. II, no. 6–7, pp. 462–469 (cf. R.s.i., 6 pp.); trad. chinoise *in*: *Tientsin University (Hautes Études)*, 1929, no. 3, pp. 61–66; cf. *Dossiers . . .*, mai 1930, vol. III, no. 5, pp. 259–264, "De transformismo", par G. Amedeo Cracco, O.F.M.; texte fr. réimpr. *in*: *Rev. quest scientif.*, janv. 1930, 4e sér., t. XVII, fasc. I, pp. 89–99 (écrit à Péking les 14 et 15 avril 1929, cf. lettre du 15 avril à L. Zanta); Œ., t. III, pp. 213–223 (Sc Ph) [103].

1930 "Sinanthropus pekinensis", *Primitive man*, t. III, pp. 46–48 (référence non contrôlée) (T).

1930 "Palaeontology of Mammifers in China", *Irish Ecclesiastical Record*, t. XXXVI, pp. 363–369 (T).

1930 "Le Paléolithique en Somalie Française et en Abyssinie", *L'anthrop.*, t. XL, pp. 331–334 (T) [104].

1930 "Le Phénomène humain", *Rev. quest. scientif.* nov., 4e sér., t. XVIII, pp. 390–406 (différent du "Phénomène humain", sept. 1928), écrit à Tientsin vers janv. 1930; Œ., t. III, pp. 227–243 (Sc Ph) [105].

1930 "Preliminary Observations on the Preloessic and Postpontian Formations in Western Shansi and Northern Shensi", en collab. avec C. C. Young, *Geological Memoirs*, mai, sér. A, no. 8, Peiping, suite des *Memoirs of the Geological Survey*, pp. 1–54, 13 fig., 9 pl. (T) [106].

1930 "On the Occurrence of a Mongolian Eocene Perissodactyle in the Red Sandstone of Sichuan, S. W. Honan", *Bull. Geol. Soc. China*, vol. IX, no. 4, pp. 331–332, 1 fig. (T) [107].

1930 "Quelques observations sur les terres jaunes (loess) de Chine et de Mongolie", *Soc. Géol. France, livre jubilaire 1830–1930,* t. II, pp. 605–612, 5 fig. (T) [108].

1930 "Les Mammifères fossiles de Nihowan (Chine)", en collab. avec J. Piveteau, *Ann. de Pal.,* t. XIX, fasc. 1–4, pp. 3–134, 42 fig., 23 pl. dont 1 double (T) [109].

1930 "P. Teilhard de Chardin et J. Piveteau offrent leur mémoire: Les Mammifères fossiles de Nihowan (Chine)", *C. R. Somm. Soc. Géol. France,* pp. 182–183 (T) [110].

1930 "Geological Observations in Northern Manchuria and Barga (Hailar)", en collab. avec É. Licent, *Bull. Geol. Soc. China,* vol. IX, no. 1, pp. 23–35, 1 carte et 3 coupes (T) [111].

1930 "Some Correlation Between the Geology of China Proper and the Geology of Mongolia", en collab. avec C. C. Young, *Bull. Geol. Soc. China,* vol. IX, no. 2, pp. 119–125, 1 carte en noir (T) [112].

1930 "Observations géologiques en Somalie française et au Harrar", *in:* "Études géologiques en Éthiopie, Somalie et Arabie méridionale", *Mém. Soc. Géol. France,* nouv. sér., t. IV, fasc. 3–4, mém. no. 14, pp. 5–12, fig. 1 à 3, et pl. 1 (fig. 1 et 2) (T) [113].

1930 "Le cañon de l'Aouache et le volcan Fantalé", en collab. avec P. Lamare, *ibid.,* pp. 13–20, fig. 4 à 9, et pl. 1 (fig. 3 à 8) (T) [115].

1930 "Observations sur les roches métamorphiques du plateau Somali près de Harrar", *ibid.,* p. 103 (T) [114].

1930 "La paléontologie des Mammifères en Chine et l'œuvre du Musée Hoangho-Paiho", *Rev. Scientif.,* 28 juin, t. LXVIII, no. 12, pp. 360–362 (T) [116].

1930 "Quelques observations biogéographiques en Chine", *C. R. somm. Soc. de Biogéographie,* 7ᵉ année, no. 60, pp. 94–96 (T) [117].

1930 "Une importante découverte en paléontologie humaine: Le Sinanthropus pekinensis", *Rev. quest. scientif.,* juillet, 4ᵉ sér., t. XVIII, fasc. 1, pp. 5–16, 1 fig.; Œ., t. II, pp. 85–95 (T) [118].

1930 "Conférence avec projections sur la géologie de la Chine et le Sinanthropus pekinensis", *C. R. somm. Soc. Géol. France,* 15 déc., pp. 207–208 (T) [119].

*1930 "Essai d'intégration de l'homme dans l'univers", 4 conférences prononcées à Chadefaud pour le groupe Marcel Légaut: 1ʳᵉ confér. (19 nov.): D.d.i., 24 pp.; 2ᵉ confér. (27 nov.): D.d.i., 14 pp., citation *in: Morale chrétienne et morale marxiste,* La Palatine, 1960, p. 140; 3ᵉ confér. (3 déc.): texte perdu dont il ne subsiste que (a) le résumé au début de la 4ᵉ confér., (b) la discuss. consécutive: D.d.i., 14 pp.; 4ᵉ confér. (10 déc.): D.d.i., 23 pp.; Œ., t. IX, sauf la 3ᵉ confér. (Ph R) [120].

1931   "L'Homme de Pékin", *Écho de l'U.S.I.C.*, Paris, janvier, 22ᵉ année, no. 1, pp. 51–52 (résumé d'une conférence.) (T) [121].

1931   "Le Sinanthropus de Péking. État actuel de nos connaissances sur le fossile et son gisement", *L'anthrop.*, t. XLI, nos. 1–2, pp. 1–11, 3 fig. (T) [122].

1931   "On an Enigmatic Pteropod-like Fossil from the Lower Cambrian of Southern Shansi, *Binoculites Grabaui*, nov. gen., nov. sp.", *Bull. Geol. Soc. China*, vol. X, pp. 179–184, 2 fig., 2 pl. (T) [123].

1931   "Some Observations on the Archaeological Material Collected by Mr. A. S. Lukashkin near Tsitsikar", *Bull. Geol. Soc. China*, vol. XI, pp. 183–200, 8 fig., 3 pl. (T) [124].

1931   "Fossil Mammals from the Late Cenozoic of Northern China", en collab. avec C. C. Young, *Pal. Sin.*, déc., sér. C, vol. 9, fasc. 1, pp. 1–88, 23 fig., 10 pl., 1 carte (T) [125].

1931 et   "Observations sur la flore et la faune entre Urumchi et Aksu
1937–   (sept. 1931)". M., s.l.n.d., 4 pp. et *in*: A. Raymond, "Résultats
1938   scientifiques d'un voyage en Asie centrale", Paris, *Rev. de géogr. phys.*, 1938, pp. 71–73 (thèse de doctorat parue d'abord *in*: *Rev. de géogr. phys. et de géol. dyn.*, vol. X, fasc. 3, 1937) (T) [127].

*1931   "L'esprit de la terre". R.d.i., 46 ou 49 pp. selon les éd. (le total de 50 étant dû à une erreur de pagination), s.i., 21 pp. (couverture beige avec titre imprimé) ou 18 pp. D.d.i., 39 pp. Pacifique, 9 mars; brève citat. *in*: *Le Moncelet*, 28 nov. 1938, p. 4; larges citat. *in*: Mgr. B. de Solages, "La pensée chrétienne face à l'évolution", extr. du *Bull. de litt. ecclés.*, oct.–déc. 1947, p. 14; id., *Le livre de l'espérance: l'âme, Dieu, la destinée: éternelles questions sous la lumière de ce temps*, Paris, Spes, 1954, pp. 171–172; *Nouvelles lettres de voyage*, pp. 184–185, et *L'Age nouveau*, 13ᵉ année, no. 106, juillet–septembre 1959, pp. 7–12; cit. *in*: *Morale chrétienne et morale marxiste*, La Palatine, 1960, pp. 135–136, 137; Œ., t. VI, 1962, pp. 23–57 avec photocopie de la 1ʳᵉ p. man. (Ph R) [128].

1932   "New Observations on the Khangai Series of Mongolia and Some Other Allied Formations", *Bull. Geol. Soc. China*, vol. XI, no. 4, pp. 395–409, 1 fig., 1 carte en noir (T) [129].

1932   "The Geology of the Weich'ang Area", *Bull. geol. Soc. China*, vol. XI, no. 19, pp. 1–46, 22 coupes et 1 carte géol. itinéraire en couleurs (T) [130].

1932   "Observations sur les changements de niveau marin dans la région d'Obock", *C. R. somm. Soc. Géol. France*, 7 nov., pp. 180–181 (T) [131].

1932   "Les Résultats scientifiques de l'expédition Citroën-centre

Asie", *La Géographie (Terre, Air, Mer)*, Paris, déc., t. LVIII, pp. 379–390, 8 fig. (T) [132].

1932 "Nouvelle étude sur le Cervus Ertborni Dub. des argiles de la Campine", en collab. avec J. Piveteau, *Bull. du Mus. royal d'hist. nat. de Belgique*, mai, vol. VIII, no. 5, pp. 1–12, 5 fig. (T) [133].

1932 "The Lithic Industry of the Sinanthropus Deposits in Choukoutien", en collab. avec W. C. Pei, *Bull. Geol. Soc. China*, vol. XI, no. 4, pp. 315–364, 36 fig., 3 pl. (T) [134].

1932 "On Some Neolithic and Possibly Palaeolithic Finds in Mongolia, Sinkiang and West China", en collab. avec. C. C. Young, *Bull. Geol. Soc. China*, vol. XII, no. 1, pp. 83–104, 21 fig. dont 1 carte dépl. (T) [135].

1932 "Observations géologiques à travers les déserts d'Asie centrale de Kalgan à Hami", *apud*: "Résultats scientifiques de l'expédition Citroën-centre Asie. IIIe Mission Haardt-Audouin-Dubreuil, 1931–32", *Rev. de géogr. phys. et de géol. dyn.*, vol. V, fasc. 4, pp. 365–396, 15 fig. dans le texte, 4 pl. et 2 cartes géol. en couleurs hors texte (T) [136].

1932 "Les Graviers plissés de Chine", *Bull. Soc. Géol. France*, séance du 19 déc., 5e sér., t. II, fasc. 8–9, pp. 527–531, 1 fig., 4 pl. (T) [137].

*1932 "Les collections paléontologiques du Musée Hoang-ho-Pai-ho. Vertébrés". D.d.i., 8 pp., s.l., mai (schéma d'un article qui n'a jamais paru) (T).

1932 "La place de l'homme dans la nature", *Rev. des étudiants de l'univ. nat. de Peiping*, 9 pp.; Œ., t. III, pp. 247–256 (Sc Ph) [138].

*1932 "La route de l'Ouest. Vers une mystique nouvelle". D.d.i., 20 pp. Pénang, 8 sept.; extr. *in*: C. Cuénot, *Teilhard de Chardin*, Paris, Éd. du Seuil, 1962, coll. "Écrivains de toujours", pp. 136–137; Œ., t. XI (Ph R) [139].

1933 "The Base of the Palaeozoic in Shansi: Metamorphism and Cycles", *Bull. Geol. Soc. China*, vol. XIII, no. 1, pp. 149–153, 2 fig. (coupes géol.) (T) [140].

1933 "Les cycles sédimentaires (Pliocènes et plus récents) dans la Chine du nord", *Bull. Ass. Géogr. Française*, no. 65, pp. 3–7, 1 fig. (T) [141].

1933 "Les Bovinés fossiles en Chine du nord", *C. R. Soc. de Biogéographie*, 10e année, no. 79, pp. 1–2 (T) [142].

1933 "The Late Cenozoic Formations of South-Eastern Shansi", en collab. avec C. C. Young, *Bull. Geol. Soc. China*, vol. XII, no. 2, pp. 207–248, 15 fig., 3 pl., 1 carte (T) [143].

1933 "Fossil Man in China. The Choukoutien Cave Deposits with a

Synopsis of Our Present Knowledge of the Late Cenozoic in China", en collab. avec. P. Davidson Black, C. C. Young, et W. C. Pei, *Mem. Geol. Surv. China*, sér. A, no. 11, pp. I–XI et 1–166, 82 fig., 3 tableaux et 6 cartes (préface, 1re et 3e parties du P. Teilhard, 2e partie de D. Black) (T) [144].

1933   "Sur la Découverte d'un rongeur du genre Paramys dans l'Éocène inférieur de Provence", en collab. avec A. de Lapparent, *C. R. somm. Soc. Géol. France*, séance du 6 févr., pp. 26–27 (T) [145].

1933   "Appendice: (I) Observations géologiques en Chine. (II) La préhistoire de l'Asie centrale", *in*: Georges Le Fèvre, *La Croisière Jaune Troisième Mission Haardt-Audouin-Dubreuil*, Paris, Plon, 1er tirage 1933, nouv. tirage 1952, pp. 357–366 (T) [146].

1933   "La signification et la valeur constructrice de la souffrance", *Le Trait d'union*, bulletin de l'U.C.M., 1er avril, no. 45, pp. 6–11; extr. *apud*: *Hymne de l'univers*: "Pensées choisies par Fernande Tardivel", éd. du Seuil, 1961, XX, XXI, XLII; Œ., t. VI, pp. 59–66, 1962 (R) [147].

1933   "L'incroyance moderne. Cause profonde et remède", *Vie intell.*, 25 octobre, pp. 218–222 (no. spécial: Enquête sur les raisons actuelles de l'incroyance); Œ., t. IX (R) [148].

1933   "Le christianisme dans le monde". D.d.i., 17 ou 13 pp. selon les éd. Pékin, mai; extr. *in*: *TC explique*; Œ., t. IX (R) [149].

*1933 et "Profession de foi" (titre fictif; *incipit*: We cannot be funda-
1957   mentally . . .). M., 2 pp., daté du 23 sept. 1933, impr. *in*: "Extraits et fragments de lettres à Lucile Swan", plaquette hors commerce, New York, 1957, et *apud*: Lucile Swan, "Memories and Letters", *The Wind and the Rain, An Easter book for 1962*, London, pp. 41–49; trad. *in*: C. Cuénot, *Teilhard de Chardin*, Paris, Éd. du Seuil, coll. "Écrivains de toujours", 1962, pp. 48–49 (Ph R) [150].

*1933   "Christologie et Évolution". D.d.i., 22 pp., s.i., 12 pp. Tien-Tsin, Noël, courte citation *apud* Viallet, *Le dépassement*, Fischbacher, 1961, p. 197; cit. *in*: R. Garaudy, "Après l'encyclique 'Pacem in Terris' communistes et catholiques", supplément aux *Cahiers du Communisme*, juill.–août 1963, nos. 7–8, pp. 8–10, cit. reproduite *in*: *Civitec Nouvelles de Chrétienté*, Paris, 19 sept. 1963, no. 407, pp. 8–9; court extr. *in*: *TC explique*; Œ, t. XI (R) [151].

1933 et "The Significance of Piedmont Gravels in Continental
1935   Geology (with an Application to Northern and Western China)", from: *Report of XVI International Geological Congress*,

Washington, 1933 preprint; issued July, 1935; vol. II, pp. 1031–1039, 3 fig., 1 carte (T) [152].

1934   "New Discoveries in Choukoutien 1933–1934", en collab. avec W. C. Pei, *Bull. Geol. Soc. China*, vol. XIII, no. 3, pp. 369–394, 9 fig., 3 pl., 1 carte (T) [153].

1934   "A Correlation of Some Miocene and Pliocene Mammalian Assemblages in North America and Asia with a Discussion of the Mio-Pliocene Boundary", en collab. avec R. A. Stirton, *Publ. Univ. Calif., Bull. Dept. Geol. Sci.*, Berkeley, vol. XXIII, no. 8, pp. 277–290, 3 pl. (T) [154].

1934   "Les fouilles préhistoriques de Péking", *Rev. quest. scientif.*, 4ᵉ sér., t. XXV, fasc. 2, pp. 181–193; Œ., t. II, pp. 99–110 (T) [155].

*1934   "L'évolution de la chasteté". D.d.i., 26 pp. s.i., 16 pp. Péking, février; Œ., t. XI (R) [156].

*1934   "Comment je crois". D.d.i., 40 pp. R.d.i., 49 ou 45 pp. selon les éd. s.i., 26 pp. Péking, 28 octobre; en projet dès le 24 juin sous le titre "Ma croyance"; large cit. *in* Mgr. B. de Solages, *Le livre de l'espérance*: *l'âme, Dieu, la destinée: éternelles questions sous la lumière de ce temps*, Paris, Spes, 1954, pp. 58–60; citation *in*: E. Kahane, *Teilhard de Chardin*, Paris, Public. de l'Union rationaliste, 1960, pp. 68, 110, 114; citation de l'Avant-propos *in*: J. P. Blanchard, *Méthodes et principes du P. Teilhard de Chardin*, Paris, La Colombe, 1961, pp. 92–93; extraits *in*: "L'équation du phénomène humain", apud: *Planète* (Paris), no. 5, 1962, p. 10; P. Chauchard, *Teilhard témoin de l'amour*, Paris, Éd. universitaires, 1962, *Carnets Teilhard*, 2, pp. 52–53 (conclus. de l'opuscule): A. Monestier, etc., *Pour comprendre Teilhard*, Paris, Minard, Lettres modernes, 1962, pp. 101–104; *Rencontre*, Besançon, no. spécial Teilhard de Chardin, 1962, p. 2; L. Barjon, "Fidélité du Père Teilhard de Chardin", *Foi vivante*, Paris, juin 1963, 4ᵉ année, no. 15, p. 75; C. Cuénot, "Situation de Teilhard de Chardin", *Bull. Soc. industr. Mulhouse*, 1963, no. 3, p. 39 (extr. de l'Avant-propos); Dom G. Frénaud, *Pensée philosophique et religieuse du Père Teilhard de Chardin*, Le Chesnay, octobre, et Paris, Club du livre civique, 1963, pp. 23, 24, 25, 29; devise initiale in P. Smulders, *La vision de Teilhard de Chardin*, Paris, Desclée, 1964, p. 129; extr. *in*: H. de Lubac, *La prière du Père Teilhard de Chardin*, Paris, Fayard, 1964, p. 148; *TC explique*; Œ., t. X (Ph R) [157].

1935   "La faune pléistocène et l'ancienneté de l'homme en Amérique du nord", *L'anthrop.*, t. XLV, pp. 483–487; Œ., t. II, pp. 113–118(T) [158].

1935 "Chronologie des alluvions pléistocènes de Java", *L'anthrop.*, t. XLV., pp. 707–708 (T) [159].

1935 "Le Cénozoïque de Chine centrale et méridionale", *C. R. somm. Soc. Géol. France*, 3 juin, pp. 150–152 (T) [160].

1935 "A Geological Reconnaissance Across the Eastern Tsinling (Between Loyang and Hsichuan, Honan)", en collab. avec. G. B. Barbour et M. N. Bien, *Bull. Geol. Surv. China*, no. 25, pp. 9–37, 16 fig., 2 pl., 1 carte en couleurs (T) [161].

1935 "The Cenozoic Sequence in the Yangtze Valley", en collab. avec C. C. Young, *Bull. Geol. Soc. China*, vol. XIV, no. 2, pp. 161–178, 12 fig. (T) [162].

1935 "On the Cenozoic formations of Kwangsi and Kwangtung", en collab. avec C. C. Young, W. C. Pei et H. C. Chang, *Bull. Geol. Soc. China*, vol. XIV, no. 2, pp. 179–210, 14 fig., 2 pl. (T) [163].

1935 "Geological Observations in the Turfan Area", Hyllningsskrift tillagnad Sven Hedin, *Geografiska Annaler*, Stockholm, pp. 446–452, 4 fig.—les 3 dern. lignes de la p. 451 et la page 452 commentent en suédois les 4 fig. et ne sont pas de Teilhard (T) [164].

1935 "La découverte du passé", *Études*, 20 nov., t. CCXXV, pp. 469–478, pages écrites pour le t. II, resté inédit, du "Livre Jubilaire de Comte Bégouën" (l'original: D.s.i., 9 pp., ou R.d.i., 14 pp., est daté de: Mer Rouge, 15 sept. 1935); Œ., t. III, pp. 259–269 (Sc Ph) [165].

1935 "Les récents progrès de la préhistoire en Chine", *L'anthrop.*, t. XLV, nos. 5–6, pp. 735–740, 2 fig. (T) [166].

1936 "Fossil Mammals from Locality 9 of Choukoutien", *Pal. Sin*, sér. C, vol. VII, fasc. 4, pp. 5–70, 30 fig., bibl., 4 pl., 3 pages en chinois non numérotées (T) [168].

1936 "On the Mammalian Remains from the Archaeological Site of Anyang", en collab. avec C. C. Young, *Pal. Sin.*, juin, sér. C, vol. XII, fasc. 1, pp. 5–78, 26 fig., 8 pl. (T) [169].

1936 "A Mongolian Amblypod in the Red Beds of Ichang (Hupeh)", en collab. avec C. C. Young, *Bull. Geol. Soc. China*, vol. XV, no. 2, pp. 217–223, 3 fig. (T) [170].

1936 "New Remains of Postschizotherium from S. E. Shansi", en collab. avec É. Licent, *Bull. Geol. Soc. China*, vol. XV, no. 3, pp. 421–427, 2 fig. (T) [171].

1936 "Observations on the Upper Siwalik Formation and Later Pleistocene Deposits in India", en collab. avec H. de Terra,

Proc. Amer. Philosophical Soc., Philadelphia, vol. LXXVI, no. 6, pp. 791–882, 14 fig. (T) [172].

1936   "Joint Geological and Prehistoric Studies in the Late Cenozoic in India", *Science*, Shanghai, nouv. sér., t. LXXXIII, pp. 233–236 (T) [173].

1936   "Sur la découverte de couches mésozoïques à poissons dans la région de Hailar", *Publ. Mus. Hoangho-Paiho*, Tientsin, no. 33, 36 pp. (T) [174].

1936   "Témoignage fraternel", *Le trait d'union*, bulletin de l'U.C.M., oct. 1936, no. 66, pp. 6–9 (no. nécrologique consacré à Marguerite-Marie Teilhard de Chardin) (B) [175].

*1936   "Esquisse d'un univers personnel". R.d.i., 56 pp. Péking, 4 mai; fragm. impr. *in*: *Présences*, 6ᵉ année, no. 2, printemps 1956, pp. 53–54; cit. *in*: *Morale chrétienne et morale marxiste*, La Palatine, 1960, pp. 135 et 145; Œ., t. VI., 1962, pp. 67–114 (Ph R) [176].
N. B. L'opuscule "Essai sur la personne". D.d.i., 8 pp., s.l.n.d [365] n'est qu'un résumé de l'"Esquisse". Dépourvu d'originalité, ce travail n'est pas de Teilhard mais d'un confrère.

*1936   "Quelques réflexions sur la conversion du monde". R.d.i., 14 pp. Péking, 9 oct.; cit. *in*: *Synthèses* (Bruxelles), 15ᵉ année, no. 172, sept. 1960, pp. 203–204; Œ., t. IX (R) [177].

1936, 1937 et 1940   "Sauvons l'humanité": I Vers. intégrale, sous le titre: "Sauvons l'humanité. Réflexions sur la crise présente". R.d.i., 34 pp. Péking, 11 nov. 1936; II. Vers. abrégée avec var. sous le titre: "La crise présente. Réflexions d'un naturaliste", *Études*, 20 oct. 1937, t. CCXXXIII, pp. 145–165 (extrait *in*: H. de Lubac, *Catholicisme. Les aspects sociaux du dogme*, Paris, éd. du Cerf, 1938, pp. 163–164); III. Réimpr. de la vers. abrégée en opuscule sous le titre: *Sauvons l'humanité*, imprimerie G. Durassié, Malakoff (Seine), pp. 5–29, préface de M. H. Bégouën datée du 11 février 1940; IV. fragm. réimpr. *in*: *La Table ronde*, juin 1955, no. 90, pp. 55–59, sous le titre: "Un front humain spirituel", et *Pensée française*, 15 nov. 1956, no. 1, pp. 7–11, sous le titre: "Les colonnes de l'avenir"; extraits *in*: Paul Chauchard, *L'humanisme et la science*, Paris, Spes, 1960, pp. 180–182; extraits présentés par Mlle Jeanne Mortier *apud*: "Les entretiens de Royaumont. Quel avenir attend l'homme?", *Rencontre internationale de Royaumont* (17–20 mai 1961) Paris, P.U.F., 1961, pp. 221–229; *Cahiers Pierre Teilhard de Chardin*, no. 3, pp. 69–97; Œ., t. IX (Ph R) [178].

1936   "Notes on Continental Geology", *Bull. Geol. Soc. China*, vol. XVI, pp. 195–220, 9 cartes en noir dans le texte (T) [179].

1937   "Eparchaean and Epi-Sinian Intervals in China", *Bull. Geol.*

Soc. China, vol. XVII, no. 1, pp. 65–82, 3 fig., 1 pl., 1 carte (T) [180].

1937 "The Post-Villafranchian Interval in North China", *Bull. Geol. Soc. China*, vol. XVII, no. 1, pp. 169–176, 1 fig. (T) [181].

1937 "Notes sur la paléontologie humaine en Asie méridionale", *L'anthrop.*, t. XLVII, nos. 1–2, pp. 22–33, 6 fig. (T) [182].

1937 "The Pleistocene of China: Stratigraphy and Correlations", *in*: G. G. MacCurdy, *Early Man*, London, Philadelphia and New York, J. B. Lippincott, pp. 211–230, 2 fig. (T) [183].

1937 "The Structural Geology of Eastern Shantung (Between Tsingtao and Yung Ch'eng)", en collab. avec Yang Kieh, *Bull. Geol. Surv. China*, no. 29, pp. 85–108, 2 pl. (T) [184].

1937 "The Proboscidians of South-Eastern Shansi (Yushê Basin)", en collab. avec M. Trassaert, *Pal. Sin.*, mars, sér. C, vol. XIII, fasc. 1, pp. 1–58, 6 fig., 13 pl. (T) [185].

1937 "The Pliocene Camelidae, Giraffidae and Cervidae of South-Eastern Shansi", en collab. avec M. Trassaert, *Pal. Sin.*, whole series, no. 102, new series C, no. 1, pp. 1–56, 19 fig., 6 pl. (T) [186].

1937 "A Map of the Younger Eruptive Rocks in China", *Bull. Geol. Surv. China*, vol. XXX, pp. 1–52, 1 fig., 2 cartes en couleurs (T) [187].

1937 "La découverte du Sinanthrope", *Études*, 5 juillet, t. CCXXXII, pp. 5–13; Œ., t. II, pp. 121–131; réimpr. *apud*: P. Grenet, *Teilhard de Chardin*, Seghers, 1961, pp. 180–190 (T) [188].

1937 "Peking Man: Our Most Apelike Relative", *Natural History*, New York, vol. XL, no. 2, pp. 514–517, 8 fig. (T) [189].

*1937 "Le phénomène spirituel". R.d.i., 29 pp. Pacifique, mars.; Œ., t. VI, 1962, pp. 115–139 (Ph) [190].

*1937 "L'énergie humaine". R.d.i., 68, 69 ou 73 pp. selon les éd. Marseille-Shanghaï, 6 août–8 sept., avec "Appendice", daté de: Péking, 20 oct., opuscule en projet dès le 3 juillet; analyse *in*: *Le Moncelet*, 21 mai 1939, no. 14, p. 6; citations *in*: *Morale chrétienne et morale marxiste*, La Palatine, 1960, pp. 140–141 et 143; Œ., t. VI, 1962, pp. 141–200 (Ph) [191].

*1937 "Rapport en vue d'obtenir un laboratoire des Hautes-études pour des recherches de 'géologie continentale' (considérée dans ses rapports avec la paléontologie humaine)". D.s.i., 5 pp.-rapp. annexé à une lettre de candidature datée de Paris (lieu fictif), 1ᵉʳ oct. 1937; large cit. *in*: L. Barjon et P. Leroy, *La carrière scientifique de Pierre Teilhard de Chardin*, Monaco, Éd. du Rocher, 1964, pp. 44–46 (T) [192].

1938 "Deuxièmes notes sur la paléontologie humaine en Asie

Méridionale", *L'anthrop.*, t. XLVIII, nos. 5–6, pp. 449–456, 3 fig. (T) [193].

1938 "The Fossils from Locality 12 of Choukoutien", *Pal. Sin.*, août, whole series, no. 114, new series C, no. 5, pp. 1–47, 36 fig., 1 pl. (T) [194].

1938 "Cavicornia of South-Eastern Shansi", en collab. avec M. Trassaert, *Pal. Sin.*, août, whole series, no. 115, new series C, no. 6, pp. 1–106, 65 fig., 4 pl. (T) [195].

1938 "Le Villafranchien d'Asie et la question du Villafranchien", *C. R. somm. Soc. Géol. France*, no. 17, pp. 325–327, 1 fig. (T) [196].

1938 "La formation des déserts en Chine et Mongolie", *in*: "La vie dans les régions désertiques nord tropicales de l'ancien monde". *Mém. Soc. de Biogéographie*, t. VI, pp. 15–20 (T) [197].

1938 "Geological and Archaeological Aspects of South-Eastern Asia", en collab. avec H. de Terra et H. L. Movius, *Nature*, London, vol. CXLII, no. 3591, pp. 275–278 (T) [198].

*1938 "Late Cenozoic Gravels and Soils in Upper Burma". D.s.i., 28 pp., 20 fig., 1 carte, s.l., mai (T) [199].

1938 et "Hérédité sociale et éducation. Notes sur la valeur humano-
1945 chrétienne de l'enseignement", *Études*, avril 1945, t. CCXLV, pp. 84–94 (écrit en 1938); Œ., t. V, pp. 41–53 (Ph R) [247].

1938– "Le phénomène humain". R.s.i., pp. I–II et 1–174, 4 fig.
1940 et Péking, juin 1938–juin 1940 (Appendice: "Quelques re-
1955 marques sur la place et la part du mal dans un monde en évolution", daté de Rome, 28 oct. 1948), 3 vers. succ. avec var., cf. lettre de Mgr. B. de Solages du 17 nov. 55 à C. Cuénot: "(. . .) Je vous précise que les 3 éditions successives du P.H. que je possède (2 dactylographiées, la 3e ronéotypée) sont en gros semblables. La 1re se reconnaît à ce qu'il n'y a pas d'avertissement en tête, la seconde à ce qu'il y en a un, la 3e à ce qu'il y a une postface. La 1re est antérieure, la 2e postérieure aux observations multiples mais de détail que nous lui avions faites *viva voce* avec le P. de Lubac. Dans la 3e il y a une simplification de l'exposé du début du livre (c'est le P. Teilhard qui me l'a dit) et des modifications aux notes, dues sans doute aux demandes de censeurs, plus la postface et l'appendice." Œ., t. I, éd. du Seuil, 1955, 348 pp., 4 fig., préface de M. N. Wildiers, fragm. de lettre à Jeanne Mortier (Péking, 13 avril 1940), extr. de l'éd. de 1955 *in*: Gaëtan Picon, *Panorama des idées contemporaines*, Paris, Galli-mard, 1957, pp. 501–506 (Sc Ph R) [200].

1939 "On Two Skulls of Machairodus from the Lower Pleistocene

Beds of Choukoutien", *Bull. Geol. Soc. China*, déc., vol. XIX, no. 3, pp. 235–256, 7 fig. (T) [201].

1939   "New Observations on the Genus *Postschizotherium*, von Koenigswald", *Bull. Geol. Soc. China*, déc., vol. XIX, no. 3, pp. 257–267, 4 fig. (T) [202].

1939   "The Miocene Cervids from Shantung", *Bull. Geol. Soc. China*, déc., vol. XIX, no. 3, pp. 269–278, 5 fig. (T) [203].

1939   "On the Presumable Existence of a World-Wide Subarctic Sheet of Human Culture at the Dawn of the Neolithic", *Bull. Geol. Soc. China*, déc., vol. XIX, no. 3, pp. 333–339, 3 fig. (T) [204].

1939   "Les industries lithiques de Somalie française", en collab. avec H. Breuil et P. Wernert, *L'anthrop.*, t. XLIX, no. 5, pp. 497–522, 13 fig. (la 1re section: "Stratigraphie et faits archéologiques", pp. 497–510, 7 fig., est du P. Teilhard) (T) [205].

1939   "La succession des faunes de Mammifères en Chine depuis le Tertiaire", *C. R. somm. Soc. de Biogéographie*, 17 mars, 16e année, no. 134, pp. 27–29 (T) [206].

1939   "La Mystique de la science", *Études*, 20 mars, t. CCXXXVIII, pp. 725–742; Œ., t. VI, 1962, pp. 201–223 (Sc Ph) [207].

1939 et   "Comment comprendre et utiliser l'art dans la ligne de
1948   l'énergie humaine", impr. sous le titre fictif: "Une opinion du R. P. Teilhard de Chardin: 'Sur l'inquiétude dans l'art d'aujourd'hui' " *in: Le transhumanisme, la semaine céphéenne*, (C.E.P.H. = Centre d'études des problèmes humains), Paris, R.s.i., no. 1, 1er juin, 1931, p. 3 (début du texte avec la mention "Extrait de l'intervention du R.P. Teilhard de Chardin au cours du déjeûner du 13 mars"; les autres numéros sont introuvables); réimpr. sans titre (moins le préambule) *in: Idées et forces*, Paris, nov.–déc. 1948, 1re année, cahier 1, pp. 32–34, et sous son véritable titre *in: Cahiers Pierre Teilhard de Chardin*, no. 3, Paris, Éd. du Seuil, 1962, pp. 101–103 (Ph) [208].

1939   "Observations sur la signification et les conditions biologiques de la recherche", *Le Moncelet*, 2 juillet, no. 17, p. 4, R.s.i. (notes prises par l'Abbé C. Gaudefroy au cours d'une conférence du P. Teilhard, en février, et revues par le Père) (Sc Ph R) [209].

1939   "Les unités humaines naturelles. Essai d'une biologie et d'une morale des races", *Études*, 5 juillet, t. CCXL, pp. 6–30 (trad. par A. C. Blanc, *in: L'avvenire dell'uomo*, 1947); Œ., t. III, pp. 273–301 (Sc Ph) [210].

*1939 "Quelques vues générales sur l'essence du christianisme". D.s.i., 4 pp. s.l., mai; Œ., t. XI (R) [211].

*1939 "L'heure de choisir—un sens possible de la guerre". D.s.i., 9 pp. Péking, Noël; Œ., t. VII, 1963, pp. 17–26 (Ph) [212].

1939– "The Past Climates of North China Since the Lower
1940 Cretaceous", *Proc. 6th Pan-Pacific Sci. Congr.* (California, 1939), vol. III, pp. 627–629 (T) [213].

1939– "The Movements of the Fauna Between Asia and North
1940 America Since the Lower Cretaceous", *Proc. 6th Pan-Pacific Sci. Congr.* (California, 1939), vol. III, pp. 647–649 (T) [214].

1939 et "La grande option", *Cahiers du monde nouv.*, 1945, vol. I, no. 3,
1945 pp. 247–263 (texte daté de Paris, 3 mars 1939); fragm. réimpr. *in*: *L'actualité dans le monde*, 1er mai 1955, no. 51, pp. 26–28; Œ., t. V, pp. 57–81 (Ph R) [215].

1940 "The Fossils from Locality 18, near Peking", *Pal. Sin.*, déc., whole series no. 124, new series C, no. 9, pp. 1–100, 51 fig., 3 pl., 1 carte (T) [216].

1940 "The Granitization of China". *Publ. Inst. de Géobiol. Pékin*, no. 1, 33 pp., et *Bull. Geol. Soc. China*, sept., vol. XIX, no. 4, pp. 341–377, 10 fig., 1 carte (T) [217].

*1940 "La parole attendue". D.s.i., 8 pp. Péking, 31 oct.; Œ., t. XI (R) [218].

1941 "Early Man in China". *Publ. Inst. de Géobiol. Pékin*, déc., no. 7, pp. V–XI et 1–100, 51 fig., 5 cartes dépliantes h.t. (T) [219].

1941 "The Fossil Mammals from Locality 13 of Choukoutien", en collab. avec W. C. Pei, *Pal. Sin.*, sept., whole series no. 126, new series C, no. 11, pp. 1–106, 78 fig., 6 pl. (T) [220].

1941 "Réflexions sur le progrès", Péking, mai 1941, plaquette impr. de 27 pp. comprenant: I. "L'avenir de l'homme vu par un paléontologiste", pp. 3–20, Péking, 1er mars 1941 (ms. daté du 22 février)—réimpr. sans l'introd. *in*: *Cité nouvelle*, éd. Pays de France, 10 juin 1941, no. 11, pp. 1107–1119, et trad. avec l'introd. par A. C. Blanc *in*: *L'avvenire dell'uomo*, 1947; II. "Sur les bases possibles d'un credo humain commun", pp. 21–27, Peking, 30 mars 1941; large citat. *in*: *Nouvelles lettres de voyage*, pp. 58–59; Œ., t. V, pp. 85–106 (Ph R) [221].

*1941 "L'atomisme de l'esprit. Un essai pour comprendre la structure de l'étoffe de l'univers". D.d.i., 39 pp., Péking, 13 sept.; extr. *in*: C. Cuénot, *Teilhard de Chardin*, Paris, Éd. du Seuil, coll. "Écrivains de toujours", 1962, pp. 98–99; Œ., t. VII, 1963, pp. 27–63 (Ph) [222].

*1941 "Éclaircissements à l'usage de ceux qui auront la charité de réviser ce livre". D.s.i., 1 p., Péking, févr. (à propos de la 1re rédaction du *Phénomène humain*) (Ph).

1942 "Chinese Fossil Mammals. A Complete Bibliography Analysed, Tabulated, Annotated and Indexed", en collab. avec P. Leroy. *Publ. Inst. de Géobiol. Pékin*, juillet, no. 8, pp. 1–142, 1 pl., 1 carte dépliante hors texte (T) [223].

1942 "New Rodents of the Pliocene and Lower Pleistocene of North China". *Publ. Inst. de Géobiol. Pékin*, nov., no. 9, pp. V–XIII et 1–101, 61 fig. (T) [224].

*1942 "Note sur la notion de perfection chrétienne", pp. 1–3: D.d.i., p. 4: D.s.i. Péking; Œ., t. XI (R) [225].

*1942 "La Montée de l'autre". D.d.i., 16 pp., Péking, 20 janv.; Œ., t. VII, 1963, pp. 65–81 (Ph) [226].

1942 et "L'esprit nouveau". D.d.i., 17 pp. Péking, 15 février 1942;
1946 impr. sous le titre: "L'esprit nouveau et le cône du temps", *in*: *Psyché*, nov. 1946, pp. 27–37 et 171–179, et réimpr. *in*: *Psyché*, janv.–févr. 1955, 10ᵉ année, nos. 99–100, pp. 48–61; Œ., t. V. pp. 109–126 (Sc Ph) [227].

*1942 "Universalisation et union: un effort pour voir clair". D.d.i., 19 pp. Péking, 20 mars.; Œ., t. VII, 1963, pp. 83–101 (Ph) [228].

*1942 "Le Christ Évoluteur ou Un développement logique de la notion de rédemption". D.d.i., 13 pp. Péking, 8 oct.; Œ., t. XI (R) [229].

*1942 et "La place de l'homme dans l'univers. Réflexions sur la com-
1957 plexité". R.s.i., 14 pp., 1 fig. Péking, 15 nov.; Œ., t. III, pp. 305–326 (Ph) [230].

1943 "Géobiologie et Geobiologia", *Geobiologia*, Péking, t. I, pp. 1–5 (T Sc Ph) [231].

1943 "The Genesis of the Western Hills of Peking", *Geobiologia*, t. I, pp. 17–49, 12 fig., 1 carte dépliante hors texte (T) [232].

1943 "Contorted Structures in the Sinian Limestone", *Geobiologia*, t. I, pp. 53–55, 1 fig., 1 pl. (T) [233].

1943 "The Lycoptera Beds and Sungari Series in Manchuria According to the Japanese Geologists", *Geobiologia*, t. I, pp. 78–81 (T) [234].

1943 "New Continental Formations in Yunnan According to M. N. Bien and C. C. Young", *Geobiologia*, t. I, pp. 82–85, 1 fig. (T) [235].

1943 "Fossil Men. Recent Discoveries and Present Problems", Peking, Henri Vetch, 15 sept. 1943, pp. V–VI et 1–28, 12 fig.; trad. fr. par Maryse Choisy, revue par l'auteur, sous le titre: "La question de l'homme fossile. Découvertes récentes et problèmes actuels": I. articles parus en févr. (pp. 126–134), mars (pp. 254–260) et avril (pp. 423–433) 1947 dans la revue *Psyché*; II. opuscule paru aux éditions *Psyché* Paris, 1948, pp. 3–34,

12 fig.; III. réimpr. dans la revue *Psyché*, janv.-févr. 1955, 10ᵉ année, nos. 99–100, pp. 12–47; IV. Œ., t. II, pp. 135–174 (T) [236].

*1943   "Super-humanité, super-Christ, super-charité. De nouvelles dimensions pour l'avenir". R.d.i., 24 pp. s.i., 14 pp. Péking, août; extr. *in*: *TC explique*; Œ., t. IX (R) [237].

*1943   "Réflexions sur le bonheur". D.d.i., 18 ou 28 pp. selon les éd. R.s.i., 13 pp. Péking, 28 déc.; fragm. impr. *in*: *La Table ronde*, juin 1955, no. 90, pp. 81–86; impr. *in extenso in*: *Cahiers Pierre Teilhard de Chardin*, no. 2, Éd. du Seuil, 1960, pp. 53–70 (Ph R) [238].

1944   "Le Néolithique de la Chine", en collab. avec W. C. Pei, *Publ. Inst. de Géobiol.* Pékin, août, no. 10, pp. IX–XIV et 1–100, 48 fig., 2 cartes; analyse et larges cit. *in*: *Le Bull. cathol. de Pékin*, impr. des Lazaristes, Péking, nov. 1944, no. 375, pp. 556–564, où il est également rendu compte de *Fossil Men*; résumé *in*: *L'anthrop.*, 1950, t. LIV, pp. 300–301 (T) [239].

*1944   "Introduction à la vie chrétienne". R.d.i., 20 pp. s.i., 13 pp. Péking, 29 juin; brève cit. *in*: Dom Charles Massabki, *Le Christ, rencontre de deux amours*, Paris, éditions de la Source, 1958, p. 139, no. 1; courtes citations *in*: Viallet, *Le dépassement*, Fischbacher, 1961, p. 162 et pp. 105–106; H. de Lubac, *La prière du Père Teilhard de Chardin*, Paris, Fayard, 1964, p. 102, n. 4; *TC explique*; Œ., t. XI (R) [240].

*1944   "La centrologie. Essai d'une dialectique de l'union". D.d.i., 31 pp., 4 fig. Péking, 13 déc.; fig. liminaire *in*: Madeleine Barthélemy-Madaule, *Bergson et Teilhard de Chardin*, Paris, Éd. du Seuil, 1963, p. 110; Œ., t. VII, 1963, pp. 103–134 (Ph R) [241].

1945   "Un problème de géologie asiatique; le faciès mongol", *Geobiologia*, Péking, t. II, pp. 1–12, 5 fig., texte antérieur au 29 mai 1944 (T) [242].

1945   "The Geology of the Western Hills—Additional Notes", *Geobiologia*, t. II, pp. 13–18, 2 fig. (T) [243].

1945   "The Geological Structure of the Shihmenchai Basin, near Shanhaikwan (North Hopei)", *Geobiologia*, t. II, pp. 19–26, 3 fig. (T) [244].

1945   "Les Félidés de Chine", en collab. avec P. Leroy. *Publ. Inst. de Géobiol.* Pékin, févr., no. 11, pp. V–VII et 1–58, 22 fig. dont 2 cartes in texte en noir (T) [245].

1945   "Les Mustélidés de Chine", en collab. avec P. Leroy. *Publ. Inst. de Géobiol.* Pékin, mars, no. 12, pp. V–VIII et 1–56, 24 fig., 2 cartes (T) [246].

*1945   "La morale peut-elle se passer de soubassements méta-
         physiques avoués ou inavoués?" D.s.i., 2 pp., Péking, 23
         avril; *TC explique*; Œ., t. XI (Ph) [248].

*1945   "L'analyse de la vie". D.d.i., 9 pp. s.l. (Pékin), 10 juin.; Œ.,
         t. VII, 1963, pp. 135–146 (Sc Ph) [249].

*1945   "Action et activation". D.d.i., 12 pp., Péking, 9 août; Œ., t.
         IX (Ph) [250].

*1945   "Christianisme et évolution (Suggestions pour servir à une
         théologie nouvelle)". D.d.i., 16 pp. ou 13 pp., s.i., 10 pp. ou 7
         pp. selon les éd. Péking, 10 nov. (en préparation–?–le 4 oct.
         sous le titre "La mystique de l'évolution"); extr. *in*: M. L.
         Guérard des Lauriers, *La démarche du Père Teilhard de Chardin*,
         Divinitas, 1959, t. III, p. 246; C. Cuénot, *Teilhard de Chardin*,
         Paris, Éd. du Seuil, 1962, coll. "Écrivains de toujours",
         pp. 139–142 et 144; Œ., t. XI (Ph R) [251].

1945 et "Vie et planètes. Que se passe-t-il en ce moment sur la terre?",
1946   Péking, Catholic Univ. Press, juin 1945, 32 pp.; réimpr. *in*:
         Études, mai 1946, t. CCXLIX, pp. 145–169; Œ., t. V, pp.
         129–156 (Sc Ph) [252].

1945–   "Un grand événement qui se dessine: la planétisation
1946   humaine", *Cahiers du monde nouveau*, août-sept., 2ᵉ année, no. 7,
         pp. 1–14 (daté de Péking, 25 déc. 1945, en projet dès le 4
         août) trad. par A. C. Blanc *in*: *L'avvenire dell'uomo*, 1947;
         Œ., t. V, pp. 159–175 (Sc Ph) [253].

1946   "Remarques sur les flexures continentales de Chine", *Bull.
         Soc. Géol. France*, 5ᵉ sér., t. XVI, pp. 497–502, 2 fig., note
         présentée à la séance du 18 nov. (T) [254].

1946   "La géologie en Extrême-Orient pendant la guerre",
         C. R. somm. Soc. Géol. France, 3 juin, no. 11, pp. 200–202 (T)
         [255].

1946   "Le christianisme et la science: P. Teilhard de Chardin"
         (titre élaboré par le périodique), *Esprit*, août-sept., 14ᵉ année,
         no. 125, fasc. 8–9, pp. 253–256 (cf. D.d.i., 4 pp., Paris, 25
         juillet 1946); Œ., t. IX (Sc R) [256].

1946   "Quelques réflexions sur le retentissement spirituel de la
         bombe atomique", *Études*, sept., t. CCL, pp. 223–230; Œ.,
         t. V, pp. 179–187 (Sc Ph) [257].

1946 et "Sur les degrés de certitude scientifique de l'idée d'évolution",
1948   *Atti del Congresso internazionale di filosofia promosso dall'istituto
         di studi filosofici*, Roma, 15–20 nov. 1946, Castellani (Milan),
         1948, t. II, pp. 537–539 (Sc Ph) [269].

*1946   "Esquisse d'une dialectique de l'esprit". D.d.i., 9 pp., 1 fig.
         Paris, 25 nov.; Œ., t. VII, 1963, pp. 147–158 (Ph) [258].

*1946   "Œcuménisme". D.d.i., 2 pp. s.l., 15 déc.; Œ., t. IX (R) [259].

1947 "Une interprétation biologique plausible de l'histoire humaine: la formation de la 'noosphère'", *Revue quest. scientif.*, janv., pp. 7-37; Œ., t. V, pp. 201-231 (Sc Ph) [260].

1947 "La foi en la paix". *Cahiers du monde nouv.*, janv. 3ᵉ année, no. 1, pp. 1-5; Œ., t. V, pp. 191-197 (Ph) [261].

1947 "L'Asie centrale, vue par le Dr Erik Norin", *Rev. scientif.*, 15 août, t. LXXXV, pp. 891-892, 1 fig. (carte schématique de l'Asie centrale) (T) [262].

1947 "Sur une mandibule de Meganthropus", *C. R. somm. Soc. Géol. France*, 1ᵉʳ déc., pp. 309-310 (T) [263].

*1947 "Place de la technique dans une biologie générale de l'humanité". D.s.i., 6 pp. s.l., 16 janv.; Œ., t. VII, 1963, pp. 159-169 (Sc Ph) [264].

*1947 "La foi en l'homme (World Congress of Faiths. Branche française, Musée Guimet)". R.d.i., 9 pp., Paris, févr.; Œ., t. V, pp. 235-243 (Ph R) [265].

*1947 "Réflexions sur le péché originel". D.d.i., 9 pp. R.d.i., 11 pp., 2 fig. Paris, 15 nov.; cit. *in*: C. Tresmontant, "Le Père Teilhard de Chardin et la théologie", *Lettre*, Paris, sept.-oct. 1962, nos. 49-50, p. 50; Œ., t. XI (R) [477].

*1947 "Réponse aux critiques du R.P. Garrigou-Lagrange, O.P". (titre fictif). D.d.i., 2 pp., s.l.n.d. (porte sur "Comment je crois", 1934); extr. *in*: H. de Lubac, *La prière du Père Teilhard de Chardin*, Paris, Fayard, 1964, p. 205 et p. 207 (Ph).

1947 et "Quelques réflexions sur les droits de l'homme", *in*: *Autour
1949 de la nouvelle Déclaration Universelle des Droits de l'Homme.* Textes réunis par l'U.N.E.S.C.O., Paris, Sagittaire, 1949, pp. 88-89 (article daté de: Paris, 22 mars 1947); Œ., t. V, pp. 247-249 (Ph) [283].

1947 et "L'apport spirituel de l'Extrême-Orient. Quelques réflexions
1950 personnelles". R.s.i., 8 pp. s.l., 10 févr. 1947; impr. *in*: *Revue de la pensée juive*, oct. 1950, 2ᵉ année, no. 5, pp. 105-113, réimpr. *in*: *Monumenta nipponica*, Tokyo, Sophia University, avril-juillet 1956, vol. XII, nos. 1-2, pp. 2-11; Œ., XI (Ph R) [266].

1947 et *Paléontologie et transformisme*, Paris, Albin Michel, 1950.
1950 Rapports et discussions du colloque intern. de Paléontologie tenu à Paris sous les auspices du C.N.R.S. en avril 1947; cf. p. 112 et surtout pp. 169-173: "Sur un cas remarquable d'orthogénèse de groupe: l'évolution des Siphnéidés", et pp. 233-235: "Évolution zoologique et invention" réimpr. *in*: Œ., t. III, pp. 329-331 (T Sc Ph) [292].

1947 et "Le rebondissement humain de l'évolution et ses consé-
1948 quences", *Rev. quest. scientif.*, CXIX, 20 avril, pp. 166-185,

15+

daté de: Saint-Germain-en-Laye, 23 sept. 1947; extr. *in*:
C. Cuénot, *Teilhard de Chardin*, Paris, Éd. du Seuil, 1962,
coll. "Écrivains de toujours", pp. 127–128; Œ., t. V, pp.
253–271 (Sc Ph) [267].

1948   "Position de l'homme et signification de la socialisation
humaine dans la nature", *L'anthrop.*, sept., t. LII, nos. 3–4,
pp. 209–219. La dactyl. est intitulée: "Agitation ou genèse?
Y a-t-il dans l'univers un axe principal d'évolution? (Un
effort pour voir clair)", et porte la mention: Paris, 20 déc.
1947; Œ., t. V, pp. 275–289 (Sc Ph) [268].

1948   "Les directions et les conditions de l'avenir", *Psyché*, oct,
1948, nos. 23–24, pp. 981–991 (daté de Paris, 30 juin);
réimpr. *in*: *Psyché*, janv.–févr. 1955, 10ᵉ année, nos. 99–100,
pp. 62–72; fragm. impr. par *Peuple du monde*, Paris, 19 févr.
1949, et *L'Arc-en-ciel*, Bruxelles, mai 1955; Œ., t. V, pp.
293–305 (Sc Ph) [270].

*1948   "Trois choses que je vois ou: Une Weltanschauung en trois
points". D.d.i., 13 pp., 1 fig., Paris, févr.; Œ., t. X (Ph) [272].

*1948   "Mise en place et structure du groupe humain". D.s.i., 3 pp.,
févr., conférence à l'École Supérieure de Guerre, dont il
subsiste un sommaire par Teilhard (Sc).

*1948   "On the Trend and Significance of Human Socialisation."
D.d.i., 7 pp. s.i., 5 pp. *Supper-conference for anthropologists*,
The Viking Fund, New York, 9 avril (diff. de l'opuscule daté
de févr. 1951); abstract: R.d.i., 3 pp. (Sc Ph) [273].

*1948   "Titres et travaux de Pierre Teilhard de Chardin". R., 25 pp.
(pp. 1–10, d.i.: Carrière scientifique; pp. 11–25: Bibliographie),
Paris, avril; extr. *in*: *Journal of Oriental Studies*, vol. III, no. 2,
juill. 1956, pp. 318–321; Œ., t. X (T) [274].

*1948 et "Ma position intellectuelle (réponse à une 'enquête', et
1955   qui n'a jamais paru)". D.s.i., 1 p., New York, avril 1948;
impr. *in*: *Les études philosophiques*, oct.–déc. 1955, nouv. sér.,
10ᵉ année, no. 4, P.U.F., pp. 580–581, sous le titre: "La
pensée du Père Teilhard de Chardin par lui-même, pour un
article qui devait lui être consacré"; P. Grenet, *Teilhard de
Chardin*, Seghers, 1961, pp. 191–193; *TC explique*; Œ., t. X
(Ph) [275].

*1948   "Sur la nature du phénomène social humain, et ses relations
cachées avec la gravité". D.s.i., 1 p. s.l. (New York), 23 avril;
Œ., t. VII, 1963, pp. 171–174 (Ph) [276].

*1948   "Note-mémento sur la structure biologique de l'humanité".
D.s.i., 2 pp. ou 3 pp. selon les éd.; Galluis (Seine-et-Oise),
3 août (Sc Ph) [277].

*1948   "Comment je vois". R.s.i., 26 pp., Paris, 12 août

(l'Appendice, pp. 25–26, est daté d'Auvergne, Les Moulins par Neuville, 26 août), extr. *in*: G. Crespy, *La Pensée théologique de Teilhard de Chardin*, Paris, Éd. Universitaires, 1961, pp. 227–231, et Au Club du Livre chrétien, 1961, *sub fine* (extr. différ.); C. Tresmontant, "Le Père Teilhard de Chardin et la théologie", *Lettre*, Paris, sept.–oct. 1962, nos. 49–50: cit. du § 25 p. 22, du § 26 p. 23, du § 27 p. 24, du § 28 p. 28, du § 29 pp. 29–30 et 39, du § 30 p. 41; C. Cuénot, "Situation de Teilhard de Chardin", *Bull. Soc. industr. Mulhouse*, 1963, no. 3, p. 7 (brève cit. de l'Avertissement); Maryse Choisy, *Teilhard et l'Inde*, Paris, Éd. Universitaires, 1964, *Carnets Teilhard, 11*, cit. du § 28 pp. 19–20, du § 30 pp. 21–23; H. de Lubac, *La prière du Teilhard de Chardin*, Paris, Fayard, p. 58, n. 1; P. Smulders, *La vision de Teilhard de Chardin*, Paris, Desclée, 1964, cit. de l'Avertissement p. 34, du § 20 pp. 122–123, p. 129, du § 24 p. 134, n. 35, et p. 252, du § 26 p. 90, du § 27 p. 91 et p. 95, n. 17, du § 28 p. 92, du § 29 p. 93, du § 30 pp. 162–163, du § 31 p. 144 et p. 246, n. 6, de la n. 32 p. 174; *TC explique*, extr. des §§ 1, 20, 21, 22, 24, 32, 33, 35; OE., t. X (Ph R) [278].

*1948   "Ce que la science nous apprend de l'évolution; conséquences pour notre apostolat" (titre du programme officiel de la session); alias: "Le néo-humanisme scientifique moderne et ses réactions sur le christianisme de la masse ouvrière", Conférence donnée à la Session d'études des Aumôniers fédéraux de l'Action catholique ouvrière, Versailles, 21 sept.; 2 versions: I. Résumé analytique par A. Millard (?), D.s.i., 5 pp. (sans résumé de la discussion); II. Notes prises par l'Abbé Pihan, D.s.i., 8 pp. (avec résumé de la discussion); Œ., t. XI (Ph R).

*1948   "Observations sur l'enseignement de la préhistoire". D.d.i., 1 p., Paris, 23 sept.; extr. *in*: C. Cuénot, *Pierre Teilhard de Chardin*, Paris, Plon, 1958, p. 333 (Sc) [279].

1948 et   "Les conditions psychologiques de l'unification humaine",
1949   *Psyché*, déc. 1948 (paru réellement en février 1949), 3ᵉ année, no. 26, pp. 1325–1332 (daté de Paris, 6 janv. 1949); réimpr. *in*: *Psyché*, janv.–février 1955, 10ᵉ année, nos. 99–100, pp. 73–80; Œ., t. VII, 1963, pp. 175–185 (Sc Ph) [281].

1949   "Les Chloritoïdes des Western Hills près Pékin", *Ann. Hébert et Haug*, t. VII, livre jubilaire Charles Jacob, pp. 381–387, 3 fig. (T) [282].

1949   "Pré-humain, humain, ultra-humain", *Idées et forces*, Paris, oct.–déc., 2ᵉ année, no. 5. pp. 59–69 (d'après divers articles impr. depuis 1946) (Sc Ph) [284].

1949   "L'humanité se meut-elle biologiquement sur elle-même?",

Rev. quest. scientif., CXX, 20 oct., pp. 498–516 (titre complété à l'encre comme suit: "Une nouvelle question de Galilée: oui ou non l'humanité", etc. . . .) daté de: Saint-Germain-en-Laye, 4 mai; Œ., t. V, pp. 319–336 (Sc Ph) [285].

*1949   "Un phénomène de contre-évolution en biologie humaine ou la peur de l'existence". D.d.i., 15 pp. s.i., 11 pp. Paris, 26 janv., 1er titre: "La peur existentielle (ou: Un aspect de la biologie humaine)"; fragm. *in*: *Cahiers Pierre Teilhard de Chardin*, no. 2, Éd. du Seuil, 1960; Œ., t. VII, 1963, pp. 187–202 (Sc Ph) [286].

*1949   "L'essence de l'idée de démocratie. Approche biologique du problème". D.d.i., 8 pp., s.i., 5 pp., Paris, 2 févr. (sous-titre: "Pour l'U.N.E.S.C.O., en réponse à une enquête"); Œ., t. V, pp. 309–315 (Ph) [287].

*1949   "Le sens de l'espèce chez l'homme". D.s.i., 4 pp. Saint-Germain-en-Laye, 31 mai (en projet dès le 22 juin 1948); discussion subséquente, D.d.i., 6 pp., Maison de la paix, 9 juin 1949, notes prises par Mme Edith Bricon; Œ., t. VII, 1963, pp. 203–210 (sans la discussion) (Sc Ph) [288].

*1949 et   "Le groupe zoologique humain. Structure et directions évolu-
1956   tives". R.s.i., pp. I–III et 1–63, 6 fig. Paris, 4 août 1949; paru en 1956 chez Albin-Michel, 172 pp., préface de Jean Piveteau, coll. "Les savants et le monde", repris sous le titre: *La place de l'homme dans la nature. Le groupe zoologique humain*: I. Paris, Union générale d'éditions, 8 rue Garancière, coll. "Le monde en 10/18", no. 33, 188 pp.; II. Paris, Éd. du Seuil, 173 pp.; Œ., t. VIII; titre primitif: "Observations géobiologiques sur la mise en place, la structure et l'ultra-développement possible de l'humanité (esquisse d'un traité ou cours d'anthropogénèse)"; La Confér. I: "Place et signification de la vie dans l'univers. Un monde qui s'enroule", D.d.i., 15 pp., est datée de Paris, déc. 1948; fragm. *in*: *Les nouvelles litt.*, no. 1487, 1er mars 1956, pp. 1 et 5; extraits apud: P. Grenet: *Teilhard de Chardin*, Seghers, 1961, pp. 194–212 (Sc Ph) [289].

*1949   "Le cœur du problème". R.d.i., 11 pp. s.i., 7 pp., 1 fig. Les Moulins, Puy-de-Dôme, 8 sept.; Œ., t. V, pp. 339–349 (Ph R) [290].

*1949   "L'avenir zoologique probable du groupe humain". D.s.i., 5 pp., conférence donnée le 24 oct., au C.I.E.F.R., Bruxelles, notes prises par E. Boné, S.J. (Sc).

1949 et   "La vision du passé. Ce qu'elle apporte à la science et ce
1951   qu'elle lui ôte", Commun. faite au 21e Congrès intern. de philos. des Sc. (VII: Sc. de la Terre), tenu à Paris du 17 au 22 oct. 1949, *Études*, CCLXIII, déc. 1949, pp. 308–315; réimpr.

avec des var. sous le titre: "La vision du passé: ce qu'elle nous apporte, et ce qu'elle nous enlève", *in*: *Actualités scient. et industr.*, Paris, Hermann, 1951, no. 1156, pp. 71–74; Œ., t. III, pp. 335–343 (Sc Ph) [291].

1950 "Qu'est-ce que la vie?", *Les nouvelles litt.*, 2 mars, 29ᵉ année, no. 1174, p. 1, col. 1 (réponse à une enquête d'André George); réimpr. *in*: Gaëtan Picon, *Panorama des idées contemporaines*, Paris, Gallimard, 1957, p. 632; Œ., t. IX (Sc Ph) [293].

1950 "La pensée religieuse devant le fait de l'évolution, débat organisé par l'U.C.S.F. en février 1950", *Bull. de l'U.C.S.F.*, juin–juillet, no. 12, pp. 19–20, R.s.i.; Œ., t. III, pp. 347–349 (Sc Ph) [294].

1950 "La carrière scientifique du P. Teilhard de Chardin", *Études*, juillet–août, t. CCLXVI, pp. 126–128; original: D.d.i., 3 pp., s.d. (printemps 1950); article non signé du P. Teilhard sur lui-même; Œ., t. X (T Sc) [295].

1950 "Le Paléolithique du Siam", *L'anthrop.*, t. LIV, nos. 5–6, pp. 547–549 (T) [307].

*1950 "Monogénisme et monophylétisme". R.s.i., 2 pp. s.l.n.d. (à propos de l'encyclique "Humani generis", 1950); Œ., t. XI (R) [296].

*1950 "Sur l'existence probable, en avant de nous, d'un 'ultra-humain' (réflexions d'un biologiste)". D.d.i., 13 pp. Paris, 6 janv.; Œ., t. V, pp. 353–364 (Sc Ph) [297].

*1950 "Comment concevoir et espérer que se réalise sur terre l'unanimisation humaine?" D.d.i., 9 pp. s.i., 6 pp. Paris, 18 janv.; Œ., t. V, pp. 367–374 (Ph) [298].

*1950 "Réflexions sur l'ultra-humain ou 'les phases d'une planète vivante'". R.d.i., 17 pp. s.i., 10 pp. Paris, 27 avril; texte abrégé sous le titre "Du préhumain à l'ultrahumain", *Almanach des Sc.*, 1951, Pierre Moray, éd. de Flore, pp. 149–155; Œ., t. V, pp. 377–385, sous le titre: "Du préhumain à l'ultra-humain ou 'les phases d'une planète vivante'" (Ph) [299] et [309].

*1950 "Le phénomène chrétien". R.s.i., 6 pp. Paris, 10 mai; Œ., t. XI (R) [300]

*1950 et "Pour y voir clair. Réflexions sur deux formes inverses d'esprit".
1955 R.s.i., 7 pp. s.l., 25 juillet; extr. impr. *in*: *Les études philoso-phiques*, oct.–déc. 1955, nouv. sér., 10ᵉ année, no. 4, P.U.F., pp. 572–579; Œ., t. VII, 1963, pp. 223–236 (Ph) [301].

*1950 "Le cœur de la matière". R.s.i., 46 pp. Les Moulins, Puy-de-Dôme, 15 août, Paris, 30 oct. 1950 (l'Appendice, pp. 35–46, contient le début de: "Le Christ dans la matière. Trois histoires comme Benson", 1916, et: "La puissance spirituelle de la matière", 1919); rééd. légèrement abrégée en 1957, R.s.i., 44 pp.;

citat. *in*: F. A. Viallet, *L'univers personnel de Teilhard de Chardin*, Paris,Amiot-Dumont,1956,*passim*;courtes cit.*apud*:Viallet,*Le dépassement*, Fischbacher, 1961, p. 163; "L'hymne à la matière" est cité par Maurice Gex, "Vers un humanisme cosmologique (III), La synthèse de Teilhard de Chardin," *Évoluer* (Yverdon), 3ᵉ année, no. 7, 2ᵉ trim. 1961, pp. 2 et 4; extr. *in*: *Hymne de l'univers*, 1961: "Pensées choisies par Fernande Tardivel", XLV, LXXVIII; extrait de la "Prière au Christ toujours plus grand" *in*: *Le Père Teilhard de Chardin, Apôtre du Christ dans l'univers,* plaquette (cf. Progr. vendu le 11 mai 1962 au concert de gala européen à Bruxelles, 1962), pp. 9–10; extraits *in*: C. Cuénot, *Teilhard de Chardin*, Paris, Éd. du Seuil, coll. "Écrivains de toujours", 1962, pp. 6–7, pp. 60–61, pp. 64–65; brève cit. *in*: C. Tresmontant, "Le Père Teilhard de Chardin et la théologie" *Lettre*, Paris, sept.–oct. 1962, nos. 49–50, p. 33; L. Barjon, "Fidélité du Père Teilhard de Chardin", *Foi vivante*, Paris et Bruxelles, juin 1963, 4ᵉ année, no. 15, pp. 75–76; F. Ferrier, "La convergence dans le 'Milieu divin'", *Cahiers de vie franciscaine*, Paris, 1963, 4ᵉ trim., no. 40, pp. 33, 34, 55; Maryse Choisy, *Teilhard et l'Inde*, Paris, Éd. Universitaires, 1964, *Carnets Teilhard*, *11*, pp. 16 et 35; *L'avenir, Recherches et Débats du Centre Catholique des Intellectuels Français*, Paris, Fayard, 1964, p. 135; P. Smulders, *La vision de Teilhard de Chardin*, Paris, Desclée, 1964, p. 15, p. 232 (n. 6), p. 240; extr. de la "Prière au Christ toujours plus grand" *in*: H. de Lubac, *La Prière du Père Teilhard de Chardin*, Paris, Fayard, 1964, pp. 55–6, et *in*: *TC explique*; Œ., t. X (Ph R B) [302].

*1950   "Le congrès universel des croyants". D.s.i., 1 p. s.l., sept. (anonyme, mais attrib. cert.: style, idées, témoignage de Mme Solange Lemaître) (Ph R) [303].

*1950   "Le goût de viver". D.d.i., 11 pp. Paris, nov.: Œ., t. VII, 1963, pp. 237–251 (Ph) [304].

*1950 et "Enquête: Nˡˡᵉˢ littéraires, 1951—"(*sic*). D.s.i., 2 pp., s.l., 2
1951   déc. cf. Marcel Brion: "Rencontre avec le Père Teilhard de Chardin", *Les nouvelles litt.*, 11 janv. 1951, pp. 1 et 4 (Sc Ph B) [305].

1951   "La structure phylétique du groupe humain", *Ann. de Pal.*, févr, t. XXXVII, pp. 49–79, 2 fig.; Œ., t. II, pp. 187–234 (T Sc Ph) [306].

1951   "Le Paléolithique du Harrar", en collab. avec H. Breuil et P. Wernert, *L'anthrop.*, t. LV, nos. 3–4, pp. 219–230, 8 fig. (T) [308].

1951   "L'évolution de la responsabilité dans le monde", *Psyché*, juillet–août, no. double spéc. 57–58, pp. 416–424, daté du 5 juin 1950 avec un abstract en anglais daté de juillet 1950; réimpr. *in*: *Psyché*, janv.–févr. 1955, 10ᵉ année, nos. 99–100, pp. 81–88; cit. *in*: *Morale chrétienne et morale marxiste*, La Palatine, 1960, p. 136 (Ph) [310].

*1951 "On the Significance and Trend of Human Socialisation". D.d.i., 2 pp. s.l., févr. (diff. de l'opuscule daté d'avril 1948) (Sc Ph) [311].

*1951 "Un seuil mental sous nos pas: du cosmos à la cosmogénèse". R.s.i., 10 pp. +1 p. non numérotée (Plan de l'essai), Paris, 15 mars 1951; extr. *in*: C. Cuénot, *Teilhard de Chardin*, Paris, Éd. du Seuil, coll. "Écrivains de toujours", 1962, pp. 83–84; Œ., t. VII, 1963, pp. 259–277; cf. aussi conférence de Paris du 8 avril "Cosmos et cosmogénèse", 14 pp. de notes prises par C. Cuénot, reproduite (avec quelques changements) *in*: C. Cuénot, "Teilhard de Chardin", *Plaisir de France*, Paris, janv. 1963, no. 291, pp. 3–5 (jusqu'à "Teilhard est à la philosophie ce que Copernic fut à l'astronomie") (Ph R) [312].

*1951 "Réflexions sur la probabilité scientifique et les conséquences religieuses d'un ultra-humain". R.s.i. (ronéotypé à la suite de l'opuscule "Un seuil mental..."), pp. 11–16, Paris, Pâques, 25 mars 1951; Œ., t. VII, 1963, pp. 279–291 (Ph R) [312, même numéro que l'opuscule précédent].

*1951 "Mémorandum au Dr. J. Huxley (à propos de son projet du 6 mars 51)". D.s.i., 1 p. (1ʳᵉ vers.), 1½ p. (2ᵉ vers.), annot. autogr., Paris, 22 mars (Sc Ph) [313].

*1951 "Note sur la réalité actuelle et la signification évolutive d'une orthogénèse humaine". D.d.i., 9 pp. Paris, 5 mai; Œ., t. III, pp. 353–362 (Sc Ph) [314].

*1951 "La convergence de l'univers". R.s.i., 9 pp. Capetown, 23 juillet; 2 types d'éd.: I. papier blanc ordin., encre noire, anonyme, daté de Capetown, 23 juil. 1951; II. papier blanc glacé, encre violette, signé P. Teilhard de Chardin, s.l.n.d.; Œ., t. VII, 1963, pp. 293–309 (Sc Ph) [315].

*1951 "Observations on the Elandsfontein Site near Hopefield." D.s.i., 2 pp., Capetown, après le 12 oct. (T) [316].

*1951 "South African Archaeological Society—"(*sic*); *incipit*: Father Teilhard said that during his too short visit to South Africa he learned a great deal... D.s.i., 2 pp., Capetown, oct. (T) [317].

*1951 "Quelques remarques 'pour y voir clair' sur l'essence du sentiment mystique". D.s.i., 2 pp., 2 fig. s.l., hiver; Œ., t. XI (R) [318].

*1951 "Transformation et prolongement en l'homme du mécanisme de l'évolution". D.s.i., 7 pp. s.l., 19 nov.; Œ., t. VII, 1963, pp. 311-323 (Sc Ph) [319].

*1951 "Un problème majeur pour l'anthropologie: y a-t-il, oui ou non, chez l'homme, prolongation et transformation du processus biologique de l'évolution?" D.s.i., 5 pp. s.l., 30 déc.; Œ., t. VII, 1963, pp. 325-332 (Sc Ph) [320].

*1951 "Notes de préhistoire Sud-africaine". D.d.i., 4 pp. s.l.n.d.; Œ.,
(ou t. II, pp. 237-242 (T) [321].
1952?)

*1952 "Observations sur les Australopithécinés". D.d.i., 4 pp. s.l.n.d. (exposé fait à l'Acad. des Sc. de New York, mars 1952); Œ., t. II, 251-255 (T) [322].

1952 "La Réflexion de l'énergie", Rev. quest. scientif., 20 oct., 65e année, XIIIe vol. de la 5e sér., t. CXXIII de la coll., pp. 481-497, 2 fig.; cf. R.s.i., 13 pp., datée de New York, 27 avril 1952, en projet dès le 1er mars.; Œ., t. VII, 1963, pp. 333-353 (Sc Ph) [323].

1952 "Hominisation et spéciation", Rev. scientif., nov.-déc., 90e année, fasc. 6, no. 3320, pp. 434-438; Œ., t. III, pp. 365-379 (T Sc Ph) [324].

1952 "Australopithèques, Pithécanthropes et structure phylétique des Hominiens", C. R. Acad. Sc., 21 janv., t. CCXXXIV, no. 4, pp. 377-379; Œ., t. II, pp. 245-248 (T) [325].

1952 "Sur la nature et la signification des Collenia précambriennes", C. R. Acad. Sc., 20 oct., t. CCXXXV, no. 16, pp. 845-847 (T) [326].

1952 et "On the Zoological Position and the Evolutionary Signifi-
1954 cance of Australopithecines", Transactions New York Ac. Sc., mars, 2e sér., vol. XIV, no. 5, pp. 208-210, 1 fig.; réimpr. dans le Yearbook of Physical Anthropology for 1952, Wenner-Gren Foundation, New York, 1954, vol. VIII, pp. 37-39 (T) [327].

*1952 Abstract of Paper "The New Advances Made by Prehistory in South Africa", Supper-conference for Anthropologists. R.s.i., 4 pp. New York (Wenner-Gren Foundation for Anthropological Research), 14 mars (le texte in extenso n'existe plus) (T) [328].

*1952 "On the Biological Meaning of Human Socialisation". R.s.i., 5 pp. New York, 15 mai (Sc Ph) [329].

1952 et "Fossil Man. On the Birth, Growth and Present Status of
1953 Our Idea of Fossil Man"—Inventory paper for the Wenner-Gren Foundation Intern. Symp. on Anthrop., New York. 9-20 juin 1952, no. 5. R.s.i., 11 pp. (Summary, D.d.i., 1 p.); impr. in: A. L. Kroeber, Anthropology Today, Chicago, University of

Chicago Press, 1953, pp. 93–100, sous le titre: "The Idea of Fossil Man" (T) [330].

*1952   "Ce que le monde attend en ce moment de l'Église de Dieu: une généralisation et un approfondissement du sens de la croix". R.s.i., 5 pp. New York (Purchase), 14 sept.; Œ., t. XI (R) [331].

1953   "La fin de l'espèce", *Psyché*, févr. 1953, 8e année, no. 76, pp. 81–87; daté de: New York, 9 déc. 1952; réimpr. *in*: *Psyché*, janv.–févr. 1955, 10e année, nos. 99–100, pp. 89–95; Œ., t. V, pp. 389–395 (Sc Ph) [332].

1953   "En regardant un cyclotron. Réflexions sur le reploiement sur soi de l'énergie humaine", *Recherches et Débats*, Paris, Fayard, avril, no. 4, pp. 123–130; cf. R.s.i., 7 pp.; extr. *in*: *Signes du temps*, Paris, oct. 1963, no. 1, nouv. série, pp. 34–36; Œ., t. VII, 1963, pp. 365–377 (Sc Ph) [333].

1953   "Réflexions sur la compression humaine", *Psyché*, sept., 8e année, no. 83, pp. 1–6, daté de New York, 18 janv.; Œ., t. VII, 1963, pp. 355–363 (Sc Ph) [334].

1953   "Sur la probabilité d'une bifurcation précoce du phylum humain au voisinage immédiat de ses origines", *C. R. Acad. Sc.*, 16–23 nov., t. CCXXXVII, no. 21, pp. 1293–1294; Œ., t. II, pp. 259–261 (T) [335].

*1953   "Contingence de l'univers et goût humain de survivre, ou comment repenser, en conformité avec les lois de l'énergétique, la notion chrétienne de création". D.d.i., 6 pp., New York, 1er mai; cit. *in*: C. Tresmontant, "Le Père Teilhard de Chardin et la théologie", *Lettre*, Paris, sept.–oct. 1962, nos. 49–50, pp. 31 et 32; Œ., t. IX (Ph R) [336].

*1953   "L'énergie d'évolution". D.d.i., 11 pp., New York, 24 mai (en projet dès le 19 déc. 1952); Œ., t. VII, 1963, pp. 379–393 (Sc Ph) [337].

*1953   "Une suite au problème des origines humaines—La multiplicité des mondes habités". D.d.i., 6 pp., s.i., 5 pp. New York, 5 juin; Œ., t. XI (Sc Ph) [338].

*1953   "L'étoffe de l'univers". D.s.i., 6 pp. En vue de Sainte-Hélène (traversée de New York au Cap), 14 juillet; Œ., t. VII, 1963, pp. 395–406 (Ph) [339].

*1953   "Le Dieu de l'évolution". D.s.i., 6 pp. Sous l'Équateur, 25 oct. (Christ-Roi); Œ., t. XI (Ph R) [340].

*1953   "L'activation de l'énergie humaine". D.d.i., 10 pp. ou 7 pp. selon les éd. New York, 6 déc.; Œ., t. VII, 1963, pp. 407–416 (Ph) [341].

1954   "Les recherches pour la découverte des origines humaines en

Afrique, au sud du Sahara", *L'anthrop.*, juin, t. LVIII, nos. 1–2, pp. 74–78; Œ., t. II, pp. 265–275 (T) [342].

*1954 et   "Un sommaire de ma perspective 'phénoménologique' du
1955   monde". D.s.i., 2 pp. New York, 14 janv. 1954; impr. *in*: *Les études philosophiques*, oct.–déc. 1955, nouv. sér., 10ᵉ année, no. 4, P.U.F., pp. 569–571, et *apud*: P. Grenet, *Teilhard de Chardin*, Seghers, 1961, pp. 216–219; *TC explique*; Œ., t. X (Ph) [343].

1954,   "Les singularités de l'espèce humaine", New York, fini à
1955 et   Pâques 1954, *Ann. de Pal.*, t. XLI, pp. 1–54 (le texte est
1956   diminué de son Appendice, "Remarques complémentaires sur la nature du point oméga ou: De la singularité du phénomène chrétien", R.s.i., 3 pp., New York, 25 mars 1954); Œ., t. II, pp. 295–375, avec l'Appendice (T Sc Ph) [344].

*1954   "Le phénomène humain (Comment, au-delà d'une 'anthropologie' philosophico-juridico-littéraire, établir une vraie science de l'homme, c'est-à-dire une anthropodynamique et une anthropogénèse?)". D.d.i., 1 p. s.l., antérieur à juin 1954 (préparé pour Jacques Rueff) (Sc Ph) [345].

*1954,   "The Antiquity and Planetary Significance of Human Cul-
1955 et   ture." D.d.i., 13 pp. New York, oct. 1954; repris, transformé
1956   et augmenté *in*: "The Antiquity and World Expansion of Human Culture": I. D.d.i., 22 p., 1 fig. New York, 26 oct. 1954; II. R.d.i., 23 pp., 1 fig., 16–22 juin 1955. Background paper no. 6 prepared for the Wenner-Gren Foundation International Symposium "Man's role in changing the face of the earth", Princeton Inn, Princeton, N.J.; III. impr. *in*: William L. Thomas, Jr. (ed.), *Man's Role in Changing the Face of the Earth*, University of Chicago Press, 1956, pp. 103–112 (Sc Ph) [346].

1955   "L'Afrique et les origines humaines", *Rev. quest. scientif.*, 20 janv., 68ᵉ année, XVIᵉ vol. de la 5ᵉ sér., t. CXXVI de la coll., pp. 5–17, daté de sept. 1954. Cf. confér. du 28 juin 1954, notes prises par Claude Cuénot, D.d.i., 5 pp.; Œ., t. II, pp. 277–291 (T) [347].

*1955 et   "Une défense de l'orthogénèse". D.d.i., 7 pp. s.i., 6 pp. s.l.n.d.
1956   (janv. 1955); impr. sous le titre: "Une défense de l'orthogénèse. À propos des figures de spéciation", *in*: *Colloques internationaux du Centre National de la Recherche Scientifique— LX. Problèmes actuels de paléontologie*. Paris, éd. du C.N.R.S., 1956, pp. 109–113; Œ., t. III, pp. 381–391 (Sc Ph) [348].

*1955   "Barrière de la mort et co-réflexion, ou de l'éveil imminent de la conscience humaine au sens de son irréversion". D.d.i., 9 pp. s.i., 7 pp. New York, 1ᵉʳ et 5 janv.; Œ., t. VII, 1963, pp. 417–429 (Ph R) [349].

*1955   "Le christique". D.d.i., 19 pp. s.i., 14 pp. New York, mars 1955 (une lettre du 13 mars le qualifie d'"à peine terminé"); rééd. 1957, R.s.i., 15 pp.; larges extr. *in: Nova et Vetera*, Fribourg et Genève, XXXIᵉ année, no. 3, juillet–sept. 1956, pp. 221–224; *in: Hymne de l'univers*, 1961: "Pensées choisies par Fernande Tardivel", LXXXI; extr. du final *in*: C. Cuénot, *Teilhard de Chardin*, Paris, Éd. du Seuil, 1962, coll. "Écrivains de toujours", pp. 66–67; brève cit. *in: Cahiers Pierre Teilhard de Chardin, no. 4*, Paris, Éd. du Seuil, 1963, pp. 31–32; *L'avenir, Recherches et Débats du Centre Catholique des Intellectuels Français*, Paris, Fayard, 1964, p. 136; P. Smulders, *La vision de Teilhard de Chardin*, Paris, Desclée, 1964, p. 213 et p. 246, n. 6; H. de Lubac, *La prière du Père Teilhard de Chardin*, Paris, Fayard, 1964, p. 98; *TC explique*; Œ., t. X (Ph R B) [350].

*1955 "Recherche, travail et adoration". D.d.i., 6 pp. New York, mars; Œ., t. XI (Ph R) [351].

II—NOTES, MÉMOIRES ET OPUSCULES MAL DATÉS

*1917 ou "Note sur la notion de transformation créatrice". M., 6 pp.
1918   D.d.i., 4 pp. s.i., 2 pp., s.l.n.d. (de peu postérieur à: "L'union créatrice", semble-t-il; Œ., t. XI (Ph) [362].

*1921   "Note sur l'essence du transformisme". D.d.i., 8p. s.l.n.d. (la
(?)   date 1935 paraît fausse; les analogies avec le no. 41: "Comment se pose aujourd'hui la question du transformisme", rendent assez probable l'année 1921) (Sc Ph) [167].

III—NOTES, MÉMOIRES ET OPUSCULES NON DATÉS

*s.d.   "À propos du spiritisme: observations sur la synthèse expéri-mentale de l'esprit". D.d.i., 4 p. s.l.n.d. (probablement ancien, vers 1920); Œ., t. XI (Ph) [363].

*s.d.   "En quoi consiste le corps humain?" M., 4 pp. D.d.i., 3 pp. s.l.n.d. (probablement avant le 5 sept. 1919, cf. "Genèse d'une pensée", p. 402, lettre de Jersey, 5 sept. 1919: "Enfin, j'ai écrit dernièrement huit pages sur la manière dont il convient de comprendre les limites du corps humain."); Œ., t. IX (Sc Ph) [364].

   N.B. Cf. aussi Section X—VARIA, *sub fine*.

IV—ALLOCUTIONS ET DISCOURS

1922   *C. R. somm. Soc. Géol. France*, t. XXII, pp. 129–131: Séance générale du 9 juin 1922: M. Marcellin Boule donne lecture de son rapport sur l'attribution du prix Viquesnel à M. l'abbé Teilhard de Chardin: "Remerciements de M. Teilhard de Chardin" (p. 131) [366].

1926   "Allocution présidentielle", *C. R. Somm. Soc. Géol. France*, t. XXVI, pp. 5–7. Séance du 18 janv. 1926 [367].

*1928   "Pour Odette et pour Jean". Plaquette impr. de 8 pp. s.l., 14 juin (allocution pour le mariage d'Odette Bacot et Jean Teilhard d'Eyry); cit. *in*: *Cahiers Pierre Teilhard de Chardin*, *no. 2*, Éd. du Seuil, 1960, pp. 144–145 (Ph R) [368].

1932 et   "Allocution prononcée devant les membres de la Croisière
1935   Jaune à la mission de Lian Tcheou (1er janv. 1932)". Titre fictif; impr. *in*: L. Audouin-Dubreuil, *Sur la route de la soie*, Paris, Plon, 1935, p. 225; fragm. cité *in*: *Paris-presse-l'Intransigeant*, 14 juin 1957, p. 2 (R) [369].

*1935   "Allocution prononcée par le R.P. Teilhard de Chardin à l'occasion de la bénédiction nuptiale de Monsieur et Madame de la Goublaye de Ménorval en l'église de Saint-Louis des Invalides le 15 Juin 1935". Plaquette impr. de 4 pp. (Ph R) [370].

*1937 et   "Spiritualistic Evolution" (titre fictif), allocution prononcée
1958   à la Villanova University à l'occasion de la réception par le P. Teilhard de la Mendel medal, Woodstock College Library, Chapbook I, April 1958, R.d.i., pp. 16–19.

1937   Jubilé de M. Marcellin Boule, 27 mai 1937. "Allocution de M. P. Teilhard de Chardin, conseiller du Service Géologique de Chine", *L'anthrop.*, t. XLVII, pp. 599–600 (B) [371].

*1947   "Au colloque de Versailles: Importance de la recherche" (titre fictif). D.d.i., 6 pp., s.l., 20 août (Réunion Internationale S.J. à Versailles, conférence du P. Teilhard) (R) [372].

*1948   "Allocution pour le mariage de Claude-Marie Haardt et de Mlle Christine Dresch en l'église Notre-Dame d'Auteuil" (titre fictif). D.s.i., 2 pp. s.l., 21 déc. (Ph R) [373].

*1949   "Allocution pour son cinquantenaire de vie religieuse" (titre fictif). Paris, 19 mars (?), les 4 dern. lignes sont citées par Auguste Demoment *in*: *Jeunesse et vocation de Pierre Teilhard de Chardin*, D., 1961, p. 97 (ouvrage inédit).

*1950   Discours prononcé ou devant être prononcé à Cahors "Depuis que l'homme est homme . . .". D.d.i., 1 p. s.l., 21 juin (Sc Ph) [374].

V—CHRONIQUES

1929   "Homo pekinensis 1. une découverte chinoise en préhistoire", *Dossiers de la Commission synodale*, Péking, déc., vol. II, no. 12, pp. 938–939 (Sc).

1930   "A Great Reward for Hard Work". *The Leader Reprints*, no. 51, pp. 13–14, Peiping, The Leaderpress (no. spécial sur Chou Kou Tien) (Sc) [380].

1947 "Un colloque scientifique sur l'évolution", *Études*, mai, t. CCLIII, pp. 257–259 (Sc) [381].

1949 "Congrès internationaux de philos. des Sc.: Colloque organisé par l'Association intern. de philos. des Sc., et tenu dans les locaux de l'U.N.E.S.C.O., sur l'évolution biologique, les 17–22 oct. 1949",*Études*, déc., t. CCLXIII, pp. 391–392 (anonyme, le 2° § seulement est du P. Teilhard, depuis "Juste une semaine avant . . .") (Sc Ph) [382].

1950 "Machines à combiner et super-cerveaux", *Études*, mars, t. CCLXIV, pp. 403–404 (Sc Ph) [383].

1950 "L'invasion de la télévision", *Études*, mai, t. CCLXV, pp. 251–252 (Sc Ph) [384].

*1952 "Le dernier symposium de la Wenner-Gren Foundation (Juin 1952). Quelques réflexions personnelles sur l'opération". D.d.i., 3 pp. New York, sept. (Sc Ph) [385].

VI—CORRESPONDANCE[1]

*Arsène-Henry (Lettres à Madame).
>Péking, 24 nov. 1943, 20 déc. 1943, dimanche matin (janv. ou févr. 1946) *in*: *Revue Teilhard de Chardin*, Bruxelles, 1er sept. 1962, no. 12, pp. 4–5 (Ph R).

*Barbour (Lettres à George Brown).
>I. Fragment s.l.n.d. (avant le 10 août 1950) *in*: George B. Barbour, "Obituary of P. Teilhard de Chardin", *Proc. Geol. Soc. London*, 20 sept. 1955, no. 1529, p. 133, et "Memorial to Pierre Teilhard de Chardin, S.J. (1881–1955)", *Proc. Vol. Geol. Soc. America*, juillet 1956, p. 170, col. 2 (B) [484].
>II. Correspondance complète, du 17 juin 1932 au 6 déc. 1954 *in*: George B. Barbour, *Sur le terrain avec Teilhard de Chardin*, Paris, Éd. du Seuil, 1965 (T Sc Ph R B).

*Bégouën (Lettres au Comte Max-Henri)
>I. Extraits (1926–1930) *in*: Max-H. Bégouën, "Témoignage", *Cahiers Pierre Teilhard de Chardin, no. 2*, Paris, Éd. du Seuil, 1960, pp. 15–27 (Ph R).
>II. Voir aussi *Lettres de voyage* (cf. *infra*).

*Blanc (Lettre à Alberto-Carlo)
>Paris, 18 juill. 1946 (et non 1945) *in*: *Notizie sull'operosità scientifica e didattica di Alberto-Carlo Blanc*, Rome, 1961, p. 28 (Sc).

*Bordet (Lettre à M. l'Abbé, Aumônier de la J.O.C.)
>Paris, 21 févr. 1951, D.s.i., 2 pp. (sur l'immortalité des âmes individuelles) (Ph R) [486].

[1] Voir aussi *infra*, XIII, 1958, C. Cuénot, *Pierre Teilhard de Chardin*.

*Breuil (Lettres à M. l'Abbé Henri) cf. *infra*, Teillard-Chambon

*Burdo (Lettre au P. Christian, S.J.)

New York, 15 févr. 1953; brève cit. *in*: L. Barjon, "L'Appel de Pâques", *Revue Teilhard de Chardin*, Bruxelles, déc. 1963, 4ᵉ année, no. 17, p. 13; H. de Lubac, *La prière du Père Teilhard de Chardin*, Paris, Fayard, 1964, p. 125 (R B).

*Carlhian (Lettre à Madame Jean)

New York, 19 juin 1953:
I. Cit. *in*: C. Tresmontant, "Le Père Teilhard de Chardin et la théologie", *Lettre*, Paris, sept.-oct. 1962, no. 49–50, p. 51.
II. Texte répandu sous le titre fictif: "Mal évolutif et péché originel", D.s.i., 2 pp. (Ph R) [495].

*Choisy (Lettres à Madame Maryse)

I. Trois lettres inédites de P. Teilhard de Chardin, fac-similé de la lettre du 15 mai 1953, extr. de la dern. lettre, écrite quelques jours avant le 10 avril 1955, extr. avec fac-similé de la lettre datée de New York, 13 mars 1954, *in*: *Psyché*, janv.-févr. 1955 (mois fictifs, éd. posthume), 10ᵉ année, nos. 99–100, pp. 9–10; fragment déjà publié *in*: Maryse Choisy, "Mon grand ami Teilhard de Chardin n'est plus", *Combat*, Paris, 18 avril 1955 (Ph R).
II. Lettre de Péking, 25 déc. 1939, très brève cit. *in*: Maryse Choisy, *Teilhard et l'Inde*, Paris, Éd. Universitaires, 1964, *Carnets Teilhard, no. 11*, p. 60 (*ibid.*, cit. de la lettre datée de New York, quelques jours avant le 10 avril 1955, pp. 36–39, et de la lettre de New York, 13 mars 1954, pp. 17–18).

*Costa (Lettre à Monsieur)

s.l. (Paris), 10 nov. 1924, D.d.i., 2 pp., connue sous le titre fictif de "Lettre à un ami" (R) [453].

*Cuénot (Lettres à Claude)

I. New York, 11 avril 1953; fragment sur la phénoménologie *in*: *La Table ronde*, Paris, juin 1955, no. 90, p. 39, et P. Chauchard *L'être humain selon Teilhard de Chardin*, Paris, Gabalda, 1959, pp. 35–36 (Ph) [494].
II. New York, 30 nov. 1952, photocopie, moins le dernier § *in*: C. Cuénot, *Teilhard de Chardin*, Paris, Éd. du Seuil, coll. "Écrivains de toujours", 1962, p. 2 (Ph).
III. New York, 21 mai 1953; fragment *in*: C. Cuénot, "Situation de Teilhard de Chardin", *Bull. Soc. industr. Mulhouse*, 1963, no. 3, p. 28 (Ph).
IV. New York, 15 févr. 1955, cit. *ibid.*, p. 9, n. 1 et pp. 28–29 (Ph).
V. New York, 25 avril 1954, *in extenso in*: C. Cuénot, "Plauderei über Teilhard de Chardin", *apud*: Die Zukunft

des Menschen in der Welt—eine Tagung über die Zukunftserwartung bei Pierre Teilhard de Chardin; Evangelische Akademie, Bad Boll, 12.-14. Juni 1964. R.s.i., pp.
42–43 (trad. allemande) (Ph R).

*Décizier (Lettre au P. Auguste, S.J.)
s.l., 23 déc. 1917; cit. *in*: C. Cuénot, "Situation de Teilhard
de Chardin", *Bull. Soc. industr. Mulhouse*, 1963, no. 3, p. 30 (R).

*Delmas (Lettre à Claude)
s.l., mars 1951; fragment *in*: Claude Delmas, "In memoriam,
le Père Teilhard de Chardin", *Combat*, Paris, 13 avril 1955 (Ph).

*Directeur du C.N.R.S. (Lettre à M. le)
Paris, 18 mars 1950, D.s.i., 1 p. sous le titre "Rapport sur les
recherches du Père Teilhard de Chardin (1949–1950)"
(T Sc B).

*Fejos (Lettre à Paul, Director of Research of the Wenner-Gren
Foundation) Johannesburg, 1er août 1951, D.s.i., 1 p.,
désignée sous le titre fictif de "My First Impressions Concerning the Possibilities for Future Work in Africa", et adressée
le 21 sept. 1951 par P. Fejos sous forme de copie circulaire
aux membres de l'American Institute of Human Paleontology
(T) [490].

*Fontoynont (Lettre au P. Victor, S.J.)
I. 15 mars 1916; extr. *in*: C. Cuénot, *Teilhard de Chardin*,
Paris, Éd. du Seuil, coll. "Écrivains de toujours", 1962,
p. 27–29 (R).
II. 15 mars 1916, 22 juillet 1916, 26 juillet 1917, *in*: H. de
Lubac, *La pensée religieuse du Père Pierre Teilhard de Chardin*,
Paris, Aubier, Éd. Montaigne, 1962, pp. 347–354 (Ph R B).

Gaudefroy (Lettres à l'Abbé Christophe)
I. Lettres de Chine, 1923–1924, *in*: C. Gaudefroy, *Les missions
géologiques du Père Teilhard de Chardin*, Semur, impr. H. Canat.
1926, pp. 3–8 (*passim*), tiré à part du *Bulletin de l'Institut
Catholique* (T) [456].
* II. Tientsin, 12 oct. 1926; cit. *in*: H. de Lubac, *La pensée
religieuse du Père Pierre Teilhard de Chardin*, Paris, Aubier, Éd,
Montaigne, 1962, p. 70–71, et Maryse Choisy, *Teilhard et
l'Inde*, Paris, Éd. Universitaires, *Carnets Teilhard, no. 11*,
pp. 7–8 (Ph).
* III. Tientsin, 27 févr. 1927; brève cit. *in*: Abbé J. Augier,
"Recherche scientifique et sacerdoce", *Catho. Journal*, Paris,
févr., no. 7, p. 18 (R).
* IV. Pékin, 14 Juillet 1934; brève cit. *in*: H. de Lubac, *La
prière du Père Teilhard de Chardin*, Paris, Fayard, 1964, p. 75,
n. 2 (R).

*   V. Voir aussi: H. de Lubac, *La pensée religieuse du Père Pierre Teilhard de Chardin*, Paris, Aubier, Éd. Montaigne, 1962, *passim* (Ph R).

*Janssens (Lettres au T.R.P. Jean-Baptiste, Général des Jésuites)
I. Paris, 25 sept. 1947, *in*: R. d'Ouince, "L'épreuve de l'obéissance dans la vie du Père Teilhard de Chardin", *apud*: *L'homme devant Dieu. Mélanges offerts au Père de Lubac*, Paris, Aubier, Éd. Montaigne, 1964, t. III, pp. 341–342 (R).
II. Capetown, 12 oct. 1951, *in*: R.P. Pierre Leroy, S.J., *Pierre Teilhard de Chardin tel que je l'ai connu*, Paris, Plon, 1958, pp. 55–60, et P. Grenet, *Teilhard de Chardin*, Paris, Seghers, 1961, pp. 213–215 (R).
III. Paris, 8 janv. 1949; très courts fragm. *in*: H. de Lubac, *La prière du Père Teilhard de Chardin*, Paris, Fayard, 1964, p. 213 (B).

*Jodot (Lettre à Paul)
Pékin, 6 avril 1932; cit. *in*: C. Cuénot, "Le Père Teilhard de Chardin entre l'Orient et l'Occident", *Le Ruban Rouge*, Paris, sept. 1960, pp. 8–9 (Article rédigé d'après les lettres inédites à Léontine Zanta (T B).

*Jouve (Lettre au P. Raymond)
Pékin, 6 juillet 1934; brève cit. *in*: H. de Lubac, *La pensée religieuse du Père Pierre Teilhard de Chardin*, Paris, Aubier, Éd. Montaigne, 1962 (R).

*Koenigswald (Lettre à Ralph von)
Peiping, 11 févr. 1936; extr. du texte original anglais *in*: Helmut de Terra, *Memories of Teilhard de Chardin*, London, Collins, 1964, p. 109 (Sc).

*Lemaître (Lettres à Madame Solange)
New York, 21 sept. 1952; cit. *in*: Mme. S. Lemaître "In memoriam", *Cahiers Pierre Teilhard de Chardin, no. 2*, Paris, Éd. du Seuil, 1960, p. 155 (B).
New York, 2 mars 1955; brève cit. *ibid.*, p. 157 (R).

*Leroy (Lettre au P. Pierre, S.J.)
Buenos Aires, 8 nov. 1951, extr. *in*: Teilhard de Chardin, *La vision du passé*, Paris, Éd. du Seuil, 1957, p. 59 (T).
Voir aussi *infra*, Barjon (L.) et Leroy (P.).

*Licent (Lettres au P. Émile S.J.), cf. *infra* Barjon (L.) et Leroy (P.).
Cit. du télégramme de fin févr. 1923 et d'un bref extr. de la carte postale de Changhaï, 17 mai 1923, *in*: R.P. Émile Licent, S.J., *Comptes-rendus de dix années (1914–1923) de séjour et d'exploration dans le bassin du Fleuve Jaune, du Pai-ho et des autres tributaires du golfe du Pei Tcheu Ly*, Tien-tsin, La Librairie française, 1924, t. III, p. 1559; extr. de la corresp. Teilhard-

Licent *in*: C. Cuénot, "Le Révérend Père Émile Licent, S.J.",
à paraître en 1965 dans le *Bulletin de l'École française d'Extrême-Orient* (T B).

*Lubac (Lettres au P. Henri de, S.J.)

I. Tientsin, 31 juill. 1930, *in*: Louis Barjon, *Mondes d'écrivains, destinées d'hommes*, Paris, Casterman, 1960 (Sc Ph).

II. Tientsin, 31 juill. 1930, *in*: H. de Lubac, *La prière du Père Teilhard de Chardin*, Paris, Fayard, 1964, p. 86 et p. 87 ("Il me semble . . . dans le monde");
Pékin, 27 juin 1932, *ibid.*, p. 131, n. 4;
Tientsin, 8 oct. 1933, *ibid.*, p. 158, n.1, p. 208, n. 2;
Pékin, 7 janv. 1934, *ibid.*, p. 199, n. 1;
Pékin, 29 avril 1934, *ibid.*, p. 169 (jusqu'à "de la Durée") et p. 190;
Pékin, 15 sept. 1934, *ibid.*, p. 154, n. 2;
Paris, 23 juin 1935, *ibid.*, p. 191;
Pékin, 15 août 1936, *ibid.*, p. 30;
Paris, 18 sept. 1948, *ibid.*, pp. 124–125;
Paris, 29 oct. 1949, *ibid.*, p. 81, n. 2, et p. 190 (depuis "Dans un Univers . . .");
cit. brèves ou très brèves (Ph R).

III. Voir aussi: H. de Lubac, *La Pensée religieuse du Père Pierre Teilhard de Chardin*, Paris, Aubier, Éd. Montaigne, 1962, *passim* (Ph R).

*Monod (Lettre à Théodore)

New York, 26 juin 1952, cit. *in*: *Christianisme social*, Paris, janv.–févr. 1960, 68ᵉ année, nos. 1–2, p. 23, et Th. Monod, *Perspectives et prospectives en écoutant Teilhard de Chardin et Gaston Berger*, *Cahiers Pierre Teilhard de Chardin, no. 4*, Paris, Éd. du Seuil, 1963, p. 79 (R).

*Mortier (Lettres à Mademoiselle Jeanne)

I. Berkeley (California), 27 juillet 1939; photocopie d'1 p. *in*: P. Grenet, *Teilhard de Chardin*, Paris, Seghers, 1961, pp. 208–209 (R).

II. Pékin, 13 avril 1940; fragment en fac-similé et transcription h.t. *in*: Teilhard de Chardin, *Le phénomène humain*, Paris, Éd. du Seuil, 1955, pp. 44–45 (B).

III. Rome, 30 oct. 1948; cit. en italien *in*: Massimo Olmi, "Il mio amico Teilhard", *L'Europeo*, 8 sept. 1963, XIXᵉ année, no. 36, p. 65 (B).

*Mounier (Lettres à Emmanuel)

I. Paris, 29 août 1947; cit. *in*: C. Cuénot, "Situation de Teilhard de Chardin", *Bull. Soc. industr. Mulhouse*, 1963, no. 3, p. 10 (Ph R).

II. Toussaint (1er nov.) 1947, publiée sous le titre: "Pour une théologie de la science moderne" *in*: *Esprit*, no. spécial ronéotypé sur: Les entretiens de Châtenay, 1er-2 nov., pp. 10–11 (R) [476].

*Needham (Lettre à Joseph)

New York, 25 oct. 1952; fragment *in*: J. Needham, "Cosmologist of the Future", *New Statesman*, U.S.A., 7 nov. 1960 (7 lignes; texte fr. traduit en anglais et légèrement adapté) (Ph).

*Oakley (Lettre à K. P.)

New York, 28 nov. 1953; très brefs fragments *in*: J. S. Weiner, *The Piltdown Forgery*, Oxford, 1955, p. 93 (T).

*Ouince (Lettre au P. René d', S.J.).

I. 21 déc. 1950, *in*: R. d'Ouince, "L'épreuve de l'obéissance dans la vie du Père Teilhard de Chardin", *apud*: *L'homme devant Dieu. Mélanges offerts au Père Henri de Lubac. III. Perspectives d'aujourd'hui*, Paris, Aubier, Éd. Montaigne, 1964, p. 343, no. 16 (R).

II. Saint-Germain-en-Laye (et non Paris), 25 juill. 1947; reproduction en photocopie de la p. 2 (moins le postscriptum) sur la couverture de: P. Smulders, *La vision de Teilhard de Chardin*, Paris, Desclée, 1964 (Ph R B).

*Parents (Lettres à ses parents, Berthe-Adèle ou Emmanuel Teilhard de Chardin, ou les deux à la fois)

I. Laval, vers le 25 mars 1901; fragment *in*: *Cité fraternelle*, Besançon, 12e année, no. 716, 25 janv. 1959, p. 4 (R B).

II. Nombreux extraits *in*: Auguste Demoment, S.J., *Jeunesse et vocation de Pierre Teilhard de Chardin*. D., 1961, 100 pp. env. (inédit).

III. Hastings, 7 juin 1911; Hastings, 2 juillet 1911, sous le titre: "Lettres du Père Teilhard sur la mort de sa sœur Françoise", *in*: H. de Lubac, *La pensée religieuse du Père Pierre Teilhard de Chardin*, Paris, Aubier, Éd. Montaigne, 1962, p. 360–361 (R B).

IV. Depuis Mongré, avril 1892, jusqu'à: Cantorbéry, 20 nov. 1914; 8 extr. de lettres sous le titre: "Lettres inédites du Père Teilhard de Chardin, enfance et jeunesse", *in*: *Jésuites de l'Assistance de France*, Lyon, 1962, no. 3, pp. 16–30 (R B).

V. Pierre Teilhard de Chardin, *Lettres d'Égypte, 1905–1908*, Paris, Aubier, Éd. Montaigne, 1963, 287 pp. (Avant-propos du R. P. Henri de Lubac, pp. 7–10) (lettres s'échelonnant du 18 août 1905 au 6 août 1908) (Sc B).

VI. 6 mars 1905, *in*: H. de Lubac, *La pensée religieuse du Père Pierre Teilhard de Chardin*, Paris, Aubier, Éd. Montaigne, 1962, p. 115, n. 3;

23 avril 1910, *ibid.*, p. 15, n. 3;

8 mai 1911, *ibid.*, pp. 40–41 (n. 8 et suite);

16 juin 1912, *ibid.*, p. 318, n. 3 (brèves cit.) (R B).

*Pelletier (Lettre au P. Félix, S.J.).

Paris, 2 juill. 1950; fragment *in*: *Figaro littéraire*, 17 sept. 1960, 15ᵉ année, no. 752, p. 10 (attribué par erreur au P. François Russo, S.J.); brève cit. *in*: L. Barjon, "L'Appel de Pâques", *apud*: *Revue Teilhard de Chardin*, Bruxelles, déc. 1963, 4ᵉ année, no. 17, p. 15 (R B).

*Ravier (Lettres au P. André, S.J.).

s.l.n.d. *in*: H. de Lubac, *La prière du Père Teilhard de Chardin*, Paris, Fayard, 1964, pp. 84–85;

17 nov. 1947, *ibid.*, p. 54;

New York, 1951 ou après, *ibid.*, p. 84;

New York, 5 janv. 1952, *ibid.*, p. 84, n. 5;

New York, 3 août 1952, *ibid.*, p. 38, n. 1;

7 juin 1953, *ibid.*, p. 179, n. 1;

New York, 14 janv. 1955, *ibid.*, pp. 53–54 (Ph R B).

*Rivière (Lettres à Madame Claude)

I. Péking, 14 déc. 1942; cit. *in*: C. Rivière, "Une grande figure de foi et d'espérance: le Père Teilhard de Chardin tel que je l'ai connu", *apud*: *Faits et idées*, Rabat, 5 oct. 1956, no. 55, p. 34 (R).

II. Péking, 14 déc. 1942, 30 mai 1943, 20 oct. 1943; courts fragments *in*: Jean Onimus, *Pierre Teilhard de Chardin ou la foi au monde*, Paris, Plon, 1963, p. 138, 139 et 154 (Ph R).

N.B. Un recueil des lettres à Madame C. Rivière est en préparation pour les Éd. du Seuil.

*Russo (Lettres au P. François, S.J.).

I. New York, 21 nov. 1952, 31 janv. 1953, 14 janv. 1954; trad. ital. de courts extraits *in*: Massimo Olmi, "Il mio amico Teilhard", *L'Europeo*, 8 sept. 1963, XIXᵉ année, no. 36, p. 60 (B).

II. New York, 8 déc. 1953; fragment *in*: Teilhard de Chardin, *L'apparition de l'homme*, Paris, Éd. du Seuil, 1956, p. 17, n. (T).

III. Berkeley (Californie), 25 juill. 1952; fragment *in*: H. de Lubac, *La pensée religieuse du Père Pierre Teilhard de Chardin*, Paris, Aubier, Éd. Montaigne, 1962, p. 98, n. 2;

New York, 21 nov. 1952; fragment *ibid.*, p. 54, p. 191, n. 3 (Ph R).

*Sahni (Lettre au Dr. M. R.)

New York, 18 nov. 1953, publiée sous le titre "Message au Dr. M. R. Sahni" *in*:

I. *Journal of the Pal. Soc. of India*, 1956, vol. I, no. 1, p. XXXII (version abrégée).

II. *Ibid., D. N. Wadia Jubilee Nr.*, 1957, vol. II, p. 23 (version *in extenso*) (T).

*Sauvage (Lettres à André)

Très courts fragments *in*: André Sauvage, "La Croisière Jaune, souvenirs", *in*: *Cahiers Pierre Teilhard de Chardin, no. 2,* Paris, Éd. du Seuil, 1960, p. 162 (fragm. datant de juill.–août 1952) et p. 164 (date inconnue) (R).

*Schurmans (Lettre au P. Maurice) Vicaire général de la Compagnie de Jésus)

1940; très brève cit. *in*: H. de Lubac, *La prière du Père Teilhard de Chardin*, Paris, Fayard, 1964, p. 30 (R).

*Sertillanges (Lettre au P. Antonin-Gilbert, en religion le P. Delmace, O.P.)

Peiping, 4 févr. 1934, sous le titre "Lettre du P. Teilhard de Chardin au P. Sertillanges après lecture de son ouvrage 'Dieu ou rien'", *in*: *Revue Teilhard de Chardin*, Bruxelles, 30 juin 1960, nos. 1 et 2, p. 12, et P. Grenet, *Teilhard de Chardin*, Paris, Seghers, 1961, pp. 178–179 (R).

*Solages (Lettre à Mgr. Bruno de)

s.l.n.d., très brève cit. *in*: H. de Lubac, *La pensée religieuse du Père Pierre Teilhard de Chardin*, Paris, Aubier, Éd. Montaigne, 1962, p. 34 (R).

*Swan (Lettres à Mrs. Lucile)

I. Extraits de lettres échelonnés de 1933 à 1950, signalés sous le titre fictif "Fragments de lettres à Lucile Swan", plaquette hors commerce, impr. de 8 p., avec introd. par Lucile Swan, New York, 1957, texte original angl.; comporte en outre la "Profession de foi" du 23 sept. 1933 (Ph R B) [501].

II. Extraits de lettres échelonnés de juillet 1933 à 1949, texte original angl., *in*: L. Swan, *Memories and Letters.—The Wind and the Rain. An Easterbook for 1962*, London, pp. 41–49; reprennent en grande partie le texte précédent (Ph R B).

III. Extraits de lettres échelonnés de 1935 à 1954, texte original angl. *in*: L. Swan, "With Teilhard de Chardin in Peking", *The Month*, London, juillet 1962, vol. CCXIV, no. 1139 (new series vol. XXVIII, no. 1), pp. 8–9, 12–15 (Ph R B).

*Teilhard de Chardin (Lettres à Berthe-Adèle et Emmanuel) cf. *supra*, Parents.

*Teilhard de Chardin (Lettres à Joseph) cf. *infra*, Teillard-Chambon.

*Teillard-Chambon (Lettres à Mademoiselle Marguerite)

I. Lettres échelonnées du 15 avril 1923 au 25 (?) juillet 1939;

s'adressant à Marguerite Teillard-Chambon, Max-Henri et Simone Bégouën, Henri Breuil, Joseph Teilhard de Chardin, *in*: Pierre Teilhard de Chardin, *Lettres de voyage* (1923-1939), Paris, Grasset, 1956, 228 pp., avec Introduction de Claude Aragonnès (pseud. de Marguerite Teillard-Chambon), pp. 11–22 (Ph R B).

II. Lettres échelonnées de Pékin, 24 septembre 1939, à New York, 1ᵉʳ avril 1955; s'adressant à Marguerite Teillard-Chambon, Max-Henri et Simone Bégouën, Henri Breuil, Joseph Teilhard de Chardin, *in*: Pierre Teilhard de Chardin, *Nouvelles lettres de voyage* (1939–1955), Paris, Grasset, 1957, 195 pp., avec Introduction de Claude Aragonnès (pseud. de Marguerite Teillard-Chambon), pp. 9–14 (Sc Ph R B).

III. Lettres échelonnées du 15 avril 1923 au 1ᵉʳ avril 1955, rassemblant les 2 vol. précédents, *in*: Pierre Teilhard de Chardin, *Lettres de voyage* (1923–55), Paris, Grasset, 1961, 370 pp.

IV. Lettres échelonnées de Clermont, 13 décembre 1914 à Jersey, 17 septembre 1919, s'adressant exclusivement à Marguerite Teilhard-Chambon, *in*: Pierre Teilhard de Chardin, *Genèse d'une Pensée. Lettres* 1914–19, Paris, Grasset, 1961, 404 pp., introductions diverses jusqu'à la p. 52 (Ph R B).

V. Lettres s'échelonnant de 1915 à 1918 publiées sous le titre: "Lettres du front (1914–1918) annotées par Claude Aragonnès", *in*: *Revue Teilhard de Chardin*, 30 juin 1960, nos. 1 et 2, pp. 2–10; à relever une lettre à Marguerite Teilhard-Chambon, du 30 sept. 1917, et une à ses parents, 25 juill. 1918, non reproduites dans *Genèse d'une pensée* (B).

VI. Lettre à Marguerite Teillard-Chambon du 13 nov. 1916, *in*: Teilhard de Chardin, *Hymne de l'univers*: "Pensées choisies par Fernande Tardivel", XL, LXXVII;
Lettre à la même, du 23 nov. 1916, *ibid.*, LIX (R B).

*Termier (Lettres à Henri)
Lettres de New York, 25 janv. 1953, 17 mars 1954 et 11 nov. 1954; extraits *in*: Teilhard de Chardin, *La vision du passé*, Paris, Éd. du Seuil, 1957, pp. 67–69 (T Sc) [493].

*Terra (Lettres à Helmut de)
I. Moulins, 3 juill. 1937; extr. du texte original angl. *in*: H. de Terra, *Memories of Teilhard de Chardin*, London, Collins, 1964, pp. 76–78 (Sc).

II. Saint-Germain-en-Laye, 12 août 1947; fragment *in*: C. Cuénot, Préface à: H. de Terra, *Mes voyages avec Teilhard*, Paris, Ed. du Seuil, 1964, texte original angl. en note et trad. fr. dans le texte (Ph).

*Tresmontant (Lettres à Claude)

    Cit. *in*: C. Tresmontant, "Le Père Teilhard de Chardin et la Théologie", *Lettre*, Paris, sept.–oct. 1962, nos. 49–50;

    New York, 14 janv. 1954, p. 35;

    New York, 20 janv. 1954, p. 35;

    New York, 8 févr. 1954, pp. 37–38;

    New York, 10 févr. 1955, p. 35 (Ph R).

*Valensin (Lettres au P. Auguste, S.J.)

    I. Paris, 12 déc. 1919; cit. *in*: Pierre Teilhard de Chardin, *Le milieu divin*, Paris, Éd. du Seuil, 1957, pp. 100–102 (R) [450].

    II. Extraits de lettres *in*: C. Tresmontant, "Le Père Teilhard de Chardin et la théologie", *Lettre*, Paris, sept.–oct. 1962, nos. 49–50;

    Paris, 19 nov. 1917 (et non 1919), pp. 18–19;

    Paris, 20 oct. 1919, p. 21;

    Paris, 17 déc. 1922, p. 36;

    Tientsin, 13 oct. 1933, p. 26 (Ph R).

    III. Courtes cit. de lettres *in*: L. Barjon, "Fidélité du Père Teilhard de Chardin", *Foi vivante*, juin 1963, 4e année, no. 15, notamment:

    Paris, 28 févr. 1920, p. 75;

    Paris, Samedi Saint 1922, p. 75;

    Paris, 16 mai 1925, p. 78;

    Paris, 19 mai 1925, pp. 78–79;

    Paris, 26 mai 1925, p. 79;

    Tientsin, 31 déc. 1926, p. 77;

    Sur *l'André-Lebon* (avant Hong-Kong), 25 févr. 1929, p. 79;

    Paris, 29 sept. 1929, p. 79 (R).

    IV. Courtes cit. de lettres *in*: R. d'Ouince, "L'épreuve de l'obéissance dans la vie du Père Teilhard de Chardin", *apud*: *L'homme devant Dieu. Mélanges offerts au Père Henri de Lubac. III. Perspectives d'aujourd'hui*, Paris, Aubier, Éd. Montaigne, 1964;

    Paris, 13 nov. 1924, p. 335, n. 5;

    Tientsin, 19 mai 1925, p. 337;

    Tientsin, 31 déc. 1926, p. 336, no. 9;

    Pao-Te (Shansi), 15 juill. (et non juin) 1929, p. 343, n. 17 et p. 344, n. 18 (R).

    V. Courtes cit. de lettres *in*: H. de Lubac, *La prière du Père Teilhard de Chardin*, Paris, Fayard, 1964;

    Paris, 21 déc. 1919, pp. 192–193 et p. 193, n. 1;

    Paris, 29 déc. 1919, pp. 130–131;

    Paris, 10 janv. 1920, p. 171 (suite de la n. 4 de la p. 170);

    Paris, 2 févr. 1920, p. 70;

Tientsin, 27 mai 1923, p. 156;

Paris, 4 juill. 1920, p. 156, n. 1;

Paris, Samedi Saint, 1922, p. 124;

Paris, 17 déc. 1922, p. 86;

Paris, 13 nov. 1924, p. 88;

Paris, 19 mai 1925, p. 82 et p. 83;

Paris, 12 juin 1925, p. 209, n. 1;

Tientsin, 31 déc. 1926, p. 83 (depuis "réaction" jusqu'à "détente intérieure"), p. 174;

Tientsin, 5 avril 1927, p. 168, n. 1;

Paris, 29 sept. 1928, p. 168, n. 1;

Sur l'*André-Lebon* (avant Hong-Kong), 25 févr. 1929, pp. 167–168;

Pao-te (Shansi), 15 juill. 1929, p. 26, n. 2;

Tientsin, 30 déc. 1929, p. 87 (depuis "Toutes les petitesses . . .");

Tientsin, 13 oct. 1933, pp. 81–82, p. 169, n. 2;

S.S. Tjinagara, 18 janv. 1936, p. 81, n. 1;

Pékin, 22 nov. 1936, p. 179 (R).

VI. Voir aussi H. de Lubac, *La pensée religieuse du Père Pierre Teilhard de Chardin*, Paris, Aubier, Éd. Montaigne, 1962, *passim* (Ph R), et L. Barjon et P. Leroy, *La carrière scientifique de Pierre Teilhard de Chardin*, Monaco, Éd. du Rocher (Sc).

Vaufrey (Lettres à Madame Marthe)

I. déc. 1929; extr. de lettre sur le premier crâne trouvé à Chou-kou-tien (avec le texte du télégramme de Pierre Teilhard de Chardin et Davidson Black, 28 août 1929), *L'anthrop.*, t. XXXIX, pp. 456–458 (Sc B) [457].

II. 21 nov. 1936; extr. imprimé sous le titre: "Deux nouveaux crânes de Sinanthrope", *L'anthrop.*, t. XLVI, p. 716 (T) [462].

III. 1937, sous le titre: "Extraits de lettres de M. P. Teilhard de Chardin (trouvailles anthropologiques en Chine)", *L'anthrop.*, t. XLVII, pp. 655–656 (T) [463].

*Viallet (Lettres à François-Albert)

I. Afrique du Sud, août–sept. 1951 (ou 1953?); fragment en photocopie et trad. all. *in*: F.-A. Viallet, *Zwischen Alpha und Omega. Teilhard de Chardin*, Nürnberg, Glock und Lutz, 1958, p. 144 (R).

II. Fragments de lettres des 2 avril 1952, 26 sept. 1952, 15 déc. 1953, 5 févr. 1954, 9 févr. 1954, *in*: F.-A. Viallet, *Le Dépassement*, Paris, Fischbacher, 1961, pp. 10, 164–165, 194–195–196, 200–201 (Ph R).

*Wespin (Lettres à Madame Dominique de) (Si les renseignements communiqués sont exacts, son nom de jeune fille serait Georgette Mathieu; elle aurait épousé successivement un baron de Wespin (Belge), un M. Wang (Chinois), puis un Polonais du nom de Barrant (?); le nom de Georges Magloire est un pseudonyme littéraire)

I. Pékin, 1944; photocopie d'1 p., s.l.n.d. *in*: *Synthèses*, Bruxelles, oct. 1957, no. 137, p. 80 (Sc) [467];
photocopie de la même p., Pékin, 1944, *in*: *Revue Teilhard de Chardin*, Bruxelles, 25 déc. 1960, nos. 3 et 4, p. 14; photocopie de la même p., *ibid.*, mars 1964, 5e année, no. 18, p. 21;

II. 1945 ou 1946, fragment *in*: *Synthèses*, déc. 1957, no. 139, p. 451 (Ph) [472].

III. Paris, 28 déc. 1946, 2 brèves cit. *in*: *Revue Teilhard de Chardin*, Bruxelles, 1er déc. 1962, no. 13, p. 36 (avec des logia de Teilhard, pp. 36–37); photocopie de la dern. p. *in*: Georges Magloire, *Album Teilhard*, Paris, Éd. universitaires, 1962, *Carnets Teilhard, no. 1* (B).

*Zanta (Lettres à Mademoiselle Léontine)

I. Aux bords du Chara-ousso-gol, Ordos oriental, 7 août 1923; extr. *in*: C. Cuénot, *Teilhard de Chardin*, Paris, Éd. du Seuil, coll. "Écrivains de toujours", 1962, pp. 45–46 (R).

II. Brèves cit. *in*: H. de Lubac, *La prière du Père Teilhard de Chardin*, Paris, Fayard, 1964;
Tientsin, 25 janv. 1924, p. 92, n. 6, p. 197, n. 2;
Mongolie orientale, 20 mai 1924, p. 84, n. 2;
Le Chambon, 22 août 1928, p. 86, n. 2;
Obock, 24 janv. 1929, p. 152, n. 1;
Pékin, 15 avril 1929, p. 168, p. 171, n. 3 (R).

III. Brèves cit. *in*: H. de Lubac, *La pensée religieuse du Père Pierre Teilhard de Chardin*, Paris, Aubier, Éd. Montaigne, 1962, *passim* (Ph R).

Destinataires inconnus ou non identifiés

Extraits de deux lettres du 24 oct. 1907 et du 12 mars 1908, *in*: *Relations d'Orient*, Bruxelles, mai 1908, pp. 178–179 (T) [448].

Large extrait d'une lettre datée de Ho-Kinn-Shien (Shansi) 30 juillet 1926, imprimée sous le titre: "Expédition scientifique en Chine", *in*: *Lettres de Jersey*, 1926–27, vol. XL (nouv. série, t. VII), impr. polyglotte Jules de Meester et Fils, Wetteren (Belgique), pp. 89–90 (B).

*Pékin, 10 mars 1945:

I. Sous le titre: "Lettre inédite en guise d'éditorial, Pékin, 1945", *in*: *Revue Teilhard de Chardin*, Bruxelles, 25 déc. 1960, nos. 3 et 4, p. 2;

II. *in*: Dominique de Wespin, "Le Père Teilhard de Chardin m'a dit . . .", *Balisage*, Louvain, mars–avril 1961, no. spécial 16–17, p. 36; texte repris avec quelques paragraphes supplémentaires *in*: *Le Phare dimanche*, Bruxelles, 2 avril 1961;

III. Sous le titre: "En guise d'éditorial, extrait d'une lettre à un ami, 10 mai 1945", *in*: *Revue Teilhard de Chardin*, Bruxelles, 20 avril 1961, no. 5, p. 2;

IV. Photocopie d'1 p. *in*: *La Messe sur le monde*, Pierre Teilhard de Chardin, *Messa della domenica*, Girolamo Frescobaldi, église Saint-Jacques, Anvers, 12 mai 1961, festival organisé par la Société Pierre Teilhard de Chardin, programme, p. 5;

V. Photocopie d'1 p. *in*: *Revue Teilhard de Chardin*, Bruxelles, 1ᵉʳ sept. 1962, p. 2 (Ph B).

*Lettre du 21 mai 1953, fragment *in*: C. Tresmontant, "Le Père Teilhard de Chardin et la Théologie", *in*: *Lettre*, Paris, sept.–oct. 1962, nos. 49–50, p. 44 (R).

*Très brefs fragm. de lettres *in*: H. de Lubac, *La prière du Père Teilhard de Chardin*, Paris, Fayard, 1964: 1924 (?), p. 172, n. 1; 17 oct. 1932, p. 150; 7 août 1950, p. 138; 5 janv. 1954, p. 19, n. 1; été 1954, p. 19, n. 1 (R B).

Abondantes citations de lettres

1958 C. Cuénot *Pierre Teilhard de Chardin. Les grandes étapes de son évolution*, Paris:

I. Club des éditeurs, coll. "Hommes et faits de l'histoire" (relié), 473 et XLI pp., 6 portraits en tête, 4 cartes en fin de vol., bibliogr. des œuvres de Teilhard;

II. Éd. Plon (brochée), 489 et XLIX pp., 45 illustr. hors texte, 22 illustr. in texte dont 6 cartes, bibliogr., index nominum, addenda et corrigenda; citations d'opuscules, photocopies de manuscrits et nombreux extraits de la correspondance; l'éd. Plon présente un texte revu, amélioré et légèrement augmenté (T Sc Ph R B).

1964 L. Barjon et P. Leroy, *La carrière scientifique de Pierre Teilhard de Chardin*, Monaco, Éd. du Rocher, 141 pp. (extraits de lettres à Pierre Leroy, Émile Licent, Auguste Valensin, etc.) (T Sc).

VII—NÉCROLOGIES

1934 Davidson Black, 1885–1934, *L'anthrop.*, t. XLIV, pp. 424–426 (Sc) [420].

1936 Henry Fairfield Osborn, 1857–1935, *L'anthrop.*, t. XLVI, pp. 704–706 (Sc) [421].

1949 Franz Weidenreich, *L'anthrop.*, t. LIII, pp. 328–330 (Sc) [422].

1951   Lucien Cuénot (1867–1951), *Études*, févr., t. CCLXVIII, pp. 255–256 (Sc) [423].

VIII—PRÉFACES

1943   Avertissement de *Geobiologia*, en collab. avec Pierre Leroy et Henri Vetch, Pékin, t. I, p. V (Sc).

*1947   Préface du R. P. Teilhard de Chardin aux lettres de Romain Rolland à "une amie catholique" [Jeanne Mortier]. D.d.i., 2 pp., Saint-Germain-en-Laye, 15 août; fragm. impr. *in: Bull. de l'Assoc. des Amis de Romain Rolland*, juin 1955, 10ᵉ année, no. 32, p. 14 (B) [424].

*1948   Préface de: *Évolution et finalité*, livre inédit de Jean Montassey (pseud. d'Olivier Costa de Beauregard). D.d.i., 3 pp. s.l., 12 févr. (Sc Ph) [425].

1951   Préface de: Marguerite-Marie Teilhard de Chardin, *L'énergie spirituelle de la souffrance*, Paris, éd. du Seuil, 1ᵉʳ trimestre 1951, pp. 9–12, préface datée de Paris, 8 janv. 1950, large citat. *in: Nouvelles lettres de voyage*, pp. 136–137; Œ., t. VII, pp. 253–257 (R B) [426].

IX—COMPTES RENDUS

1921   "Ueber einen bei Ehringsdorf in der Nähe von Weimar gefundenen Unterkiefer des *Homo primigenius*, par G. Schwalbe, *L'anthrop.*, t. XXXI, pp. 531–533 (T) [386].

1921   "Diluviale Menschenfunde in Obercassel bei Bonn", par Max Verworn, R. Bonnet et G. Steinmann, *L'anthrop.*, t. XXXI, pp. 533–536 (T) [387].

1921   "Les hommes fossiles. À propos d'un livre récent", *Études*, 20 mars, t. CLXVI, pp. 570–577—C.R. de: *Les hommes fossiles, éléments de paléontologie humaine*, par Marcellin Boule; Œ., t. II, pp. 41–50 (T) [388].

1922   "Fossil Man", *The Living Age*, Boston, vol. CCXXI, pp. 415–419 (trad. de: "Les hommes fossiles. À propos d'un livre récent") (T) [48].

1922   "Die menschlichen Skeletreste aus dem Kampfe'schen Bruch im Travertin von Ehringsdorf bei Weimar", par Hans Virchow, *L'anthrop.*, t. XXXII, pp. 129–132 (T) [389].

1922   "The Origin and Evolution of the Human Dentition. A Palaeontological Review", par William K. Gregory, *L'anthrop.*, t. XXXII, pp. 285–288 (T) [390].

1922   "Les religions de la préhistoire. L'âge paléolithique", par Th. Mainage, *L'anthrop.*, t. XXXII, pp. 525–526 (T) [391].

1922 "The Status of the Dingo", par F. Wood-Jones, *L'anthrop.*, t. XXXII, pp. 546-547 (T) [392].

1922 "On the Occurrence of Aboriginal Stone Implements of Unusual Types in the Tablelands of Central Australia", par W. Howchin, *L'anthrop.*, t. XXXII, pp. 547-548 (T) [393].

1923 "Der diluviale Menschenfund von Obercassel bei Bonn", par M. Verworn, R. Bonnet, G. Steinmann, *L'anthrop.*, t. XXXIII, pp. 206-208 (T) [394].

1928 "La Grotte de l'Observatoire à Monaco", par M. Boule et L. de Villeneuve, *L'anthrop.*, t. XXXVIII, pp. 150-153 (T) [395].

1928 "L'exigence idéaliste et le fait de l'évolution", par Édouard Le Roy, *La Vie Cathol. en France et à l'Étranger*, 5ᵉ année, no. 203, samedi 18 août, p. 5, sous le titre: "La pensée dans la science" et le pseud. de Max Bégouën, attribution garantie par une lettre du 1ᵉʳ sept. 1928 (Sc Ph) [396].

1939 "La préhistoire", par A. Vayson de Pradenne, *Études*, 20 févr., t. CCXXXVIII, pp. 564-565, extr. du C.R. *in*: *Le Moncelet*, 5 mars 1939, no. 9, p. 8 (Sc) [397].

1939– "Note préliminaire sur les formations cénozoïques et plus
1940 récentes de la chaine annamitique septentrionale et du Haut-Laos (stratigéographie, préhistoire, anthropologie)", par J. Fromaget et E. Saurin, *L'anthrop.*, t. XLIX, pp. 137-138 (T) [398].

1939– "Études sur l'époque glaciaire dans l'Inde et sur les cultures
1940 humaines trouvées en association (Studies on the Ice Age in India and Associated Human Cultures)", par H. de Terra et T. T. Paterson, *L'anthrop.*, t. XLIX, pp. 729-731 (T) [399].— Trad. et adapt. angl. sous le titre: "The Quaternary Sequence in North India According to Dr. de Terra", *Geobiologia*, Peking, 1943, t. I, pp. 97-101 [430].

1943 "The Genesis of the Japanese Islands as Seen by Dr. T. Kobayashi", *Geobiologia*, t. I, pp. 63-72, 2 cartes in texte (T) [400].

1943 "The Continental Basement of the Western Tarim Basin According to Dr. Erik Norin," *Geobiologia*, t. I, pp. 73-77, 1 carte in texte (T) [401].

1943 "The Flora and Climate of Northeastern China During the Miocene According to Dr. Ralph W. Chaney", *Geobiologia*, t. I, pp. 86-91, 1 carte in texte (T) [402].

1943 "The Pleistocene of Hsikang According to Dr. J. G. Andersson", *Geobiologia*, t. I, pp. 92-94 (T) [403].

1943 "The Pleistocene Sequence of Taiwan (Formosa) According to Dr. Hayasaka", *Geobiologia*, t. I, pp. 95-96 (T) [404].

1943 "Quantitative Zoology According to G. G. Simpson", *Geobiologia*, t. I, pp. 139–141 (T) [405].

*1944 "History of the Conflict Between Religion and Science", par J. W. Draper. D.s.i., 1 p. Pékin, 1944 (et non 1940, cf. ligne 13); brève cit. *in*: C. Cuénot, "Situation de Teilhard de Chardin", *Bull. Soc. industr. Mulhouse*, 1963, no. 3, p. 21 (Ph R) [406].

1947 "Les hommes fossiles, éléments de paléontologie humaine", par M. Boule et H. Vallois, *Études*, janv., t. CCLII, pp. 122–123 (T) [407].

1949 "La planète au pillage", par F. Osborn, *Études*, déc., t. CCLXIII, pp. 402–403 (T) [408].

*1950 "Catalyse et biologie", par Frédéric Gillot. D.s.i., 1 p., 10 févr. (T) [409].

1950 "La Genèse des montagnes", par M. Roubault, *Études*, févr., t. CCLXIV, pp. 279–280 (T) [410].

1950 "Rythme et modalités de l'évolution", par G. G. Simpson, *Études*, mai, CCLXV, p. 278 (Sc Ph) [411].

1950 "Les Australopithèques et le chaînon manquant (ou "missing link") de l'évolution", C.R. de "Finding the Missing Link", par R. Broom, *Études*, juin, t. CCLXV, pp. 340–345; Œ., t. II, pp. 177–183 (T) [412].

1950 "Sa Majesté le pétrole", par Georges Le Fèvre, *Études*, juillet–août, t. CCLXVI, p. 130 (T).

1950 "Géologie de l'Afrique", par Raymond Furon, *Études*, juillet–août, t. CCLXVI, pp. 132–133 (T).

1950 "L'évolution rédemptrice du P. Teilhard de Chardin", par ***, *Études*, sept., t. CCLXVI, p. 284 (R) [413].

1950 "Essai sur la théorie psychologique de la vie", par Docteur Tilicheef, *Études*, sept., t. CCLXVI, p. 285 (Sc Ph).

1951 "Rythme et modalités de l'évolution", par G. G. Simpson, *L'anthrop.*, janv., t. LIV, nos. 5–6, pp. 460–461 (Sc Ph) [414].

1951 "Qu'est-ce que la vie?", par E. Schrödinger, *Études*, févr., t. CCLXVIII, pp. 275–276 (Sc Ph) [415].

1953 "Histoire géologique de la biosphère", par H. et G. Termier, *Études*, juin, t. CCLXXVII, pp. 425–426 (T) [416].

1955 "Formation des continents et progression de la vie", par H. et G. Termier, *Études*, mars, t. CCLXXXIV, p. 419 (T) [417].

1955 "Problématique de l'évolution", par François Meyer.—Observations du P. Teilhard de Chardin, *Bull de l'U.C.S.F.*, nouv. sér., no. 25, mars-avril. R.s.i., pp. 15–17 (Sc Ph) [418].

1955 "Problématique de l'évolution", par François Meyer, *Études*, mai, t. CCLXXXV, p. 279 (Sc Ph) [419].

X—VARIA

*1896 "Comptes rendus de la Congrégation des Grands du Collège Notre-Dame de Mongré, Villefranche (Rhône)". Cahier manuscrit, archives de la province des R.P. Jésuites de Lyon, pp. 220–226 (oct.–déc.) (R B) [447].

*1915–
1925 "Notes et esquisses". M., 9 cahiers dont Mgr B. de Solages vient de nous envoyer la description bibliographique, cf. Addenda p. 483; brèves cit. allant du 15 sept. 1916 au 27 avril 1918 *in*: Madeleine Barthélemy-Madaule, *Bergson et Teilhard de Chardin*, Paris, Éd. du Seuil, 1963, *passim* (Ph).

*1917 "Le sens de la croix" (brouillon). M., 2 p. s.l., 24 déc. (R) [449].

*1917 "Note sur la nature synthétique de l'esprit et la réalité d'un centre d'union des monades" (titre fictif). M. de quelques pp., Champigneul (Marne), 10 nov. (Ph).

*1921 "Un mot d'explication sur mon attitude vis-à-vis de l'Église officielle". D.d.i., 4 p. s.l., 5 janv. (R) [451].

*1921–
1922 "Notes de cours" (titre fictif). Notes prises par Jean Cuvillier à l'Institut Catholique de Paris pendant l'année scolaire 1921–1922 (T).

1925 Bref résumé d'une "Allocution à l'ouverture de la réunion extraordinaire de 1925, en Alsace", *C. R. somm. Soc. Géol. France,* Séance d'ouverture du vendredi 11 sept., p. 182 (B) [454].

1928 "*Canis sinensis* Schlosser et *Canis procyonides*" (titre fictif), *C. R. somm. Soc. Biogéographie,* 17 févr., 5ᵉ année, no. 35, p. 10 (T).

*1931 "La seule tactique digne des plus hautes traditions de la Compagnie" (titre fictif), extrait d'une brève note confidentielle, 9 lignes, s.l., janv. (R).

1931 "Mammalian Palaeontology. Survey of Pliocene Formations in North China" (informal address before the Osborn Research Club on February 10), *Natural History. The Journal of the American Museum of Natural History*, New York, mai–juin, t. XXXI, no. 3, pp. 338, col. 2, et 339, col. 1, avec 1 photo d'Henri Breuil et de Teilhard; reproduit par H. F. Osborn, "Explorations, Researches and Publications of Pierre Teilhard de Chardin, 1911–1931", *American Museum Novitates*, New York, 25 août, no. 485, p. 7 (avec la photo p. 8; le résumé de l'allocution de Teilhard commence au 3ᵉ §, "A good deal of work had been done . . ." (T) [126 et 458].

1931 "Twenty-three of the Chief Fossil Collecting Areas of China, 1885–1931, as Indicated by Teilhard", *in*: H. F. Osborn, "Explorations . . .", pp. 12–13, 1 carte hors texte en noir (T).

*1932   "Orient et Occident ou la mystique de la personnalité". M.,
ou   3 pp. conférer. à l'Éc. Norm. Sup.; notes prises par Claude
1933   Cuénot; impr. in: C. Cuénot, Pierre Teilhard de Chardin, Paris,
        Plon, 1958, pp. 174–175 (Ph R) [459].

1933–   Note of Editor in: Gordon T. Bowles, "A Preliminary Report
1934   of Archaeological Investigations on the Sino-Tibetan Border
        of Szechwan", Bull. Geol. Soc. China, vol. XIII, no. 1, p. 123
        (cf. lettre à H. Breuil datée de: Tientsin, 25 juin 1934) (T)
        [460].

1934   Bref résumé d'une "Allocution en souvenir de Davidson
        Black", Proceedings of the Special Meeting on May 11, 1934,
        Bull. Geol. Soc. China, vol. XIII, no. 3, p. 322 (Sc) [461].

*1937   "China gave a Lead to 'Missing Link'", New York Times, 19
        mars, 1 col. + 1 début de col., interview de Teilhard par
        William L. Laurence; les déclarations de Teilhard sont
        déformées; autre interview, rectifiant le précédent, de peu
        postérieur dans le Toronto Star (Canada) (Sc).

1938–   "Conférence du P. Teilhard de Chardin sur la Chine, la
1939   Birmanie et Java", 17 déc. 1938; analyse in: Le Moncelet, 12
        janv. 1939, no. 6, pp. 4–5, R.s.i. (T) [464].

1939   "Le féminin et l'univers". R.s.i., 3 p., avril ou mai, conférence
        devant "L'Union spirituelle des femmes", notes prises par
        Mme Pellé-Douel (Ph).

*1939– "Carnet de retraites". M., comprenant sûrement les retraites de
1943   1939, de 1940 (oct.), de 1942, de 1943 (à Péking). Nous
        n'avons pu obtenir jusqu'ici aucune description biblio-
        graphique de ce texte sûrement manuscrit et dont l'existence
        a été brusquement révélée par H. de Lubac, La prière du Père
        Teilhard de Chardin, Paris, Fayard, 1964, qui contient de très
        brèves cit.:
        1939, pp. 94, 95, 99;
        1940, pp. 48, n. 2, 84 (cf. n. 3), 89, 90, n. 1 et 3, 94–95, 96,
        n. 3, 96–97, 99, 107, 124, 129–130;
        1942, pp. 90, n. 1;
        1943, pp. 89, 99 (R).

1939–   "Entretiens et propos de P. Teilhard de Chardin" in: Georges
1946 et Magloire, "Teilhard de Chardin tel que je l'ai connu",
1957   Synthèses, 12e année, no. 132, mai 1957, pp. 422–429; no. 134,
        juillet 1957, pp. 193–200; no. 137, oct. 1957, pp. 77–83; no.
        139, déc. 1957, pp. 450–455 (articles rassemblès en 1 vol. par
        les Éd. Synthèses, Bruxelles, 1958); voir aussi Raoul Crubbe,
        "Une conférence de Mme Dominique de Wespin: P. Teil-
        hard tel que je l'ai connu", in: Le Phare dimanche, Bruxelles,
        le 14 févr. 1960, 15e année, no. 737, p. 5 (Sc Ph R) [468].

*1939– "Souvenirs d'enfance" (titre fictif) *in*: Georges Magloire, "Le
1946 et Monologue de Sarcenat", *Le Phare dimanche*, Bruxelles, 13
1959   sept., 1 p. (R B).

*1939– "Nouveaux souvenirs d'enfance" (titre fictif) *in*: Georges
1946 et Magloire, "Sarcenat, berceau des Teilhard de Chardin", extr.
1959   de *Synthèses*, Bruxelles, sept., no. 160, 8 p., 5 photos h.t.
         (B R).

*1939–1946–1950, publié en 1960 "Instantanés du P. Teilhard", *in*:
         Dernière heure, Bruxelles, 28 avril 1960, 3 relations d'entretiens
         (Peking 1939 et 1946, Paris, 1950) rédigées par Mme Domi-
         nique de Wespin (Ph R).

*1943 et "Logia" (titre fictif) *in*: Dominique de Wespin, "Aimons-nous
1962   les uns les autres", *Revue Teilhard de Chardin*, Bruxelles, 1er
         déc. 1962, no. 13, p. 2 (Ph B).

*1944–   Cahiers manuscrits constituant un "Journal":
1955   XIII (sic, =no. 1) (17×22), 18 juillet 1944–27 octobre 1945
         (Pékin, rue Labrousse), pp. 1–162+, en tête, une p. non
         numérotée;
         XIV (=no. 2) (17×22), 27 oct. 1945–6 avril 1947 (*ibid.*),
         151 pp.+, en tête, 2 pp. non numérotées;
         XV (=no. 3) (17×22), 6 avril 1947–31 déc. 1948 (Paris,
         Études), pp. 1 à 183 avec numérotation continue, pp. 184–185
         blanches, pp. 186–189 avec des notes+1 p. en tête non
         numérotée avec l'inscription "Paris. Rue Monsieur 1947";
         XVI (=no. 4) (17×22), 30 sept.–5 nov. 1948 (Rome), 1er
         janv.–6 août 1949 (Paris, *Études*), p. 1 à 77 inclus; à partir de
         la fin, numérotation à l'envers de 1 à 19 inclus+1 p. de
         couverture à la fin;
         XVII (=no. 5) (17×22), 10 août 1949–31 oct. 1950 (Paris,
         Études), en tête 2 pp. non numérotées, puis pagination 1 à 68
         inclus. Par erreur la pagination reprend à 59 (au lieu de 69)
         jusqu'à 173 inclus. Sont blanches les pages 163 et 165;
         XVIII (=no. 6) (17×22), 1er nov. 1950 (Paris, *Études*), le 19
         juin 1952 (Purchase), 168 pp.;
         XIX (=no. 7) (17×22), 23 juin 1952 (*Purchase*), 18 juin 1953
         (Park Avenue, New York), 72 pp.+3 pp.;
         XX (=no. 8) (17×22), Retraite 1952 (*Purchase*) puis notes:
         24 juin 1953–8 oct. 1954, 72 pp. +3 pp. numérotées 3, 2, 1+1
         p. non numérotée;
         XXI (=no. 9) (19×25), 10 oct. 1954–7 avril 1955 (Hotel
         Fourteen, New York), 35 pp. continues de 1 à 35+p. 120+
         +p. 121+p. 123 (et quelques notes au crayon sur la p. de
         gauche). La dernière p. (p. 35; 7 avril 1955) a été publiée *in*:
         L'avenir de l'homme, 1959, p. 404;

Brèves cit. du *Journal in*: C. Cuénot, *Teilhard de Chardin*, Paris, Éd. du Seuil, 1962, coll. "Écrivains de toujours" (s.d. p. 61, 1947 et 1948 p. 159, 1950 p. 163); Madeleine Barthélemy-Madaule, *Bergson et Teilhard de Chardin*, Paris, Éd. du Seuil, 1963, *passim* (du 15 févr. 1945 au 24 déc. 1947); C. Cuénot, "Situation de Teilhard de Chardin", *Bull. Soc. industr. Mulhouse*, 1963, no. 3, pp. 11 et 12.

N.B. La numérotation de 1 à 9 est posthume. Les cahiers antérieurs, laissés à Péking, sont probablement perdus (Sc Ph R B) [469].

*1944–
1954
"Carnet de retraites" (couverture noire). M. à double entrée: notes de retraites pp. 1–42, et notes diverses (extraits du Nouveau Testament pp. 1–14), comprenant:

Retraite 21–29 oct. 1944 (Pékin, rue Labrousse);
Retraite 20–28 oct. 1945 (*ibid.*);
Retraite 17–24 août 1946 (Le Châtelard, Rhône);
Retraite 30 août–7 sept. 1948 (Les Moulins);
Retraite 25 août–2 sept. 1949 (*ibid.*);
Retraite 27 sept.–4 oct. 1950 (*ibid.*);
Retraite 28 sept.–8 oct. 1953 (S.S. *Tjisedane*, South Atlantic);
Retraite 19–26 août 1954 (Purchase).

N.B. La retraite du 23 au 30 juin 1952 (Purchase, près de New York) est consignée dans le *Journal*, Cahier 8, pp. 1–5. Extr. des notes de retraites *apud*: *Hymne de l'univers* "Pensées choisies par Fernande Tardivel", XXVI; brèves cit. *in*: L. Barjon, "L'appel de Pâques", *Revue Teilhard de Chardin*, Bruxelles, déc. 1963, 4e année, no. 17 (Pékin, 1944: pp. 13, 14, 15; Le Châtelard, 1946, Les Moulins, 1948: p. 15); H. de Lubac, *La prière du Père Teilhard de Chardin*, Paris, Fayard, 1964:

1944, pp. 90, 94, 96, 98, 100;
1945 pp. 94–95, 95, 96, 99, n. 1, 100;
1946 p. 100;
1948 pp. 95, 99, 124, 126, n. 1;
1950, p. 93, n. 2;
1954, pp. 94, 100 (R) [470].

*1945 et
après

1952
Cahiers manuscrits "Notes de lectures":
I   (17 × 22), 1945, 105 pp.;
II (17 × 22), 1945, 93 pp.;
III (19 × 25), s.d. (postérieur à 1952), 51 pp. (T Sc Ph R) [471].

*1945–
1946
"Conversations avec Grootaers" (titre fictif), *in*: Journal de Willem A. Grootaers, D.s.i., cf. 27 mars, 1er avril, 10 mai, 28 juin, 27 août, 4 oct., 19 oct., 27 oct., 4 nov., 7 nov., 1er déc.

1945, 2 janv., 16 janv. 1946, pp. 6 à 15 (y compris des résumés de conférences et d'articles) (Ph R).

*1946   "Sommaire des titres scientifiques de P. Teilhard de Chardin". D.s.i., 1 p. s.l.n.d. (sans doute Paris, 1er oct.)—rédigé pour le C.N.R.S. (T B).

*1946   "Objet de recherche". D.s.i., $\frac{1}{2}$ p., Paris, 1er oct., figure à la p. 3 de la Notice individuelle remplie pour le C.N.R.S. (T).

*1946   "Notes prises au cours d'une conférence du R.P. Teilhard de Chardin sur le règne de Dieu dans le cadre des exercices de S. Ignace". D.s.i., 3 pp., Le Châtelard, juillet–août 1946, notes prises par M. l'Abbé A. Lahogue (R).

1946   "L'homme et la Paléontologie", Congrès de l'Union Française Universitaire, Besançon, 14 août 1946:
1) Résumé par R. R. sous le titre: "Au Congrès de l'Union Française Universitaire. Une heure avec le R. P. Teilhard de Chardin", *Le Franc-Comtois*, Besançon, 16 août 1946, p. 1, 2 col.;
2) Notes prises par Jean Orcel, 2 pp., D.s.i., sous le titre: "Quelques notes prises pendant la conférence faite par le Père Teilhard au cours des vacances de l'U.F.U. à Besançon, 14 août 1946" (Sc Ph).

*1946–   "Conversations avec Roger Lévy". M., 5 pp., notes prises par
1947   Roger Lévy et extraits de ses carnets (conversations des 22 mai et 4 juin 1946, du 25 janv. 1947) (B).

*1947   "Cosmologie et théologie". D.d.i., 1 p. Paris, 19 janv., *in*: *Bulletin de liaison entre scientifiques s.j.*, débat entre le P. Teilhard de Chardin, le P. Dominique Dubarle et l'abbé Semat, après un exposé du P. Dubarle (Ph R).

*1947   "Équipe 'Science et conscience': Débat entre le Père Teilhard de Chardin et Gabriel Marcel". D.s.i., 6 pp. Paris, 21 janv., sténogr. comportant: I. un Exposé du P. Teilhard de Chardin sur la question: "Dans quelle mesure l'organisation matérielle de l'humanité l'entraîne-t-elle vers un point de maturation spirituelle?" II. des Considérations de Gabriel Marcel autour de cette donnée, suivies d'une discussion entre le Père Teilhard, le P. Dominique Dubarle, O.P., et Gabriel Marcel; cf. aussi notes prises par L. Roinet, M., 2 p., et par le P. Teilhard, M., 2 p., fragment (Ph) [473].

*1947?   "Communication. Anthropologie? Sur la place à donner en biologie au phénomène humain" (*sic*). M., 2 pp. s.l.n.d. (6 avril? 1947); photocopie *in*: C. Cuénot, *Pierre Teilhard de Chardin*, Paris, Plon, 1958, pp. 346–347 (Sc Ph) [474].

*1947   "L'apport spirituel de l'Extrême-Orient" (titre fictif). D.d.i.,

1 p., avant juin, conférence à l'Institut catholique de Paris, notes prises par M. l'Abbé R. Girault (Ph).

*1947 "Point de vue du P. Teilhard de Chardin à propos d'une conférence de Louis Lavelle au Centre Catholique des Intellectuels Français 'Pourquoi un monde?'". D.d.i., 2 pp. Paris, mai, résumé en quelques lignes *in*: *Bulletin de liaison entre scientifiques s.j.*, juin, no. 4, p. 12 (dactylographié); les précisions manuscrites consignées par le P. Teilhard sur le texte *in extenso* (janv. 1947, hiver 1947) sont probablement tardives et en tout cas erronées (Ph) [475].

*Entre 1947 et 1951, publié en 1961.   Schéma (l'évolution vers Oméga) *apud*: Viallet, *Le dépassement*, Fischbacher, p. 215 (photogravure d'un dessin de Teilhard).

*1948 "Foi humaine—foi spirituelle", conférence prononcée à Paris, 12 rue de l'Abbé-Grégoire, le 18 janv.: 1° M., 1 p. (notes prises par L. Roinet); 2° M., 13 pp. (carnet couverture rose, notes prises par Mme Solange Lemaître, texte plus complet et très différent (Ph R) [478].

*1948 "Mystique orientale et mystique de l'ouest", M., 1 p., confér. prononcée à Paris, 19 rue Brey, le 4 juillet (notes prises par L. Roinet; publ. *in*: C. Cuénot, *Pierre Teilhard de Chardin*, Paris, Plon, 1958, p. 361) (Ph R) [479].

*1948 "Notre enquête sur les lectures spirituelles". D.d.i., 7 pp. s.l.n.d., interview de Teilhard per Robert Barrat, sept.? (Ph R).

*1948– "Réponses au Questionnaire du C.N.R.S." R.s.i. et M., ½ p.
1949– (questionnaires ronéotypés, réponses manuscrites) (T Sc B).
1950–
1951–
1952

*1949 "La peur existentielle", M., 1 p., confér. prononcée à Paris, 20, place des Vosges, le 29 janv. (notes prises par L. Roinet) (Ph) [480].

*1949 "L'ultra-humain". M., 1 p., confér. prononcée à Paris, 61, rue Madame, le 16 oct. (notes prises par L. Roinet) (Ph R) [481].

*1950 "L'avenir zoologique probable du groupe humain". D.s.i., 5 pp., confér. donnée le 24 oct. 1950 au C.I.E.F.R. (Bruxelles) (notes prises par Édouard Boné, S.J.) (Sc).

*après "Conversation avec Marguerite Teillard-Chambon" (titre
1950 fictif). 3 pp. environ, date incertaine, mais probablement après 1950 (Ph).

*1950– "Entretiens avec Claude Cuénot" (titre fictif), Paris, 3 avril,
1954 12 juillet, 25 déc. 1950, 17 avril, 6 juin 1951, 29 juin, 7 juillet 1954. M., 17 pp. (notes prises par C. Cuénot); extr. *in*: C.

Cuénot, *Teilhard de Chardin*, Paris, Éd. du Seuil, 1962, coll. "Écrivains de toujours", pp. 147–148 (entretien du 23 sept. 1950); Massimo Olmi, "Il mio amico Teilhard", *L'Europeo*, 8 sept. 1963, XIXe année, no. 36, p. 62 (entretiens du 3 avril 1950 et du 7 juillet 1954, trad. italienne); C. Cuénot, "Situation de Teilhard de Chardin", *Bull. Soc. industr. Mulhouse*, 1963, no. 3, p. 30 (entretien du 7 juillet 1954); C. Cuénot, "Plauderei über Teilhard de Chardin", *in*: Die Zukunft des Menschen in der Welt—eine Tagung über die Zukunftserwartung bei Pierre Teilhard de Chardin.—Evangelische Akademie, Bad Boll, 12.–14. Juni 1964. R.s.i., pp. 41–42 (entretiens du 3 avril 1950 et du 7 juillet 1954, trad. allemande) (Sc Ph R) [482].

*1951   Notes pour la Semaine des Intellectuels Catholiques Français (séance préparatoire du 8 mai ?) "Biologie et transcendance" (titre fictif). D.s.i., ½ p. s.l.n.d., sûrement antérieur à la séance inaugurale du 24 mai 1951.—N'a pas été imprimé dans *Espoir humain et espérance chrétienne*, Paris, Pierre Horay, éd. de Flore (Sc Ph) [483].

*1951   "Teilhard 1951 (S.A.)" (*sic*). M., 90 pp., carnet de notes scientifiques 1er voyage en Afrique du Sud, South Africa, couverture bleue, oblong, 12 × 18 (T Sc Ph) [487].

*1951   "Commission chargée de réunir et de présenter (faire valoir) les preuves ou indices d'un déplacement biologique de l'humanité sur elle-même". M., 1 p. s.l.n.d. (écrit à bord du *Carnavon Castle*, postérieur au 12 juillet 1951) (Sc Ph) [488].

*1951   "Teilhard de Chardin's note on a discovery he made in the ancient deposits of the Vaal River at Harrisdale near Barkly West", August 25th, 1951 (5 lignes autographes, avec figures et légendes autographes) (T).

*1951   "Comparative Observations on South Africa and Eastern Asia (Northern China)". M., 4 pp. s.l.n.d. (brouillon de conférence à la South African Archaeological Society, Capetown, oct.) (T Sc) [491].

*1951 ou "Faire un 'lexique' de mes termes (notions)" (*sic*). M., 1 p.
après   s.l.n.d. (1951 ou de peu postérieur à 1951) (liste de concepts
1951?   teilhardiens).—Photocopie *in*: C. Cuénot, *Pierre Teilhard de Chardin*, Plon, 1958, p. 353, et C. Cuénot, *Lexique Teilhard de Chardin*, Éd. du Seuil, 1963 (avec transcription) (Ph) [485].

*1952   "Notes scientif." (*sic*). M., 31 pp. (cahier de notes scientifiques: voyage à travers les États-Unis, couverture bleue) (T) [492].

1952   "The Psychological Conditions of Human Unification", *Cross Currents*, Fall, 1952, pp. 1–5, cf. p. 443, 1948 et 1949.

*1953   "Afrique du sud, 1953" (*sic*). M., 69 pp. (carnet de notes scientifiques, 2ᵉ voyage en Afrique du Sud, couverture brune, oblong, 13,5 × 21,5) (T Sc Ph) [496].

*1954   Notes manuscrites sur H. et G. Termier, *Formation des continents et progression de la vie*, Paris, Masson. M., 1 p., recto-verso (simple brouillon) (T) [497].

*1954 et   "Le royaume de Dieu" (titre fictif).—Propos tenus en juin ou
1955   juillet 1954 à Monique Galy, *in*: M. Galy, "Pour le R.P. Teilhard de Chardin la doctrine de Saint Paul s'applique à l'ère atomique", *Samedi-Soir*, 21 avril 1955, no. 512, p. 2 (1§) (R).

*1954 et   "Propos du Père Teilhard de Chardin" (titre fictif). Paris, 21
1959   juin 1954, *in*: Jean Guitton, *Journal*, Paris, Plon, 1959, pp. 235–236 (R).

*1954   "Entretiens avec Fernand Lafargue" (titre fictif). Paris, juillet 1954.—Notes prises par F. Lafargue et schéma autographe de la philosophie teilhardienne par le Père (Ph R) [498].

*1954   Inscription sur le livre d'or de l'Hostellerie Chavant, Uzerche (Corrèze), juillet (quelques lignes) [499].

*s.d. et   "Le peuplement de l'Asie". D.s.i., 2 pp. s.l.n.d. (brouillon
1955   datant des dernières années du Père), impr. *in*: *Bull. Soc. Études Indochinoises*, 4ᵉ trim. 1955, nouv. série, t. XXX, no. 4, pp. 351–353 (nombreuses coquilles) (T) [500].

*s.d. et   "Instantanés du P. Teilhard", *Dernière heure*, Bruxelles, 28
1960   avril 1960, 1 col., par Dominique de Wespin (logia de Teilhard) (Ph).

*s.d. et   "Logia et citations diverses" (titre fictif), *in*: Georges Magloire
1961–   (pseud. de Dominique de Wespin) et Hubert Cuypers,
1964   *Présence de Pierre Teilhard de Chardin—l'homme, la pensée*, Paris, Éd. Universitaires, 1961 et Nouvel Office d'Édition, 1964 (cf. notamment les souvenirs de jeunesse, pp. 13–20 de l'éd. de 1964) (B).

*s.d.   "L'éducation de l'amour". D.d.i., 5 p. s.l.n.d. (la 1ᵉʳ p. manque; *incipit* de la 2ᵉ p.: "Mais l'un des points essentiels . . .") (Ph) [503].

*s.d.   "Note sur l'union physique entre l'humanité du Christ et les fidèles, au cours de la sanctification". D.d.i., 7 p., s.l.n.d. (probablement ancien; texte incomplet de la dern. page); Œ., t. XI (R) [504].

*s.d.   "Le problème du mal, réponse à un ami". D.d.i., 4 p. s.l.n.d. (Ph R) [505].

*s.d.   "Réflexions sur la gravité". M., 2 p. s.l.n.d. (probablement ancien) (Ph R) [506].

*s.d.   (dernières années) et 1961 "Litanies au Sacré-cœur" (titre fictif). M., 2 p.; litanies écrites sur l'image du Sacré-Cœur qui a été trouvée à la mort de Teilhard, sur sa table de travail; publié en photocopie et en transcription *in*: Georges Crespy, *La pensée théologique de Teilhard de Chardin*, Paris, Au Club du Livre chrétien, 1961, *sub fine* (R).

XI—OUVRAGES INSPIRÉS, OU RÉCRITS ET REFONDUS, OU SIMPLEMENT REVUS PAR TEILHARD DE CHARDIN

1932   Young (Chung-chien), "On the Artiodactyla from the *Sinanthropus* Site at Chouk'outien", *Pal. Sin.*, 30 juin, sér. C, vol. VIII, fasc. 2, pp. 1–158, 32 fig. dans le texte, pl. I–XXIX. —cf. p. 2 "I am also especially indebted to Père Teilhard de Chardin, the Honorary Adviser to the Survey, with whom I have had many profitable discussions and who has helped me over many difficulties during the present study. Dr. Black also kindly went over my manuscript and made many interesting improvements"; cf. lettres de Teilhard à H. Breuil, Peiping, 8 mai 1932, p. 4; "J'ai dû récrire entièrement un mémoire de Young sur les Artiodactyles de C K T, prêt maintenant,—et intéressant: on va imprimer"; et à Stehlin, Peiping, 5 mai 1932: "Young va publier les Artiodactyles de Choukoutien dans un Mémoire (sous presse) qui vous intéressera (je l'ai très sérieusement revu et refondu)" (T) [507].

1936   Pei (Wen-chung), "On the Mammalian Remains from Locality 3 at Choukoutien", *Pal. Sin.*, sér. C, vol. VII, fasc. 5, 120 pp., 59 fig. in texte et VI pl.—cf. lettre de Teilhard à C. C. Young, Rawalpindi, 4 oct. 1935: "I bring back with me his (Pei's) memoir on Locality 3. I had no time for finishing the revision (. . .)" et à H. Breuil, Peiping, avril 1936; "Moi je suis occupé par la révision du mémoire de Pei sur la localité 3" (T).

1939   Bergounioux (F. M.), "Recherches préhistoriques en Extrême-Orient d'après le R.P. Teilhard de Chardin", *Bull. de litt. ecclés.*, Toulouse, avril-juin, no. 2, pp. 92–99 (mise au point des questions de préhistoire exposées par le P. Teilhard le 27 févr., à la Faculté des lettres: cours de préhistoire sur les fouilles de Chou-Kou-Tien et le *Sinanthropus*; le 28 févr., à l'Institut cathol.: cours de géologie sur le Quaternaire de Chine et d'Extrême-Orient; le 29 févr., à l'Institut cathol.: conférences sur les recherches préhistoriques en Birmanie) (T) [466].

1939   Pei (Wen-chung), "New Fossil Material and Artifacts Collected from the Choukoutien Region During the Years 1937 to 1939", *Bull. Geol. Soc. China*, déc., vol. XIX, no. 3, pp. 207–234, 1 pl. (6 fig.)—cf. lettre de Teilhard à H. Breuil, Peiping, 16 févr. 1940: "Nous venons de sortir un numéro du Bulletin entièrement écrit (ou ré-écrit) par moi: surtout paléontologique, sauf le dernier article sur le Méso–ou Néo–lithique, qui vous intéressera" (T).

1939   Young (Chung-chien), "On a new sauropoda, with notes on other fragmentary reptiles from Szechuan", *ibid.*, pp. 279–315, 25 fig.—cf. même lettre (T).

1939   Young (Chung-chien), "New Fossils from Wanhsien (Szechuan)", *ibid.*, pp. 317–331, 7 fig.—cf. même lettre (T).

1939   Breuil (Henri), "Bone and Antler Industry of the Choukoutien *Sinanthropus* Site", *Pal. Sin.*, new series D, no. 6: Préface (pp. I–IV) revue et mise à jour par P. Teilhard de Chardin.—cf. lettre de W. C. Pei à H. Breuil, datée de Peiping, 19 avril 1939 (T) [465].

1939   Terra (Helmut de) et Paterson (T.T.), "Studies on the Ice Age in India and Associated Human Cultures", *Carnegie Institution of Washington*, no. 493, 354 pp.—cf. Teilhard *in*: "Sommaire des titres scientifiques du P. Teilhard de Chardin", 1946: "En ce qui concerne l'Inde septentrionale et centrale, et la Birmanie mes observations ont été incorporées dans les mémoires publiés en Amérique par le Dr de Terra" (T).

1943   Terra (Helmut de), "The Pleistocene of Burma", pp. 271–239, *in*: Helmut de Terra et Hallam L. Movius, Jr., "Research on Early Man in Burma", *Transactions of the American Philosophical Society*, Philadelphia, new ser., vol. XXXII, 3ᵉ partie.— cf. p. 267, col 2: "As on a previous occasion, Père Teilhard has given generously of his time and energy by joining this party for a duration of five months. It is difficult to express in words the admiration and gratitude which the expedition members entertain toward their distinguished associate and friend whose encouragement and vision has been felt as a never-failing source of inspiration. He placed a brief summary of his observations at the disposal of the expedition leader which he felt should be incorporated in any form in this volume. This was done in the first part where some of the sections are to be regarded as the joint outcome of our cooperation in the field".—cf. aussi Teilhard *in*: "Sommaire des titres scientifiques de P. Teilhard de Chardin", 1946, *loc. cit.* (T).

*1945   Foreword. D.d.i., 2 pp., quelques corrections autographes par Teilhard. s.l.n.d. projet de préface inédit à *Geobiologia*, Péking,

t. II (*incipit*: "Owing to the difficulties of the times, this second number of *Geobiologia* can hardly compare with the first . . .")—cf. lettre de Pierre Leroy à Claude Cuénot du 14 juin 1960: "le Foreword du tome II, de *Geobiologia* (1945) n'a pas été imprimé. Il a été composé et rédigé par Henri Vetch, notre éditeur: revu et corrigé et annoté par Teilhard" (T).

*1950   Lejay (Pierre), "Rapport sur les titres du P. Pierre Teilhard de Chardin". D.d.i., 7 pp., corr. autogr. de Teilhard. s.l.n.d. (Paris avant le 22 mai 1950) (Sc B).

XII—PUBLICATION POSTHUME DES ŒUVRES
Éditions du Seuil

1955   *Le phénomène humain* (T. I.).
1956   *L'apparition de l'homme* (T. II).
1957   *La vision du passé* (T. III).
1957   *Le milieu divin* (T. IV).
1959   *L'avenir de l'homme* (T. V.).
1961   *Hymne de l'univers* (hors série).
1962   *L'énergie humaine* (T. VI).
1963   *L'activation de l'énergie* (T. VII).
1963   *La place de l'homme dans la nature* (*Le groupe zoologique humain*) (classé primitivement hors série, puis T. VIII).
1965   *Élévations et prières* (hors série).
1965   *Teilhard de Chardin explique sa pensée*. *Textes choisis* (anthologie par Jean-Pierre Demoulin) (hors série).
1965   *Science et Christ* (T. IX).
?   *Le cœur de la matière* (T. X).
?   *Christianisme et évolution* (T. XI.).

Autres Éditeurs

1956   *Le groupe zoologique humain. Structures et directions évolutives,* Albin-Michel, 1956 (repris par les Éd. du Seuil sous le titre: *La place de l'homme dans la nature*).
1965   *Écrits du temps de la guerre 1916–1919,* Grasset.

N.B. Voir aussi Section VI.—CORRESPONDANCE: *Lettres d'Égypte* p. 458, *Genèse d'une pensée* p. 461, *Lettres de voyage* p. 461.

XIII—ANTHOLOGIES, MORCEAUX CHOISIS, RECUEILS DE TEXTES

1955   Numéro spécial: Textes de Pierre Teilhard de Chardin, *Psyché*, Paris, janv.-févr. (mois fictifs: éd. posthume), 10ᵉ année, nos. 99–100; 3 lettres inédites et réimpression de: "La question de l'homme fossile", 1948; "L'esprit nouveau et le cône du temps", 1946; "Les directions et les conditions de l'avenir", 1948; "Les conditions psychologiques de l'unification humaine", 1948–49; "L'évolution de la responsabilité dans le monde", 1951; "La fin de l'espèce", 1953 (T Sc Ph) [353].

1955   Numéro spécial: Textes de Pierre Teilhard de Chardin et études sur lui, *Les études philosophiques*, oct.–déc., nouv. sér., 10ᵉ année, no. 4; "Un sommaire de ma perspective phénoménologique du monde", 1954: *in extenso*; "Pour y voir clair. Réflexions sur deux formes inverses d'esprit", 1950: extraits; "'Ma position intellectuelle', Réponse à une 'enquête', et qui n'a jamais paru", 1948: *in extenso* (Ph) [354].

1955   Nombreuses citations d'imprimés *in*: Claude Tresmontant, *Études de métaphysique biblique*, Paris, Gabalda, pp. 91–126 (Ph) [376].

1955   Numéro spécial: Textes de Pierre Teilhard de Chardin et études sur lui, *La Table ronde*, Paris, juin, no. 90; fragments de: *La nostalgie du front*, 1917; *La messe sur le monde*, 1923; *Le milieu divin*, 1926; *Sauvons l'humanité*, 1936; *Réflexions sur le bonheur*, 1943 (Ph R B) [352].

*1956   Nombreuses citations d'imprimés et d'inédits (opuscules et correspondance) *in*: Louis Barjon, S. J., *Le Père Teilhard de Chardin*, Paris, D.d.i. et s.i., 500 pp. en 2 vol. (demeuré inédit) (T Sc Ph R B).

1956   Nombreuses citations d'imprimés et d'inédits *in*: Claude Tresmontant, *Introduction à la pensée de Teilhard de Chardin*, Paris, Éd. du Seuil, 134 pp., cf. R. P. Philippe de la Trinité, O.C.D., "Teilhard de Chardin: Synthèse ou confusion", *in*: *Divinitas*, Rome, 1959, 3ᵉ année, fasc. 2, pp. 285–329 (Ph R) [377].

1957   Textes choisis *in*: Gaëtan Picon, *Panorama des idées contemporaines*, Paris, Gallimard, 1957.—extr. du *Phénomène humain*, pp. 501–506; de *Qu'est-ce que la vie?* p. 632 (Ph).

1958   Nombreuses citations d'imprimés et d'inédits (opuscules et correspondance) *in*: C. Cuénot, *Pierre Teilhard de Chardin. Les grandes étapes de son évolution*, Paris, Plon, 489 pp.; cf. *supra*, Section VI. CORRESPONDANCE (T Sc Ph R B).

1958   *Construire la terre.*—Cahiers Pierre Teilhard de Chardin, no. 1.— extr. et adapt. de: *Sauvons l'humanité*, 1936; *L'esprit de la terre*, 1931; *L'énergie humaine*, 1937; *Réflexions sur le progrès*, 1941; *Sur les bases possibles d'un credo humain commun*, 1941;—Intr. de Max-H. Bégouën, texte en 5 langues (fr., angl., all., russe, arabe), Paris, Èd. du Seuil, déc. 1958, 187 pp. (Ph) [379]. N.B. Les *Cahiers Pierre Teilhard de Chardin* contiennent des inédits de Teilhard (2, *Réflexions sur le bonheur*, 1960; 3, *Pierre*

Teilhard de Chardin et la politique africaine, 1962; 4, *La parole attendue,* 1963).

1959 "Quelques pages choisies de Teilhard de Chardin", *in*: Édouard Lescaze, *De l'étoile à l'homme. Introduction à la pensée de Teilhard de Chardin,* Genève, *Les Cahiers de "Foi et Vérité",* fasc. 35 (série 10, no. 1), pp. 25–30 (extr. de *L'apparition de l'homme* et du *Milieu divin* (Ph R).

1960 Nombreuses citations d'opuscules *in*: C. Cuénot, "La morale et l'homme selon Pierre Teilhard de Chardin", *apud*: *Morale chrétienne et morale marxiste,* Paris et Genève, La Palatine, coll. "Christianisme et actualité", no. 6, pp. 117–147 (Ph R).

1960 Jean Laloup, *Anthologie de littérature scientifique,* Paris, Casterman (extraits des œuvres de Teilhard, pp. 66–67, 70–71, 72, 101–102, 120, 190, 205–206) (Sc Ph).

1961 Textes choisis *in*: Abbé Paul Grenet, *Teilhard de Chardin, un évolutionniste chrétien,* Paris, Seghers, coll. "Savants du monde entier", pp. 161–219 (Sc Ph R).

1962 Diverses citations d'inédits *in*: Anonyme (P. Philippe de la Trinité), "Pierre Teilhard de Chardin e il suo pensiero sul piano filosofico e religioso", *L'Osservatore romano,* Città del Vaticano, 30 juin–1er juill. 1962, CIIe année, no. 148 (31022), p. 2; cf. *La Croix,* Paris, 13 juill. 1962 (Ph R).

1962 Nombreuses citations d'inédits (opuscules et correspondance) *in*: C. Tresmontant, "Le Père Teilhard de Chardin et la théologie", *Lettre,* Paris, sept.–oct., nos. 49–50, pp. 1–53 (Ph R).

1962 Nombreuses citations d'imprimés et d'inédits (opuscules et correspondance) *in*: C. Cuénot, *Teilhard de Chardin,* Paris, Éd. du Seuil, 1962, coll. "Écrivains de toujours", 192 pp.

1962 "Anthologie" en appendice à: Henri Fesquet, *Le catholicisme religion de demain,* Paris, Grasset, coll. "Église et temps présent", pp. 278–294.

1962 Nombreuses mais brèves cit. d'imprimés et d'inédits (opuscules et correspondance) *in*: Henri de Lubac, *La pensée religieuse du Père Teilhard de Chardin,* Paris, Aubier, Éd. Montaigne, 1962, 375 pp. (cit. beaucoup plus longues dans les Appendices I, II, III, pp. 347–361).

1963 Citations d'inédits (opuscules et correspondance) *in*: Louis Barjon, "Fidélité chrétienne et religieuse du Père Teilhard de Chardin", *Foi vivante,* Bruxelles et Paris, avril-juin 1963, IVe année, no. 15, pp. 70–82.

1963 Nombreuses cit. d'imprimés et d'inédits (opuscules et correspondance) *in*: C. Cuénot, "Maximum de l'homme, maximum de Dieu ou la spiritualité de Teilhard de Chardin", *Rencontre,* Besançon, no. 1, pp. 13–17, no. 2, p. 9 et pp. 12–15.

1963 "Appendice" *in*: Monique Périgord, *Évolution et temporalité chez Teilhard*, Paris, Éd. Universitaires, Carnets Teilhard, no. 9, pp. 48–62 (extraits d'œuvres, portant sur le temps et l'instant).

1963 Anthologie des textes majeurs de Teilhard concernant Marie *in*: "La Vierge Marie dans la montée humaine", *Cahiers marials*, avril 1963, pp. 149–153.

1964 Nombreuses cit. d'imprimés et d'inédits (opuscules) *in*: Pierre Smulders, S.J., *La vision de Teilhard de Chardin. Essai de réflexion théologique,* Paris, Desclée de Brouwer, 275 pp.

1964 Nombreuses mais brèves cit. d'inédits (opuscules et correspondance) *in*: Henri de Lubac, S.J., *La prière du Père Teilhard de Chardin*, Paris, Fayard, coll. "Le Signe", 223 pp.

1965 Rideau (R.P. Émile, S.J.), *La pensée du Père Teilhard de Chardin*, Paris, Éd. du Seuil (choix de textes à la fin; nombreuses cit. dans le texte).
Voir aussi Section XII, *Hymne de l'univers* et *Teilhard de Chardin explique sa pensée.*

XIV—TRADUCTIONS ANGLAISES

1959 *The Phenomenon of Man*, London, Collins, 320 pp., New York, Harper, 318 pp. *Introduction by Sir Julian Huxley*, pp. 11–28 (London, December 1958). English translation by Bernard Wall (cf. *Translator's note* p. 9). *Index* (British edition, pp. 315–320; American edition, pp. 313–318). 1 photo hors texte (British edition only).

1960 *Le Milieu Divin, An Essay on the Interior Life*, London, Collins, 160 pp. *Index* pp. 157–160. *Note*, by Bernard Wall, General Editor of the English edition of the works of Teilhard de Chardin, p. 7. Publié sous le titre: *The Divine Milieu, An Essay on the Interior Life*, New York, Harper, 144 pp.

1962 *Letters from a Traveller*, London, Collins, 380 pp., New York, Harper. *General Editor's Note*, by Bernard Wall, p. 5. *The Thinker*, by Sir Julian Huxley, pp. 13–14. *The Man,* by Pierre Leroy, S.J., pp. 15–47. *The Traveller,* by Claude Aragonnès, pp. 49–62. *Index*, pp. 367–380. 1 carte, 4 photographies hors texte.

1964 *Le Milieu Divin, An Essay on the Interior Life.* Pocket edition, London, Collins, Fontana Books, 160 pp. *Note*, by Bernard Wall, p. 9. *Teilhard de Chardin: The Man*, by Pierre Leroy, S.J., pp. 13–42. *Index*, pp. 157–160.

1964 *The Future of Man*, London, Collins, 319 pp. New York, Harper and Row. Translated from the French by Norman Denny. *Translator's Note*, by Norman Denny, pp. 9–10. *Index*, pp. 313–319.

ADDENDA

I—NOTES, MÉMOIRES ET OPUSCULES BIEN DATÉS

p. 439

*1944   "Introduction à la vie chrétienne"; à la p. suivante, Teilhard propose le titre "Introduction au christianisme".

X—VARIA

p. 469

*1915–
1925
   "Notes et esquisses". Nous transcrivons purement et simplement la description bibliographique que Mgr B. de Solages a bien voulu nous adresser le 20. XI. 64: "Cahiers manuscrits dont plusieurs portent, de la main du P. Teilhard "Notes et Esquisses". Ces cahiers se suivent, les interruptions qu'il y a entre eux ne dépassent guère celles qu'il y a à l'intérieur d'un même cahier. Tout ceci est naturel chez un homme en guerre. Ce sont des cahiers d'écolier de même dimension, mais pas toujours les mêmes, 17cm × 22cm, 5 (à quelque chose près). Le 4ème et le 6ème n'ont pas (ou plus) de couverture. La couverture des 3 premiers et du 5ème porte "Teilhard", "Pierre Teilhard" ou "Teilhard de Chardin caporal brancardier 4ème mixte T.Z. 1ère Cie S.P. 131".
Le 1er cahier du 26 août 1915 au 22 sept. 1916, 75 pp. écrites.
Le 2ème cahier du 5. X. 1916 au 2. XII. 1916, 20 pp. écrites.
Le 3ème cahier du 2. XII. 1916 au 10. XI. 1917, 18 pp. écrites.
Le 4ème cahier du 6. XII. 1917 au 13. V. 1918, 66 pp. écrites.
Le 5ème cahier du 18. IX. 1918 au 6. I. 1919, 56 pp. écrites, précédées de 5 pp. détachées du 14. V. 1918 au 7. VII. 1918.
Le 6ème cahier du 5. I. 1919 au 21. V. 1919, 64 pp. écrites.
Le 7ème cahier du 20 mai 1919 au 25. II. 1920, 72 pp. écrites.
Le 8ème cahier du 28. II. 1920 au 26. II. 1922, 113 pp. écrites.
Le 9ème cahier du 12. III. 1922 au 17. VII. 1925, 99 pp. écrites.
   Ces cahiers ont été laissés (abandonnés) par le Père Teilhard à Mlle M. Teillard-Chambon en 1925, en partant pour la Chine. Il ne les lui a jamais redemandés.

p. 472

*1944–   Cahiers manuscrits constituant un "Journal"; ajouter à la
1955   suite de la ligne 7:
    in: C. Cuénot, "Brief an meine evangelischen Freunde", *apud*:
    Die Zukunft des Menschen in der Welt—eine Tagung über
    die Zukunftserwartung bei Pierre Teilhard de Chardin;
    Evangelische Akademie, Bad Boll, 12.–14. Juni 1964. R.s.i.,
    p. 49 (notes des 29 janv. 1946 et 15 févr. 1948 en trad.
    allemande) (R).

XIII—ANTHOLOGIES, MORCEAUX CHOISIS, RECUEILS DE TEXTES

p. 482

1964   Nombreuses cit. d'imprimés et d'inédits (opuscules) *in*:
    Jean-Pierre Demoulin, *Teilhard de Chardin,* Centre belge
    Teilhard de Chardin, 32 rue Berckmans, Bruxelles 6, 32 pp.

XIV—TRADUCTIONS ANGLAISES

p. 482

1965   *Hymn to the Universe.* London, Collins; New York, Harper &
    Row (translation of *Hymne de l'Univers*).
    The Making of a Mind. London, Collins; New York, Harper &
    Row (translation of *La genèse d'une pensée*).

Index

The bold figures indicate the more important passages—decisive role played by the person concerned, a description of the person or a quotation from him.

Dodds, John W., 355
Dollo, Louis, 34, 56
Dominic, St, 404
Dompierre d'Hornoy, Berthe-Adèle de (wife of Emmanuel Teilhard de Chardin), 1
Doncœur, Paul, S.J., 7, 33 (n. 26)
Dostoievski, F., 236
Draper, John William, 237
Drennan (South African scientist), 317 (n.)
Dreyer, T. F., 331 (n.)
Dubarle, D., O.P., 251, 257–8, 259, 260
Dubois (Dutch palaeontologist), 175, 191
Duhamel, Georges, 111
Duns Scotus, 399
Durban, 317

East Indies, 160, 161, 162, 165
East London (South Africa), 318
Egypt, 8–10
El Faiyum, 8, 10
Elias, 407
Emerson, Professor, 285
England, 6, 17, 21, 31, 56, 139, 147, 151, 162, 219, 248, 278, 303
Ethiopia, 89–94
Evans, Sir Arthur, 236

Fan (Founder of the Fan Institute), 231 (n.)
Faral, Edmond, 359
Fejos, Paul, 287, 288, 310, 328 (n.), 329, 332, 335 (n.), 336, 355, 361, 388
Feng, Colonel, 48
Fenneman, Nevin, 78
Fessard, 209
Field (grandson of Henry Field), 109, 223
Flanders, 23, 26
Foerster, F., 236
Fontoynont, Victor, S.J., 7
Fourtau, René, 9
France, 30, 79, 85, 86, 108, 137 ff., 143, 150–1, 152, 165, 197, 204, 205, 206, 207, 218–21, 239, 240 (n.), 245 (n.), 247, 250, 359, 365, 366, 390, 394. *See also* Paris, Auvergne
Francis of Assisi, St, 385, 400, 403
Franquet, R., 33
Freud, 312
French West Africa, 390 (n.)
Frick, Childs, 155, 225, 280
Fromaget, Jacques, 198

Galileo, 261, 360
Galton-Darwin, Charles, 304
Ganne, Père, S.J., 108

Gannon, Fr, S.J. (President of Fordham University), 282
Gannon, Robert I., S.J., 309, 387
Gap, 11
Garaudy, Roger, 390 (n.)
Garrigou-Lagrange, Père, O.P., 269
Garrod, Miss Dorothy, 31 (n.), 56, 164
Gaudefroy, Abbé C., 32, 33, 136, 139, 219, 221 (n. 5)
Gentilly, 87, 88
George, André, 386
Geraghty, Martin, S.J., 388
Germain, Gabriel, 59–60
Gex, Maurice, 306 (n.)
Gide, André, 59–60, 236, 237
Gilson, Étienne, 360
Glacier Park, Montana, 341, 343
Gobi Desert, 54, 68, 102–3, 125, 126, 129, 154
Gobineau, Arthur de, 237
Goldschmidt-Rothschild, Marianne de, 249
Goodwin, John, 314, 315, 317 (n.)
Goublaye de Ménorval, M. and Mme de, 144, 378 (n.)
Gouhier, Henri, 276
Grabau, A. W., 71, 72, 74, 77, 156–7, 160, 163, 168, 174, 241
Graham, Professor, 102, 160, 163
Grandmaison, Léonce de, S.J., 13
Granger, Walter, 32, 51, 73, 102, 154, 165, 218, 219, 280
Greene, Graham, 236, 264
Greene, Roger, 173
Gregory, William King, 111, 155
Grew, U.S. Ambassador to Japan, 311
Grousset, René, 142, 296–7, 298
Guillaume (palaeontologist), 277
Guillaume, Baron, 302
Guitton, Jean, 364–5
Gusdorf, George, 398, 399
Guyénot, E., 275
Guyot de Salins, General, 22, 25

Haardt, Claude, 104, 105, 128 (n.)
Haardt, Georges-Marie, 105, 111, 128, 131–2, 135, 143, 152
Haardt, Mme Georges-Marie, 104–6
Hackin, Joseph, 129, 139
Haiti, 311
Haldane, J. B. S., 254, 277
Hankow, 182
Hanoi, 138
Harar, 89, 92, 276
Harbin, 129, 144
Harvard University, 282, 283, 311, 355
Hastings, Ore Place, 10–11, 12, 35; Museum, 12
Haug, E., 30 (n. 22), 339